Art in Hungary 1956–1980

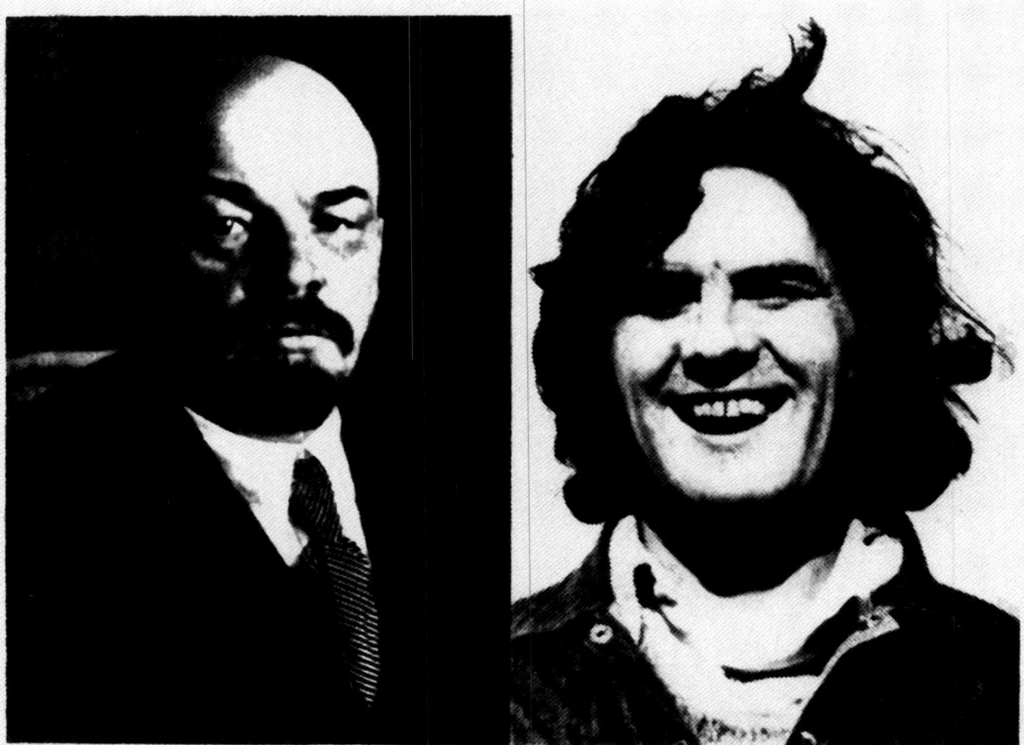

You are the one who made me glad

Art in Hungary 1956–1980

Doublespeak and Beyond

Edited by
Edit Sasvári
Sándor Hornyik
Hedvig Turai

Thames & Hudson

Institutions

Discourses

Disguises

Speech Acts

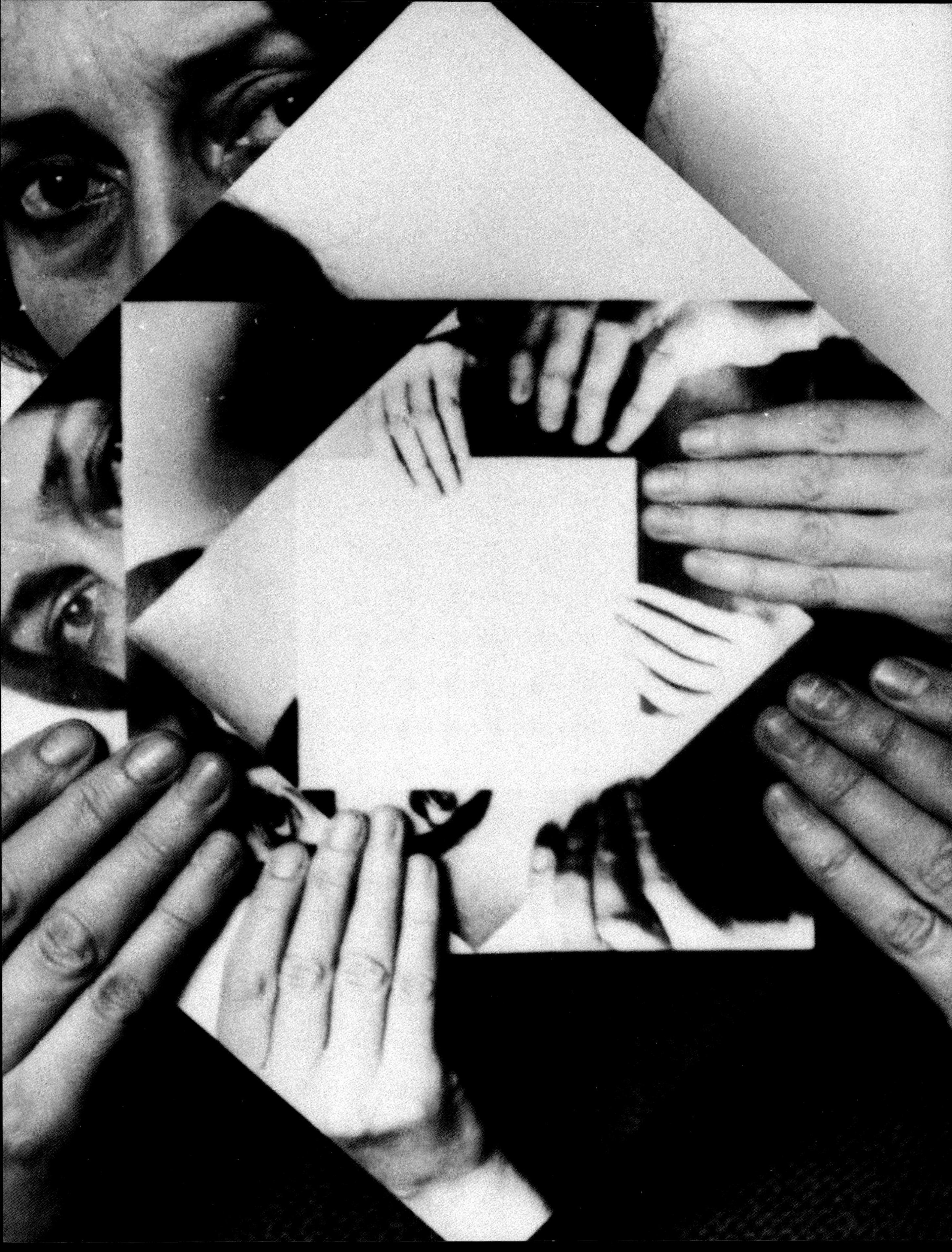

Autonomy and Doublespeak

Art in Hungary in the 1960s and 1970s

Edit Sasvári

In 1960, Lajos Kassák, the internationally respected seventy-three-year-old doyen of the historical avant-garde in Hungary, was invited to have an individual exhibition at the renowned Galerie Denise René in Paris. The Hungarian state gave the go-ahead to the exhibition, but Kassák was not allowed to travel to Paris. State officials replaced the artist at the opening, representing the Hungarian political system rather than art.[1]

The date marks the beginning of the period under discussion here, and this brief story also illustrates the contradictoriness that typified the situation in which Hungarian art found itself for the two decades to come. It testifies to the difference between Hungary and Western bourgeois societies in terms of the status (namely, in Hungary, the absence) of the individual and the institutional autonomy of art and artists. It also demonstrates the state's unbounded ambition to control and its use of doublespeak and double standards, which characterized Hungary as it formed the core of a political/social consensus.[2] Eschewing this consensual system of doublespeak both in person and in the spirit of their work was a unique achievement of the Hungarian neo-avant-garde, as all but a fraction of Hungarian artists conformed.[3]

Studies on the Eastern European neo-avant-garde[4] in the 1960s–70s usually emphasize two things: produced in East-Central Europe, this art was synchronous and on a par with Western contemporary art; additionally, this achievement was made within the framework of a totalitarian regime suppressing artistic freedom, which demanded high levels of human and ethical courage from the artists. Although these two tenets do contain a kernel of truth, the problem is that the accomplishments of the Hungarian neo-avant-garde are examined primarily in terms of the relationship between Eastern and Western art, largely ignoring the more problematic East-Central European context. Restricting the analysis to East–West relations risks basing research and interpretation on formal analogies and remaining within a self-justifying framework. What I mean by self-justification is the reassuring recognition of familiar analogies of Western art in unofficial Eastern art. This over-simplifies the matter. For it is the acknowledgment of the local context that allows one to perceive the tension in the situation in which the neo-avant-garde was condemned by the communist authorities as a product of capitalist cultural imperialism, while the predominantly conservative public rejected it as a foreign form, alien to the spirit of national culture. The combination of state and popular rejection isolated new avant-garde artists struggling for their independence, while also putting them at risk of being caught up in false confrontations between the communist authorities and national conservatism.[5]

The question is whether the analogous development of East-Central European and Western contemporary art can be accepted as an unequivocal fact. Should we take into account that the comparable aesthetic forms of the period were created in fundamentally different situations and reacted to different relationships, and therefore call for different interpretations?

It seems self-evident that autonomy – i.e. self-governance, independent of outside coercion – is a relevant issue in any examination of the local context of East European art. *Theorie der Avantgarde* by Peter Bürger is a good starting point in this respect, particularly because his theory was developed in the middle of the period in question (the work was published in West Germany in 1974).[6] Bürger examines the relationship between bourgeois capitalist society and art. One of the fundamental tenets of the work is that the autonomy of the institution of art in the broadest sense is the key to modernity and avant-gardism in a bourgeois society. He convincingly argues that the precondition of autonomy is the separation of the system of art institutions from social practice; put more simply, the institutional system of modern art should not have to serve extra-artistic goals, for instance, political goals. It follows that full autonomy enables art to focus on its internal aesthetic issues. The main characteristic of classical avant-gardism, however, is dissatisfaction with the autonomous but isolated institution of art and the attempt to escape it. If one accepts this line of argument, the question arises how one can interpret this contradiction in the case of a renewed Hungarian modernity and the neo-avant-garde in the 1960s and 1970s in a society controlled by a Soviet-type regime, where the institution of art was anything but autonomous? Several answers are possible. For instance, the goals of the neo-avant-garde may have differed significantly from those of the classical avant-garde. In that case, however, is one justified in calling it (neo-)avant-garde? Alternatively, one should consider whether the Hungarian neo-avant-garde was different in content from its Western counterpart due to the different conditions. While Western neo-avant-gardism arose (for the most part) in liberal democracies, Hungary was a Soviet-type state from the end of the Second World War through to 1989.

Bürger clearly distinguishes aestheticist and avant-garde strains within the radical art of the first half of the twentieth century. Whereas aestheticism, which emphasized beauty and art-for-art's-sake over socio-political intent, was produced through the autonomy of the institution of art, the avant-garde movement attacked this autonomy. In this construction, the aestheticizing forms of modernism were opposed to avant-gardism. This separation between the concepts of modernism and avant-gardism was not as clear in the Hungarian usage, partly because the people representing the two were often identical. Lajos Kassák, for instance, was a representative of constructivist painting as well as dada poetry in the 1910s and 1920s. Furthermore, Bürger does not consider the Western neo-avant-garde emerging in the 1960s to be a true avant-garde movement because it more or less accepted the autonomy of the institution of art. What makes the interpretation of the East European neo-avant-garde more challenging is that the acceptance of the institutional system of art does not apply here, as autonomy did not exist, and the neo-avant-garde was opposed to an entire totalitarian political system. In fact, the terms 'unofficial' or 'prohibited' art are often used in Hungarian scholarship. Both expressions applied only to the local political status of neo-avant-gardism. Piotr Piotrowski suggests that autonomous modernism became avant-garde art in East-Central Europe in a political sense, precisely because it critiqued the communist institution of art. What these concepts share is a common ground for aesthetic modernism and avant-garde art on the basis of their political position. For the sake of simplicity, the terms East-Central European neo-avant-garde or neo-avant-garde in Hungary will be the preferred usage in this volume.

We may begin then by stating that the Hungarian neo-avant-garde did not oppose the non-existent institutional autonomy of art institutions, but rather struggled to achieve autonomy due to the general restrictions on liberty and the lack of autonomy within the institutional system. In contrast to Bürger's interpretation of autonomy in the context of Western European art, what the issue of autonomy primarily meant to the neo-avant-garde in Eastern Europe was the recognition by society, and ultimately by the authorities, of the subjective autonomy of art. The artists considered the art institutions of the socialist regime to be part of the machinery of totalitarianism, which they rejected wholesale. The real question, therefore, is how this fact affects the interpretation of the East European avant-garde.

Let's return to the opening story of our study for a moment in the interest of a more nuanced understanding. So, Lajos Kassák is one of the most important figures of Hungarian abstract painting and at the same time the embodiment of the richly diverse idea of avant-gardism. On the other hand, abstract art is strictly rejected by the Soviet doctrine as a worthless product of the culture of 'declining capitalism'. Nevertheless, the Hungarian state participates in the exhibition honouring Kassák's abstract painting in Paris in 1960, though the artist is prohibited from attending his own exhibition. Instead of Kassák, representatives of the state cultural bureaucracy are present. Where is the logic in this?

Nowhere.

By the 1960s, Hungarian cultural policy and even the political regime as a whole had gradually come to give up the Marxist–Leninist notion that society would be transformed into an ideologically coherent structure. It is the incoherence of Hungary and other East-Central European regimes that makes it so difficult to understand the context of art, namely the relationship between the art of the region and power aiming at total control.

The intellectual and mental state of Hungary at the time was characterized by what may be called doublespeak. This was essentially a consequence of the dual ambition of the communist leadership to meet Soviet expectations (Hungary was under military occupation!) and to enable the Western relationships that provided the sole opportunities for development. This was obviously an impossible task. The situation was only made worse by the memory of the 1956 anti-Stalinist revolution in Hungary, brutally crushed by the Soviet military. Since the János Kádár regime was installed by force by the Soviets after they had quashed the revolution, its legitimacy was fragile and its political survival depended on the collective pretence that the revolution and its defeat had never happened. The regime offered a certain quality of life in exchange for this collective amnesia, but needed Western help to deliver it, so it attempted to develop the best possible relationships with the West. Yet Soviet control was still in operation during this period, if in a changing form. This caused the Hungarian communist leadership to adopt doublespeak, showing one face to the 'friendly' Soviet Union, which wanted to hold it on a short leash, and another to the 'hostile' West, from which it hoped to receive assistance. This difficult task generated plenty of tension in domestic politics: how can the Communist Party avoid losing face and make society accept the ideologically enforced system, when this ideology is rather obviously being replaced by utilitarian pragmatism? While the Kádár regime could not resolve this contradiction, it managed it rather skilfully for about thirty years (1956–88). This was, in fact, the true political achievement of the Kádár regime. The result was unfortunately a profoundly corrupt, opportunistic society.

In other words, doublespeak was a symptomatic reflection of the dysfunction and structural crisis of the totalitarian systems that presented themselves as monolithically unified. It was a contradiction between the ideology and the survival practices of the socialist regimes that eroded the East European system in the long run. The structural crisis was due to the Soviet-style system's inability to develop without relying on Western models of research, production and organization. Consequently, the Eastern bloc partly adopted the techniques of the West, though filtering them and attempting to make them compatible with the Soviet model. In the long run, this absurd situation would undermine the operation of the entire system.

Wedged between the two world orders yet having to find a way to develop, the majority of East European communist powers – including the Hungarian leadership – were forced to engage in constant self-correction, which eventually gave those within these systems – those active in the economy, scholarship and art – more room to manoeuvre. The constant shifts in the position and assessment of the intelligentsia and art during the socialist period are more easily understood in the light of this process of self-correction.

To sum up: the Stalinist model did not allow and, in fact, severely sanctioned doublespeak, but the East European states began to abandon the totalitarian model in the late 1950s and attempted to mirror, as much as the local ideological frameworks permitted, the freedoms embodied in the market and the multi-party system in Western democracies. This phenomenon, which was articulated in the economic, political and cultural conditions of various East European countries in different ways, could not be openly acknowledged, so the communist authorities, with their demand for total control, played a double game: they both permitted and prohibited attempts to adopt certain models of capitalist society. This contradictory logic enabled the appearance of certain presumably innocent Western European elements in official, state-funded culture from the mid-1960s onwards.

Eastern Europe's cultural and intellectual dependence on the Soviet Union manifested itself in models of Marxism conforming to the Soviet system and reflecting local power equations, often representing the narrow elite of those in power. There were, however, forces committed to democracy in East European societies: economists, scholars and artists with an interest in a Western orientation and development. The confrontation of these two fronts, and the constant renegotiation of the balance between them, supply the dynamic of doublespeak. The contradictions of this dual orientation were always on the agenda in the 1960s–70s and provided the basic pattern that determined, to various degrees, life and culture in East European societies.

Very few people refused to participate in this consensual discourse of opportunism, which was dictated by career ambitions, and those who did abstain paid the price. Besides having to withstand pressure from the authorities, they had to suffer the social majority's ill-will due to their own bad consciences about their opportunism. This made it easy for the state authorities to put neo-avant-garde artists under pressure throughout the 1970s. Some of them emigrated to the West and those who stayed became isolated. Of course, such circumstances made building relationships with the West vital both for those who left and those who stayed in Hungary. The communist authorities eyed this Western network with suspicion, and the fundamentally conservative nationalist, non-communist public disliked it as well. It is a measure of the pettiness of the Hungarian political leadership that even though neo-avant-garde art would have been an ideal export product with which to display a positive image to the West, the powers that be never attempted to pursue this.

The context to what follows is that the situation in Hungary was dominated by communist power in the 1960s–70s, which had a strong influence on society as a whole, including artists. Yet one should also ask whether this context, which differs from its Western counterpart, is simply a consequence of the socialist system. Could it be traced back, perhaps, to earlier periods in East-Central European history?

Examining the classical modernist and avant-garde movements of the 1910s and 1920s, one finds that East-Central European countries were wedged between two cultural centres, both of which were sources of powerful positive artistic impulses. There were West European French, German and Italian influences from one side and robust Russian impulses from the other. The influence of the West largely drove aesthetic modernization, and its limited radicalization in the 1920s was actually a result of Russian influence. Avant-gardism attained a revolutionary, social reformist and even utopian character in Russia, but the Russian public could not be receptive to its aesthetic language in the long run. The development of the avant-garde in the West was more successful in this respect because its prolonged continuity enabled the spirit of modernity to transform the cultural tastes and increase the awareness of a broader public. This became discernible around the 1960s. In the Soviet Union, however, the utopian avant-garde became politically marginalized and its development was tragically cut short by Stalinism.

What makes this even more complex is the dominance of the nineteenth-century national concept of culture in East-Central European countries – whereby art is meant to serve the cause of the nation – which persisted even in the first half of the twentieth century when classical modernism was emerging. When one attempts to position modernist and avant-garde initiatives within this conservative nationalist construction, it is difficult to identify them even as a secondary scene because the two approaches to art are so antagonistic. This is what poses the greatest challenge in terms of the issue of context. As a result, the modernist movements of the region fit better into a broader network: the history of the *international* networks of modernist movements, in which participants mutually legitimize each other to some extent by serving the same radical ideas. By contrast, the *national* concept of culture bases cultural legitimacy on its national framework and character – or, put more eloquently, its service to the nation. The nation funds culture, which in turn serves the nation. (It is rather easy to see the profound similarity between this and the communist version: power funds culture and culture in turn serves power.) Although this interpretation of national culture has survived in the countries of the region to this day, it is highly problematic in several respects: firstly, it is fundamentally opposed to the autonomy of the – imaginary or real – institutional system of art; and, secondly, it was in fact the largely international character of classical modernism and avant-gardism that provided the unique dynamic of their rapid development. It is no accident that modernist and avant-gardist movements subsided after the appearance of dictatorial regimes in the 1930s and remained dormant until the post-war period.

To avoid oversimplifying the issue, one ought to acknowledge that part of the population saw positive traits in communism, however ambivalent they were in their assessment. The Soviet-style system unquestionably tried to modernize, but this entailed the forcible transformation of the economy, which took the form of an unrealistically excessive industrialization beyond the country's capacity and the forcible collectivization of agriculture. Even so, by the 1960s this process of modernization had raised the standard of living for society as a whole. Moreover, the communists' broad democratizing efforts after the Second World War seemed promising to the majority of the population, given the prior experiences of fascism and its racial ideology, and the semi-feudal caste system of the Horthy regime in the interwar period (Miklós Horthy was regent of the Kingdom of Hungary in 1920–44, prior to the occupation of Hungary first by German forces and then more permanently by Soviet forces towards the end of the war). This, however, led to an unpopular new hierarchical social structure, a transformed society with limited freedom managed by a bureaucratic party and state apparatus based on centralized Stalinist control.

Quite significantly, the majority considered the communist authorities to be foreign due to the Soviet occupation, which sustained and revived the traditional conservative national feelings. It became increasingly clear in the period in question that the potential political opposition to Soviet control was the national conservative faction, which could not become a political formation or party until the late 1980s.[7] This line of thought adds some nuance to the view of the socialist system and may indicate the political force-field in which the Party's cultural policy had to manoeuvre.

Three layers can be distinguished in the Hungarian art scene of the 1960s–70s: what was known as official art, in conformity with the regime; national conservative art that flirted with modernist forms; and neo-avant-garde art, which was marginalized and therefore sought its place within international contemporary art rather than the Hungarian art scene.[8] Those in power expected conformist artists not merely to praise the regime, as direct propaganda became ineffective after the brutal suppression of the anti-Stalinist uprising by the Soviet military in 1956. The requirement was now to identify with the Communist Party leadership and its policies, and to find relatively independent ways to aid aesthetically the problems the Party leadership faced in relation to the difficult task of building socialism. The main problem inherent in Party policy was how to create an authentic political image between 'orthodox' loyalty to the Soviets and a 'liberal' openness to the West. As partners of the Party, regime-conformist artists were supposed to endow current ideology with an aesthetically appealing authentic image. The Stalinist cultural doctrine of the 1950s stipulated a realism influenced by the nineteenth-century academic model, but this stylistic requirement gradually became relaxed in the period in question. So, representatives of official art had a range of aesthetic options, and they had to test the limits of their movement: their experiments either pushed the boundaries towards a more radically leftist, modernist art than the official one or re-envisioned artistic possibilities in the spirit of the traditional rhetoric of national identity. Accessibility replaced realism as the main expectation. Accessibility meant, more specifically, that the work should allow everyone to grasp the artist's wholehearted commitment to the Communist Party in power. Paradoxically, however, the only people who could identify, from a work's actual formal appearance, whether it conformed to the Party's propaganda objectives were those already very familiar with these patterns of thought. Therefore, the one constant in the process was the expectation for artists to demonstrate identification with the current Party line. Although they were not free to choose any aesthetic strategy, the options became subject to trial and assessment, i.e. they became negotiable. This, in turn, meant that regime-conformist artists, as members of the cultural elite, were engaged in communication and even debate with the Party's cultural leadership.

The leading representatives of regime-conformist art were also responsible for the highest level of art education. As professors at colleges of art, they were primarily in charge of selecting the next generation of artists who would serve the Party's ideology. The period under discussion here includes approximately three such generations. Young people were not educated about issues in contemporary international art at these institutions; not only were their teachers often unfamiliar with international developments, but there was an attempt to block access to this information.

The audience of the 'stars' who served the objectives of the Party leadership was inescapably large: their monumental works adorned public places and buildings, and they were the highlights of museums and publications. The new governments after the political transition in 1989 gradually removed these artists' works from public spaces, and they are no longer on display in the museums. They are increasingly sinking into oblivion.

Although the overwhelming majority of the artists felt awkward about working hand-in-glove with the powers that be, they were afraid to adopt an oppositional stance. In the course of the twenty years under discussion here, such artists came up with innumerable but mostly uninteresting variations on avoiding taking a stand. The basis of their approach was a clichéd, derivative realism following local traditions, which was mixed with certain aesthetic elements of post-impressionism, cubism or classical modernism. These works were not that different stylistically from those of Party favourites, but were more restrained and ambiguous in content. The conservative character of the works helped legitimize the state's institutional system of art. The state generously funded its artistic elite, and the great majority of the uncommitted were kept afloat with modest state funding through various channels. Many artists only had contact with lower-ranking local representatives of the Party, typically in connection with some minor conflict or career advancement. Most of them embraced national conservatism and, like the majority of the population, considered communists (just like the international process of modernization) an unavoidable evil. They made a living in the low- and intermediate-level institutions of art education and taught in a conservative spirit, often with a measure of openness to the aesthetic of classical modernity, which was covered in a growing number of Hungarian publications. They were rarely interested in the issues of contemporary international art and had limited access to relevant information.

Those in power saw the neo-avant-garde 'crowd' as an obscure and incomprehensible oppositional political group with which no dialogue was possible or desirable. The group was regarded as so insignificant that limiting their access to the public sphere seemed sufficient and there was no need to abolish them. Clearly, the representatives of the neo-avant-garde subculture were in no hurry to start a dialogue with the establishment in this situation. On the contrary, they unequivocally rejected it and focused on participating in the transformation of international art through the channels of Western avant-garde, doing so against all odds (their challenges included marginalization, financial difficulties, lack of information and control based on a network of informants). From their perspective, Eastern European art appeared to be stagnant in the 1960s and 1970s compared to the dynamic of its Western counterpart.

Members of the Hungarian neo-avant-garde often did not have a degree and became receptive to issues in contemporary international art despite their lack of formal education. They made an effort to find information about art and this process of self-training enabled them to join the network of international art. Art historians committed to contemporary art had a major role in this. In the 1970s, it became easier to obtain Western art publications, which proved beneficial to the rise of the second generation of the Hungarian neo-avant-garde.

Being confined to a rather closed subculture, the neo-avant-garde could not count on a broad audience. Exhibitions and actions took place within a small circle. Since their events were routinely banned by the authorities, they usually held exhibitions and actions without asking for a permit and held them at out-of-the-way cultural sites, where the manager of the institution was willing to take this risk. They could not publish high-quality reproductions, which also limited their public exposure and dissemination. When the Hungarian media covered their work, however sporadically, it was always negative coverage. Since the main strategy of the neo-avant-garde artists was to become part of the circulation of international contemporary art, the development of Western contacts compensated for their marginalization in Hungary. Building such Western contacts was actually illegal and entailed a certain degree of risk, so the neo-avant-garde circles were suffused by a conspiratorial spirit. Legal foreign contacts were only possible through official Hungarian channels; since they had no contact with the official sphere, this was out of the question.

Western interest in the Hungarian neo-avant-garde manifested itself in two ways: firstly, there was an appreciation and also an openness to potential integration, though this was coloured by the privileged position of the institutional system of contemporary Western art and by a sense that the appearance of such art in Eastern and East-Central Europe in the 1960s and 1970s was a sign of the universality of Western art and culture. Secondly, the West also treated the East-Central European neo-avant-garde as a political opposition to communism, which it could use for political purposes in the spirit of an East–West confrontation, which kept repression by the communist regime on the agenda.

Of course, one barely scratches the surface of a very complex historical situation with such a simplified sketch. In fact, social and personal relationships were nearly always far more nuanced and contradictory in specific cases. Let me offer a single illustrative example: the Biennale del Dissenso (Biennial of Dissent) in 1977. The event was organized by the Italians, building on the institution of the Venice Biennale. Positioned between the Venice Biennales (in our case, the years 1976 and 1978), the Biennale del Dissenso was a special event that distinguished itself from the traditional concept of the Biennale: it strove to highlight the unofficial or critical art of the Soviet bloc in an independent international space. The organizers wanted to give an overview of this largely unknown genre of the art and culture, including film, literature, religion and science, of the region. This enterprise was a unique event and perhaps the most ambitious effort to create an international forum for learning about and assessing Eastern European art that was critical of the regimes.

The Biennale del Dissenso occurred in a force-field of political interest throughout its existence. Carlo Ripa di Meana, the main organizer, was a leftist Italian aristocrat, who had spent a long time in Prague in the 1950s and had first-hand knowledge of East European conditions. The conception of this Biennale was formulated with the backing of the Partito Socialista Italiano (Italian Socialist Party) in 1977. It would be logical to expect the Italian right to be the ones driving this initiative in order to undermine the political legitimacy of the Soviet bloc. In fact, it was the relatively small socialist party, which was in a rather precarious position, that wanted to show that it could be critical of Soviet politics and, despite being a leftist party, it was not a satellite to the Soviet Union. Characteristically, the rightist Christian Democrats opposed the conception of the Biennale del Dissenso because Italian big business had an interest in relationships and contracts with the Soviet Union (such as Fiat's investment in the Togliatti Lada car factory in Russia) and hoped to avoid tension. The political situation was quite tense within Italy at the time: the Partito Comunista Italiano (Italian Communist Party), which was the largest national communist party in Western Europe, won over one-third of the votes in the election in 1976. The Italian communists had internal debates about the plans for the Biennale, and the party was unable to agree a clear position regarding the event. This situation shows how ambivalent West European intellectuals, and particularly the leftists among them, were about the conflict between Soviet-style regimes and the emerging opposition of intellectuals there.

By the mid-1970s, the international political climate of the cold war had changed in some respects. These were the years when human rights came to the forefront of the confrontation, on the initiative of the United States. So, the conception and process of the Biennale del Dissenso was also informed by current human-rights issues. The main question was whether art was, in fact, free in the Soviet states that claimed to have been de-Stalinized. By posing this question, Italian parties representing various shades of leftist politics tried to demonstrate their critical stance towards Soviet-type communist goals and assure the public that they would not install a Soviet-style political system if elected.

Unofficial and critical art of East European countries had to present itself in this rather complex political constellation. As indicated earlier, there were two parallel strains in the assessment of Hungarian unofficial art: political and aesthetic. The Biennale del Dissenso is a striking example of how the

West's interest in East European art could be motivated solely by its own political interests. The Biennale (often called the notorious 'dissident Biennale' in the political jargon of the Eastern bloc) endowed East European art with a political brand, which in turn raised the question whether the West needed East European dissidents, including avant-garde artists, given the realities of the thaw in cold-war politics. And if it did, what was its objective? And did East European intellectuals and artists fighting for cultural freedom have any interest in risking their way of life at home to achieve the Biennale organizers' goals, which must have seemed elusive and vague to them?[9] The Biennale del Dissenso was a large-scale, unique event, which offered a major forum to East European oppositional art despite all its problems, but eventually led to a very fragmentary presentation. The majority of the artists did not trust such highly politicized initiatives.

In terms of Western relations, participants in the unofficial scene tried to build relationships they hoped would help ensure the acknowledgment of their artistic achievements. Interest in the region and in Hungarian art began to rise significantly in West Germany in the 1970s; to take just a few examples, the volume *Aktuelle Kunst in Osteuropa* (1972) by Klaus Groh introduced seventy-eight artists from the region,[10] and Dieter Honisch, as director of the Neue Nationalgalerie in West Berlin, began to cover artists from the region and the Hungarian scene systematically in 1975.

After the political transition, the aesthetic reassessment and growing appreciation of East European art by the West began in the 2000s, when East-Central European art had a chance to become integrated into the aesthetic canon represented by museums and into the elite art trade with little interest in political content. This process began in the form of private initiatives, but did not offer a high-quality professional analysis or a reassessment of the unofficial art of the 1960s and 1970s in a broader context.

The assessment of neo-avant-garde art also changed within Hungary after the political transition. Two approaches developed: neo-avant-garde works of the 1960s and 1970s were included in the Hungarian art trade and were aesthetically appreciated by a very well-informed but narrow circle of collectors. Inclusion in Hungarian galleries gave a new impetus to a systematic professional inventory of neo-avant-garde art, typically commissioned by galleries. At the same time, the dominant right-wing national establishment has valued and appropriated anything that can be construed as critical of communism and used in its projects praising anti-communist opposition in the service of short-term political goals. This, however, does not help with understanding and interpreting the unofficial art of the 1960s and 1970s or the culture of the period as a whole.[11] While the accomplishments of the Hungarian neo-avant-garde are at risk of being appropriated by short-term political agendas or the interests of the art trade, a coherent reassessment is as challenging as it is necessary. Therefore, one still has to live with two parallel interpretations, one in the aesthetic context and another in the political one. For now, there seems to be no escaping this dual dialogue.

1 Edit Sasvári, '"Our culture cannot be different at home and abroad." Lajos Kassák's exhibition in Paris in 1960', *Művészettörténeti Értesítő*, Vol. 59, No. 1, 2010. http://akademiai.com/doi/abs/10.1556/MuvErt.59.2010.1.4 (1 August 2017).

2 The spirit and practice of doublespeak permeated Hungarian society in countless ways: the country's leadership communicated different things in domestic and foreign policy. The economy gradually transitioned from a Stalinist planned economy to a constantly changing 'liberalized' mixed economy, which could never be justified by the regime, but it nevertheless expected society's tacit agreement. People spoke very differently in private, in the media, in literature and in the theatre, and a method of 'reading between the lines' came to be established, whereby certain signs in the text could be deciphered in a number of contradictory ways.

3 This is a sensitive question. In any given case, it is very difficult to establish a rigid boundary between the rejection of the consensual spirit that permeated society as a whole and a less risky passive bystander position. We do not wish to engage in such moralizing in this book, and we claim that it was a matter of principle for the neo-avant-garde not to participate in doublespeak.

4 The growth and development of the avant-garde in the West during the twentieth century was not interrupted by massive political unrest. By contrast, the totalitarian regimes that emerged in Eastern and East-Central Europe in the 1930s prevented the further activities of the avant-garde in this region, and avant-garde art that was independent of such regimes did not reappear until the 1960s. This interruption and restoration of development makes it necessary in the context of East-Central European art to distinguish between the classical avant-gardism of the 1930s and the neo-avant-garde of the 1960s.

5 Neither the communists nor the nationalists constituted a democratically elected political party. National conservative political forces could not form parties in Hungary in the 1960s and 1970s. The communists were ruling from a minority position under the protection of the Soviet military power present in the country, while the overwhelming majority of the population adopted a national conservative attitude and represented an informal political power. A complex system of relationships evolved during the years of coexistence between the communists and the nationalists, based on a degree of mutual adaptation. The neo-avant-garde wanted to remain outside of this network of relationships.

6 Peter Bürger, *Theory of the Avant-Garde*. Minneapolis: University of Minnesota Press, 1984. Originally published as *Theorie der Avantgarde*. Frankfurt am Main: Suhrkamp, 1974.

7 The political developments after the transition away from Soviet influence in 1989 have also confirmed the incredible endurance and mass base of the conservative national faction during the Kádár era.

8 This categorization seems plausible enough, but it must be noted that it corresponds precisely to the categorization by communist cultural policy: the system of the 'Three Ts', for *támogat*, *tűr* and *tilt*, the Hungarian equivalents of 'supported', 'tolerated' and 'prohibited', was introduced in 1957 (see also Júlia Perczel, 'The Art Sphere as a Grey Zone', pp. 59–75). One's feeling of awkwardness about using these categories becomes even more acute when one realizes that the communist categories of the Three Ts imitate the Three Vs of Nazi cultural policy (*Volksfreund*, *Volksfremd* and *Volksfeind*; friend, foreigner and enemy of the people).

9 Edit Sasvári, 'Eastern Europe under Western Eyes. The "Dissident Biennale", Venice, 1977', in Beata Hock (ed.), 'Doing Culture under State-Socialism: Actors, Events, and Interconnections', *Comparativ, Zeitschrift für Globalgeschichte und Vergleichende Gesellschaftsforschung, Leipziger Universitätsverlag*, Vol. 14, No. 4, 2014, 12–22.

10 Klaus Groh, *Aktuelle Kunst in Osteuropa* [Current Art in Eastern Europe]. Cologne: DuMont-Schauberg, 1972.

11 Neo-avant-garde works usually do not make it clear what specific political position their oppositional stance represents. Is it more radically leftist than the regime or more liberal, more democratic, in the bourgeois sense? Interpretations of the works are open in this respect, which enables them to function as objects of subjective political projections.

Institutions

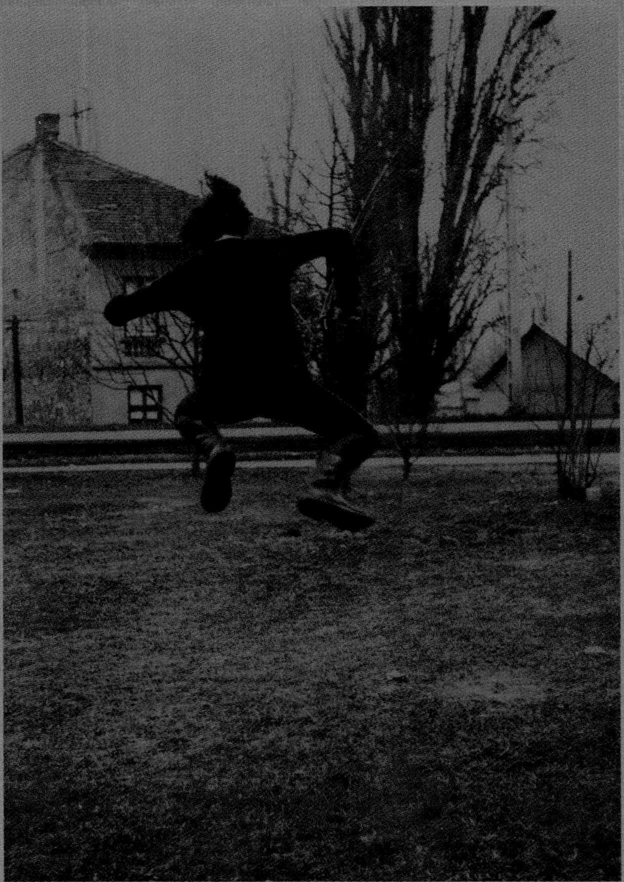

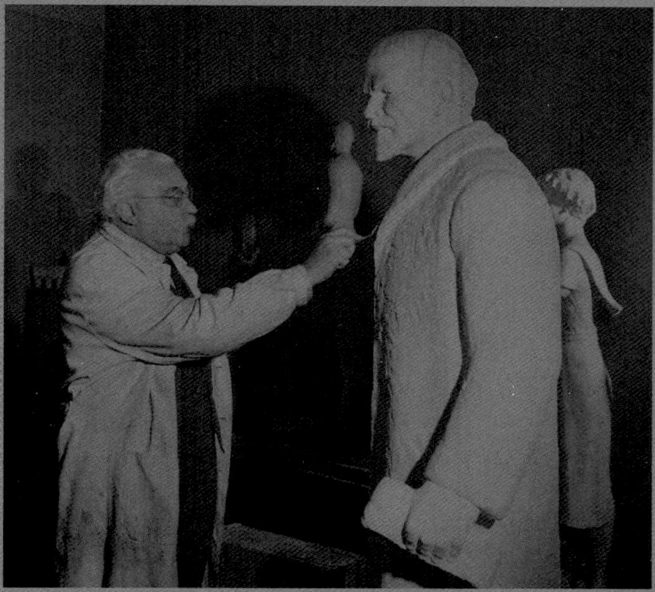

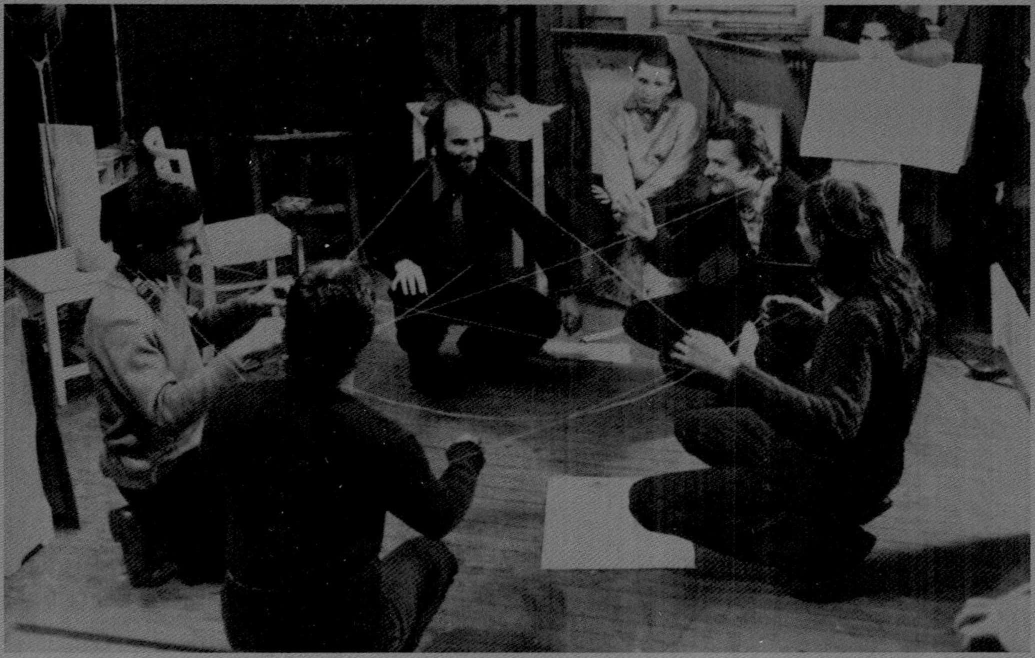

1. Jenö Benedek Sr, *What I Saw in the Soviet Union*, 1950, oil on canvas, 135 × 225 cm, Szépművészeti Múzeum – Magyar Nemzeti Galéria, Budapest

1

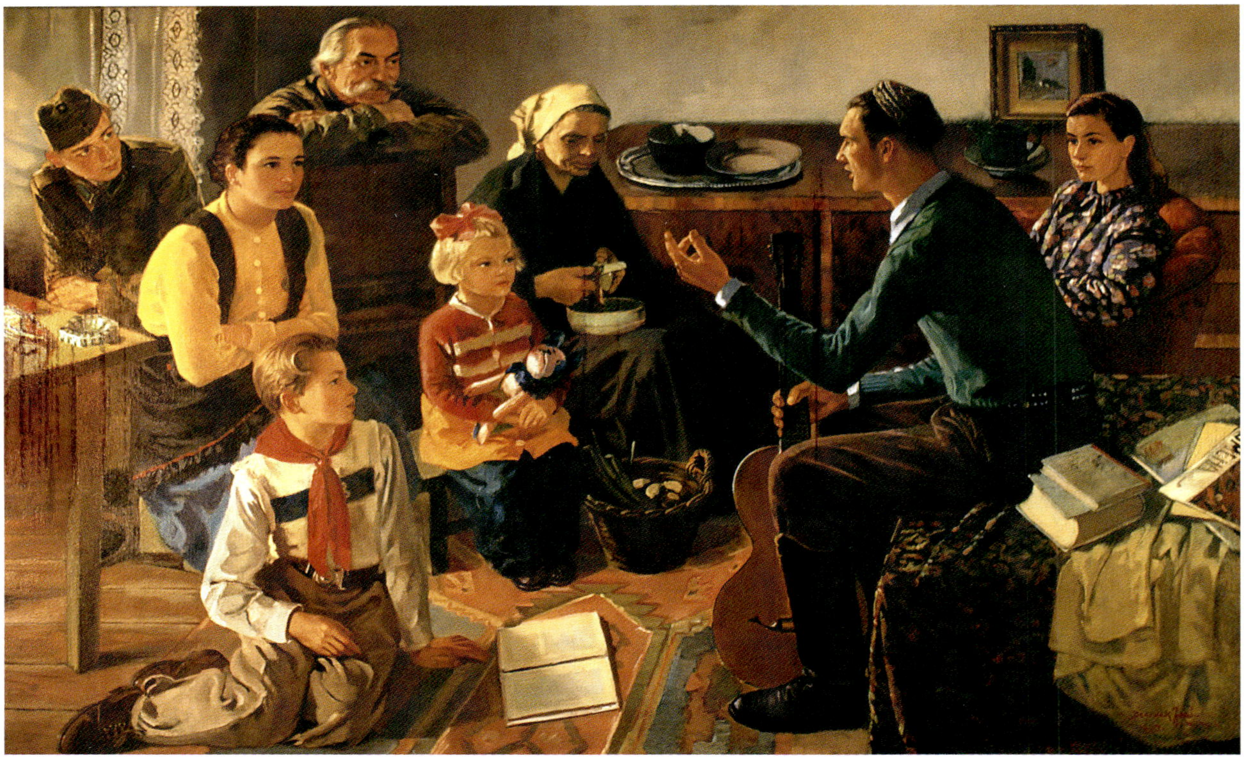

Péter György

Under Eastern Eyes

For the least glimmer of truth is conditioned by politics.
— Michel Foucault, *The History of Sexuality I*

In *Csak semmi pánik* (No Panic), a Hungarian feature film made in 1982 in the manner of Bud Spencer and Terence Hill,[1] a then well-known Hungarian actor plays a policeman reminiscent of the Spencer character. He ends a long, clumsily choreographed 'fight' scene in a trashed apartment, which quite obviously belongs to a member of the intelligentsia, by picking up a slim volume from a table, with a bemused expression on his face. The camera shows the cover in extreme close-up, and the viewer has ample time to read the title, *Művészetpolitikánk időszerű kérdései* (Current Issues in Our Politics of Art),[2] a collection of studies published by the press of the Magyar Szocialista Munkáspárt (MSZMP, Hungarian Socialist Workers' Party). He jams the book into the hand of a villain hanging from a chandelier, as if to say, 'Let him figure out where he is living.' The volume includes a piece by György Aczél, one of the key figures of Hungarian cultural politics during the regime of János Kádár (the General Secretary of the MSZMP, and therefore the country's leader, from 1956 to 1988), and the villain actually leafs through the pages of the book.

This genre movie was a bad copy of Western pop culture, and more specifically of Italian comedies.[3] As such, it could be described as a mere commodity according to the ethical and aesthetic criteria of the socialist art universe, and one that violated the fundamental principles of Marxist aesthetics and the regime's doctrine on several counts – yet film production was part of the state apparatus, so that particular scene could be seen as a moment of self-awareness by the state. The briefly glimpsed message was clear to the majority of the Hungarian audience: we all know where we are living, what is expected of us, what we expect of the authorities, and how tenuous the borderline is between us and them, between those in power and those disempowered. The Hungarian viewer was delighted to see in this film, which could be thought of as a concession to 'Western' culture, that ideological norms did not have to be taken literally when the regime itself did not do so.

One might well fear that an outsider, who reads about this belatedly in English without any internal first-hand experience of state socialism, will not obviously grasp the intimate, amiable cynicism of the scene, the jovial insolence of the actor protected partly by his popularity, the ironic gesture of the (pseudo)autonomy of the 'loyal outsider'. Yet I think it is understandable why this example is placed at the beginning of a volume that looks at cultural-political doublespeak and contemporary art in Hungary in the 1960s and 1970s. This brief episode precisely summarizes the basic issue of the book.

The studies and essays in this volume are permeated by the cultural specificity of a 'Ferry-land' – to use the poet Endre Ady's term, an initially lethally self-ironic expression, now worn into a cliché in Hungarian culture, to explain the country's predicament of floating between Eastern and Western influence.[4] The relevance of the term has survived the changing political contexts over the long term. Doublespeak is the language game of dual identity: the impossible desire to find the way

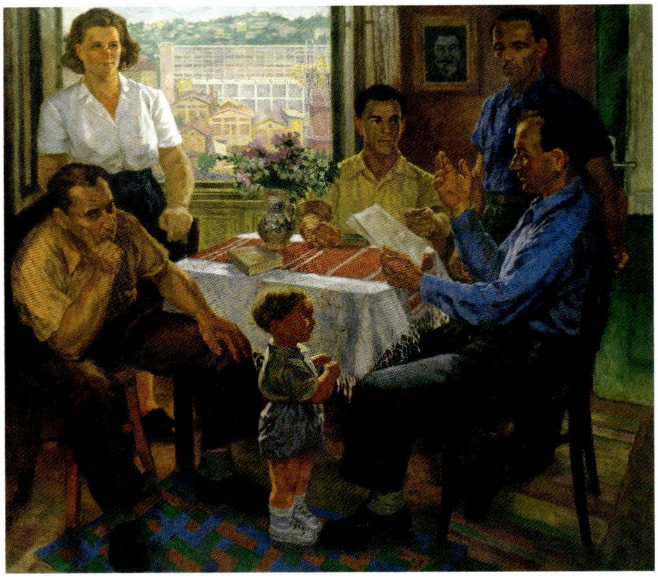

2

2. Béla Bán, *Comrade Kónyi, Stakhanovite of the Ganz Electric Factory*, 1953, oil on canvas, 160 × 180 cm, Szépművészeti Múzeum – Magyar Nemzeti Galéria, Budapest

3. Jenő Kerényi, *Ostapenko Monument*, 1951, bronze, h. 430 cm, Budapest (taken down and moved to Memento Park, Budapest)

4. Sándor Mikus, *Stalin Monument*, 1951, bronze, h. 800 cm, Budapest (demolished in 1956)

3

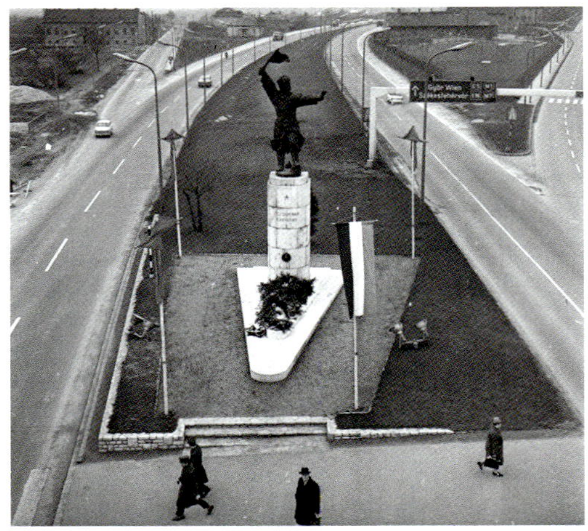

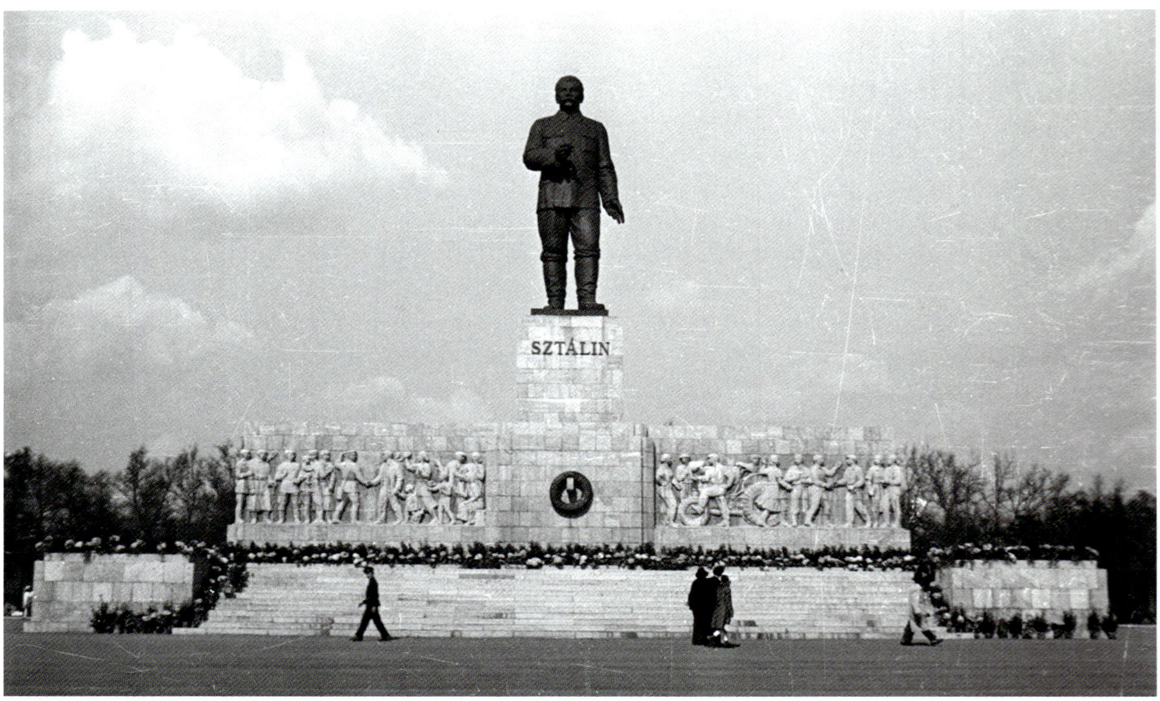

4

between a West that is alternately a source of hope and disappointment, and an East sometimes treated as a cultural resource, and sometimes despised (fig. 1).

This was the framework inherited by communist Stalinist ideology, which the apparatus had to work with, and which only became more complicated after 1945, when the East was no longer primarily a territory of a nostalgic dream of 'Hungarian identity' going back to an imaginary prehistory. The East was now the reality of the contemporary political establishment: Hungary's liberating and occupying country was the Soviet Union. In other words, the East became the name of the new chronotopos, the contemporary present and the looming future, rather than the 'heroic past'. This duality, the sudden intermingling of radical revolutionary change and the geopolitical traditions of Hungary that had been formed over time, determined the perspectives of Marxism and the ideological norms of the MSZMP employing the tradition of critical theory.[5] The fundamental and eventually insurmountable problem determining the perspectives of contemporary art and culture was the conflation and inseparability of Russian/Soviet Marxism and the Stalinist culture of the Soviet Union gaining power and influence over western territories after the Second World War.[6] The passing decades forced ideological programmes and historical developments alongside each other. What illustrates this especially well is the fact that the serious tensions generated by post-war geopolitical transformations could largely be fought out, with the exception of a few local wars, in the cultural cold war (fig. 2).

The hope of world revolution and its political programme dictated by Lenin – that there would be a direct, global social transformation – was replaced by the Stalinist model of 'socialism in one country', which was achieved through coercion. This changed in 1945; the revolution took a step westward with Stalin.[7] In a divided Europe, a geographical and social space fatally determined by cold-war geopolitics, the countries that came under the influence of the victorious Soviet Union could react to this force in various ways, depending on their histories. What happened in the area of Poland given to the Soviet Union following its division after the Molotov–Ribbentrop pact could not be overshadowed even by the horrors of German occupation. Therefore, the relationship of socialist Poland[8] to Stalinism was radically different both to that of divided Germany, determined by the reality and political myth of anti-fascism,[9] and to that of Hungary. A top-down Stalinist revolution was forced onto each country in the Soviet zone, but there are numerous differences between local interpretations, as shown by the studies of the present volume. Stalinist or post-Stalinist occupation and the radical political and cultural revolution governed from above in the spirit of Marxist eschatology were the same reality; however, researching the period without looking at the variation of local aesthetic choices – the alternative and countercultures – would be limited to a reconstruction of the broader framework.[10]

It is clearly impossible to summarize the radicalism of Stalinist revolution briefly; suffice to say that it had a new relationship to the political community at its centre. 'For millennia, man remained what he was for Aristotle: a living animal with the additional capacity for a political existence; modern man is an animal whose politics places his existence as a living being in question.'[11] Foucault's text, dating from 1976, precisely marks the fundamental schism between the worlds of liberal capitalism and socialism. The modern human being occupied with his or her own meaning, significance, role, ego and sexuality: this was the privilege of the post-war West and the basis of its global allure. In this respect, socialism was pre- or postmodern, since the basis of the anthropological and pedagogical turn was the political Self and life, that is, the Ego subordinated to the community and the future.[12] The concept of the *Novyi Chelovek* – the New Man, an ideal Soviet who was a strong, learned, selfless and disciplined adherent to the tenets of socialism, and free of all nationalist sentiment – simply did not recognize the exclusivity and telos of the culture of narcissism, the *l'art pour l'art* revolution of self-liberation (fig. 3).

Within this paradigm, a plethora of social realities appeared: complex microhistories, local variants of geopolitical aesthetic norms, varying details, habits and styles of central control with an array of differences invisible at first glance to Western eyes. Russian/

Soviet Marxism was based on a Western eschatological system of ideas, the adaptation and transfer of which followed a more long-term and therefore more complex logic than a simple following of the steps required by the Stalinist superpower in its contemporary political manoeuvres. Hungarian society and the communists in power had a hard time finding their own bearings in this constantly changing system of relations, let alone able to guide others. Marxism and the idea of leftist salvation, the world of the Soviet Union inscrutable to Hungarian eyes, were strange to the numerous layers and cultural communities within Hungarian society. The constant interpretation and ironic critique of this context were a recurrent aesthetic opportunity for those living in the milieu of the contemporary art of the day, as shown in the example above as well as in countless other references and parables in film (fig. 4).

The everyday and the sociocultural reality of Stalinism was unknown to Hungarian society, including to those on the left who believed in the idea of it. It was familiar only to those who read a few important reports and travelogues[13] and, later, to the small elite of Moscow exiles who would play a leading role in the MDP (Magyar Dolgozók Pártja, Hungarian Workers' Party). Direct 'experiences of the Soviet Union', however, often triggered radical transformations, as in the case of the writer István Örkény, an upper-middle-class Hungarian of Jewish origin who became a POW after being called up for forced labour service, turned into a communist, and wrote a diary novel, *The People of the Camps*. Similarly, Ferenc Mérei, who had studied with two pioneers of child psychology, Jean Piaget and Henri Wallon, returned home as an officer of the Red Army and a committed disciple of pedagogy. He played a crucial part in the progressive reform of Hungarian child psychology until being marginalized in 1952 in line with the Soviet reassessment of pedagogy.[14]

Leaders of the anti-Stalinist factions[15] of the Hungarian communists learned to their cost how right they had been in their critique during the interwar period. They were immediately arrested in 1945–46. (A remark in the anonymously authored blurb of the 1989 edition of Lajos Nagy's travelogue is just as applicable to them: 'In hindsight, reading the travelogue today, what is truly unbelievable for us, is that our own future was not before us in time but next to us in space.')

In other words, the Stalinist version of Western Marxism that arrived in Hungary from the East – the grand theory filled with tactical moves determined by the necessities of imperial rule – played a major part in the complete disappearance of the political structures of the Miklós Horthy regime (1920–44) and the Ference Szálasi era (1944–45), and 1945 meant a radical break on an unprecedented scale. The Hungarian political system had fallen apart by 1944, and the next year, the *Stunde Null* (Zero Hour, the end of the Second World War in Europe) threatened one part of society with the complete obliteration of the past, while the new country in the making became the promised land for others. Short-term political teleology and political-philosophical eschatology were, in fact, two sides of the same coin. It was this duality that shaped the framework of contemporary art and culture for decades to come. So, socialist realism, the art of socialism, was not simply a style, a variant of classic realism adapted to socialist themes; it was no less than the very cultural framework for the application

5

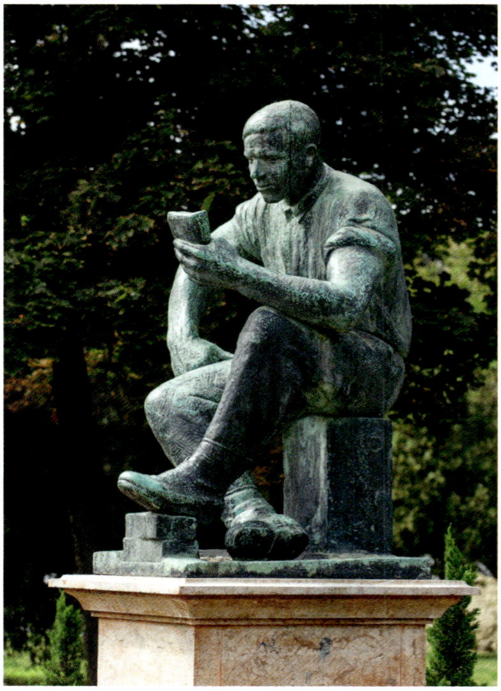

of Stalinism: a unified system of art – text, image, and space – that produced a new sensory and ideological reality everywhere, every single day (fig. 5). Accessible mass culture served as far more than entertainment: it was the representation and promise of the irreversibility and universalism of the revolutionary transformation, its pedagogical about-turn and a new era of communal existence. The hyper-intellectual shapers of socialist mass culture – stage and film directors, screenwriters and playwrights – were fully aware of this role.[16] The pettiness and therefore unavoidably comic character of the revolutionary new life, once translated into conditions in Hungary, became an inescapable given just as the regulated sizes of artworks did. So, concepts of art legitimized by political-technological apparatuses,[17] such as institutions, convictions, routines, types of knowledge, rights and sources, determined the framework for representing the new world (fig. 6).

At the same time, the model constantly represented by the Party, that of Russian/Soviet culture, became filled with heroes; the heroic and everyday life became inseparable, as life was determined by the constant presence of the Soviet mission and history, which permeated the entire space and every moment.[18] The characters of the Russian author Vassily Azhaev's novel *Far from Moscow*, including the author himself,[19] had to follow models of heroism, if not by choice, while they were building the Baikal–Amur Mainline in a re-education camp in 1937. Military characters created by Emmanuil Kazakevich[20] and Vera Panova[21] lived the same way: they felt they were at the frontline even when they had long been in the hinterland. Finally, *Life and Fate* and *Everything Flows*, Vassily Grossman's two novels critical of the Soviet regime, which have been translated into many languages, also attempt to record the total transformation of life and the need to live with irresolvable conflicts time and time again.

In Hungary, however, the apparatus for ideological rule and the political appropriation of the entire social sphere was lacking. And the real everyday life of socialism, its fragments and chaos, kept resurfacing from beneath the schemas. In a society regulated by a planned economy and a teleological eschatological order, it was not evident how fragile the regime was. This is shown clearly by how unexpected were the events of 1956, the year of the uprisings against Soviet state control in Germany, Poland and Hungary.

The Soviet new-world experience was something about which Hungarian society and its communist elite – except for a few taciturn Moscow émigrés – knew precious little. The irrevocably new world was grandiose on a scale incomprehensible to Hungarian senses, as proven by the view of the new Moscow,[22] which was a stern challenge to progressive architects who had no first-hand experience of the Soviet Union. When József Révai, the

6

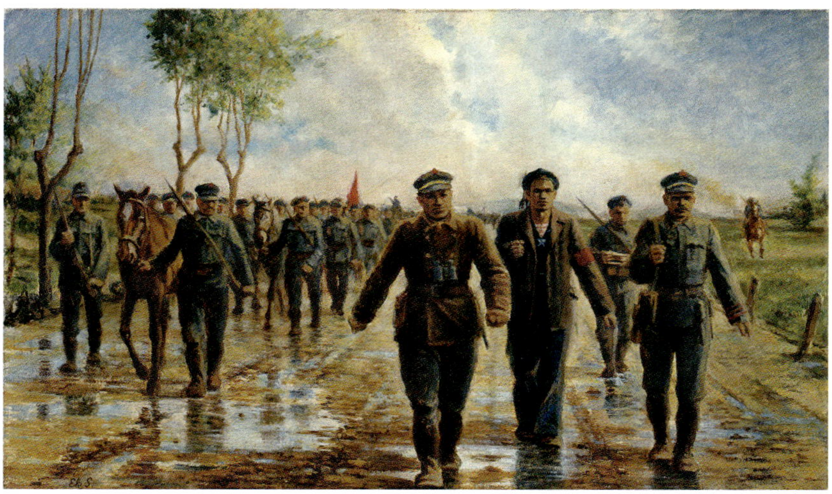

5. András Beck, *Reading Worker*, 1951, bronze, h. 150 cm, Budapest

6. Sándor Ék, *Comrade Rákosi on the Salgótarján Front in 1919*, 1951, oil on canvas, 71 × 115 cm, Szépművészeti Múzeum – Magyar Nemzeti Galéria, Budapest

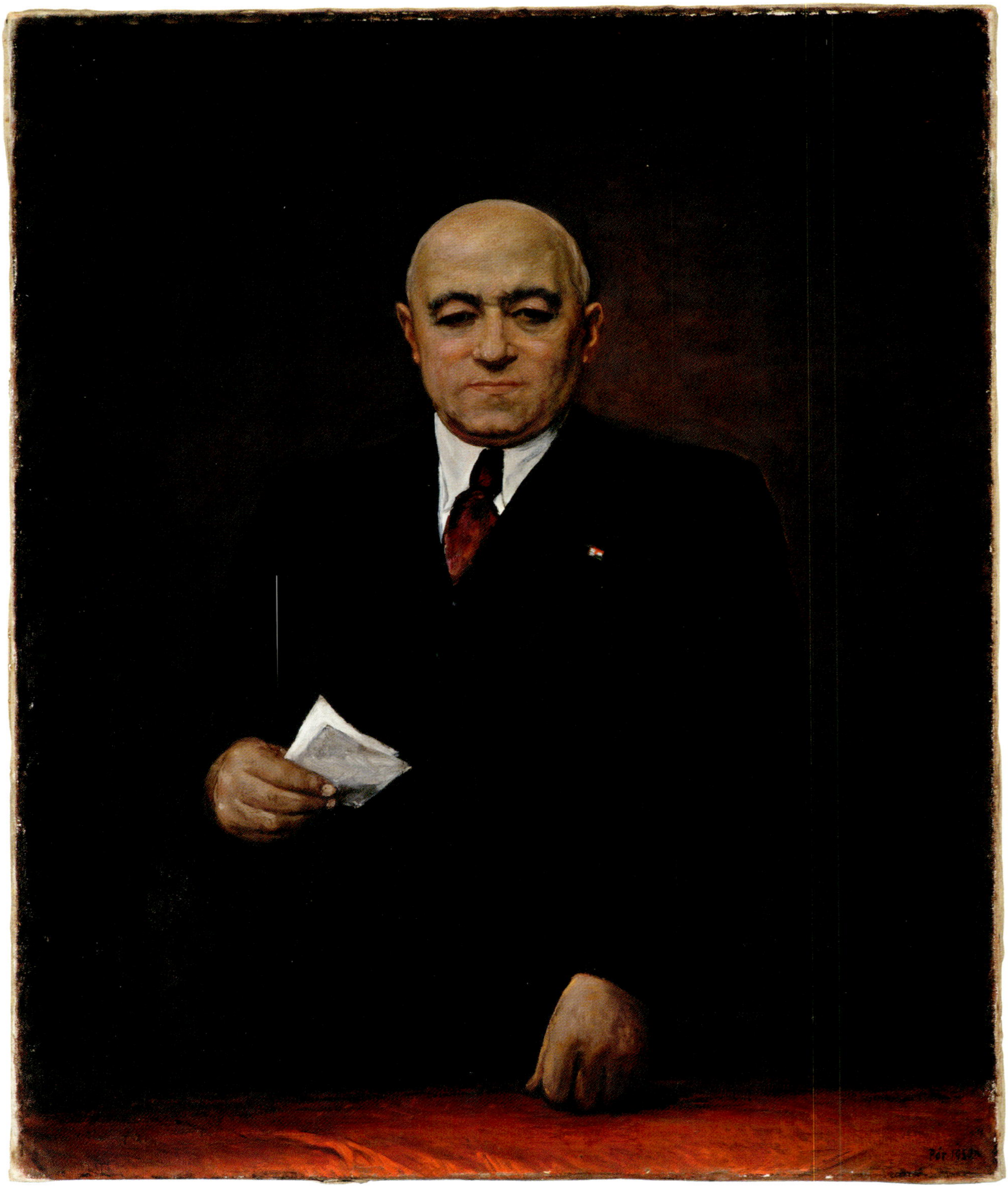

7

7. Bertalan Pór, *Mátyás Rákosi*, 1952, oil on canvas, 130 × 105.5 cm, Szépművészeti Múzeum – Magyar Nemzeti Galéria, Budapest

8. (overleaf) Aurél Bernáth, *Stalingrad Docks*, 1952, oil on canvas, 84.5 × 120 cm, Szépművészeti Múzeum – Magyar Nemzeti Galéria, Budapest

one-time avant-garde poet and excellent scholar of literary theory and history, returned to Hungary from his Moscow exile in 1950 as a communist cultural policymaker, he unambiguously declared the geopolitical consequences of the given power relations at the opening of the 'I. Magyar Képzőművészeti Kiállítás' (First Hungarian Fine Art Exhibition), which blatantly announced the new world and a new calendar in its title. From this point on Hungary would belong to the new socialist world east of the Elbe and west of Magadan in the Far East, which was to be the new context of Hungary. This was an enormous, strange space, the homelessness of which became the shared experience of the hundreds of millions who grew up in it (fig. 7).

Yet, the traditional geopolitical scale, institutions and concepts of Hungarian culture were unsuited to the internalization of socialist realism, which was playing a world historical role on the Soviet scale, so doublespeak remained an unavoidable given throughout. Consequently, it is as if Hungarian art never truly understood the reality of the grand emptiness of socialism and only saw socialist realism as coercion, and therefore only saw the limits of its possibilities.

This volume allows the reader to follow the traces of duality caused by this coercion: the basic issue is the abyss between the small scale typical of Hungarian contemporary art, and the unfamiliar grand scale synonymous with Soviet art. The presence of constraints and coercion raises problems relating to the question of domesticating the Soviet scale and mentality within Hungarian art, and to the authenticity of the cultural transfer. Apart from a few exceptions, Hungarian art of the 1950s and the 1960s–1970s did not go through a real aesthetic experience of creating the New Man: therefore, for the Hungarian artist, the position of the 'outsider' – with a cautiously suspicious and ironic approach – remained the dominant mode. The often-horrible reality of socialism and the art of socialist realism came into contact and conflict time and time again. The reality of the culture of Stalinism, in terms of the scale,[23] pedagogy[24] and eschatology that form its implacable programme,[25] was equally unknown to the groups within Hungarian society that observed the building of communism with alarm, to those who followed it with interest, and to those who engaged in it (fig. 8).

The Communist Party controlled a top-down cultural revolution built on the aesthetic paradigm of socialist realism, which was meant to permeate society as a whole to an unprecedented degree; the question was how it managed to implement this paradigm in actual social reality.[26] Socialist culture created a new framework in which the main role was no longer played by high vs low culture or market distribution, but rather a new system of aesthetic norms. It is worth mentioning that Zoltán Kodály, who was quite distant from the ideas of communism, was enormously successful in the era of state socialism not only as a composer, but also as a writer of pedagogical programmes for schools.

Hungary was confronted with a country unfathomably large, and this was traumatic in and of itself. Hungarians simply did not know the social and geographical space, the demography and sensory reality that were the bearings for the political reality that came to apply to their country. The political metaphor of 'Ferry-land' became sensory reality.

So, doublespeak was produced by the change of identity represented by political and geographical borders. The elite of the *ancien régime*, the official Hungary of the Horthy era, identified itself with the West, whatever happened. On 23 June 1941, after the German attack, Molotov called in László Kristóffy, Hungary's ambassador to Moscow, and stated that as long as Hungary remained neutral the Soviet Union would be open to a post-war renegotiation of the case of Transylvania, which Hungary had lost to Romania as a result of the Treaty of Trianon following the First World War. This was the most important and, in the end, the worst-resolved issue of the Horthy era. Despite this overture from the Soviet Union, the geopolitical identity of Hungary was firmly with the West at the time, even if the concept of the West happened to apply to a Europe conquered by Nazi Germany. Consequently, the government of Hungary entered the war against the Soviet Union: it was a mere two years before the illusion of regaining the previously lost territories, returned to Hungary by Hitler in the Vienna Accords, would evaporate. Viewed from a Hungarian perspective, the war that forged

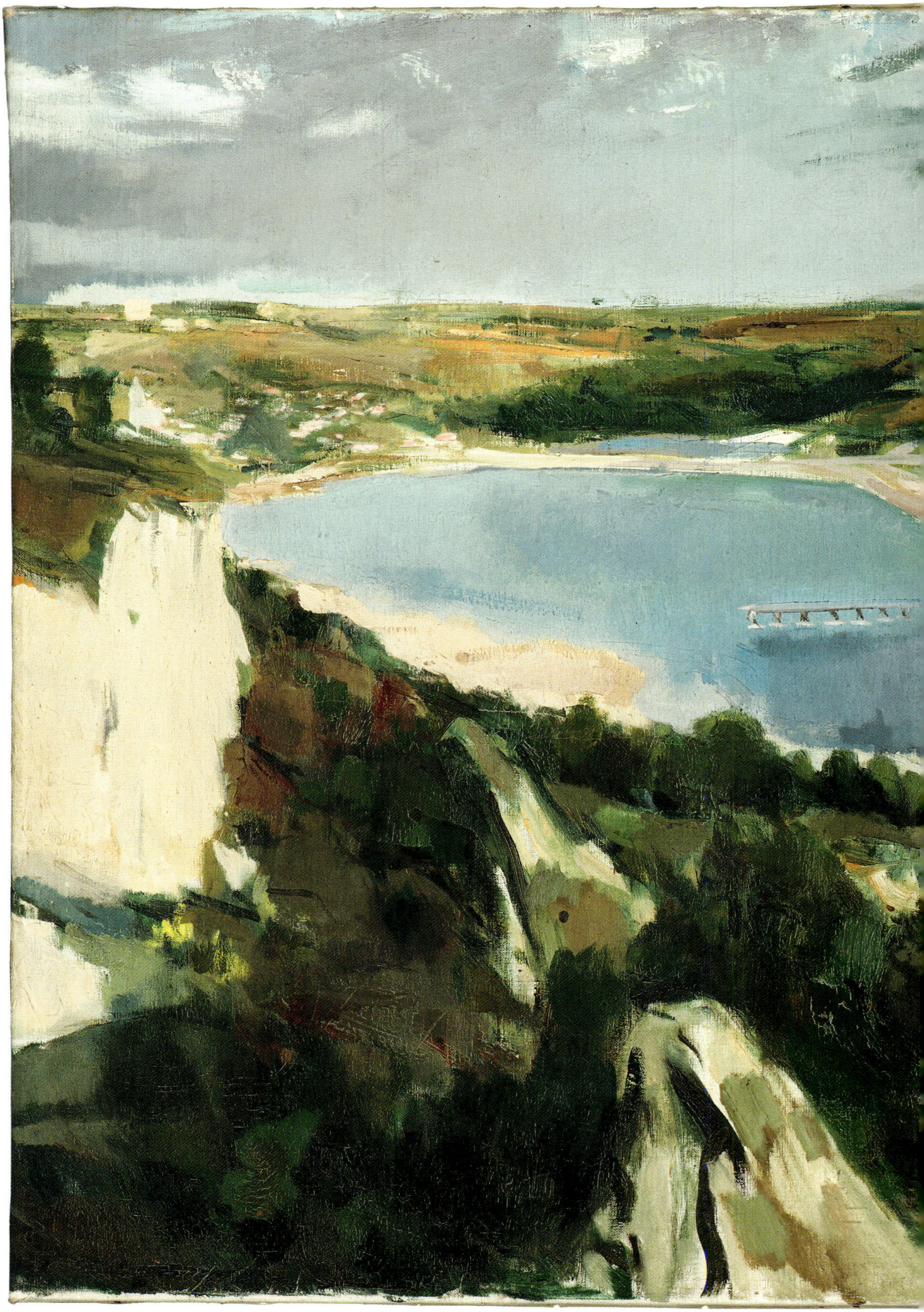

8

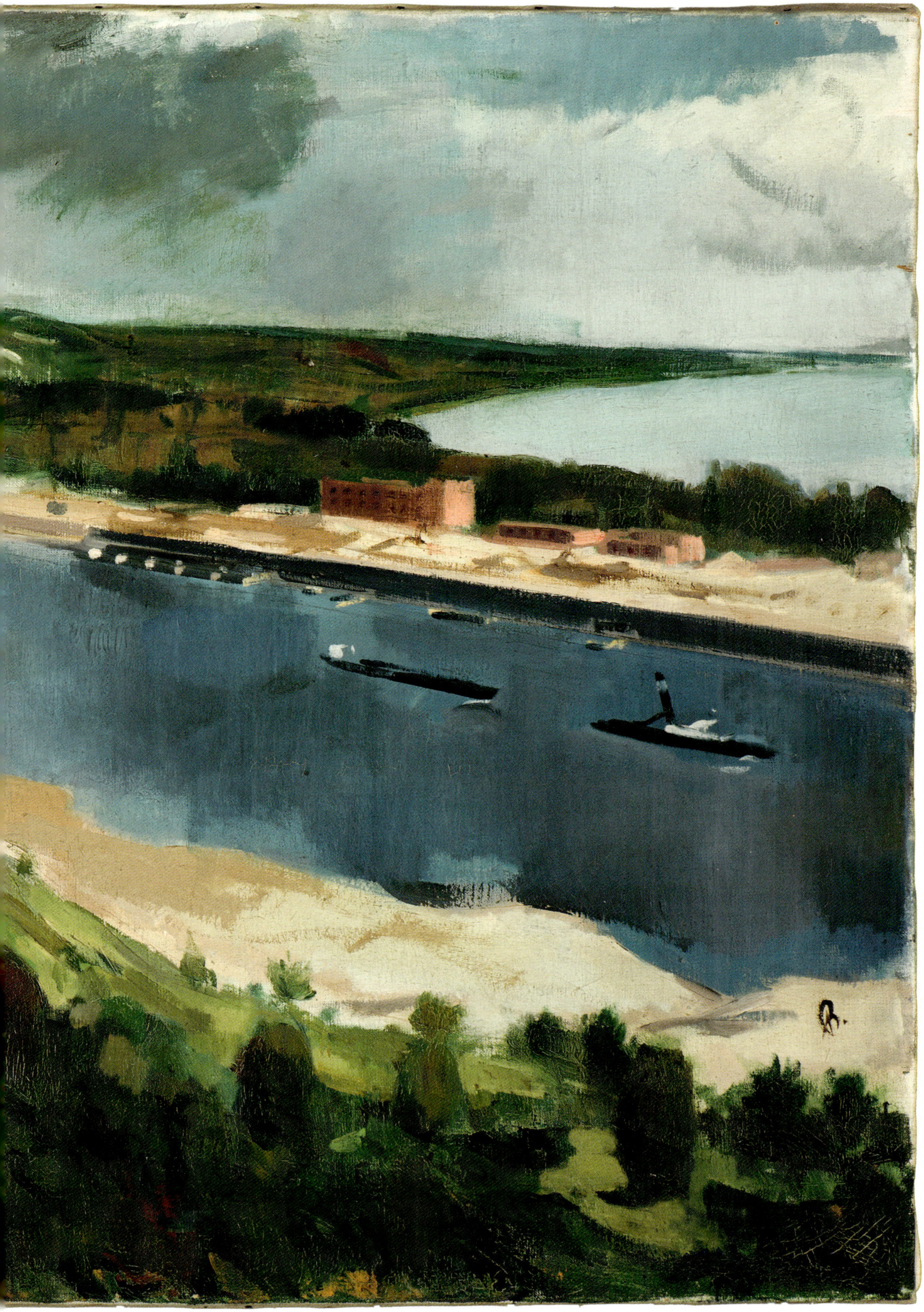

9

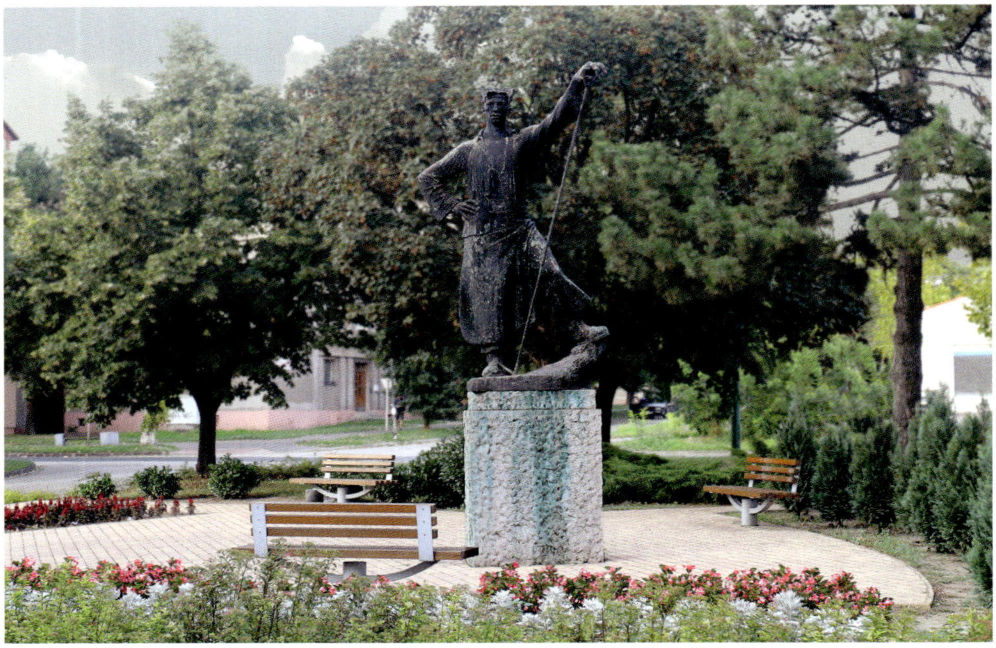

9. József Somogyi, *Smelter*, 1953, bronze, h. 168 cm, Dunaújváros

10. Endre Domanovszky, *Worker-Peasant Alliance*, 1955, fresco, 300 × 1700 cm, Dunai Vasmü (Danube Ironworks), Dunaújváros

10

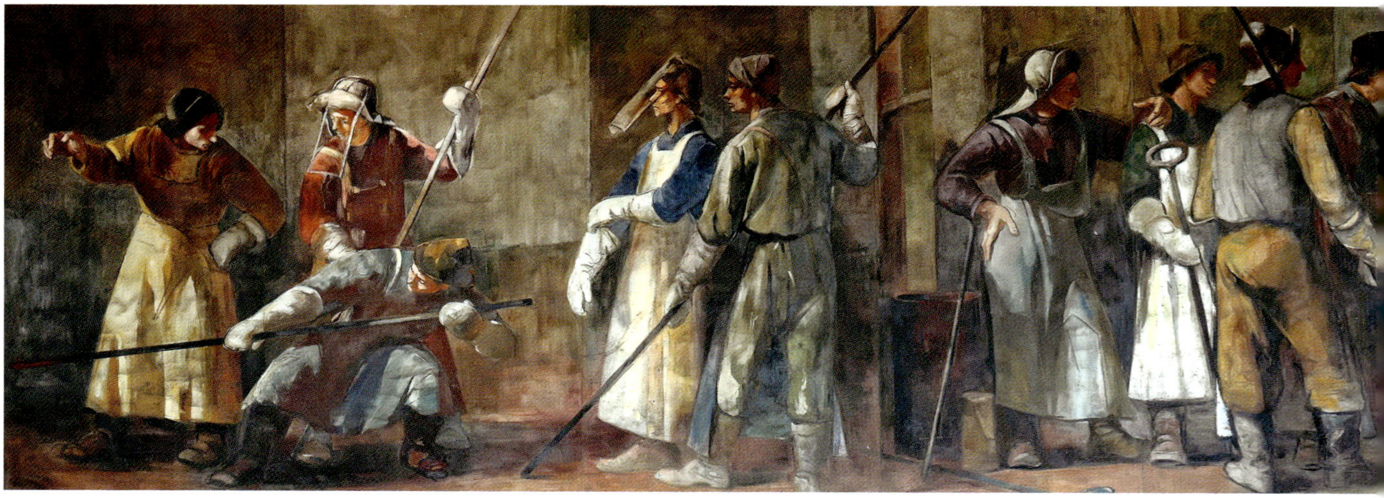

a cathartic unity in Stalin's Soviet Union brought a shameful final ruin that was thoroughly senseless, and could not be talked about after 1945 (fig. 9).

Other than to the new generation of the communist elite, both socialism and its art were a coercion, accepted by a Hungarian society that was helpless in the face of terror under Mátyás Rákosi (the de facto communist leader in 1949–56), and with its bad conscience about the destruction of the half-million Hungarian citizens labelled Jewish and transported to Auschwitz in 1944 with the active participation of the Hungarian authorities (see Daniel Véri, 'The Holocaust and the Arts', pp. 209–49). Behind Hungarian socialist realism there was nothing comparable to the self-evident shared experience of the peoples who had lived in the tsarist empire (that is, Ukrainians, Belorussians, Crimean Tatars, Chechens, Kazakhs, Georgians, Armenians and Turkmens). In fact, the Hungarian variant of socialist realism was merely a norm dictated by the MDP, which had to represent the present and the future for a society filled with silence, trauma, fear, self-loathing and disdain. The greatest aesthetic problem was the cultural transfer of Soviet heroism, pride and certainty, when those characteristics could not be adapted to suit existing Hungarian culture. The heroism, radical pedagogical overhaul and workers' pride that were fundamental to Soviet socialist realism were unknown to the aesthetic, pedagogical and artistic traditions, and institutional knowledge, that were linked to Hungarian leftist progressive movements (fig. 10).

It was not heroism, but rather a kind of minimalism – the reality and miniature utopia of safety and reliability, and the clarity and poetry of everyday life – that was at the centre of Hungarian socialist realism. Contemporary Hungarian art at the border of the figurative and the nonfigurative was dominated by deconstruction, which technically meant that smaller than life-size images dominated.

In other words, in terms of the representation of workers' pride in a truly powerful art, there were no Hungarian equivalents – in size or scale, approach or theme – to the works of Russians such as Georgy Nissky, who painted enormous industrial landscapes far beyond the limits of formal socialist realism; Dmitry Zhilinsky (*Gymnasts of the Soviet Union*, 1964–65), who can be interpreted from a pop-art perspective and represented the self-evidently proud identity of the political body in a picture 268 × 216 cm in size; or Viktor Popkov, who created a monumental painting of construction workers at the Bratsk Hydroelectric Power Station (1960). The oeuvres of Ilya Kabakov and Erik Bulatov, who operated in the grey zone at the edges of official art, or of Dmitri Prigov, Komar and Melamid, operating in the milieu of unofficial art, all took shape in opposition to and in conversation with the large scale of official Soviet art and ultimately in a comparable size. The Hungarian alternative pedagogy of art,

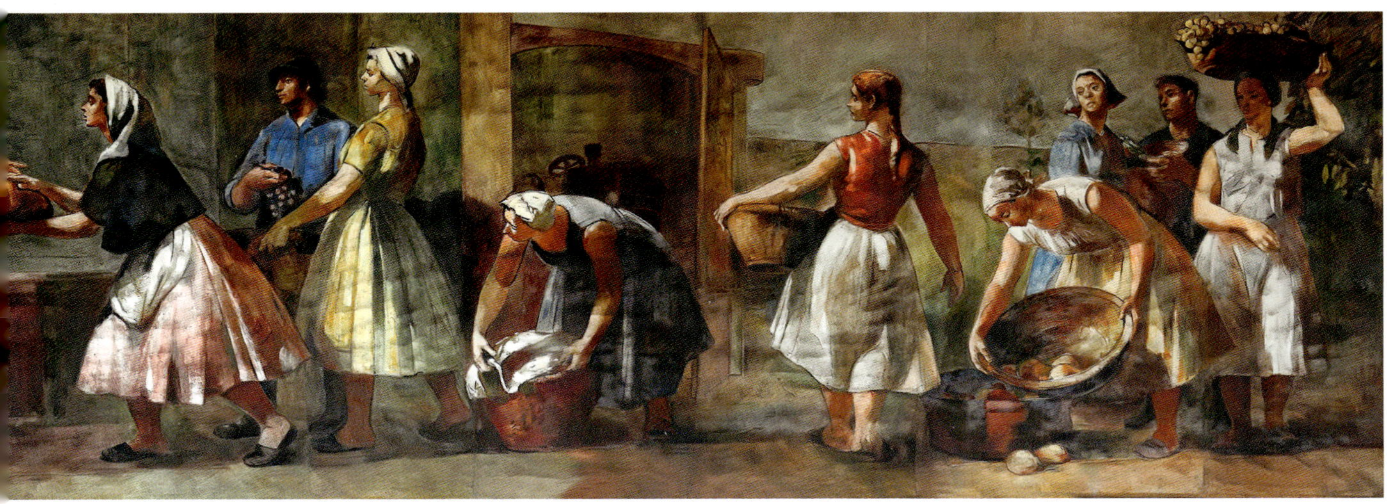

11

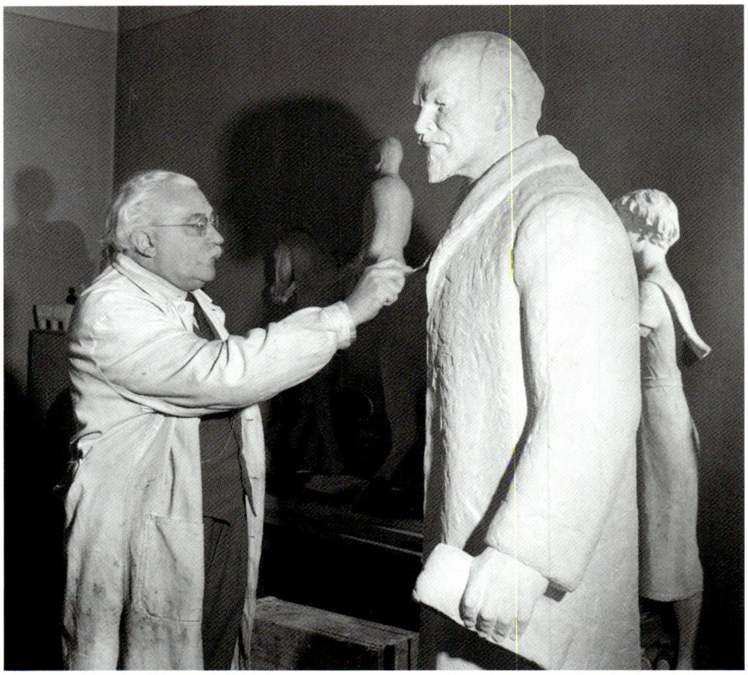

12

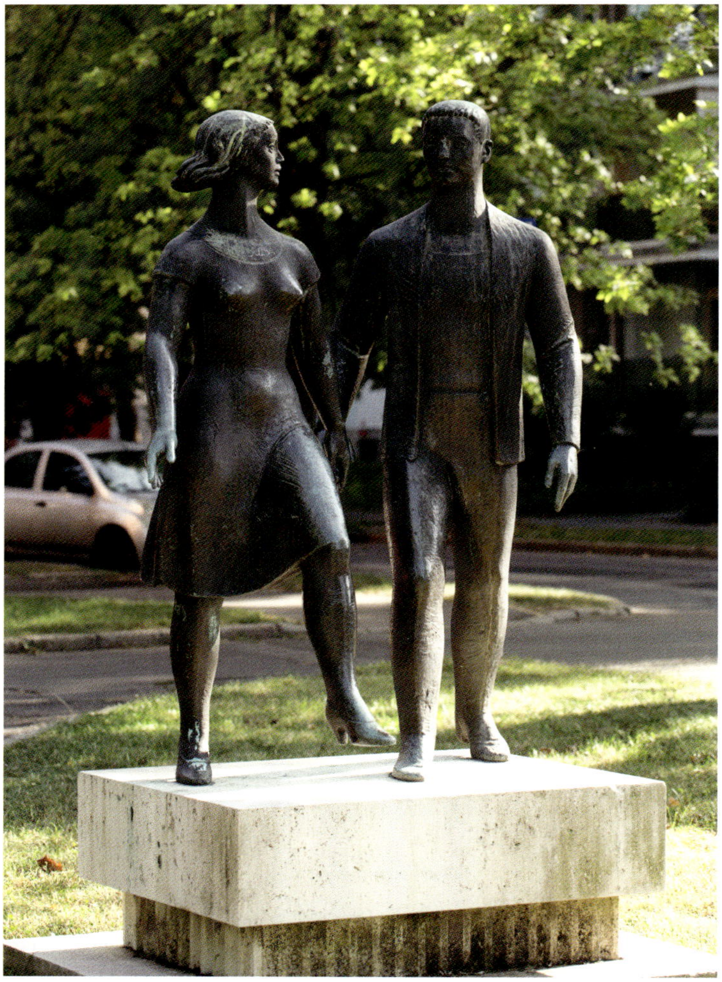

11. Pál Pátzay in his studio with the model of his Lenin statue, 1964, Budapest

12. Sándor Mikus, *Youth*, 1965, bronze, h. 170 cm, Miskolc

13. Endre Domanovszky, *Dispute*, 1968, gobelin, 300 × 1500 cm, Miskolci Egyetem, Miskolc

which is an exceptionally important milieu of contemporary art and counterculture, had conceptual media art at its centre, an approach and programme far from direct political art. Constructive pedagogy, one of the still authoritative and stellar intellectual achievements of the Hungarian neo-avant-garde, put individual creativity at its centre, and even if the narrow neo-avant-garde community was a cooperative milieu, its programme was certainly no political reality. The size, or more precisely the smallness, of the neo-avant-garde scene determined the social existence and meaning of this community. The neo-avant-garde milieu and network, like any culture, had to fulfil a complex system of conditions; they had to reflect simultaneously on their position in the hierarchy and on the internal public sphere of the subculture, and the two were, of course, inseparable.[27]

Neo-avant-garde film and photographic art were suited to this metapolitical, individual, self-fulfilling pedagogy with their practice of medial self-reflection at the margins of which political issues faded in and out of view. The feeling of liberation and tragic self-knowledge, the body abandoned both in its suffering and pleasure, is displayed time and time again as personality torn into shreds and imprints of an inexpressible life without a story. It is the victims of a society that fell apart before it was built who appear in the frames of the films *Self-Fashion Show*, made in 1976 by Tibor Hajas, and Tamás Szentjóby's *Centaur*, made a year earlier (see Katalin Székely, 'The Influx of Images', pp. 331–55).

By the 1960s and 1970s, the direct political counterculture and art which aimed to create alternative community strategies became or remained peripheral. Meanwhile, socialist realism or the art of socialism – and then finally the ideology-free thesis of art in socialism – became the dominant experiences. The 1950s were suffused with the fear or hope of turning ideological rule into an aesthetic canon, but the Hungarian uprising in 1956 instantly showed that the doctrine of collective art had become formal and empty. The switching of geopolitical sides and maintenance of a pseudo-Western orientation in this small, humble territory of the enormous post-Stalinist Soviet bloc – namely the desire to become 'the happiest barrack in the socialist camp', as it was known – seemed to provide hope of a suitable political compromise (fig. 11).

Consequently, the cultural paradigm of state socialism was valid to varying degrees east of the Oder–Neisse border. The 'Western' orientation of Hungarian society merely entailed the cautious criticism and silent, if unmistakeable, ignoring of the collectivist ideology of state socialism; the contemporary neo-avant-garde never moved beyond the programme of modern narcissism so clearly seen by Foucault.[28]

13

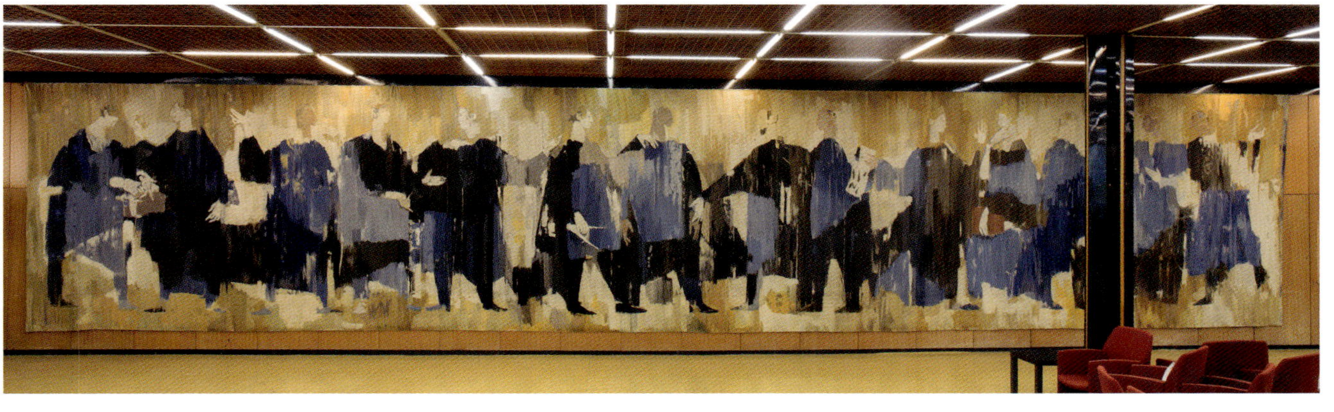

Doublespeak posited, or alternately ignored, geopolitical aesthetic norms, so it worked in different ways in individual countries: it meant something completely different in the Soviet Union, in the German Democratic Republic, and in Hungary for that matter. At the same time, there were two unstated rules, paradigms understandable as tacit knowledge and a shared tradition, that survived right until 1989, irrespective of the local dialect and forms of emptiness (fig. 12).

One was the identity of state socialism and the anthropology of the New Man, and the other was the concealment and annulment of the orders of historicity, of the longer, non-Soviet history of a region, through political norms. Subsequently both tacit, consensual rules lost their aesthetic background, their validity reflected by contemporary art. The doctrine of the art of socialism had become empty around 1985, at a time when the regime still had years ahead. This was the real Hungarian characteristic: the regime that survived itself gave an opportunity to establish new contractual relations between apparatuses and concepts, institutions and works (fig. 13).

Artists could gradually put aside the questions and frameworks that had been posed by state socialism and then left unanswered; it seemed that the last years of the regime were dominated by a subtle chaos in the wake of politics by direct order and its illusion of freedom. One of the most characteristic Western cultural transfers of the final years of the regime was the adoption of *Neue Wilde*, the New Sensibility, the carefree infantilism of neo-expressionism.[29] The group organized by the outstanding, highly talented art historian Lóránd Hegyi, impeccably meeting all norms of curatorial behaviour, had exhibitions that were organized in increasingly important state galleries and museums, the institutions of a regime that has lost its ideological convictions. This practically moved the artists of the New Sensibility out of the social space that existed, if in its ruins and emptiness, until a number of chance events and peculiar confluences made the civilization of state socialism disappear in 1989, just as the border of the distinct territory that maintained it. Painter Ákos Birkás's words in 1980 offer a very precise diagnosis of how the last contemporary movement of the regime ended: 'The point, however, is that the representative Hungarian art did not emerge as avant-garde art, but rather a new variant of traditionally marketable Hungarian kitsch. The most celebrated genre will be the disco version of operetta.'[30] Indeed.

For by this time it was quite clear – in terms of Ferry-land – that the market was now west of Hungary. East of Hungary, it seemed, there was once again nothing.

Note on essay title: One may recall here Joseph Conrad's wonderful novel *Under Western Eyes* (1911) for more than a pun. Written in English by a Slavic author who knew tsarist Russia quite well and moved to the West, and having a relationship to the work of Dostoyevsky, the novel still feels current. The relationship between the allegorical figure of the secret agent and doublespeak would merit a study of its own.

1 Screenplay by István Bujtor, directed by Sándor G. Szőnyi, starring István Bujtor. http://videa.hu/videok/film-animacio/csak-semmi-panik-teljes-film-akcio-bujtor-csopi-ICNBSaTiUE8JqDwh (15 March 2017). Bud Spencer and Terence Hill, despite their pseudonyms, were an Italian acting duo who became famous worldwide, particularly for their Spaghetti Westerns.
2 Péter Agárdi (ed.), *Művészetpolitikánk időszerű kérdései* [The Current Questions of Our Cultural Policy]. Budapest: Kossuth Kiadó, 1977.
3 Instead of offering a possible interpretation of the various Spencer and Hill films, the Hungarian version mostly adopted the choreographed fistfights and the two-detective premise; it could be understood both as an empty parody and as a touristic film of the beaches of Lake Balaton in Hungary, which did not detract from its popularity. This shows the depth of the cultural transfer and its broad and complex system of relations I mention in this essay. Various other aspects of this are analysed in several studies later in this volume.
4 Endre Ady, *Ismeretlen Korvin-kódex margójára, Sírás és panaszkodás* [On the Margins of an Unknown Corvin Codex; Crying and Lamentation], 1905.
5 See, for instance, the reception of Georg Lukács in Hungary or the case of his contemporary political assessment. After 1989, in spite of the largely extant Budapest School consisting of Lukács disciples and the Lukács Archive operating as part of the Hungarian Academy of Sciences, Lukács simply dropped out of contemporary intellectual fashion, and his interpretation is sadly impoverished in Hungary, which is at least partly incomprehensible in retrospect.
6 Stephen Kotkin, *Magnetic Mountain, Stalinism as a Civilization*. Berkeley: University of California Press, 1995; Jochen Hellbeck, *Revolution on My Mind, Writing Under Stalin*. Cambridge: Harvard University Press, 2006; Evgeny Dobrenko and Eric Naiman (eds), *The Landscape of Stalinism: The Art and Ideology of Soviet Space*. Seattle: University of Washington Press, 2003. For the reception of Kotkin's book, see Igal Halfin and Jochen Hellbeck, 'Rethinking the Stalinist Subject: Stephen Kotkin's Magnetic Mountain and the State of Soviet Historical Studies', *Jahrbücher für Geschichte Osteuropas*, Vol. 44, No. 3, 1996, 456–63.
7 Richard C. Raack, *Stalin's drive to the West 1938–1945: The Origins of the Cold War*. Stanford: Stanford University Press, 1995; Vojtech Mastny, *The Cold War and Soviet Insecurity, The Stalin Years*. New York: Oxford University Press, 1996.
8 Cf. Jan T. Gross, *Revolution from Abroad: The Soviet Conquest of Poland, Western Ukraine and Western Belorussia*. Expanded edition, with a new preface of the author. Princeton: Princeton University Press, 2002.
9 Cf. Gareth Pritchard, *Making of the GDR, 1945–1953*. Manchester: Manchester University Press, 2004.
10 Cf. Piotr Piotrowski, 'How to Write a History of Central-east European Art', *Third Text*, Vol. 23. No. 1, 2009, 5–14; Piotr Piotrowski, *In the Shadow of Yalta: Art and Avant-garde in Eastern Europe, 1945–1989*. London: Reaktion Books, 2009; Piotr Piotrowski, 'The Global NETwork: An Approach to Comparative Art History', in Thomas DaCosta Kaufmann, Catherine Dossin and Béatrice Joyeux Prunel (eds), *Circulations in the Global Art History of Art*. Burlington: Ashgate, 2015.
11 Michel Foucault, *The History of Sexuality: An Introduction*, trans. Robert Hurley. New York and London: Knopf/Doubleday, [1976] 2012, 143.
12 Vasily Grossman, *Life and Fate*, trans. Robert Chandler. New York: New York Review Books Classics, 2006.

13 Lajos Nagy, *Tízezer kilométer Szovjetoroszország földjén* [Ten Thousand Kilometers in the Land of the Soviet Russia] appeared serially in the weekly *Szabadság* in 1934, and was collected in a volume as late as 1989. Gyula Illyés's *Oroszország* [Russia] was published by the journal *Nyugat* in 1934, then republished numerous times after 1945. André Gide, whose *Retour de l'URSS* was published in 1936, was excommunicated by Western Marxists; Tibor Déry translated it into Hungarian, for which he was charged with communist propaganda and sentenced to several months in prison, so clearly neither the prosecutor nor the judge opened the anti-communist travel diary. Yet the protagonist of Déry's *chef-d'oeuvre, The Unfinished Sentence* (unpublished until 1945), is a working-class woman who leaves for, or rather flees to, the Soviet Union at the end of the novel: to the land of salvation and promise. Tibor Déry: *Befejezetlen mondat* [Unfinished Sentence]. Budapest: Szépirodalmi Könyvkiadó, 1980. On Déry and communist aesthetics, see Dávid Szolláth, *A kommunista aszkétizmus esztétikája* [The Aesthetic of Communist Asceticism]. Budapest: Balassi Kiadó, 2011.

14 Zsolt K. Horváth, 'Egy munkaszolgálatos fényképre' [On a Photo from Forced Labour Service], *Beszélő*, 24 May 2014. http://beszelo.c3.hu/online a cikk/egy-munkaszolgalatos-fenykepre (17 March 2017); Zsolt K. Horváth, 'A demokrácia pedagógiai megalapozásának kisérlete 1945-ben. Mérei Ferenc: Gyermeklélektani tanulmány' [An Attempt to Create a Pedagogical Basis for Democracy in 1945: Ferenc Mérei's Study on Child Psychology], in Balázs Böcskei and Miklós Sebők (eds), *50 könyv, amit minden baloldalinak ismernie kell* [50 Books that Every Leftist Must Know]. Budapest: Kossuth Kiadó, 2015. http://www.demokratikusneveles.hu/index.php/19-demokratikus-neveles/366-k-horvath-zsolt-merei-ferenc-a-gyermek-vilagnezete (17 March 2017).

15 It was in 1924 that the influential faction of Pál Demény (1901–1991), which had a large membership although its role was restricted in the Horthy era, deviated from the illegal Kommunisták Magyarországi Pártja (KMP, Party of Communists in Hungary) controlled from Moscow. Demény was arrested in 1938 and released in 1940. On 13 February 1945 he was once again arrested on Mátyás Rákosi's orders, and he was released on 13 October 1956, a few days before the revolution. He became a Member of Parliament for the Magyar Szocialista Párt (Hungarian Socialist Party) after 1989. Aladár Weisshaus (1887–1963) participated in the organization of the illegal KMP with Rákosi, was in prison in 1924–25, then expelled from the party, and estabished his own faction. He was arrested in 1946 and was released in 1956. Before his death, he requested membership in the MSZMP, but the state party refused him.

16 Zoltán Várkonyi was an emblematic figure of the creation of a legitimized mass culture. Rector of the Szinház- és Filmművészeti Föiskola (Theatre and Film Academy), he was a master of popular films and successful theatre productions. He was a true 'engineer of consciousness', and remained a communist out of conviction to his death. See Magdolna Jákfalvi (ed.), *Várkonyi 100, Tanulmányok Várkonyi Zoltánról* [Várkonyi 100, Studies on Zoltán Várkonyi]. Budapest: Balassi Kiadó/Szinház és Filmművészeti Egyetem, 2013. The significance of the socialist entertainment industry can be measured by figures such as these: *Majd a papa* [Papa Takes Care of It], a musical play by István Kállai and Szabolcs Fényes featuring comic scenes in the life of a working-class intellectual, was performed 751 times in 1958 and it was seen by 326,823 people all over Hungary.

17 Michel Foucault, 'The Confession of the Flesh', in Colin Gordon (ed.), *Power/Knowledge*. New York: Pantheon Books, 1980, 194–228; Giorgio Agamben, *What is an Apparatus? And Other Essays*, trans. David Kishnik and Stefan Pedatella. Stanford: Stanford University Press, 2009.

18 See this in such masterpieces of the time as Oleg Pavlov, *Captain of the Steppe, And Other Stories*, 2013. I am afraid the work and life of the members of the Pussy Riot group is also a dismally good example of the self-evident tradition of the necessarily heroic life in Russia.

19 Azhaev was arrested in 1935 and was released early from the Gulag in 1937 for good behavior and could remain in the Zone. His novel *Daleko ot Moskvy*, which was based on his own experiences, appeared in 1948 and was awarded the Stalin Prize in 1949. See Thomas Lahusen, *How Life Writes the Book: The Real Socialism and Socialist Realism in Stalin's Russia*. Ithaca: Cornell University Press, 1997.

20 *Tavasz az Oderán*. Budapest: Új Magyar Könyvkiadó, 1951 [*Spring on the Oder: A novel in three parts*, Foreign Languages Publishing House, 1953]; *Csillag, Két ember a sztyeppén*. Budapest: Zrinyi Katonai Kiadó, 1963 [*Star: A Story*, Foreign Languages Publishing House, 1952].

21 Vera Panova, *Fehér vonat* [White Train]. Budapest: Új Magyar Könyvkiadó, 1949.

22 Katerina Clark, 'Socialist Realism and the Sacralising of Space', in Evgeny Dobrenko and Erik Naiman (eds), *The Landscape of Stalinism, the Art and Ideology of Soviet Space*. Seattle: University of Washington Press, 2003, 3–19.

23 Rachel Wells, *Scale in Contemporary Sculpture, Enlargement, Miniaturization and Life-Size*. Aldershot: Ashgate, 2013.

24 V. I. Malinin, 'Makarenko and Stalinisim', *Russian Education and Society*, Vol. 36, No. 8, 1994, 61–75; Peter Fritzsche and Jochen Hellbeck, 'The New Man in Stalinist Russia and in Nazi Germany', in Michael Geyer and Sheila Fitzpatrick (eds), *Beyond Totalitarianism: Stalinism and Nazism compared*. New York: Cambridge University Press, 2009, 302–24; Anton Makarenko, *Az új ember kovácsa – Pedagógiai hőskölteméný* [Pedagogical Poem], I–II. Budapest: Új Magyar Könyvkiadó, 1947; Ferenc Mérei, 'Makarenko hőskölteményéről' [On Makarenko's Pedagogical Poem], *Társadalmi Szemle*, no. 11, 1947, 828–38; Ferenc Mérei, 'Utópia és valóság a magyar nevelésben' [Utopia and Reality in Hungarian Education], *Embernevelés*, No. 2, 1949, 48–73.

25 Igal Halfin, *From Darkness to Light: Class, Consciousness and Salvation in Revolutionary Russia*. Pittsburgh: University of Pittsburgh Press, 2000.

26 Cf. Evgeny Dobrenko, *Political Economy of Socialist Realism*. New Haven and London: Yale University Press, 2007.

27 Michel Foucault, *The Hermeneutics of the Subject: Lectures at the Collége de France 1981–1982*. London: Palgrave Macmillan, 2005, 179.

28 The relationships between the artists and critics of the era mirror each other. The articulation of the same experience was recorded in a film made in 1986, in the immediate semi-past, in which progressive art historians committed to the neo-avant-garde attempt at objective self (interpretation). Outstanding intellects jointly expressed their guilty conscience and dissatisfaction on assessing the sum of the alternative art they had also supported. The conversation, which appeared in a volume in 2016 and has now become a documentary source, precisely records the cost of not having political self-consciousness: the independence of the regime also generated a distance from politics, which led to that emptiness of medial self-reflection they also mention in the conversation. Cf: Dóra Maurer and László Beke, *Látlelet és prognózis: Új magyar művészet a hatvanas hetvenes években* [Diagnosis and Prognosis: New Hungarian Art in the Sixties and Seventies]. Budapest: SUMUS, 2017.

29 See the 'Új szenzibilitás' [New Sensibility] exhibitions organized by Lóránd Hegyi (Fészek Galéria, 1981, Óbudai Pincegaléria, 1983, Budapest Galéria, 1985, Pécsi Galéria, 1987). See also 'Frissen festve' [Freshly Painted], 1984, Ernst Múzeum, 'Eklektika' [Eclectics], Magyar Nemzeti Galéria, 1986.

30 In Maurer and Beke, *Látlelet és prognózis*, 101. For the best summary of Hegyi's theoretical work, see *Élmény és fikció. Modernizmus – avantgárd – transzavantgárd* [Experience and Fiction. Modernism – Avant-garde – Transavant-garde]. Pécs: Jelenkor, 1991.

1. Lajos Kassák, International network of the journal *MA* (Today) on the back cover of its 15 October 1922 issue, print, 31 × 31 cm, Petőfi Irodalmi Múzeum – Kassák Múzeum, Budapest

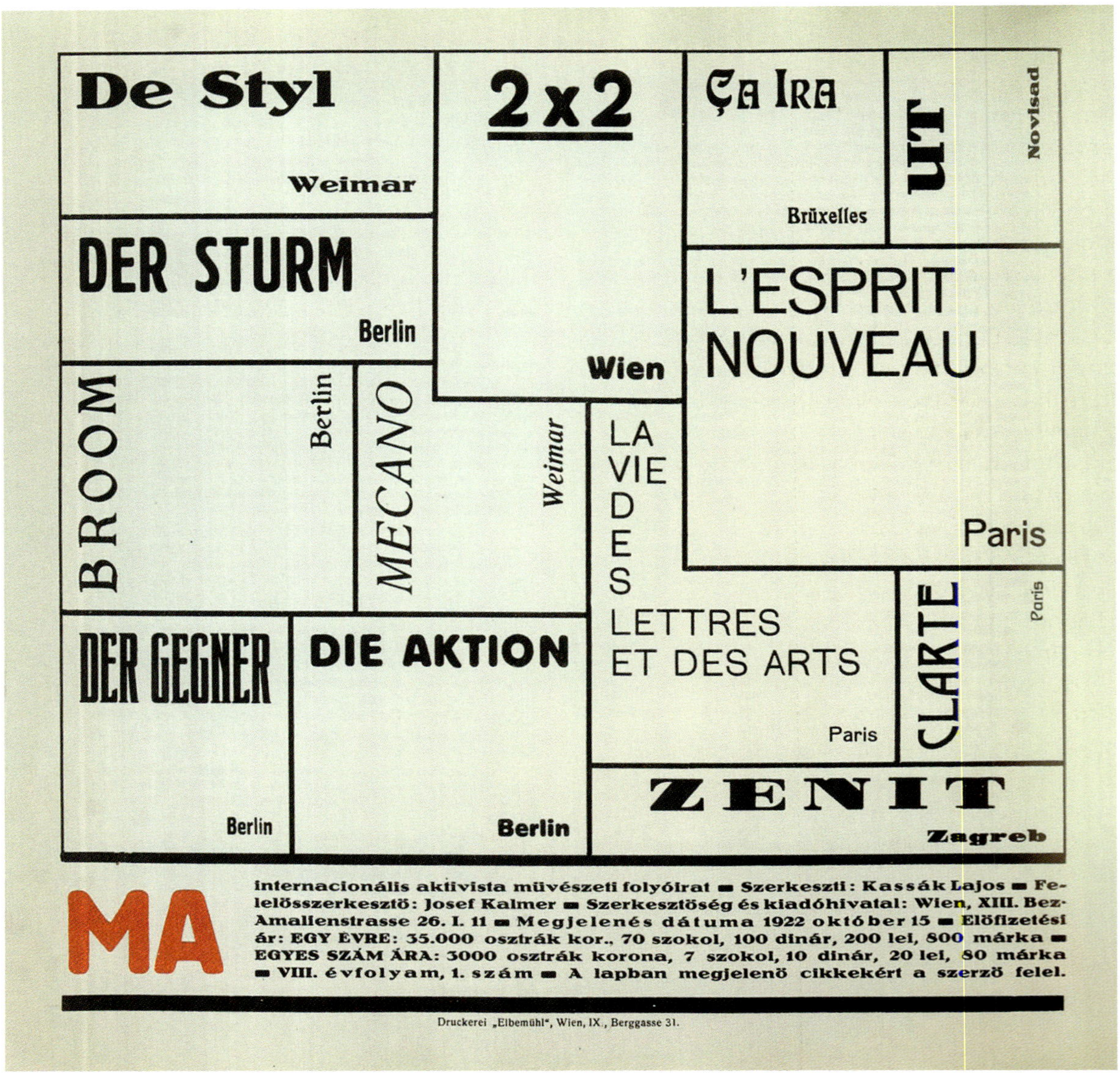

1

Gábor Dobó and Merse Pál Szeredi

Hungarian Culture +/- Europe

Positions and Self-images of Avant-garde and Modernist Movements in Hungary, 1915–68

Discontinuity, the roles of intellectuals, 'Europe' and the Hungarian avant-garde

This book proves that twentieth-century Hungarian art has multiple histories and parallel or intersecting paths. There is no single master narrative that can tell the story of the twentieth-century East-Central European avant-garde and modernism and, more specifically, the story of the avant-garde and modernism in Hungary.[1] The same applies to East-Central European cultural and political relations more generally. The possible roles and careers of intellectuals, and their sense of culture, have no discernible characteristics that are uniquely East-Central European or Hungarian while remaining valid for the period as a whole.[2] Should one insist on some generalizable observation about twentieth-century Hungarian culture, it would be about discontinuity, by which we mean both a lack of continuity and the breaking up of relationships. Relations between twentieth-century Hungarian avant-garde and modernist trends and the Hungarian cultural environment are arguably discontinuous, as avant-garde artists' relationship with the Hungarian public was interrupted time and time again by censorship, political persecution and restrictions placed upon the public sphere. Consequently, avant-garde ideas and radical political and artistic programmes were not sustained in contemporary cultural discourse and, in contrast to Western European art history, had a small, limited or extremely belated effect on later art movements. Discontinuity also characterizes twentieth-century Hungarian culture, and specifically the avant-garde trends, in yet another way: the 'project' of Hungarian culture was to attempt to bridge the (assumed) abyss between itself and the whole of Europe.

Avant-garde and intellectual careers in Hungary in the twentieth century

Due to the existence of a restricted public sphere and an institutionalized cultural life closed to radical artistic and political initiatives, early avant-garde movements died out in Hungary by the late 1920s, which is not a phenomenon unique to that country. The careers of Hungarian cultural actors with ties to the avant-garde traversed the various regimes of the 1910s to the 1960s, but tended to ascend only after the conclusion of their avant-garde period. A number of the artists, including Pál Pátzay and Sándor Bortnyik, who were important figures in the historical avant-garde and modernism became beneficiaries and even shapers of post-war Stalinism. Others had important roles in the cultural politics of the 1950s, such as József Révai, who used to publish avant-garde poetry as a teenager in Lajos Kassák's circle in the 1910s, and belonged to the highest echelons of Party leadership after the post-war advent of Stalinism in Hungary. By contrast, there were artists whose behaviour was more consistent: working from the time of the historical avant-garde to the 1960s, they maintained a connection to the avant-garde, and did not accept a role in cultural politics after the rise of Stalinism. Of the latter type, it was undoubtedly Kassák who had the greatest influence, being considered a 'master' by generation after generation, even though his oeuvre was never part of the cultural mainstream.

The twentieth-century history of the Hungarian avant-garde and modernism can be considered discontinuous when compared to similar movements in other countries. Compared to Hungary, the figures of the historical avant-garde and modernism, and the lessons of those movements, were integrated more organically into the cultural traditions of France, the East-Central European and Balkan regions, and later into the cultural politics of the newly established post-war states.[3]

The avant-garde manifestoes as programmes of discontinuity

The self-image of Hungarian avant-garde and modernist movements was based on discontinuity in the first place. The movements tended to announce themselves to the public with a founding proclamation, through a journal or other publication, that would become the central institution of the movement, or with some other demonstrative, collective appearance (for instance, an exhibition). Their founding or programmatic texts often distanced them from the 'past' and earlier trends of art, but their self-interpretation also positioned them as part of a discontinuous story.[4]

Participants and historians often describe, in retrospect, the history of the twentieth-century Hungarian avant-garde as an 'underground stream', a metaphor suggesting that the efforts keep surfacing, disappearing and changing course throughout the century. Furthermore, this phenomenon is often told as a secret story based on the personal relationships that occurred within the Hungarian avant-garde: master–disciple relations, informally and often illegally circulated information, allusions, acts of homage, and gestures of bequest and initiation.

The problem of discontinuity was also traditionally present in the relationship of Hungarian intellectuals to Europe in the twentieth century. The concept of 'Europe' would always appear as a distant island to which Hungarian intellectuals were seeking a bridge or, alternatively, wanted to turn away from, insisting on the assumed 'Eastern' roots of Hungarian culture (Turanism). Avant-garde artists wanted to rise above the relationships built on the difference between Hungarian culture and 'Europe', and the 'new artists' imagined the position of the avant-garde as part of a supranational, non-hierarchical system. Hungarian intellectuals in the interwar period related to Europe in what can be best described as a dynamic that emphasized either the particular or the universal traits of Hungarian culture.[5] In other words, was Hungarian culture part of an imagined universal culture or was it an island in the world? The avant-garde position was closer to the former interpretation; it denied the ethnic and nationalistic interpretations of culture and considered art to be the cause of humankind as a whole.

The responsibility of articulation: the Romantic seer and the role of the avant-garde artist

The major participants in twentieth-century Hungarian culture believed in the responsibility of articulation. There was little difference in this regard between avant-garde artists, moderate modernists and those artists who were closer to the official culture of the various regimes. Except for short interludes, Hungary was ruled by oppressive political systems throughout the twentieth century. Artists operated in the restrictive framework of censorship and self-censorship, varying in nature and severity over the different periods. Regimes paid significant attention to the participants of cultural life, which resulted in a controlled cultural politics and a system of centrally financed culture. Twentieth-century Hungarian political systems sensed the important role artists could play in shaping public opinion (though often overrating it). Artists, too, sensed the importance of their social roles, particularly through the articulation of their viewpoints. Artists and intellectuals close to the ruling elite and those critical of the establishment both shared the view that it was an artist's duty to take a position on public affairs and social issues.[6] This behaviour originated in the idea of the artist as 'seer', a concept constructed in the French Revolution and particularly influential in East-Central Europe. There is a great Romantic tradition of the artist as visionary prophet in Hungary. Since the early nineteenth century, Hungarian artists had considered the attainment of national independence and the expanded use of the Hungarian language in literature, philosophy and politics to be one of the chief tasks of Hungarian authors. The avant-garde, in turn, dealt with political issues programmatically. They did not simply understand artistic activity as a social role, but actually aimed to dissolve the border between the cultural and political fields.

Internationalism and isolation

Internationalism and the responsibility of articulation: Kassák's notion of the avant-garde during the First World War

The history of the Hungarian avant-garde began with Lajos Kassák's journal *A Tett* (The Action), published in 1915–16. This journal had at least two traits that would characterize the Hungarian historical avant-garde and the neo-avant-garde artists and artist groups later on, too: an internationalist attitude and transgressive statements on political issues made in one's capacity as an intellectual. The internationalism of Kassák and his circle was a radical political position in the case of *A Tett*. The mission of the journal suggested that 'modern' art was leftist and antimilitaristic. Kassák's response to First World War propaganda was an anti-war project that rose above 'self-serving racial or national goals'.[7] The international issue of *A Tett* in August 1916 was no less than a provocation: Kassák published poems and short stories by authors from countries at war with the Austro-Hungarian Monarchy in his journal. At the same time, representatives of openly pro-war and nationalist Futurism could also appear in the journal, alongside Serbian sculptor Ivan Meštrović with his celebration of southern Slavic heroism. So, the purpose of the journal was to capture the spectrum of artistic attitudes in relation to war, rather than being anti- or pro-war. *A Tett* was banned in October 1916 by the censorship authorities on account of its material 'endangering military interests'; they treated Kassák's decision to include artists of the Entente countries as a provocation and treason.[8]

Supranationalism and discontinuity: Hungarian artists in avant-garde networks in the 1920s

Certain artists of the Hungarian avant-garde became part of the international art circuit when they left Hungary (usually not entirely by choice). Numerous leftist intellectuals fled the country in fear of reprisals by the right-wing government that came to power after the fall of the Hungarian Republic of Councils in 1919. Most of them left for Berlin, 'capital of the united states of Europe',[9] where they came into contact with the influential art trends of the era, at times becoming the dominant figures in the movements. The case of László Moholy-Nagy is exemplary in this respect: after a short period in Hungary, his career took a sharp upward turn in 1923, when Walter Gropius appointed him professor at the Bauhaus in Weimar, Germany. As an 'engineer-artist' identifying with the constructivist principles of supranationalism, Moholy-Nagy considered the creation of a new egalitarian society to be the goal of artistic and technical research. His statement in 1924 emphasizes that 'the enormously significant cultural potential' and 'civilizational structures' of Western Europe may open Hungarians' eyes to the need to avoid both 'a romantic sliding back into the culture of the past' and 'nationalistic separation from those factors which shape the world today'.[10] Those leaving the country after the fall of the Republic of Councils and having the greatest international influence (such as Moholy-Nagy or Marcel Breuer) subsequently had little to no effect on cultural life in Hungary in the interwar period. When the history of twentieth-century Hungarian culture is called discontinuous, the term also refers to this recurrent pattern: the impact of intellectuals (artists as well as numerous philosophers and natural scientists) who left Hungary and became internationally important was absent or significantly delayed in their homeland, where it failed to shape Hungarian cultural and academic life.

The history of Kassák's avant-garde movement in the 1920s reveals a different position. After the fall of the Republic of Councils, Kassák fled to Vienna and during the next few years established relationships with the outstanding figures and movements of the international avant-garde, and he published 'supranationalist' dadaist and constructivist works in his journal *MA* (Today), published between 1920 and 1925 in Vienna (fig. 1). He had a dual aim: to be integrated into the international art scene, and to take on the role of a cultural mediator and educator to acquaint the Hungarian public with international examples of 'new art'. Kassák was not only contemplating his own career abroad but also fulfilling a cultural mission. However, he considered his Vienna exile temporary and returned to Hungary as soon as it was possible, thanks to a general amnesty put in place by Miklós Horthy's regime in 1926 (fig. 2).

His manifesto to reform the mentality of society and the living conditions of the working class through art appeared in Hungarian in the journals *MA* and *Dokumentum* (Document, published in 1926–27 in Budapest), addressing a Hungarian audience. It received, however, no response. Kassák's journals were banned in Hungary until 1926 and could only make a significant impact in the former Hungarian territories, primarily in Czechoslovakian and Romanian cities with Hungarian populations. The international network Kassák and his colleagues had built in the 1920s did not make an impact on cultural life in Hungary. Kassák's name would appear in the Hungarian press of the 1920s almost exclusively in the context of cabaret sketches and cartoons; his characteristic, easily caricatured figure (with his long hair and distinctive clothes) became part of popular public discourse.

The avant-garde artists who returned to Hungary after 1926 – and Kassák more than anyone else – laboured to create an alternative culture. Their work focused on local problems and increasingly on pragmatic political and social issues. In 1928, Kassák launched his journal *Munka* (Work) for young workers and engaged in intense consciousness-raising work, building communities and creating culture. This workers' culture, which was not founded on bourgeois tradition, but rather aimed to create a cultural language that could authentically express the workers' attitudes and worldview, began a new chapter in Hungary. This was the intellectual milieu in which the socio-photography movement began and this is where artists like Sándor Trauner, Victor Vasarely and Robert Capa began their path to future world fame.

Nationalism and Europe: modernism in 'neo-Baroque' Hungary in the 1930s

Historian Gyula Szekfű coined the expression 'neo-Baroque society' in 1934 to describe the *ressentiment* (the envy or hatred generating conflict between social strata and groups), authoritarianism and overly theatrical political posturing of the Hungarian regime led by Governor Miklós Horthy in 1920–44.[11] This definition also applies to modernist activities supported by official cultural politics in the 1930s. These were primarily conducted by neo-classical artists and groups that positioned themselves critically towards avant-garde ideas, yet reinterpreted and used the forms of early twentieth-century art movements. Their works typically mixed the glorious moments of Hungarian history and the representation of idealized progress and modernity with elements of Christian tradition and Hungarian folklore, so they were eminently suitable to aid the self-representation of the regime.

The so-called Római Iskola (Roman School), inspired by the ideas of art historian Tibor Gerevich, was characteristic of the type of modernist initiatives that found national support. Gerevich was the curator of a fellowship programme in the Collegium Hungaricum of Rome, which was set up following a bilateral treaty between Hungary and Italy in 1927. Young artists were granted study trips to Rome by the fellowship programme, which was used as a tool by Gerevich to create the 'Roman Hungarian style' among the fellows.[12] The formal and ideological precursor of the new style was *Novecento*, the Italian interpretation of neo-classicism, which aimed to unite modernism with a revival of Roman classical art.[13] Gerevich presented contemporary Italian painting as the model for Hungarian artists, rather than the 'aesthetic chaos' of cubism

2. Lajos Kassák, *Picture-Architecture (Dynamic Composition)*, 1924, tempera on cardboard, 54 × 43 cm, Petőfi Irodalmi Múzeum – Kassák Múzeum, Budapest

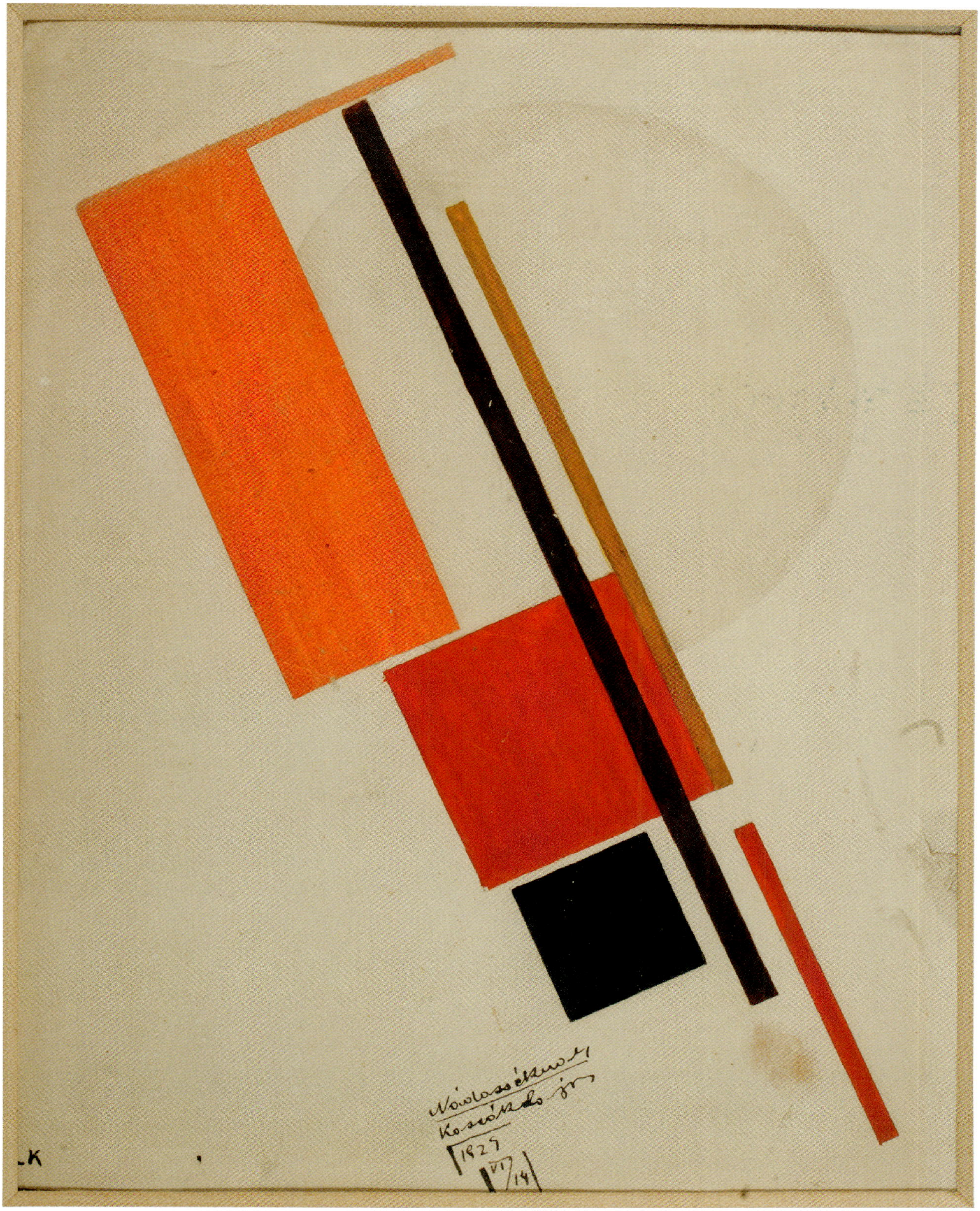

2

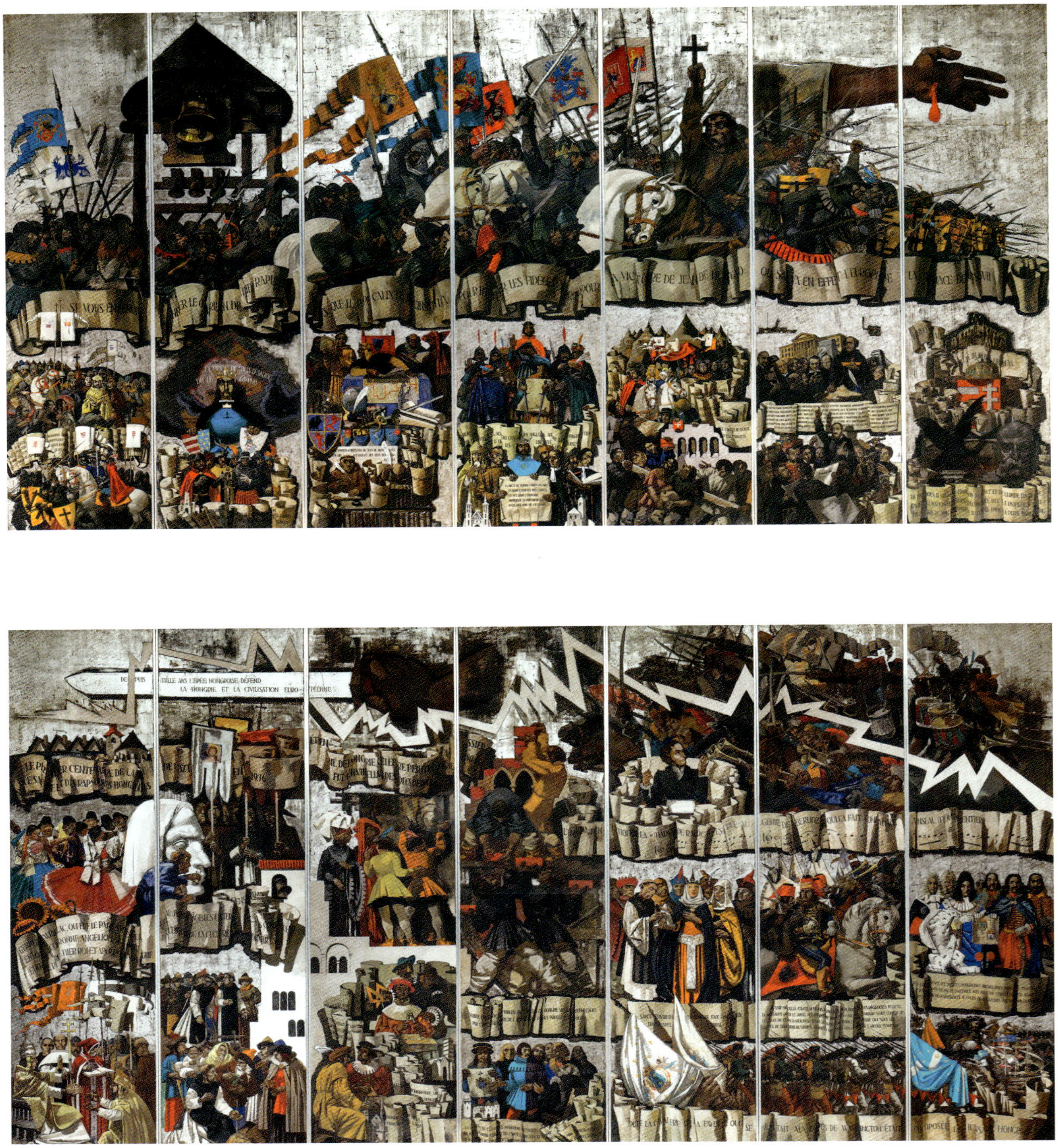

3

3. Vilmos Aba-Novák, *Hungarian-French Historical Relations*, Panels from the Hungarian Pavilion at the Paris 'International Exposition of Art and Technology in Modern Life' in 1937 (detail), tempera on fibreboard, 14 pieces, 200 × 780 cm, Szent István Király Múzeum, Székesfehérvár

4. Pál Molnár C., *Hungarian Resurrection ('I believe in God, the Father almighty...')*, *c.* 1937, oil on canvas, 150 × 110 cm, Yosyp Bokshay Transcarpathian Regional Museum, Uzhhorod

and German expressionism. In contrast to cosmopolitism (Francophone modernism) and internationalism (the avant-garde), the 'Roman Hungarian style' proclaimed a 'new European consciousness' on a Christian basis, which was also opposed to the earlier orthodox nationalist principles that governed official cultural politics in the 1920s. Gerevich's programme – much like *Novecento* – focused on the balance of 'tradition and modernity' and national and international trends.

The Horthy regime – the kingless kingdom restored after the First World War – avowed continuity with the thousand-year-old Christian tradition, so the neo-classicism envisioned by Gerevich uniting Christian (that is European) and national elements of style was perfectly suited to its political propaganda. The cultural political establishment commissioned the decoration of the Hungarian Pavilion of the 1937 Paris Expo from the artists of the Római Iskola. This event was especially important in Hungarian politics, since this was the first appearance of 'truncated' Hungary at the Expo following the Treaty of Trianon of 1920. (Hungary, a loser in the First World War, lost about two-thirds of its territory in the treaty concocted by the Entente powers.) The entrance to the pavilion was framed by sculptures of Saint Stephen, the first Christian Hungarian king, and of the Virgin Mary, 'the great lady of the Hungarians'. A white marble statue of Governor Horthy and the monumental painting *Hungarian-French Historical Relations* by Vilmos Aba-Novák were displayed in the main hall (fig. 3). The painting enumerates the key events of Hungarian and French history, politics and culture in a narrative that lends itself to being read like a comic strip. Given its topic, the painting was also the first time that the Horthy regime had publicly addressed the national trauma caused by the Trianon peace treaty. Pál Molnár-C. (the C. is short for Contat, his mother's name) symbolized the revival of the Hungarian nation in his painting *Hungarian Resurrection*, which was given a central space in the pavilion: its cross-shaped branch, newly growing from a desiccated tree, represented the regime's favoured vision of the future (fig. 4).

The gradual shift to the political right was accompanied by analogous processes in the field of art. The formerly envisioned 'new European consciousness' was replaced by nationalism: the Eucharistic World Congress in Budapest and Saint Stephen's jubilee in 1938 heralded a new era. The neo-Baroque visuality of the *arrière-garde* (i.e. aggressively favouring obsolete forms) replaced both Christian modernist principles and the last avant-garde initiatives in Hungarian public life.

4

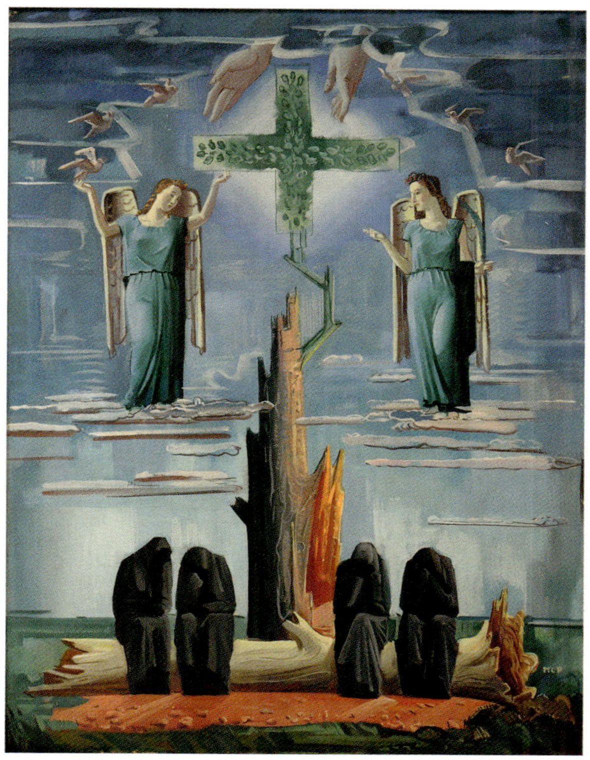

A pan-European illusion: the 'Európai Iskola'

One of the most important art initiatives of the years after the Second World War was the Európai Iskola (European School) established in October 1945 with a manifesto signed by Árpád Mezei, Imre Pán, Ernő Kállai, Pál Gegesi Kiss and Lajos Kassák, which organized exhibitions and lectures on literature and philosophy, and published books. In the brief democratic period of the post-war coalition era the prevailing mood was optimism and a new sense of freedom unknown for many years. This was productive for the avant-garde art networks, which were being rebuilt from their ruins. The Európai Iskola was formed as a loose network of artists who represented a broad range of avant-garde painting techniques in the manner of the École de Paris: figurative painting drawing on an expressionist tradition, constructivist abstraction and various interpretations of surrealism. As indicated by their choice of name, the group's objective was to move past the horizon of Hungarian national culture and the traditional French orientation of Hungarian culture. The founders believed it was possible to create a pan-European movement that would rally the artists of the continent behind shared slogans, because 'European culture' was not merely a 'sum of national cultures'.[14] The creators of the Európai Iskola imagined cultural transfer as a bidirectional and mutually influencing process when they sought to realize Western and Eastern influences simultaneously.

A precursor to the Európai Iskola was the work of two outstanding artists of the generation whose career was launched in the late 1920s. Lajos Vajda and Dezső Korniss met in Paris in the early 1930s, and they began collecting folklore motifs in and around Szentendre, a settlement near Budapest with a sizable Greek Orthodox Serbian minority population (fig. 5). Their project was conducted in parallel with Béla Bartók and Zoltán Kodály's collection of folksongs and folk music. Like Bartók, Vajda and Korniss found inspiration in the motifs and universal meanings of folklore, which often provided starting points for their works. Yet, their 'constructive surrealist' paintings, which combined these motifs through montage technique, were driven by Vajda's visionary intentions. 'Our aim', he wrote in a letter,

> *is to create a distinctly East-Central-European new art through the influence of the two great European cultural centres (French and Russian). Hungary's geographical position in Europe predestines it to be a link between the West (French) and the East (Russian). We want to fuse together the cultural (artistic) expression of two types of European people as understood in the two poles; we want to build bridges.*[15]

Vajda and Korniss drew on the earlier metaphor of the 'Ferry-land' mediating between East and West, originally created by leading Hungarian modernist poet Endre Ady. Escaping both the official cultural politics of the Horthy era and the internationalism of the *Munka* circle led by Kassák, they envisioned an established East-Central-European language of form and cultural milieu, and inspired both the founders of the Európai Iskola and the artists the group exhibited in the post-war period (fig. 6).

5. Lajos Vajda, *Houses of Szentendre with Crucifix*, 1937, tempera on paper, collage, 46 × 62 cm, Ferenczy Múzeumi Centrum, Szentendre

6. Dezső Korniss, *Cricket Wedding*, 1949, oil on canvas, 121 × 300 cm, Ferenczy Múzeumi Centrum, Szentendre

7. Tamás Lossonczy, *In the Storm*, 1944, oil on canvas, 53 × 63 cm, Szépművészeti Múzeum – Magyar Nemzeti Galéria, Budapest

8. Margit Anna, *Tin Christ*, 1947, oil on canvas, 60 × 40 cm, Kolozsváry Collection, Győr

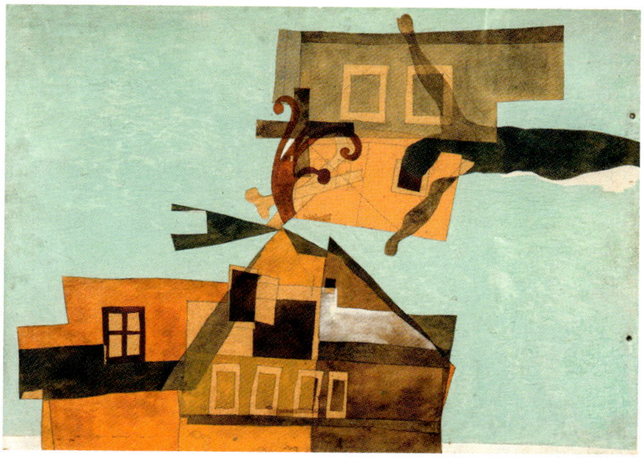

5

6

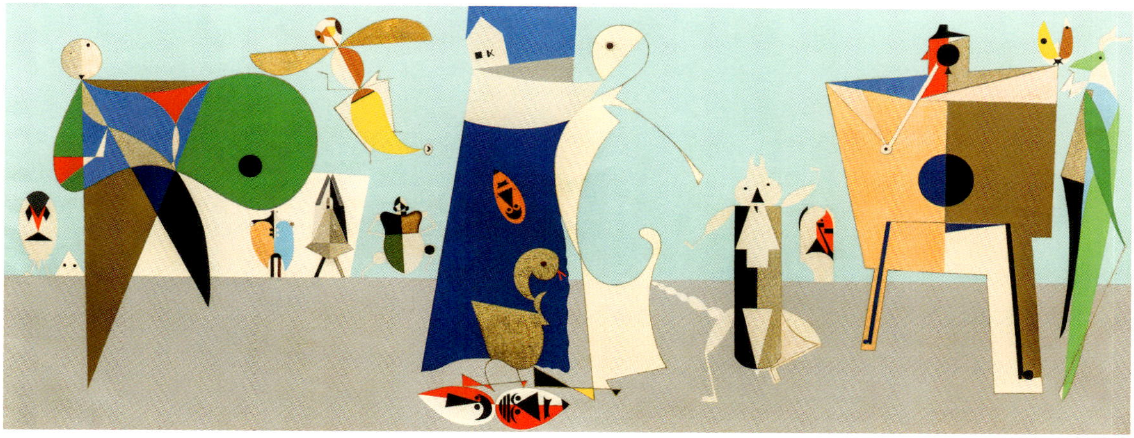

7

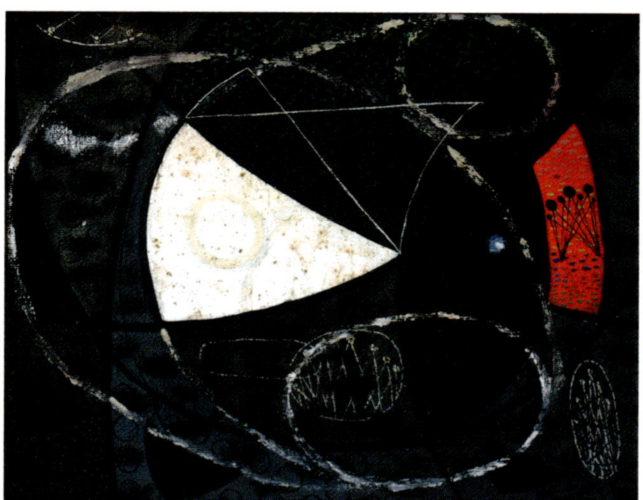

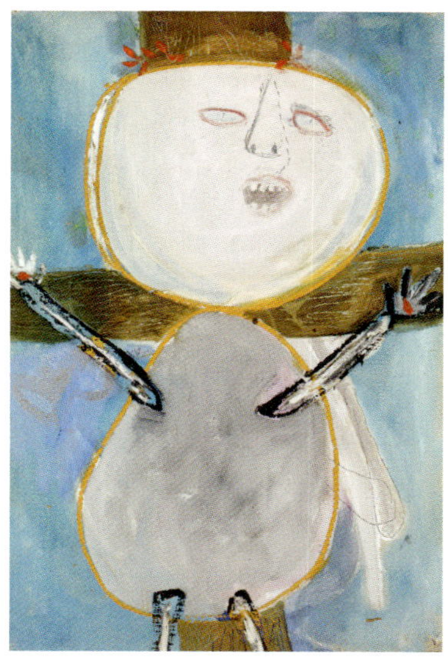

8

The founding manifesto of the Európai Iskola emphasized the role of Hungarian culture as a mediator between East and West:

Europe and its age-old ideal lies now in ruins. We have up until now understood the European ideal as the Western European ideal. But from now on, we need to think of Europe as a whole. The new Europe can only be built from a synthesis of West and East. In AD 1945 everyone has to decide whether they have a right to be designated a European or not. We have to create a vital European School, which formulates the new relationship between life, man and community. This is the decisive task of the activity of the first 'European School'.[16]

The utopian image of a future transnational European synthesis proclaimed by the manifesto may be compared to the preamble to the founding charters of the United Nations accepted a mere few months earlier, in the summer of 1945.[17] It must be emphasized that the Európai Iskola wanted to actively shape European culture as a whole, rising above both the national and stylistic divisions of European culture. Nevertheless, Európai Iskola's own programme linked it to the theory and practice of surrealism above all. According to one of its key theorists, Árpád Mezei, the surrealist method is what can 'dissolve the conflicts between good and bad, true and false and can thereby make the world finally truly habitable'.[18]

Several of the Hungarian artists joining the group came from the 'constructive surrealist' circle around Vajda and Korniss (Margit Anna, Endre Bálint, Béla Bán and Júlia Vajda), yet the exhibitions were dominated by abstract artists (Tihamér Gyarmathy, Tamás Lossonczy, Ferenc Martyn and Endre Rozsda) with a French orientation who had first-hand knowledge of Abstraction-Création, the group formed in Paris in 1931, and the surrealist groups in the same city (figs 7–9). Led by critic and former Bauhaus collaborator Ernő Kállai, these abstract artists even set up their own subgroup in 1946 with its own exhibition space named Galéria a 4 Világtájhoz (Four Corners of the World Gallery).[19] From 1946 on, the Európai Iskola regularly organized individual and group exhibitions, displaying not only their own works, but also those of their 'forerunners', the Hungarian avant-garde artists of the interwar period (Lajos Vajda, Imre Ámos and Gyula Derkovits). The European connection also materialized in an international exhibition programme that was powerfully shaped by their French orientation. The exhibitions of the Európai Iskola presenting international art in 1946–47 could only be arranged with the assistance of direct Parisian contacts. Even if these seemingly random contacts left a mark on the exhibition series, it still testifies to the ambition of the Európai Iskola to present the possibility of a systematic renewal of modern art in Budapest in the post-war period. Pán and Mezei were helped by the painter Marcel Jean, who lived in Budapest during the Second World War, and by Béla Bán and Endre Bálint, who were visiting Paris at the time. It was Corneille and Jacques Doucet (members of the later CoBrA group) of the contemporary French art world and the Swiss Paul Klee who were presented in individual exhibitions, but there were also two representative exhibitions of leading artists of the Paris galleries in 1947 (such as Picasso, Laurens, Matisse and Miró), showing their original and, more often, reproduced graphic works. The exhibitions were accompanied by the publication of essays by Hungarian and European authors with surrealist ties (Guillaume Apollinaire, André Breton, Herbert Read, Picasso, Paul Éluard, and Alfred Jarry) in a series launched by Pán and Mezei. The Európai Iskola also wished to exhibit East-Central-European surrealist groups in Budapest; since these groups operated in isolation from each other, they relied on André Breton as a mediator. The only show actually realized in Budapest was that of the Czech surrealist artist group Skupina Ra, but the exhibition demonstrated that the Európai Iskola was not alone in the region in trying to create a network of artists and intellectuals that could break through 'national limits'. They also had plans for presenting surrealists from Bucharest (Gherasim Luca, Dolfi Trost), but this became impossible due to changes in cultural politics.[20]

Theorists specializing in socialist realism (Georg Lukács) and bourgeois modernism (Aurél Bernáth) launched a full-blown aesthetic attack against the Európai Iskola and abstraction on the eve of the Stalinist turn in cultural politics under Mátyás Rákosi

(1945–56).[21] The Európai Iskola dissolved itself in December 1948 due to criticism and attacks in the press, but its roughly three-year history, defined by the illusion of a pan-European cultural programme, was an episode of Hungarian art that was as rich as it was brief. The official visual language of the Rákosi-era completely eliminated the formal influence of surrealism and abstraction, and the Európai Iskola and its impact only survived as an undercurrent, a kind of legendary, hermetic, private culture. Younger generations had a chance to learn about the attitude of 'a need for the avant-garde' in unofficial venues such as Lajos Kassák's and the painter Jenő Gadányi's apartments in the outskirts of Budapest, Dezső Korniss's atelier apartment in the city centre or in the home of Endre Bálint, József Jakovits and Júlia Vajda in the Rottenbiller utca.[22] For decades, Júlia Vajda stored the paintings left behind by her late husband, Lajos Vajda, in a drawer underneath a sofa bed in her apartment. These works played a crucial, emblematic role in the aesthetics and politics of the Európai Iskola. Consequently, the apartment became the desired and unattainable 'island of freedom', and simultaneously a secret place and foreign body in the visual art scene of Budapest and Hungary ruled by the socialist realist doctrine of the Rákosi era.

The new cultural politics erased the pan-European programme proclaimed by the founders of the Európai Iskola – the Mezei-Pán brothers, Ernő Kállai and Lajos Kassák – almost without a trace; it was replaced by a Soviet orientation and later by a programme of international socialist art. Some of the former members of the Európai Iskola (including Béla Bán and Tamás Lossonczy) accepted the doctrine of socialist realism and experimented with it in the 1950s, only to return to their modernist principles later on. Those who were unable completely to give up a modernist language of forms had two options: seemingly adapting to the official realist style in order to continue their abstract art in the solitude of their atelier (Endre Rozsda, Ferenc Martyn) or a complete withdrawal from the art world created by the regime, choosing the tactic of internal aesthetic exile (Tihamér Gyarmathy).

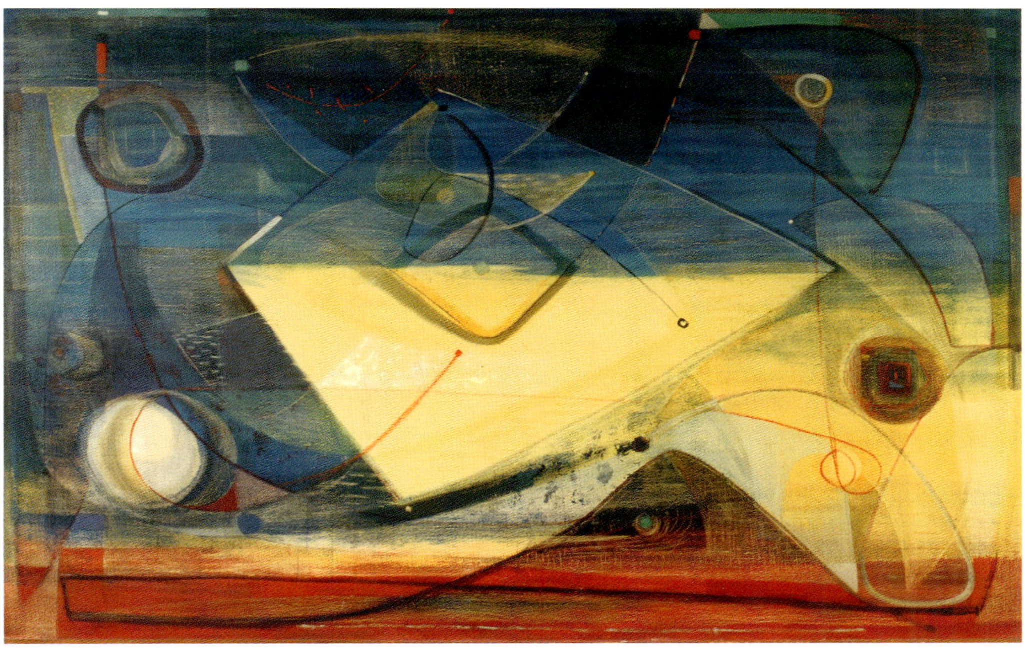

9

9. Tihamér Gyarmathy, *Dynamic Composition*, 1946, oil on canvas, 130 × 196 cm, Szépművészeti Múzeum – Magyar Nemzeti Galéria, Budapest

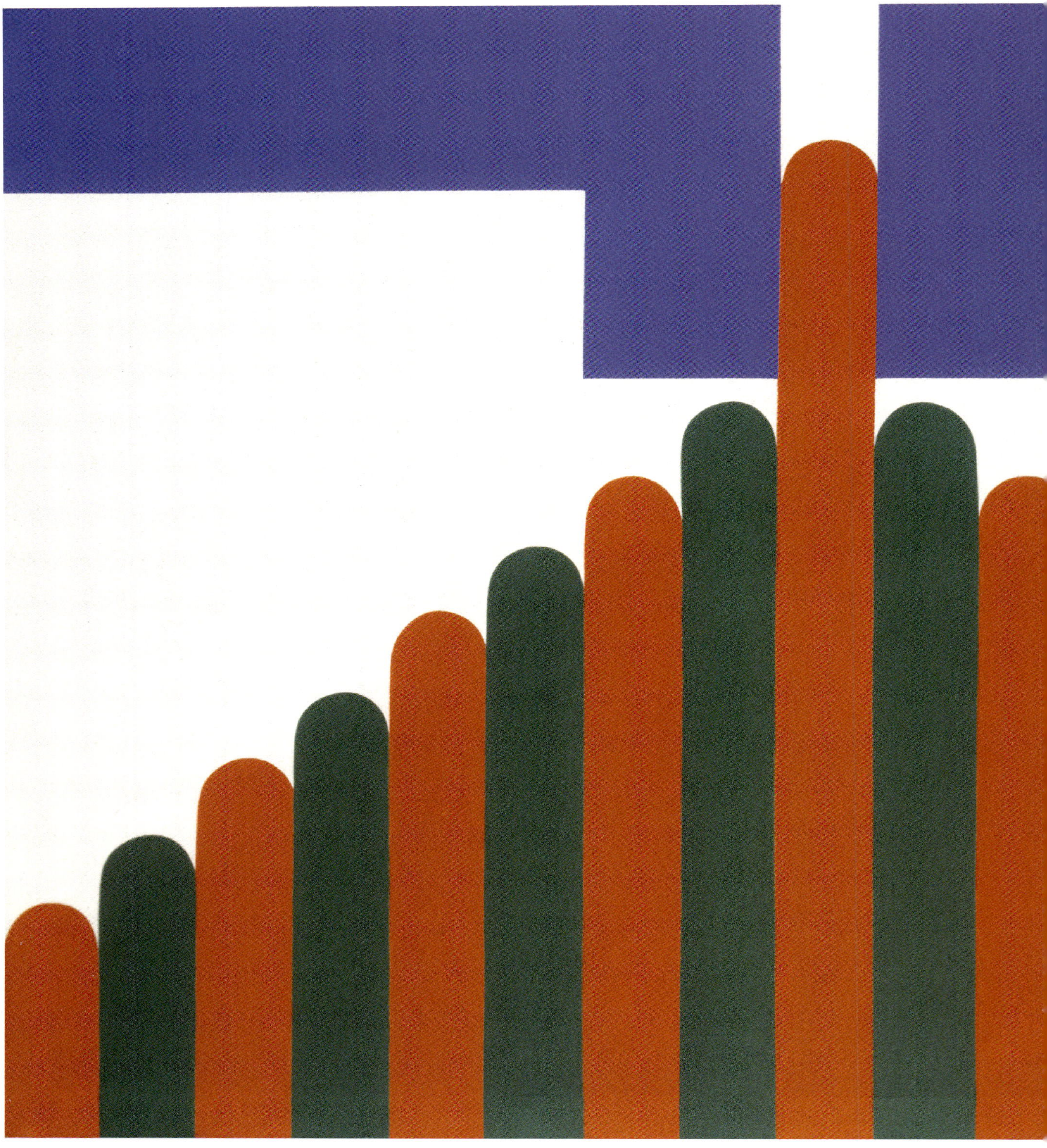

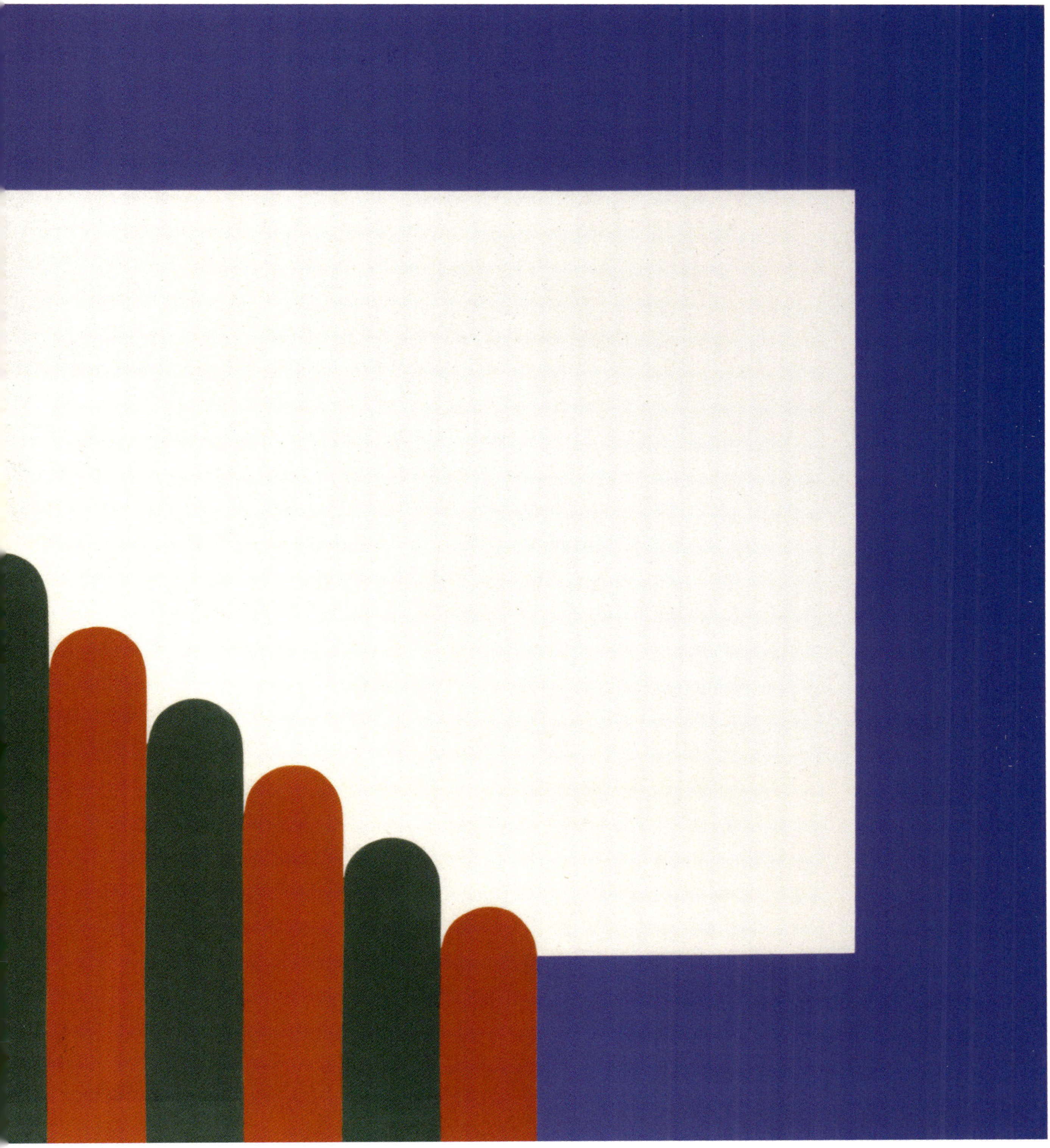

12

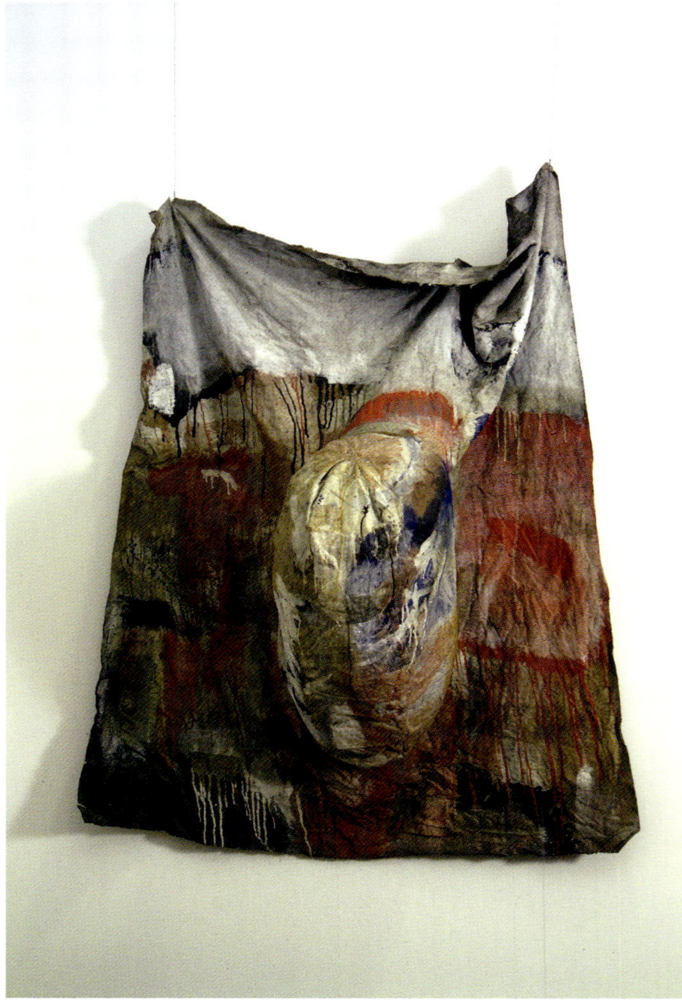

11

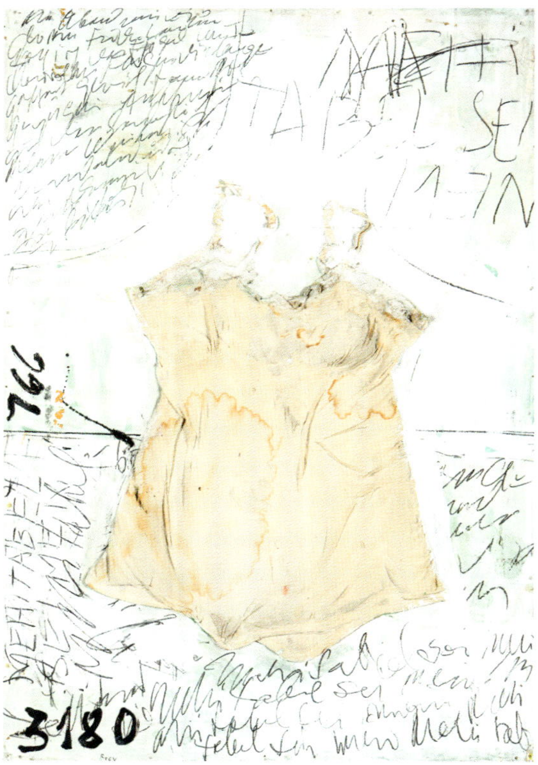

10. (previous pages) Imre Bak, *Blue Frame*, 1968, oil on canvas, 120 × 222 cm, Szépművészeti Múzeum – Magyar Nemzeti Galéria, Budapest

11. Krisztián Frey, *3180 (Slip)*, 1966, oil on fibreboard, mixed media, 123 × 84 cm, Szépművészeti Múzeum – Magyar Nemzeti Galéria, Budapest

12. Gyula Konkoly, *Softened Egg*, 1968, mixed media, canvas, 125 × 125 cm, Szépművészeti Múzeum – Magyar Nemzeti Galéria, Budapest

The illusion of synchronicity: the 'Iparterv' exhibitions

Following in the footsteps of the pre-1948 Hungarian avant-garde, as opposed to the 'internationalism' of socialist realism, the next initiative that would take on the relationship of Hungarian culture and (Western) European art dates from the late 1960s. This was the first 'Iparterv' group exhibition organized by the newly graduated art historian Péter Sinkovits in December 1968. Works by eleven young artists were displayed in the lobby of the headquarters of the state-owned Ipari Épülettervező Vállalat (Industrial Architecture Company) in the city centre. Sinkovits wished to establish the European position of Hungarian art created behind the Iron Curtain, suggesting that the artists produced works that were 'influenced by the most significant contemporary European and American artists' and 'attempted to make connections to current artistic processes in the world'.[23] In other words, Western trends functioned as the ideal that Eastern versions must adapt to and catch up with to achieve the desired state of synchronicity.

Sinkovits's simultaneous reference to artists of the historical Hungarian avant-garde and to contemporary international trends clearly served the purpose of using the exhibition to restore an interrupted dialogue. The works on display, even though they expressed the dominant post-war trends and techniques in Western visual arts, and reflected on them with a previously unprecedented concentration, actually had some precursors.[24] This latest presentation of modernism was made possible by the Kádár regime's softened stance on cultural politics from the mid-1960s and its ideology of opening to the West; it was also influenced by the art historical study of the avant-garde (primarily the Kassák circle, Lajos Vajda and the Európai Iskola) in the interwar period and the post-war coalition years.[25]

The exhibition was dominated by works formally or thematically related to an 'American type of abstraction' (abstract expressionism, gestural painting and hard-edge painting) and pop art. The Western orientation cannot be ignored, but 'one need not deny influences, since each of us has something extra as an individual'.[26] Sinkovits stressed the connection between the avant-garde and the new avant-garde artists of the late 1960s in terms of ideas and the disconnection in terms of the movement: young artists, he claimed, were 'in some sense representatives of new traditions', yet partly 're-introducers of avant-garde initiatives'.[27] He implied that the avant-garde as an attitude had not become an organic part of culture in Hungary, neither in the years after the First World War nor after the Second World War, so the 'third generation' had to build from scratch once again. That was why such disparate tendencies and attitudes were present together in the 'Iparterv' exhibitions, which would never be exhibited side by side in a clearer and nuanced Western art world.[28] The aspects of new painting represented by Imre Bak, István Nádler, Tamás Hencze, Ilona Keserü, László Lakner and Endre Tót, and the neo-dada works by Gyula Konkoly and, partly, Krisztián Frey, were in sharp contrast to the distinct East-Central-European interpretations of pop art – which alluded to the political role of artists – that were on display one year later, in 1969, at the second 'Iparterv' exhibition (figs 10–12).[29]

The radical artists of the period were also exhibited at this second show; this is where Tamás Szentjóby exhibited his works that he classified as 'pop objects'. Although Szentjóby's favoured interpretation of his objects *Cooling Water* (p. 322, fig. 4) and *A New Unit of Measurement* (p. 281, fig. 8), which were made in 1965, was more general and closer to dada (especially Duchamp) and the radical anti-art stand of Fluxus, the works still attained a distinctly political meaning in the given context. According to this political interpretation, *Cooling Water* (hot water poured into a chemist's flask) was a provocative repetition of the Party slogan of the 'thaw' after 1963, and *A New Unit of Measurement* (a horizontally placed metal pipe about half a metre in length) was the symbol of the police state, the rubber baton or lead-weighted truncheon.[30]

Two more recent works of his, which reflected on the reprisals following the Prague Spring period of liberalization in Czechoslovakia, 1968, had a more direct political meaning. The brick of *Czechoslovakian Radio* evoked the members of the opposition in Prague, who provoked the police units by 'listening' to bricks wrapped in newspaper after listening to the radio had been banned. Given its unambiguous symbolism, *Portable Trench for Three* could also be interpreted as an aggressive political provocation (fig. 13; see also Klara Kemp-Welch, 'Soft-spoken Encounters', pp. 273–89).

Miklós Erdély did not participate in either exhibition, but he planned to include his photomontage series *Oath* in the catalogue, which was to be published later. The photos show Erdély with his hand raised for the oath with a quotation by Erwin Schrödinger superimposed on his chest, the latter explaining the basis of quantum physics, and questioning the rationalism and naive realism of the modern scientific worldview (p. 334, fig. 2). Erdély recalled the reason for the eventual exclusion of the series from the catalogue: Gyula Konkoly, the artist editing the catalogue, said, 'either this is valid – your work – and then all the others in the catalogue aren't, or this isn't valid and then the rest stay'.[31]

Both exhibitions were closed down by the Képző- és Iparművészeti Lektorátus (Supervisory Body for Arts and Crafts) a few days after opening. Yet their impact was outstanding, partly because of the prohibition, partly because of successful self-documentation: 'Iparterv' became the 'myth' of the new Hungarian avant-garde, and artists starting their careers in the early and mid-1960s were later referred to as the 'Iparterv generation'.[32] Sinkovits collected the works on display at the two exhibitions in the illegal publication *Dokumentum* 69–70 (Document 69–70) in 1970, reflecting on the title of the Kassel 'documenta'. Once again, he emphasized his earlier claim that the young artists exhibiting their works 'did not continue traditions in any direct way, but were trying to orient themselves in the current state of art in the world, moving synchronously with the most progressive avant-garde initiatives'.[33] The censorship authorities reacted to the publication with an intense counterattack against artists from the group. Gyula Konkoly, editor and publisher of the illegal publication, decided to leave the country on the day after publication. Such a decision was far from unique: as cultural politics turned increasingly icy once again, many of the artists who had been introduced at the 'Iparterv' exhibitions would emigrate to Paris or Switzerland, and Ludmil Siskov and Krisztián Frey would leave for West Germany, between 1970 and 1976.

13

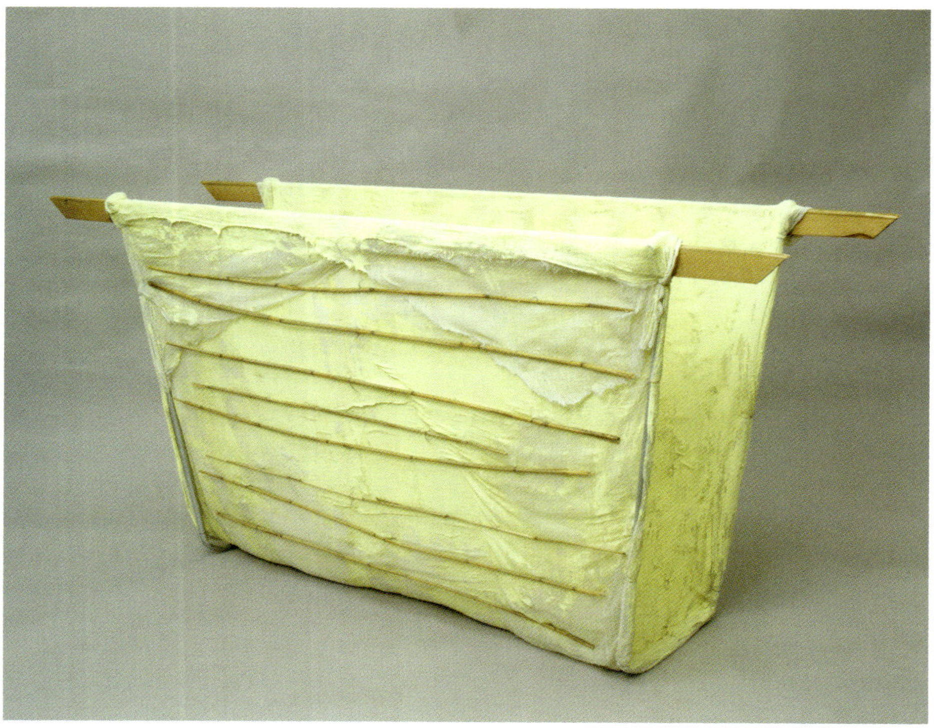

13. Tamás Szentjóby, *Portable Trench for Three*, 1969, wood, aluminium, gauze, sulphur dust, cane, mixed media, 93 × 180 × 60 cm, Szépművészeti Múzeum – Magyar Nemzeti Galéria, Budapest

Conclusion

The story of twentieth-century Hungarian avant-garde and modernist art is a story of short-lived movements, exiles, bans, suppressions and manoeuvres in cultural politics. As a result, retrospective accounts of the subject have frequently given rise to opportunities for creating legends (by the major players themselves), anecdotes, mystification and repression. By contrast, one can tell the story of twentieth-century Hungarian avant-garde and modernist art through emphasizing the discontinuities and the embeddedness of each movement in a given historical context, while also discovering patterns that characterize Hungarian art and the intelligentsia. Such patterns include the following: Hungarian artists reflect on their sense of isolation (e.g. the avant-garde émigrés in the 1920s), they deal with the position of Hungarian culture within a European one (e.g. the avant-garde of the 1910s, the Római Iskola and the Európai Iskola), and they consider articulation an eminent task of the artist (e.g. artists of the historical avant-garde and the 'Iparterv' exhibitions). Such an approach to the history of Hungarian art resists the exoticizing, orientalist 'Western gaze' as well as the self-referential narratives restricted to a Hungarian framework. Taking the historical context into account and highlighting the patterns observable over the course of history enable one to discuss Hungarian art as a story of movements self-reflexively dealing with their own traditions, yet sensitive to international trends, and creating distinctive strategies against political oppression.

1 We have followed the Introduction of *The Oxford Handbook of Modernisms* in our use of the terms 'modernity' and 'modernism': 'When "modernity" is the prior term, "Modernism" – of whatever kind – becomes its expression....[However] if Modernism expresses modernity in some sense, then this notion is to be conceived not on a base-superstructure model but on the principle of multiple interactions across social and geographical locations and of a non-linear, non-progressivist view of temporality.' Peter Brooker, Andrzej Gasiorek, Deborah Longworth and Andrew Thacker (eds), *The Oxford Handbook of Modernisms*. Oxford: Oxford University Press, 2010, 3–4. In this text, we use the term avant-garde to refer to the variant of modernism that proposes a radical artistic and political programme.

2 See, for example, Timothy O. Benson (ed.), *Central European Avant-Gardes: Exchange and Transformation, 1910–1930*. London and Los Angeles: MIT Press/LACMA, 2002; György C. Kálmán, 'Strange Interferences: Modernism and Conservativism vs Avant-Garde, Hungary, 1910s', *Hungarian Studies*, Vol. 26, No. 1, 2012, 107–122; 'Europe 1880–1940', in Peter Brooker, Sascha Bru and Andrew Thacker (eds), *The Oxford Critical and Cultural History of Modernist Magazines*, Vol. III, Part I–II. Oxford: Oxford University Press, 2013. On the theoretical outcomes of the issue, see Per Bäckström and Benedikt Hjartarson (eds), *Decentring the Avant-Garde*. Leiden and Boston: Brill, 2014; Piotr Piotrowski, *In the Shadow of Yalta: Art and the Avant-garde in Eastern Europe, 1945–1989*. London: Reaktion Books, 2011.

3 On this issue, see, for example, Klara Kemp-Welch, *Antipolitics in Central European Art: Reticence as Dissidence under Post-Totalitarian Rule, 1956–1989*. London and New York: I. B. Tauris, 2013.

4 On theoretical aspects of the issue, see Peter Bürger, 'Avant-Garde and Neo-Avant-Garde: An Attempt to Answer Certain Critics of Theory of the Avant-Garde', *New Literary History*, Vol. 41, No. 4, 2010, 695–715.

5 On this issue, see Jenő Szűcs, 'The Three Historical Regions of Europe: An Outline', *Acta Historica Academiae Scientiarum Hungaricae*, Vol. 29, Nos 2–4, 1983, 131–84; Larry Wolff, *Inventing Eastern Europe: The Map of Civilization on the Mind of the Enlightenment*. Stanford: Stanford University Press, 1994; Robert Bideleux and Ian Jeffries, *A History of Eastern Europe: Crisis and Change*. London and New York: Routledge, 1998; Adrian Webb, *The Routledge Companion to Central and Eastern Europe since 1919*. London and New York: Routledge, 2008; Stefano Bianchini, *Le sfide della modernità: Idee, politiche e percorsi dell'Europa orientale nel XIX e XX secolo*. Rubbettino: Soveria Mannelli, 2009; Stefano Bottoni, *Un altro Novecento: L'Europa orientale dal 1919 a oggi*. Roma: Carocci, 2011.

6 Pierre Bourdieu, *The Rules of Art: Genesis and Structure of the Literary Field*. Redwood City: Stanford University Press, 1996.

7 Lajos Kassák, 'Programme' (1916), trans. John Bátki, in Timothy O. Benson and Éva Forgács (eds), *Between Worlds: A Sourcebook of Central European Avant-Gardes*. London and Los Angeles: MIT Press/LACMA, 160–61.

8 See Gábor Dobó and Merse Pál Szeredi (eds), *Signal to the World: War – Avant-Garde – Kassák*. Budapest: Kassák Foundation, 2016.

9 Herwarth Walden (1923), quoted by Hubert van den Berg and Lidia Głuchowska, 'The Inter-, Trans- and Postnationality of the Historical Avant-Garde: Introduction', in *Transnationality, Internationalism and Nationhood: European Avant-garde in the First Half of the Twentieth Century*. Leuven and Walpole: Peeters, 2013, xiii.

10 Krisztina Passuth, *Moholy-Nagy*. London: Thames & Hudson, 1985.

11 See Irene Raab Epstein, *Gyula Szekfü: A Study in the Political Basis of Hungarian Historiography*. London and New York: Routledge, 1974.

12 Tibor Gerevich, 'Római magyar művészek' [Hungarian Artists in Rome], *Magyar Művészet*, Vol. 7, No. 4, 1931, 189.

13 Julianna P. Szűcs, *A Római Iskola* [The School of Rome]. Budapest: Corvina, 1987, 12–13.

14 Pál Kiss, Árpád Mezei and Imre Pán, *Az Európai Iskola* (Az Európai Iskola Könyvtára, 21–24) [The European School (The Library of the European School, 21–24)]. Budapest: Független Nyomda, 1947, 2. See also Gábor Pataki (ed.), *Cricket Wedding: The European School, The Hungarian Avant-Garde 1945–1949* (exhibition catalogue). Leiden and Budapest: Stichting Européer, 2002; Marianna Kolozsváry and Krisztina Passuth (eds), *European School: The Art of Freedom – The Freedom of Art* (exhibition catalogue). Paris: Institut Hongrois de Paris, 2011.

15 Lajos Vajda, letter to Júlia Vajda, Szentendre, 11 August 1936, in Stefánia Mándy, *Vajda Lajos*. Budapest: Corvina, 1983, 181–83.

16 Imre Pán, *Bevezetés Európába* (Index Röpirat és Vitairat-Könyvtár, 3–4) [Introduction to Europe (Index Pamphlet and Debate Library, 3–4)]. Budapest: Művészbolt, 1946, inside cover.

17 Attila Horányi, 'Taten und Einsätze: Der Modernismus der Európai Iskola', in Hans Knoll (ed.), *Die zweite Öffentlichkeit: Kunst in Ungarn im 20. Jahrhundert*. Dresden: Verlag der Kunst, 1999, 112–37.

18 Péter György and Gábor Pataki, *Az Európai Iskola és az Elvont Művészek Csoportja* [The European School and the Group of Abstract Artists]. Budapest: Corvina, 1990, 44.

19 On 'bioromanticism', Ernő Kállai's distinctive interpretation of abstraction, see Monika Wucher, 'Rereading Bioromanticism', in Oliver A. I. Botar and Isabel Wünsche (eds), *Biocentrism and Modernism*. Farnham and Burlington: Ashgate, 2011, 47–60; Gábor Pataki (ed.), 'Ernst/Ernő Kállai und die Kunstkritik in Deutschland und Ungarn', *Acta Historiae Artium*, Vol. 36, Nos 1–4, 1993, 150–236.

20 György and Pataki, *Az Európai Iskola*, 53.

21 Gábor Pataki, '"Van alkonyat, mely olyan, mint a hajnal": Képzőművészeti viták, 1948–1949' ['Some Twilights are Like Dawns': Debates in Visual Arts, 1948–1949], in Gyula Kozák, Gábor Pataki, János M. Rainer and Éva Standeisky (eds), *A fordulat évei: Politika, képzőművészet, építészet 1947–1949* [The Years of the Turning Point: Politics, Visual Arts and Architecture 1947–1949]. Budapest: 1956-os Intézet, 1998, 217–37.

22 Péter György, *Az elsüllyedt sziget* [The Sunken Island]. Budapest: Képzőművészeti Kiadó, 1994, 25.

23 Péter Sinkovits, 'Introduction to Iparterv I', in *Iparterv 68–80: Exhibition in the Meeting Hall of Iparterv* (exhibition catalogue). Budapest: Iparterv, 1980, 22.

24 Bürger, 'Avant-Garde and Neo-Avant-Garde'; Péter Kovács (ed.), *A huszadik század magyar művészete: Régi és új avantgárd (1967–1975) / Hungarian Art of the Twentieth Century: Early and New Avantgarde (1967–1975)* (exhibition catalogue). Székesfehérvár: Szent István Király Múzeum, 1987.

25 Lajos Németh, *Modern Art in Hungary*. Budapest: Corvina, 1969.

26 László Beke, '12 years Iparterv', in *Iparterv 68–80: Exhibition in the Meeting Hall of Iparterv* (exhibition catalogue). Budapest: Iparterv, 1980, 9.

27 Sinkovits, 'Introduction to Iparterv I', 22.

28 Sándor Hornyik, 'Veszélyes kiegészítések? Megjegyzések a magyar neoavantgárd elméletéhez' [Dangerous Supplements? Notes on the Theory of the Hungarian Neo-avant-garde], in Ágnes Berecz, Mária L. Molnár and Erzsébet Tatai (eds), *Nulla dies sine linea. Tanulmányok Passuth Krisztina hetvenedik születésnapjára* [Nulla dies sine linea: Studies for the 70th Birthday of Krisztina Passuth]. Budapest: Praesens, 2007, 171–77.

29 David Crowley, 'Pop Effects in Eastern Europe under Communist Rule', in Jessica Morgan and Flavia Frigeri (eds), *The World Goes Pop* (exhibition catalogue). London: Tate, 2015, 29–37; Dávid Fehér, 'Pop Beyond Pop: Some Exhibitions of the Hungarian "Iparterv-Circle"', in Annika Öhrner (ed.), *Art in Transfer in the Era of Pop: Curatorial Practices and Transnational Strategies*. Stockholm: Södertörn University, 2017, 345–74.

30 For more details on the context of Tamás Szentjóby's artworks, see Emese Kürti, 'Esoteric Avant-garde. The Concept/Conceptual Paradigm', *Exindex*, 4 August 2014, http://exindex.hu/index.php?l=en&page=3&id=934 and Emese Kürti, '"A szocialista realizmus gyöngyszemei". Posztfluxus jelenségek Magyarországon' ["The Pearls of Socialist Realism". Post-Fluxus Tendencies in Hungary], *Exindex*, 26 May 2016, http://exindex.hu/index.php?l=hu&page=3&id=992.

31 Miklós Peternák, 'Beszélgetés Erdély Miklóssal (1983 tavaszán)' [A Conversation with Miklós Erdély (Spring 1983)], *Árgus*, Vol. 2, No. 5, 1991, 78.

32 Júlia Fabényi, István Hajdu and Péter Sinkovits (eds), *Groupe IPARTERV: Le progrès de l'illusion: The Third Generation of the Hungarian Avant-Garde, 1968–1969* (exhibition catalogue). Paris: Institut Hongrois de Paris, 2010.

33 Péter Sinkovits, 'Dokumentum 69–70 (Introduction)', in *Iparterv 68-80. Exhibition in the Meeting Hall of Iparterv* (exhibition catalogue). Budapest: Iparterv, 1980, 55.

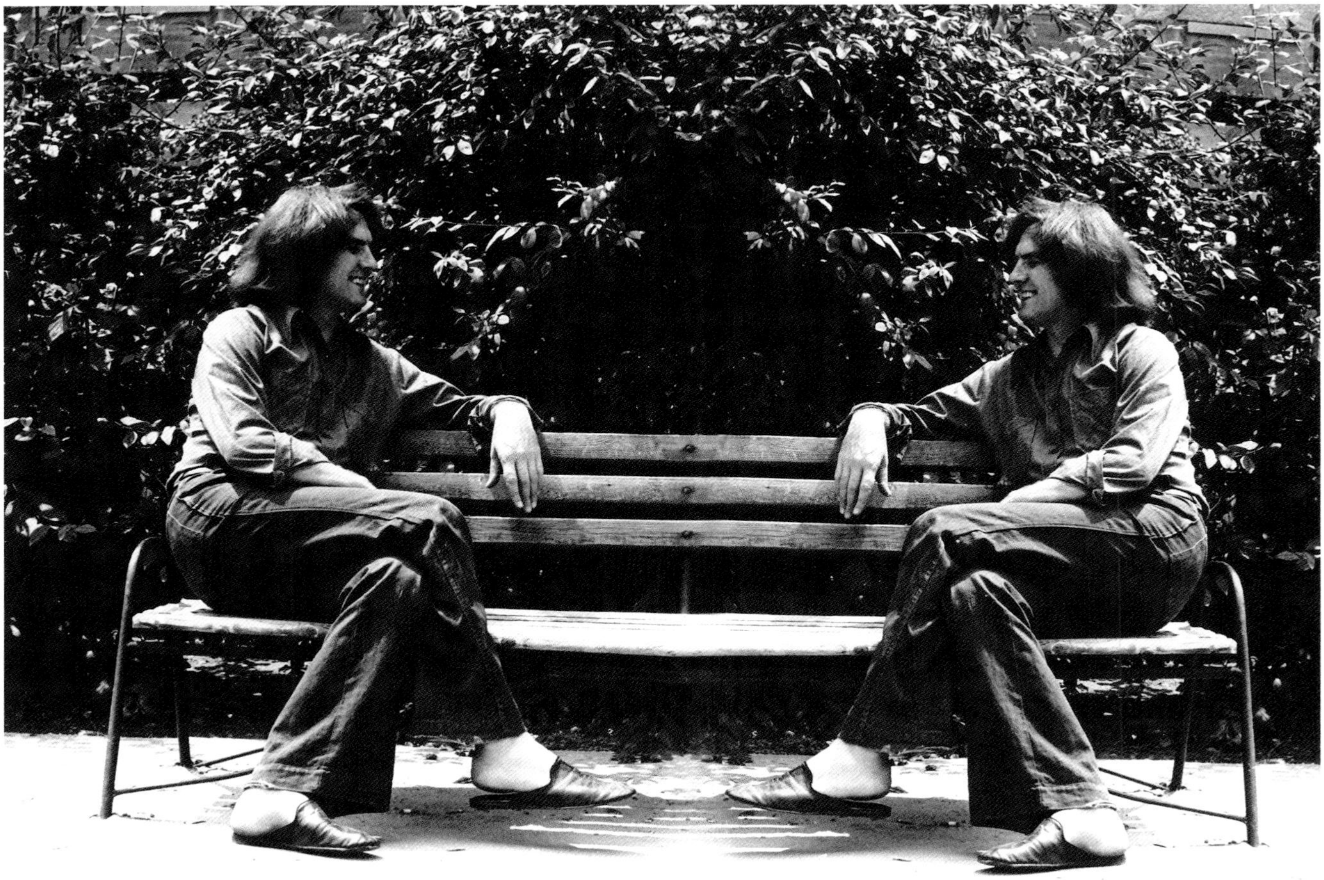

1

1. Endre Tót, *I am glad if I can gaze at you*, 1973–76, silver gelatine print, 18 × 24 cm, acb Galéria, Budapest

The Art Sphere as a Grey Zone

Techniques of Power and the Context of Artistic Practices

Whoever is not with us is against us. Whoever is not against us is with us. The former was the motto of Mátyás Rákosi, leader of the Stalinist dictatorship in Hungary in 1949–56, whereas its revision was proclaimed by János Kádár, General Secretary of the Magyar Szocialista Munkáspárt (MSZMP, Hungarian Socialist Workers' Party), the ruling state party in the socialist system, 1956–88. The difference between the two sentences shows not only that the long-term sustainability of dictatorship motivated the regime to relax its regulatory control of society (expanding, as it were, its definition of social belonging), but also the fact that the basis of the system, its dependence on Soviet Communist Party directives, was unchanged. This shift in the techniques of power, which could be interpreted as a kind of 'softening', occurred in each country of the Eastern bloc, though in different manners, at different times and with different dynamics. In each case, it led to the creation of 'grey zones'.

This thaw began in Hungary relatively early in comparison to the Soviet bloc as a whole. After suppressing the 1956 revolution against the communist state in Hungary, the newly established regime wished to break with the Stalinist terror of the previous era –in full accord with Moscow's directives – and introduced a softer, subtler and more sustainable system of power. As Péter György argues, the regime furthered this by offering a tacit deal to society.[1] In this deal, the Party ignored (or rather suppressed) the oppressions, traumas and sins of the past (the Second World War and the Holocaust, in which Hungary aided the Nazis [see Daniel Véri, 'The Holocaust and the Arts', pp. 209–27], as well as the Stalinist dictatorship), and promised a gradual rise in the standard of living. In return, the state expected society to respect that it had turned the 1956 revolution into a taboo subject and generally to refrain from political life and addressing political issues.

Since the regime made a form of political behaviour the subject of a political deal, apolitical conduct was elevated into a political act, namely one of accepting the regime. The notions of being reconciled and being broken were getting blurred. This is how the socialist state regime inflicted long-term damage on the democratic modes of conduct, as it drove its citizens to repress any feeling of oppression – and interpretation of that oppression – and motivated them to develop strategies of survival and advancement within the framework of the status quo. After the horrors of the prior two decades, and the subsequent internments and disenfranchisement, the regime suggested making individual compromises for the sake of peace and quiet; in other words, to focus on one's own advancement rather than on interpreting and criticizing the regime. Individual political views and compromises made for the sake of survival were relegated to personal issues by the required apolitical attitude, and asking about them became taboo even among close acquaintances. All of this helped sustain the rules of the game constructed by the regime, since the more successful compromises one could achieve in one's individual life, the more opportunities one could have within the system, and the harder it became to reflect on the regime's actions and the nature of the deal.

Thus, state power was continuously able to recreate itself in individual lives by managing to coerce society as a whole into accepting the rules of advancement. In this newer system of oppression, people had to resolve or put up with fundamental contradictions that citizens of Western democracies would have a hard time perceiving. The concept of the grey zone may help to understand and interpret the conditions relating to artists' activities at the time, such as the issues and dilemmas regarding their livelihood, censorship and contact with the Western art world. The notion of the grey zone allows one to move beyond the dichotomies of victim/suppressor, sell-out/rebel, Good/Evil or us/them. Being overly reductive, those black-and-white categorizations cannot address the highly complex mechanisms of the system's operation. The following basic understanding may lead to a more sensitive approach: the strict boundaries of the Stalinist dictatorship gave way to a more relaxed framework of rules and implementation of power in the Kádár regime, in relation to which the practice of art under the socialist state regime can be construed as a grey zone.

The concept of the grey zone was introduced by the Italian writer Primo Levi in his characterization of the micro-society of concentration camps. Partly as a result of the mixed role of prisoner-functionaries, certain groups of prisoners with relative privilege emerged even among the victims in the Nazi death camps. Membership of these groups increased one's chances of survival and blurred the boundaries between us and them. As Levi writes: 'the enemy was all around but also inside, the "we" lost its limits, the contenders were not two, one could not discern a single frontier but rather many confused, perhaps innumerable frontiers, which stretched between each of us.'[2] He continues a little later: 'It is naive, absurd, and historically false to believe that an infernal system such as National Socialism sanctifies its victims: on the contrary, it degrades them, it makes them resemble itself, and this all the more when they are available, blank, and lacking a political or moral armature.'[3]

Levi's concept of the grey zone has since been employed to interpret countless social conflicts and violent oppressive regimes from the Vichy government of occupied France during the Second World War through South African apartheid to South American military dictatorships.[4] The Czech sociologist Jiřina Šiklová wrote a particularly relevant study in 1990 on the application of the term to East-Central European art in the 1960s–70s.[5] While discussing the role of the Czechoslovakian intelligentsia after 1968, when the Soviet Union sent troops in to occupy the country in response to its political liberalization, she refers to the grey zone as a sphere of mobility and a form of conduct within the given social and political framework. She states that there were few people truly loyal to the Party and just as few who were real dissidents, so social processes were largely determined by two other roles: by the consumerist, apolitical and largely passive behaviour of the majority of the population, and by the activity of those existing in the grey zone. She included in the latter group those professionals who kept their jobs at the universities and research institutes after 1968, but who shared the politic sentiments of those fired, with whom they also remained in (often supportive) contact. The researchers, artists and intellectuals who belonged to the grey zone did not cooperate with the regime directly, yet in their acceptance of its rewards and exploitation of the advantages of institutional positions (a permanent job, the opportunity to travel, fellowships, professional training and advancement), they did not merely make their lives easier, but also contributed to sustaining the power structure. Moreover, because they were not actively engaged in politics, they had more time to build their professional careers, which further expanded their range of possibilities compared to those who chose the path of direct political resistance or internal exile.

Individual compromises with the regimes in the Soviet bloc and the moral assessment of them are still highly sensitive issues. This is partly because the period before the political transition from Soviet influence at the end of the 1980s is still historically close, but also due to the fact that discussions of this issue are still primarily determined by current power balances in party and professional politics, which prevents nuanced discussion. Therefore, expanding Šiklová's concept of the grey zone from a specific role to an interpretive framework for the entirety of the art field of state socialism offers not only a chance for refining dichotomies, but also an opportunity for starting a new approach, which primarily aims at understanding the nature of oppression rather than morally evaluating or denouncing the participants.

The rise of Stalinism in Hungary in 1949, when the Hungarian People's Republic was created by the Soviet-influenced MSZMP, brought art under Party control. Unlike in the Western system based considerably on the free trade of art, involving buying and selling by collectors, in the Eastern bloc predominantly the state regulated art, based on the ideological principle that art was not a commodity. A system of managing and financing the visual and applied arts through clearly delineated roles and spheres of responsibility was set up in Hungary by the mid-1960s and regulated the art scene until the political transition.[6] The centralized system of state institutions that controlled all cultural processes at every stage was governed by political and ideological preferences and had four basic pillars. The Művelődésügyi Minisztérium (Ministry of Culture) was where general directives and regulations were crafted. The Magyar Népköztársaság Művészeti Alapja (simply called Művészeti Alap – Art Fund of the Hungarian People's Republic) coordinated the most important regulatory issues relating to the livelihood of artists and the creation of artworks. The Soviet-style Magyar Képző- és Iparművészek Szövetsége (Association of Hungarian Artists) functioned as a kind of professional advisory institution; whereas the Képző- és Iparművészeti Lektorátus (Supervisory Body for Arts and Crafts) functioned as an independent institution of censorship, having separated from the review department of the Művészeti Alap.

Only the members of the Művészeti Alap counted officially as artists in Hungary. There was technically no unemployment in the years of state socialism, and anyone who was not officially employed risked imprisonment as they were regarded as deliberately avoiding work, and therefore a danger to the good of society. As long as they were members of the Művészeti Alap, the state ensured the livelihood of artists in a centrally regulated way. Thus membership of the organization was mandatory if one wished to make a living as a creative artist and receive state funds related to art.

An extremely small minority opted out of participation in the art institutions of the regime, taking jobs clearly distinct from their creative activities. These included, among others, people imprisoned for their activities in the 1956 revolution and those expelled from or never admitted to university or professional institutes. Reflecting on the regime's principle of 'whoever is not against us is with us', it expected artists to join this network of institutions.

One of the forms of state-ensured livelihood was what was known as the 'Képcsarnok purchase'. The Képcsarnok Vállalat (Art Gallery Company) operated a system of 'state art trade' with regular and frequent submissions, where artists were supposed to submit works conforming to the latest criteria of style, subject and size. The pictures admitted were then sold to the public at various locations across the country. Since there was no market in the Western sense, it was the state that kept artists afloat with purchases in a market that was artificially generated. The centralized management of art affairs and the sale of artworks as symbolic 'welfare' goods were instruments of power that had multiple benefits. With the accumulation of material goods and the growth of consumption guaranteed by the state, the socialist state could make good on its promise to raise the standard of living through the paternalistic support of art. At the same time, most of the artists, despite their ironic attitude to the 'state art market', had to rely on this opportunity in the absence of an alternative outlet for sales, and therefore had a compliant role in strategic matters of state power. Finally, the enormous influx of pictures created earnings for the state.

Another important source of artists' income was what was known as the 'two-million purchase' held two or three times a year, spending first two, later three and six-million Hungarian forints. While the Képcsarnok sales primarily targeted the population, and covered the smaller size and lower price range artworks, this purchase was invented for the higher price range artworks and typically involved museum collections and state institutions.[7]

Naturally, the socialist state art market only motivated part of the production, while the other part, namely official commissions, were more significant not only because they meant state representation, but also in terms of income and artistic prestige. In these commissions, preference was clearly given to those who had proven their political loyalty, for example, as professors at the Magyar Képzőművészeti Főiskola (Hungarian Academy of Fine Arts) or by accepting various official positions.

The result was a situation in which boundaries were blurred, and – due to the fact that earning a livelihood was guaranteed if your art conformed to state expectations – the overwhelming majority of artists separated their political views and their professional activities in the interest of making a living. For example, membership of the Művészeti Alap and relations with state art institutions were not seen as political statements. Paradoxically, precisely because this very separation was the basis of the Kádárian deal offered, this is what made politics inseparable from any other (professional or aesthetic) consideration. As art historian Géza Perneczky points out, the case of Miklós Erdély illustrates this contradiction well: when Erdély wrote a study in the mid-1960s arguing that political demonstrations would become the most important means of artistic expression in the future, he submitted the article to the journal *Valóság*, positioned as an intellectual niche publication within the cultural political establishment.[8]

Although the choices of separation had been made, these dilemmas related to livelihood were so profound that artists – as numerous memoirs indicate – often experienced their participation in painting for Képcsarnok as a form of tension or even as a 'schizophrenic' state, since the work they produced for Képcsarnok sales were mainly – and especially in the earlier period of the regime – incompatible with their own artistic inquiries.[9] The stylistic criteria of Képcsarnok shifted with time; while the early 1960s were dominated by a strict rejection of abstraction, the domesticated abstract and semi-abstract tendencies became the new stylistic criteria of Képcsarnok by the 1980s concurrently with the appearance of the latest enemies – actionism and conceptualism – around 1968. These changes gave artists more stylistic freedom.

For example, when an exhibition was held at the Műcsarnok (the Kunsthalle, or Budapest Palace of Exhibitions), the representative exhibition venue of the Magyar Képző- és Iparművészek Szövetsége, in 1971, a group of nonfigurative artists also applied on the condition that none of them would be rejected by the jury. They succeeded, and those involved experienced this as an emblematic case of a collective promotion of interests.[10] This compromise was no less beneficial for the cultural political establishment. Exhibiting members of the new generation who had already been to the West proved how open the regime was, and it fitted well with the attempt to transform socialist realism into socialist modernism by integrating new nonfigurative tendencies that could be interpreted as neo-constructivist.

Behind the protective shield of official art membership, artists also attempted to make money in various other ways. Applied art projects such as graphic work for exhibitions, advertisements or book illustrations, or even teaching, were such additional sources of income. The regular income of a life partner or spouse was also crucial for many, but private purchases and contacts with collectors also intensified in the late 1960s.

The writer Imre Kertész evokes the compromises of the era quite vividly:

I once said that so-called Socialism for me was the petite madeleine cake that, dipped into Proust's tea, evoked in him the flavor of bygone years. For reasons having to do with the language I spoke, I decided, after the suppression of the 1956 revolt, to remain in Hungary. Thus I was able to observe, not as a child this time but as an adult, how a dictatorship functions. I saw how an entire nation could be made to deny its ideals, and watched the early, cautious moves toward accommodation. I understood that hope is an instrument of evil, and the Kantian categorical imperative – ethics in general – is but the pliable handmaiden of self-preservation...By the nineteen-sixties, the dictatorship in Hungary had reached a state of consolidation that could almost be called a societal consensus....In the miry depths of this consensus, one either gave up the struggle or found the winding paths to inner freedom.[11]

In order to win over artists and intellectuals, the regime provided financial security in a structure that severely limited artistic reflection on – or even knowledge of – the operation of power. At the same time, it also relied on the application of coercive but informal instruments of power, particularly in situations where boundaries were less than transparent.

As Jeremy Morris and Abel Polese have emphatically claimed, the reliance on social capital is a crucial condition of the establishment and resilience of the grey zone.[12] In terms of using power within the grey zone of the socialist state art institutions, this corresponded to the frequent informal compromises, unofficial paths and techniques of informal pressure within formal frameworks of organization. Nothing illustrates this better than the way censorship worked.

The principle of differentiating between degrees of censorship appeared as early as the directives of cultural policy adopted by the Party in 1958. It was formally the Magyar Képző- és Iparművészeti Lektorátus that implemented this through a system of supported, tolerated and banned works known as the 'Three Ts' (for the Hungarian equivalents '*támogat – tűr – tilt*'; see also Edit Sasvári, 'Autonomy and Doublespeak', pp. 8–17). Socialist realist works were worthy of support, works trying to undermine socialist state order had to be banned, and the middle category offered the possibility of a kind of stylistic experimentation for works that were compatible with the idea of socialism or were not hostile to it. However, these categories did not offer any specific reference point to the juries evaluating the works, since the criteria of socialist realism had gradually loosened by the late 1950s and early 1960s. As the official system of aesthetic expectations integrated the traditions of early twentieth-century Hungarian and French painting (domesticating first the tradition established by the art colony at Nagybánya in the late nineteenth century, then expressionist, cubist and other modernist tendencies), the criteria for supported, tolerated and banned works was in constant flux. Exhibiting artists could directly and indirectly influence the composition of the jury, which generated mutual favours between jury members and artists. As a result, even though these categories formally existed, in reality there was a refinement of the parameters of permission and prohibition and, in turn, there was increasing potential for negotiation between the artists and the authorities.[13] This was advantageous for the authorities because they could attempt to corrupt individual artists by employing non-public, oral forms of control and compromise, such as allusions and blackmail, in the course of making particular deals.

One of the important oral techniques for the informal use of power involved the concealment of the hierarchical relationship; the person representing the powers-that-be would attempt to present the situation as an interaction between equals. This technique would typically prolong the discourse and extend its content to the personal and private. This may have led to a violation of the subordinated party's sphere of intimacy and even to blackmail (for instance, implicitly or explicitly touching on the future prospects of their children or close relatives, and their opportunities for travel and employment).
It is this penetration of privacy by power that Miklós Erdély reflects on in his photographic work, *Two People Who Have Had a Decisive Influence on My Life* (1972, p. 240, fig. 9), depicting textile artist Zsuzsa Szenes, the artist's wife, and János Kádár, General Secretary of the Party, which incidentally resulted in the disqualification of Erdély's wife from state commissions for a while (see also Edit András, 'Out of Private Public Opinion into Shared Personal Opinion', pp. 229–49).[14]

Another chief characteristic of this technique was the use of a language overburdened with allusions and implications, in which nearly every word and sentence referred to something else, usually something personal. This was made both necessary and possible by the concealment of the true balance of power, by the impossibility of articulating the rules. As the writer Péter Nádas explains:

It's as if a sentence only had a context, but you couldn't utter the sentence itself. Less than a decade passed after the defeated revolution, and the smartest minds of the Hungarian intelligentsia stood there completely stupefied by their own double-decker sentences, as if János Kádár had not been forced by the Russians to retroactively call them in, but as if they had actually wished them to return and subjugate all Hungarians in the interest of universal good. [They managed to make people accept] that the reality of weapons was stronger than the freedom of thought, and therefore inarticulate sign language was more important for survival than articulate speech.[15]

To sum up, one of the things that contributed to the roughly outlined grey zone in Hungarian art of the 1960s–70s was the use of an informal instrument of power that created the semblance of a particular relationship between state power and individuals within a dictatorial regime: the pretence of a relationship between equals and of well-meaning paternalistic relations. Communication continuously sustained the appearance that mutually beneficial deals could be made between the parties. The panels that were developed in this process were not supplementary devices of control, but rather pillars of the regime, which helped foster individual deals and hybrid models, ceaselessly crossing the lines of force connecting the seemingly fundamental markers and dichotomies (Party membership, the status of banned or supported artist) within the increasingly pliable institutional environment.

When artists dealt with this type of power in their works, they employed various registers of irony to reflect on how it took advantage of fluctuating, blurred, and re-codable meanings. Especially after the appearance of conceptual art in Hungary in the early 1970s, some artists reacted to the workings of the state by twisting and re-contextualizing the visual symbols of the regime and exaggerating its linguistics to the point of absurdity. Since the avant-garde programmatically dealt with politics, it was primarily artists in neo-avant-garde circles who exploited this possibility of reflection. Examples of this include Endre Tót's photo series *I am glad if...* in the early to mid-1970s,

2

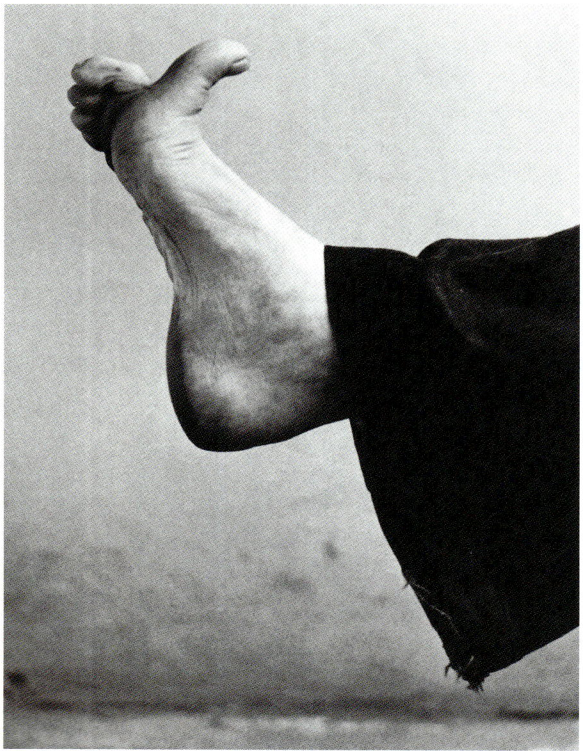

2. Endre Tót, *I am glad if I can do this*, 1973–76, silver gelatine print, 12 × 9 cm, acb Galéria, Budapest

3. Endre Tót, *I am glad if I can jump a little*, 1973–76, silver gelatine print, 12 × 9 cm, acb Galéria, Budapest

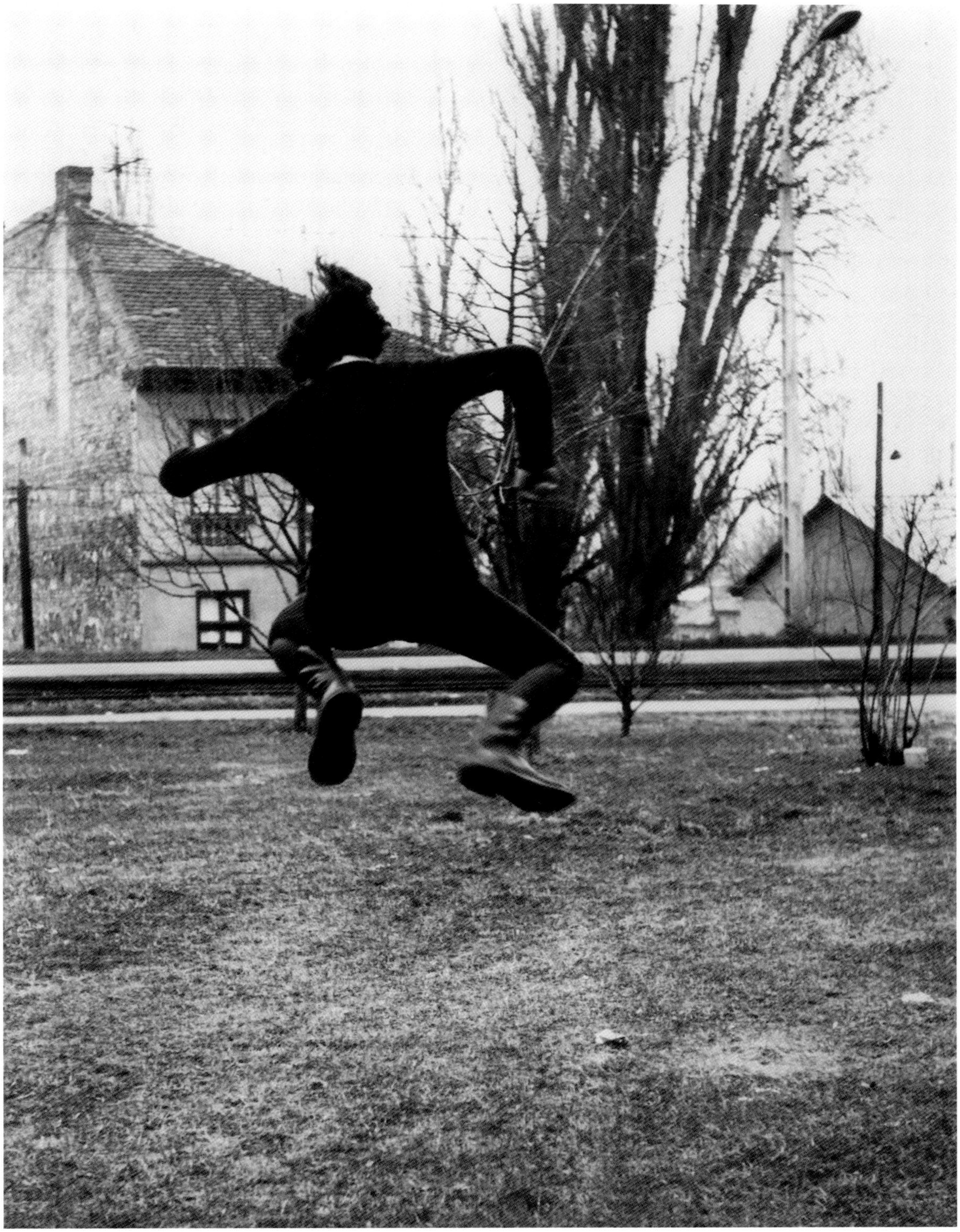

3

which depicts trivial acts and situations as a state of happiness to reflect on society's shift to increasingly petit-bourgeois values (see also Edit András, 'Out of Private Public Opinion into Shared Personal Opinion', pp. 229–49). The absurdity of the images is ironic, but it also exudes bitterness over the extreme constraints of fundamental action and the elevation of the most banal activities to the level of the symbolic (*I am glad if I can take a step*, *I am glad if I can look at you*, *I am glad if I can jump a little*, *I am glad if I can write one sentence after another*, *I am glad if I can photograph my shadow*; figs 1–3; see also pp. 241–43, figs 11–13).[16] The action objects by Tamás Szentjóby in the 1960s were also ironic reflections on the use of language by the regime, wherein there is an aesthetic and political force field between objects and their names (*Portable Trench for Three* – p. 54, fig. 13; *Cooling Water* – p. 322, fig. 4; and *A New Unit of Measurement* – p. 281, fig. 8).

The multimedia artist Sándor Pinczehelyi re-contextualized the symbols of communism and socialism in a similarly ironic manner with his gesture of laying out cobblestones in the form of the pentagram (fig. 4) in Dóra Maurer's action, *What Can One Do With a Paving Stone?* (p. 237, fig. 7). Irony was at work in the personification and animation of these symbols in György Galántai's performance *Homage to Vera Mukhina on Heroes' Square* in May 1980. Others expressed far more bitter registers of irony. István Harasztÿ's *Cage* (fig. 6) and Albert Kováts's *Ubu* series (fig. 5) represented the treacherous lies of the regime and the illusion of freedom with far more general symbols and cultural references. Yet others tried to create an autonomous territory for their art by refusing to deal with the operations of power even in the form of critical reflection, or attempted to leave the system by joining non-European and non-modern cultural traditions. Sándor Molnár, for instance, developed a special kind of painting yoga on the basis of lyrical abstraction and abstract expressionism.

Privacy, which was of heightened importance in the life of intellectuals and artists in the 1960s, was a characteristic aspect of the grey zone. In accordance with Kádár's deal, state power respected privacy; yet, despite this declared principle, a significant part of the intelligentsia was under surveillance, circles of friends were infiltrated by informers, and the information obtained in this manner was exploited in the informal use of power. That said, the private sphere expanded in the 1960s compared to the era of the Stalinist dictatorship[17] and – due to the strict control of the public sphere – it came to include social functions (exhibitions, concerts, lectures and debates) that would belong to the public sphere in a democratic society. At the same time, a particular defence mechanism emerged as a correlative of the informal use of power: partly as a technical necessity in response to surveillance (those under surveillance were usually aware of or suspected the fact), spoken communication and allusive language also characterized the private sphere, where they aided concealment through coded information, but also functioned as a secret subcultural language and shared knowledge that became an important component of identity and the foundation of a sense of belonging.

The development of private space was closely connected to changes in the cultural political climate and to fluctuations in the attitude to the West. Control was quite strict during the first five years after the 1956 revolution and the consequent reprisals. Only those travelling on state business or who had the highest political connections could visit Western countries. Only a very limited range of Western art publications could be found, primarily journals in the foreign language bookshop in Váci utca, one of the principle shopping streets in Budapest. A French book exhibition in 1959 attests to the conditions at the beginning of the period: the exhibition, which toured countries of the Eastern bloc under the watchful eye of the French Minister of Cultural Affairs André Malraux, essentially evaporated by the end of the tour as the exhibited material kept going missing. This emphasizes the scarcity of Western material, which was why events held in private spaces and by invitation-only were so important in the late 1950s and early 1960s: they allowed a measure of cultural transfer and access to information. The Budapest 'salons' of Pál Petrigalla and Dr László Végh were particularly crucial for information about visual art; the former salon referred to a small apartment

4. Sándor Pinczehelyi, *Star (cobblestone)*, 1972, black and white photos mounted on fibreboard, 6 × 50 × 60 cm, Paksi Képtár, Paks

5. Albert Kováts, *Father Ubu*, 1967, oil on canvas, 60 × 50 cm, Private collection

6. István Harasztÿ, *Cage*, 1972, steel, brass, electronics, 62 × 34 × 50 cm, Szent István Király Múzeum, Székesfehérvár

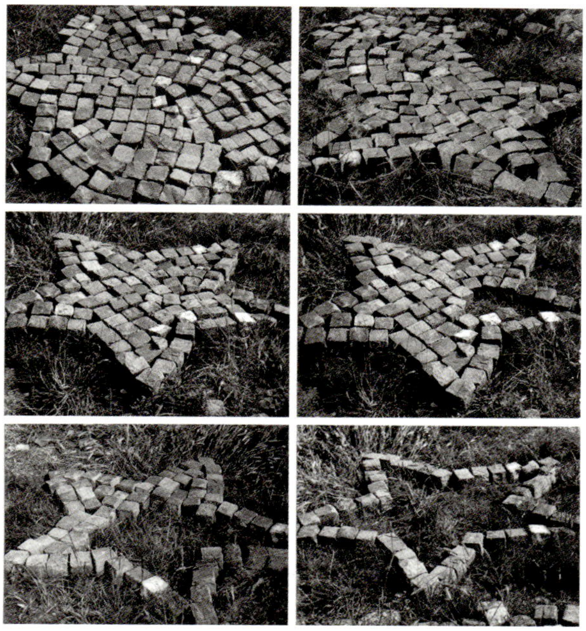

4

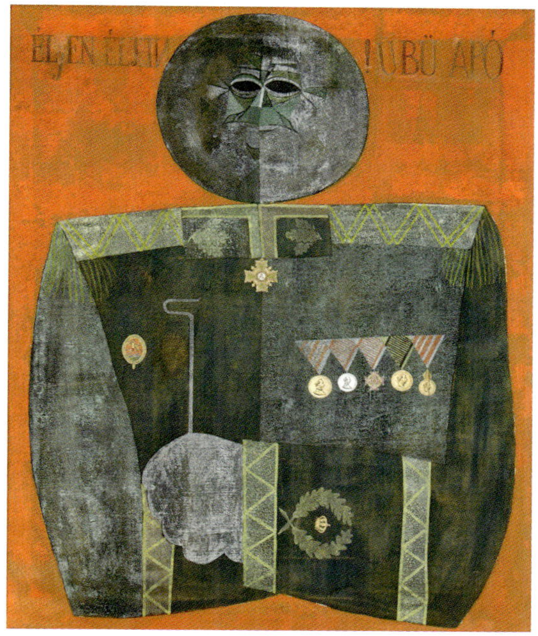

5

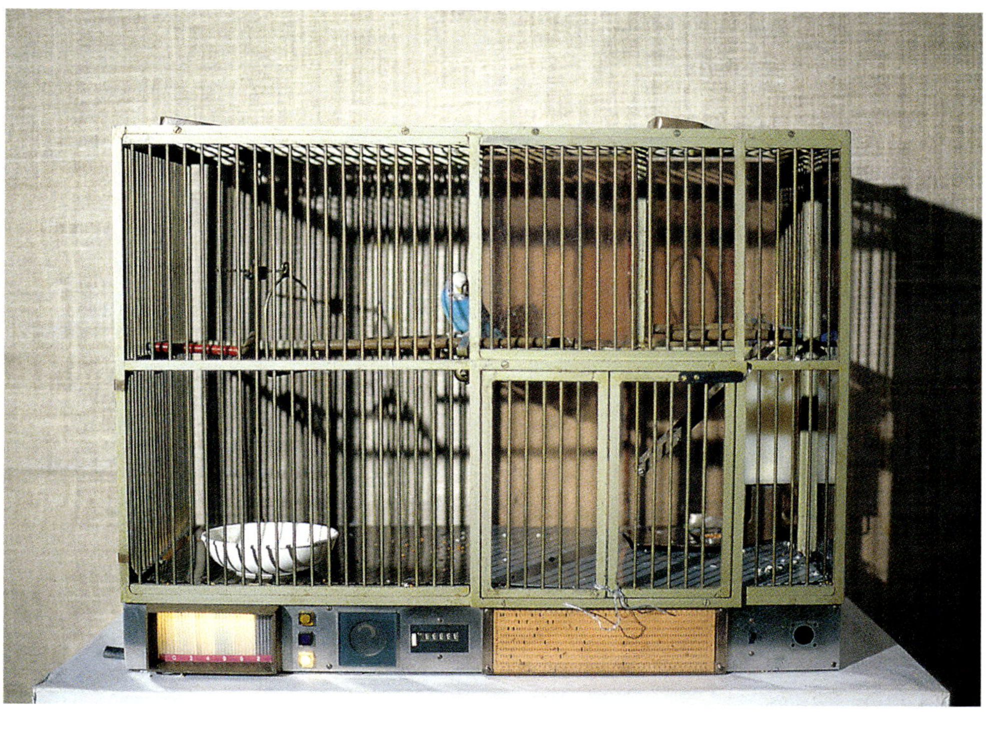

6

in Vécsey utca, while the latter was a single room on Rákóczi tér.[18] Petrigalla organized a series of events entailing listening to records and chamber exhibitions, and his apartment served as a meeting place for various intellectuals and artists' groups.[19] People found out about them through the grapevine, and admission was also conditional on such personal networks. At the same time, Végh's room was a workshop of learning about avant-garde music and shaped the attitudes of the emerging neo-avant-garde generation.[20] A similar salon, or rather debating group, was the circle of friends surrounding painter Sándor Molnár, a devotee of the Gnostic philosophy of Béla Hamvas (a writer and philosopher, who from 1948 was discouraged from participating in public affairs and went into internal exile) (fig. 7). Members of this circle (Imre Bak, István Nádler and Pál Deim) began to take an interest in the new American geometric abstraction of the mid-1960s. Meeting at Molnár's apartment in the Zugló district in 1958–63, the members set up a self-education group, trying to learn about Hungarian and international avant-garde initiatives. They also strove to survey European avant-garde art from Bauhaus to Jean Bazaine and French lyrical abstraction in the form of producing translations and arranging debates about them.[21]

The hunger for information did not apply to Western culture alone; in fact, it was not until the late 1960s that the regime gradually came to accept the art of the Európai Iskola (European School), which strove to integrate regional, Eastern European and Western European traditions organically during its activities in 1945–48. Of the most influential artists of Európai Iskola, Lajos Kassák, Dezső Korniss and Endre Bálint (fig. 8) were not admitted to the state organization of artists, Magyar Képző- és Iparművészek Szövetsége, until 1967; once admitted, they were at least theoretically allowed to have major state exhibitions and receive funding for them, although Kassák's 'Picture architecture' exhibition on the eightieth birthday of the artist was still granted only in self-financed form. Besides, there were contexts in which a reference to artists of the Európai Iskola could produce tension or serve as a pretext for rejection even in the late 1970s. When 'fellow traveller' Miklós Szüts intended to substitute as a gesture of respect a painting by Endre Bálint for his own work at the exhibition of the Fiatal Képzőművészek Stúdiója (Young Artists' Studio) in 1978, the jury objected.

Artists of the Európai Iskola would become masters of the new generation of artists coming of age in the 1960s outside the framework of official training. This was an alternative socialization, as it were, through individual contact and studio visits (for instance, Lajos Kassák was a personal mentor for János Fajó, Endre Bálint for Lili Ország (fig. 9), Dezső Korniss for Endre Tót, and Ferenc Martyn for Ilona Keserü).

Overall, as sociologist Ferenc Hammer notes,

The multitude of personal private spheres that slowly grew into a network was an important event in the transformation of the public sphere in the sixties not only in a topographic sense; the networks actually began to function as a system of values and norms that integrated the personal, but also rose above it as a larger 'social fact'.[22]

From the mid-1960s on, the goal of state power was not so much to prohibit, but rather to influence and control the Western orientation of the new generations. After Hungary allowed greater freedom of movement in 1963, there was a growing range of opportunities for gaining Western experiences. The majority of artists could make trips to the West once every two or three years with a tourist passport and the $70 currency exchange allowance; this included nearly every member of the young neo-avant-garde generation, who encountered pop art and hard-edge painting there in the mid-1960s, and a rising number of them began to exhibit in the West as well.[23]

Besides West German art historians Klaus Honnef and Jürgen Weichardt, the most important Western contact for the neo-avant-garde generation was Dieter Honisch. After meeting Imre Bak and István Nádler in Stuttgart in 1968, he gave numerous exhibition and fellowship opportunities to Hungarian neo-constructivist and neo-avant-garde artists in his capacity as the director of the Museum Folkwang, Essen, from the early 1970s onwards (fig. 10). Evenings and art events (e.g. private film premieres) organized by Western (particularly the British, German, French and

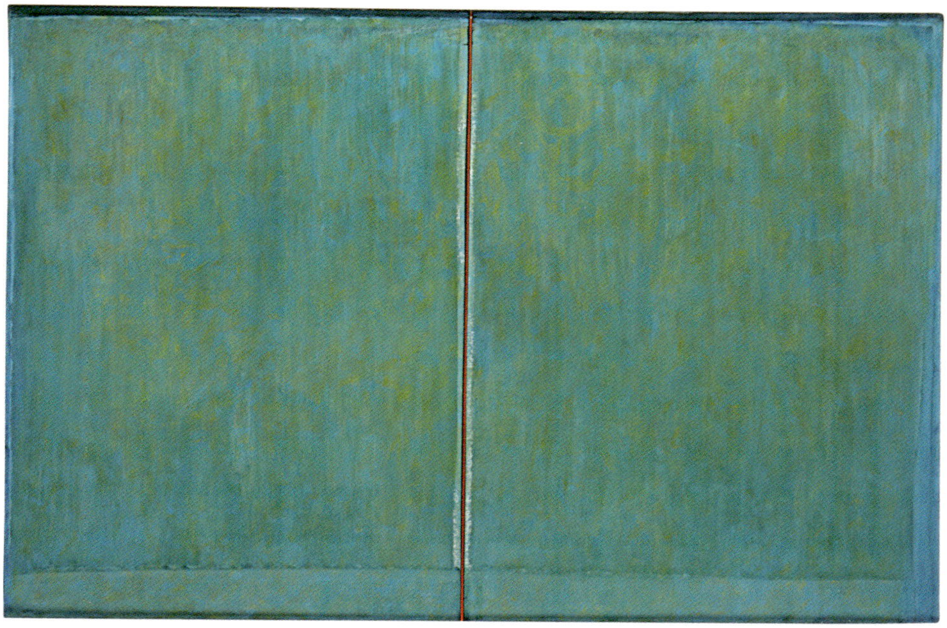

7

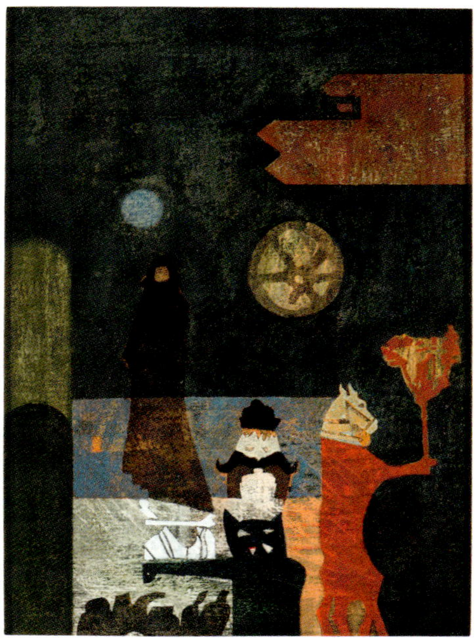

8

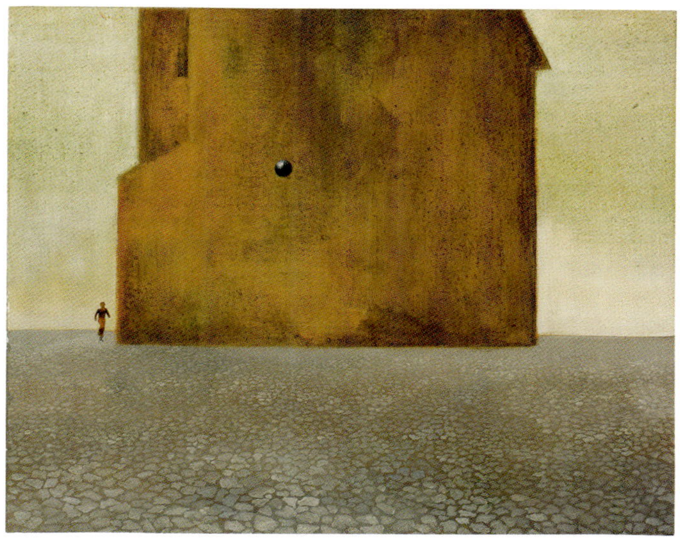

9

7. Sándor Molnár, *Principle*, 1968, oil, acrylic, canvas, lath, 98 × 134 cm, Szépművészeti Múzeum – Magyar Nemzeti Galéria, Budapest

8. Endre Bálint, *Grotesque Burial*, 1963, oil on canvas, 92 × 66 cm, Szépművészeti Múzeum – Magyar Nemzeti Galéria, Budapest

9. Lili Ország, *Great Wall II (Ballplayers)*, 1955, oil on canvas, 55 × 65 cm, Antal-Lusztig Collection, Debrecen

American) embassies in Budapest became especially important for neo-avant-garde artists, art historians and the critics of official papers in the 1970s, because of the networking opportunities they provided.

However, the expansion of opportunities to encounter contemporary Western art did not mean that the works resulting from the impact of such encounters could actually be exhibited in Hungary in the 1960s. Despite the atmosphere of a thaw, even exhibitions deliberately organized in marginal venues, away from the mainstream institutions, were closed down without further ado before the opening or after a few days. Such cases included 'Reptéri kiállítás' (Airport Exhibition) in the cultural club of the Ferihegy airport in 1966, the 'Iparterv' exhibitions (see also Gábor Dobó and Merse Pál Szeredi, 'Hungarian Culture +/- Europe', pp. 39–57, for more information on the 'Iparterv' exhibitions) organized by art historian Péter Sinkovits in the lobby of an office for industrial planning in 1968 and 1969, and the 'R' exhibition initiated by artist and exhibition organizer Attila Csáji in a club in one of the halls of residence at the Budapesti Műszaki Egyetem (Budapest University of Technology) in 1970, where the Szürenon and Iparterv groups were presented on a common platform.[24] The last of these revealed the complexity and contradictions of the state's cultural policy especially well, since the Magyar Képző- és Iparművészeti Lektorátus resolved to ban the exhibition, but it was opened by the vice-director of the Magyar Nemzeti Galéria (Hungarian National Gallery),

10

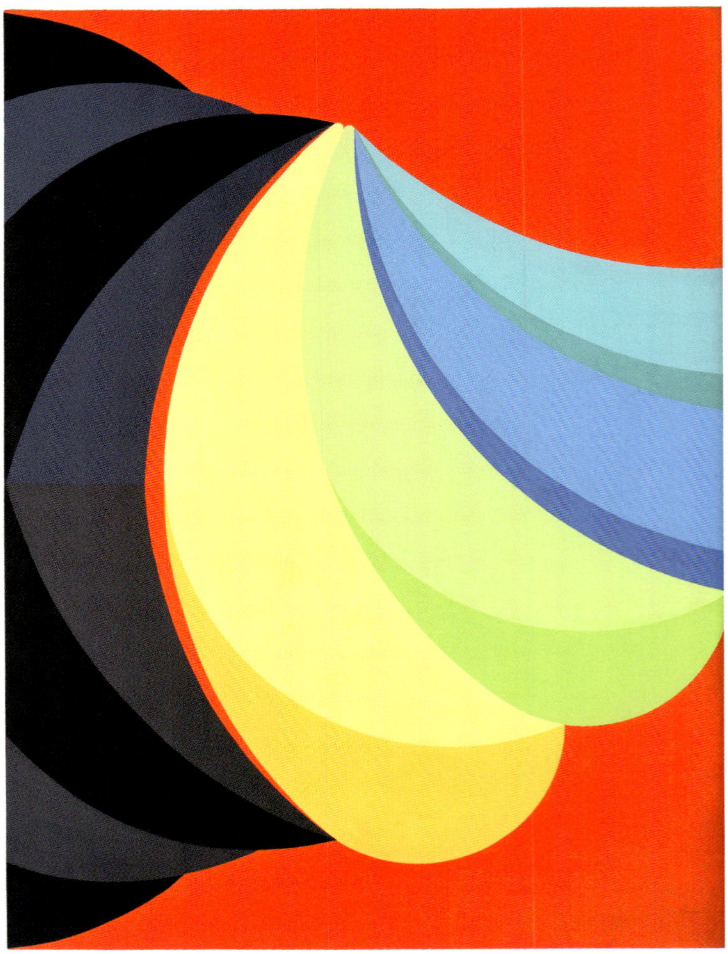

10. István Nádler, *Violence*, 1968, caseine tempera, acrylic, canvas, 199.5 × 150 cm, Ludwig Múzeum – Kortárs Művészeti Múzeum, Budapest

11. The exhibition 'K 358/72'. Pictured: András Orvos and György Szemadám (in the centre), Árpád Fenyvesi Tóth and Ottó Mezei (right), György Galántai (on the balcony), 1972, the Balatonboglári Kápolnaműterem of György Galántai (György Galántai's Balatonboglár Chapel Studio)

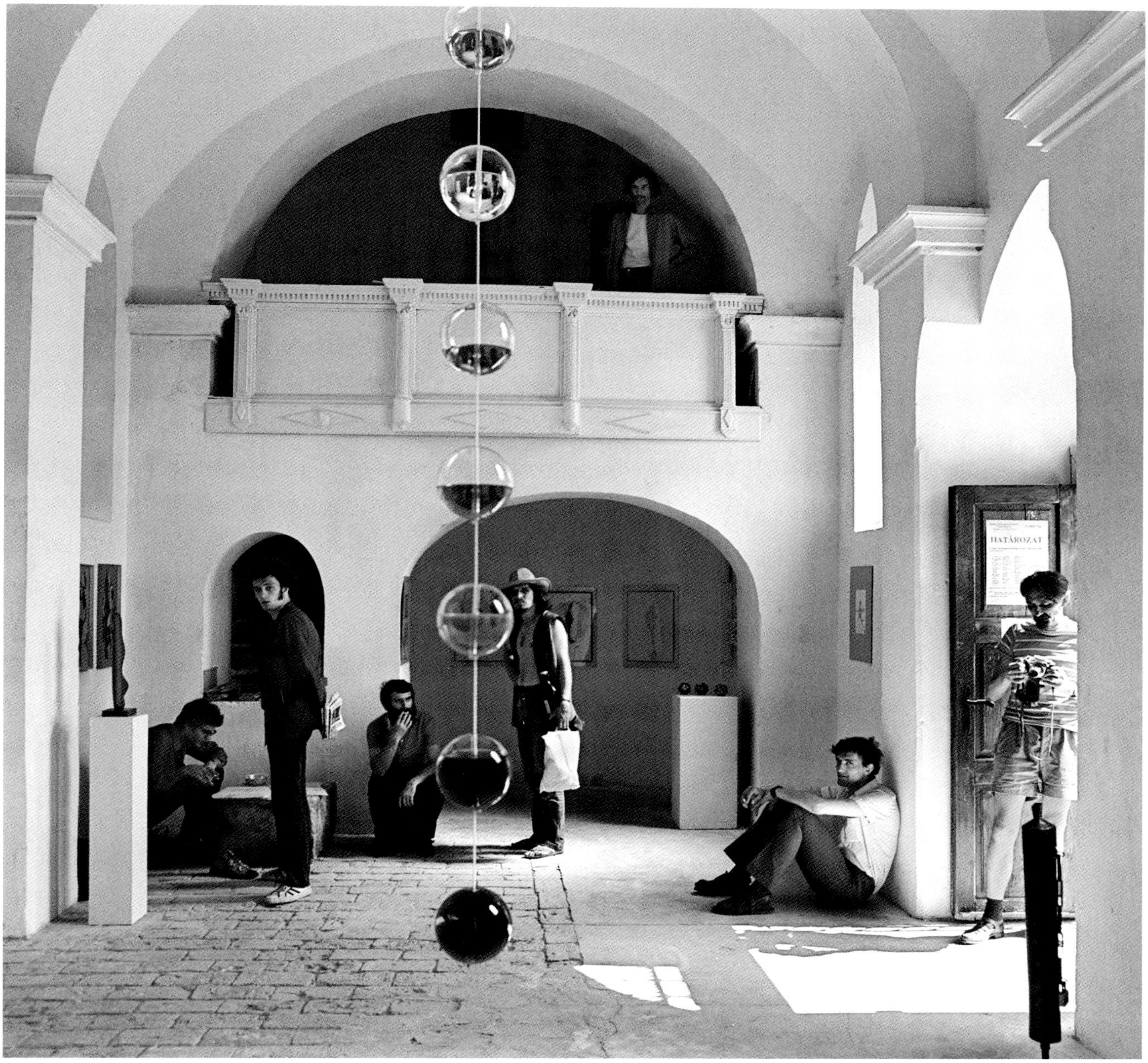

11

and was attended both by the director of the Képző- és Iparművészeti Lektorátus and by György Aczél, who oversaw cultural life as a whole in his capacity as secretary of the Central Committee of the MSZMP.[25] Exhibitions held in another peripheral venue, György Galántai's Balatonboglári Kápolnaműterem (the Balatonboglár Chapel Studio of György Galántai; see Maja Fowkes and Reuben Fowkes, 'Liberty Controlled', pp. 77–93, and Klara Kemp-Welch, 'Soft-spoken Encounters', pp. 273–89) in 1970–73, belonged to the grey zone of the exhibition scene in a broader sense. These exhibitions managed to organize modernist and neo-avant-garde events legally by exploiting loopholes in the jury selection system (fig. 11).[26]

Artistic practices that reflected upon the state control of cultural networking described above also emerged in the early 1970s as a development of Fluxus and conceptual art. The majority of them used, or rather exploited, the main communication channel that symbolized state control, namely the postal services. While the American and West European variants of mail art (and the related network art) that flourished in the 1960s offered primarily a critique of capitalism and the art market, their counterparts in the Eastern bloc – where there was an expectation that letters would be screened and diverted – reflected on the controlled flow of information and thereby inescapably critiqued socialism. Partly because of the internationalist attitude of the avant-garde, the neo-avant-garde generation of artists that emerged in the early 1960s was quite substantially involved in a wave of defections in the 1970s, which added a further political layer to Hungarian mail art.[27] The most significant works in this respect are the postcard series *Rain* and *Zero* and artist's stamps by Endre Tót (fig. 12) and György Galántai's extensive mail-art activities (mail-art works, action correspondence with the authorities on non-artistic matters and stamp pictures). Mail art and network art often entailed art-management tasks as well. One exceptional Hungarian example was László Beke's project *Imagination/Idea* in 1971, in the framework of which he invited artists – as if in a prelude to Hungarian conceptual art – to send him their artistic project plans on paper through the mail. Another example was the grand NET project initiated by the Polish artists Jarosław Kozłowski and Andrzej Kostołowski at the end of 1971, which attempted to connect artists and art historians in the Eastern bloc and beyond the Iron Curtain, and to create an extended transnational art network.[28]

The emergence of the flexible and negotiable boundaries of the grey zone were facilitated by the state's use of both formal organizations and informal modes of pressure to ensure the conformity and loyalty of artists after the defeat of the 1956 revolution. This technique, however, affected the operation of the regime in turn, disintegrating the fabric of power in ever more vivid ways by the end of the period. Additionally, a new attitude emerged in the 1980s concurrently with the development of a democratic political opposition: negotiating with state power and conforming to informal techniques of power that continuously blurred the boundaries between the private and public were abandoned, and communication with the regime was now kept intentionally formal. This distancing in communication and in contact was a necessary condition for developing a systematic and increasingly broad critique of the techniques of power that were used within state socialism.

12. Endre Tót: *First-class Rain/Second-class Rain*, 1979–94, acrylic on photo canvas, 42 × 51 cm, Ludwig Múzeum – Kortárs Művészeti Múzeum, Budapest

12

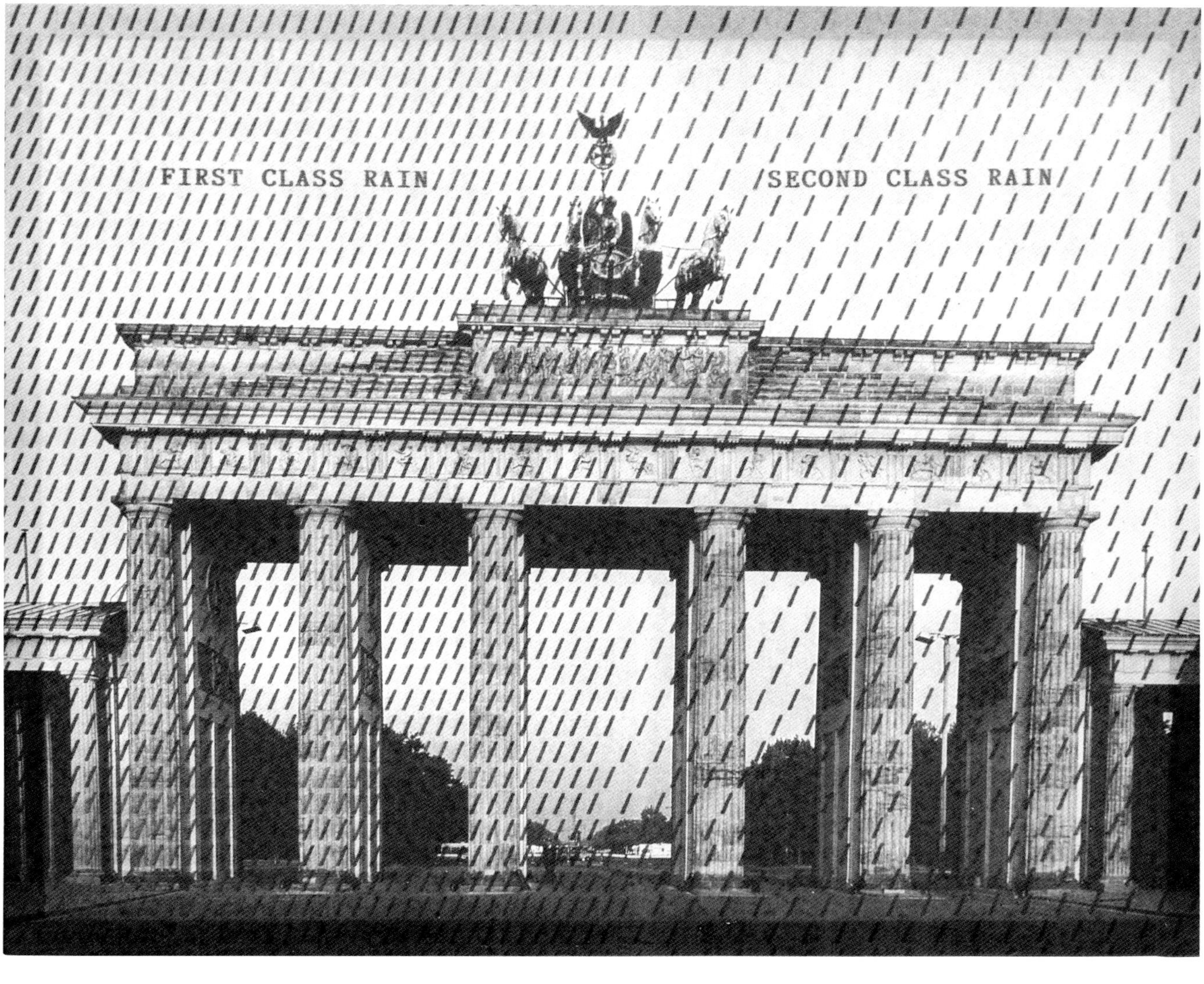

1 Péter György, *Apám helyett* [Instead of My Father]. Budapest: Magvető Kiadó, 2011, 54–57.
2 Primo Levi, *The Drowned and the Saved*, trans. Raymond Rosenthal. New York: Simon & Schuster, 1988, 38.
3 *Ibid.*, 40.
4 Most recently, GREYZONE Starting Grant Project, led by Mihaela Mihai and funded by the European Commission through the European Research Council, started in 2016. http://blogs.sps.ed.ac.uk/greyzone (23 June 2017).
5 Jiřina Šiklová, 'The "Grey Zone" and the Future of Dissent in Czechoslovakia', *Social Research*, Vol. 57, No. 2, Summer 1990, 347–63.
6 György Horváth, *A művészek bevonulása: A képzőművészet politikai irányításának és igazgatásának története 1945–1992* [The Entry of the Artists: The Story of the Political Control and Management of the Visual Arts 1945–1992]. Budapest: Corvina Kiadó, 2015, 251.
7 *Ibid.*, 256–63.
8 Géza Perneczky, 'Produktivitásra ítélve? Az Iparterv-csoport és ami utána következett Magyarországon' [Sentenced to Productivity? The Iparterv Group and What Followed It in Hungary], *Balkon*, Vol. 4, Nos 1–2, 1996, 5–22.
9 András Zwickl, 'Beszélgetés Keserü Ilonával' [A Conversation with Ilona Keserü], and Edit Szentesi, 'Beszélgetés Lakner Lászlóval' [A Conversation with László Lakner], in Ildikó Nagy (ed.), *Hatvanas évek: új törekvések a magyar képzőművészetben* [The Sixties: New Strivings in Hungarian Visual Art] (exhibition catalogue). Budapest: Képzőművészeti Kiadó – Magyar Nemzeti Galéria – Ludwig Múzeum, 1991, 139–50 and 125–38.
10 Gábor Bellák, 'Beszélgetés Bak Imrével' [A Conversation with Imre Bak], in Nagy, *Hatvanas évek*, 175–83.
11 Imre Kertész, 'Imre Kertész – Nobel Lecture: Heureka', trans. Ivan Sanders. *Nobelprize.org*. Nobel Media AB 2014. http://www.nobelprize.org/nobel_prizes/literature/laureates/2002/kertesz-lecture-e.html (20 April 2017).
12 Jeremy Morris and Abel Polese, 'Introduction: Informality – enduring practices, entwined livelihoods', in Jeremy Morris and Abe Polese (eds), *The Informal Post-socialist Economy: Embedded Practices and Livelihoods*. New York: Routledge, 2015, 1–19.
13 Sándor Révész, *Aczél és korunk* [Aczél and Our Age]. Budapest: Sík Kiadó, 1997, 75–85.
14 László Beke, 'A magyar konceptuális művészet szubjektív története' [A Subjective History of Hungarian Conceptual Art], in Pál Deréky and András Müllner (eds), *Né/ma? Tanulmányok a magyar neoavantgárd köréből* [Mute? Studies on the Hungarian Avant-garde]. Budapest: Ráció Kiadó, 2004, 227–39.
15 Péter Nádas, 'Az elvarázsolt párbeszéd: Révész Sándor Aczél és korunk című könyvéről' [The Enchanted Conversation: On Aczél and Our Age by Sándor Révész], *Nappali ház*, Vol. 9, No. 2, 1997, 3–15, 9.
16 Klara Kemp-Welch, 'Affirmation and Irony in Endre Tót's Actions of the 1970s', in Liniara Dovydaityte Kaunas (ed.), *Art History & Criticism 3, Art and Politics: Case-Studies from Eastern Europe*. Kaunas: Vytautas Magnus University, 2007, 136–44.
17 Ferenc Hammer, 'Az éjszakai élet mint populáris nyilvánosság a szocializmusban' [Night Life as a Popular Public Sphere in Socialism], in *...nem kellett élt vasalni a farmerbe. Mindennapi élet a szocializmusban* [...You Didn't Have to Iron a Crease into Your Jeans: Everyday Life in Socialism]. *MaDok füzetek* 8. Budapest: Néprajzi Múzeum, 2013, 82–104.
18 For more detail on Pál Petrigalla's salon, see Lóránt Bódi, 'Művészeti és közösségi élet Petrigalla Pál szalonjában 1959–1970' [Art and Community Life in Pál Petrigalla's salon 1959–1970], *Új Forrás*, Vol. 43, No. 6, 2011, 49–65.
19 Those exhibiting at Petrigalla's apartment in 1963–65 included Gábor Attalai, Imre Bak and István Nádler, Csaba Koncz and Sándor Csutoros, Attila Csáji, István Ventilla and István Lugossy, Elek Lisziák, and Péter Molnár and Kálmán Kecskeméti.
20 Through the art of Christian Wolff, Pierre Boulez, György Kurtág, Karlheinz Stockhausen and Edgard Varèse. For further information on the salon of László Végh, see Emese Kürti, 'Glissando és húrtépés: Kortárs zene az underground magánterekben, 1958–1970' [Glissando and Plucking Strings: Contemporary Music and Neo-Avant-garde in the Underground Spaces], Budapest: L'Harmattan, 2018.
21 The name of the Zuglói kör artists' group does not originate from this period. For information on Zuglói kör, see Flóra Barkóczi's and József Mélyi's contributions to this book (pp. 95–109 and 161–77), and Gábor Andrási, 'A Zuglói kör (1958–1968). Egy művészcsoport a 60-as évekből' [The Zuglói kör (1958–1968): An Artists' Group in the 1960s], *Ars Hungarica*, Vol. 19, No. 1, 1991, 47–64.

22 Hammer, 'Az éjszakai élet', 92.

23 For instance, Imre Bak and István Nádler, Galerie Müller, Stuttgart, 1968; Dóra Maurer, Galleria il Collezionista, Bologna, 1966; László Lakner, Künstler aus Ungarn, Baukunst Galerie, Cologne, 1970.

24 The name 'Szürenon' is derived from a combination of the words 'surrealism' and 'non-figuration', and also of 'sur' and 'non'. The goal of the group, which was founded by Attila Csáji, was to provide a forum for those artists who wished to address local artistic issues, reject official stylistic criteria and integrate Western stylistic approaches and regional specificities. Its first exhibition, held in 1969, featured the work of Gyula Bocz, Attila Csáji, Sándor Csutoros, István Harasztÿ, László Haris, István Ilyés, Gábor Karátson, Ferenc Lantos, Oszkár Papp, Gyula Pauer, Péter Prutkay, Péter Türk and Pál Veress. Csáji also helped organize exhibitions both in Hungary (for example, the Szürenon exhibition at the Kassák Művelődési Otthon [Kassák Culture Centre], 1969, an exhibition at the József Attila Művelődési Ház [Attila József Culture House] in the Angyalföld district of Budapest in the same year, and, initially, the exhibitions at György Galántai's Balatonboglár Chapel Studio), and abroad, contributing to the introduction of the Hungarian avant-garde to Poland and Yugoslavia in 1970–72. The most important of the latter was probably an exhibition in Poland co-organized with János Brendel in 1970, which was a collaboration between the Arsenal in Poznan, Museum Pomorse in Kosalin and the National Museum in Szczecin, jointly introducing the latest initiatives in Hungarian art.

25 Edit Sasvári, 'A balatonboglári kápolnatárlatok kultúrpolitikai háttere' [The Cultural Political Background of the Balatonboglár Chapel Studio Exhibitions], in Júlia Klaniczay and Edit Sasvári (eds), *Törvénytelen avantgárd: Galántai György balatonboglári kápolnaműterme, 1970–1973* [Illegal Avant-garde: The Balatonboglár Chapel Studio of György Galántai, 1970–1973]. Budapest: Artpool-Balassi, 2003, 9–39, especially 24.

26 Exhibitions classified as 'private studio displays' and open for no more than three days did not have to be submitted to the Képző- és Iparművészeti Lektorátus for jury review.

27 Defectors in the generation of artists coming of age in the late 1960s: Gábor Altorjay, Germany, 1966; Gyula Konkoly, France, 1970; Ludmil Siskov, Austria, 1969; Krisztián Frey, Switzerland, 1970; László Lakner, Germany, 1974; Tamás Szentjóby, a Swiss citizen through his mother, 1975; László Najmányi, France, Canada and the United States, 1979; Gergely Molnár, Western Europe, United States and Canada, 1978; András Halász, France and the United States, 1979; Orsolya Drozdik, United States, 1978; László Méhes, France, 1979; Endre Tót, Germany, 1978.

28 For more detail, see Flóra Barkóczi, 'Creative (Dis)Courses', pp. 95–109, and Klara Kemp-Welch, 'Soft-spoken Encounters', pp. 273–89; and Klara Kemp-Welch, 'NET: Jarosław Kozłowski in Conversation with Klara Kemp-Welch', *Artmargins*, Vol. 1, Nos 2–3, 2012, 14–35.

1

RUDOLF SIKORA, akademický maliar v spolupráci s VILIAMOM JAKUBÍKOM, akademickým maliarom, dovoľujú si Vám oznámiť presné údaje základov novej budovy Slovenskej národnej galérie, Rázusovo nábrežie 2

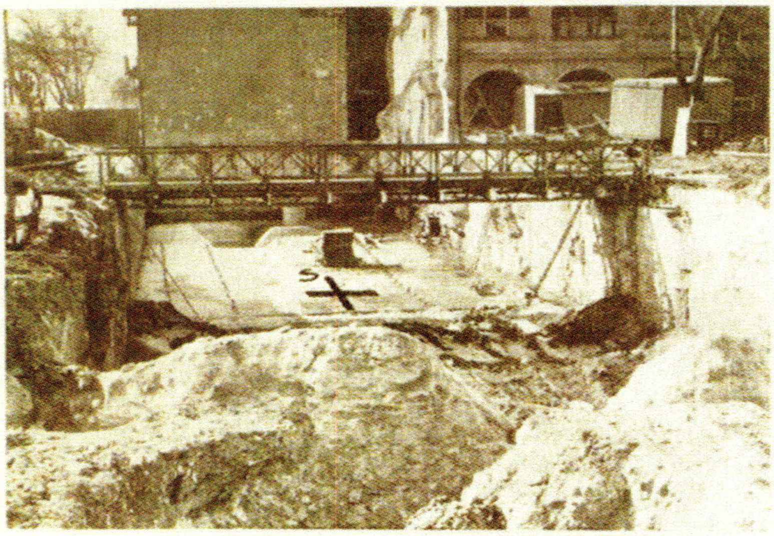

Bod S ležiaci v strede základov (jamy) má súradnice: λ = 17° 06′ 37,2″ vých. zem. dĺžky
φ = 48° 08′ 26,3″ sev. zem. šírky

Nadmorská výška H v bode S = 133,75 m nad hladinou Baltického mora.

Rozmery základov (jamy): dĺžka = 74,00 m
šírka = 14,00 m
hĺbka = 4,50 m

Astronomické zameranie previedol v priebehu februára 1971 geodet Ing. Boleslav Boška.

1. Rudolf Sikora, *Foundations of a New Building of the Slovenská Národná Galéria* (Slovak National Gallery), 1971, flyer, 27 × 11.7 cm, Private collection

Liberty Controlled

Institutional Settings of the East European Neo-avant-garde

A black-and-white flyer containing precise geographic coordinates about a building that was to be constructed at the intersection of 17°06'37.2" longitude and 48°08'26.3" latitude, rising to 133.75 metres (439 ft) above the level of the Baltic Sea, was printed and disseminated in Bratislava, Czechoslovakia, in February 1971. The accompanying photograph on which the exact location was marked also revealed that only the groundwork had begun, with accurate geodetic measurements supplied giving the size of foundations, which were 74 metres long, 14 meters wide and 4.5 metres deep (245 × 46 × 15 ft) (fig. 1). The flyer was the work of artist Rudolf Sikora who, in collaboration with his colleague Viliam Jakubík, decided to make a public announcement about the building of a new wing of the Slovenská Národná Galéria (Slovak National Gallery), which was to host the expanding collection of the country's preeminent artworks.[1] Although it was inaugurated in spring 1977, its doors would remain firmly closed to Sikora and his neo-avant-garde circle until after the fall of communism. In fact, the artist had only one solo exhibition, held at the Galéria Mladých (Gallery of Youth) in Bratislava in 1970 before the repressive 'normalization' period kicked in following the crushing of the Prague Spring of 1968, as a consequence of which the institutional landscape was drastically reconfigured.[2] The factuality and concreteness on which the artists insisted in their document revealed that all they had at their disposal was the stoic, rational and accurate observation of the given situation.

A poster exhibited in the Galerija Studentskog Centra (Student Centre Gallery) in Zagreb, Yugoslavia, in November 1971 illustrated a rather different cultural climate. It was a single work that constituted the entire solo exhibition of Goran Trbuljak, showing a photographic portrait of the artist and a written statement underneath that read, 'I do not want to show anything new nor original', while the data giving the opening hours, dates of the exhibition and the gallery address included on it pointed to the fact that the work itself was also intended as an advertising poster (fig. 2).

This fittingly dematerialized intervention and conceptual confrontation with the institutional system was so successful that a year and a half later Trbuljak was offered a solo show in Zagreb's Galerija Suvremene Umjetnosti (Gallery of Contemporary Art). For this, he developed further his stance towards institutional art structures and produced a single statement claiming that 'The fact that someone was given an opportunity to make an exhibition is more important than what will actually be shown there.'[3] This episode from Croatian art history indicates the situation in which artists and art historians operated, since due to the more liberal socialist path Yugoslavia had taken, they were free to organize events of this type and accommodate critical approaches towards their own practices. At the same time, however, there was no encroachment into the political realm outside the institutional system. Both Sikora and Trbuljak addressed the existing gallery structures in unadorned ways and both were also, as will be shown later, engaged in experimenting with alternative exhibition spaces in the early 1970s.

The formulation of a critical attitude towards the institutional system of the Hungarian art world, that both revealed the ways in which its functioning circumscribed the activities of artists and proposed an effective counter strategy, could be found in the *Pseudo* series by Gyula Pauer. The Hungarian artist also chose the ephemeral form of a printed flyer in order to circulate his *First Pseudo Manifesto* during a two-day exhibition in October 1970 that flew under the radar of art censorship by being framed as scenery for a film shot at the Attila József Culture House in Budapest (fig. 3).[4] Pauer outlined the agenda of *Pseudo* as an exploration of the 'false, deceptive, unreal, and seemingly real', referring to the 'circumstances' of artistic production in socialist Hungary and the deceptions perpetrated by the ruling ideology.[5] More explicit expression of his critical outlook appeared in his *Second Pseudo Manifesto* of 1972, which alerted his audience to the fact that 'what is sold to you as art is only a tool in the economic and ideological manipulations of the prevailing authority', and provocatively suggested that 'if you are manipulated, manipulate back!'[6]

Critics recognized the '180-degree turn' away from the artist's previous practice as a sculptor of abstract and organic forms and towards the new approaches entailed by *Pseudo*, while his exposure of the fake veneer of authenticity of the art scene alienated the artist from the structures of the official art system.[7] Indicatively, until *Pseudo* Pauer had functioned within the economy of the socialist art world, taking part in official symposia and exhibitions, while entertaining hopes of commissions for public sculpture; subsequently, however, he was obliged to seek new outlets for his work in off-site venues as well as in less tightly controlled state-funded spaces, such as houses of culture and theatres (see also Klara Kemp-Welch, 'Soft-spoken Encounters', pp. 273–89, for further discussion of the *Pseudo* project).

Across Eastern Europe the neo-avant-garde was characterized by a desire to experiment with innovative artistic forms and test the boundaries of the established institutional structures, mirroring the revolutionary mood of 1968. At the same time, the neo-avant-garde was obliged to negotiate its position within the complex systems of control and containment devised by the socialist state. This essay examines the sites of dissemination of nonconformist artistic practices within institutional settings, which were developed through a process of arbitration between the divergent interests of artists and the state authorities. While considering the modus operandi of particular spaces, it assesses the balance between confrontation and accommodation, attempts at appropriation from both sides, the avoidance of issues of open conflict and the seeking of a 'happy medium' through mutual concessions. Examples of the diverse sites that saw the emergence of conceptual artistic practices in Poland, Czechoslovakia and Yugoslavia in the early 1970s provide a comparison for the situation in Hungary. The essay examines the wide range of exhibition strategies in relation to specific social, political and cultural conditions, while also inspecting the ways in which the given institutional landscape was critically addressed. Finally, focusing on the metamorphosis of the gallery system in response to neo-avant-garde strivings, it investigates the degree of autonomy found in their programming, the limits posed by socialist institutional frameworks, and attempts to evade the system.

In Eastern Europe at the end of the 1960s, the art-world structures that artists were obliged to confront and negotiate in their professional life still carried the strong imprint of the far-reaching changes enacted during the period of Stalinization. Moreover, although the domination of the Soviet-imported style of socialist realism was strongly felt in artistic production only during the early 1950s, the legacy of the remaking of the whole system of museums and galleries, journals, art education, artist organizations and arts funding was to be a lasting factor in the history of East European art. Even in Yugoslavia, which after the Tito–Stalin split of 1948 distanced itself from the Soviet model, favouring instead a depoliticized high modernism, the art institutions developed in the late 1940s were enduring elements of the art world during the whole socialist period. As art historian Leonida Kovač has insisted, the Soviet artistic model

2. Goran Trbuljak, *'I do not want to show anything new nor original'*, 1971, paper, print, 59.6 × 42 cm, Marinko Sudac Collection, Zagreb

3. Gyula Pauer's exhibition in the József Attila Művelődési Ház (Attila József Culture House), 1970, Budapest

3

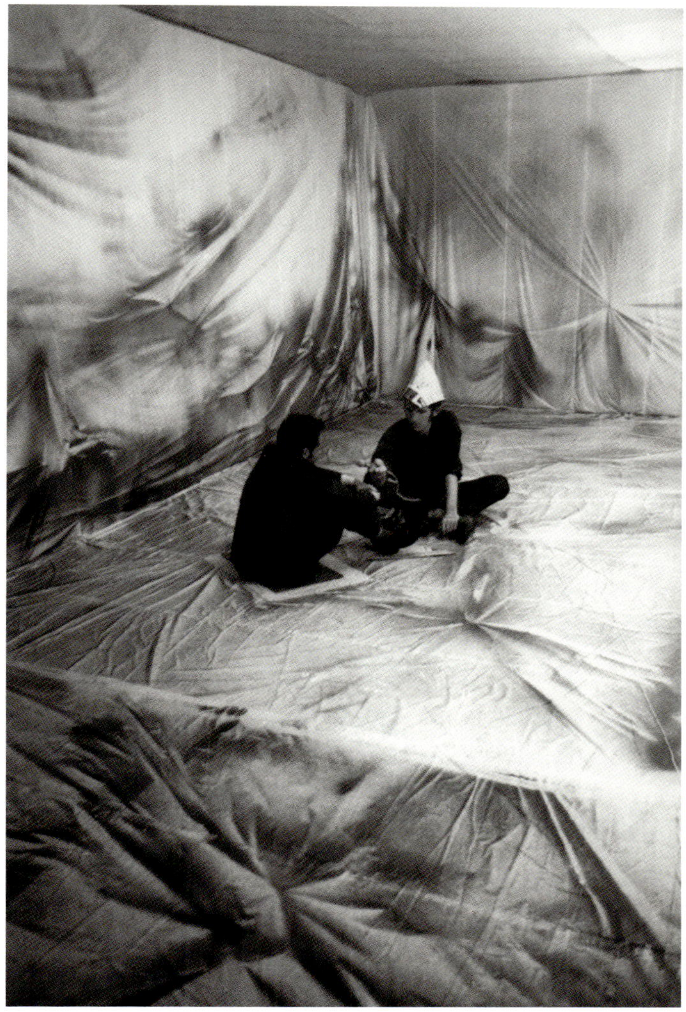

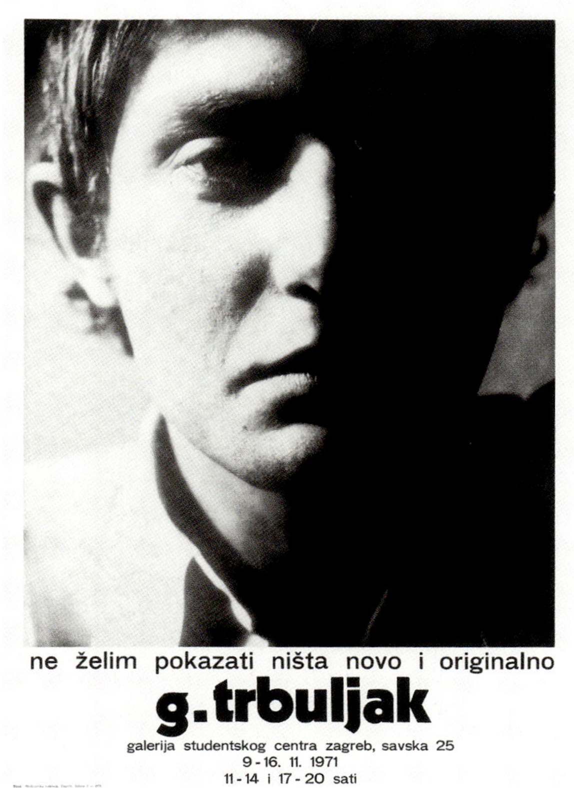

2

should be considered as a 'specific form of the totalitarian organisation of the world of art that was gradually implemented in all the socialist countries'.[8] Her enumeration of the components of the top-down reorganization of the institutional field of art included a 'unified, monopolistic association of artists', the centralization of the organization of artistic life, control of the media, establishment of a hierarchy of exhibitions, the design of a system of state prizes, a return to 'traditional teaching methods' in the academy with the introduction of 'master workshops', and the creation of a 'central "scientific" institution charged with the theoretical explanation of the problems of artistic creativity'.[9]

The period of the 1960s, in addition to fluctuations in official policy towards particular artistic movements, saw some diversification of the institutional structure of the art world, although overall the authorities maintained their tight grip on the mechanisms of artistic production and display. In Hungary, despite a number of institutional reconfigurations in the wake of the suppression of the Hungarian Revolution of 1956 and new leader János Kádár's compromise-seeking maxim that 'who is not against us is with us', the official art system of the post-Stalinist era was characterized more by continuity than change. Although professionalized and established as a separate institution in 1963, the Képző- és Iparművészeti Lektorátus (Supervisory Body for Arts and Crafts) continued to have a gate-keeping role in deciding on the permissibility of exhibitions. The Magyar Képző- és Iparművészek Szövetsége (Association of Hungarian Artists), purged and reorganized after the 1956 revolution, was also joined on the institutional horizon in 1958 by the Fiatal Képzőművészek Stúdiója (Young Artists' Studio), which under a liberal-minded leadership from 1964 to 1967 pushed for a series of reforms in the art world; their most notable success being to organize an exhibition at the Ernst Múzeum without pre-submitting the works to an official jury for approval.[10] Another sign of the slight easing of relations between the Party and the art world was the introduction of the practice of 'self-financed exhibitions' in the early 1960s, which offered a conciliatory alternative to the outright banning of exhibitions that did not fully meet these criteria.[11] Nevertheless, for the new generation of neo-avant-garde artists that emerged in the middle of the decade, the restrictions embedded in the system were a spur to critically address its limitations.

Military intervention by Warsaw Pact troops to end the Czechoslovak Spring in August 1968 extinguished the hopes of leftist intellectuals and artists that state socialism in Eastern Europe could be reformed into a more humane system that was truer to the original Marxist ideal. In Czechoslovakia itself, the era of 'normalization' geared up after the adoption by the Komunistická strana Československa (KSČ, Czechoslovak Communist Party) of the policy document 'A Lesson from the Crisis Development in the Party and Society' in December 1970. This set off a series of purges and repressive measures from which the artistic sphere was not immune. Specifically these measures included the expelling of artists associated with the experimental attitude of the 1960s from the artist's union, the exclusion of their work from acquisition for public collections, the refusal of permission to take part in exhibitions at home and abroad, and also the banning of articles that dealt with their work.[12] Remarkably, neo-avant-garde artists faced in the 1970s a situation not unlike that described by art theorist Jindřich Chalupecký in his 1949 text, 'The Intellectual under Socialism', where 'people who previously had not been taken seriously by anyone – suddenly gained key positions in various official functions and public positions', while those with 'integrity became speechless'.[13]

The systemic change of the Czechoslovak art world was a gradual process that took several years and lasted until society was, as dissident theorist Milan Šimečka put it, 'returned to order' under firm Communist Party control.[14] It was accompanied by the endorsement of 'private citizenship' that involved staying away from potentially hazardous public affairs and focusing instead on everyday life within the family, work and small circles of friends.[15] It was in this atmosphere, in which the public sphere was inaccessible and the private domain still unrestrained, that Rudolf Sikora organized the 'First Open Studio' (fig. 4), a group exhibition which opened on 19 November 1970 at the artist's house in Bratislava.[16] The eighteen artists who participated in the event

4

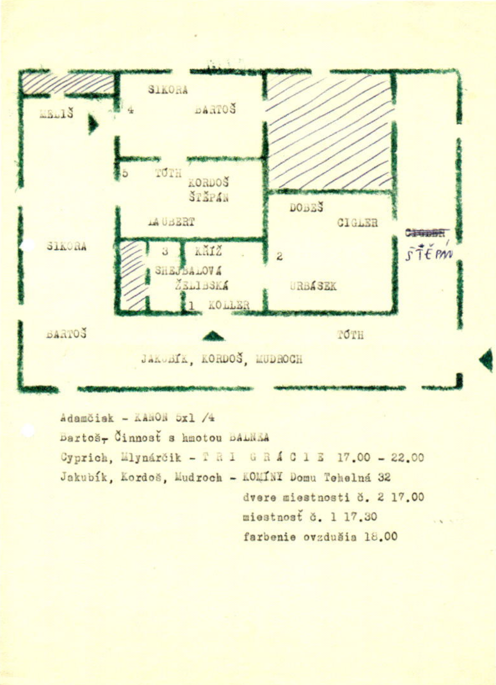

5

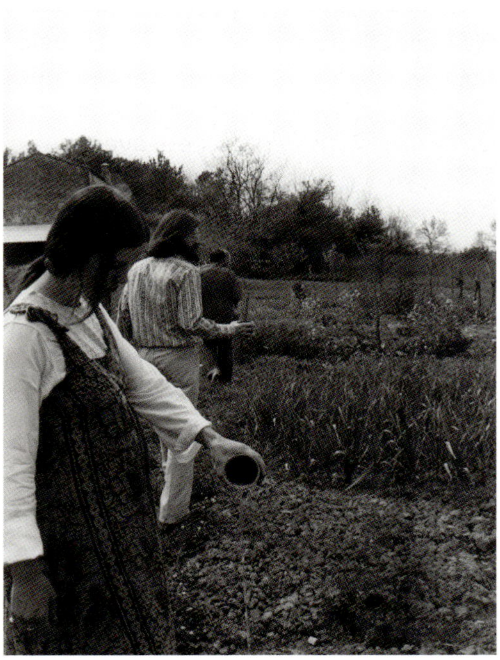

4. Floorplan of Rudolf Sikora's house in Tehelná Street, Bratislava, where the 'First Open Studio' was held, 1970, typed text, pen, paper, 29.7 × 20.9 cm, Marinko Sudac Collection, Zagreb

5. Šempas Family Commune in the Vipava Valley, Slovenia, 1977, Marinko Sudac Collection, Zagreb

were demonstrating their defiance towards the institutional banning of art festivals, exhibitions and symposia by resorting to private space. A lecture was given by Chalupecký, whose influential position within the Czechoslovak neo-avant-garde art scene derived both from his writings and his role as head of the Galerie Václava Špály (Václav Špála Gallery) in Prague from 1965 until 1970, before it was taken over by the official Svaz československých výtvarných umělců (Union of Czechoslovak Fine Artists). The exhibition in Sikora's house marked the beginning of the unofficial art scene in Slovakia and was such a success that it remained the first and only edition of the 'open studio', as it came to the attention of the authorities who forbade further similar events.[17]

The neo-avant-garde tendencies that appeared in the late 1960s and early 1970s in a Yugoslav context are referred to as 'New Art Practice', which art historian Ljiljana Kolešnik has summarized as the 'giving up of the artwork, redefinition of social function of art and social construction of the authorial subject', as well as a 'critical approach to social reality'.[18] Significantly, one more characteristic was 'resistance towards institutionalized models of artistic activity', the deliberateness of which clearly sets it apart from the necessity to use non-institutional settings, to which artists in normalization-era Czechoslovakia had to resort. Among numerous examples as to how far the artists were prepared to take their challenge to institutional frameworks in the context of Yugoslav art is the Haustor gallery, set up in the entrance hall of a residential building in Frankopanska Street in the centre of Zagreb by the small circle around Goran Trbuljak and Braco Dimitrijević, who organized several exhibitions there during 1970 and 1971. The reason for this enterprise were the artists' wish to 'democratize art by leaving the circle of specialized, socially and educationally defined gallery spectators' and make it available to passers-by, while at the same time they wanted to 'emancipate themselves from the gallery system in order to be able to show their works without depending on the annual programme and exhibition policies of galleries'.[19] This was the venue for the international conceptual art exhibition 'At the Moment', organized by Nena and Braco

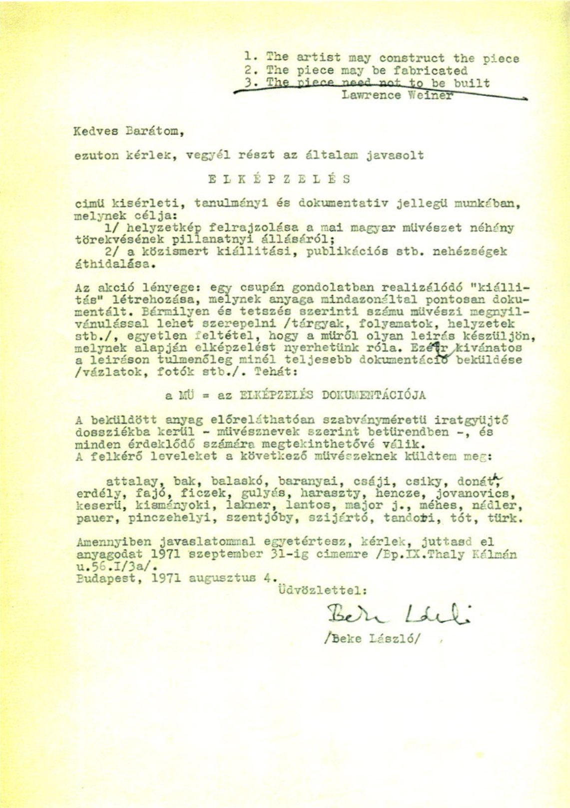

1. The artist may construct the piece
2. The piece may be fabricated
3. The piece need not to be built
Lawrence Weiner

Kedves Barátom,

ezuton kérlek, vegyél részt az általam javasolt

E L K É P Z E L É S

cimü kisérleti, tanulmányi és dokumentativ jellegü munkában, melynek célja:
1/ helyzetkép felrajzolása a mai magyar müvészet néhány törekvésének pillanatnyi állásáról;
2/ a közismert kiállitási, publikációs stb. nehézségek áthidalása.

Az akció lényege: egy csupán gondolatban realizálódó "kiállitás" létrehozása, melynek anyaga mindazonáltal pontosan dokumentált. Bármilyen és tetszés szerinti számu müvészi megnyilvánulással lehet szerepelni /tárgyak, folyamatok, helyzetek stb./, egyetlen feltétel, hogy a müről olyan leirás készüljön, melynek alapján elképzelést nyerhetünk róla. Ezért kivánatos a leiráson tulmenőleg minél teljesebb dokumentáció beküldése /vázlatok, fotók stb./. Tehát:

a MÜ = az ELKÉPZELÉS DOKUMENTÁCIÓJA

A beküldött anyag előreláthatóan szabványméretü iratgyüjtő dossziékba kerül - müvésznevek szerint betürendben -, és minden érdeklődő számára megtekinthetővé válik.
A felkérő leveleket a következő müvészeknek küldtem meg:

attalay, bak, balaskó, baranyai, csáji, csiky, donáth, erdély, fajó, ficzek, gulyás, haraszty, hencze, jovanovics, keserü, kismányoki, lakner, lantos, major j., méhes, nádler, pauer, pinczehelyi, szentjóby, szijártó, tandori, tót, türk.

Amennyiben javaslatommal egyetértesz, kérlek, juttasd el anyagodat 1971 szeptember 31-ig cimemre /Bp.IX.Thaly Kálmán u.56.I/3a/.
Budapest, 1971 augusztus 4.
Üdvözlettel:
/Beke László/

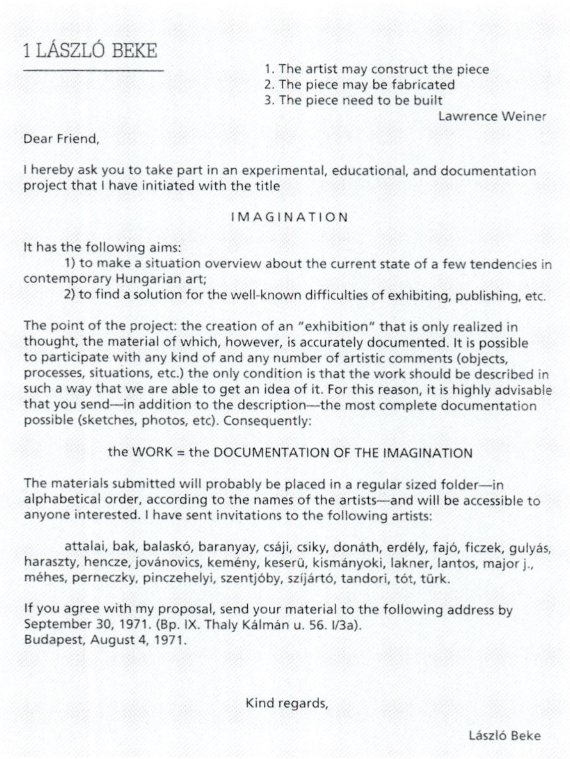

1 LÁSZLÓ BEKE

1. The artist may construct the piece
2. The piece may be fabricated
3. The piece need to be built
Lawrence Weiner

Dear Friend,

I hereby ask you to take part in an experimental, educational, and documentation project that I have initiated with the title

IMAGINATION

It has the following aims:
1) to make a situation overview about the current state of a few tendencies in contemporary Hungarian art;
2) to find a solution for the well-known difficulties of exhibiting, publishing, etc.

The point of the project: the creation of an "exhibition" that is only realized in thought, the material of which, however, is accurately documented. It is possible to participate with any kind of and any number of artistic comments (objects, processes, situations, etc.) the only condition is that the work should be described in such a way that we are able to get an idea of it. For this reason, it is highly advisable that you send—in addition to the description—the most complete documentation possible (sketches, photos, etc). Consequently:

the WORK = the DOCUMENTATION OF THE IMAGINATION

The materials submitted will probably be placed in a regular sized folder—in alphabetical order, according to the names of the artists—and will be accessible to anyone interested. I have sent invitations to the following artists:

attalai, bak, balaskó, baranyay, csáji, csiky, donáth, erdély, fajó, ficzek, gulyás, haraszty, hencze, jovánovics, kemény, keserü, kismányoki, lakner, lantos, major j., méhes, perneczky, pinczehelyi, szentjóby, szijártó, tandori, tót, türk.

If you agree with my proposal, send your material to the following address by September 30, 1971. (Bp. IX. Thaly Kálmán u. 56. I/3a).
Budapest, August 4, 1971.

Kind regards,

László Beke

Dimitrijević on 23 April 1971, which, although it lasted only three hours, was considered one of the most important displays of this innovative trend.[20] This ad hoc exhibition became more 'institutionalized' when it was taken to the Belgrade Studentski Kulturni Centar (Students Cultural Centre) a few months later and presented under the title 'In Another Moment'.[21]

The appearance of home-grown Yugoslav conceptual art is regularly linked to the activities of OHO Group in Slovenia, who in the later part of the 1960s engaged in practices that ranged from *arte povera*, land art and performative practices, heading towards more dematerialized expressions in the early 1970s characterized by a countercultural and new-age spirit. Their remarkable acceptance by Yugoslav art critics and presentations in the leading art venues across the federal state, which culminated in participation in the seminal conceptual art exhibition 'Information' at the Museum of Modern Art in New York in 1970,[22] did not deter them from expressing their critical attitude not only towards the institutional art system, but society in general.[23] Namely, in April 1971 the artists from the OHO Group decided to abandon their urban life and establish a rural commune in which they could practise their preferred way of life in harmony with the cosmic laws, which could be regarded as an ultimate form of critique (fig. 5).[24]

The form that the debut of conceptual art took in Hungary was indicative of the type of cultural policy implemented in that particular socialist state. In August 1971, art historian László Beke invited twenty-eight artists to respond to his proposal that 'the WORK = the DOCUMENTATION OF IMAGINATION', using the notion of *elképzelés* that in English corresponds to both 'imagination' and 'idea', while the suggested medium was a sheet of paper (fig. 6).[25] The original plan was to hold the exhibition in the regional István Király Múzeum in Székesfehérvár, which held an 'exceptional' status as at that time 'hardly any exhibition space could develop a progressive profile'.[26] However the Képző- és Iparművészeti Lektorátus had classified the proposal as belonging to the category of 'self-financed', so this format was abandoned. Instead, Beke organized the works in several folders that could be viewed in his flat in Budapest, the

7

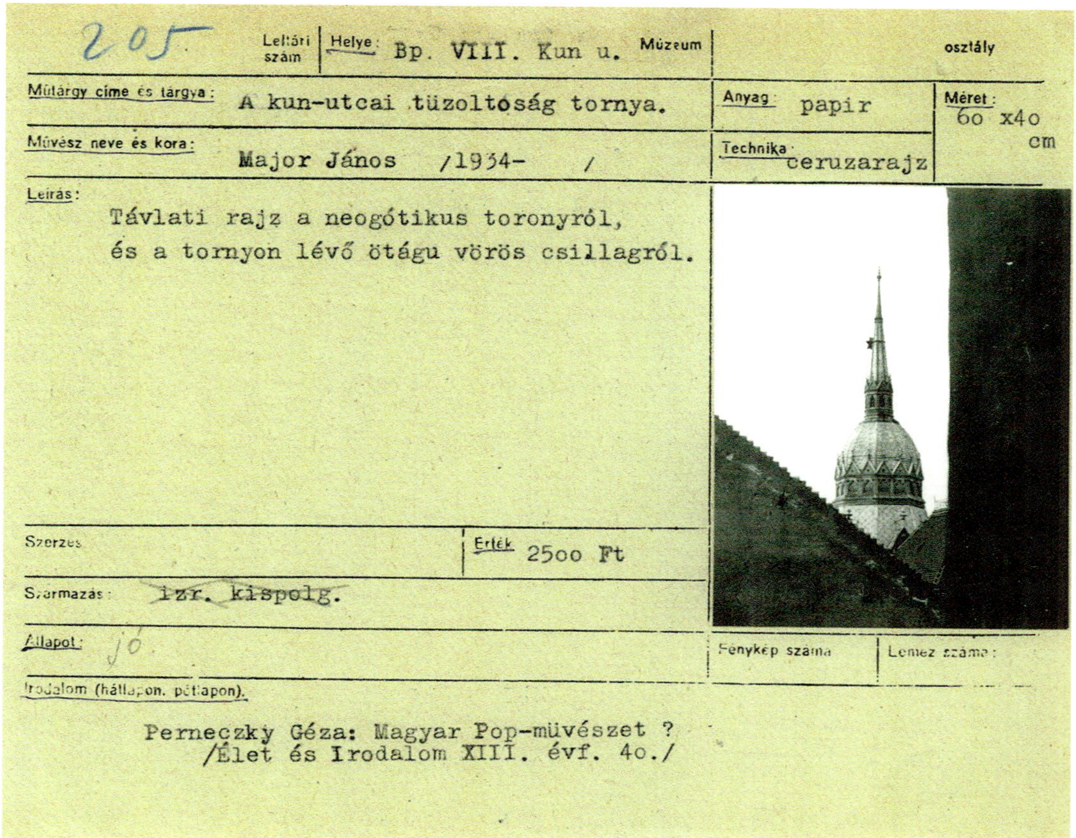
205 Leltári szám | Helye: Bp. VIII. Kun u. Múzeum | osztály

Műtárgy címe és tárgya: A kun-utcai tüzoltóság tornya. | Anyag: papir | Méret: 60 x40 cm

Művész neve és kora: Major János /1934- / | Technika: ceruzarajz

Leirás: Távlati rajz a neogótikus toronyról, és a tornyon lévő ötágu vörös csillagról.

Szerzés | Érték 2500 Ft

Származás: ~~izr. kispolg.~~

Állapot: jó

Fénykép száma | Lemez száma:

Irodalom (hátlapon, pótlapon).

Perneczky Géza: Magyar Pop-müvészet ?
/Élet és Irodalom XIII. évf. 40./

8

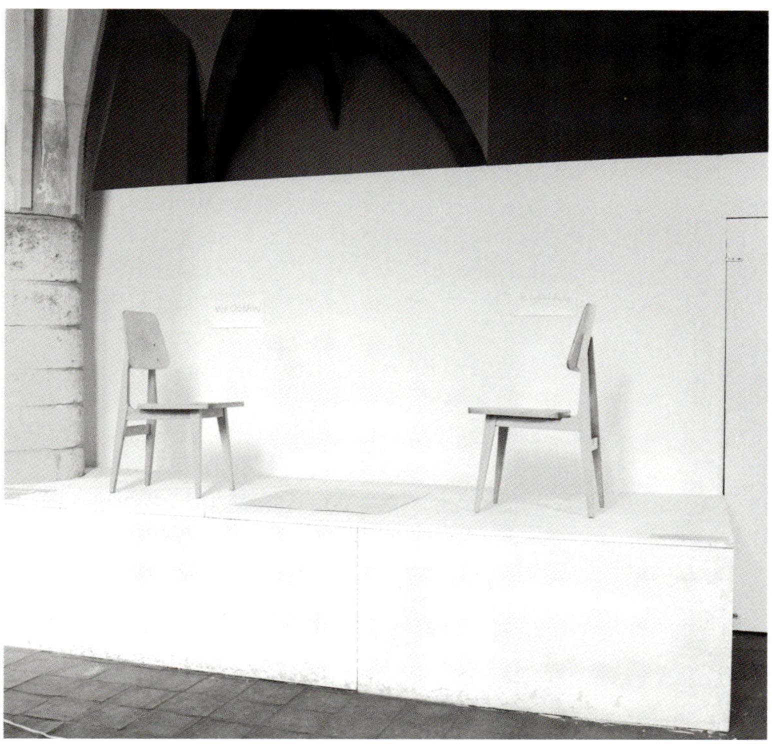

6. László Beke, *Imagination/Idea*, 1970, paper, pen, typed text, 29.7 × 21 cm, Private collection

7. János Major, *The Tower of the Kun Street Fire Station* (Part of Gyula Pauer's 'art collection' in László Beke's *Imagination/Idea* project), 1971, paper, index card, photo, 15.5 × 19.6 cm, Private collection

8. Włodzimierz Borowski, *Dialogue*, Wroclaw '70 Symposium, 1970, installation

opportunity for which was taken by about eighty visitors. Further dissemination of the project came from his essay published in samizdat edition, in which he analysed the received materials.[27] There was a wait of almost four decades until it was made more publicly available with the publication of a book that also appeared in English in 2014. The smooth operational logic of the supervisory body, which did not forbid the exhibition but just made it more difficult to realize, had in effect the result that this type of art stayed within a very narrow group of art professionals.

Gyula Pauer introduced an additional twist to the curatorial strategy of this project. He was invited to participate, but turned his contribution into another call for proposals addressed to sixteen artists from the same circle. Pauer asked them to fill out truthfully museum index cards with data relating to what they regarded as their 'best work of art', explaining that the 'museum card is the only document that reliably proves the existence and the identity of an art object' (fig. 7).[28] Aiming to use the contributions as a 'pseudo exhibition', Pauer commented on the innovative practices of conceptual artistic production while at the same time directing attention to the preeminent role of art institutions in validating artistic achievements. In comparison with Yugoslav artists who intervened directly in the infrastructure of art institutions, in this case the conceptual context of the interactions remained an activity that existed only on paper.

The appearance of conceptual art in Poland also crystallized the limits of compromise between the most experimental wing of the neo-avant-garde and the Party-approved art authorities. Over a series of encounters in 1970, the potential for existing structures to foster the realization of the most ambitious goals of conceptual art and accommodate radical artistic ideas within the cultural landscape of actually existing socialism was severely tested. The first site of contestation was the Wrocław '70 Symposium, notable for revealing for the 'first time the existence of significant conceptual tendencies in Polish art'.[29] The ideologically tinged occasion marked the twenty-fifth anniversary of regaining the formerly German-ruled territories of Poland. Its stated aim to create 'prominent artworks within the organism of Wrocław', through a collaboration between artists and industrial plants, initially attracted much support from official bodies, Party committees and city authorities. Organized by curator and theorist Jerzy Ludwiński, in practice the project became a platform for conceptual art practices that were unacceptable to its sponsors and commissioners, with the result that of the forty finalists whose proposals were selected by the organizational board, only one was actually realized as planned in a city space for the Victory Day celebrations on 9 May 1970.[30]

One of the most interesting proposals generated by the project was Włodzimierz Borowski's *Dialogue*, the concept of which was to connect Wrocław and Elbląg by aligning two 'maximally enlarged' chairs in the public space of the two cities, objects that were to be produced by an industrial plant in Elbąg that also sponsored the town's Biennial of Spatial Forms (fig. 8). The ironic comment the work made about the over-enthusiastic encouragement of collaborations between artists and industry in modernizing Poland, and the artist's conceptual approach that opted for 'the exchange of ideas rather than their monumental scale materialisation', highlighted the barriers to a meaningful 'dialogue' with the socialist state.[31] Gatherings such as the symposium also had an international dimension, and Hungarian artists were present either as visitors or participants in biennials and artist meetings across Poland during the period.[32]

Jerzy Ludwiński was also the leader of the Galeria Pod Mona Lisa, which from 1967 to 1971 operated under the auspices of Wrocław's International Press and Book Club. One of a number of institutions in the city catering to the needs of the cultural intelligentsia, this 35m^2 (377 sq. ft) entrance hall in front of the club's reading room provided a niche for the curator to explore the potential of a 'micro-institution', 'a mentally flexible gallery' that challenged audiences while criticizing the 'official rituals' of the art world.[33] After a series of increasingly radical exhibitions, culminating in 'Concept Art' in December 1970 – which was dematerialized to the degree that instead of artworks, the pages of the exhibition catalogue were exhibited and also distributed as loose sheets in an envelope – pressure was

9. 'Concept Art', exhibition view, Galeria pod Moną Lisa, Wrocław, 1970, Ossolineum Collection, Wrocław

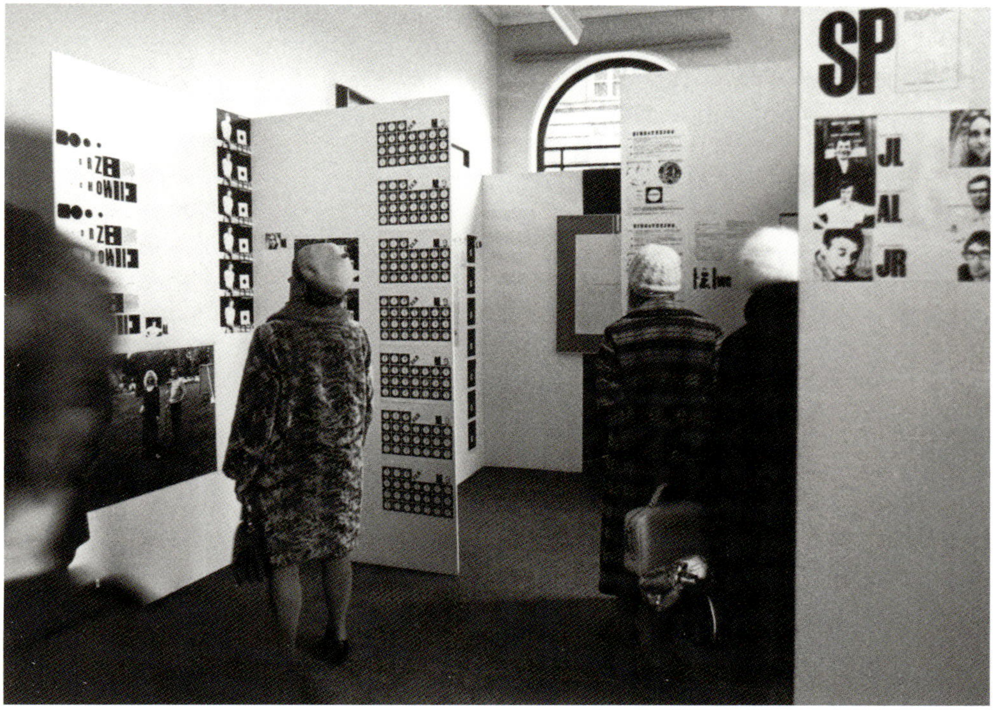

9

put on the director of the Book Club, Maria Berny, to curtail Ludwiński's activities, which offended the sensibilities of both Marxist and modernist critics (fig. 9). Ludwiński's refusal to accede to the demand that the gallery's programme be divided fifty-fifty with the local artists' union resulted in the termination of their collaboration, while the denouement also demonstrates the importance of the support of political powerbrokers for the survival of neo-avant-garde activities.

A similarly precarious situation was faced by the Galeria Foksal in Warsaw, which was founded in 1966 on the initiative of three art critics and conceived as an 'autonomous and isolated place' dedicated to 'the creation and production of "living" art'.[34] In institutional terms, however, the gallery was dependent on the Pracownie Sztuk Plastycznych (PSP, Fine Arts Studios), a state-run organization responsible for commissioning propaganda art from artists. As a consequence, while the gallery was allowed to make use of the umbrella organization's substantial material resources, it also had to submit its exhibition programme to the PSP director for approval.[35] The contradictions between the gallery's artistic programme and the institutional context were a recurrent topic of debate, exposing the ethical pitfalls of the unwritten social contract between the Party and the art world in Poland, which offered material support in exchange for an avoidance of politics and self-confinement to high modernist aesthetics. This culminated in 1970 with a rancorous split between the founders of the Galeria Foksal over the failure to implement the 'New Foksal Gallery Regulations' that had been drawn up by theorist Anka Ptaszkowska in 1969. These were designed to update the gallery's mission in the spirit of an institutional critique that pointed beyond the safety of the 'defined borders' of the exhibition space towards the more risky, conceptual intent to become an informational office for the 'free transmission of meaning'.[36] (For more on the Galeria Foksal, see Klara Kemp-Welch, 'Soft-spoken Encounters', pp. 273–89.)

In a recent interview about his role as head of the Student Centre Gallery in Zagreb at the turn of the decade, Želimir Koščević emphasized the importance of the 'openness of the programme and the freedom to act'.[37] Indeed, the exhibitions held in the gallery in the late 1960s and early 1970s testify to this, as they were instrumental in the inauguration of the new generation of artists that would became associated with the New Art Practice.[38] What is more, the notion of 'freedom' was especially expressed in curatorial undertakings, for instance in his 'Exhibition of Men and Women' held in 1969, where the only exhibits were the visitors to the opening, while the introductory text stated: 'In this exhibition you are the work, you are the figuration, you are the socialist realism' (fig. 10).[39] A similar attitude was expressed in 'Postal Delivery', consisting of the mail-art section of the Paris Biennale of Youth in 1971, which Koščević decided to present unpacked. This could be taken as another marker of difference when compared to neighbouring countries, where mail art served as a main 'form of communication' with the international scene.[40] Significantly, one of the main reasons the Student Centre Gallery could maintain such activity was thanks to the sympathy it enjoyed from Božo Bek, an official socialist cadre who was the director of the Zagreb Gallery of Contemporary Art and 'held an extremely important ideological influence within the city of Zagreb', while at the same time being 'supportive' of progressive artistic practices.[41]

Student cultural institutions in Zagreb, Novi Sad and Belgrade acted as seminal sites for experimentation and the presentation of innovative artistic trends. In Novi Sad, an active role was played by the Tribina Mladih (Youth Forum), which in the period 1968–74 was characterized by 'multicultural, experimental, new leftist and international' practices that 'challenged the dominant discourse of moderate modernism' in Yugoslavia.[42] As a platform through which the 'left critique of socialism'[43] was tested from perspectives ranging from Maoist to Situationist, and where aesthetics and ethics overlapped, the Tribina Mladih gradually attracted attention from Party hardliners. As art historian Nebojša Milenković observed, the 'sophisticated guardians of social and public morality' wanted to discipline the Tribina and bring it 'under strict social control and oversight', but the job of doing this fell to other 'artists, writers – cultural apparatchiks who actually defended their own undeservedly obtained privileges and earnings'.[44]

The gallery of the Student Cultural Centre in Belgrade was another locality where neo-avant-garde art was practised, and it continued its experimental programme for longer than similar centres in other Yugoslav republics, whose activities were gradually neutralized. The myth of artistic freedom in such centres was addressed by art theorist Miško Šuvaković, who referred to an episode from the Belgrade centre's 'April Meetings' festival in 1974, which the organizers considered a huge

10

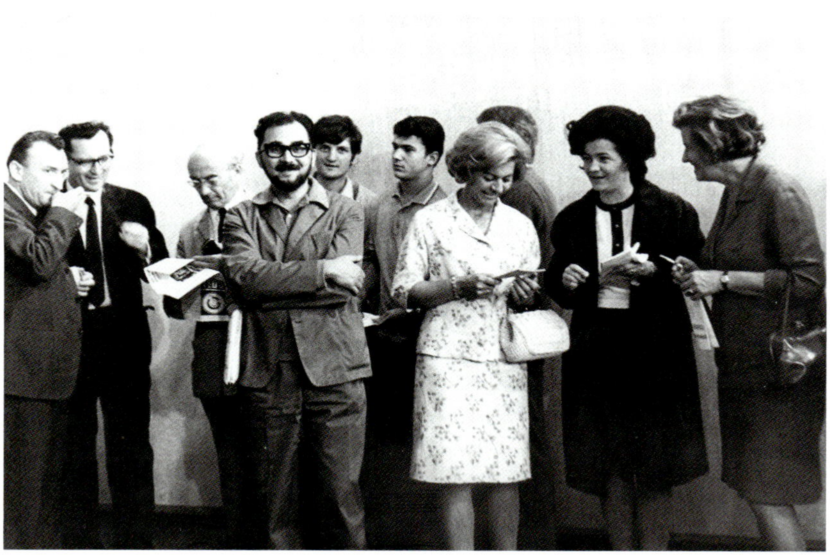

10. The 'Exhibition of Men and Women' at the Studentski Centar u Zagrebu (Student Centre of the University of Zagreb), 1969

11. Participating artists of the exhibition 'R', Budapesti Műszaki Egyetem (Budapest University of Technology), 1970

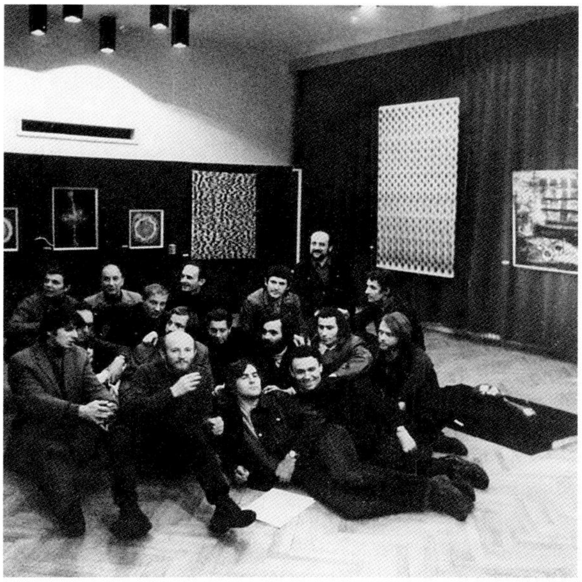

11

success, boasting that in a 'socialist country a completely open international festival' could take place, since it was attended by Joseph Beuys, Barbara Rose and Achille Bonito Oliva; the latter, however, remarked that the setting was essentially a 'reservation, which is completely closed and isolated from the culture in which it takes place'.[45] According to Šuvaković, 'delicate, careful, bureaucratically well performed centring, enclosing and isolating' strategies were employed to control the activities of student cultural centres, while across the republics their 'critical subversive practices' were to be 'neutralized, without banning them, by transferring them' to another social environment.[46] In other words, although the student cultural organizations were state-funded and generally had autonomy over their programmes, their position was marked by a policy of 'ghettoisation of critical art practices and thinking, limiting their effects on a narrow segment of urban student youth'.[47]

The chronology of Hungarian 'concept art' can also be read as a record of the spaces that were sought out by neo-avant-garde artists to show their work, and of the cat-and-mouse game they played with the authorities.[48] A group show entitled 'New Endeavours' at the Kommunista Ifjúsági Szövetség Club (KISZ Club, Communist Youth Organization Club), located at the offices of the Hungarian airline Malév, was, for example, banned by the Képző- és Iparművészeti Lektorátus in 1966, although exhibitions by Endre Tót and Gyula Pauer in the KISZ Club of the Központi Fizikai Kutató Intézet (KFKI, Central Physics Research Centre) in 1968 went ahead as planned; two landmark exhibitions were held in the unlikely venue of the Culture Hall of the Iparterv (Industrial Planning Office; see also Gábor Dobó and Merse Pál Szeredi, 'Hungarian Culture +/- Europe', pp. 39–57) in 1968 and 1969, while a Fluxus concert planned by László Beke and Tamás St Auby (Szentjóby) for the Egyetemi Színpad (University Stage) in May 1973 was forbidden.

Along with private flats, cellars, the halls of houses of culture, communist youth clubs and offices of the Patriotic Popular Front, artists also made ad hoc use of the semi-public and less systematically supervised spaces of student clubs and theatres, student dormitories and cafés (see also Júlia Perczel, 'The Art Sphere as a Grey Zone', pp. 59–75, and Flóra Barkóczi, 'Creative (Dis)Courses', pp. 95–109). In that sense, a typical fate befell the 'R' exhibition of December 1970, which despite bringing together one of the earliest and broadest surveys of Hungarian neo-avant-garde art, was held in the student club of the R Building of the Budapesti Műszaki Egyetem (Budapest University of Technology) and lasted only three days (fig. 11). After the crackdown on neo-avant-garde activities culminating in the closure of the neo-avant-garde retreat of the Balatonboglári Kápolnaműteren of György Galántai (György Galántai's Balatonboglár Chapel Studio) at the end of August 1973, experimental art events increasingly took place within the less anarchic context of professional artist clubs that were equipped with a members-only bar, performance and exhibition spaces, and which fulfilled the dual role of functioning as a 'safety valve' while making it easy to 'keep the avant-garde art world under surveillance'.[49]

Nevertheless, as László Beke has put it, despite the fact that it 'was actually closed to the public', from 1973 to 1976 the Fiatal Művészek Klubja (FMK, Young Artists' Club) was still the most important example of an '"alternative" institution' in the Budapest art scene (see also Klara Kemp-Welch, 'Soft-spoken Encounters', pp. 273–89).[50] Opened in 1960 in the basement and ground floor of a villa on Andrássy Avenue under the aegis of the district office of the KISZ that occupied the upper storeys and also had a say in its management, the FMK was in practice self-run and from the 1970s it became a meeting place for the second public sphere, or parallel artistic culture of the unofficial art circuit. The attitude of the FMK to the cultural politics of the mid-1970s can be glimpsed in a police informer's report on the club members' reactions to the visit of György Aczél, the leading ideologue of the Party in the Kádár era. His participation in a four-hour-long question-and-answer session on Marxism in February 1976 before an audience of a hundred artists and intellectuals provoked numerous frank exchanges that were duly noted, including a challenging question from György Galántai asking why it was that 'committed artists' are supported 'even if they are completely talentless', and 'state commissions' only go to those that draw 'Lenin or the five-pointed star on their works'.[51] The Party's control of finances in the socialist art world was an additional instrument that complemented the use of administrative and directly repressive measures.

The passing of the moment of conceptual art, with its ambition to challenge the restrictive structures of art and society, can also be deduced from the more self-referential topics of a number of the FMK exhibitions in the period, such as 'Image/Poem' in 1974, which set out to examine the 'the role of writing in art, as well as the role of the (visual) image in poetry'.[52] Material for this conceptual exhibition was sourced from both Hungarian and international artists, and also presented through a samizdat publication put together by Beke and artist Dora Maurer. The FMK also provided the venue for the parting shot of unreconstructed avant-gardist Tamás St Auby before his enforced emigration in 1975: a self-curated retrospective exhibition he conceived to 'tie up loose ends in my life here' and consisting of 150 items including 'picture poetry, photos, objects, [and] environments' (fig. 12).[52] This exhibition could be taken as indicative of the transition to a phase of the (self)-historicization of that stream of art, while the fact that, unlike the original events, it was officially allowed to take place demonstrates that the authorities had realized that, as the artist put it, 'a banned exhibition would have a greater influence on the general atmosphere than the exhibition itself'.[54]

As a result of the multifaceted limitations that were imposed on the institutional terrain of the neo-avant-garde – and in the spirit of experimentation that was so characteristic of such practices – many art events took place in the countryside, either within organized frameworks or as more individual excursions and undertakings. This phenomenon is observable across the Eastern bloc; however, in Yugoslavia, where certain institutions were available to the artists, open-air activities were least typical, with OHO Group's founding of a rural commune representing an exception. Since art events in the countryside required the mobilization of artists typically coming from capitals or large cities, they often had a collective character. In her analysis of participatory practices under socialism, art historian Claire Bishop repeatedly emphasized that the reason for organizing events in the countryside in Eastern Europe was 'to avoid surveillance'.[55] Ending her substantial chapter on Czech neo-avant-garde action art that took place in nature with a question, 'how many of these actions would have been created if the artists had had the chance to openly exhibit in galleries?', art historian Pavlína Morganová also confirmed the need for an exodus to the countryside during the 'normalization' period, and also connected it to the Czech tradition of hiking and nature excursions as 'part of

12

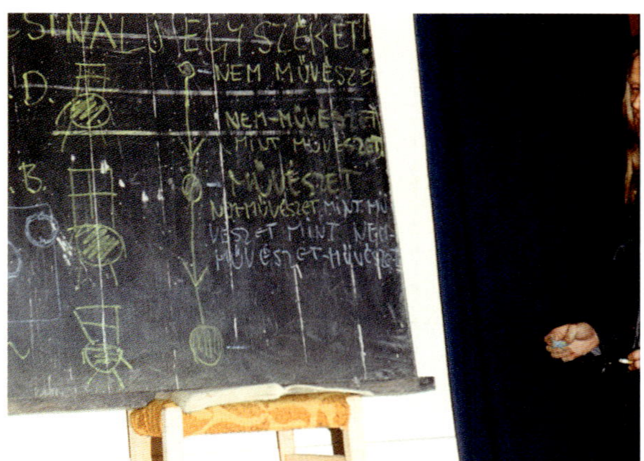

12. Tamás Szentjóby, *Make a Chair! – Homage to George Brecht* (lecture), Young Artists' Club, Budapest, 1975

13. Exhibition in the Balatonboglár Chapel Studio of György Galántai (depicted: Kálmán Szijártó and Sándor Pinczehelyi), 1973

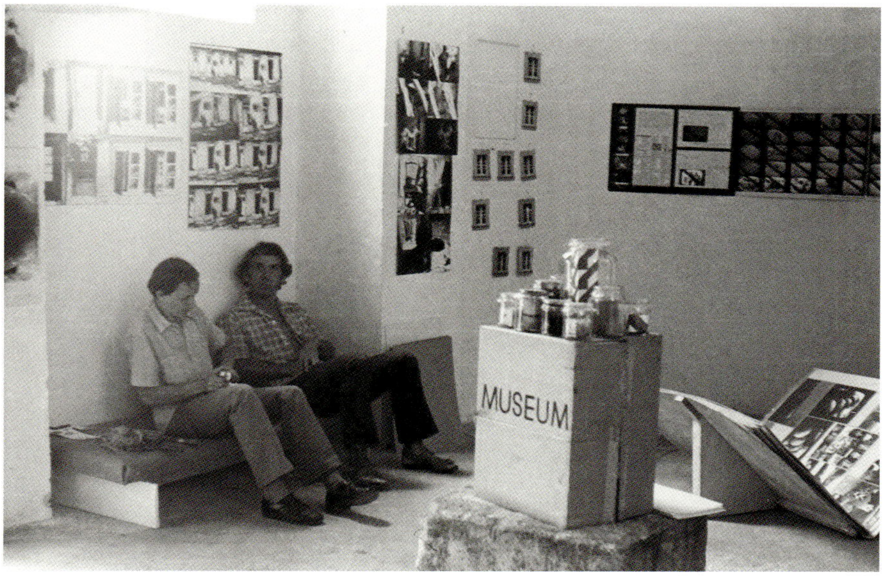

13

the alternative lifestyle during the totalitarian years'.[56] Collective artistic actions were even more present in the Slovak context during the normalization years, and in addition to being a 'reaction to political situation', they took many different approaches and forms.[57] Significantly, these manifestations, although collective, were individually organized and typically one-off events without state support.

In contrast, the artistic activities in the countryside in Poland were organized within an official framework, as the interests of the authorities and the neo-avant-garde coalesced to a certain extent around the establishing of a series of '*plenar*' (*plein-air*) meetings in the 1960s and 1970s. These were a specific form of outdoor art event that was more ambitious than a traditional artist colony and addressed particular themes through a wide variety of interventions and happenings, symposia and exhibitions. For the Party, the *plenar* was a means to use culture to cement the 'regained territories' within the new borders of socialist Poland: the majority of them were organized in lands that were appended to the country in 1945. For artists and curators, it offered a less-controlled setting and the material conditions in which to realize experimental artworks.

Disputes over conceptual art came into the open at the Osieki *plenar* of 1970, the invitation list for which was unusually not subject to censorship and included most of the artists from the Wrocław '70 Symposium, with the leitmotif provided by Ludwiński in his lecture on 'Art in the Post-Artistic Period'.[58] The vociferousness of the official reaction, reflected in aggressive press reports and a refusal to finance the next *plenar*, demonstrated that conceptual art practices, in their rejection of the 'traditional model of an artist and artistic output' in favour of the notions of 'process and idea', were a 'type of poetics which both deterred and disturbed' the authorities.[59]

In Hungary, many significant neo-avant-garde conceptual works were realized in the non-urban context of the Balatonboglár Chapel Studio, which in the summer months from 1970 until its closure in 1973 provided an unparalleled platform for experimental artistic approaches. It was not just the distance from the capital that accounted for the freer conditions, but also the institutional specificities of the space: a disused chapel rented as a studio by the artist György Galántai, which became a venue for ever more ambitious collective programmes (figs 13 and 14). As the critical position of artists became more pronounced, with the transfer of several banned neo-avant-garde art projects from Budapest to the Chapel Studio and the activating of unofficial neo-avant-garde networks across the Eastern bloc, the authorities used bureaucratic measures to harass Galántai, such as by imposing substantial fines for not keeping to safety regulations, before closing it for infringing rules on the display of 'propaganda materials' in August 1973.[60] Despite this dramatic denouement, until then the activities of the Chapel Studio had been more or less tolerated, and Galántai himself had essayed a rapprochement with the authorities, on one occasion submitting an exhibition programme to be juried and even attempting 'to evade the administrative method used against us by providing an ideological illusion of Marxist truth'.[61] When the authorities decided to move against the Balatonboglár Chapel Studio, they brought to bear the whole weight of propaganda machinery: their insinuations that the summer gatherings were depraved and that 'nobody was painting, drawing or sculpting' informed a vitriolic condemnation in the official press.[62]

The institutional landscape *c.* 1970 varied significantly across the Central European states of the Eastern bloc, but two points were constant. On the one hand, the communist parties had a clear set of official rules that were not to be broken, while, on the other, a young generation of artists took it upon themselves to test the boundaries and experiment with the potential that dematerialized art practice had to offer by turning a material disadvantage into a conceptual advantage. The meeting of the two sides seemed to function with least conflict in the socio-political environments of Poland and Yugoslavia, where state support for artistic infrastructures was contingent on a reciprocal disengagement from direct political topics on the part of artists. Nevertheless, the nonconformist attitude displayed by conceptual artists proved too experimental for the liking of the authorities there as well, so many neo-avant-garde centres were neutralized within a short lifespan. The crude normalization era in Czechoslovakia had the strongest impact on the institutional setting of the neo-avant-garde, which responded by moving either into the private sphere or out into the countryside, marking a dramatic turn from the freer atmosphere of the 1960s. In Hungary, the inconsistent reaction of the authorities, which wavered between banning and tolerating experimental art practices, made it possible for temporary outlets to emerge for the expression of the neo-avant-garde agenda. Ultimately, the search for alternative spaces, the evasion of both direct and more subtle control mechanisms, and attempts to carve out islands of relative autonomy within the institutional terrain of socialist art worlds had political, aesthetic and existential implications for all art practitioners.

14. Dóra Maurer, *Spatial Confusion* from the series *'Once We Went To…'* (Miklós Erdély, György Jovánovics, Tamás Szentjóby, Tibor Gáyor), photo taken at the Balatonboglár Chapel Studio of György Galántai in 1972, Vintage Galéria, Budapest

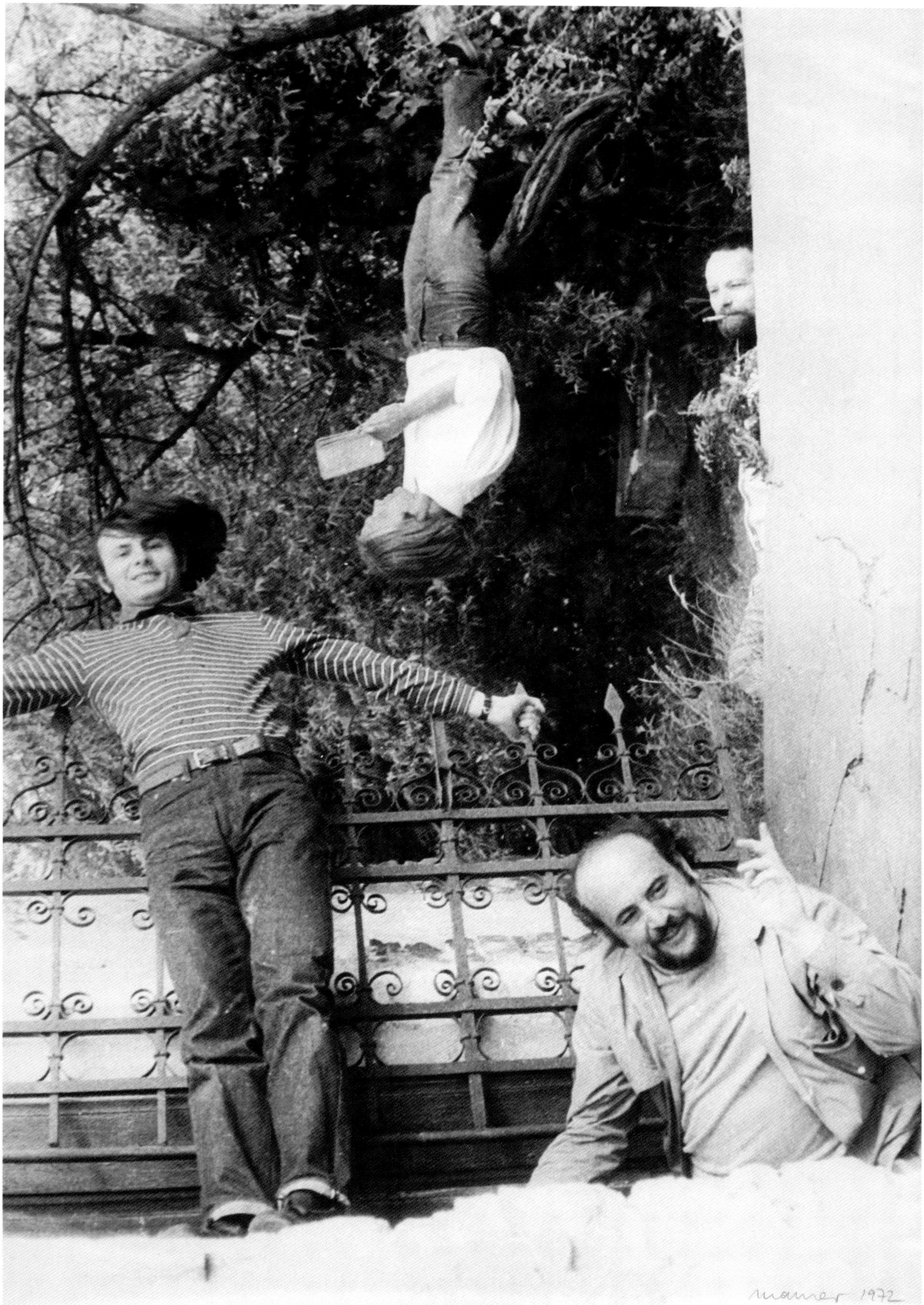

16

1 Helena Musilová (ed.), *Rudolf Sikora: Against Myself*. Prague: National Gallery, 2006.
2 See the chapter on Rudolf Sikora in Maja Fowkes, *The Green Bloc: Neo-avant-garde Art and Ecology under Socialism*. Budapest: CEU Press, 2015.
3 Branka Stipančić, *Goran Trbuljak*. Zagreb: Muzej Suvremene Umjetnosti, 1996.
4 The film was made by János Gulyás, a student at the Színház- és Filmművészeti Főiskola (Theatre and Film Academy). See 'Pseudo Exhibition', in Dóra Hegyi, Sándor Hornyik and Zsuzsa László (eds), *Parallel Chronologies: 'Other' Revolutionary Traditions: How Art Becomes Public. An Exhibition in Newspaper Format*. Budapest: Tranzit Hungary Public Benefit Association, 2011, 26–27. http://tranzit.org/exhibitionarchive/pseudo-exhibition (4 August 2017).
5 English translation in Hans D. Christ and Iris Dressler (eds), *Subversive Practices: Art under Conditions of Political Repression: 60s–80s/South America/Europe*. Berlin: HatjeCantz, 2010, 173–74.
6 'Gyula Pauer: *Pseudo advertisement*', in Hegyi, Hornyik and László, *Parallel Chronologies*, 31.
7 Annamária Szőke, '"Évekig tartott, amíg kialakítottam a magam művészi világát"' ['It Took Years for Me to Form My Own Artistic World'], in Annamária Szőke (ed.), *Pauer*. Budapest: MTA Művészettörténeti Kutatóintézet, 2005, 20.
8 Leonida Kovač, 'Are we still Modern?', in Jasmina Bavoljak (ed.), *Reflections of Time 1945–1955*. Zagreb: Galerija Klovićevi Dvor, 2012, 353.
9 *Ibid.*
10 See Edit Sasvári, 'A Moment of Experimental Democracy in the Kádár Era: György Galántai's Chapel Studio in Balatonboglár and the Social Milieu of Counter-Culture in Hungary in the 1960s and 1970s', in Ivana Bago, Antonia Majača and Vesna Vuković (eds), *Removed from the Crowd: Unexpected Encounters I*. Zagreb: Blok, 2015, 88–92.
11 Notably this policy only applied to smaller spaces and specifically excluded the major venues; the Ministry of Culture had the final say as to whether an exhibition qualified or not; and proposals that offended public morals or were deemed politically unacceptable were still not permitted. See Edit Sasvári, 'Resurgence and Rejection: Lajos Kassák's Self-Financed Exhibition in Adolf Fényes Showroom, Budapest', *Acta Historiae Artium*, special issue on 'The Long Sixties' edited by Edit András and Hedvig Turai, Vol. 56, No. 1, 2015, 238–39.
12 Aurel Hrabušický (ed.), *Slovenské vizuálne umenie 1970–1985* [Slovak Visual Arts 1970–1985]. Bratislava: Slovenská Národná Galéria, 2002, 236.
13 Jindřich Chalupecký, 'The Intellectual under Socialism', in Laura Hoptman and Tomáš Pospiszyl (eds), *Primary Documents: A Sourcebook for Eastern and Central European Art since the 1950s*. New York: Museum of Modern Art, 2002, 30.
14 Milan Šimečka, *Restoration of Order: Normalization of Czechoslovakia*. London: Verso, 1984.
15 See Paulina Bren, *The Greengrocer and His TV: The Culture of Communism after the 1968 Prague Spring*. Ithaca: Cornell University Press, 2010.
16 Marián Mudroch (ed.), *1. Otvorený ateliér* [First Open Studio]. Bratislava: SCCAN, 2000.
17 Interview with Rudolf Sikora, Bratislava, 24 May 2016.
18 Ljiljana Kolešnik, 'Conflicting Visions of Modernity and the Post-war Modern Art', in Ljiljana Kolešnik (ed.), *Socialism and Modernity: Art, Culture, Politics 1950–1974*. Zagreb: Museum of Contemporary Art, 2012, 156.
19 Nena Baljković, 'Braco Dimitrijević – Goran Trbuljak', in Marijan Susovski (ed.), *New Artistic Practice in Yugoslavia: 1966–1978*. Zagreb: Gallery of Contemporary Art, 1978.
20 The participating artists were Giovanni Anselmo, Robert Barry, Stanley Brouwn, Daniel Buren, Victor Burgin, Jan Dibbets, Braco Dimitrijević, ER Group, Barry Flanagan, Douglas Huebler, Alain Kirill, Jannis Kounellis, John Latham, Group Kod, Sol LeWitt, OHO Group, Goran Trbuljak, Lawrence Weiner, Ian Wilson. Ješa Denegri, 'Art in the Past Decade', in Susovski, *New Artistic Practice in Yugoslavia*, 11.
21 Prelom Kolektiv (ed.), *The Case of Belgrade's Students' Cultural Centre in the 1970s*. Belgrade: Prelom Kolektiv, n.d.
22 Kynaston McShine, *Information*. New York: Museum of Modern Art, 1970.
23 Igor Španjol (ed.), *OHO – A Retrospective*. Ljubljana: Moderna Galerija, 2007.
24 See the chapter on the OHO Group in Maja Fowkes, *The Green Bloc*.
25 Dóra Hegyi, Zsuzsa László and Eszter Szakács (eds), *Imagination/Idea: The Beginning of Hungarian Conceptual Art – The László Beke Collection 1971*. Budapest: tranzit.hu, 2014. In fact, over the course of several months while the material was collected, three more artists joined the call, making the final number thirty-one.
26 Hegyi, Hornyik and László, *Parallel Chronologies*, 9. This is regularly put down to the museum curators Márta Kovalovszky and Péter Kovács, as well as to its location outside Budapest, where venues were more firmly controlled.
27 For reprints, see Hegyi, László and Szakács, *Imagination/Idea*.
28 'The Collection of Gyula Pauer', in Hegyi, László and Szakács, *Imagination/Idea*, 183.
29 Piotr Piotrowski, *In the Shadow of Yalta: Art and the Avant-garde in Eastern Europe, 1945–1989*. London: Reaktion Books, 2009, 294.

30 The work in question was Henryk Stażewski's *Infinite Vertical Composition* (1970); see Jolanta Gromadzka, 'The Wrocław '70 Visual Arts Symposium', in Dorota Monkiewicz (ed.), *The Wild West: A History of Wrocław's Avant-Garde*. Warsaw: Zachęta/National Gallery of Art, 2015, 101–103.
31 Sylwia Serafinowicz and Dorota Monkiewicz, 'The Open Wrocław', in Monkiewicz, *The Wild West*, 141.
32 See also Magdalena Radomska, 'PERMAFO's Hungarian "Points of Support"', in Anna Markowska (ed.), *PERMAFO 1970–1981*. Wrocław: Wrocław Contemporary Museum, 2013, 120–25.
33 Jerzy Ludwiński quoted in 'It Begins in Wrocław ... Wanda Gołowska and Jan Chwałczyk in Conversation with Magdalena Ziółkowska', in Magdalena Ziółkowska (ed.), *Notes from the Future of Art: Selected Writings by Jerzy Ludwiński*. Eindhoven: Van Abbe Museum, 2007, 165.
34 Piotrowski, *In the Shadow of Yalta*, 295–96.
35 Luiza Nader, 'Transgressing the Imagination: The Zalesie Ball in 1968', in Claire Bishop and Marta Dziewańska (eds), *1968–1989: Political Upheaval and Artistic Change*. Warsaw: Museum of Modern Art in Warsaw, 2009, 103, footnote 24.
36 Nader, 'Transgressing the Imagination', 102.
37 WHW interview with Želimir Koščević, *Galerija Nova Newspaper*, Vol. 18, No. 12, 2008, 14.
38 Želimir Koščević (ed.), *Student Centre Gallery Zagreb: 1961–1973*. Zagreb: Studentski Centar Sveučilišta u Zagrebu, 1975.
39 *Ibid.*, 87.
40 László Beke in interview with Eszter Szakács in Hegyi, László and Szakács, *Imagination/Idea*, vi.
41 WHW interview with Želimir Koščević, *Galerija Nova Newspaper*, 15.
42 Branka Ćurčić, 'The Novi Sad Neo Avant-Garde of the 1960s and 1970s', in Zorana Dojić and Jelena Vesić (eds), *Political Practices of (Post-)Yugoslav Art: Retrospective 01*. Belgrade: Prelom Kolektiv, 2010, 176.
43 Maja and Reuben Fowkes, 'Remains of Utopia: Neo-Marxist Affinities of the East European Neo-avant-garde', *Acta Historiae Artium*, No. 56, 2015, 333–42.
44 Nebojša Milenkovć, 'Invisible Art', in Nebojša Milenković, Gordana Nikolić and Luka Kulić (eds), *Examples of Invisible Art*. Novi Sad: Museum of Contemporary Art of Vojvodina, 2012, 17.
45 Miško Šuvaković, 'Students' Cultural Centres as Reservations', in Prelom Kolektiv, *The Case of Belgrade's Students' Cultural Centre*, 99.
46 *Ibid.*
47 Kolešnik, 'Conflicting Visions', 157.
48 Miklós Peternák, *concept.hu: The Influence of Conceptual Art in Hungary*. Paks: Paksi Képtár, 2014, 67; and 'Kronológia 1966–81', available at http://www.c3.hu/collection/koncept/frame.html (6 October 2016).
49 See the footnote to György Galántai's biography, available online at http://www.galantai.hu/appendix/eletrajz.html (5 August 2017).
50 László Beke, 'Dulden, verbieten, unterstützen: Kunst zwischen 1970 und 1975', in Hans Knoll (ed.), *Die zweite Öffentlichkeit: Kunst in Ungarnim 20. Jahrhundert* [The Second Public: Art in Hungary in the Twentieth Century]. Dresden: Verlag der Kunst, 1999, 217.
51 Police informer report, ÁBTL 3. 1. 2. M-39271/2, 239–247, published in *2000 Irodalmi és Társadalmi havi lap*, No. 10, 2006, and available online at http://ketezer.hu/2006/10/az-aczelt-megedzik (6 October 2016).
52 'KÉP/VERS tájékoztató a FMK 1974. febr. 22-i programjához' ['Image/Poem' information about the FMK programme of 22 February 1974], available at http://www.c3.hu/collection/koncept/footnote/f12.html (6 October 2016).
53 Tamás St Auby, 'Make a Chair! (Hommage à George Brecht)', text of a lecture given at the Young Artists' Club, 6 June 1975, reprinted in Hegyi, Hornyik and László, *Parallel Chronologies*, 43.
54 *Ibid.*
55 Claire Bishop, *Artificial Hells: Participatory Art and the Politics of Spectatorship*. London: Verso, 2012, 143.
56 Pavlína Morganová, *Czech Action Art: Happenings, Actions, Events, Land Art, Body Art and Performance Art behind the Iron Curtain*. Prague: Charles University/Karolinum Press, 2014, 151.
57 Daniela Čarná, *Out of the City: Land Art*. Bratislava: City Gallery, 2007, 13.
58 Jerzy Ludwiński, 'Art in the Post-Artistic Age', in Ziółkowska, *Notes from the Future of Art*, 17–27.
59 Luiza Nader, 'Towards Criticism of the Visual: the 8th Meeting of Artists and Theoreticians of Art in Osieki', in *Avant-Garde in Plein-Air: Osieki and Łazy 1963–1981*. Koszalin: Museum of Koszalin, 2008, 89.
60 Edit Sasvári, 'A balatonboglári kápolnatárlatok kultúrpolitikai háttere' [The Cultural-political Background of the Balatonboglár Chapel Exhibitions], in Júlia Klaniczay and Edit Sasvári (eds), *Törvénytelen avantgárd: Galántai György balatonboglári kápolnaműterme 1970–1973* [Illegal Avant-garde: The Balatonboglár Chapel Studio of György Galántai 1970–1973]. Budapest: Artpool-Balassi, 2003, 35.
61 [György Galántai], 'The Pre-Story of Artpool: Chapel Studio of György Galántai Balatonboglár, 1970–1973', in György Galántai and Júlia Klaniczay, *Artpool: The Experimental Art Archive of East-Central Europe*. Budapest: Artpool, 2013, 32.
62 László Szabó, 'Happening a kriptában' [Happening in the Crypt], *Népszabadság*, 16 December 1973. Reprinted in Klaniczay and Sasvári, *Törvénytelen avantgárd*, 185–86, trans. Reuben Fowkes.

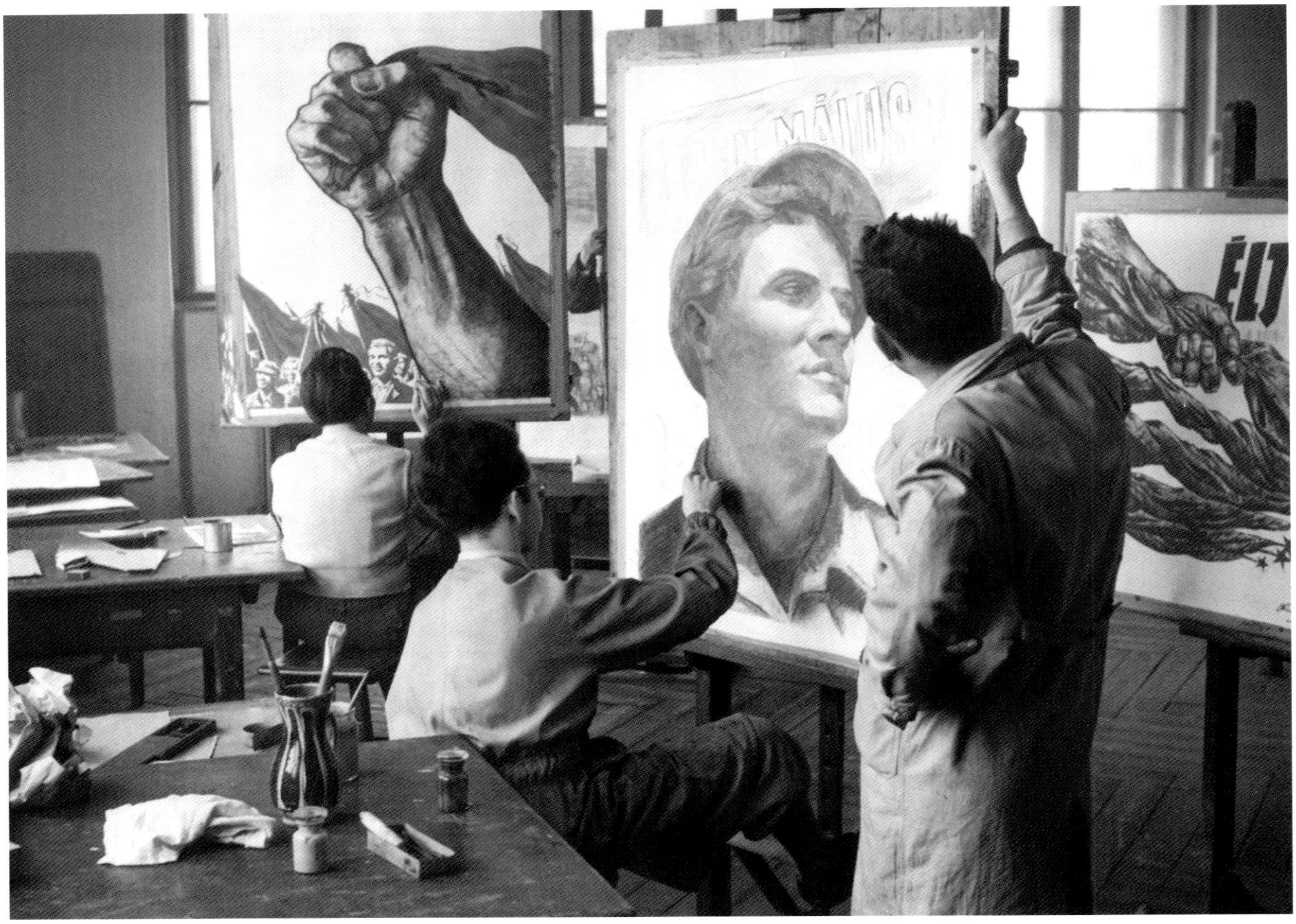

1

1. Magyar Képzőművészeti Főiskola (Hungarian Academy of Fine Arts), 1960s

Flóra Barkóczi

Creative (Dis)Courses

The Forms, Methods and Locations of Alternative Art Pedagogy in Hungary

The visual arts of any given period are intertwined with issues related to artists' education. The system, approaches, institutions and teachers of art education have always left their mark on developments in art, particularly in Eastern Europe. In Hungary in the 1960s–70s, if young people wanted to become professional artists and to integrate into the state system of art, they could only do so within an institutional structure based on solid nineteenth-century conservative traditions and following Marxist-Leninist ideology.

The training system was heavily centralized and politicized in Hungary in the years of socialism from the end of the Second World War to 1989. Its key institutions – the Képző- és Iparművészeti Gimnázium (Secondary School of Fine and Applied Arts) and the Magyar Képzőművészeti Főiskola (Hungarian Academy of Fine Arts) – both operated in the capital, Budapest (figs 1 and 2). Both schools were regarded as elite institutions to which one was admitted only after a series of competitive exams, yet the majority of the students were disappointed by them. Neither the spirit and pedagogical methods of the colleges, nor the knowledge they provided, showed any awareness of the explosion that was taking place in international art in the 1960s–70s. In order to keep up with the dynamic developments in contemporary art, a student artist had to rely almost exclusively on themselves and undertake a form of self-education. This dual orientation meant that students simultaneously had to conform to the expectations of an ideologically governed college education, totally isolated from international contemporary art, and to realize their own needs and desires. It was the personal, internal demands that shaped the colourful scene of alternative art education during the decades of socialism.

Artists' training in the state system

From the late 1950s to the late 1970s, the principles of art education kept shifting in Hungary with changes in the political situation. The dogma of socialist realism still played a major role in the cultural politics of the 1960s, but no longer as exclusively as in the 1950s, and there was a degree of relative freedom within the state system of education as well (figs 3 and 4). The most important instruments of socialist education were the state educational institutions, which required a growing number of teachers. This training of teachers en masse resulted in an odd situation in the 1960s: graduates of the Magyar Képzőművészeti Főiskola received degrees for art education (as 'teachers of drawing') rather than art. This was linked to a shift in emphasis from autonomous artistic activities, and an elite culture in general, to an expansion of the social role of art. Politics, and more specifically the politics of education, focused on the culture of the environment and visual education for society as a whole, and the educational reforms of the 1960s and 1970s were meant to serve this policy. This change in emphasis was an international phenomenon rather than a peculiarly Hungarian one, and recast the role of the artist within society across the world.

The Magyar Képzőművészeti Főiskola was the only state institution of higher education that trained artists in the 1960s–70s. This situation, which would not change until the political transition at the end of the 1980s, prevented competition, and eliminated any institutional motivation for development and renewal.[1] The director of the Magyar Képzőművészeti Főiskola was Endre Domanovszky in 1956–74; as a painter, he was one of the key figures in interwar modernism and became a prominent socialist realist in the 1950s. The curriculum and teaching methods embraced the ideas of academic realism and the post-Nagybánya tradition (following the style of the artists' colony at Nagybánya that was an influential *plein air* movement from the end of the nineteenth century until the 1930s). Yet students could also encounter a more up-to-date approach to art, departing from academism, through teachers like Jenő Barcsay, Aurél Bernáth, Gyula Hincz and Károly Koffán. A number of artists (such as Tibor Csernus and Béla Kondor) who were influential in the 1960s were their former students, while figures of the young generation, such as László Lakner and Ákos Szabó, were former students of Aurél Bernáth in particular.

A number of significant artists gave up on the prospect of earning a degree in art in the state system after multiple applications and rejections. These included Tibor Csiky, who became a geometric abstract sculptor after graduating in mathematics and physics and then teaching Hungarian language and literature; István Harasztÿ, who trained himself in art having been an engine fitter; and Gyula Pauer, who developed his radical conceptual programme (called *Pseudo*).

Intermediate forms

The training of so-called 'amateur' artists took place in the Népművészeti Intézet (Institute of Folk Art) established in 1951 and modelled on the Soviet Folk Art Centre, Dom narodnogo tvorchestva. It was subsequently renamed the Népművelési Intézet (Institute of Public Education) in 1956. The concept of popular education began to make its mark in

2 & 3. Magyar Képzőművészeti Főiskola (Hungarian Academy of Fine Arts), 1960s

4. Jenő Barcsay's anatomy lesson at the Hungarian Academy of Fine Arts, 1960s

5. Péter Forgács's course, held at a primary school in Budapest, animation after Ferenc Lantos's book *Természet – Látás – Alkotás* (Nature – Vision – Creation), *c.* 1977–78

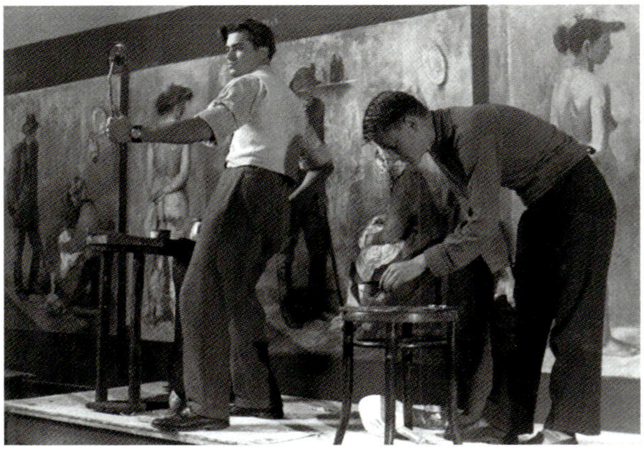

2

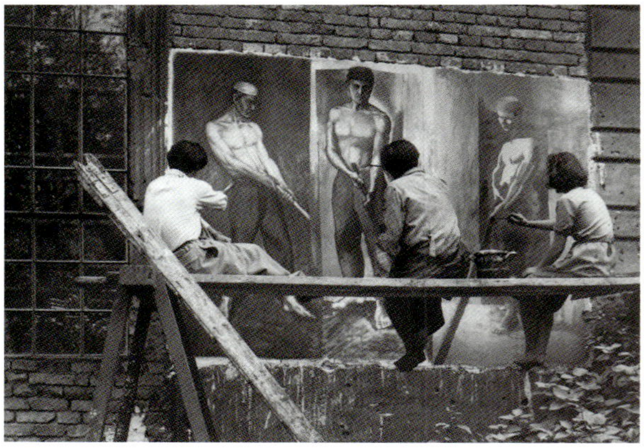

3

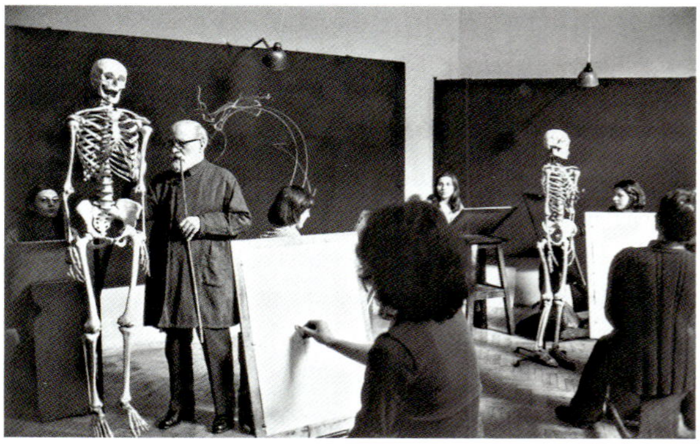

4

Hungary in the 1950s and primarily included extracurricular cultural activities. The main task of the institute was to educate and orientate the receptive masses while aiming to popularize a uniform 'socialist culture'. This included popular science, library work, amateur art and science projects, workshops and various leisure activities. The institute had to manage, coordinate and support the art activities of the trade unions, associations and cultural centres; and it had to scout for and train talented 'amateur artists' and educate art professionals. The term 'amateur', which had a pejorative connotation, was reserved for those participants in the art scene who did not have a college degree. At the same time, the label 'amateur' was a badge of honour outside the official scene, as it lent an aura of independence to artists outside the system.

The Népművelési Intézet ran hundreds of workshops,[2] cultural centres, creative camps and artists' colonies in the country, motivated partly by the desire to break Budapest's near-monopoly on culture. Although the role of popular education was closely connected to the programme of socialist indoctrination, the Népművelési Intézet could function as a less controlled and somewhat freer space, thanks to some enlightened members of the institute, such as Pál Bánszky, who headed the Vizuális Művészeti Osztály (Department of Visual Art), painter Imre Bak and sociologist Iván Vitányi. Bak, who began working as a neo-avant-garde visual artist in the mid-1960s, helped the Népművelési Intézet play an important role in the dissemination of contemporary art. He was on the staff of the Módszertani Intézet (Institute of Methodology) at the Vizuális Művészeti Osztály in 1974–79 and visited cultural centres all over Hungary in that capacity. He gave talks to art teachers, those involved in popular education and amateur artists, typically discussing issues relating to contemporary Hungarian and Western visual art, topics that were almost completely unknown to people living in the Hungarian countryside.

The institute also held sway over the structural transformations of art institutions: it established the system of 'small galleries' in the mid-1970s. Unlike art galleries in the West, these sites had no commercial activities, since there was, in fact, no commercial art trade in Hungary during that period. Yet, these mini-institutions became crucial sites for experimentation in contemporary art. For example, neo-constructivist artist János Fajó ran a small gallery named the Józsefvárosi Galéria from 1976, which became a home for contemporary exhibitions and various innovative programmes involving applied art, visual art and visual culture.

A number of progressive artists came into contact with the Népművelési Intézet in the 1970s: on behalf of the institute, Péter Forgács, who worked primarily as a performance artist in the second half of the 1970s, held experimental art events at a primary school from 1974 (fig. 5); until he emigrated in 1976, the institute also supported Péter Halász's productions at the neo-avant-garde theatre, Kassák Ház Stúdió (Kassák House Studio).[3]

5

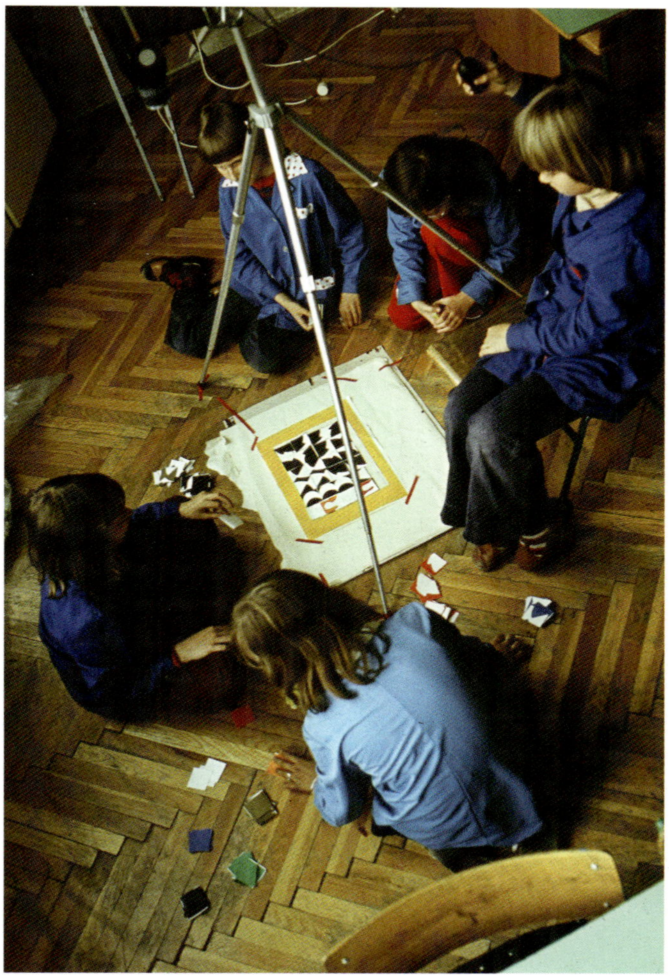

Alternative forms of art training

The restrictions and conservatism of official art training pushed young visual artists towards alternative forms of self-education. Fluxus, which appeared in Hungary in the mid-1960s, as well as later developments in conceptual art had a major influence on this trend, since they strengthened the already existing concepts of self-education and alternative pedagogy in Hungary. The mid-1960s also saw an upward swing in travel to and contacts with the West, which also contributed to Hungarian artists' increasing familiarity with new Western models of creativity and pedagogy. For instance, the work of Joseph Beuys became a point of reference for a number of Hungarian visual artists in the 1970s, and artists could meet the French Fluxus artist Robert Filliou in person at the Fiatal Művészek Klubja (FMK, Young Artists' Club) in Budapest in 1976 . It was there that Filliou's work *Poïpoïdrome* – originally planned in 1963 – was realized for the first time; the installation, which the artist called the 'institute of permanent creation', was meant to be both a monument to and a workshop of creative production and alternative pedagogy.

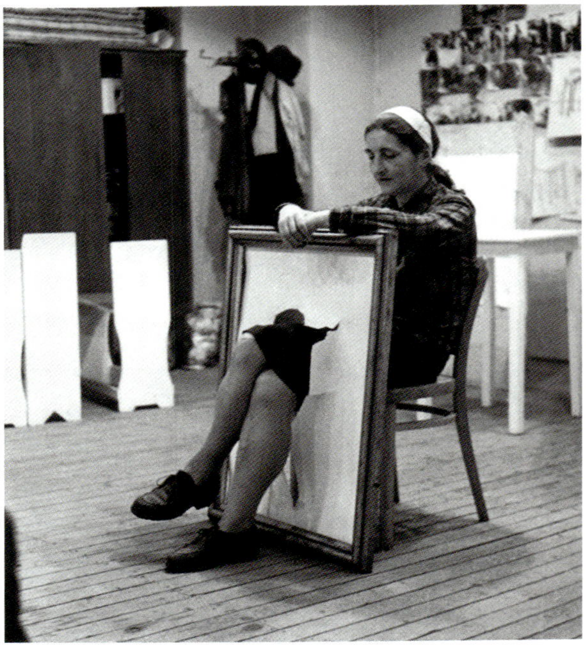

6

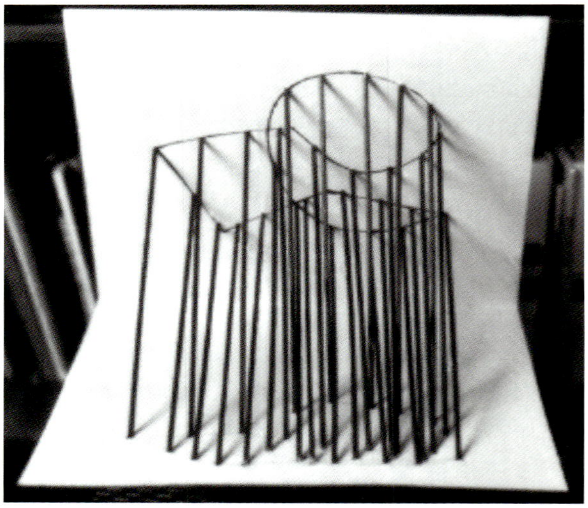

7

The workshop as a site of art education

The first initiatives of alternative art pedagogy in Hungary date from the 1970s and were linked to artists who were already active in contemporary art at the time. While Imre Bak tried to acquaint a relatively broad public with the latest developments in contemporary visual art through the channels of the Népművelési Intézet, alternative art pedagogy was based on intimacy, transpired in closed circles and reached only few people. Miklós Erdély and Dóra Maurer's projects were no exception (see Géza Boros, 'Taboo and Trauma: 1956', pp. 193–207, for more on Miklós Erdély's early career). They launched their first joint workshop in the mid-1970s at the Ganz-MÁVAG Művelődési Ház (Ganz-MÁVAG Culture House). Erdély and Maurer's courses were mostly attended by the young avant-garde generation of the 1970s–80s. Their pedagogical activities were based on an experience in 1971, when they attended composer Mauricio Kagel's

6. Model at the Creativity Exercises workshop, Ganz-MÁVAG Müvelődési Ház (Ganz-MÁVAG Culture House), Budapest, 1976

7. A piece from Dóra Maurer's drawing course, Ganz-MÁVAG Müvelődési Ház (Ganz-MÁVAG Culture House), Budapest, 1975–77

8. Active-passive exercise at the Creativity Exercises workshop, Ganz-MÁVAG Müvelődési Ház (Ganz-MÁVAG Culture House), Budapest, 1976–77

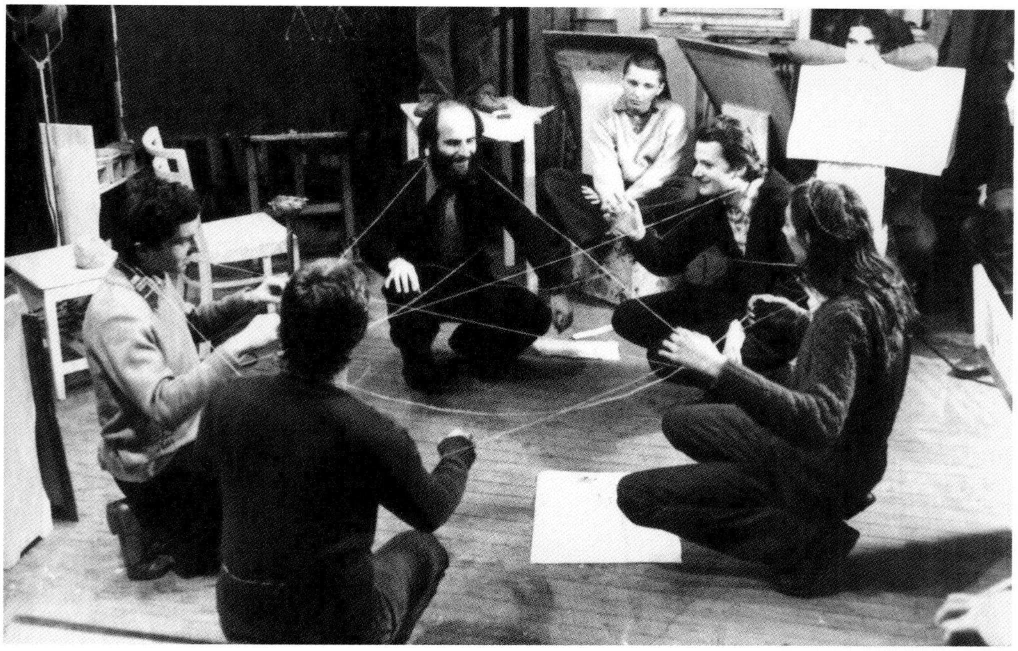

8

course at the Kunstzone art fair in Munich.[4] Experiencing the creative exercises, combined with musical experimentation and movement, made such an impact on them that they launched their own movement-based workshop, 'Mozgástervezési és kivitelezési gyakorlatok' (Motion Planning and Performing Exercises), in Budapest in 1975. It was Tamás Papp, a popular educator at the Ganz-MÁVAG Művelődési Ház in the 1970s, who approached Erdély and Maurer about running the workshop. Thanks to Papp, the place became an important institution for the avant-garde projects of the period.

Erdély and Maurer's courses broke with earlier traditions of art education and replaced the classical drawing of models and scenes with exercises developing creative thinking, experimental methods and tasks aimed at fostering the experience of community. Dóra Maurer also ran a drawing workshop in 1975–77 at Ganz MÁVAG Művelődési Ház (fig. 7). She commuted between Budapest and Vienna in the mid-1970s (she had Austrian and Hungarian dual citizenship), so her Western European experiences also contributed to the appearance of cutting-edge forms of art dissemination, previously unknown in Hungary, in a cultural centre in Budapest. Maurer once said that her work as a workshop leader was simply 'instinctively consistent pedagogical practice',[5] which is related to the fact that her art pedagogy stemmed from her own creative activities and remained closely interlinked with it throughout. According to her recollection, their courses were terminated in 1977 due to a scandalous photo exhibition in which pictures of naked bodies were displayed. The exhibition was organized by the members of the Dziga Vertov Fotó- és Amatőrfilm Szakkör (Dziga Vertov Amateur Photo and Film Workshop), which was based at the cultural centre. Erdély and Maurer's contracts were not renewed after that event, but Erdély continued to run workshops at other locations.

Erdély, who was known as a representative of Fluxus, conceptual art and actionism, had begun but never completed his studies as a sculptor at the Magyar Képzőművészeti Főiskola. He became a legendary figure of Hungarian visual arts in the 1960s, 1970s and 1980s. This was due to his charismatic personality and inspiring mind, but also to his unique methods, primarily based on the principles of holistic and interdisciplinary thought. After his aforementioned

9. INDIGO group, The exhibiton 'Coal and Charcoal Drawing', Marczibányi Téri Ifjúsági Ház (Marczibányi Square Youth Centre), Budapest, 1978

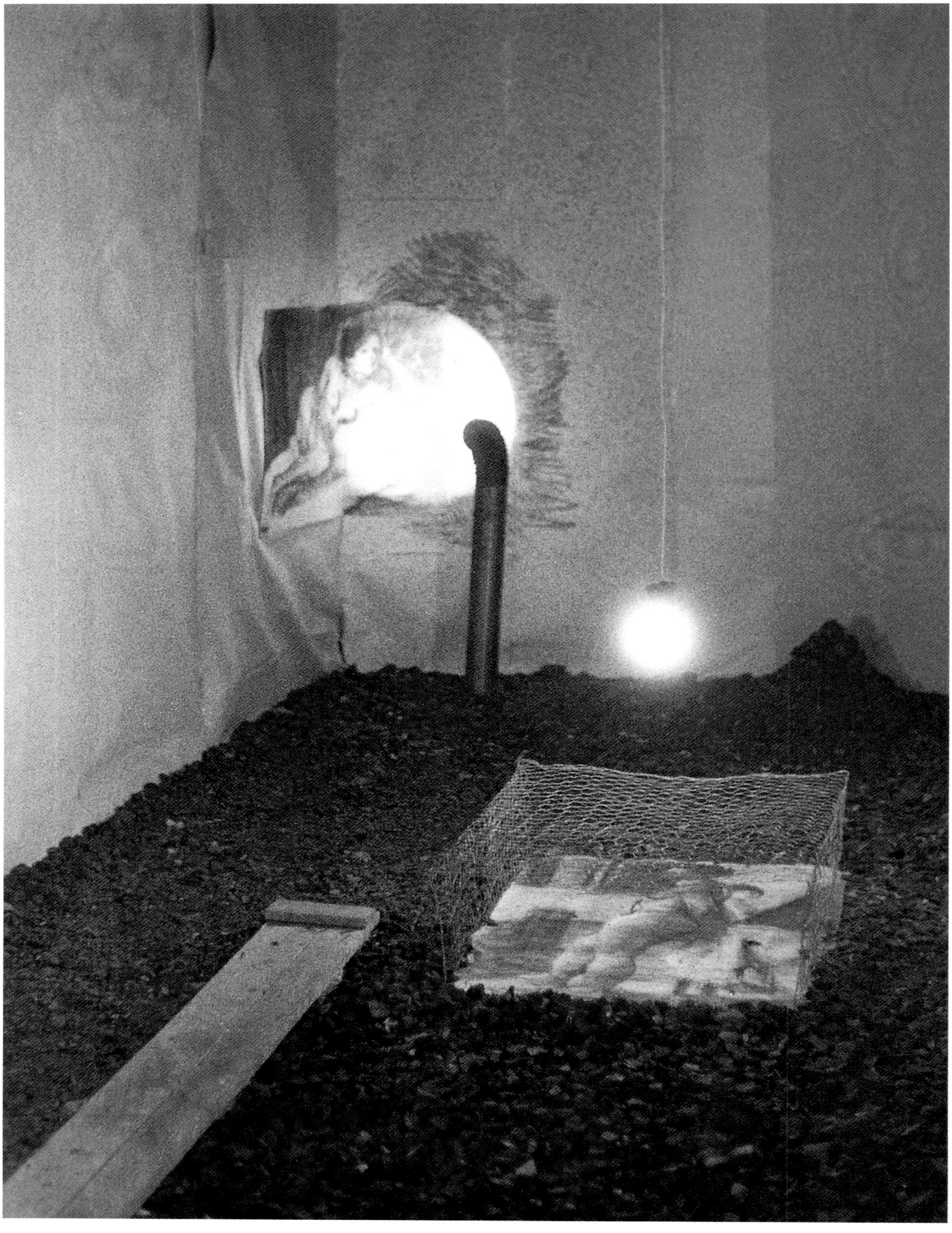

'Mozgástervezési és kivitelezési gyakorlatok' and 'Kreativitási gyakorlatok' (Creativity Exercises, figs 6 and 8), Erdély led two more workshops, the titles of which expressed his pioneering approach quite vividly: 'Fantáziafejlesztő gyakorlatok' (Fantasy-developing Exercises, 1977–78) and 'Interdiszciplináris gondolkodás' (Interdisciplinary Thinking, 1978–86). Erdély used innovative methods to develop the course concepts, including brainstorming as a basis for the project-based and informal teaching, which aimed to engage learners in a collaborative process based on active participation and thinking together, rather than a unidirectional transfer of knowledge by the teacher. The current issues of contemporary art (performativity, conceptuality) and new media (action, video) were also included in the course content. Erdély's pedagogy was not based on drawing models and scenes, which developed copying skills, but rather on exercises that could be actively shaped by the participants and fostered creative thinking, interdisciplinarity and skills of creative collaboration. Although Erdély tended to use the concept of creativity ironically, he was familiar with the theories of creativity that arose in Western Europe in the early 1950s, some of which were published in Hungarian translation in the 1970s.

Around 1978, Erdély's art pedagogy shifted from thinking to artistic representation and public display: the workshop named 'Interdiszciplináris gondolkodás', functioned less as an art course than as an artists' group, later called INDIGO. The workshop was attended mostly by students of the Magyar Képzőművészeti Főiskola, who were eager to display their works publicly. They organized several thematic shows centred on various media and concepts of art. The exhibition 'Coal and Charcoal' explored coal, but departed from traditional charcoal drawing and included not only discarded charcoal drawings by students of the academy, but also hundreds of kilograms of coal, some of which was in fancifully tall heaps, stove pipes and sugar-filled balloons (fig. 9). The starting point for the exhibition was a short story about poverty by Franz Kafka ('The Bucket Rider'), but the goal was to present as many layers of the meaning of coal (social, physical and chemical) as possible. Such exhibitions would be preceded by brainstorming sessions, the memory of which is preserved on index cards that might also be considered materials of conceptual thinking. The emphasis on a collaborative creative process did not fade in the thematic exhibitions, as Erdély considered exhibitions a device for displaying the interdisciplinary, critical and creative thinking of the group.

INDIGO attracted the attention of the powers-that-be in 1980, when the exhibition 'Aquarelle' was closed down after an inquiry ordered by the management of the Bercsényi Kollégium of the Műegyetem (Bercsényi Dormitory, University of Technology), the location of the exhibition. By focusing on watercolour, the exhibition ironically reacted to the expressive tendencies in painting emerging at the turn of the 1970s and 1980s; it became a target of censorial attention due to works by Ildikó Enyedi and Miklós Peternák. Enyedi's *Attempt at Disproving the Four Colour Theorem* reflected on the problem of colouring the regions of a map by using four different colours. However, the Soviet Union, as represented in her map, was right under Italy's boot, which seemed to trample on its socialist ally. Miklós Peternák presented a photographic work in which the text 'we are on strike' appeared on the wall of a Polish shipyard. An arrow and the word 'painting' superimposed on the photo identified the text itself as a painting and thereby art.

In the wider East-Central European region, Oskar Hansen was engaged in pedagogical activities just as significant as those of Erdély during the same period. An architect, painter and urbanist best known for his theory of Open Form, Hansen aimed to develop a new structure that could be freely shaped, opposing the standard, allegedly closed system of architecture. Hansen's theory inspired countless visual artists in Poland from the 1950s onwards, including KwieKulik (the duo Zofia Kulik and Przemysław Kwiek) and Grzegorz Kowalski. Unlike Erdély, who also had a degree in architecture, Hansen had the opportunity to teach in an official capacity at the Akademia Sztuk Pięknych (Academy of Fine Arts) in Warsaw, which testifies to the Polish system being that much more open. His methods spread widely thanks to his students, unlike the practices of Erdély's workshops, which only reached a small circle. And yet, Erdély's effect on art education in Hungary has remained powerful to this day; a number of people who had previously attended Erdély's workshops joined the faculty of the Magyar Képzőművészeti Egyetem (Hungarian University of Fine Arts) after the political transition and integrated his approach into their own educational practice.

Artists' groups as an alternative environment for art education

The story of Miklós Erdély's workshops vividly illustrates how the lack of up-to-date art education at the academy drove students away from an intensely individual type of art training to alternative forms of learning, and to creating and thinking in groups. INDIGO as a group testifies not only to Erdély's pedagogical role, but also to the significance of collaborative creativity during that era. The neo-avant-garde artist groups that emerged in the 1960s were typically held together by a shared interest in a given medium or genre. The Zuglói kör (Zuglói Circle) was such a group, with members such as Imre Bak, Pál Deim, István Nádler and Sándor Molnár sharing an interest in abstract art (see also József Mélyi, 'Abstract Boundaries', pp. 161–77). The group included young artists, freshly graduated from the Magyar Képzőművészeti Főiskola, who gathered around Sándor Molnár and regularly met at his apartment in the Zugló district of Budapest. They met as an intellectual circle rather than a creative group in 1958–68, holding discussions and readings and

10

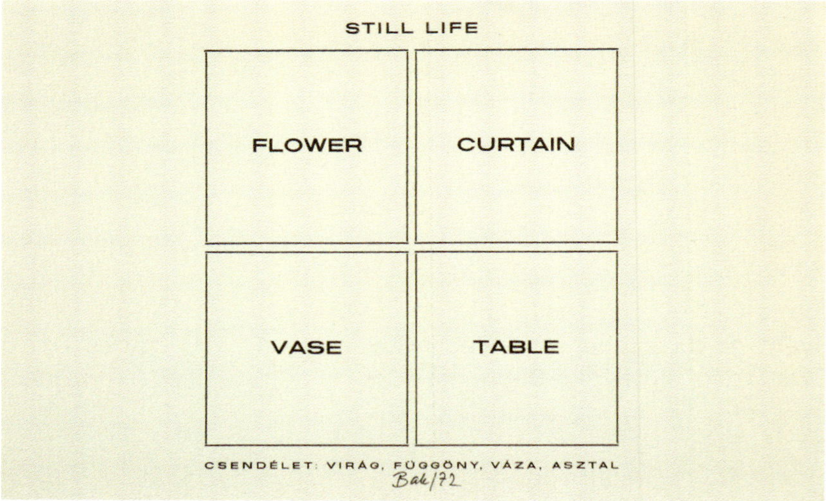

11

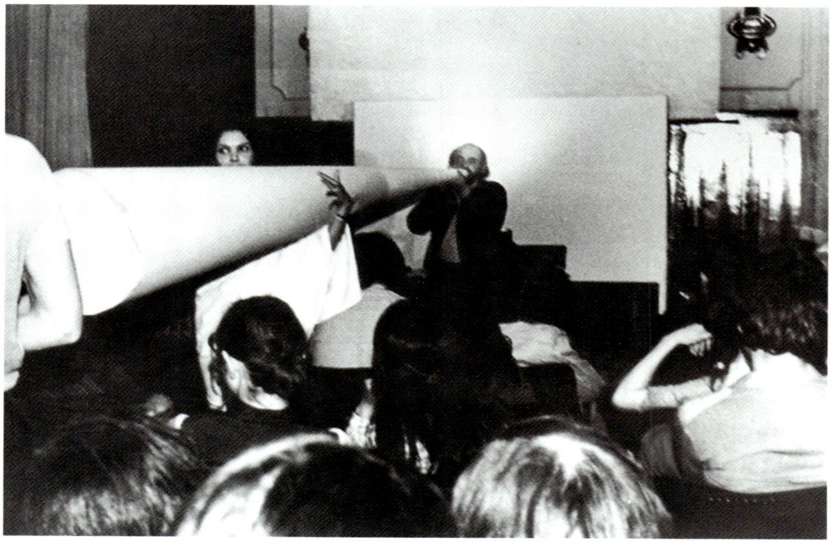

10. Imre Bak, *Still Life*, 1972, paper, ink, 50 × 70 cm, Vintage Galéria, Budapest

11. Miklós Erdély, *CETI (Communication with Extra-terrestrial Intelligence), action within the programme 'Here comes the boogeyman! Actions in learning and general orientation practices'*, Ganz-MÁVAG Művelődési Ház (Ganz-MÁVAG Culture House), Budapest, 2 May 1973

occasionally showing their works at one of the alternative venues of the period, the apartment of Pál Petrigalla (see also Júlia Perczel, 'The Art Sphere as a Grey Zone', pp. 59–75).

The members of another creative group, the Pesti Műhely (Budapest Workshop), were former members of the Zuglói kör. The Pesti Műhely's programme was developed by Imre Bak, already on the staff of the Népművelési Intézet, and two collaborators, János Fajó and István Nádler, in 1971, and it operated until 1981 as an intellectual and creative workshop as well as a publishing house. Bak, Fajó and Nádler drew on constructionist traditions for their unique formal language, and their work showed the influence of structuralism and hard-edge painting as early as the 1960s (fig. 10). The Pesti Műhely experimented primarily with applied genres and reproduction techniques, through which they aimed to disseminate artworks. All of this was also connected to Imre Bak's work for the Népművelési Intézet, as he distributed prints (including works by Lajos Kassák, Jenő Barcsay, Ferenc Martyn, Dezső Korniss, Tamás Lossonczy and Gyula Hincz) during his visits to cultural centres in the countryside.[6]

The Pécsi Műhely (Pécs Workshop), formed by the students of Ferenc Lantos, an avant-garde teacher at the Pécsi Művészeti Szakközépiskola (Pécs Secondary School of Fine Arts), provided a similar intellectual environment. Members of the group (Ferenc Ficzek, Károly Halász, Károly Kismányoki, Sándor Pinczehelyi and Kálmán Szíjártó), which was active between 1968 and 1980, worked on renewing avant-garde and constructivist traditions in Pécs, thereby establishing a second avant-garde centre of art in the country beside Budapest. In the early 1970s, the Pécsi Műhely primarily engaged in land-art actions, but several of the artists also turned to photography under the influence of conceptual art (see also Katalin Székely, 'The Influx of Images', pp. 33–55). The pedagogical role of Ferenc Lantos was not limited to holding the group together, but also contributed significantly to the development of the local formal language of the Pécsi Műhely: Lantos looked at abstract art within a wider system of visual arts, aiming to create a potential new approach to socialist art. This attitude would profoundly influence the oeuvres of the members of the Pécsi Műhely as well.

Besides groups led by emblematic artists of the period, there were also cases of the spontaneous creation of self-organized groups. The formation of the Rózsa Presszó Circle in 1976, for example, was motivated by dissatisfaction with the rigid curriculum of the Magyar Képzőművészeti Főiskola. When classes ended, students would walk over to the Rózsa Presszó café across from the college building to continue their discussions about contemporary art and to work on joint art actions and events. The artists, who mostly attended the Graphics Department, were interested in expanding the genre of graphic arts and its range of media (combining drawing with silkscreen, text and photo), as the academy provided no opportunity for that. The students chose titles by Beuys as their motto ('Rose for Direct Democracy'/'We Won't Do it without the Rose'), which conveniently suited the site of their meetings, where they gave readings and debated contemporary art, conceptual art, Fluxus and Western visual art events.

The Ganz-MÁVAG Művelődési Ház, the location of Erdély and Maurer's workshops, was also the site of various popular science talks and events involving other avant-garde figures. One of these was the Fluxus event *Here comes the boogeyman! Actions in learning and general orientation practices* in 1973 with László Beke, Miklós Erdély and Tamás Szentjóby as participants (fig. 11). The Fiatal Művészek Klubja, which was founded in 1960, had a similar function and operated under similar conditions. The FMK was an important meeting place for young visual artists in or freshly out of college in the 1960s and 1970s, where exhibitions, popular science talks, readings, performances and international gatherings were held. The club was monitored by the regime, and events deemed overly avant-garde or oppositional were banned. Another location for professional discourse and the exchange of ideas was the Fiatal Képzőművészek Stúdiója (Young Artists' Studio), established by the state in 1958. The studio's original goal was to help early-career artists: it was an official organization and a branch of the Magyar Népköztársaság Művészeti Alapja (Art Fund of the Hungarian People's Republic)

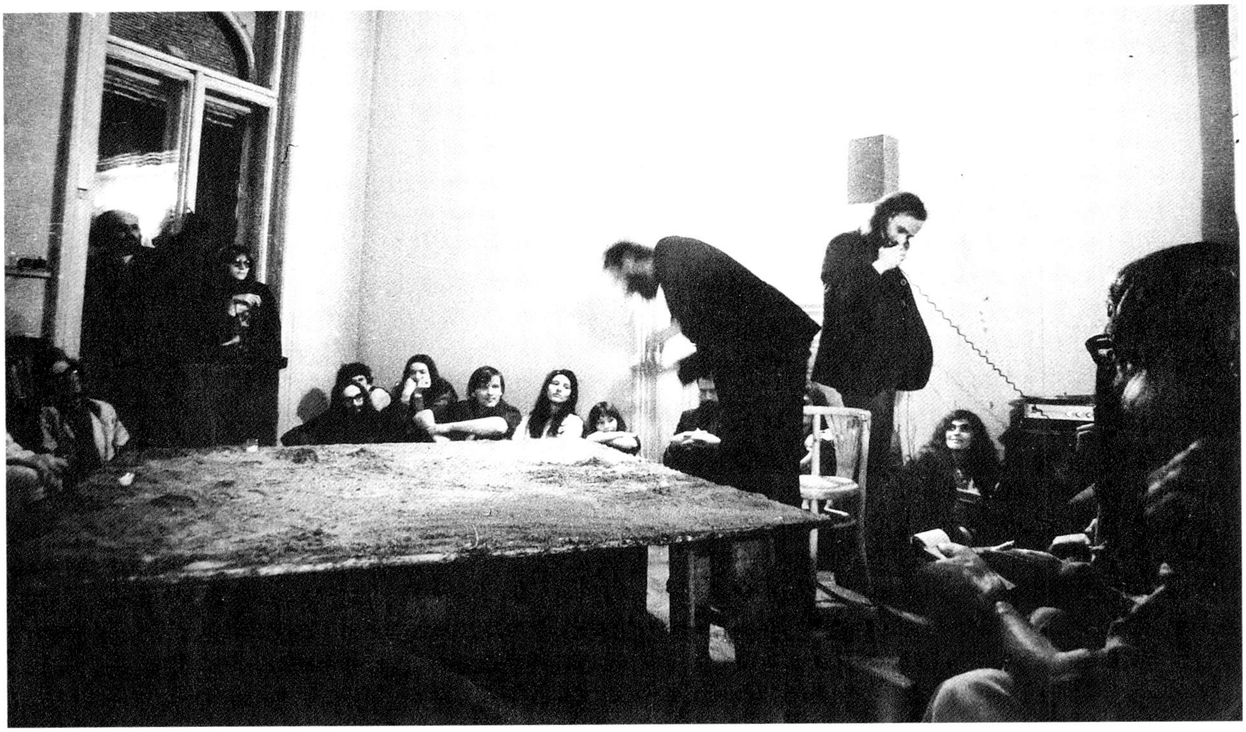

in the 1960s and 1970s; it was home not only to annual group exhibitions but also individual exhibitions by members of the studio from 1972 onwards.

The private apartments of a number of visual artists began to play a significant role in the 1960s: Lajos Kassák's home in Óbuda became a frequent meeting place for young people involved in the avant-garde (including Imre Bak, István Nádler, Tamás Hencze and János Fajó). Kassák was an important master for this generation despite lacking a formal teaching position (see also Gábor Dobó and Merse Pál Szeredi, 'Hungarian Culture +/- Europe', pp. 39–57).

Young people who were eager to combine or contrast folk culture and avant-garde traditions (for instance, Ilona Keserü, Tibor Csiky, Tamás Hencze and Endre Tót) formed a similar circle around Dezső Korniss. György Galántai's Balatonboglári Kápolnaműterem (Balatonboglár Chapel Studio) also offered space for the development of avant-garde art in the early 1970s, acting as a location for a series of exhibitions and art events for four years (1970–73), with most participants being young artists who graduated from the academy (see Maja Fowkes and Reuben Fowkes, 'Liberty Controlled', pp. 77–93, and Klara Kemp-Welch, 'Soft-spoken Encounters', pp. 273–89).

Theatrical groups worked quite similarly to those of the neo-avant-garde visual arts in the same period. The amateur theatre company Kassák Ház Stúdió (see also Katalin Székely, 'The Influx of Images', pp. 331–55) was founded by Péter Halász and Anna Koós in 1969 on the outskirts of Budapest, at the Kassák Művelődési Ház (Kassák Culture House) in the Zugló district (fig. 12). Group members had received no training on the official courses at the Színház- és Filmművészeti Főiskola and emphasized self-education, developing their productions in response to audience feedback after performances. Each member of the company could participate in shaping productions. Kassák Ház Stúdió's productions were provocative from the very start, and its permit was revoked by the censorship authorities in 1972 in response to obscene and politically allusive scenes in the play *The Village Museum Killers*; it was accused of misleading the supervising committee by omitting the scenes in question at the dress rehearsals visited by the authorities. After the revocation of Kassák Ház Stúdió's permit, they performed in the Dohány Street Apartment Theatre and other private apartments for several years and illegally at various events abroad. The company appeared in Wrocław, Poland, for instance, at the Open Theatre Festival in 1973, putting on a performance without a permit in a college dormitory in order to evade official paperwork. According to the members' own description, the performance consisted of the following: 'semi-nudity, drawing blood, drinking bloody milk, boiling milk, chopping off male heads, incarnation, pietà, nursing babies and a dwarf'.[7] After the emigration of Péter Halász and members of the company in 1976, they continued in Western Europe and later in New York under the name Squat Theater. The theatre of Halász, who saw the American Robert Wilson as someone to emulate, completely revised the concept of theatre and the role of the actor in Hungary: the actor appeared on stage no longer as a 'player', but as a real person.[8]

Alternative forms of education appeared in other East-Central European countries besides Hungary in the 1960s–70s, and they were frequently linked to neo-avant-garde art practice. Jiří Valoch, Milan Adamčiak and Július Koller all operated on the borderline of official and alternative culture in Czechoslovakia, reinterpreting the role of the 'amateur artist' in one way or another. Milan Knížák, who was in touch with several international Fluxus artists, established the Aktual group in 1963 in Prague. The Grupa šestorice autora operated in Zagreb in 1975–81, working in public spaces due to the limited opportunities for exhibition. The majority of the group members had not received any official art training and were mostly involved in areas at the margins of the visual arts (amateur film, amateur photography, visual poetry, etc.). A comparable formation in Poland in the 1960s was Grupa ZERO-61, whose collaborative works involved painting, photo and film. Another Polish group, called NET, began as an avant-garde community originated in the spirit of Fluxus; it was launched with a manifesto in 1972 by Jarosław Kozłowski (linked to Foksal Gallery in Warsaw), Andrzej Kostołowski and Andrzej Turowski as an alternative to the academy there (see also Júlia Perczel's 'The Art Sphere as a Grey Zone', pp. 59–75, and Klara Kemp-Welch, 'Soft-spoken Encounters', pp. 273–89).

13

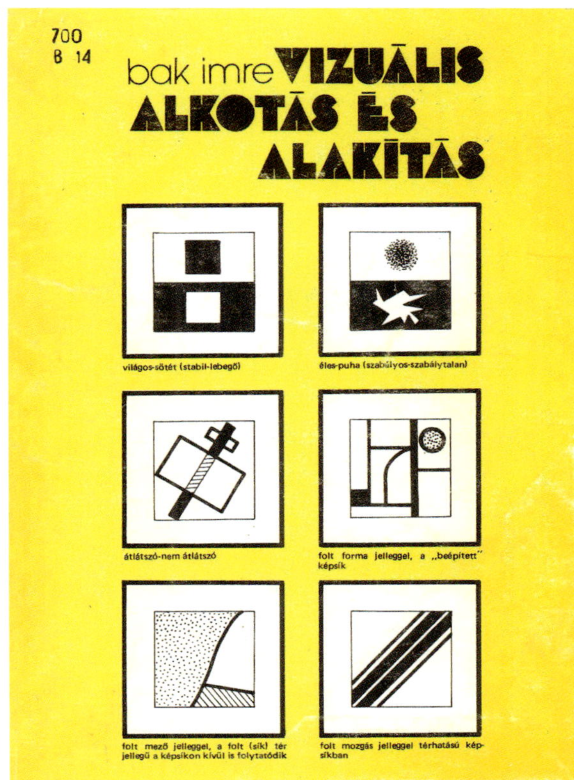

12. Dohány Street Apartment Theatre, *Sand Table*, theatre play, Budapest, 1975

13. Imre Bak, *Visual Creation and Shaping* (book cover), Népművelési Propaganda Iroda, Budapest, 1977

Options offered by individually initiated art pedagogy programmes

Artists attempted to expand the possibilities of the visual arts partly by forming artist groups, workshops and communities, and also by developing either complex or focused pedagogical programmes. As part of his responsibilities at the Népművelési Intézet, Imre Bak developed a curriculum for art education at secondary schools and cultural centres in Hungary. The curriculum was published in book form by the Népművelési Intézet under the title *Vizuális Alkotás és Alakítás* (Visual Creation and Shaping), and contains the course content for a three-semester visual arts workshop (fig. 13).[9] Bak's book was modelled on Bauhaus publications and was published with the intention of expanding knowledge of contemporary art. It featured international artists like Jackson Pollock, Jasper Johns and Frank Stella – whose names were never mentioned in the official courses at the Magyar Képzőművészeti Főiskola. The book's design also conveyed an avant-garde approach, with typography and explanatory illustrations having affinity with Bak's works at the time, such as his *Do it yourself!* notebook, a collection of images calling for interaction and based on conceptual ideas (fig. 14). Although the book had a small print run, it reached students at numerous cultural centres and schools thanks to Bak's distribution activities.

At roughly the same time, in 1974–76, Gábor Bódy developed a pedagogical programme called *Film School*, one of the most influential and internationally well-known works on Hungarian experimental film and video art in the 1970s–80s (fig. 15). The three-part instructional film series was made for Iskolatelevízió (School Television), and each part covered a topic of media studies. The methodology, pedagogy and film language of the series were influenced by neo-avant-garde aesthetics, as was Bódy's video oeuvre more generally. His video works, which were driven by semiotic and art-theory problems, were pioneering in Central Europe. Bódy's work in practical education continued in Western Europe in the 1980s thanks to his international success as a filmmaker: he taught at the Deutsche Film und Fernsehakademie in West Berlin in 1982–84.

Another complex pedagogical utopia was connected to Tamás Szentjóby, who was already living in Switzerland by this time. Szentjóby published his model, called the International Parallel Union of Telecommunication (IPUT) under the title *Parallel Course/Study Track* in 1968 (see also Emese Kürti, 'Poetry in Action', pp. 291–313). According to his own interpretation, the concept of a 'parallel course' referred to a system of instruction proceeding in parallel with traditional education, and to an alternative reality existing alongside socialism. Szentjóby considered public and collaborative creativity to be both the aim

14

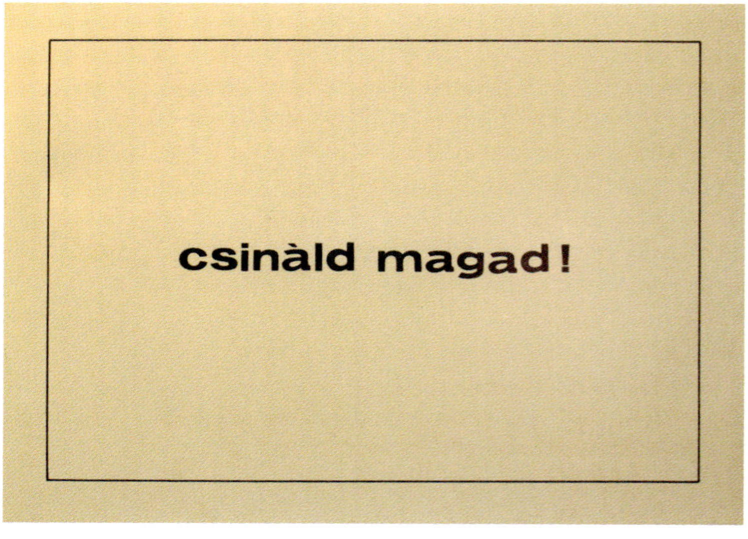

14. Imre Bak, *Do it yourself!*, 1973, leaflet cover (self-published), 11 × 15 cm

15. (overleaf) Gábor Bódy, *Film School*, 1976, 16 mm film, 82', Magyar Nemzeti Filmarchivum, Budapest

and the methodology of the *Parallel Course*, and his programme's synthesis of practical philosophy, politics and pedagogy was driven by the core principles of direct democracy or direct representation.[10] *Parallel Course* was inspired by the ideas of the international Fluxus movement and the New Left: he was familiar with the works of Joseph Beuys and Robert Filliou, who were similarly drawing on both modern Western and ancient Far Eastern philosophies.[11]

Beuys's Free International University at 'documenta' in 1977 provided a framework for Szentjóby to present his action *Make a Chair! (Hommage à George Brecht)*. The action, which was first performed at the FMK in 1975 (p. 88, fig. 12), builds on the art of Marcel Duchamp and George Brecht and defines the concept of art through a denial of both traditional art practice and the aesthetic concept of art, summed up in three statements: '1. Non-art as art (Marcel Duchamp) 2. Non-art as art as art as non-art (George Brecht) 3. Make a Chair! (Szentjóby)'.[12] Szentjóby's neo-avant-garde action not only reflects critically on Duchamp's concept of the readymade and on American artist Joseph Kosuth's conceptual art (*One and Three Chairs*), but also on Fluxus artist George Brecht's *Three Chair Events* in 1961, in which he called for immediate direct action.

Though differing in their methods and approaches, the alternative pedagogical initiatives in Hungary in the 1960s and 1970s all aimed at educating and informing citizens. Imre Bak carried out this transfer of knowledge in the form of popular science talks to a provincial and amateur audience; by contrast, János Fajó – who was connected to Bak in many ways – ran his own graphic arts workshop, in which media, such as folders of reproduced graphic works, were used democratically and made accessible to the general public. Tamás Szentjóby's utopian yet ironic approach is a counterpoint to Bak and Fajó's activities, as he proposed a globally valid programme heavily influenced by Fluxus without defining a target audience. The programme, which encouraged the broadest possible social access to creativity, was only known to the narrowest neo-avant-garde circles. Comparable in spirit and framework to Szentjóby's programme, Miklós Erdély and Dóra Maurer led courses and, later, artist groups with the intention of developing the thinking and creative behaviour of young visual artists with an interest in the avant-garde. As well having distinct aesthetic and political characteristics, these alternative pedagogical programmes reveal much about the era, since they tried to achieve their objectives while navigating circumstances imposed by the socialist system.

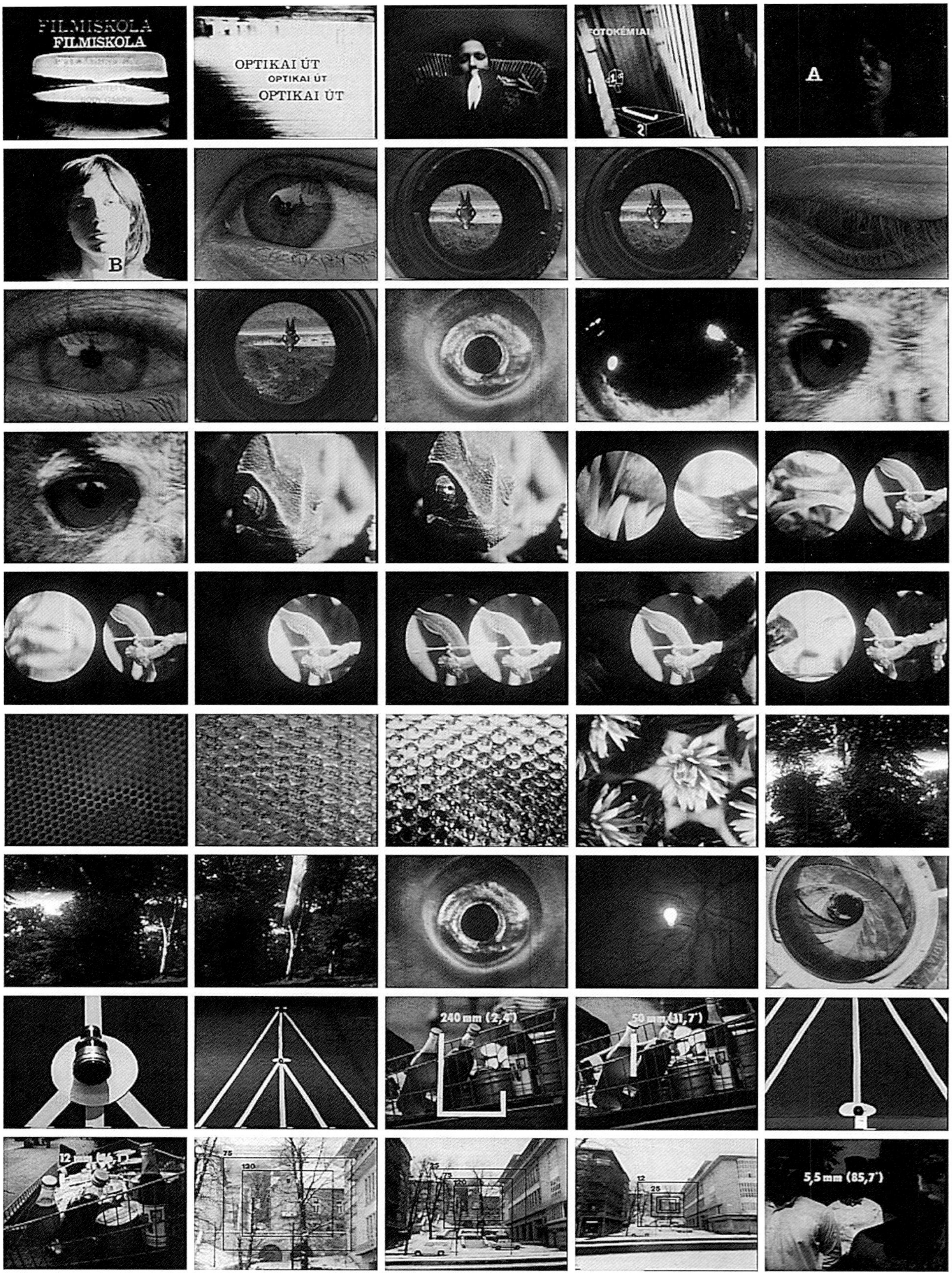
FILMISKOLA
FILMISKOLA
OPTIKAI ÚT
OPTIKAI ÚT
OPTIKAI ÚT
FOTOKÉMIAI
A
B
240 mm (2,4')
50 mm (11,7')
5,5 mm (85,7')

1 There were three institutions of higher education in the broader sphere of the arts in Hungary in this era besides the Magyar Képzőművészeti Főiskola: the Színház- és Filmművészeti Főiskola (Theatre and Film Academy), Magyar Iparművészeti Főiskola (Hungarian Academy of Applied Arts) and Liszt Ferenc Zeneművészeti Főiskola (Ferenc Liszt Music Academy), all situated in Budapest.

2 Pál Bánszky (ed.), *Az amatőr képzőművészeti mozgalom fejlődése: Tartalmi-szemléleti kérdések napjainkban* [The Development of the Amateur Visual Art Movement: Current Issues of Content and Method]. Budapest: Népművelési Intézet, 1975, 10.

3 Júlia Klaniczay and Edit Sasvári (eds), *Törvénytelen avantgárd: Galántai György balatonboglári kápolnaműterme, 1970–1973* [Illegal Avant-garde: The Balatonboglár Chapel Studio of György Galántai 1970–1973]. Budapest: Artpool–Balassi, 2003, 363.

4 Sándor Hornyik and Annamária Szőke (eds), *Kreativitási gyakorlatok, FAFEJ, INDIGO. Erdély Miklós művészetpedagógiai tevékenysége 1975–1986* [Creativity Exercises, FAFEJ, INDIGO. Miklós Erdély's art pedagogical activities 1975–1986]. Budapest: MTA MKI/Gondolat/2B/EMA, 2008.

5 Dóra Maurer, 'Tanulmány-vázlat vizuális nevelés ügyben' [Notes for a Study on the Issue of Visual Education], in T*anulmányok a vizuális nevelés köréből* [Studies on Visual Education]. Budapest: MTA Vizuális Kultúrakutató Munkabizottság, 1978, 139.

6 Imre Bak, interviewed by the author, 24 March 2016.

7 'A Kassák Színház kronológiája' [Chronology of the Kassák Theatre], Artpool, http://www.artpool.hu/AI/al11/KHS-3.html (21 July 2017).

8 Magdolna Jákfalvi, 'A Halász Péter Archívum' [The Péter Halász Archive], in *Színházi Kreativitási Eszközök: Színészképzés és neoavantgárd hagyomány* [Theatrical Devices of Creativity: Actor Training and the Neo-avant-garde Tradition]. Budapest: Balassi Kiadó, 2013, 21.

9 Imre Bak, *Vizuális Alkotás és Alakítás* [Visual Creation and Shaping]. Budapest: Népművelési Propaganda Iroda, 1976.

10 Emese Kürti, 'Pedagogy on Reality: Tamás Szentjóby's Parallel Course/Study Track Program', in Dóra Hegyi, Zsuzsa László and Franciska Zólyom (eds), *Creativity Exercises*, Sternberg Press, 2018.

11 Joseph Beuys's project: *Freie Hochschule für Kreativität und Interdisziplinäre Forschung*; Robert Filliou's text: *Teaching and Learning as Performing Art*.

12 Sándor Hornyik, 'A nem-művészet, mint nem-művészetelmélet: A TNPU kiállítása a Ludwig Múzeumban' [Non-art as non-art-theory: The Exhibition of IPUT at Ludwig Museum]. *Exindex*, 2013, http://exindex.hu/print.php?l=hu&page=3&id=887#_ftn3 (21 July 2017).

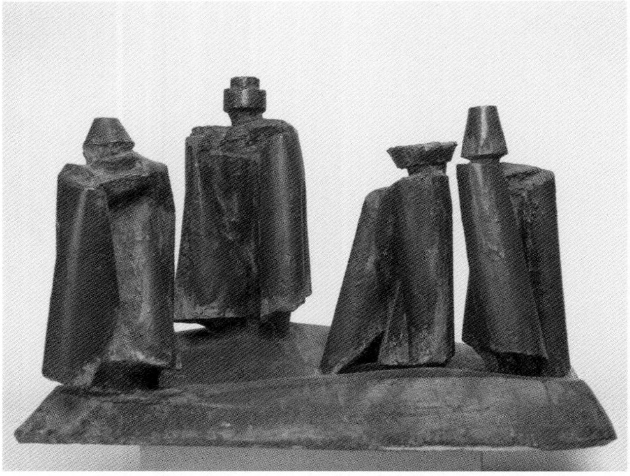

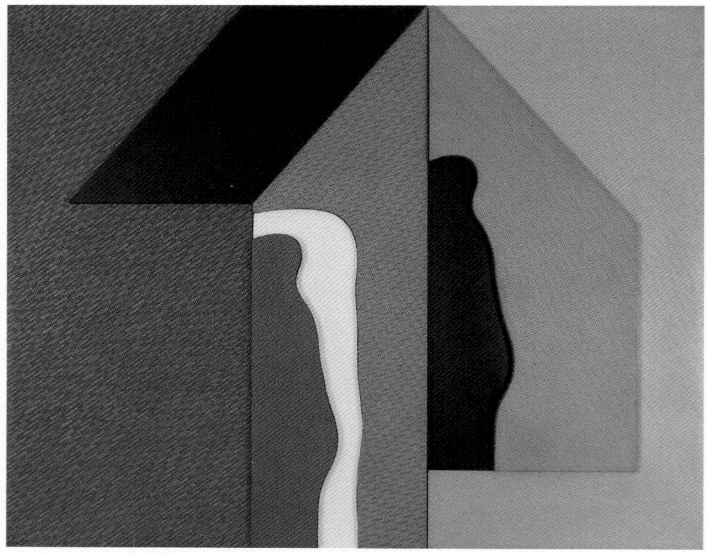

Discourses

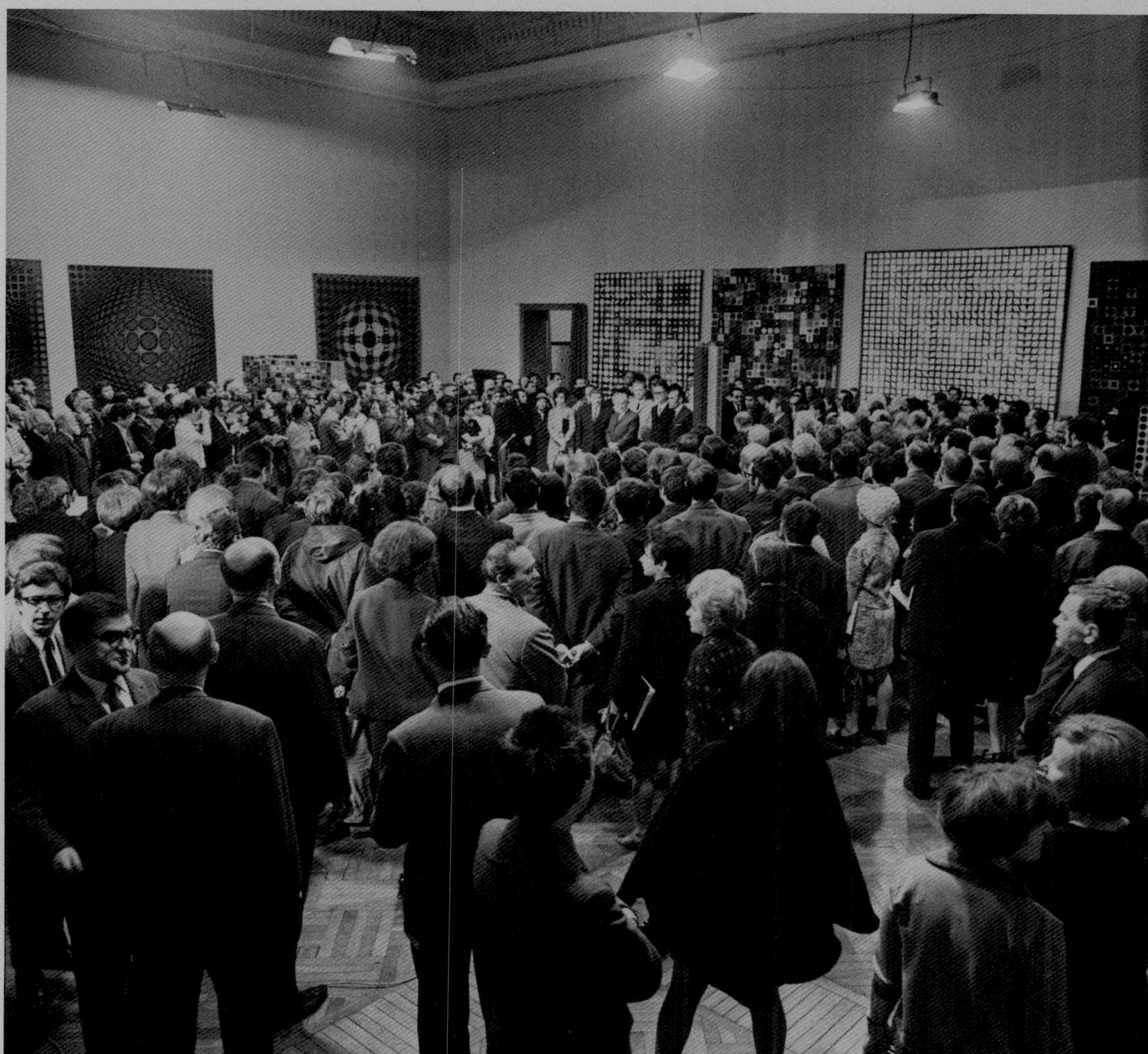

1. Jenő Barcsay, *Women*, 1964, mosaic, 300 × 720 cm, Miskolci Egyetem, Miskolc

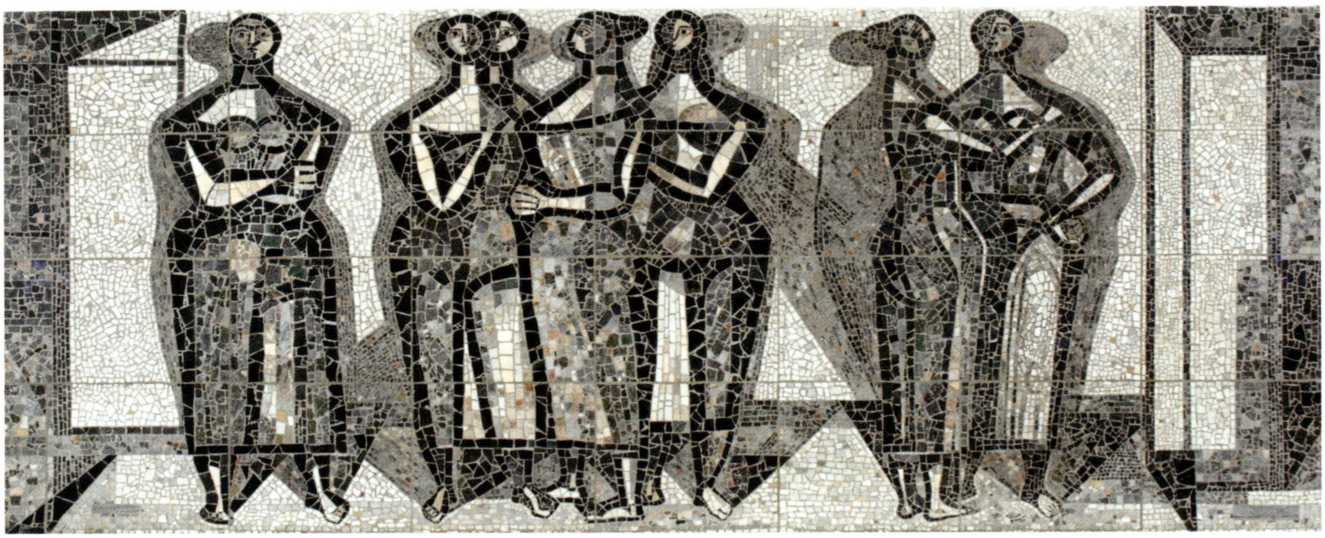

1

Sándor Hornyik

Reforming Socialist Realism

Encounters of Eastern Modernization and Western Modernism

In Hungary, like in other countries of the Eastern European region, the reforms of socialist realist orthodoxy, in the vein of Maxim Gorky and Andrei Zhdanov, began after Stalin's death (1953) and accelerated in earnest after the 20th Congress of the Soviet Communist Party (1956).[1] The reform process, which had cultural implications, was shaped in Hungary by the geopolitical strategies of the political thaw, and by the Kádár regime's need for legitimacy, following the quashing of the 1956 revolution against Soviet-imposed policies. The government wished to make a gesture to the West in terms of foreign policy, while internally it sought a compromise with the Hungarian artist community through personal political and aesthetic deals. So, a Khrushchevian politics of the thaw did not leave the arts untouched, and the Hungarian art community expressed a desire for modernization and an abandonment of socialist realist orthodoxy. Although these processes did not result in a radical break with Soviet artistic doctrine, formal experiments were officially deemed legitimate in 1958 as long as they remained within the reformed framework of socialist realism.[2]

After the reprisals following the 1956 revolution, the Party leadership in Hungary aimed at political consolidation through a 'deal' with society from the early 1960s onwards; János Kádár, General Secretary of the Magyar Szocialista Munkáspárt (MSZMP, Hungarian Socialist Workers' Party), put it most succinctly in his famous sentence: 'Whoever is not against us is with us.' What this meant for artists was a degree of creative freedom for those who did not criticize the regime openly, unless their view contradicted the tenets of the Party. In other words, the orthodox doctrine of socialist realism was no longer in force in this new political situation, but realism remained the expected form of expression. The works had to conform to the Party's art policies and the principles of socialist education,[3] that is, the propaganda that was used in service of social transformation. Aesthetic changes could not affect the principles and ideological character of socialist realism, so the socialist agenda and the canon of realism were still considered valid. What did change, however, was a relation to realism. The imperative of being 'up-to-date' had gained so much ground by the mid-1960s in the discourse and culture of socialist realism that it contributed to the deconstruction of realism.[4] The photographic realism expected in the early 1950s was continuously loosened, fragmented and abstracted by artists who used the various techniques and compositional methods of the historical avant-garde. The dissolution of realist painting through the integration of cubism, expressionism and magic realism was perhaps more spectacular, but expressionism and abstraction spread even to public sculpture, the most ideologically policed area of art in the 1960s. So, the reassessment of realism opened the way to a cautious modernization, which essentially meant an adaptation of Western aesthetic trends in Hungary.

Consequently, the late 1950s saw the rise of a peculiar mixture of Soviet-type modernization and the culture of Western modernism in art, which was promoted by the official aesthetic discourse of the 'contemporary' (*sovremennost* in Russian). This process entailed the reassessment of such oeuvres as Pablo Picasso's, who had been branded a 'formalist' during the Stalinist era despite his well-known commitment to the left. In the second half of the 1950s, however, he was celebrated as a critical realist and, indeed, the Hungarian government courted the world-famous artist in the 1960s.

The modernizing ambitions of a socialist aesthetic that recycled avant-garde formal innovations correspond to the capitalist strategy of recuperation, as defined by Guy Debord: that is, an appropriation and alternative use of the originally subversive avant-garde mentality and creativity for the sake of the capitalist aesthetic and political system.[5] Socialist cultural policy also used the cultural technique of recuperation later, in the late 1960s, as socialist realism was disintegrating and slowly fading. By this time, though, the objective was a socialist modernity that would remain loyal to the regime's socialist humanism, yet seek its forms in constructivism and modern natural and social science theories. This aesthetic and political process is discernible in the mid-1970s shift from the phraseology and ideology of socialist realism to the discourse of 'socialist visual culture', which aimed to utilize the results of semiotics, psychology, sociology and neo-constructivist art.

Before a Soviet-type communist cultural policy was made into law in 1949, there had been virtually no artistic and art historical tradition of socialist realism in Hungary and the Eastern bloc. The ideology of socialist realism was almost exclusively a result of direct adaptation of the Soviet model under political pressure: the newly nationalized institutional system of art initially had room for only strictly thematic and propagandistic works of art. Party ideologues in Hungary, however, tried to adapt the 'introduction' of socialist realism in its role as official art to the country's art traditions in order to gain some legitimacy for the 'foreign' style among artists and the non-communist majority of the population. Interestingly enough, the Hungarian model of socialist realism was, in fact, a late nineteenth-century academic painter in Munich, namely Mihály Munkácsy. This thoroughly bourgeois painter might have been chosen because his subjects often included marginalized, poor characters, whom he painted without any kind of critical edge, but rather in the style of '*Armeleutemalerei*' (genre painting representing poor people and circumstances) suited to a bourgeois and aristocratic taste for voyeurism. The Munkácsy tradition and Soviet socialist realism as ideals of realism both failed in the long run. Young followers of Munkácsy and imitators of the Soviet model lacked invention, even by the standards of Hungarian Marxist critics, and those respected artists of the period who cooperated with the communist establishment stood by the post-avant-garde bourgeois modernism of the interwar period.[6]

Representatives of official Hungarian art – neo-classicism generated from certain elements of the Renaissance and expressionism – between the two world wars had the professional skills and political flexibility to meet official socialist and realist expectations, so they could keep their professorial and teaching positions. Their artistic and political strategy was clearly working: Aurél Bernáth, for example, taught at the Magyar Képzőművészeti Főiskola (Hungarian Academy of Fine Arts) before Sovietization and kept his job after 1949, and his post-impressionist painting style, which was not adapted to the Soviet model, initially counted as 'formalist', but became accepted after 1953. The official criticism of Stalinist schematism and the revision of the criteria of 'formalism' brought a more accepting official cultural policy, which began to tolerate the bourgeois modernism of Bernáth, and even the critical realist (Neue Sachlichkeit) and expressionist formal cultures of the interwar period began to be integrated in the second half of the 1950s. The recuperation of expressionism, as defined by Debord, allowed the shift from the former academic painter Mihály Munkácsy to a new model for Hungarian socialist realism: Gyula Derkovits, an actual communist artist, who had created a decidedly anti-capitalist art, mocking the bourgeoisie and idealizing the proletariat, in the interwar period.

Derkovits represented the symbolic figures of the working class and the bourgeoisie with the most modern painterly devices of the 1920s by Hungarian standards; his reassessment and socialist realist recycling were in sync with the emergence of two distinct new artistic trends in the late 1950s in Hungary, which could not only compete with classic Western modernism, but also seemed compatible with the Soviet reform of the arts and could have a place within official cultural policy. One of the two was the new 'constructivism' of Jenő Barcsay and Gyula Hincz, rooted in the bourgeois modernism of the interwar period and influenced by École de Paris aesthetics.[7] The other was the 'magic realism' of the students of Aurél Bernáth mentioned above; this also explored the possibilities of a modern realism like the followers of Renato Guttuso, Diego Rivera and Aleksandr Dejneka in the German Democratic Republic and the Soviet Union. In a formal sense, it was mostly Picasso's and Braque's painting that Barcsay, Hincz and their numerous 'semi-abstract' followers were adapting to suit political expectations in the arts.[8] Bernáth disciples Tibor Csernus, László Lakner and Ákos Szabó, however, gained legitimacy in terms of cultural policy through the tradition of modern critical realism that ranged from the Mexican muralists to the German Neue Sachlichkeit and its key figures such as Käthe Kollwitz and Georg Grosz.[9] While Yugoslavia and Poland allowed neo-constructivist aesthetics to work unhindered as early as the mid-1950s, the abstract and post-cubist approach could initially only appear in Hungary indirectly, in the guise of refreshing and updating socialist realist figurativeness. Contrary to the path of constructivism, Csernus and his followers almost instantly faced severe orthodox criticism concerning their surreal decadence, which would drive all of them abroad and out of Hungarian culture in the 1960s.

It was in the writings of Lajos Németh,[10] an art historian committed to aesthetic and political reforms, that the catchwords of aesthetic modernization appeared most visibly in Hungary: cherishing national traditions, a combination of monumentality and expressiveness, and a new realism, which aims at a contemporary reflection in accord with a worldview based on modern natural science.[11] These trends evolved in parallel with reforms in Moscow, where there was support for impressionistic folk realism and the pronouncement of a 'contemporary style', which amounted to a rehabilitation of the expressionism of Dejneka and the cubism of the Russian Bubnovy Valet (Jack of Diamonds) group, and the Soviet integration of the aesthetics of Picasso, Guttuso and Diego Rivera, who were held up as positive examples in official East German and Hungarian art journals as well.[12]

The political limits of this aesthetic modernization were determined by the principle of coexistence, which shifted the cold-war fight to the arenas of culture and technology in the mid-1950s. As the discourses of opening up to the West and innovation came to the fore, the possibilities of an international critical realism began to take shape from Mexico, through Rome, Paris and Berlin, to the Soviet Union.[13] The united aesthetic front, which entailed the reclaiming and recycling of various avant-garde traditions, led to the deconstruction of the visual culture of classic socialist realism, which revealed itself most obviously in the prominent French communist philosopher Roger Garaudy's concept of 'realism without shores' in the mid-1960s.[14] The concept originated from the French cultural sphere and the history of ideas prevalent in that milieu, and the fact that it was vigorously critiqued in Moscow and Budapest illustrates how reform and modernization were accompanied by debates, which were in turn significantly affected by geopolitical events (such as the Berlin Wall, Cuban Missile Crisis and Vietnam War). The conservative, partisan, anti-capitalist position of cultural policy opposing aesthetic reforms still saw signs of decadence in avant-garde 'formalism', which could only be transformed into critical realism via the brutality of the represented subject or the artist's committed socialist humanism, as shown in the works of Hans Grundig and Renato Guttuso.

Yet, it was the allegedly decadent formalist and existentialist works of Bernáth's innovative students – the magic realist painters Csernus, Lakner and Szabó – that were censored and removed from national exhibitions by the strict 'guardians' of orthodox socialist realism, namely the conservative wing of the cultural policy establishment, in the first third of the 1960s (as a Hungarian version of the Manezh Affair).[15] By contrast, one of the lesser known followers, György Korga, who was their contemporary but studied with Gyula Hincz, slipped through the jury's selection process – which was effectively a tool of censorship – and his individual show received illuminating reviews. It was in reference to this exhibition in 1964 that the revealingly pejorative term of 'surnaturalism' – coined from decadent surrealism and bombastic naturalism – was born in order to denigrate the style of Csernus and his followers. In fact, the pictures exhibited by Korga reflected the latest topics of socialist humanism, being inspired by the cold war and depicting apocalyptic nuclear disasters, which made them a huge success with the general public, thanks to their current relevance and virtuoso execution. The works were suffused with the kind of anti-capitalism and humanism that was characteristic of the newly fashionable surrealist and committed socialist poetry, which represented the existential anxiety of the nuclear age through the traditional themes of folk culture. Yet one of the leading conservative critics of the period found the pathos of Korga's works too disingenuous and bombastic when compared to the tragic expressivity of Hans and Lea Grundig, the communist painters of the German Democratic Republic.[16] She deplored the absence of a socialist and humanist ethos that goes beyond merely revelling in virtuoso representations of naturalist details (like Korga's model, Csernus, does) and encourages the anti-capitalist peace struggle and the building of socialism.

The rhetoric of aesthetic reform that supported 'formal experimentation' (a favoured official catchword at the time) was intensifying in the second half of the 1960s, a process not unrelated to improving relations with the West, the success of Hungarian economic reforms and the rise of the standard of living. Doublespeak and a dual orientation (socialist topics coupled with up-to-date, i.e. Western, forms; see Péter György's essay 'Under Eastern Eyes', pp. 21–37) did not transform socialist visual culture through young artists exploring new paths of realism. Instead, the older masters, who had a major say in education and the distribution of state commissions, smuggled their own earlier interwar bourgeois modernist style and culture into the representation of socialism, which the cultural leadership of the Party was only too happy to accept. Even Barcsay's and Hincz's formally more innovative post-cubism became accepted by the early 1960s in the wake of the recuperation of Domanovszky's post-expressionist and Bernáth's post-impressionist formal culture (which almost imperceptibly relaxed the photographic objectivity and accessible didacticism of orthodox socialist realism), the reception of Picasso, and the increasingly powerful socialist imperative of modernity. In fact, their fundamentally figurative 'constructivism', which integrated a degree of abstraction and reflected certain compromises, became one of the key models of a socialist realism in transition and of a process of modernization. With its natural science allusions, monumentality and optimistic, positive tone, the allegedly constructivist formal repertoire of Barcsay and Hincz's work was actually a better fit for

2

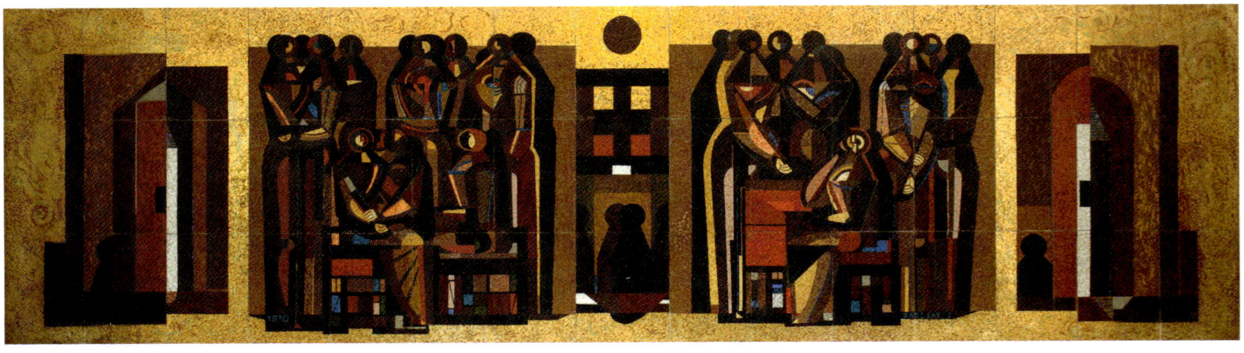

the new spirit of socialist humanism in the 1960s–70s than an overly abstract and ghostly surnaturalism was.

A one-time member of the Európai Iskola (European School), an artist group trying to bring the spirit of the École de Paris to Budapest (1945–48; see Gábor Dobó and Merse Pál Szeredi, 'Hungarian Culture +/- Europe', pp. 39–57), Jenő Barcsay emerged as one of the figures chosen for Hungarian state representation in the early 1960s. He had extensive material on display at the Hungarian Pavilion of the 1964 Venice Biennale, and a large mosaic (*Women*, 1964, fig. 1) was commissioned for the lobby of the Miskolci Nehézipari Műszaki Egyetem (Technical University of Miskolc). Barcsay delivered this public commission by developing sketches he had made in the late 1940s without substantially altering their cubist aesthetic. The mosaic was a success, as shown by subsequent commissions, in which the forms of geometric abstraction increasingly predominated, something that no longer contradicted socialist humanist ideology thanks to the recycling of constructivism. By the early 1970s, Barcsay could, in fact, begin to drop the figurative forms, which arguably functioned as realist compromises in his earlier works. The reason he could do this was that socialist realism had given way to socialist modernism, which no longer rejected abstract forms. Barcsay even got his own museum, founded in Szentendre in 1978. His largest mosaic can be found here, in the library of the 'city of art'; its women can be interpreted both as heroic representatives of communist workers and as late, 'constructivist' descendants of classic muses (fig. 2).

Gyula Hincz, Barcsay's contemporary and fellow artist, also built a significant career on harmonizing Western aesthetics and Eastern politics – significant enough to propel him to the presidency of the Magyar Iparművészeti Főiskola (Hungarian Academy of Applied Arts). Unlike Barcsay, however, Hincz did not employ a single style for his entire oeuvre; he switched from one to the next in response to the political and intellectual expectations of each successive period from neo-classicism through post-expressionism to a Picasso-inspired post-cubism, which he could also successfully adapt to the discourse of socialist realism during the process of aesthetic modernization. A characteristic example of this move is the enormous tapestry in the Debreceni Egyetem (University of Debrecen), placed in one of the largest public spaces of the university and representing the cosmic beauty of education as a modern socialist spectacle.[17] *Science* (1967, fig. 3), representing the allegorical triumph of science in a public space, expresses itself in a monumental realist style like Barcsay's, but it has closer intellectual affinities with biomorphic modernism and its organic associations than with the technophilia of constructivism.[18]

2. Jenő Barcsay, *Szentendre Mosaic*, 1970, mosaic, 300 × 1100 cm, Pest Megyei Művelődési Központ és Könyvtár, Szentendre

3. Gyula Hincz, *Science*, 1967, tapestry, 210 × 756 cm, Debreceni Egyetem, Debrecen

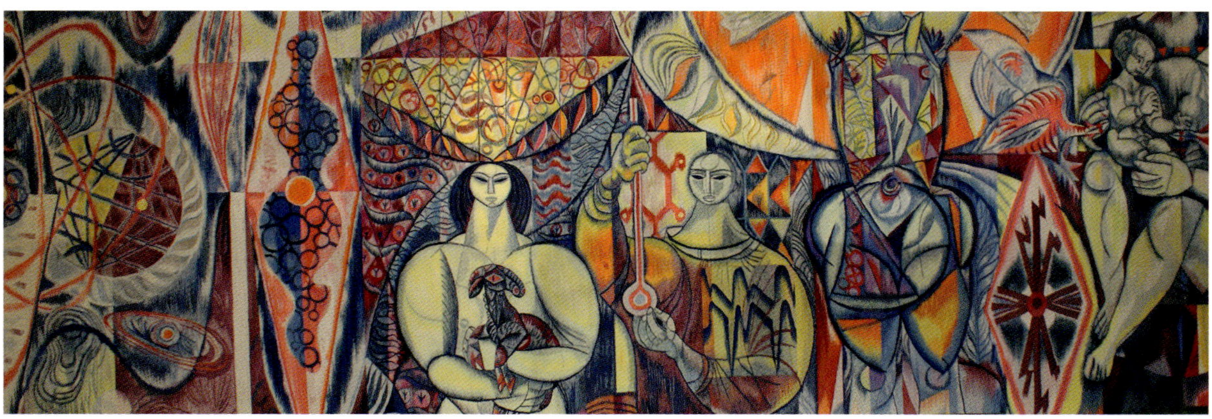

3

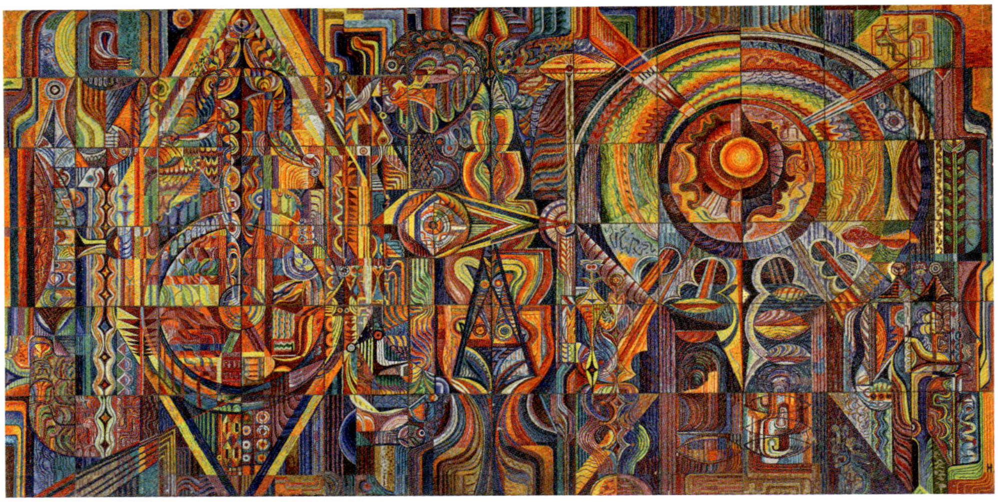

4

How systematically the official aesthetic credo was modernized is demonstrated well by the parallel developments found in Barcsay's and Hincz's work in the late 1960s: Hincz also shifts to abstract compositions in public space, such as the enormous, completely nonfigurative mosaic in the lobby of Budapesti Kertészeti Egyetem (Budapest Horticultural University), which brings the scientific technological optimism of smaller abstract geometric graphic works on cosmic themes (a combination of atomic and astronomical structures) to a monumental scale (fig. 4).

The growing dominance of 'constructivist' aesthetic ideology was also instrumental in Béla Kondor's characteristically socialist career in the 1960s, thanks to the support offered by reformist critics. Besides his fundamentally traditional, realist approach to art, Kondor's career was also substantially boosted by his working-class origins and the fact that he was a young artist acculturated within the state socialist regime, and consequently had no ties to the supposedly reactionary bourgeois culture.[19] Critics compared Barcsay's young student to Picasso at the beginning of his career, as early as the second half of the 1950s, and lauded the optimism and sacralizing heroism of his *Human Couple* (1959, fig. 5) as a possible course of renewing the socialist realist representation of the worker. *Angel of Revolution* (1959), a similarly formed figure in his first solo show in 1960, still evoked dangerous political connotations, since its title conjured up the 1956 revolution (which was officially labelled a counterrevolution). As a result, the work was removed from the exhibition held at Fényes Adolf Terem (Adolf Fényes Showroom). This made the young artist, who was already famous for not mincing his words, quite popular with many of the intellectuals averse to the ideology of the party-state.[20] The most spectacular specimen of Kondor's nearly cynical pragmatism could not be displayed at the exhibition either: *Launch of the Artificial Grasshopper* (1958, fig. 6) was an ironic reflection on the success of the first Sputnik satellite with a grotesque representation of the Soviet officer who was its mysterious designer (Sergei Korolev).

Even Kondor's ideologically impeccable figures provoked conservative criticism's charges of surrealism due to their proportions and unrealistic motifs (angel wings and nonfunctional mechanical and architectural constructions). So, Kondor's art was accompanied by constant debates, in which reformist critics tried to justify the socialist commitment of his works through analogies with Picasso, Guttuso and Bernard Buffet. Even so, the state authorities were hard pressed to gloss over specific references like the 1956 revolution or Sputnik, since their support of art was conditional on their political and aesthetic legitimacy being unquestioned. By evoking politically sensitive topics, Kondor violated this tacit aesthetic and political deal, but he changed his strategy after the years of 'silencing' that followed his exhibition in 1960 (he had no opportunity for another solo show from 1960 to 1963): his irony and cynicism became subtler and more abstract. His painting *Wasp King* (1963), for example, was paradigmatic in banishing the figure of the constructor into a mythic world, an abstract fairy-tale space with medieval associations, thereby depoliticizing the figure holding a wasp-like helicopter in his hand. In the same spirit of compromise, Kondor did not reject even quite schematic themes (building socialism) as long as he could integrate them into his own painting, which reinterpreted classic culture and mythology from the vantage point of modern technology and the imperative of modernization. At the same time, his work was celebrated by reformist criticism, which was increasingly attuned to modern and innovative voices, as a modern socialist reinterpretation of Renaissance, humanist and 'realist' culture (in the sense of Albrecht Dürer, Martin Schongauer and Matthias Grünewald) from the mid-1960s.

One can detect a similar logic of recuperation and 'partisan' reinterpretation being applied to Tibor Csernus's oeuvre. His first surnaturalist work – *Saint-Tropez* (1959, fig. 7), subtly combining anti-capitalist critique, impressionist pictorial culture and surrealist technique (grattage and décalcomania) – was a great success, but then he developed an increasingly strong interest in the kind of experimentation for its own sake that was denounced in Hungarian criticism for its 'formalist decadence' and 'anti-humanist existentialism'. Like Kondor, Csernus was 'banned' from solo shows at the

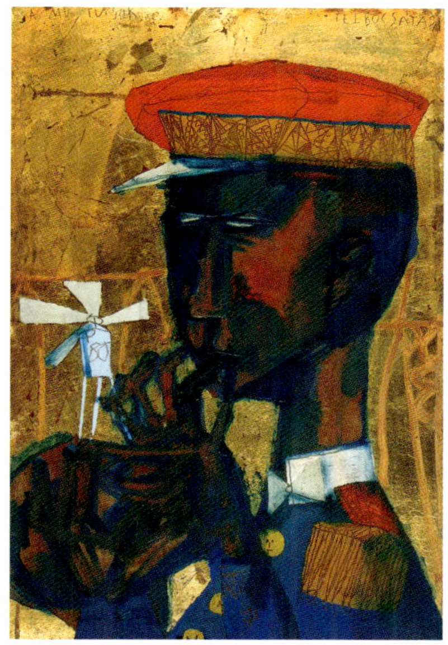

6

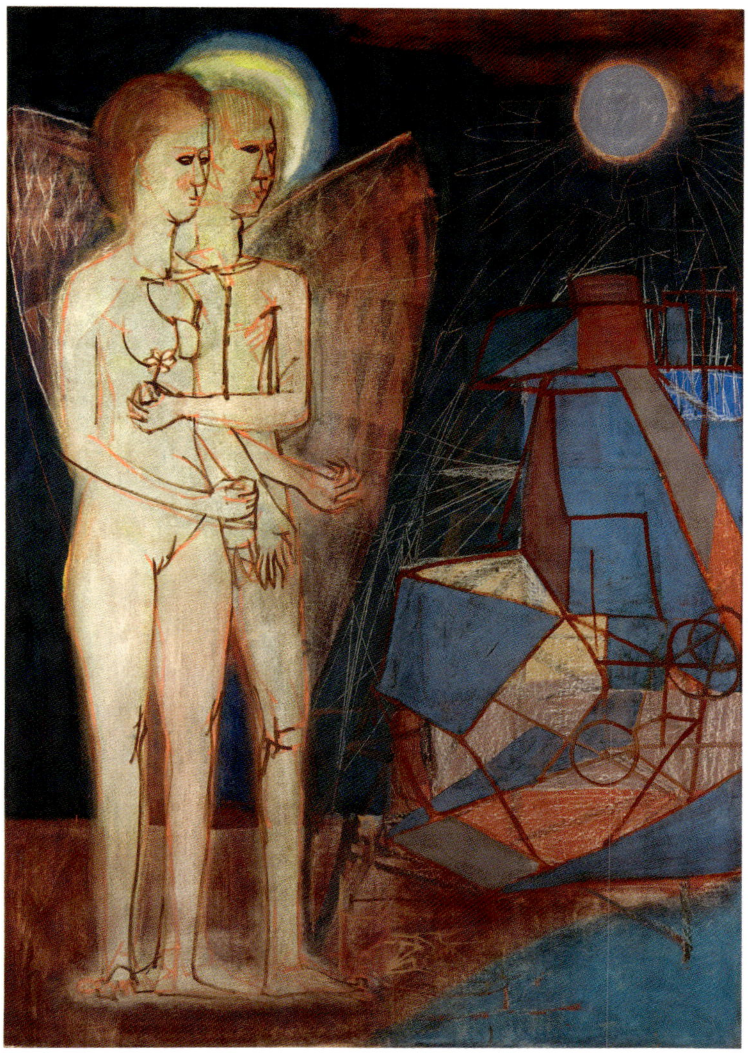

5

4. Gyula Hincz, *Cosmos*, 1970, mosaic, 400 × 1000 cm, Szent István Egyetem, Budapest

5. Béla Kondor, *Human Couple*, 1959, oil on canvas, 197 × 137.5 cm, Szépművészeti Múzeum – Magyar Nemzeti Galéria, Budapest

6. Béla Kondor, *Launch of the Artificial Grasshopper*, 1958, oil and gold on plywood, 46 × 30 cm, location unknown

same time. By the logic of doublespeak and dual orientation, however, his exhibition at the Galerie Lambert in Paris was approved by cultural authorities in 1963 after some debate, since his surnaturalist works could do no further damage to the aesthetics of an evolving Hungarian socialist culture.[21] *Lehel Square Market* (1962, fig. 8), in which genre painting is almost completely deconstructed by decalcomania, is quite likely to have been passed over in the jury selection for the Hungarian national exhibition for similar reasons: namely, the 'grand' realism of an accessible socialist spectacle was swept away by the microrealism of pictoriality and the manipulations of the surface. In *Model Makers* (1963, fig. 9), however, reformist criticism could foreground the 'positive' socialist theme, which could be tied to peaceful cold-war rivalry.[22] The space race was one of the key fronts of this rivalry, and the Soviet Union was still leading even in the early 1960s, so an airplane-modelling course could popularize the primacy of the socialist ethos and socialist technology.

Csernus, who had been staying in Paris since his 1964 exhibition in that city, could even exhibit *Reeds* (1964, fig. 10) in Hungary in 1965, although it could be interpreted as a profound, if somewhat allegorical, critique of socialist

7

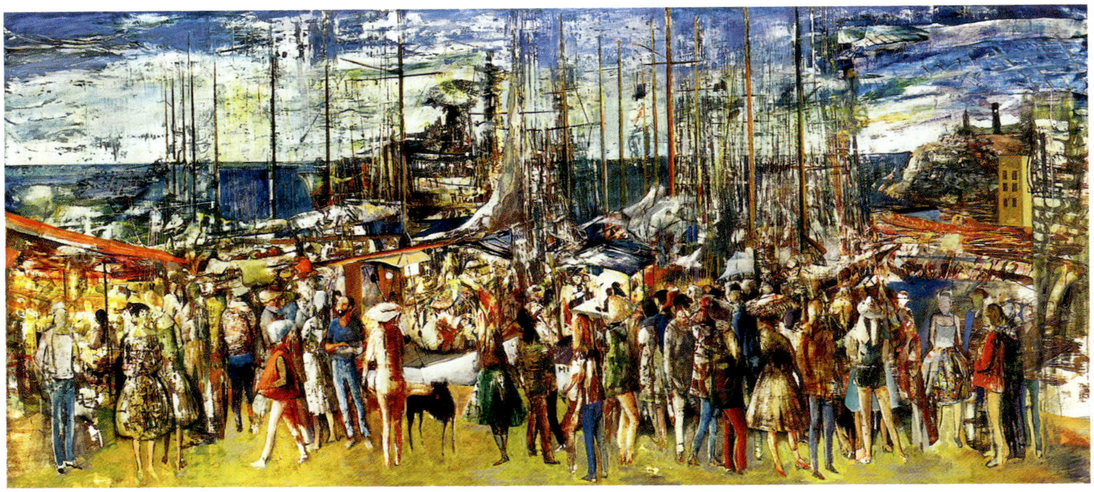

8

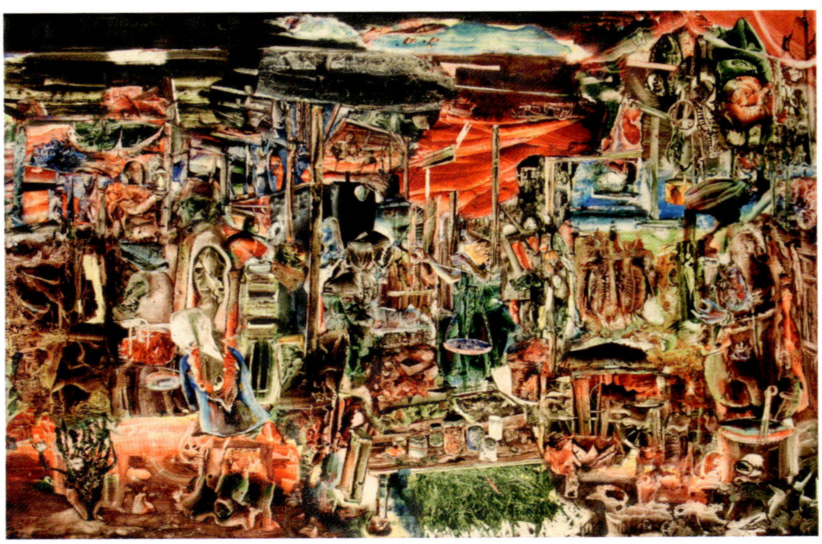

realism. A bathing platform rises from a swampy Lake Balaton landscape suffocating in trash; it evokes classical reminiscences of the Parnassus and the pantheon of Grand Art. Csernus's interpretation is no apotheosis of socialist culture and socialist art; the figures sunbathing on the platform seem to be in different stages of decomposition. This kind of critical reading of socialist realism, the representation of an impoverished reality instead of ideas, was characteristic of his socialist genre paintings too, which were rejected by the juries of exhibitions; instead of representing factories, they show markets and waste collection plants, and the critics found the negative energies of decay, destruction and chaos too strong in them. Therefore, the official exhibition of *Reeds* may symbolically demonstrate that the demand for modernity and innovation – that is, the imperative of the modern socialist realism of Guttuso, Garaudy, Dmitrieva and Németh – was strong enough in the mid-1960s to override the earlier Zhdanovian and Stalinist paradigms of optimism and accessibility.

Public sculpture, which was not only costlier than painting but appeared before a larger public and was therefore strictly censored, took longer to respond to these changes. The Stalin statue toppled during the 1956 revolution

9

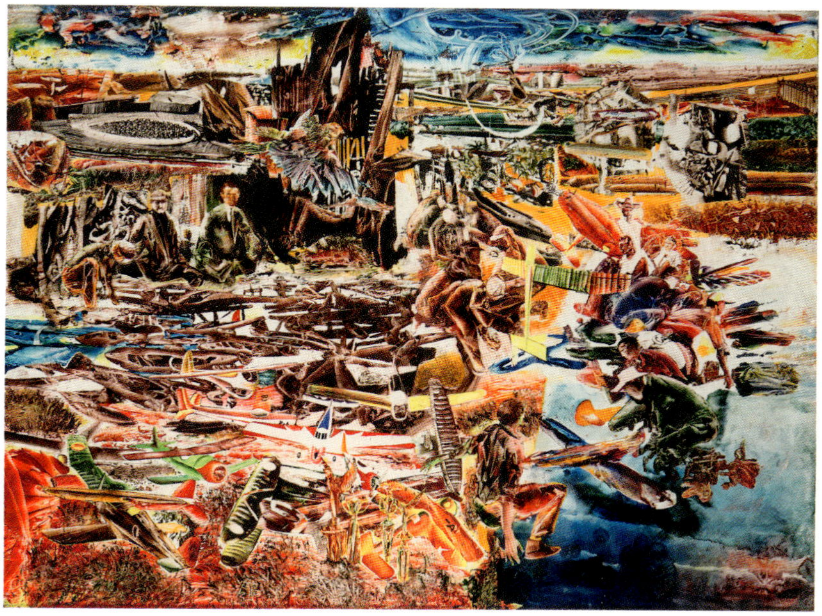

10

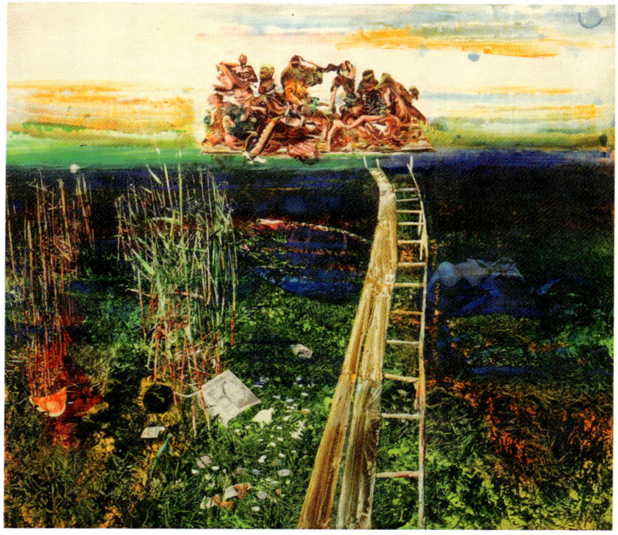

7. Tibor Csernus, *Saint-Tropez*, 1959, oil on canvas, 115 × 250 cm, Private collection

8. Tibor Csernus, *Lehel Square Market*, 1962, oil on canvas, 137 × 188.5 cm, Szépművészeti Múzeum – Magyar Nemzeti Galéria, Budapest

9. Tibor Csernus, *Model Makers*, 1963, oil on canvas, 140 × 182 cm, Szépművészeti Múzeum – Magyar Nemzeti Galéria, Budapest

10. Tibor Csernus, *Reeds*, 1964, oil on canvas, 134 × 152 cm, Kiscelli Múzeum – Fővárosi Képtár, Budapest

symbolically represented thematic, classicist art, and once that was discredited, a new Hungarian public sculpture reflecting the spirit of socialism had to be invented. It was mainly Agamemnon Makrisz's, Jenő Kerényi's and József Somogyi's realism infused with expressionist and impressionist formal elements that represented this new direction. The secret of cautious stylistic modernization must have been that it was affirmed both from the East and the West. It met the requirements of the 'contemporary style' as defined by Dmitrieva, but its modernity also received Western accolades that could be exploited within the discourse in Hungary, as in the case of Kerényi and Somogyi's *Dance* (1958, fig. 11) being awarded the Grande Prize at the Brussels World's Fair. The press commentary on the sculpture was namely that even the West acknowledges the achievements of new Hungarian socialist art.

More innovative works, like Tamás Vígh's *Memorial of the Regulation of the River Tisza* (1967, fig. 12), with its depiction of legendary nineteenth-century engineer Pál Vásárhelyi and pick-and-shovel men, could not be presented in public, despite the fact that they conformed thematically to the expectations of the regime. Vígh's theme was current: rebuilding and modernization. In his memorial, he even found an accessible way to convey the dialectical conflict between modern engineers and the peasantry guarding its traditions.[23] Yet, reviewers found the sculptor's artistic choices for the engineer's figure too abstract and expressionist, and he allegedly dressed the peasants in a cubist sheepskin cape (*suba*) bordering on abstraction, so the public display of the work was denied.

József Somogyi faced similar problems when one of his most famous sculptures was unveiled in Hódmezővásárhely. Locals began a furious dispute in response to his statue of the late nineteenth-century agricultural socialist peasant leader János Szántó Kovács in 1965 (fig. 13). Instead of a realist portrait of a renowned historical figure of the town, they got an idealized stature symbolizing agrarian peasantry. Somogyi no longer wanted to conform to the earlier orthodox and populist socialist realist canon that adjusted art to the average person's needs.[24] It is a testimony to his modernization strategy

11

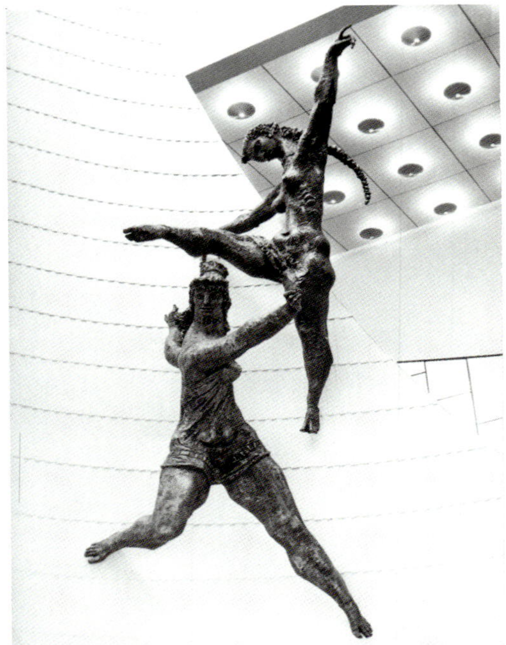

12

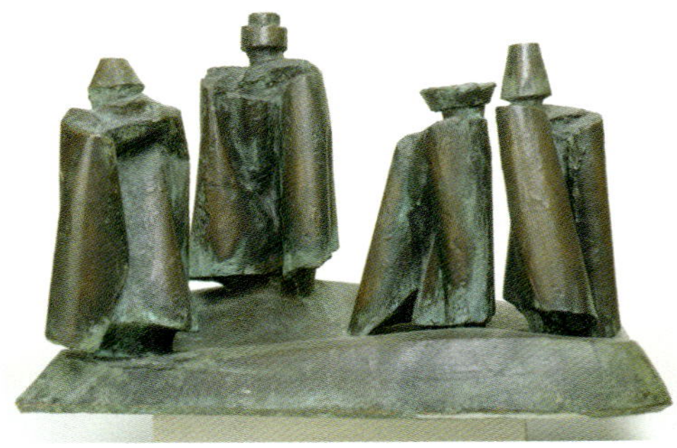

11. Jenő Kerényi – József Somogyi, *Dance*, Brussels, Hungarian Pavilion of the World's Fair, 1958, aluminium (today in Namur, Belgium)

12. Tamás Vigh, *People of the Great Plain* (detail of the *Memorial of the Regulation of the River Tisza*), 1967, bronze, 53 × 67 × 44 cm, Szépművészeti Múzeum – Magyar Nemzeti Galéria, Budapes

13. József Somogyi, *János Szántó Kovács*, 1965, bronze, h. 290 cm, Hódmezővásárhely

14. Tibor Vilt, *Singing Children*, 1960, limestone, 700 × 700 cm, Eszterházy Károly Egyetem Gyakorló Általános, Közép-, Alapfokú Művészeti Iskola és Pedagógiai Intézet, Eger

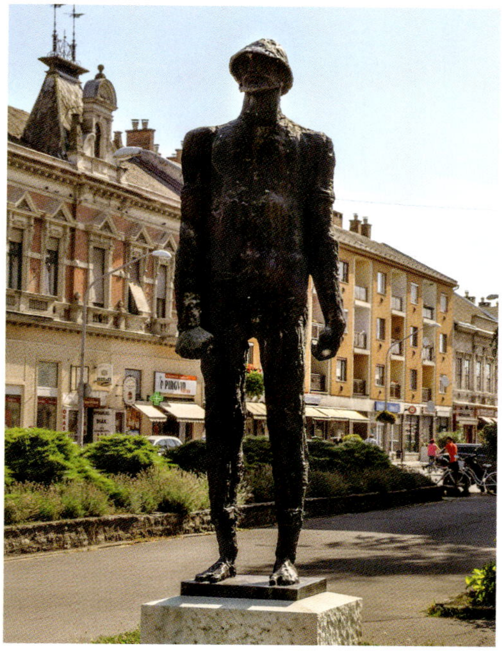

13

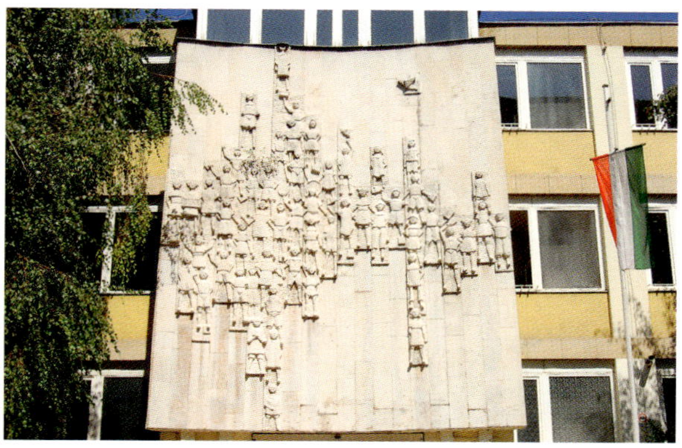

14

that the cultural policy establishment would also admit later that Somogyi had developed a formal language that was more than a simple offshoot of Western styles; it was characteristically Hungarian, simultaneously national and socialist, and was capable of rivalling modern Western realist sculpture in aesthetic terms. Indeed, it was as a result of his new style developed in the mid-1960s that Somogyi would become one of the regime's busiest creators of public sculpture and later the rector of Magyar Képzőművészeti Főiskola.

Tibor Vilt, one of the best-known sculptors of the period, had grown up on the bourgeois modernism of the interwar era and the surrealism of the Európai Iskola just like Hincz and Barcsay. It is quite symbolic that he could 'experiment' with abstraction primarily on small sculptures, whereas his public sculptures reflect a conservative taste, now classicist, now rather realist in character: *Soviet Heroic Monument* (1965) in Pesterzsébet, for example, was made to meet the orthodox requirements of socialist realism. Interestingly, more artistically daring and independent compositions could be realized in less busy or even hidden public places, which clearly shows the logic of dual thinking. Vilt's relief *Singing Children* (1960, fig. 14) – situated on the wall of a primary school in Eger, in the countryside – seems a bold, abstract composition from a distance; up close, however, the rows of children's heads reveal a plastic work that fulfils all criteria of realism and symbolizes the community spirit and educational power of socialism. This visual language, based on compromise, and this allusive and associative type of expression were prevalent in the 1960–70s. Another key modernist figure in the sculpture of the era was Erzsébet Schaár, whose *Scientists* (1968–70, fig. 15) was placed in Tihany, far from Budapest. The faces and hands of the figures were formed realistically, while the blocks of their bodies evoke the visual culture of geometric abstraction, which may also be motivated thematically as a reflection of the rationalism of science and its power of abstraction.

Doublethink also features prominently in the reformist criticism of the era, which would carefully position the works thematically within Soviet ideology, while comparing Hungarian artists to the outstanding figures of Western

15

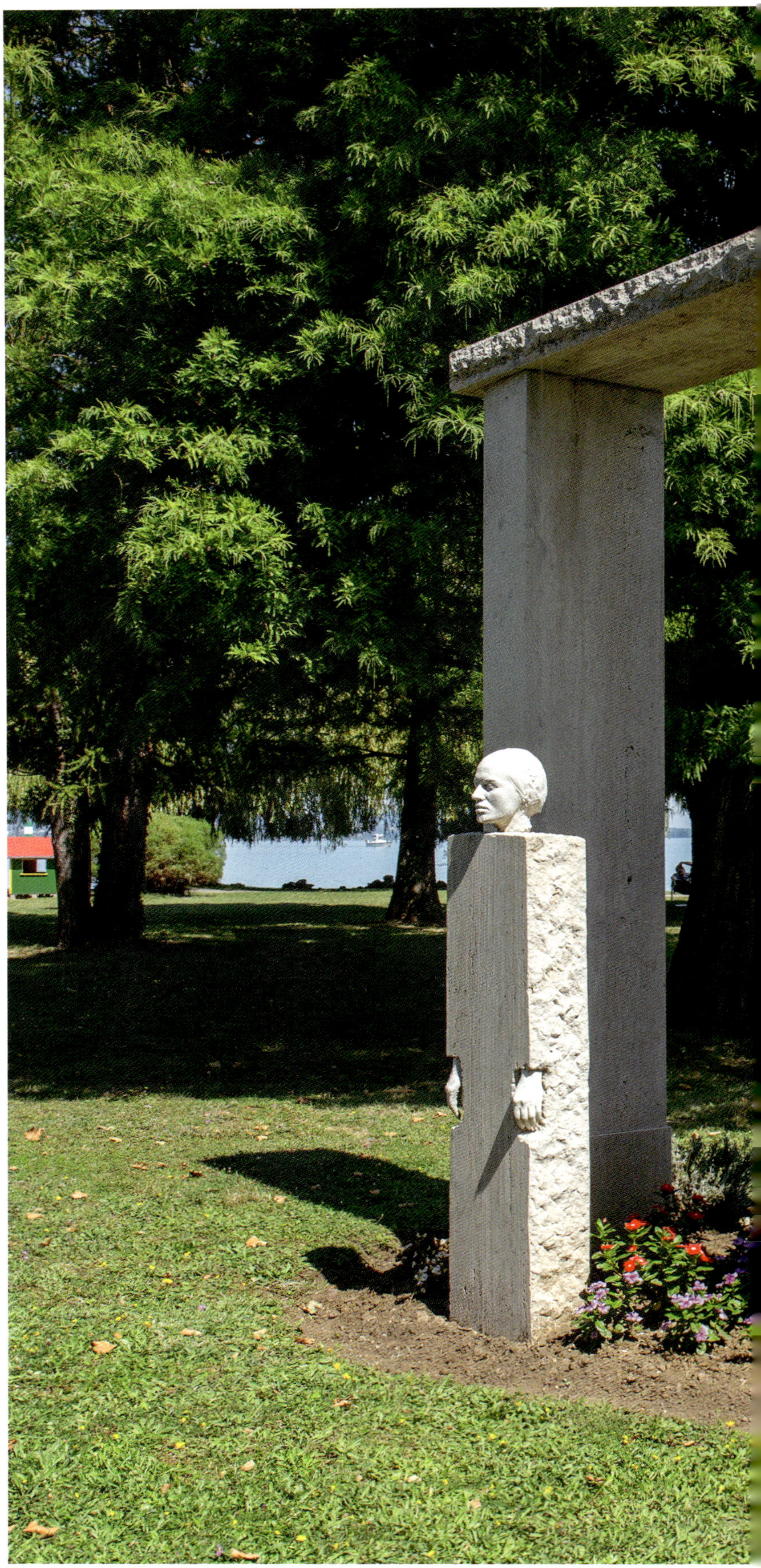

15. Erzsébet Schaár, *Scientists*, 1968–70, limestone, h. 300 cm, MTA – Balatoni Limnológiai Intézet (MTA – Balaton Limnological Institute), Tihany

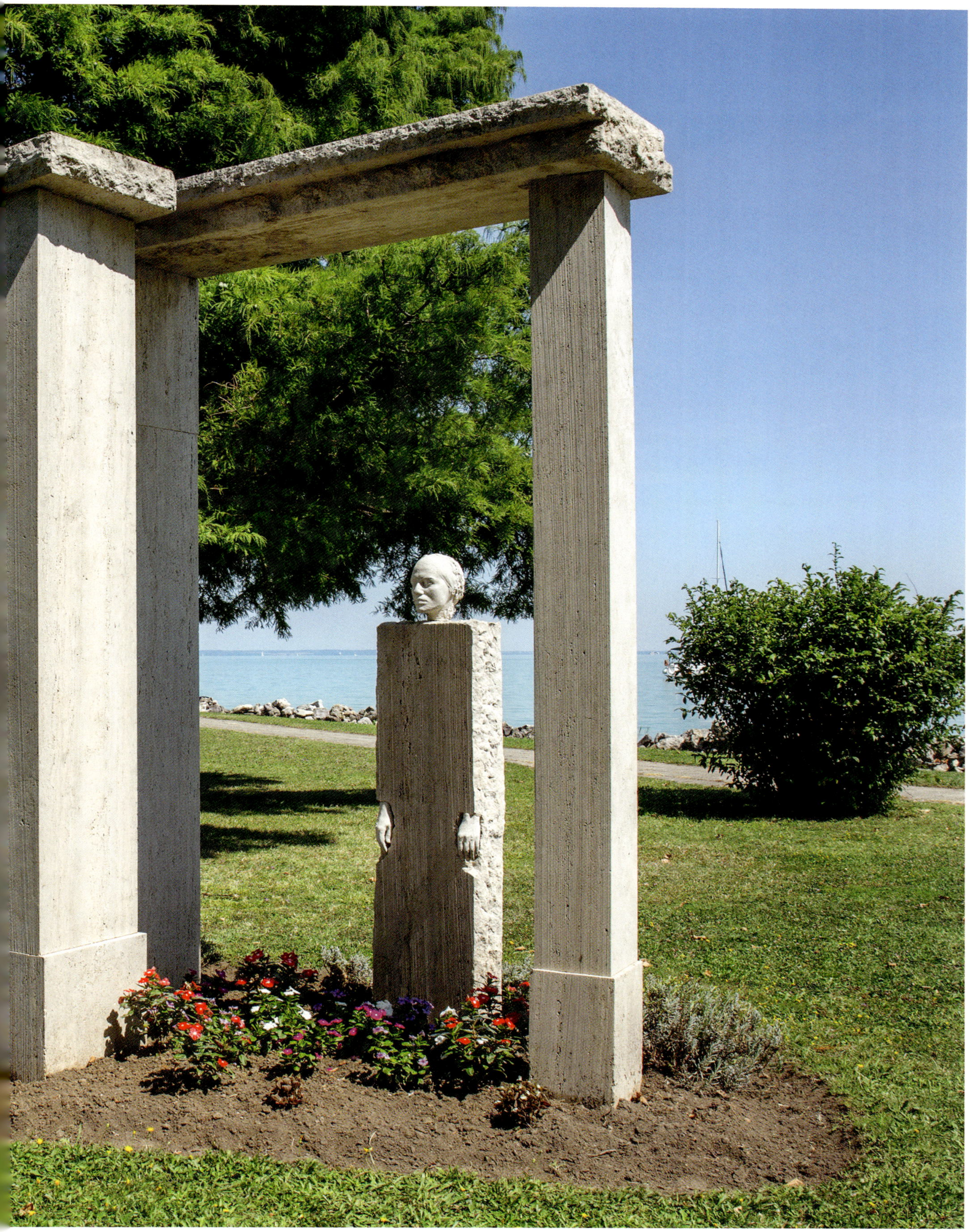

modernism. Somogyi was connected to the French sculptor Germaine Richier, the other two modern realists – Vilt and Schaár – were linked to Alberto Giacometti and Marisol Escobar, and Tamás Vígh was often discussed in relation to Henry Moore. All of these Western sculptors were acceptable in socialist and anti-capitalist terms, yet they were also modern and European role models. So, a European horizon and aesthetic internationalism were important for reformist criticism, while the conservative factions of cultural policy held up the Soviet model, accessibility, and the culture of the proletariat above all. Aurél Bernáth's mural painting was a good match with this conservative taste that was also fairly typical of the Party elite: a perfect example is one of the later imposing commissions, *Workers' State* (1968–72, fig. 16), an apotheosis of communism that was the jewel of the Budapest Party headquarters. For unlike Csernus's *Reeds*, this painting is not a grotesque tableau, but rather a seemingly harmonious way of positioning the Party and its leadership within the aesthetic framework of a post-impressionist modernization of the Renaissance. In other words, in the year 1968, Bernáth created the apotheosis of the rise and reign of the working class according to socialist realist orthodoxy, which is an exemplary realization of socialist spectacle, in Debord's and Dobrenko's sense, since it is centred on learning and education. As a respected professor of the Magyar Képzőművészeti Főiskola and an influential artist, Bernáth could even afford to paint executed prime minister Imre Nagy, a symbolic figure of the 1956 revolution otherwise shrouded in silence, who appeared among famous writers and politicians in this spectacle akin to a waxworks display. Of course, the Party secretary János Kádár appears in the mural as well, playing chess, while chief cultural ideologue and policymaker György Aczél looks over his shoulder. Bernáth put the two men, the most important and influential figures of the regime, in the same position as donors in Renaissance mural painting, a choice that may be interpreted either as a gesture of loyalty or subtle irony.

Yet, it is no longer just aesthetic modernization that is reflected in the toleration of Hincz's and Schaár's abstraction in public

16

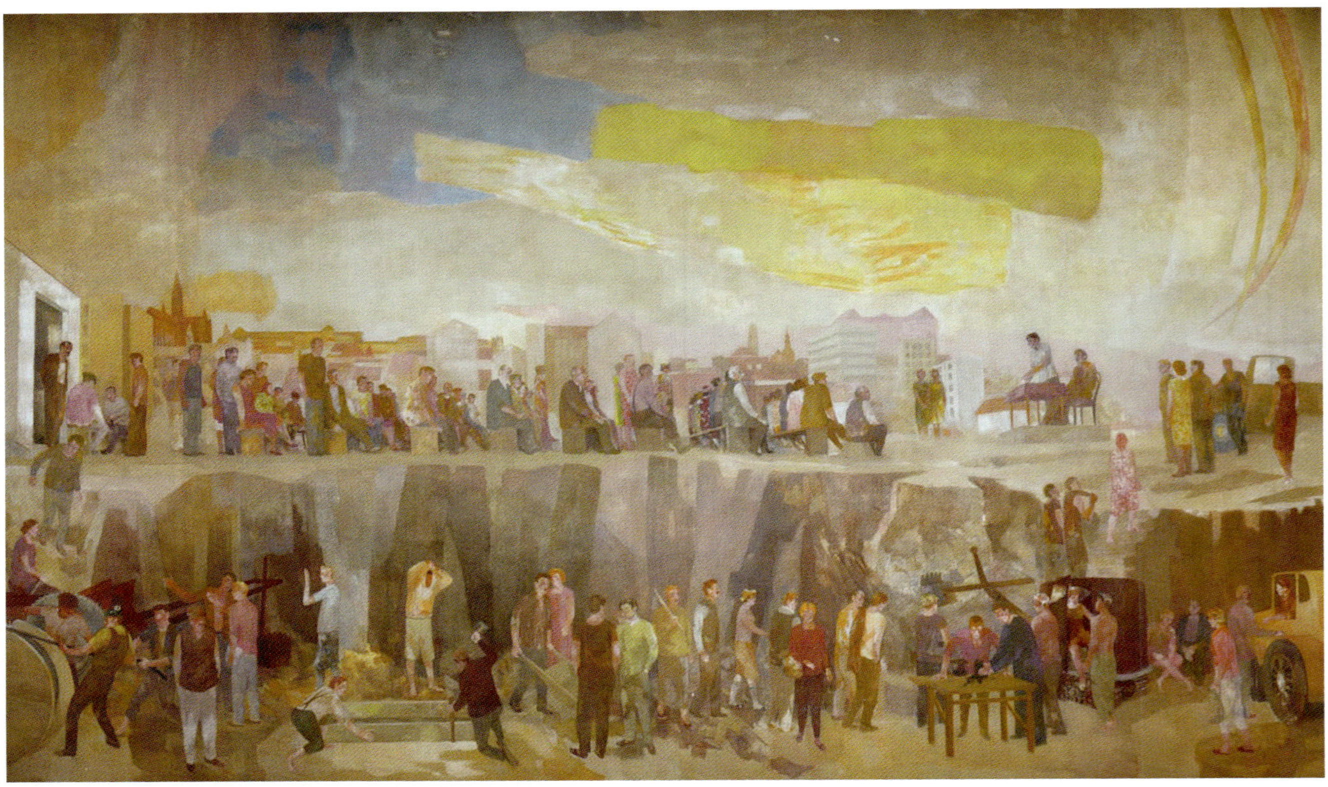

spaces and the anecdotal intimacy of Bernáth's monumentality, but also an increasingly clear shift in political function. Namely, the ideological questions of visual art basically disappeared from the agenda in the late 1960s, as the mass media (especially television) and science became the most important media for agitprop and socialist education. The modern-sounding term 'visual culture' became the new catchword, so the narrative fresco and the symbolic monument, and socialist realism altogether, slowly slid into obsolescence even in official aesthetic and political circles. At the same time, the fact that cultural policy had been able to maintain the discursive hegemony of socialist realism for a decade and a half could be claimed as its undisputed success. As for artists, since the late 1950s they had not seen the term socialist realism as more than a type of 'floating signifier', a term that could refer to anything thematically socialist as long as it did not break with the tradition of figurative representation.[25] Doublethink and dual orientation were realized in the case of artists through conforming to ideological expectations, while attempting to represent aesthetically their innovative, though mostly realist, culture of painting. Béla Kondor, for instance, followed in Barcsay's footsteps in his efforts to fuse Picasso's and Dürer's art, and Csernus, as a disciple of Bernáth, tried to find a common ground for the works of Édouard Manet and Max Ernst. Like Csernus, László Lakner was first fascinated by Max Ernst's surrealism, before his interest shifted to American versions of realism, Charles Sheeler's precisionism and Ivan Albright's magic realism. László Gyémánt, who was Lakner's friend and another gifted follower of Csernus fashionable at the time, was enthralled by Salvador Dalí's and Ernst Fuchs's fantastic realism. An excellent exemplar of this alternative canon, which overlaps – however ironically – with Soviet-type socialist realism, is Gyula Konkoly's painting *The Academy of Fine Arts Visited by the Muse* (1964, fig. 17), where the 'blotted' muse (made with the technique of decalcomania) and the socialist realist painter meet in an atelier that counts as a (counter)cultural cabinet of curiosities, evoking works by Manet, Zola, Velázquez, Rodin and de Chirico.

17

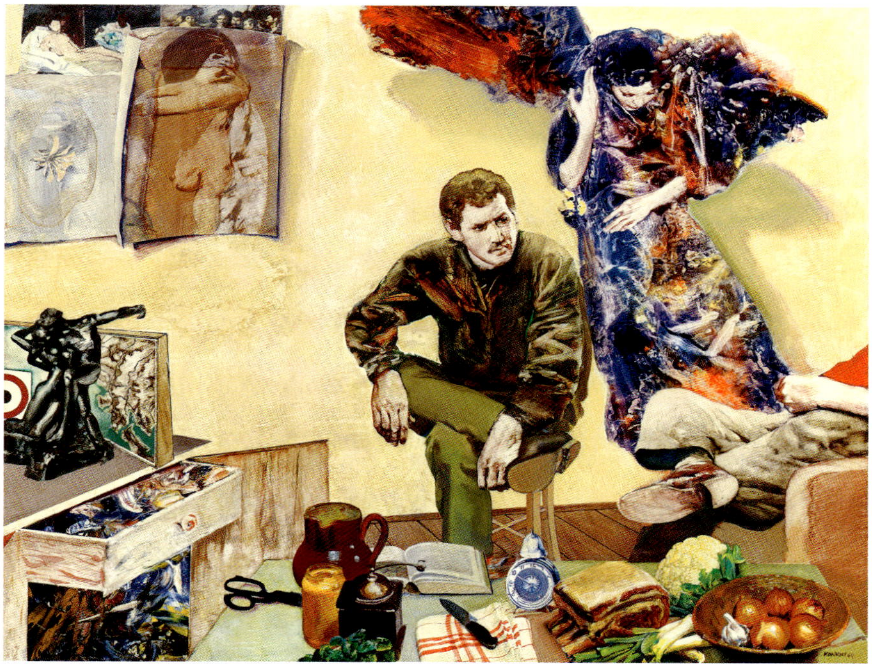

16. Aurél Bernáth, *Workers' State*, 1968–72, secco, 800 × 1200 cm, Országgyülés Irodaháza (Office of the National Assembly), Budapest

17. Gyula Konkoly, *The Academy of Fine Arts Visited by the Muse*, 1964, oil on canvas, 110 × 140 cm, Private collection

18. László Lakner, *Dockyard Workers*, 1960, oil on canvas, 105 × 130 cm, Private collection

19. László Lakner, *Dockyard Welders*, 1959, oil on canvas, 98.5 × 132 cm, Private collection

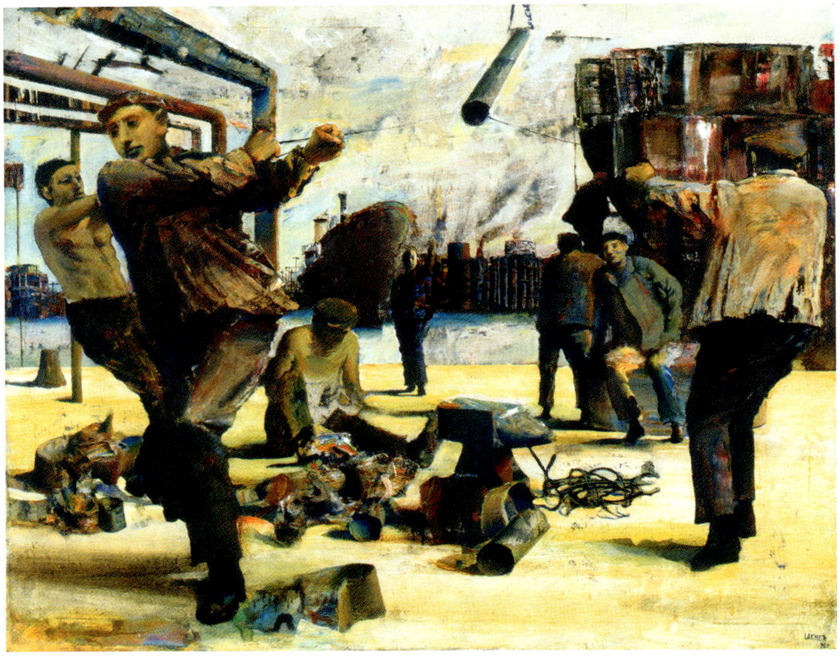

18

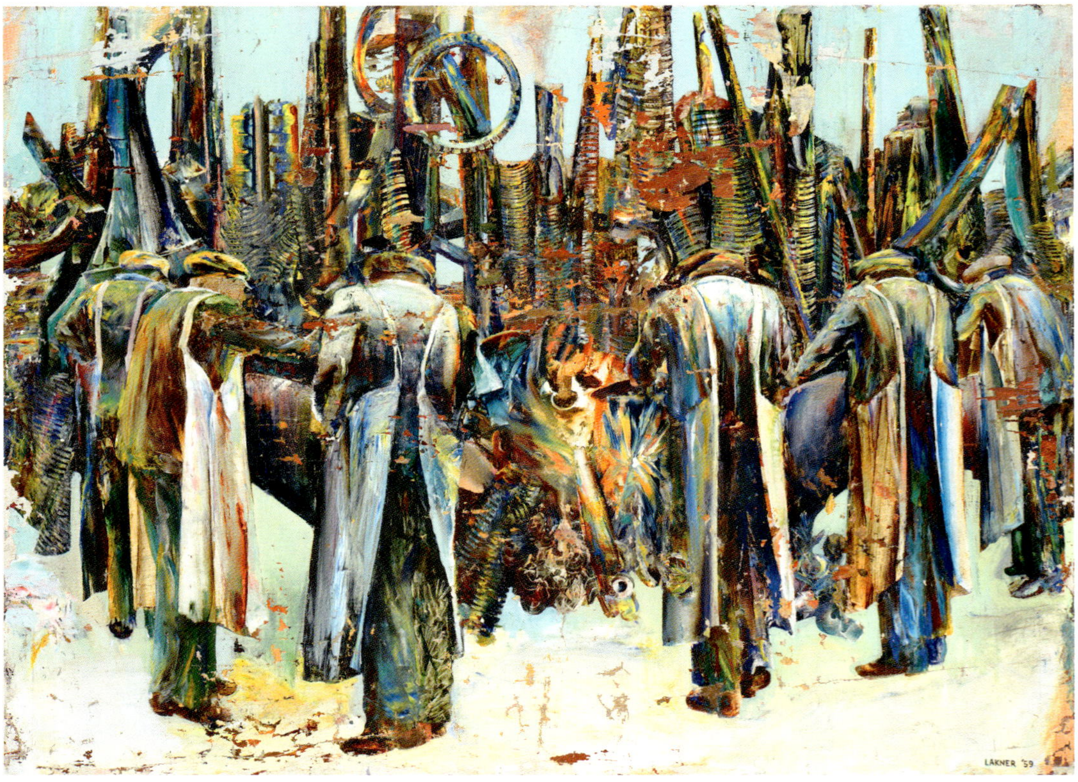

19

Whereas Konkoly did not wish to graduate with this work in 1964 – he did not submit it to the conservative jury at the academy – Lakner had still insisted on completing his degree in 1960, since that was a precondition of state recognition of an artist's existence, so he produced works that would be acceptable both to his master, Bernáth, and to the more partisan taste of his conservative colleagues. Thus, he submitted *Dockyard Workers* (1960, fig. 18) instead of *Dockyard Welders* (1959, fig. 19); Max Ernst's and Tibor Csernus's inspiration was less evident in the former, which also approximated a representation of factory work that could be tolerated from a socialist perspective. Whereas expressionist modernization was a kind of surface change in sculpture, without altering the solid core of thematic socialism, 'formalism' caused far greater problems in two-dimensional painting, especially in the early 1960s, when the orthodox conservatives took much stronger positions in the various juries. Both Kondor and Csernus made a living by illustrating books at this time, while Lakner and Gyémánt designed film posters and submitted magic realist still lifes to Képcsarnok, because they received no significant state exhibition opportunities or public sculpture commissions.[26] Ákos Szabó's graduation project *Cantata profana* (1960) at a primary school in Budapest (at the periphery of official representation) was a rare exception, and was exciting on account of its topic – it was inspired by Bartók and the issue of folk modernization, and the Bartókian synthesis of Hungarian folk culture and European modernism had been an important reference point for aesthetic modernization from the mid-1950s onwards. The work, which barely deconstructed realism but conjured up associations of the 1956 revolution in the depiction of a fleeing boy, was received unfavourably, so Szabó spent the rest of his career painting apolitical interiors, as if symbolically retreating into an interior space. This is evident in the case of the virtuoso painting *Farewell* (1962, fig. 20), which parallels magic realism and offers a surreal apotheosis of an urban bourgeois culture cultivating its own culture.

The policy of opening and the deconstruction of socialist realism also brought a slow canonization of Bernáth's and Barcsay's surrealist contemporaries, Endre Bálint and Dezső Korniss, who had experimented with a Bartókian combination of Hungarian folk culture and European modernism; yet the second half of the 1960s was aesthetically still rather under the sign of the state's triumphant celebration of Barcsay's and Hincz's 'constructivism' (i.e. more open to compromises).[27] Kondor's career also suited this constructivist aesthetic, thanks to a combination of socialist themes and modern, neo-realist visuality. Kondor earned the most support from the official cultural policy establishment with works such as *Rebuilding Felszabadulás Square* (1963), but the modern icons of housing-estate blocks and airplanes appear even in his works on biblical themes, while the surrealist richness of detail and mythical, existentialist apolitical character of his graphic works created a school no less than Csernus's surnaturalism did. While Csernus could not be enticed to return, Kondor's state recognition extended to being chosen as one of the representatives of Hungary at the Venice Biennale in 1968. The two other modern 'socialist realists' were Tibor Vilt, experimenting with expressionist and abstract forms, and Ignác Kokas, who blended lyrical abstraction and the realism of the Alföld School. All three of them were working on the borderlines of realism, surrealism and expressionism, and the success and official recognition of all three in Hungary could be attributed in no small measure to the cosmic dimensions of their thought and the universality of their reflections on humanity (much like Hincz's) even in 1968.[28] Yet, Kondor's brilliant copperplate etching *Venice Biennale of Greatest Hits* (1968, fig. 21), cynically mocking the appearance in Venice and the new trends witnessed there, clearly shows the obsolescence of his, Vilt's and Kokas's classic modernism and pessimistic humanism in juxtaposition to the latest Western intellectual trends and media. In terms of the history of ideas, Kondor and the similarly highly cultured Vilt were shaped by French existentialism above all, whereas pop art, conceptual art and actionism were on the rise in the West, with the attendant critiques of autonomous art, a consumer society of spectacle and colonialism.

Consequently, Kondor could not be a partner for the representatives of the new abstraction in Hungary, for those working on Hungarian versions of the latest Western modernist trends (hard-edge painting and post-painterly abstraction); he was not invited to their exhibitions, not that he would have gone, given his disdain for the reductive spirit of the new abstraction. In fact, the 1970s brought official recognition for the abstract, geometric and structuralist trends, since they focused on the autonomous, aesthetic and visual problems of art. In a concurrent process, socialist realism, which was constantly losing its function of communicative agitprop, was being replaced by the new phenomenon of socialist modernism, which could draw on and recycle abstract and constructivist traditions most of all.

Although the young followers of Lajos Kassák, Korniss, Barcsay and Hincz were working in the spirit of hard-edge and post-painterly abstraction, they also claimed the old avant-garde as a tradition. The artists of the Pesti Műhely (Budapest Workshop) founded by Imre Bak and János Fajó, for example, published silkscreen albums of not only Kassák, but also Max Bill, Nicolas Schöffer and Victor Vasarely in the first half of the 1970s, and while the cultural authorities interpreted them as labouring on the creation of modern socialist visual culture, they aimed to produce an apolitical, modernist, contemporary Hungarian art (see also Flóra Barkóczi, 'Creative (Dis)Courses', pp. 95–109, for a discussion of the Pesti Műhely, Bak and Fajó). Imre Bak, and the others joining him – István Nádler, András Mengyán, Tamás Hencze and Ilona Keserü (with the exception of Fajó) – were actually not representatives of a new constructivism, but experimented with characteristically Hungarian versions of hard-edge, concrete art, op art and lyrical abstraction. Bak merged the aesthetics of hard-edge, folk art and an increasingly fashionable semiotics in his *Sun – Human – Face II* (1976, fig. 22) in which he intended to fuse Eastern philosophies and theories of the modern psychology of vision. Despite this authorial intention, the humanist spirit of the work was an excellent fit with the discourse of socialist realism transformed into socialist modernism.

Bak was also active in visual art education, working at the Népművelési Intézet (Institute of Public Education), while Fajó began to run a gallery in the outskirts of Budapest in 1976, where he popularized modernist visuality within the state-sanctioned limits. This was a time when even neo-avant-garde artists like Miklós Erdély exploited, if somewhat ironically, the intellectual and institutional frameworks of the new constructivism and socialist modernism:

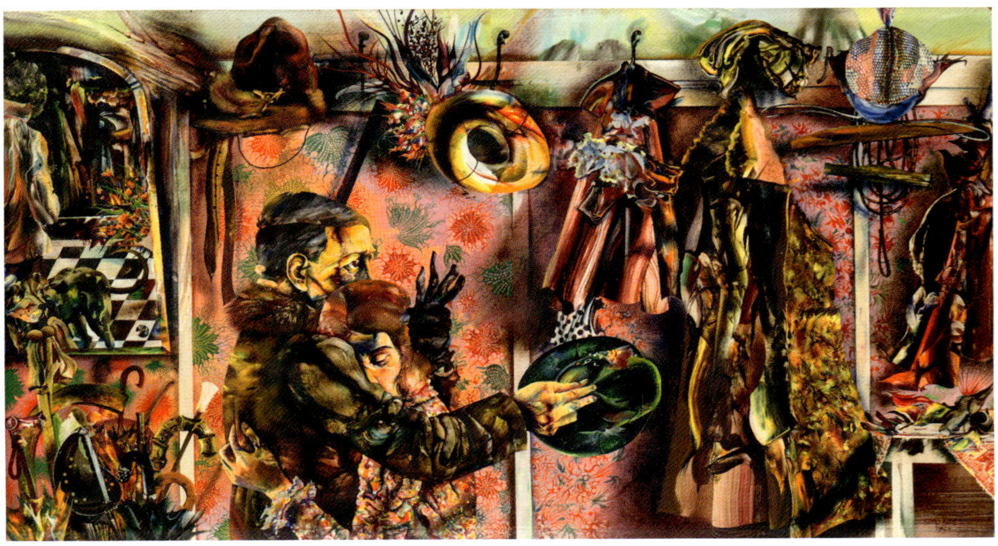

20

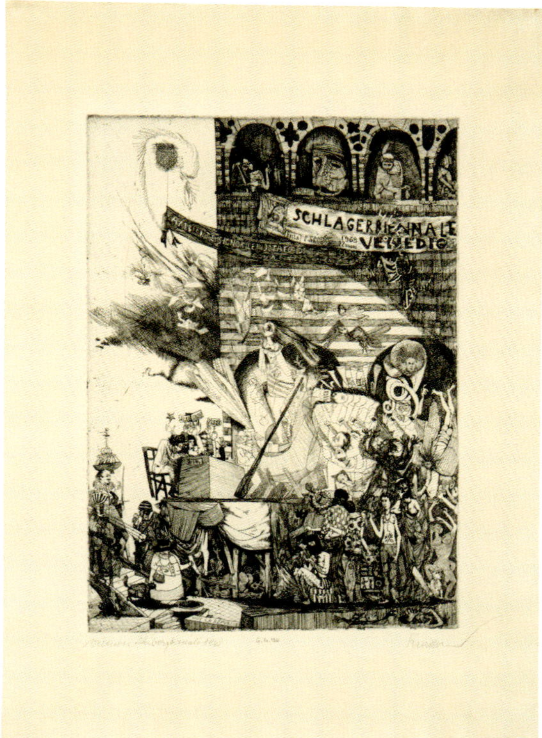

21

Józsefvárosi Galéria provided a home for the exhibition of the 'Kreativitási gyakorlatok' (Creativity Exercises) workshop run by Erdély and Dóra Maurer, who followed Kondor and Csernus's surreal realism early in her career until she turned towards geometric abstraction via conceptual art. The 'Kreativitás – Vizualitás' (Creativity – Visuality) exhibition in 1976 presented the work of a community, forged from the young workshop participants, that was committed to developing a new, creative and innovative socialist human being, though only nominally (that is by appropriating and redirecting the concept of creativity). Erdély and Maurer exploited the state initiative of modernizing socialist culture, which aimed to use the latest methods (including the psychology of creativity) in education as well, while their alternative pedagogy no longer formed the participants' consciousness in the spirit of socialist realism turned socialist modernism, but in the neo-avant-garde spirit of conceptual art and actionism.

20. Ákos Szabó, *Farewell*, 1962, tempera and watercolour on fibreboard, 70 × 125.5 cm, Szépművészeti Múzeum – Magyar Nemzeti Galéria, Budapest

21. Béla Kondor, *Venice Biennale of Greatest Hits*, 1968, etching, 41 × 29 cm, Szépművészeti Múzeum – Magyar Nemzeti Galéria, Budapest

22. (overleaf) Imre Bak, *Sun – Human – Face II*, 1976, tempera on canvas, 105 × 220 cm, Tate Modern, London

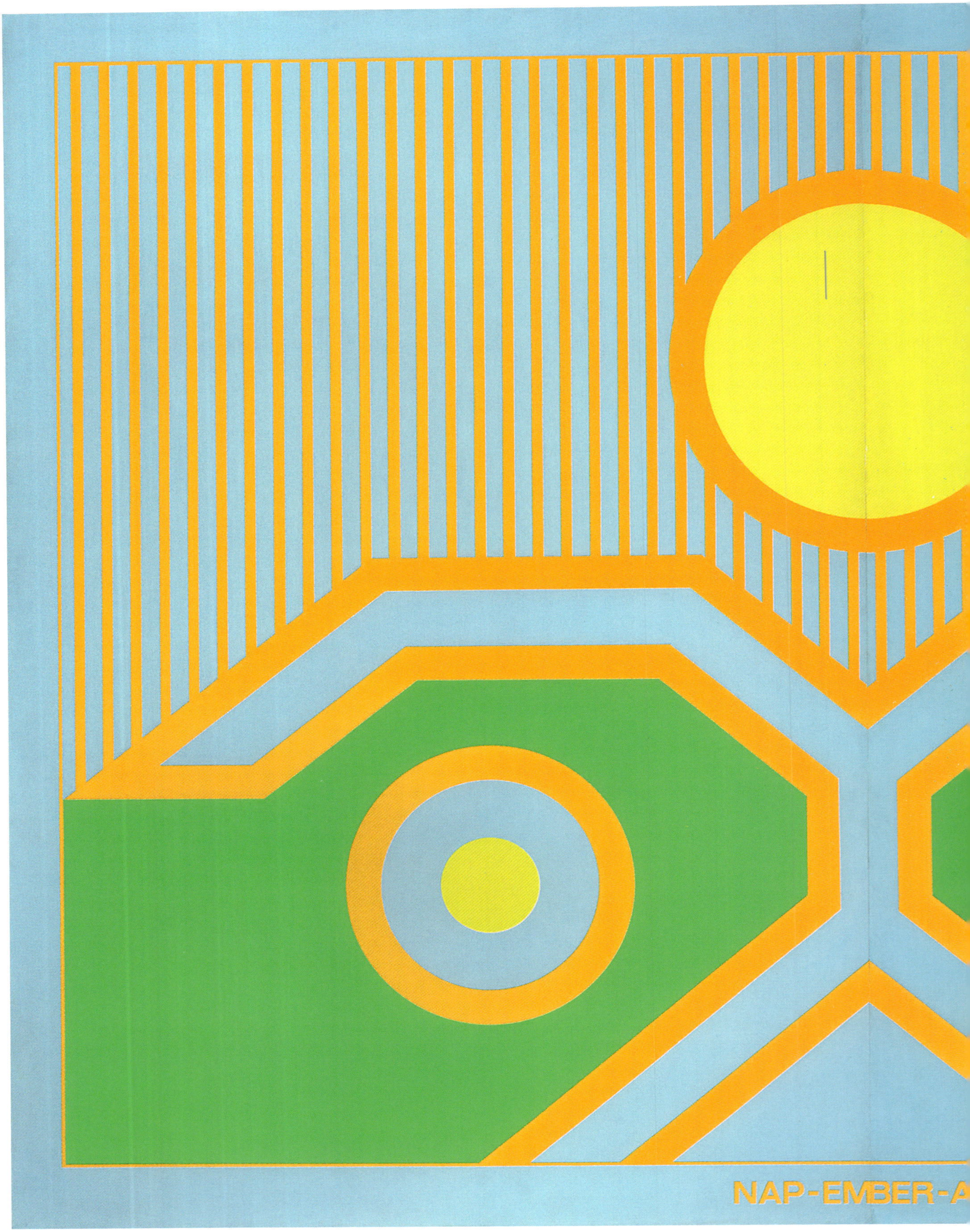
NAP-EMBER-A

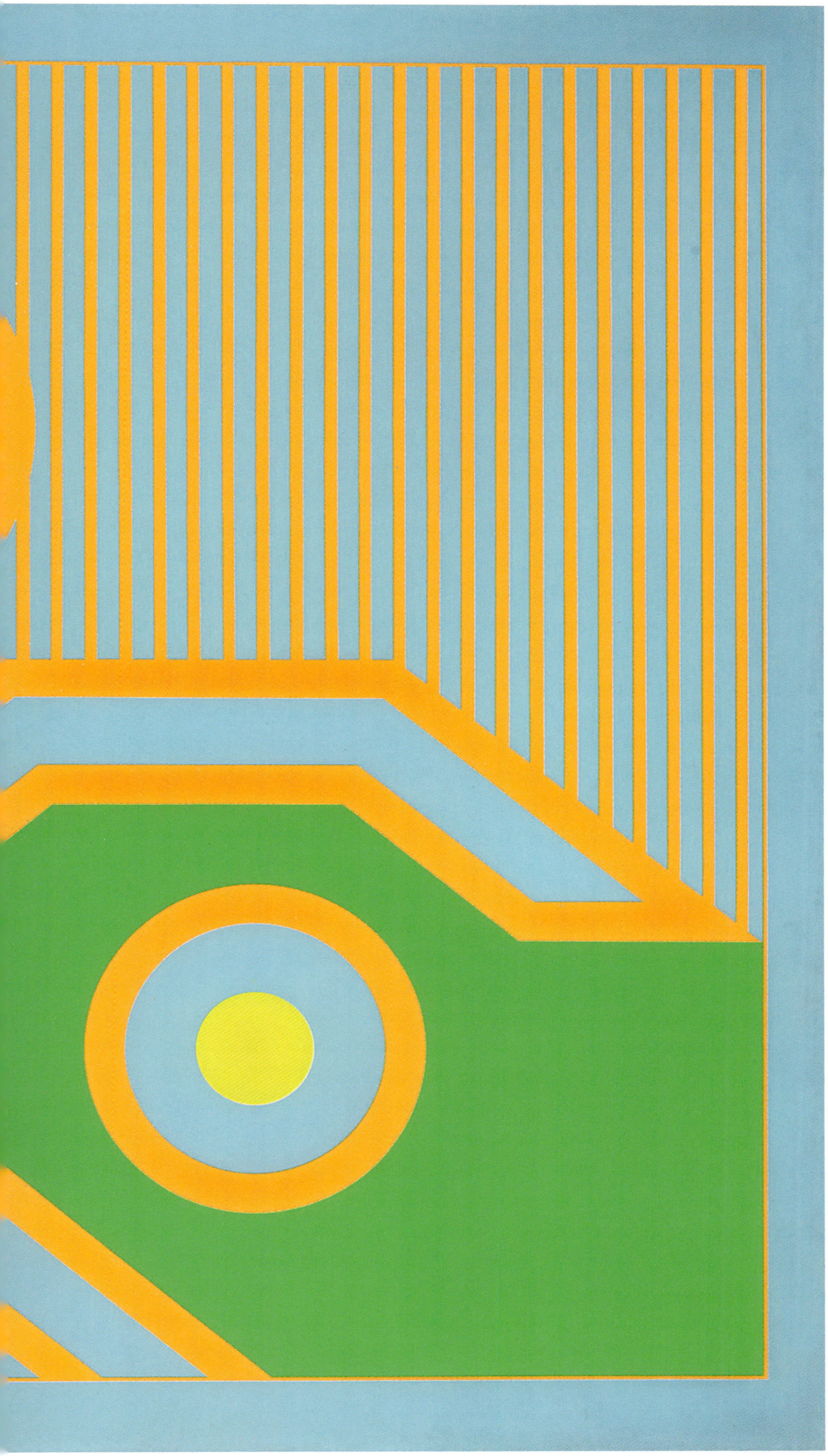

1 The orthodox meaning of 'socialist realism', based on Maxim Gorky's ideas about its educational function, is the realistic and optimistic representation of an idealized state of Soviet workers. After the Second World War, Andrei Zhdanov transformed Gorky's ideas into the Zhdanov Doctrine, which divides the world into two camps headed by the 'imperialistic' United States and the 'democratic' Soviet Union.

2 The volume *Principles of the Cultural Policy of the Hungarian Socialist Workers' Party*, published in 1958, declares the approved course of art to be a realism allowing more artistic freedom, yet faithful to the ideas of socialism. Abstraction and nonfigurativeness were not prohibited in art in principle, but abstract works could not be publicly shown in Hungary until the mid-1960s, unlike in Poland and Yugoslavia.

3 I am using the term 'socialist education' in the extended sense preferred by Evgeny Dobrenko, since socialist realism and the socialist reality permeated or even concealed by socialist realist symbols and products can be interpreted in Guy Debord and Dobrenko's terms as a spectacle the very objective of which is the production of the socialist subject. Visual art played a crucial role in this education, interpreted as 'production process', at least in the 1950s–60s before the dramatic rise of television. Evgeny Dobrenko, *Political Economy of Socialist Realism*. New Haven: Yale University Press, 2007.

4 I find the Derridian term of deconstruction appropriate because the modernization of the formal, rhetorical and stylistic constructions of socialist realist discourse and visual culture ultimately led to the dissolution and transformation of orthodox socialist realism by the internal logic of modernization.

5 According to Debord, recuperation is a process through which the society of the spectacle incorporates the revolutionary and subversive ideas to become more effective and powerful. For a detailed analysis of capitalist recuperation, see Luc Boltanski and Eve Chiapello, *The New Spirit of Capitalism*. London: Verso, 2005.

6 Gyula Derkovits, who passed away in 1934, transformed from a 'formalist' into a socialist realism artist and also employed the formal repertoire of modernism. In the mid-1950s, he was established as a model that contemporary artists should emulate. His rehabilitation is most clearly indicated by the fact that the state fellowship established for young artists in 1955 was named after him.

7 Barcsay's painting cannot be identified as constructivist in the avant-garde interpretation of the term in the 1920s–30s. It was, however, labelled as constructivist in Hungarian criticism and art history because it experimented with the decomposition of the view into its geometrical components in a version of cubist and geometric abstract aesthetics. 'Semi-abstract' was another popular term for this trend of the period, whereas 'state abstract' became prevalent after the political transition. Piotr Piotrowski calls this constructivist tendency – quite significant in Hungary, Yugoslavia and Poland alike – neo-constructivist and implies that its apolitical modernism is the key to its success. Cf. Piotr Piotrowski, *In the Shadow of Yalta: The Avant-Garde in Eastern Europe, 1945–1989*. London: Reaktion Books, 2009, 105–46.

8 On the connections between de-Stalinization after 1953 and 1956 and the reassessment of Picasso, see Piotr Bernatowicz and Vojtech Lahoda, 'Picasso and Central Europe after 1945', in Christoph Grunenberg and Lynda Morris (eds), *Picasso – Peace and Freedom*. Liverpool: Tate, 2010, 44–51.

9 Cf. Jérôme Bazin, 'Socialist Realism and Its International Models', *Vingtieme Siècle*, No. 109, 2011, 72–87.

10 Lajos Németh (1929–1991) was head of the subdepartment of visual arts at the Hungarian communist party (Magyar Dolgozók Pártja, Hungarian Workers' Party) from 1954 to 1956. He did not join the re-established communist party (MSZMP) after the quelling of the 1956 revolution, and moved on to an academic career: he worked at a state research institute and taught art history at Eötvös Loránd Tudomány Egyetem (Eötvös Loránd University), Budapest.

11 Lajos Németh, 'Megjegyzések képzőművészetünk helyzetéről' [Notes on the State of Our Visual Art], *Új Írás*, Vol. 1, No. 8, 1961, 738–44. Németh was the first to write a comprehensive study on modern and contemporary Hungarian art; it reflected the reformist attitude and even began a cautious canonization of surrealism and abstraction: *Modern Art in Hungary*. Budapest: Corvina, 1969.

12 In an article that triggered the debate about 'contemporary style', Nina Dmitrieva, one of the most influential Soviet art historians and critics of the period, thought the future of socialist realism lay in the attainment of a modern style that was not only monumental but also expressive; it would not just illustrate but also make one think, and would offer an objective representation instead of schematic idealization. Nina Dmitrieva, 'K voprosu sovremennom stile' [On the Question of Contemporary Style], *Tvorchestvo*, Vol. 39, No. 6, 1958, 6–9.

13 Cf. Susan E. Reid, '(Socialist) Realism Unbound: The Effects of International Encounters on Soviet Art Practice and Discourse in the Khrushchev Thaw', in Matthew Bown and Matteo Lafranconi (eds), *Socialist Realisms: Soviet Painting, 1920–1970*. Milan: Skira, 2012, 261–76.

14 Roger Garaudy, *D'un réalisme sans rivages: Picasso, Saint-John Perse, Kafka*. Paris: Plon, 1963.

15 While Russian art history identifies the conservative aesthetic turn with the 1962 scandal of the Manezh exhibition – Khrushchev's harsh criticism of the incomprehensible formalism of young artists – the corresponding process in Hungarian art history may be the systematic rejection of Csernus and his fellow artists by the national exhibition jury. Cf. Nóra Aradi, 'A IX. kiállítás zsűrizésének munkájáról' [On the Jury's Work of the IXth Exhibition], *Művészet*, Vol. 2, No. 5, 1962, 4–7. Nóra Aradi is the most knowledgeable, conservative partisan critic of the period, who summed up her communist view of modern art in *Absztrakt művészet* [Abstract Art]. Budapest: Kossuth Kiadó, 1964. (See also József Mélyi, 'Abstract Boundaries', pp. 161–77.) On the Manezh Affair, see Susan E. Reid, 'In the Name of the People: The Manezh Affair Revisited', *Kritika*, Vol. 6, No. 4, 2005, 673–716.

16 Anna Oelmacher, 'Fiatal festő képei a Mednyánszky-teremben' [Pictures by a Young Painter in Mednyánszky Show Room], *Magyar Nemzet*, 5 March 1964, 9.

17 Drawing on Guy Debord and Jean Baudrillard, Evgeny Dobrenko considers the socialist spectacle an interpretive framework combining elements of reality and fiction, which transmits official ideology to subjects primarily in the form of images, spectacles and social events (such as art debates). Dobrenko, *Political Economy of Socialist Realism*.

18 Hincz was quite familiar with the oeuvre of Ernő Kállai, one of the chief theorists of the Európai Iskola, who discovered the 'hidden face of nature' in abstraction, a notion that parallels the partiality to biological forms in the aesthetics of surrealist and abstract art. Oliver A. I. Botar and Isabel Wünsche, *Biocentrism and Modernism*. Burlington: Ashgate, 2011.

19 The interpretation of socialism as a 'cultural revolution' may explain Kondor's success and state recognition, even if Kondor himself was sceptical about the achievements of socialism. Sheila Fitzpatrick, *The Cultural Front: Power and Culture in Revolutionary Russia*. Ithaca and London: Cornell University Press, 1992.

20 The picture was rejected by the jury during the mandatory official selection process prior to the opening. Kondor, however, insisted on showing the work. Nóra Aradi, head of the Department of Visual Arts at the Művelődésügyi Minisztérium (Ministry of Culture), personally removed the picture on the day of the opening. Even though the work only indirectly alluded to 1956, it contradicted official policy by not approaching it as a counterrevolution.

21 It was primarily his master, Aurél Bernáth, who lobbied for his appearance abroad. Bernáth was not only on good terms with György Aczél, the highest ranking figure in cultural policy, but was also a member of the Művészeti Tanács (Art Council), the professional body advising the Művelődésügyi Minisztérium on any aesthetic-political disputes.

22 Sándor Láncz, 'A székesfehérvári Téli Tárlat' [Winter Exhibition in Székesfehérvár], *Művészet*, Vol. 4, No. 5, 1964, 29.

23 The Stalinist and Zhdanovian cultural revolution, that is the Sovietization of culture, drew quite heavily on popular and accessible themes and narratives. See Katerina Clark, *The Soviet Novel: History as Ritual*. Chicago: University of Chicago Press, 1981.

24 On relations between Stalinism, socialist realism and middlebrow taste, see Evgeny Dobrenko, 'The Disaster of Middlebrow Taste, or Who Invented Socialist Realism?', in Thomas Lahusen and Evgeny Dobrenko (eds), *Socialist Realism Without Shores*. Durham: Duke UP, 1997, 135–64.

25 I follow Laclau and Mouffe's use of the term 'floating signifier' in a broader political sense, extending its linguistic sense. Ernesto Laclau and Chantal Mouffe, *Hegemony and Socialist Strategy*. London: Verso, 1985.

26 Contemporary visual art was only sold legally in Hungary by the galleries and shops of the Képcsarnok Vállalat (Art Gallery Company). Pictures could be submitted to Képcsarnok twice a month, and their potential purchase and further circulation was determined by a jury applying official cultural policy. See also Júlia Perczel, 'The Art Sphere as a Grey Zone', pp. 59–77.

27 This official success was no doubt related to the West European rediscovery and popularity of Russian and Hungarian constructivism (Lajos Kassák, László Moholy-Nagy, György Kepes, Victor Vasarely).

28 The humanist and mythic themes of their art and the cosmic horizon of their visual culture can be understood not only as a reflection of the scientific and technical revolution, but also as evidence of their compromise with the socialist regime. This compromise basically meant that the artist's formal exploration could not extend to representing the shortcomings of the surrounding tangible reality or to reflecting of the faults of the current political regime. Cf. Péter György, *Kádár köpönyege* [Kádár's Cloak]. Budapest: Magvető, 2005.

1. Tibor Csernus, *Újpest Quay*, 1957, oil on canvas, 140 × 150 cm, Szépművészeti Múzeum – Magyar Nemzeti Galéria, Budapest

1

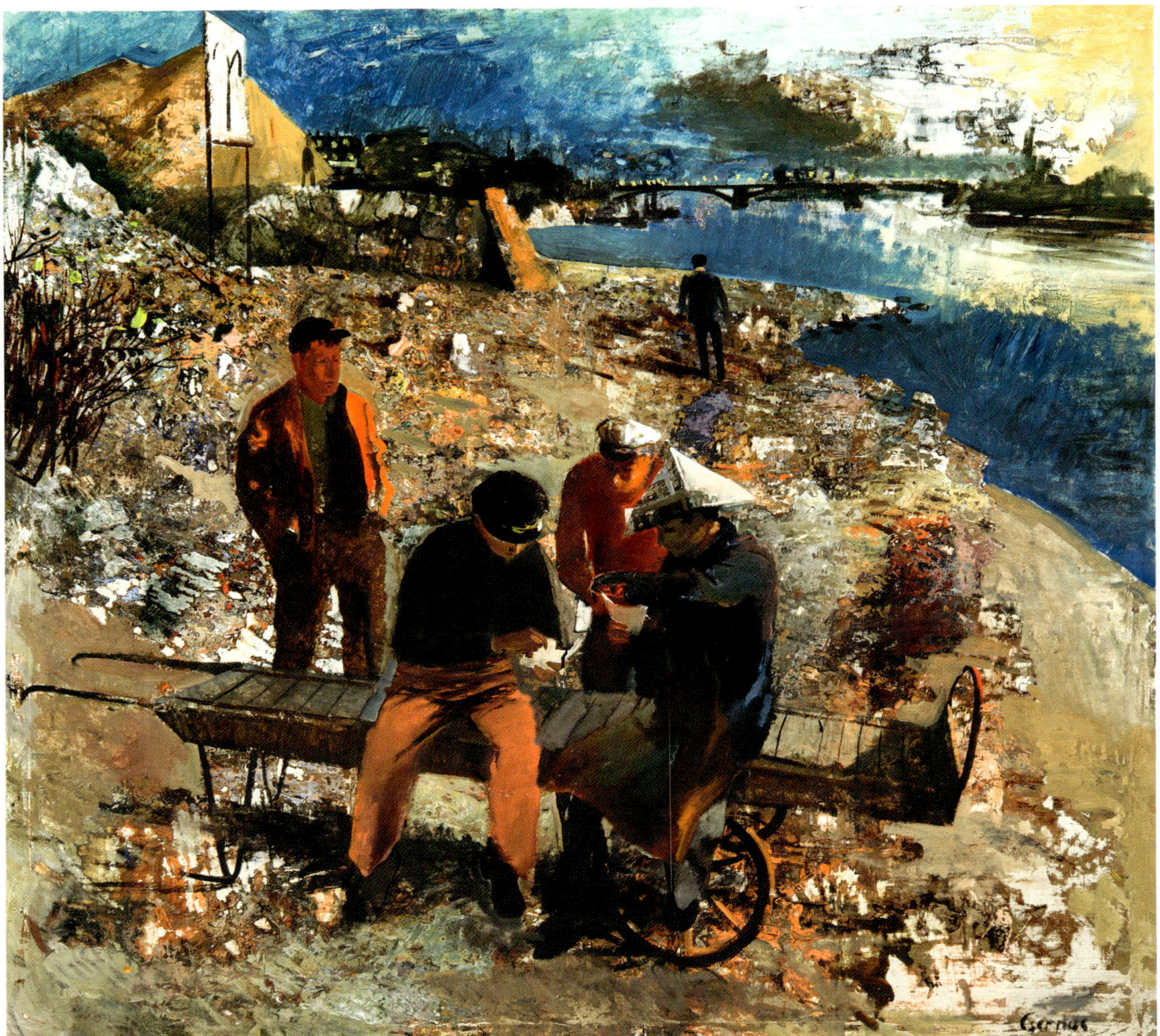

Dávid Fehér

(Dis)figuring Reality

New Forms of Figuration in Hungarian Painting, 1957–75

The 'medial turn' of painting in the East and West

The narrative of the cold-war art world, built on the opposition of 'Western' abstraction and 'Eastern' realism, came into dispute in the late 1950s as a result of a lengthy process.[1] The dominance of abstract expressionism and *art informel* (expressive abstract painting using informal, improvised methods and random gestures) was replaced, first in the UK and the US, then in Western Europe (and various other places in the world) in the early 1960s, by a more figural approach that tended to reflect on the visuality of mass media and the culture of everyday objects. One may call this phenomenon the 'medial turn' (or pivotal cultural shift) in painting,[2] which blurred the lines between painted and mediatized images, between the unique and the reproduced, and between high and low culture. At the same time, the declining dominance of socialist realism in the East-Central European art scenes (where it had never had any theoretically pure representation in any case) often gave way to a figural painting that was modernist in spirit and post-cubist in character.

Besides these post-cubist tendencies, other variants of figural painting also appeared in Eastern Europe, and some were comparable to those found in Western European and American works, marking a medial turn in painting and pointing to the international trends of pop art. Official cultural policy viewed these developments ambivalently: being figural, they were occasionally quite close to the cultural authorities' expectations of realism, yet their Western orientation, experimental techniques and provocative system of forms and motifs also made them controversial. Accordingly, the new developments of figural painting in the early 1960s are difficult to fit into the categories of official vs oppositional, supported vs banned, which appear in many narratives of the period, both then and now.

The development of figurative painting in Hungary is distinctive even within the region. It appeared in the late 1950s (for a period that can be defined as 1957–64) under the name of surnaturalism as a trend in painting related to magic realism; in the mid-1960s, however, several of the former surnaturalist artists moved closer to narrative figuration related to the international trends of pop art (1964–69). With the emergence of conceptual art at the end of the decade, a rising number of artists turned from pop art to analytical, yet politically and socially sensitive, photorealist painting (1969–75). This shift characterized a distinct circle of artists who belong to the same generation and a half (Tibor Csernus, László Lakner, Gyula Konkoly, László Gyémánt and László Méhes). Insofar as the path from surrealism to photorealism can be described as a linear story, it is unique among the realist tendencies in the region.

Although the new figurative trends of Hungarian painting in the 1960s are partly analogous to 'realist' developments in Western Europe and North America (pop art and new realism), the differences are significant, since the social milieus in which the works were produced were completely unlike. The artists wanted to deconstruct socialist realism by creating East European alternatives to Western figural trends.[3] What is exceptional in this is that the artists did not break with realist painting and, as a result, they occupied a peculiar position between the frontlines of the official cultural policy's preferred realist language and the creative strategies (such as abstraction and happenings) condemned in that period. They represented a 'third way', even if typically from a critical stance, in opposition to the political status quo.

Their artistic goal was usually the depiction of Hungarian social reality without idealization: the dark, frequently depressive paintings are diagnoses, as it were, of daily life in Hungary in the Kádár era (i.e. from 1956 onwards); the richly layered irony of the works and their allusive web of motifs refer to the *human condition* of the period. In this sense, the paintings are significant not only by virtue of their painterly complexity, but also as crucial documents.

Surnaturalism: images of reality confounded (1957–64)

It is a recurring statement in the historical surveys of surnaturalism, as it was somewhat ironically named by contemporary criticism,[4] that the majority of its artists attended the class of Aurél Bernáth, a respected professor of painting at the Magyar Képzőművészeti Főiskola (Hungarian Academy of Fine Arts) in Budapest (see also Sándor Hornyik, 'Reforming Socialist Realism', pp. 113–35, for a discussion of Aurél Bernáth, Tibor Csernus, László Lakner and surnaturalism). Bernáth had been an important figure of modern painting in the interwar years. The relaxed, figural, painterly character of his art was coupled with a rejection of abstraction, but he did not become a socialist realist, strictly speaking, since he infused the typical repertoire of socialist realist motifs with a peculiar lyricism. Besides Bernáth, there were other teachers of painting at the academy in the 1950s – Róbert Berény, István Szőnyi – with ties to the Gresham Circle, a group of painters in the interwar period of Hungarian art whose work expressed a bourgeois mentality (and who took their name from their meeting place, the café of the art nouveau Gresham Palace in Budapest). Bernáth and Szőnyi accordingly kept their distance from socialist realist orthodoxy in the 1950s, but often painted works that featured socialist realist themes, since they were high-profile artists in the official art scene. Tibor Csernus, one of Aurél Bernáth's best students, who was one of the officially recognized young talents of the regime early in his career, recalled decades later:

As a matter of fact, socialist realism – thanks to Bernáth's, Berény's and Szőnyi's struggles – was no insurmountable threat. It was practically the three of them who defended figurative art as justified at the academy, but they refused to accept the adoption of Zhdanov's theories [Andrei Zhdanov developed the Stalinist cultural doctrine by which the content of artistic creations had to conform to the Party line]. Of course, they never said 'Let's ignore Zhdanov,' because that would have been a police matter rather than an aesthetic one at the time. Yet it was clear enough from what they implied to their students that they did not consider ideological pictures produced in the spirit of Zhdanovian aesthetics to be works of art. When correcting works, they dropped comments like Bonnard, Cézanne, or Degas did a better job of depicting the world than, say, an Aleksandr Gerasimov. […] This whole socialist realism seemed like squaring the circle; so let's paint after nature, as we see things, but the theme should show the Soviet Union twenty years from now. Or if I paint a worker, I shouldn't show him in stained trousers, as I see him, but I should paint the elegant man that this worker becomes when socialism has fulfilled all its promises.[5]

An important detail in the birth of the surnaturalist movement was young Tibor Csernus's trip to Paris in 1957–58, in the period of transition after the fall of the 1956 revolution against Soviet policies in Hungary. Simon Hantaï, who had been living in Paris since 1949 and was a highly respected artist in the French art scene, introduced Csernus to the French (post-)surrealist trends and to Max Ernst's technical experiments with surfaces (grattage, frottage and décalcomania). These experiences in Paris informed Csernus's synthesis of Bernáth's approach to painting and a surrealist painting technique based on automatisms, which simultaneously intensified descriptive painting into an absurd vision, while still evoking socialist realism.[6] Csernus's painting *Újpest Quay* (1957, fig. 1) positions the figures of workers standing on the riverbank in a hazy blue landscape reminiscent of the relaxed painting of his master, Aurél Bernáth, but the stony bank is formed by scratching and experimental surface techniques. This was a unique juxtaposition of the tradition of the representational painting of the interwar period, the themes of socialist realism and Max Ernst's surrealist treatment of the surface. After his stay in France, Csernus created overfilled compositions built up of realistic visual fragments, creating a peculiar form of horror vacui, i.e. kenophobia or the fear of empty space (*Lehel Square Market*, 1962, p. 121, fig. 8). He transforms the ordinary view into a mutability filled to the brim with amorphous motifs and forms, thereby flipping Bernáth's poetic representations of the atmosphere and his relaxed figural painting into their opposites. As a result, official criticism condemned Csernus for his 'irrationalism', which was incompatible with the spirit of socialist realism, and his 'serious engagement' with surrealism, a term used like a slur in the official discourses of the period.

The epitome of Csernus's surnaturalist period – and Hungarian surnaturalism in general – is *Reeds* (1964, p. 121, fig. 10), made right before the artist emigrated to France. The work, which employs references to classic painting (e.g. a group of people alluding to *Le Déjeuner sur l'herbe* by Édouard Manet), depicts a pier on a lake shore and a group sitting in a twilight landscape, but the intensive (absurd) use of colour and the Max Ernstian formal systems modelled with a razor blade make the composition visionary. The 'microrealism' of details adds up to something nonrealistic. Csernus takes verisimilitude to the point of absurdity by using direct prints of objects and by transposing various print products mechanically (using solvent). Among the pieces of trash lying in the grass in the lowest segment of the image, one glimpses the cover of the Italian communist magazine *Vie Nouve* and the packaging of a packet of 'Franco-American' macaroni as reversed direct prints. Csernus probably employed the technique of 'image transfer' used by the American Robert Rauschenberg in his series illustrating Dante's Inferno (*XXXIV Drawings for Dante's Inferno*, 1958–60), which was on show at the Venice Biennale, where Rauschenberg won the Grand Prize that year. In the context of Csernus's works, Rauschenberg's technique seems a development of surrealist image construction with its use of mechanical prints and other automatisms, assisting the artist with juxtaposing reality and irreality, creating an absurd, 'schizophrenic' visual world. The magazine cover and food packaging transposed to the surface of the painting also suggest a medium-conscious attitude gesturing towards pop art, while the contrast between the motifs and their surroundings underscores the unbridgeable gap between the media images flowing in from the West and reality in Hungary.

Young artists with whom Tibor Csernus was in touch – László Lakner, Ákos Szabó, Ferenc Kóka, László Gyémánt, Gyula Konkoly and others, most of them students of Bernáth – began to experiment with surnaturalist methods in the late 1950s. Within this circle, members of which became central figures of the new figuration of the 1960s, Lakner's position was markedly different from that of Csernus. Although Max Ernst's works, which he knew from reproductions, and French tachism – which used dabs, splashes and improvised brushwork – were important reference points for Lakner, the American influence on his early works was even stronger. He got to know the American trompe l'oeil school (John Frederick Peto and others), precisionist painting (Charles Sheeler) and magic realists like Ivan Albright and Andrew Wyeth from Western books and magazines. His post-1956 works were, in turn, comparable to those of Ben Shahn. The streets with ruined brick walls after the quashed revolution, with the occasional passersby, posters of Lenin and mass demonstrations (*Street 1956*, 1957; *Demonstration*, 1957) all resonated with Ben Shahn's social realism. Lakner was still in the academy when he began to seek a characteristically leftist new figuration that would resonate with social and political processes, and could offer an alternative to the dominant image-making regime of socialist realism. The figure of the newsvendor appears in one of his early works, holding a magazine with a stylized image of Lenin's head on the cover (*Newsvendor*, 1958, fig. 2). The realist representation of press publications and the ghostly faces evoke the depressing social conditions after the fall of the revolution as well as the state media's propaganda. At the same time, the manner of representation can be compared to examples of proto-pop like Peter Blake's inventive depictions of magazine covers and comics (*Children Reading Comics*, 1954; *On the Balcony*, 1955–57),[8] or Andy Warhol's early drawings on leftist themes inspired by Ben Shahn (*Communist Speaker*, 1950s; *Crowd with Communist Flags*, 1950s).[9] It is virtually certain that the young Lakner could not have known these works, yet his path towards pop art was quite similar to that of his Western contemporaries working in a different social milieu.

László Lakner's graduation paintings and the jury panel's debate about them at the Magyar Képzőművészeti Főiskola were symptomatic of the conditions of Hungarian cultural policy and its expectations of art. Of Lakner's three graduation works, it was *Dockyard Workers* (1960, p. 128, fig. 18) that was the centre of attention. Although the painting evokes the clichés of socialist realism, the professors at the academy found it problematic due to its 'foreign attitude' and 'mixing of surrealist and naturalist elements'. They were bewildered by the tension between the technical excellence of execution, the figurative painting depicting predominantly leftist themes and the surrealist ('irrationalist') affinities lurking in the details of the painting. There are barely any surrealist devices in this painting, but *Dockyard Welders* (1959, p. 128, fig. 19) – the first version of the picture, which was not shown publicly – had the 'forest' motif of Max Ernst's paintings in the background. It is as if Lakner projected details of socialist realism, surrealism and reminiscences of classic art onto one another,[10] evoking but also overwriting the expectations of socialist realism and creating an absurd constellation.

The painterly sensitivity to photography and print media is stronger in Lakner's works than in that of Csernus. He used photos as early as his graduation work *Dockyard Workers*, but it was outside the academy that he first began to use documents and photographic prototypes in paintings. (It was general practice in the period for artists to create different types of work in official environments, such as the academy, and 'at home' experimental works were mostly shown to a relatively narrow informal public.) *Construction* (1959, fig. 3), which uses surrealist devices (nonrealistic colours, collage technique) to represent a characteristically socialist realist theme, is probably based on a photo by Henri Cartier-Bresson. Yet the historic piece of the period with respect to the use of photo documents is the painting *Seamstresses Listen to Hitler's Speech* (1960, fig. 4; see also Daniel Véri, 'The Holocaust and the Arts', pp. 209–27). Its precursor is a documentary photograph from 1937, showing a group of women listening to Hitler delivering a speech, which the artist found in the April 1960 issue of *Magnum*.[11] The painting was rejected by the jury, so Lakner could not exhibit it at the most important Budapest show of young artists, the annual exhibition of the Fiatal Képzőművészek Stúdiója (Young Artists' Studio), in 1961. Posing questions about the perpetrators' responsibility for the trauma of the Holocaust, it ran counter to the official politics of memory. In its probing of political problems (including the politics of memory itself), its historical and social sensitivity to taboo topics, and its medium-conscious approach to painting, *Seamstresses Listen to Hitler's Speech* offers a significant parallel to Gerhard Richter's photo-painting, which had East German roots, though it developed later in West Germany.

Among the surnaturalists, László Gyémánt's works also testify to an interest in American art, and more specifically magic realism. Gyémánt is also ironic in his evocation of a cliché of socialist realism in his early painting, *Construction* (1960, fig. 5). The composition, mixing naturalist and surrealist modes of expression, is dominated by empty scaffolds, with virtually no view of a building among them: the building is just a semblance without any perceptible solidity, and the set conceals stagnation, decay and the vacuousness of the utopia. Gyémánt's graduation work, *Carnival of Survivors* (1963, fig. 6), which he cautiously presented to the jury as *Carnival of Peace*, also provoked a fierce debate, primarily due to the surrealist treatment of facture and the

2. László Lakner, *Newsvendor*, 1958, tempera on paper, 40 × 30 cm, Private collection

3. László Lakner, *Construction*, 1959, tempera, collage, paper, 38.6 × 24.6 cm, Private collection

4. László Lakner, *Seamstresses Listen to Hitler's Speech*, 1960, oil on canvas, 70 × 100.5 cm, Deposit of Roberto Tosi (Rome) in the Szépművészeti Múzeum, Budapest

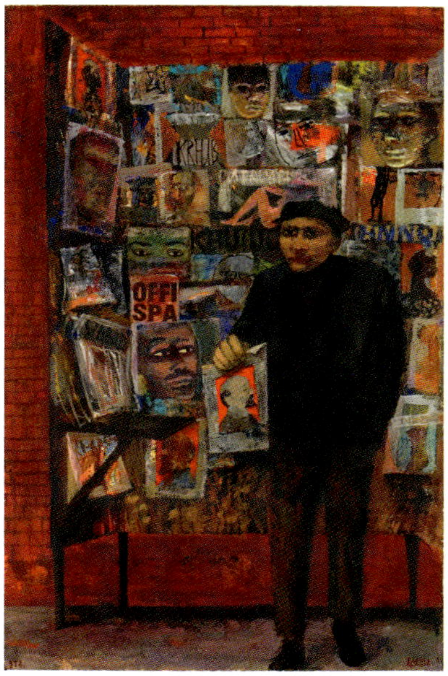

2

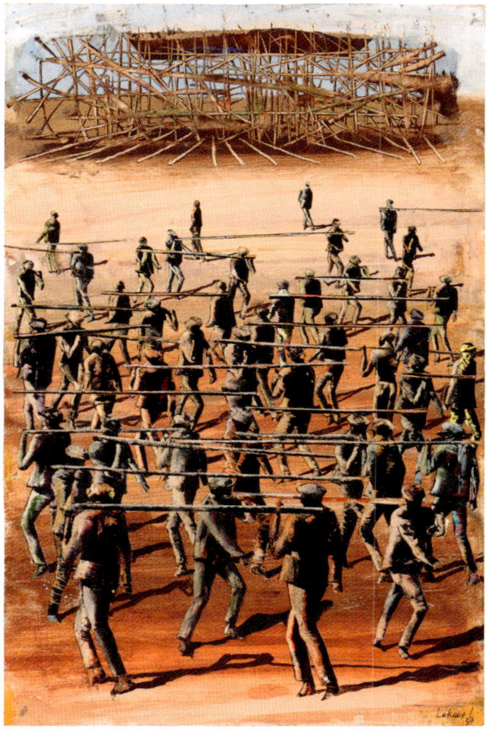

3

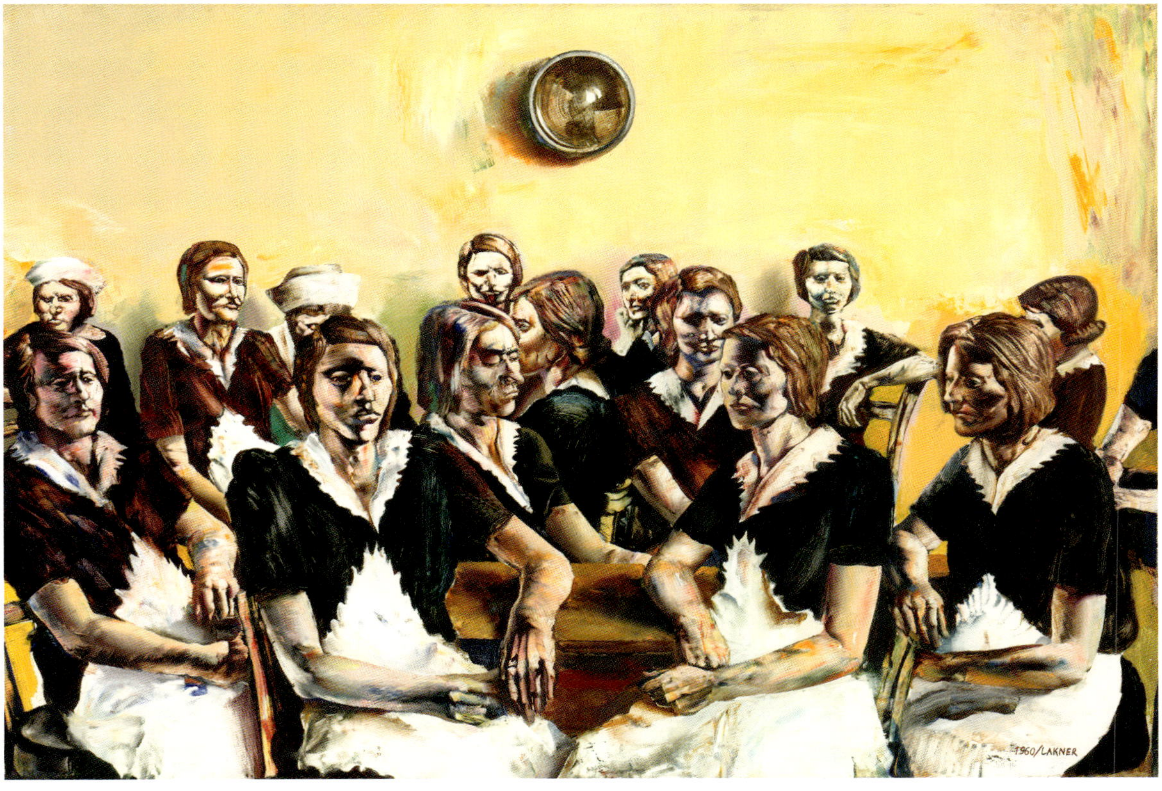

4

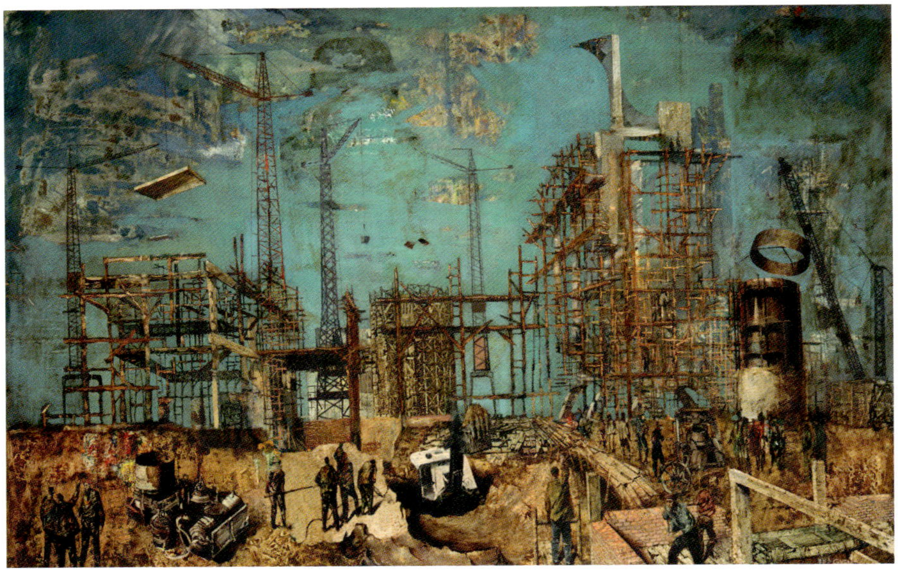

5

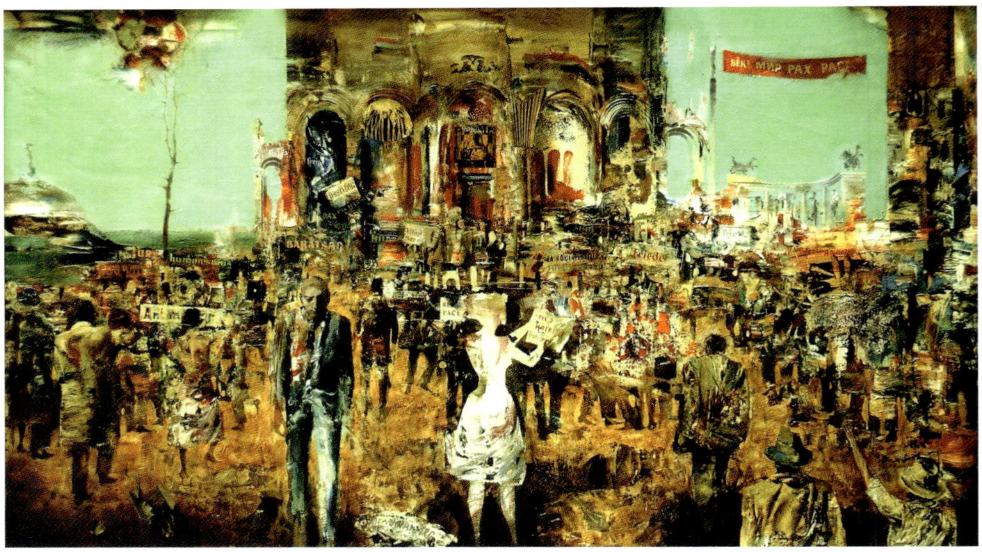

6

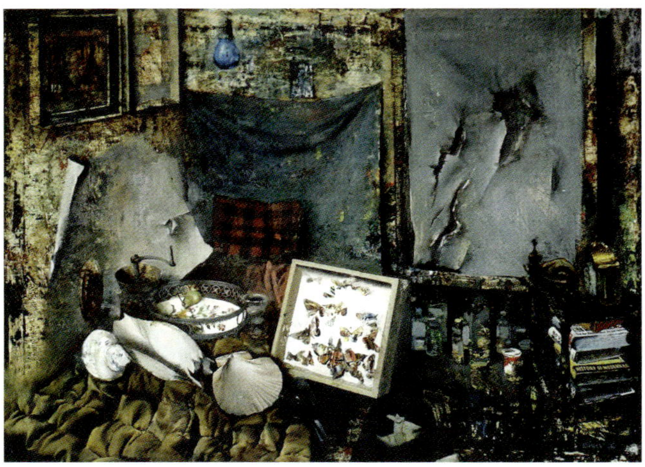

7

5. László Gyémánt, *Construction*, 1960, oil on fibreboard, 93 × 140 cm, Szépművészeti Múzeum – Magyar Nemzeti Galéria, Budapest

6. László Gyémánt, *Carnival of Survivors*, 1963, oil on canvas, collage, 83 × 143 cm, Private collection

7. László Gyémánt, *The By-products of Time*, 1963–65, oil on canvas, 90 × 120 cm, Private collection

attendant 'problems of worldview'. At the same time, the jury was puzzled and confounded by its narrative figural style of painting coupled with unquestionable technical skill. The crowd scene set among the ruins of a stylized Budapest – juxtaposing realistic human figures, collage elements and texts – is filled with cryptic allusions. The concrete readings (the associations of the Second World War and the defeated 1956 revolution) and their traumatic aspects – which were taboo in the Kádár era – are literally overwritten by the universal slogans ('humanism', 'friendship', and 'peace'), displaying clichéd messages of socialist realism, but also degrading them to empty catchwords scattered on the surface.

In the early 1960s, Gyémánt also comes closer to a realist language of painting with photographic character. His painting *The By-products of Time* (1963–65, fig. 7) combines the surnaturalist scratching of the facture with trompe l'oeil. Still-life elements (a butterfly collection, a revolver and torn drapery) and the crumbling sections of wall exude a sense of claustrophobia and depression. The magic realist representation of memento mori appears as a gauge of the general mood, raising existential questions in a coded allegory of a hopeless situation, and the towering stack of English books about the history of modern art adds a broader art historical context to the composition. The latter refers both to the constantly changing definition of art and to Western works that kept arriving in the form of reproductions, and they also raise the question of how Gyémánt's still-life, which calls classic traditions to mind, positions itself towards the modernist canon conveyed in books. What is the relationship between locality and internationality and between realism and the modernist abstraction included in the books?

The Academy of Fine Arts Visited by the Muse (1964, p. 127, fig. 17), a surnaturalist painting by Gyula Konkoly (see also Géza Boros, 'Taboo and Trauma: 1956', pp. 193–207), who was younger than Lakner and Gyémánt, can be read as an *ars poetica* – a treatise on the art of composition – too. Its Rodin copy and trompe l'oeil-type reproductions (Manet, Velázquez) conjure up iconic figures of figural art, but there is a counterpoint to these realistic details in the execution, bordering on the abstract (the figure of the muse evokes French tachism), juxtaposing different modes of image-making and putting the painting in a broader art historical context. The representation of the reproductions, however, promises a visual language already akin to pop art.

Towards 'International Pop' (1964–69)

Although a number of other artists can also be classified under the general label of surnaturalism (Ferenc Kóka, György Korga) and some used socialist realist iconography ironically (Ákos Szabó's painting *Asphalt Pourers* in 1960 is a case in point), it was the works of László Lakner, László Gyémánt and Gyula Konkoly where the painting of motifs in a photographic manner became emphatic. They moved closer to a montage-like composition of the image based on a juxtaposition of photographically painted elements, characteristic of pop art as well. Both Hungarian and international scholarship dates the decisive step in the internationalization of pop art to 1964. This was the year Robert Rauschenberg won the Grand Prize of the Venice Biennale, when his work went on 'tour' around the world, and this was also the time of the first international travelling exhibitions of American pop art. These events not only laid the foundations of the international dominance of American pop art,[12] but also had consequences in Hungarian art and other local scenes. Research projects rethinking the history of pop art on a global horizon examined primarily the flow of art-related information (through travel, magazines, reproductions and correspondence) and the international expansion of traditionally British and American concepts of 'pop art', which were replaced by the broader umbrella terms of 'international pop' and 'global pop'.[13] There are undoubtedly numerous tendencies that were prevalent in East-Central Europe that can be connected to the loud, psychedelic visuality of 'international pop', especially in graphic design. However, works that can be stylistically linked to pop art tend not to engage with the phenomena of capitalist consumer societies (those being non-existent in the region); instead, they rethink the relation to mediatised images in the context of cold-war politics and the dictatorial societies of East-Central Europe.

Besides Czechoslovakia in the 1960s (in the work of Jiří Kolář, Július Koller, Alex Mlynárčik, Stano Filko and Jana Želibská), tendencies linked to pop art became the most dominant in Hungary within the East-Central European region.[14] The most important arc of this development was the continuation and enhancement of surnaturalism. László Lakner, who was the first to turn to pop art, was soon followed by Gyula Konkoly and László Gyémánt (and Tibor Csernus also moved in the same direction after his stay in Paris). Although the term pop art was in use in Hungary and other East European countries during the period in question, one should use it with discernment and not refer to it as a borrowed style. The dynamic of a 'foreign style' and 'local context' can be described with the concept of cultural transfer.[15] Although László Lakner saw Robert Rauschenberg's works in the US Pavilion of the Venice Biennale in 1964 and Gyula Konkoly saw the 'Pop etc.' exhibition in the Museum des 20. Jahrhunderts in Vienna the same year,[16] their surnaturalist painting employing realistic collage effects and including photo-like details had gestured towards pop art's montage-like image construction years before the turn to pop.

Artists seeking an authentic realist language as an alternative to socialist realism had to confront Western 'new realist' trends around 1963–64. Hungarian works that have Pop-art affinities partly followed up on works in the late 1950s that sought a way out of socialist realism through painting with a photographic character. At the same time, they are analogous to new interpretations of realism prevalent in the West as well. In East and West alike, artists raised questions about the epistemological challenges related to a pervasiveness of media images, and found the answer in a medium-conscious realist form of painting. Realism on a monumental scale served the fetishization or mockery of the visual world of a profusion of consumer goods in the West, which replaced an equally monumental abstract painting. In Eastern Europe, a figuration close to pop art was an alternative to local official discourses of realism. Significantly, the gesture of decontextualizing press images and transforming them into artworks (particularly easel paintings) is crucial in both cases, for press images were the tools of manipulation and propaganda on both sides of the cold war.[17]

The 'new figuration' in Hungary had important parallels not only in American examples, but also the realist trends in Europe, which took account of the European traditions of realism: these often engaged with historical-political issues, at times employing photographic precursors. These included French figuration narrative, Belgian and Dutch *nieuwe figuratie* (new figuration), and especially West German capitalist realism. The artists of the latter, Gerhard Richter and Sigmar Polke, who had East European (East German) roots, created a confrontation between socialist realist rhetoric and the visual world of a capitalist culture industry (and American pop art reproducing it), projecting the Eastern and Western blocs' view of realism onto each other. The starting point for Hungarian artists who can be linked to pop art was a figural painting style that undercut the schemes of socialist realism. Similar to capitalist realists, they set up confrontations between Eastern and Western interpretations of realism in their realist paintings. This kind of figuration was a middle path between banned and supported art because it was legible in terms of the figurative painting dominant in Hungary, but it was still not entirely compatible with it. Lakner and Gyémánt's works appeared in state institutions yet they did not become supported; they existed in a grey zone, which only occasionally shifted from banned and tolerated to moderately supported (see Júlia Perczel, 'The Art Sphere as a Grey Zone', pp. 59–75).

The principle of composition that might be called handpainted montage, which is superficially similar to Rauschenberg's silkscreen printed montage compositions, became increasingly emphatic in Lakner's photo-based painting around 1963–64. The painting *News* (1964, fig. 8) multiplies the figure of Muhammad Ali, evoking the circulation of press images from the West, yet it does not break with surnaturalist painting techniques. The same applies to Gyula Konkoly's painting *Fallow Ragout* (1965, fig. 9), which cites a broad range of printed reproductions from Marilyn Monroe to a work by Vincent van Gogh. The works juxtapose diverse techniques of painting, from surrealist grattage through tachist gestures to a naturalist representation of figures and texts evoking posters and packaging. Gyémánt projects brand logos ('Coca-Cola', 'Triumph') upon the ruin of the Colosseum painted in

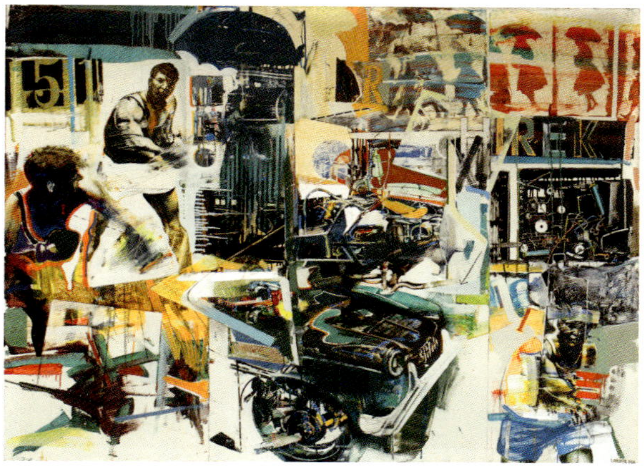

8

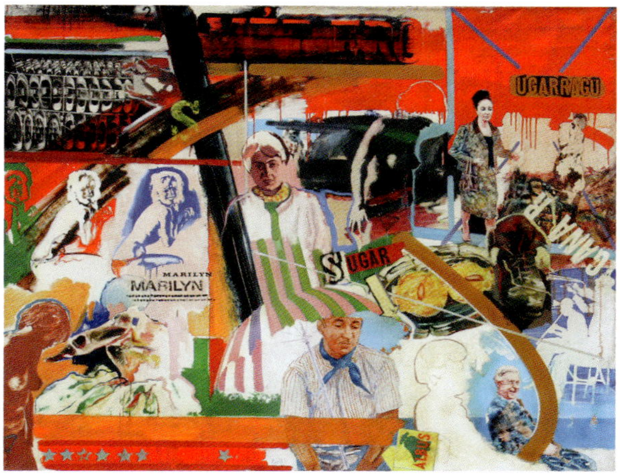

9

8. László Lakner, *News*, 1964, oil on canvas, 130 × 150 cm, Private collection

9. Gyula Konkoly, *Fallow Ragout*, 1965, oil on canvas, 150 × 170 cm, Tragor Ignác Múzeum, Vác

surnaturalist style, asking about the fate of European culture and the effects of the international spread of American products from a peculiarly East European position (*Cosmopolis*, 1965, fig. 10). However, the positive context of American motifs became more emphatic in Gyémánt's art at this time, which was also 'problematic' for the official ideology that treated America as the enemy. His painting of Abraham Lincoln (*Death of a President*, 1967) is a coded reference to the Kennedy assassination, and he also paints the Moon landing two years later (*Neil Armstrong*, 1969), but jazz and pop motifs emerge as his central themes (*Blues in the Night*, 1968; *Beatles*, 1969), although he does not give up surnaturalism even in the late 1960s. His works couple typical American themes of pop art with a surrealist treatment of facture.

Unlike that of Gyémánt, Lakner's position was often highly critical of America. In his paintings that resonated with current political events, the leftist critique of the Vietnam War is a recurring topic, which was not only comparable to the positions of New Left opinion leaders of the West, but was paradoxically also compatible with the pro-Vietnam official political stance of Hungary. Consequently, his painting *Saigon (The Protest of the Buddhist Monks of Saigon)* (1965, fig. 11) was shown at the group exhibition 'A magyar képzőművészek a fasizmus ellen' (Hungarian Artists Against Fascism) of the Magyar Nemzeti Galéria (Hungarian National Gallery) in the year of its making.[18] The work, inspired by the press photo of a Buddhist monk setting himself on fire in Saigon, presents protest as a sequence based on phases of motion. The painting evokes an artistic style associated with America, while also expressing a critique of America's position as an 'aggressor'. The figure who is tied up and vulnerable or, in other works by Lakner, the revolutionary facing execution are recurring motifs that could refer to the claustrophobic conditions of Hungary in the period, while they can also be tied to the artist's works and memories related to the revolution of 1956. Konkoly also evokes the Vietnam War in his painting *Oh Africa: Don't Go There* (1966, fig. 12), but he does not take a stand; instead, he juxtaposes the clichéd compositions of the posters criticizing the Vietnam War and completely unrelated motifs (an African

10

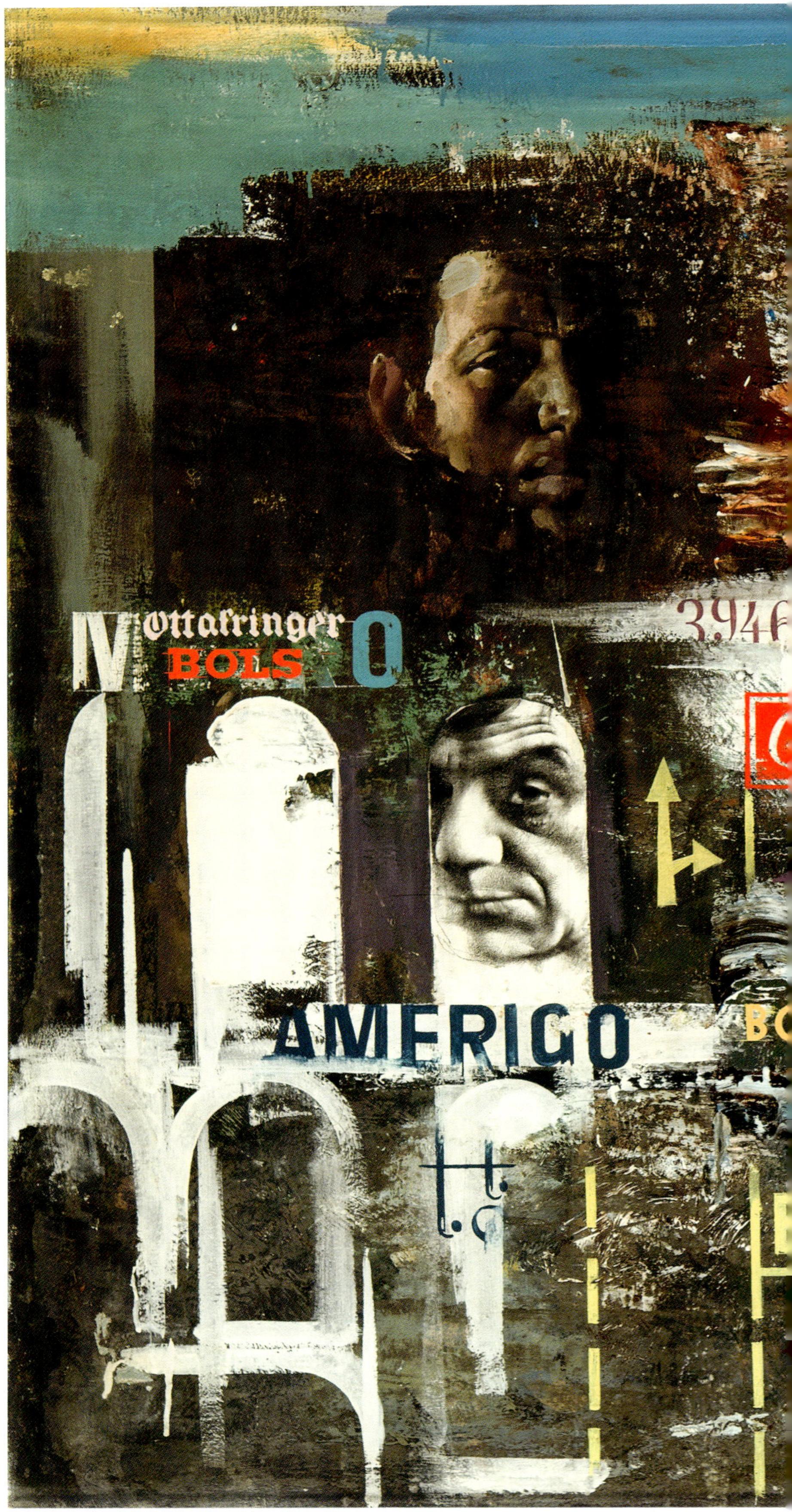

10. László Gyémánt, *Cosmopolis*, 1965, oil on canvas, 90 × 120 cm, Szépművészeti Múzeum – Magyar Nemzeti Galéria, Budapest

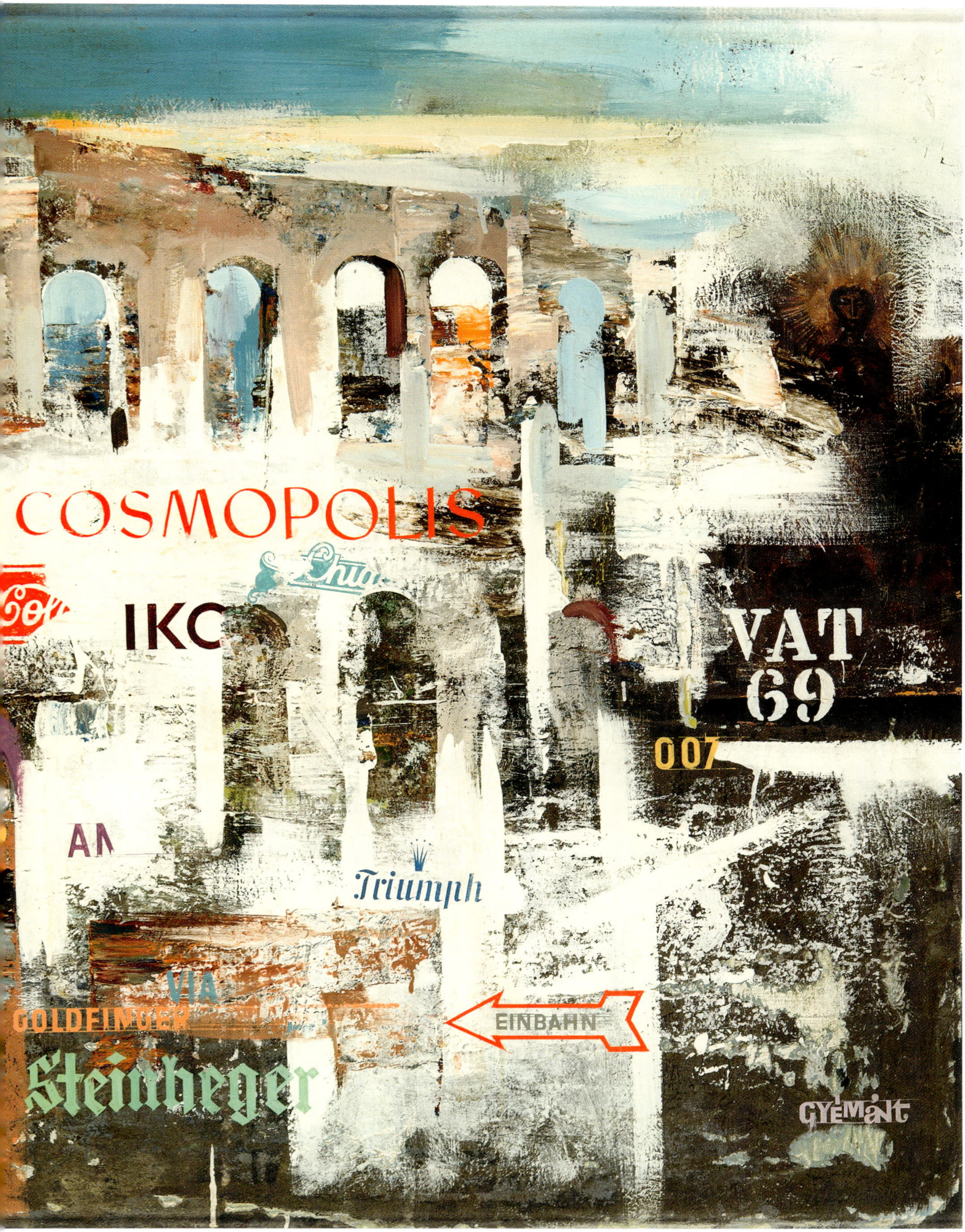
COSMOPOLIS
IKC
VAT
69
007
AN
Triumph
VIA
EINBAHN
Steinbeger
GYEMANT

11

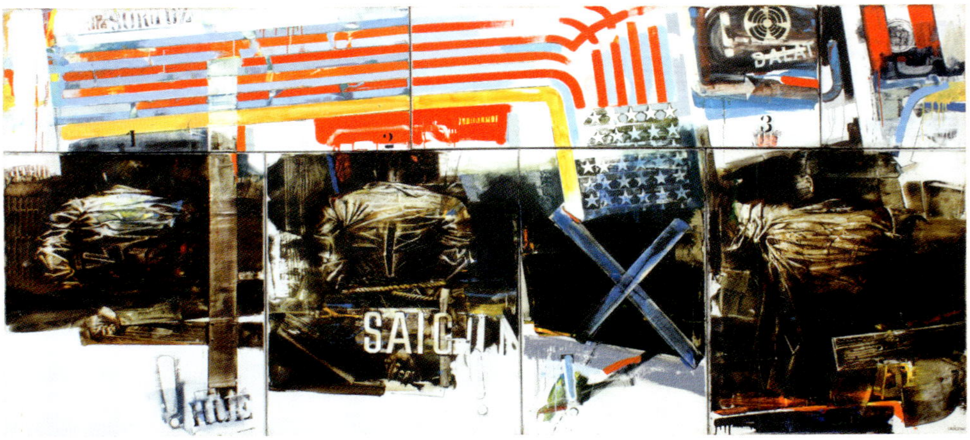

man, a male figure from Velázquez). The pentagram in the painting is composed of colour strip sequences, which are reminiscent of American pop art and hard-edge painting, and a painterly gesture in red appears above the star. The motif can be linked to abstract expressionism, but the red colour can be associated with the socialist regime opposed to abstraction (in Hungary) and to that extent it refers to the dichotomies and tensions of the cold war and to the contradictory relations of abstraction and figuration. Konkoly's representation of the worker (*Portrait of P. S. Porcelain Factory Worker*, 1966, fig. 13) allows similar associations, as it simultaneously invokes American abstract expressionism and pop art while continuing earlier ambivalent surnaturalist representations of the worker.

Art historical references infused with existential and political content become increasingly important in Lakner's art: Rembrandt's deep browns and olive tones, for example, can be read as metaphors of a bleak human situation cut off from light (*Rembrandt Studies*, 1966).[19] Such references underscore that Lakner was reflecting on the state and fate of realist easel painting: he always substituted hand-painted repetitions for mechanical reproduction processes, thereby creating complex narrative structures. He rethought the surnaturalist construction of the image in the context of contemporary painting, creating – to use his own later expression – a 'historical Pop Art'.[20] This is the case in his monumental painting *Metamorphosis* (1964–67), in which a figure with an animal head transitions in three (dialectical) phases into a sarcastically smiling human figure, evoking Rembrandt's late self-portrait but simultaneously recalling Heartfield's montage,[21] Francis Bacon's representation of the figure, British pop art and a surnaturalist treatment of the surface. At the same time, the work itself, which depicts a Kafkaesque metamorphosis, reflects on historical traumas (in a coded language) as the artist confirms: 'this is a parable about the founding experience of my generation after '45 and '56: the assimilation of yesterday's tigers into lambs, into innocent citizens'.[22] The sarcastically smiling but silenced antihero of *Obediently* (1966, fig. 14), the reduced version of the composition, has a sack pulled over his head; the painting refers to the ambivalent modus vivendi of the dictatorial regime, as the artist later commented: it is 'a painting with a hidden current relevance, with symbols of Hungarian "goulash communism," the world of comrades blindly following the "great friend," yet also winking westward'.[23] The grotesque human figure refers to a grotesque (social) situation. The painting can be compared to Peter Blake's interpretation of pop art, but this is no more than a surface projection, since the subject of the picture is the schizophrenic everyday world and oppressive mood of a depressive, claustrophobic milieu: the Kafkaesque universe of socialist bureaucracy.

The reception of the works reveals how contradictory the situation was in cultural policy. The jury approved László Lakner's *Metamorphosis* for the annual exhibition of Fiatal Képzőművészek Stúdiója in 1967,

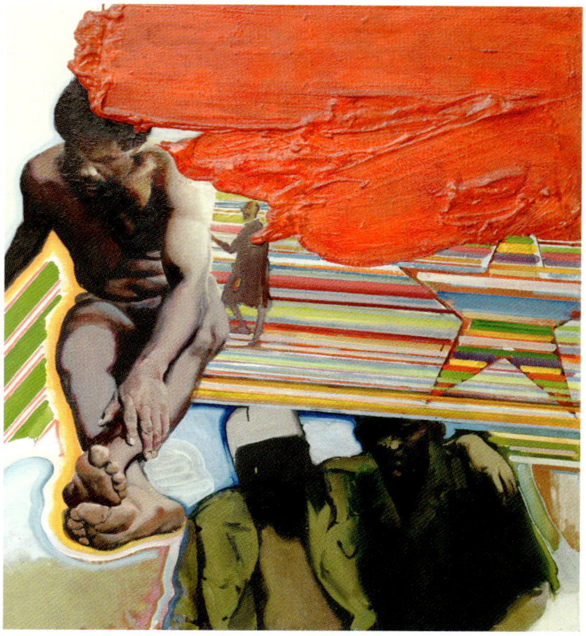

12

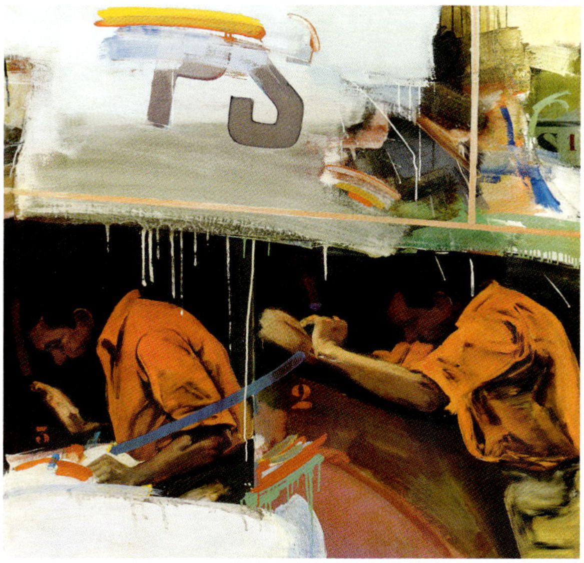

13

11. László Lakner, *Saigon (The Protest of the Buddhist Monks of Saigon)*, 1965, oil on canvas, 100 × 240 cm, Thúry György Múzeum, Nagykanizsa

12. Gyula Konkoly, *Oh Africa: Don't Go There*, 1966, oil on fibreboard, mixed media, 125 × 109 cm, Nudelman Collection, Budapest

13. Gyula Konkoly, *Portrait of P. S. Porcelain Factory Worker*, 1966, oil on fibreboard, mixed media, 125 × 125 cm, Private collection

whereas the monumental work *Let Me Sink Upwards (Portrait of E. M. Waving)* (1967, fig. 15) by his contemporary, Sándor Altorjai, who also began his career as a surnaturalist, was rejected. The work, which combined aspects of both French *nouveau réalisme* (new realism) and Rauschenberg's combine painting, was probably rejected for reasons of content rather than style: it subversively used the topic of the traumatic past of Miklós Erdély, the artist of Jewish origins depicted in the work (in other words, it violated the taboo of Jewish identity).[24] Altorjai's starting point was also surnaturalism – the work mixes collage elements with surrealist methods of painting – but he did not move towards pop art in the 1960s; he developed a bitingly ironic, intentionally damaged and ruined grotesque language of painting that also reflected on the provincial circumstances of Hungarian society (for instance, *Two Halfwits*, 1968, *The Old Girl Dropped Her Hearing Aid*, 1978–79).

The 'Iparterv' exhibitions in 1968 and 1969 were central events of the late 1960s (see also Gábor Dobó and Merse Pál Szeredi, 'Hungarian Culture +/- Europe', pp. 39–57).[25] These semi-official exhibitions were the first time a circle of artists who represented different approaches presented themselves jointly, thanks to a shared interest in Western trends and a commitment to progressive values. Of the former surnaturalists, László Lakner, Gyula Konkoly and László Méhes had work shown at these exhibitions (the latter in 1969). Although the first 'Iparterv' exhibition was the central event of Hungarian discourses that can be associated with pop art, it was a conclusion rather than a beginning in terms of pop art. Konkoly turned from figural painting to a 'softened' plastic language inspired by Claes Oldenburg (see for example Konkoly's work *Cage: Academic Study*, 1968), then to conceptual art; as for Lakner, the painterly enlargement of photographic details became increasingly crucial in his work, which was coupled with a keen analytical interest inspired by Michelangelo Antonioni's 1966 film *Blowup* and the Canadian philosopher Marshall McLuhan's media theories.

14. László Lakner, *Obediently*, 1966, oil on canvas, collage, 78.5 × 119 cm, Szent István Király Múzeum, Székesfehérvár

15. Sándor Altorjai, *Let Me Sink Upwards (Portrait of E. M. Waving)*, 1967, collage, oil on fibreboard, mixed media, 305 × 342 cm, Szépművészeti Múzeum – Magyar Nemzeti Galéria, Budapest

16. László Méhes, *Everyday*, 1969, oil on fibreboard, 80 × 120 cm, location unknown

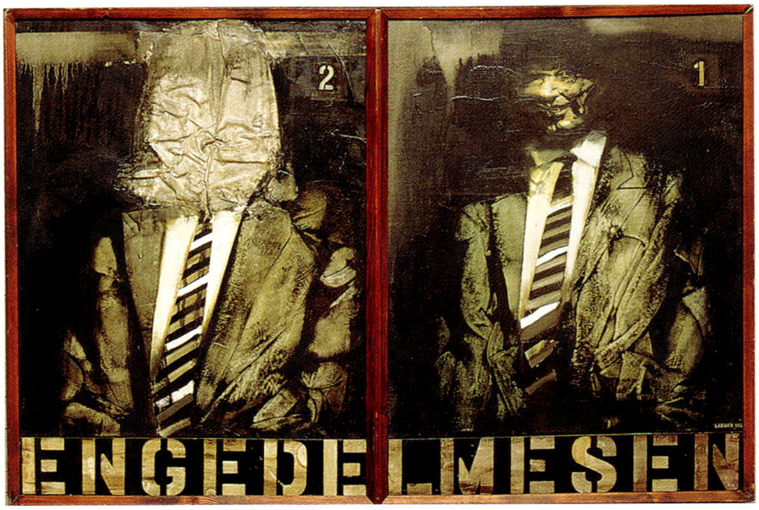

14

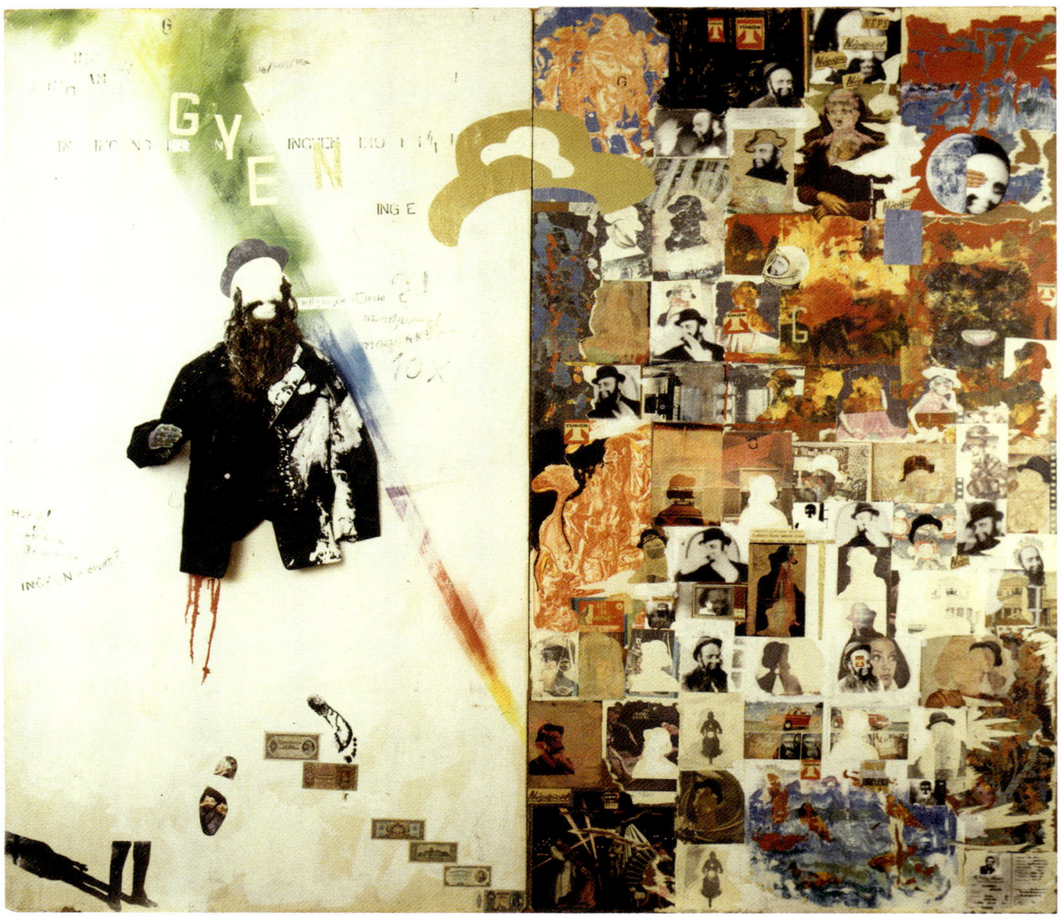

15

Political photorealism (1969–75)

The first photorealist painting in Hungary, *Everyday* (1969, fig. 16) by László Méhes, was displayed at the second 'Iparterv' exhibition in 1969.[26] When Méhes found his way to photorealism, it was mainly not a result of learning about the analogous American developments. He followed his own path from surnaturalist image construction through painting with pop art affinities to photorealism. Photographic effects became increasingly dominant in his montage compositions painted after photographs, and he began to create paper works consistently imitating the characteristics of solarized photographs in 1968 (for example, *Portrait of Csita*, 1968). *Everyday* neutrally enlarges an ordinary scene in Budapest – a man is reading the paper in a tram, and an elderly woman is sitting across from him. Méhes consistently imitates the characteristics of the photographic image: the burned, hardened spots of overexposed details, the surface of inappropriately developed film, as in the sequence of coloured spectral segments at the right edge of the frame. The spoiled photo appears as the image of unidealized 'real reality' and, to that extent, it flips the seeming verisimilitude and actual falsehood of the socialist realist representation of reality into its opposite.[27] Méhes does not examine the 'spectacular' images of the metropolis and the realities and hyperrealities of consumer societies (like American photorealists such as Richard Estes), but rather assesses the critical potential and political contexts of the realist image. He consciously plays with the political associations of realist depiction: *Construction* (1970) uses trompe l'oeil to imitate a clichéd socialist realistic painting in a period when the official canon had not equalled Zhdanovian socialist realism for over a decade.[28] Méhes had a choir of young pioneers open his exhibition held at Csepel Galéria on the outskirts of Budapest in 1972, thereby playing with levels of meaning in the displayed realist works: the members of the choir and the

16

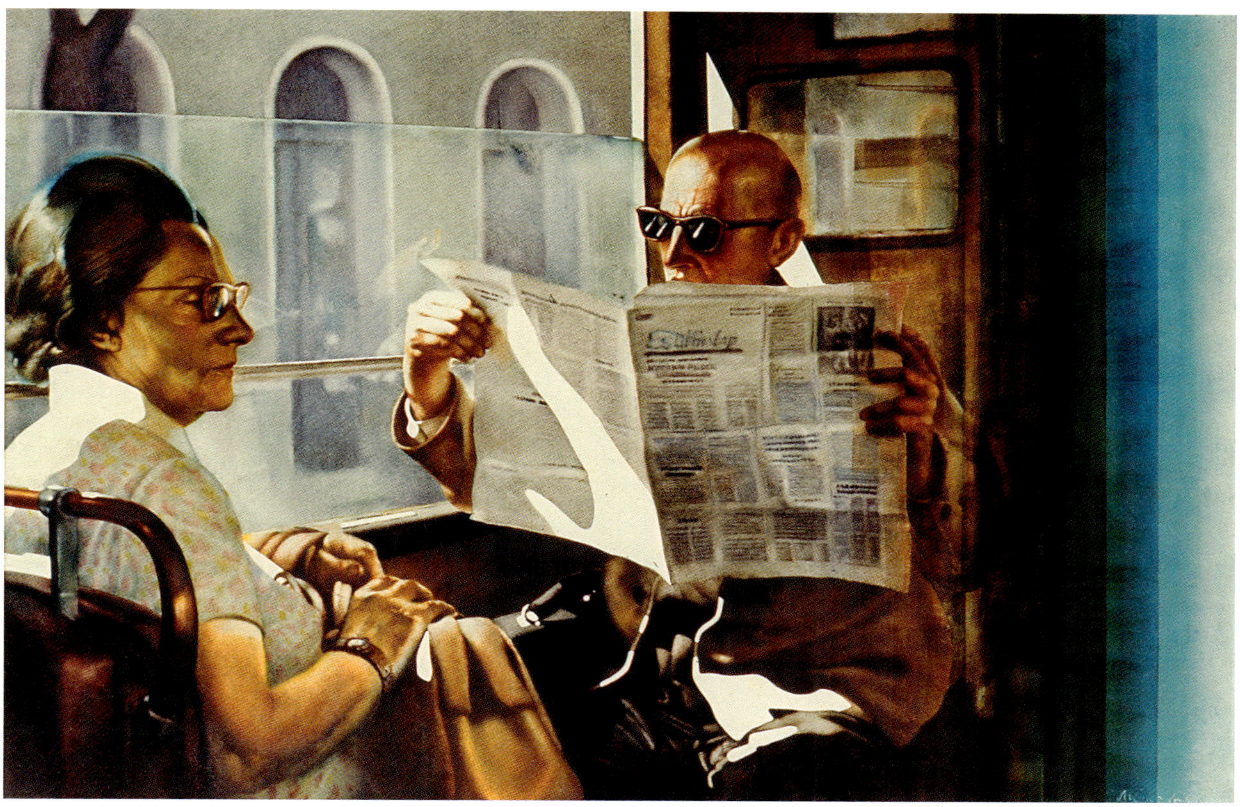

17

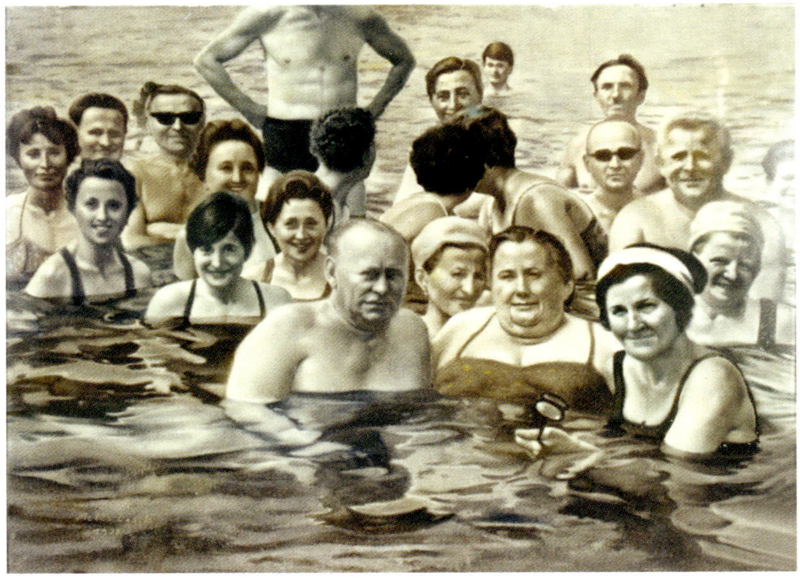

18

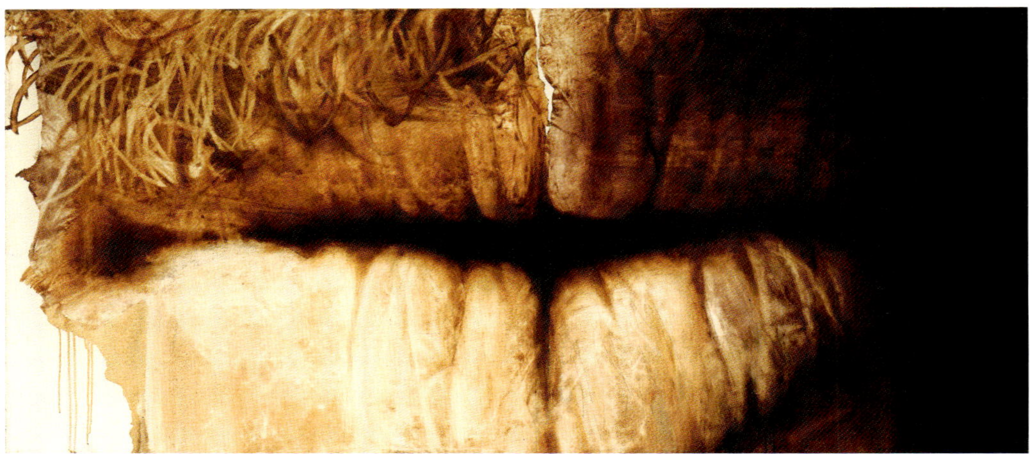

workers who had no sense of the irony with their naive admiration for the painter's brilliant solutions, and the gaze of the professional audience in the know and fully aware of the irony. Official criticism was also helpless in the face of these pictures displayed without commentary, as their irony was difficult to pin down and allowed diverse interpretations. Still, the style of realist painting represented by Méhes did not become officially supported.

The first pieces of Méhes's *Lukewarm Water* series (1970–75, fig. 17) had already been shown in Csepel. The paintings, which show petits bourgeois and workers bathing in the lukewarm water, continue the theme of *Everyday* in reflecting the unidealized everydays of a society as metaphors of a softening dictatorship. The vulnerability of the human figures stripped naked before the alienating camera-eye casts a shadow over the pseudo-kitsch effect of the pink-and-green glasses and over the seeming idyll of the paintings created after faulty, decomposed amateur photos. The ironic, grotesque or even absurd character of the works evokes the spirit of the surnaturalist paintings of the early 1960s, but there is an increasing emphasis on theoretical inquiry into the nature of the image and visual representation.

The same applied to László Lakner's photorealist series. Lakner gradually shifted towards a quasi-photographic representation and came close to photorealism at the time Méhes made his first photorealist works: the

17. László Méhes, *Lukewarm Water I*, 1970, oil on fibreboard, 60 × 80 cm, Szépművészeti Múzeum – Magyar Nemzeti Galéria, Budapest

18. László Lakner, *Mouth*, 1968–69, oil on canvas, 92 × 200 cm, Kiscelli Múzeum – Fővárosi Képtár, Budapest

19. László Lakner, *Chinese Postcard*, 1972, oil on canvas, 200 × 150 cm, Private collection

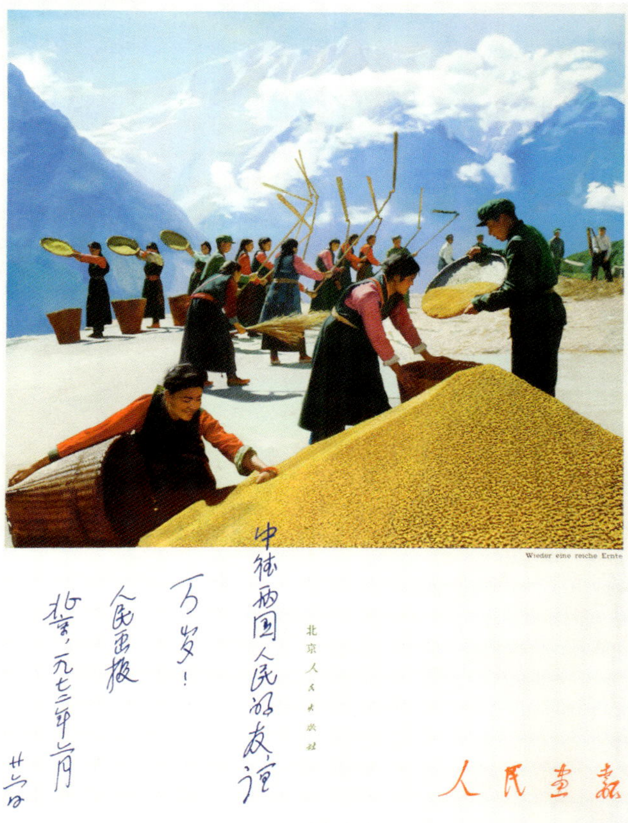

19

X-ray-like depiction of *Bones* (1968) and a large painting entitled *Mouth* (1968–69, fig. 18), based on a photo in *Stern* magazine. Text fragments and dual structures juxtaposing originals and copies are important components of Lakner's monumental paintings of objects; in the long run, these led to the theoretical analysis of word and image, and manual as well as technical reproduction. In the late 1960s Lakner turned to text and photo-based conceptual works, experimental films and book objects, and began *Collected Documents*, a series of photorealist paintings. Following up on the problem probed in *Seamstresses Listen to Hitler's Speech* in 1960, he took up sensitive questions of individual and collective memory, much like Gerhard Richter at the same time. The relationship of realism and leftist politics is a recurring theme in the series. Laknermade objects out of tied-up book objects and painted them in a style that is a species of trompe l'oeil. The oeuvre of leftist philosopher Georg Lukács became a central motif. Lakner tied up Lukács's volume on the theory of realism and then painted it in a realist style, thereby making it unreadable, while also fetishizing it. Lakner's other paintings on 'leftist' themes, in which a new leftist interest was in conflict with the critique of actually existing socialism, are characterized by a similar contradictoriness. Lakner painted the documents of the history of the Hungarian Soviet Republic and the cover of Marx's *Das Kapital* in photorealist style,[29] reaching back to the roots of (Hungarian) communism, confronting the early communist utopia with its later state. His photorealist series, which depicts a barricade from 1968 (*Barricade, Memorial of Revolutions*, 1970), the drawings depicting the arrest of the Baader–Meinhof group (*Baader–Meinhof* series, 1972) and the painting *Chinese Postcard* (1972, fig. 19) also exhibit new leftist interests. The last of these shows a postcard sent by a Maoist newspaper in reply to the author's letter. The carefully arranged composition of the postcard evokes the elevated rhetoric of socialist realism. Lakner enlarged and painted the picture, thereby putting it in quotation marks, as it were, creating a socialist realist composition both 'cancelled out and preserved'.

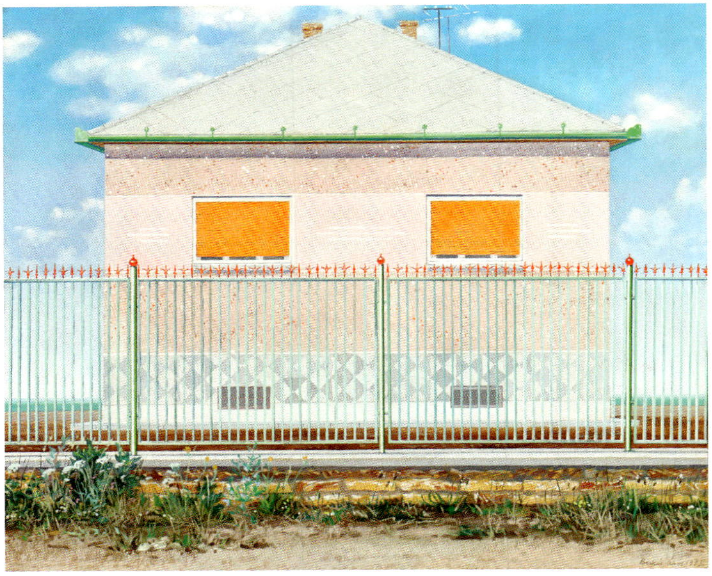

20

21

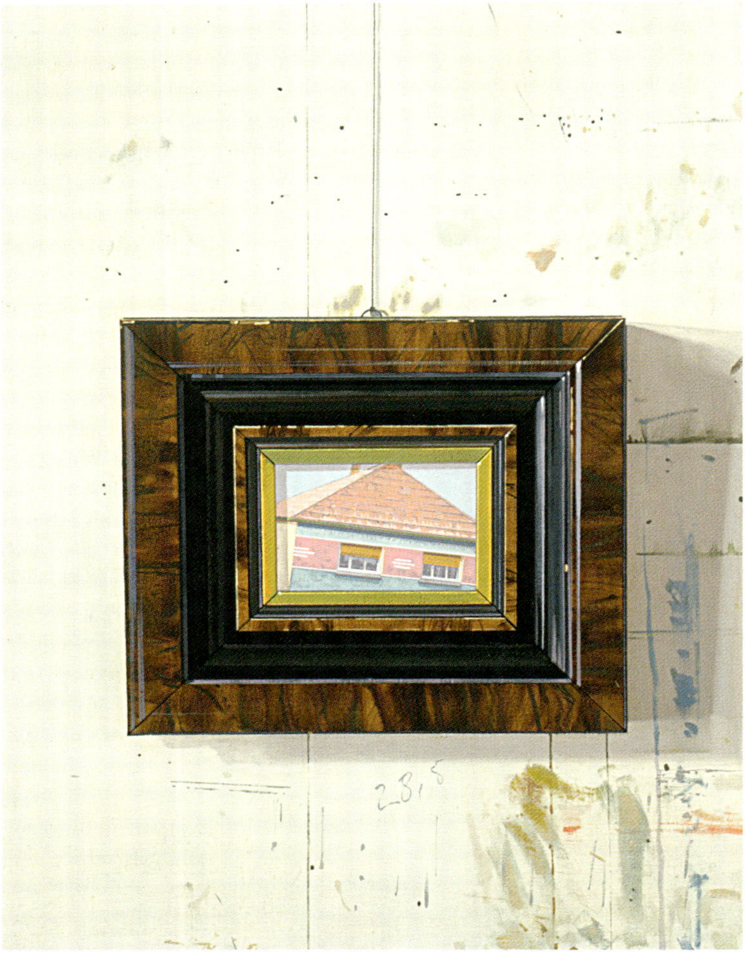

20. Ákos Birkás, *New House*, 1973, oil on canvas, 100 × 120 cm, Private collection

21. Ákos Birkás, *Wall and Picture*, 1973, oil on canvas, 80.5 × 60.5 cm, Szépművészeti Múzeum – Magyar Nemzeti Galéria, Budapest

22. Lóránt Méhes, *Identity Card*, 1972, oil on canvas, 60 × 80 cm, Private collection

In the early 1970s, other artists besides László Lakner and László Méhes turned to photorealist painting. Although this 'second wave' that came a few years later did not actually traverse the path from surnaturalism through pop art, the artists still were connected to this tradition. Ákos Birkás painted portraits reflecting existentialist interests and the influence of Giacometti's paintings in the 1960s, but turned to conceptualism and photo-based painting in the early 1970s (fig. 20). He painted detached houses typical of Hungarian villages in the 1970s, contrasting the era's dated cult of folk art with the interiors and external look of buildings representing the actual taste of ordinary people during that period. The compositions often take the form of a picture within the picture, like Lakner's conceptual trompe l'oeil paintings, probing the nature of realism and easel painting (fig. 21). Birkás said:

In 1972–75, I painted photo-based pictures. These had little to do with what is called photorealism, the painterly analysis you see in Franz Gertsch's or Chuck Close's pictures at the time. Let's put it this way, I was interested in articulating an 'aesthetic reality' opposed to the learned approach and the official ideology in my paintings: they represented new houses, typical details of the interior, and scenes composed of photos.[30]

He was clearly separating Western photorealist painting from the characteristics of photo-based realism in the Eastern bloc with its political connotations. This is true more generally of the majority of artists who opted for photo-based realism: the goal of painting photos of everyday topics was the display of an unidealized 'aesthetic reality' that could be opposed to official ideology.

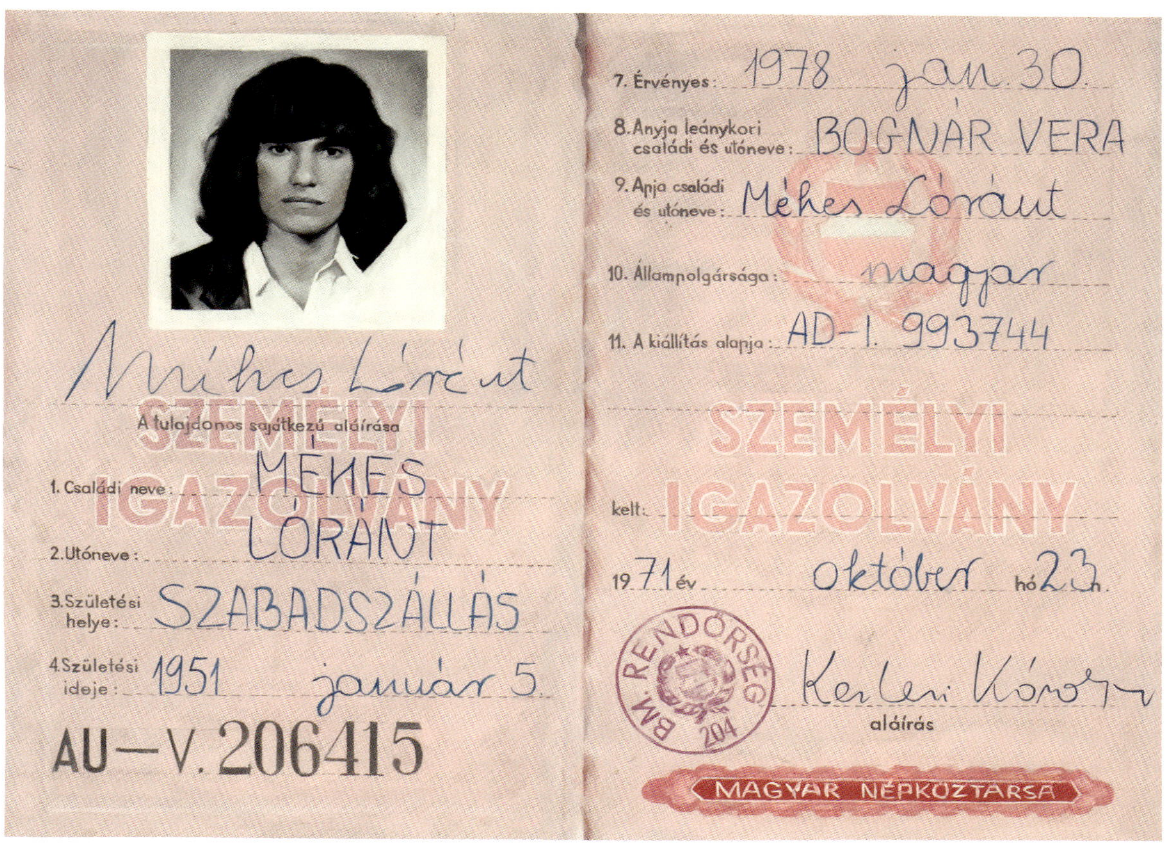

22

In this respect, two of the young artists who emerged in the early 1970s are exceptionally significant: Lóránt Méhes and László Fehér, for whom László Méhes's and László Lakner's paintings were a determining influence in the 1960s. Lóránt Méhes – no relation to László Méhes – created an early photorealist painting (*Modern Painting. Dad*, 1973), in which a faulty grey photo of his father is counterposed to the words '*modern festészet*' (modern painting) written on the surface in red block letters, probing the relationship of modernity and realism. In another early work, he painted his ID card (*Identity Card*, 1972, fig. 22). The stark look of the document enlarged in a conceptualist manner is a metaphor of surveillance and ideological control, which the artist, who looks like a hippy, confronts with a gaze filled with repressed impulses.

Underpass I (1975, fig. 23), which provoked a scandal when it was shown at the Magyar Képzőművészeti Főiskola, was painted by László Fehér a year after his graduation. The completely unadorned representation of a stark everyday reality was fiercely rejected by the institution, which prevented the artist from continuing his postgraduate studies. Fehér's painting, based on a crumpled and creased black-and-white photo, shows passersby walking up the stairs of an underpass in Budapest. The unidealized greyness, the trompe l'oeil effects of the painted creases and the replacement of the bright urban views (familiar as clichés of American photorealism) by a ruined and worn urban view appear as the critique of a hopeless East European existence. The motif of the stairs connecting darkness and light, however, gestures beyond the specific historical situation and becomes emblematic of the human condition characterizing socialist Hungary (like László Méhes's *Lukewarm Water* pictures).[31] An early series by Fehér, *Excerpts from the Brigade Diary* (1975, fig. 24), showing anonymous 'Stakhanovists' and based on blurry press photos, offers a ruthless vision of reality that turns the idealizing socialist realist representation of the worker into its opposite. The work fits into the long process that begins with the – often photo-based – surnaturalist representation of the worker in the late 1950s and leads to ironic-critical photorealist paintings of socialist brigades.[32]

The issue of personal memory becomes increasingly important in Fehér's paintings depicting everyday details of socialist Hungary, including people looking through the closed windows of the underground (*Underground*, 1976), grotesque situations (*Genre Painting*, 1979), family memories and unmaintained Jewish cemeteries. His works gesture towards a medium-conscious, photo-based, post-conceptual painting linking the photorealism of the 1970s and new directions in painting in the 1980s.[33] Although a number of important photorealist works date from after 1975 (see the works of Károly Kelemen, István Nyári, Imre Kocsis and Bernáth/y among others), a long process came to an end in the mid-1970s not only internationally but also in Hungary,[34] though the chief figures of this genre, which had begun in the late 1950s, were no longer living in Hungary.[35]

The topographic extension of the history of pop art and photorealism and the revision of the schematic opposition of 'banned' and 'supported' works in narratives of the Eastern bloc became important research topics in the 2010s. In light of recent comparative exhibitions, even a cursory overview of the arc from surnaturalism through pop art to photorealism in Hungary over a decade and a half warrants a revision of the earlier frequent yet erroneous notion that certain tendencies in East-Central-European art were 'imported'. One can speak of a cultural transfer or an international orientation and outlook, yet the apparent similarities of style conceal fundamentally different discourses and connections. Just like there was no pop art in Hungary in the strictest sense of the word, there was no photorealism either; it would be better to refer to a trend of socially and politically sensitive figurative painting, with its own internal connections and history, that can be positioned in the global history of 'popisms' and 'realisms', and is a significant precursor to current trends in figural painting.

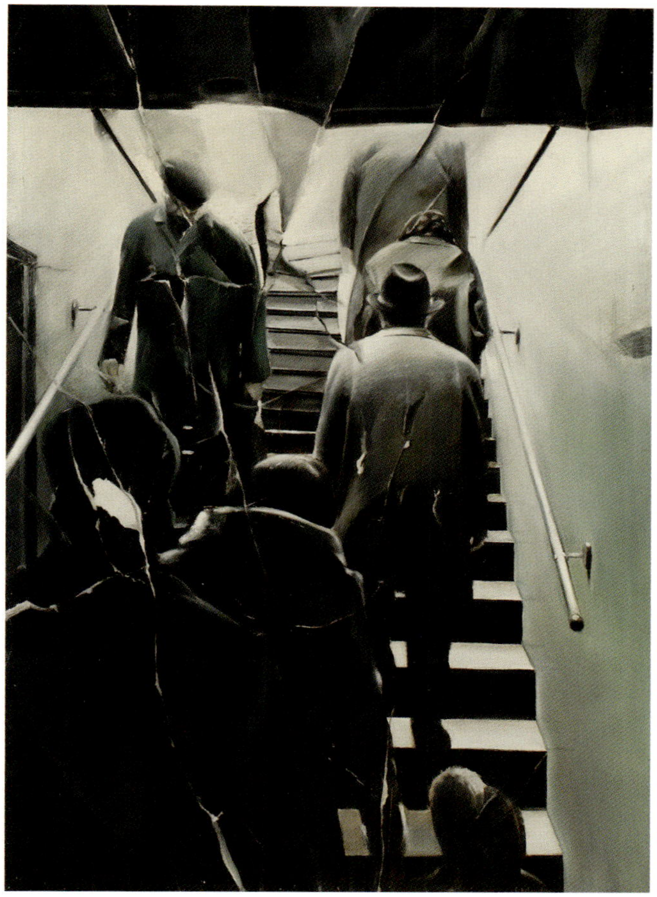

23

24

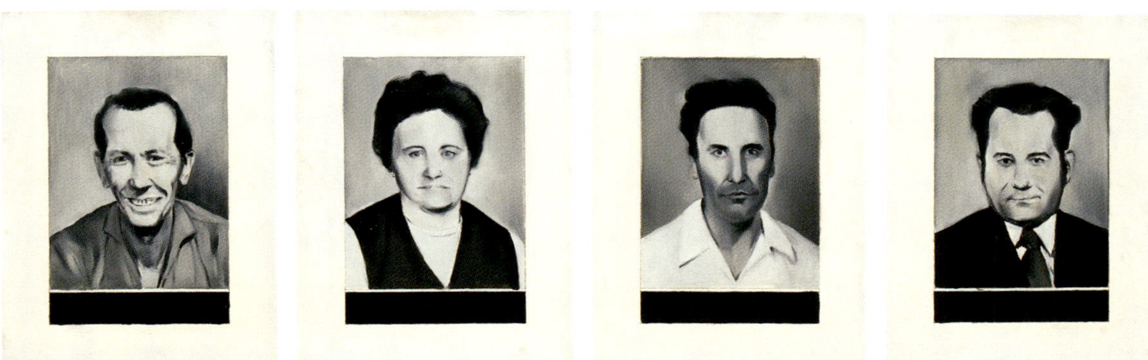

23. László Fehér, *Underpass I*, 1975, oil on fibreboard, 241 × 170 cm, Kiscelli Múzeum – Fővárosi Képtár, Budapest

24. László Fehér, *Excerpts from the Brigade Diary*, 1975, oil on plywood, each 62 × 46 cm, Private collection

1 On the problematic status of opposing abstraction and figuration in East–West terms, see John J. Curley, *A Conspiracy of Images: Andy Warhol, Gerhard Richter and the Art of the Cold War*. New Haven and London: Yale University Press, 2013, 10 ff.

2 The above phenomena were also accompanied by other 'medial turns' in the early 1960s in the international art scene, which can be linked primarily to the emergence of photo-, event- and language-based arts (e.g. Fluxus, conceptual art). The styles related to Fluxus and pop art evolved in parallel not only in the US and Western Europe but also in Eastern Europe.

3 Piotr Piotrowski also emphasizes the importance of a (negative) dialogue with socialist realism, when he adopts the general reference 'Un-Socialist Realism'. Piotr Piotrowski, *In the Shadow of Yalta: Art and Avant-garde in Eastern Europe, 1945–1989*. London: Reaktion Books, 2009, 147–77 (especially 166).

4 Géza Perneczky, 'A magyar "szür-naturalizmus" problémája' [The Problem of Hungarian Surnaturalism], in *Tanulmányút a pávakertbe* [Study Tour to Peacock Garden]. Budapest: Magvető, 1969, 78–102 (originally published in *Új Írás* in 1966).

5 Tibor Csernus, 'Pályakezdés: A művész emlékezései' [Starting a Career: Memories of an Artist] (excerpts from Tibor Kis's interview with Csernus Tibor, 1996), in Zsuzsa Varga (ed.), *Csernus Tibor*. Budapest: Helikon–EMA, 2000, 9.

6 Sándor Hornyik, 'Aesthetics in the Shadow of Politics: Surnaturalism and Magical Socialist Realism in Hungary in the Early Sixties', *Acta Historiae Artium*, Vol. 56, No. 1, 2015, 324–32 (especially 324–26).

7 For a more detailed analysis of *Reeds*, see Sándor Hornyik, 'A szürnaturalista kísérlet: Csernus Tibor és a szocialista realizmus' [The Surnaturalist Experiment: Tibor Csernus and Socialist Realism], *Ars Hungarica*, Vol. 37, No. 3, 2011, 14–18.

8 Dávid Fehér, *Lakner László*. Budapest: Hungart, 2013, 37.

9 On early Warhol and Ben Shahn see: Curley, *A Conspiracy of Images*, 55 ff.

10 *Dockyard Workers* paraphrases *Flagellation* by Piero della Francesca. See Lakner's statement on this in Edit Szentesi, 'Beszélgetés Lakner Lászlóval' [A Conversation with László Lakner], in Ildikó Nagy (ed.), *Hatvanas évek: új törek a magyar képzőművészetben* [The Sixties: New Strivings in Hungarian Visual Art] (exhibition catalogue). Budapest: Képzőművészeti Kiadó – Magyar Nemzeti Galéria – Ludwig Múzeum, 1991, 128–29, and Hornyik's analysis in Hornyik, 'Aesthetics in the Shadow of Politics, 327–28.

11 For a detailed history and interpretation of the work and for additional related literature, see Dávid Fehér, *László Lakner: Seamstresses Listen to Hitler's Speech* (exhibition catalogue). Budapest: Szépművészeti Múzeum, 2011.

12 See Hiroko Ikegami, *The Great Migrator: Robert Rauschenberg and the Global Rise of American Art*. Cambridge: MIT Press, 2010.

13 'International Pop', 11 April–29 August 2015 (curators: Darsie Alexander and Bartholomew Ryan); 'The World Goes Pop', Tate Modern, London, 17 September 2015–24 January 2016 (curators: Jessica Morgan and Flavia Frigeri).

14 Estonian artists appearing in the late 1960s (Sirje Helme: *Popkunst Forever. Estonian Pop Art at the Turn of the 1960s and 1970s*, Eesti Kunstimuuseum, KUMU, Tallinn, 2010) and Yugoslav tendencies related to pop art (in the work of Boris Bućan, Marko Pogačnik, Dušan Otašević and others) are equally significant.

15 Dávid Fehér, 'Where is the Light? Transformations of Pop Art in Hungary', in Darsie Alexander and Bartholomew Ryan (eds), *International Pop* (exhibition catalogue). Minneapolis: Walker Art Center, 2015, 135–52; and also see the debate provoked by Katalin Keserü, *Variations on Pop Art: Chapters in the History of Hungarian Art Between 1950 and 1990*. Budapest: Új Művészet Kiadó, 1993, and the eponymous exhibition (e.g. 'Katalin Timár: Is Your Pop Our Pop? The History of Art as a Self-Colonizing Tool', *Artmargins online*, 15 March 2002, http://www.artmargins.com/index.php/archive/323-is-your-pop-our-pop-the-history-of-art-as-a-self-colonizing-tool (20 August 2015).

16 'Pop etc.', Museum des 20. Jahrhunderts, Wien, 19 September–31 October 1964.

17 Cf. Curley, *A Conspiracy of Images*, 8.

18 Zsuzsa D. Fehér (ed.), *A magyar képzőművészek a fasizmus ellen* [Hungarian Artists against Fascism] (exhibition catalogue). Budapest: Magyar Nemzeti Galéria, 1965, 16.

19 Fehér, 'Where Is the Light?', 135 ff.

20 Marina Varga, 'Kísérleti helyzetek: Nyomkövetés Lakner Lászlóval: pop art, fotórealizmus és concept' [Experimental Situations: Tracking the Traces with László Lakner: Pop Art, Photorealism and Concept]. *Műértő*, June 2015, 11.

21 The human figure with an animal head recalls John Heartfield's montage *Zum Krisen-Parteitag der SPD* from 1931. (John Heartfield had a solo show in the Ernst Múzeum in Budapest in 1965.)

22 Varga, 'Kísérleti helyzetek', 11.

23 Quoted in János Brendel, *László Lakner: Das Frühwerk: Budapest, 1959–1973*. Budapest and Essen: Új Művészet Kiadó/Niessen Buch und Offsetdruckerei GmbH, 2000, 42.

24 For a more detailed discussion of the work, see Fehér, 'Where Is the Light?', 142.

25 *Groupe Iparterv – Le Progrès de l'Illusion. La troisième génération de l'avant-garde hongroise*. Paris: Institut Hongroise de Paris, 2010. In relation to pop art see Dávid Fehér, 'Pop Beyond Pop: Some Exhibitions of the Hungarian "Iparterv-Circle"', in Annika Öhrner (ed.), *Art in Transfer in the Era of Pop: Curatorial Practices and Transnational Strategies*. Stockholm: Södertörn University, 2017, 345–74.

26 For a historical summary of early Hungarian examples of photorealism, see Dávid Fehér, 'Painted Reality: The Beginnings of Photorealism in Hungary', in Nikolett Erőss (ed.), *East of Eden: Photorealism: Versions of Reality* (exhibition catalogue). Budapest: Ludwig Múzeum/Kortárs Művészeti Múzeum, 2012, 14–39.

27 Hungarian artists' first encounters with photorealist image construction can indeed be linked to socialist realism; *Stakhanovist at the Furniture Factory* (1950) by László Félegyházi and *Letter from the Front* (1947) by Aleksandr Ivanovich Laktionov come to mind.

28 Cf. László Beke, 'The Strange Afterlife of Socialist Realism', in Péter György and Hedvig Turai (eds), *Art and Society in the Age of Stalin*. Budapest: Corvina Kiadó, 1992, 122.

29 On this and on Lakner's 'leftist' works, see Dávid Fehér, 'Consonants of Karl Marx. Left vs Left in the Hungarian Neo-avantgarde: The Case of László Lakner', *Acta Historiae Artium*, Vol. 56, No. 1, 2015, 343–53.

30 Edit Sasvári, 'Ist es ein Gebäude oder ein weg?' [Is It a Building or a Way?], in Krisztina Szipőcs (ed.), *Birkás Ákos: Művek/Works 1975–2006* (exhibition catalogue). Budapest: Ludwig Múzeum/ Kortárs Művészeti Múzeum, 2006, 119.

31 Cf. Éva Forgács, *László Fehér*. Budapest: Új Művészet Könyvek, 1993, 5–9.

32 For example, László Lakner's painting *The Honoured Socialist Brigade of Ganz-MÁVAG* in 1972.

33 Cf. Lóránd Hegyi, 'Glimpses of Human Existence: Comments on the Art of László Fehér', in Rainer Fuchs (ed.), *László Fehér: Erinnerungen an Reales* (exhibition catalogue). Vienna: Museum Moderner Kunst Stiftung Ludwig Wien, 1997, 19–29.

34 While the European reception of pop art 'peaked' at the Kassel 'documenta' of 1968, that of photorealism peaked at the 'documenta' of 1972, organized by Harald Szeemann and entitled *Befragung der Realität (Questioning Reality)*. In the second half of the 1970s, new realist tendencies in painting were already receiving less attention internationally.

35 Tibor Csernus emigrated to Paris in 1964, Ákos Szabó in 1965 and Gyula Konkoly in 1970; László Gyémánt moved to London in 1970 and only returned in 1982; László Lakner has been living in (West) Germany since 1974; László Méhes did not emigrate to Paris until 1979 (after a prolonged stay there in 1972–73), but he gave up photorealist painting around 1975.

1. Ferenc Martyn, *Composition*, 1948, oil on canvas, 80 × 100 cm, Szépművészeti Múzeum – Magyar Nemzeti Galéria, Budapest

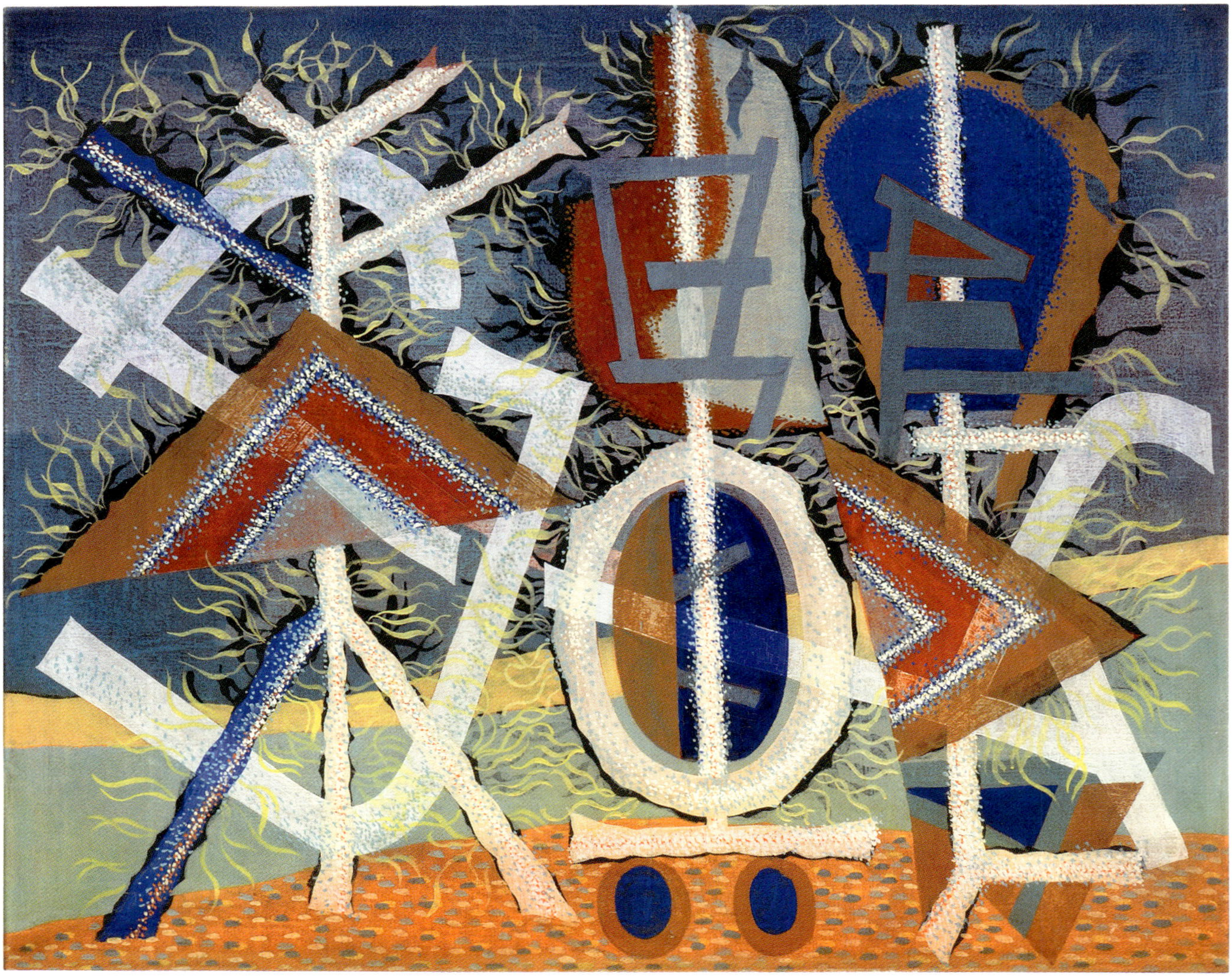

1

Abstract Boundaries

The Changing Principles of Art Policy in 1958–68

Looking back on the Hungary of the 1950s and 1960s with the hindsight of over fifty years, the official standpoint on abstract art seems to have been clear: official art policy appears to have interpreted abstraction as an unambiguously negative and therefore prohibited concept. Upon closer inspection, however, the picture becomes more nuanced. One can see the rippling boundaries of official art, their constant shift from a strict rejection or cautious toleration of 'Western' tendencies, and the Janus-faced rejection of abstraction as autonomous art and its acceptance as 'decoration' in design and architecture. In fact, the attitude to abstract art can be grasped best in terms of other concepts, such as realism and the shifting position on socialist realism. The period examined here is approximately a decade, from the late 1950s to the late 1960s. It begins with the ideological rigidity that set in after the brief thaw following the 1956 revolution against Soviet-style control, and it ends with the last years of the 1960s, when the issue of abstract art quietly vanished from ideological debates.

Everywhere across the world, hostility to abstraction was a conservative objection to the experimental spirit of the avant-garde. Yet, in Hungary in the 1950s, it was also complemented by official prohibition, which was not merely a function of Marxist dogma but also a device of populist politics. At the same time, the attitude towards abstraction involved a fundamental characteristic of Kádár's Hungary (1956–88): a restricted access to lifestyles on the Western model, which was at least partly manifested in the acceptance of modern visual elements of the Western world. Changes in the quality of life were detectable in objects that were born of the Western style: modern pictures and aspects of the cultural environment that slowly and almost secretly integrated into everyday life. While abstraction in the visual arts was lampooned in caricatures and satirical texts, this integration is detectable in Hungarian feature films in the early 1960s. In addition to being a symbol of socialist progress, modernity was a safety valve in János Kádár's politics in a specifically Hungarian context: it served to deflect and contain the critique of the Soviet-type socialist regime through aesthetic sublimation. (Over the course of ten years, this process reached the point in 1966 where the set of *Táncdalfesztivál* [Song Contest], the most popular talent show on Hungarian television, consisted of abstract elements reminiscent of Bridget Riley's works.) While the official standpoint on abstract visual art remained negative until the end of the 1960s, numerous Hungarian visual artists exploited the possibilities of this political safety valve and included abstract motifs in their decorative works in public spaces and in works of applied art. The entire decade is dogged by ambivalence: it is an amalgamation of official political pressure and aesthetic laxness, populism and modernity, and prohibition and access to information. The conservative/modern duality of the cultural environment in Hungary,[1] though in numerous respects similar to the dynamic of the Western scene, can be traced in the changing course of official prohibition.

One cannot understand how abstract art was interpreted by cultural politics after 1956 without reference to the debates that transpired in the second half of the 1940s. Like in other countries in the sphere of Soviet political interest, abstraction was branded as formalism in Hungary in 1947–48, following the Soviet model that made it a rejected or even banned tendency in art. One of the intellects driving this approach was Georg Lukács, a top ideological authority of the emerging new regime. Lukács, who otherwise rarely discussed the visual arts, devoted a major study to this issue.[2] He expressed his opposition to the spread of 'confused bourgeois ideas' and – with regard to abstraction – to Ernő Kállai, a notable figure of East-Central European art theory in the interwar years, and his favoured scientific worldview, which had significantly influenced numerous artists. Lukács's main arguments would be familiar from an earlier debate on expressionism,[3] namely, that abstraction, which was not a style, went against the classical, realist and humanist traditions of European art. Lukács did not hold any official position in the Communist Party at the time, but Hungary's Stalinist authorities still needed his support as he was the only internationally recognized Marxist thinker who returned to Hungary after the Second World War.

The aesthetic objections and the subsequent, increasingly strident political attacks on abstraction after 1947–48 marginalized the work of various avant-garde groups and artists championing different types of abstraction. For instance, Aurél Bernáth (see Sándor Hornyik, 'Reforming Socialist Realism', pp. 113–35, and Dávid Fehér, '(Dis) figuring Reality', pp. 137–59), an advocate of the conservative traditions of Hungarian painting – which he supported in his capacity as department chair at the Magyar Képzőművészeti Főiskola (Hungarian Academy of Fine Arts) – attacked abstract art in the name of figurative painting representing reality. The Európai Iskola (European School; see Gábor Dobó and Merse Pál Szeredi, 'Hungarian Culture +/- Europe', pp. 39–57, and Júlia Perczel, 'The Art Sphere as a Grey Zone', pp. 59–75) was not the only group to be forced to close down; the Elvont Művészek Csoportja (Group of Abstract Artists), with members such as Tihamér Gyarmathy, Tamás Lossonczy and Ferenc Martyn (fig. 1),[4] also had to cease activities. The denouncement of abstraction was already playing a major role in the marginalization of autonomous art initiatives by the mid-1950s. The general cultural thaw following Stalin's death in 1953 did not change the situation; the rehabilitation of nonfigurative and surrealist artists belonging to a variety of trends or movements was practically out of the question until the 1956 revolution. It seemed possible for a brief moment after the revolution that the authorities that controlled cultural politics might strengthen autonomy in order to correct the mistakes of the early 1950s, of which even representatives of the communist regime were now aware. The exhibition 'Konstruktív törekvések' (Constructive Tendencies) held at Nemzeti Szalon (National Salon) in Budapest in 1957, served primarily the 'rehabilitation' of Cézanne, Hungarian cubism and expressionist activism. 'Tavaszi Tárlat' (Spring Exhibition) was held at Műcsarnok (Kunsthalle) in Budapest in same year, in the illusory spirit of a return to the brief thaw before 1956.

One of the four juries set up for the selection of works for the latter exhibition was specifically devoted to modernists labelled 'constructivists', a label that covered artists creating abstract works. The exhibition was part of a broader plan for institutional reform,[5] and it was meant to provide an opportunity to exhibit for abstract artists who had been marginalized by cultural politics, and to give them long-term, if somewhat restricted, opportunities for sales. Artists who had been working without any hope of exhibiting for years now had their artworks on display but their various forms of lyrical and geometric abstract experiments would bear the brunt of hostile criticism, even though the exhibition attracted great public interest.

Plans for relaxing strict institutional control had been shelved by the fall of 1957, partly as a result of public denouncements of the 'Tavaszi Tárlat'. The department of visual arts in the Művelődésügyi Minisztérium (Ministry of Culture), headed by thirty-three-year-old hardliner Nóra Aradi,[6] seized full control. Consequently, abstract art was once again excommunicated after this brief interlude, even as the reprisals following the 1956 revolution were in progress. At the same time, there was an attempt to fill the concept of socialist realism with new content as a corrective. While the representatives of abstract art in Poland and Yugoslavia had limited or complete access to the public sphere, Hungary and other countries of the region toed the Soviet line in this respect as well.

The concept of the 'two-front battle', which was prominent in political discourse in the wake of the 1956 revolution, was similarly central to the principles of the Kádár regime's art policies. The concept referred to a simultaneous rejection of leftist dogmatism and attempts to revive the ideas of the interwar years. In terms of art, this meant empty naturalism or petit bourgeois kitsch on the one hand and the supposed anti-humanity of abstraction on the other. 'Those who popularized an obsolete naturalism and anti-human trends after the counter-revolution were not justified in claiming to do so in the spirit of artistic freedom,' wrote Nóra Aradi.[7] Yet the criticism in the official art press was lopsided: its most avowed claim in 1958 was that abstraction was the greatest enemy of socialist realism; meanwhile, the fight against naturalism and kitsch was left to the future and to visual education. The system was seeking to reclaim its clear boundaries and to return to the Stalinist guideline of art that was 'socialist in content, national in form'. The new modified political stance after the revolution claimed that the new culture was now offering a synthesis of populist and national characteristics with humanism on a higher level. Abstract artists who were 'isolated from society' and had 'abandoned reality' by constructing their own world did not fit into this framework. According to the official position, abstraction was opposed to socialist humanism and expressed the inhumanity and anti-humanism of capitalism.[8] The official terms, drawn from the ideological vocabulary of earlier years, for this tendency were 'abstract aristocracy' and 'the artistically inferior speculation' of parasites. So, the official attitude combined anti-avant-garde clichés that were over half a century old and the veneer of ideology.

Nóra Aradi thought one of the most important lessons of the 1958 Venice Biennale (the first that was held in the brand-new Hungarian pavilion, rebuilt in the same year) was that 'the insanities called modern' had lost their mass base internationally as well.[9] While her criticism, in the spirit of the cold war, primarily targeted Western artistic tendencies, other reviews were returning to the debates of the late 1940s, when the assessment of abstraction was linked to a demand for content accessible to the public.[10] The expression 'experimental art', occasionally used in Western Europe, also appeared in Hungarian political terminology at the same time; this could refer to modernist, constructivist abstract art or to the artistic use of similarly prohibited surrealist elements. 'Although our so-called experimental attempts are more moderate, they are no less fanatical than most of the experiments on display at the Biennale,' Nóra Aradi remarked critically in reference to Hungarian artists. Broadly, the sentence was connected with the increasingly prominent critical Western views that saw signs of the dehumanization of art in abstraction and modernism. Specifically, she must have been referring to the Hungarian artists who had been on the jury for the abstract section of the 'Tavaszi Tárlat', such as Tihamér Gyarmathy (fig. 2), who consistently stood by abstract art during his internal exile throughout the 1950s. The rhythmic multi-plane system of geometric elements in his works began to include occasional stylized figures in the late 1950s (*Nuclear Destruction*, 1960), which were less akin to socialist realism than to French surrealism and Pablo Picasso's work.

As abstraction flourished abroad and the works of American abstract expressionists poured into Europe, some advocated allowing 'experimental art' at least minimal exposure, if for no other reason than to know one's enemy. Lajos Vayer, an art historian specializing in the Renaissance, was the Hungarian commissioner for the Venice Biennale. He claimed that even though 'bourgeois decadence, and the resulting bleak and pointless future of art and the pestilence of the art trade are exposed to the public and increasingly to the critics by the "works" that make a mockery of art at the Biennale – this does not suffice to show the path towards development'.[11]

Art policy saw the key to development as the collaboration between architecture and visual art, which was to take advantage of the

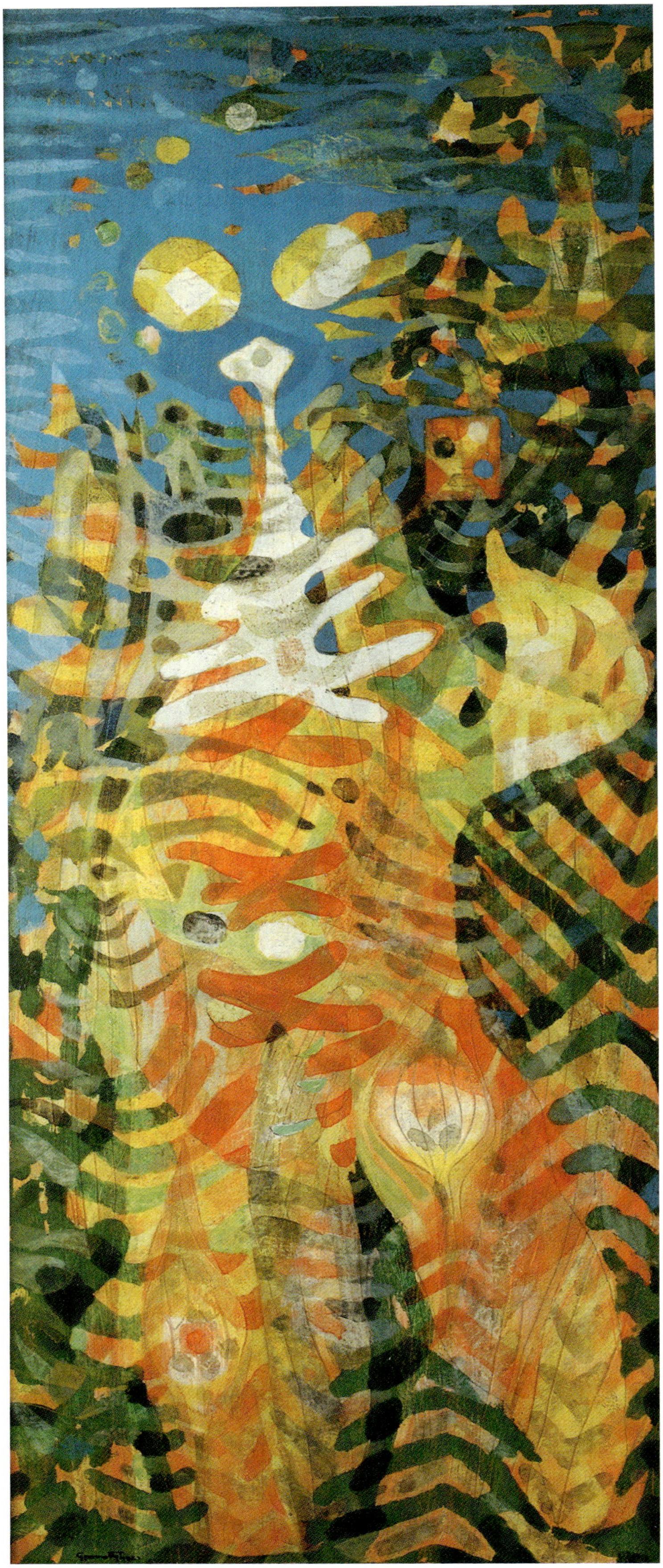

2. Tihamér Gyarmathy, *Metamorphosis*, 1960, oil on fibreboard, 122 × 50 cm, Private collection

possibilities of communal art – in a politically and ideologically revised sense – as opposed to initiatives of autonomous, i.e. independent and individualistic, art.[12] This essentially meant that the only option for the development of experimental art, at least in terms of officially sanctioned work, was architectural decoration. (In fact, a panel painting at the Hungarian Pavilion of the 1958 Brussels World's Fair was allowed to remain on display, despite the objections of the Művelődésügyi Minisztérium, when the organizers classified it as decoration.[13]) Nonfigurative mural works and abstract elements that could be used as decoration simultaneously functioned as loopholes for artists and, in terms of state assessment, external to art proper. Theory preceded practice in the late 1950s, when a handful of public buildings in the regional towns (in Dunaújváros and Tiszaújváros, for example) had abstract mosaics or ceramic murals installed, but such commissions did not become frequent in Hungary until the mid-1960s. So, design became the escape route from the dogmatic dead end of art policy in the solidifying Kádár regime. This was concurrent with the aesthetic trend that aimed to dissolve rigid political boundaries, and which entailed the showing of French and Italian films in the cinema and the appearance of images of Western European cities in the magazines. Through the accounts of Hungarian actors, musicians and singers returning from Western (primarily Italian and French) tours, the public could also learn about the way that abstract forms were being used to dominate the modern environment, and could adopt the surface elements for use at home.

The explorations of Hungarian official art in the late 1950s had some solid points of orientation, the most solid of all being the statement that abstraction and (socialist) realism were mutually exclusive concepts – in conformity with the Soviet position most steadfastly represented by a prominent figure of Soviet art policy, Vladimir Kemenov.[14] Ideologues such as Nóra Aradi and Gábor Ö. Pogány, director of the Magyar Nemzeti Galéria (Hungarian National Gallery), who applied cold-war political rhetoric to art were vocal supporters of this position in Hungary. Yet the same Gábor Ö. Pogány called Lajos Kassák the greatest abstract artist in the catalogue of Kassák's exhibition at the Galerie Denise René in Paris and lauded him in a review. The Hungarian media only occasionally covered Western art exhibitions and even then through an ideological filter; they always positioned abstraction as a counterpoint to socially embedded 'communal' art. While French visual arts remained an important reference point, what actually reached a restricted public in Hungary was limited to a few marginal realist groups – primarily the works of those artists connected to the Salon Populiste who had contact with Hungarian artists.[15] All forms of abstraction – as well as surrealism – were shrouded in silence. Of the older avant-garde artists, neither Lajos Kassák, who experimented with lyrical abstraction in 1957–60, nor Dezső Korniss, who used various calligraphic elements in his works in this period, could appear in the public sphere in Hungary at the time (see also Gábor Dobó and Merse Pál Szeredi, 'Hungarian Culture +/- Europe', pp. 39–57).[16] Korniss stood by his artistic principles unwaveringly, continuously producing calligraphic pictures, which had their precursors in his 'drip' works in the 1940s, between 1958 and 1963. While the works of the late 1950s were closer to action painting, gestures soon arranged themselves into scripts in his paintings (for instance, in *Calligraphy*, 1963).

At the end of the 1950s, the top priority for official art policy was not the task of marginalizing elderly artists, but rather the effort to prevent the spread of modern Western art trends among the young. Behind the veneer of seeming laxness at the Magyar Képzőművészeti Főiskola, there lurked the critique and prohibition of Western art. The surrealist and magic realist influences in the works of Tibor Csernus or László Lakner were subject to especially severe ideologically motivated criticism (see also Sándor Hornyik, 'Reforming Socialist Realism', pp. 113–35). It attests to the ambivalence of art policy that the very same visual elements that could be found dangerous in a painting or at an exhibition were acceptable on a book cover classified as belonging to design and applied art. For instance, Tibor Csernus's cover design for one of the most popular Hungarian books of the period, *Generation of Rust* by Endre Fejes, was reminiscent of surrealism.

Yet the authorities found it increasingly difficult to maintain the strategy of strict prohibition in the period of the general thaw, and specifically the cultural thaw represented particularly by György Aczél on the Central Committee of the ruling Magyar Szocialista Munkáspárt (MSZMP, Hungarian Socialist Workers' Party), that followed the reprisals against participants in the 1956 revolution. Following the initiatives related to de-Stalinization in the mid-1950s, the cultural policy of the early 1960s was one of a cautious reassessment of the past. Young artists were quickly handed various opportunities in the spirit of creating a new socialist culture. (Such activities happened in every branch of culture, and representatives of different disciplines were, at that time, allowed to launch joint institutions: the young stage director Miklós Szinetár, composer Emil Petrovics and literary historian Tamás Ungvári could found a musical theatre company in the early 1960s, and this was also how István Szabó, the future Oscar winner, could make several feature films in his twenties.) The thaw also entailed a revival of the Bartókian programme of the interwar period (in which there was a modernist approach, inspired by composer Béla Bartók's synthesis of Hungarian folk culture and European modernism) and the cautious relaxing of the restrictions on artistic freedom (including the occasional Western study trip) in order to prevent the exodus of the intelligentsia. This context increasingly undermined the art policy advocated by hardliners like Nóra Aradi, which focused on maintaining boundaries and insisted on the fundamental tenet of the ban of abstraction. Although the situation was similar in other socialist countries, the impact of the thaw was different in each place, as vividly demonstrated by the regional, and particularly Polish, aftermath of a large exhibition held in Moscow in late 1958 entitled 'Art of the Socialist Countries': soon afterwards, the Polish Communist Party would issue a rather amusing directive permitting no more than 'fifteen per cent of abstraction' in any exhibition of visual arts.[17] By the turn of the 1950s and 1960s, there was a paramount and pressing need to reassess the avant-garde traditions of the interwar period and to mark the boundaries of an inescapably experimental art being created by a new generation that had come of age after the war – art that was distanced from the dogmatic spirit of the 1950s, though it was still called socialist realism.

Debates in journals, particularly literary journals, became an important tool of Aczél's cultural policy in the early 1960s; state power influenced and controlled the debates, while using them as safety valves. One of the most influential debates in the area of the visual arts dealt primarily with the issue of abstraction and became known as the *Új Írás* (New Writing) debate, named after the journal. The intensely discussed debate, which aimed at a reassessment of the position of abstract art, was triggered by an article published by the reformist art historian Lajos Németh in 1961.[18] In his discussion of abstraction, Németh returned to the platform of the reform initiatives of the 'Tavaszi Tárlat' exhibition held four years earlier: the '"Tavaszi Tárlat" [...] proved that our visual art rejected the 1949–56 period and [...] wanted to return to the pre-1949 foundations. Yet the image presented by the "Tavaszi Tárlat" was subsequently modified as the extreme naturalists and the abstracts were once again marginalized and nonfigurative projects were relegated to architectural decoration.' At the same time, Németh lamented the loss of Bartókian cultural standards and used the fashionable concept of modernity (which had also been reassessed in Moscow by that time) to criticize disconnection from the international tendencies of modern art: 'The modernity of our visual art is surely at least half a century behind Bartók's modernity, even though Bartók has been dead for a decade and a half. And whoever accepts *Allegro Barbaro* cannot view Picasso's black period in bewilderment.'[19] Németh professed a view that had not been publicly espoused since 1948, namely that experimental efforts must not be repressed through administrative measures; on the contrary, opportunities need to be offered for making them known: 'Korniss arranged a highly successful exhibition in Western Europe, and the television in Amsterdam showed his picture among Picasso's and Braque's, so an open discussion of his art is the least he deserves.'[20] When discussing young artists, Németh's article once again touches on the problem of official prohibition;

he asks why the perhaps most talented Hungarian painters, Béla Kondor and Tibor Csernus, are only allowed to work as illustrators.

Lajos Németh's pamphlet immediately made waves. Critics loyal to the regime brandished the decade-old concept of socialist realism to question the ideological commitment of the art historian and asked whether Németh chose public debate in order to defeat abstraction in the open or because he saw nonfigurative trends as the future of socialist art. Nóra Aradi, who had already lost her position at the Művelődésügyi Minisztérium by 1961 as a result of conflicts with György Aczél, reacted to the critical questions with exceptional rancour: she castigated the artists who were choosing 'a dangerous path' as proponents of existentialist philosophy, a term which had negative connotations, in terms of cultural policy, in the late 1950s and early 1960s (to the point of annihilating the ideological opponent). Aradi nearly self-evidently connected abstraction with vacuity and bluffing, and with the charge that revisionist artists in Hungary – even though they received commissions for architectural decoration and ornamental works – failed to appreciate state funding while not hesitating to exploit it. A similarly stilted and hostile tone was struck by Gábor Ö. Pogány, director of Magyar Nemzeti Galéria and the most important representative of official art policy in the 1960s besides Aradi: 'As Socialist art becomes stronger, it renders all types of nonfigurative foolhardiness anachronistic.'[21] The expression 'nonfigurative foolhardiness' referred primarily to the work of those who stood by abstraction for decades despite its prohibition; they included Ferenc Martyn and Tamás Lossonczy, who had been severely criticized in the late 1940s, then briefly tried to conform to the expectations of cultural policy in the early 1950s only to sharply turn against them once again. After a trip to Paris, Martyn returned to geometric abstraction in the early 1960s, while Lossonczy returned to the surrealist bio-romantic approach he had developed by combining figurative and nonfigurative elements in the interwar period, as demonstrated by his painting *Great Purifying Storm* completed in 1962 (fig. 3).

3

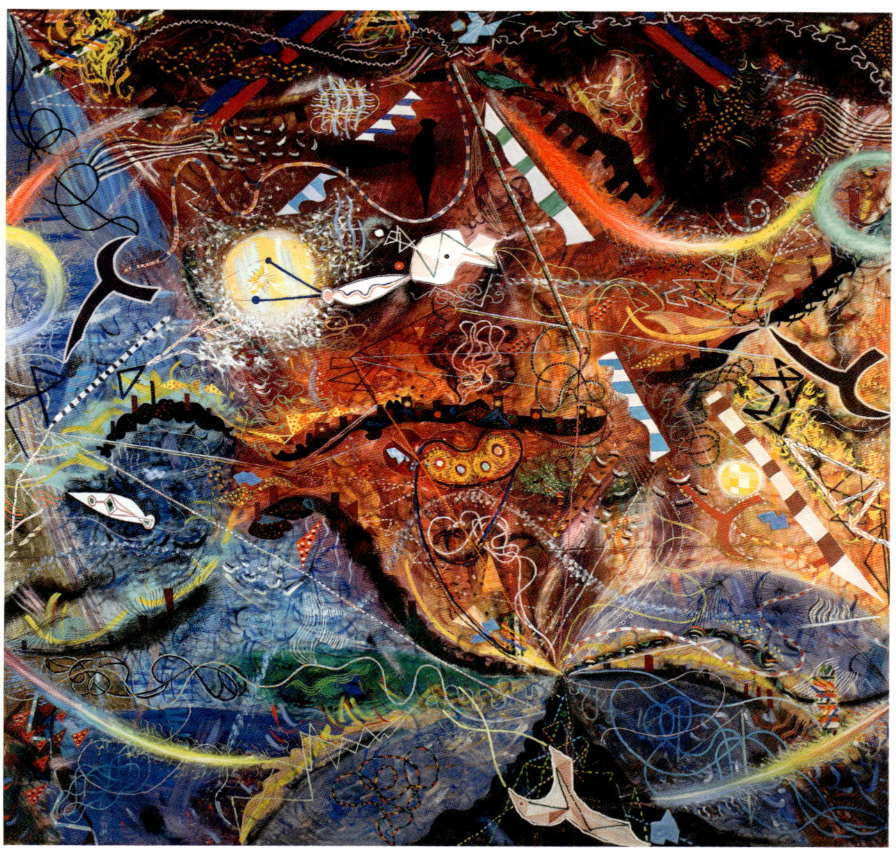

3. Tamás Lossonczy, *Great Purifying Storm*, 1962, oil on canvas, 300 × 300 cm, Szépművészeti Múzeum – Magyar Nemzeti Galéria, Budapest

The debate ended in 1963, when uttering the claim that experimental art was justified was no longer deemed sacrilege, due to the general political thaw and its effect on cultural policy. Ferenc Lantos (fig. 4), an abstract artist working in Pécs, who moved from figurative realist painting to geometric abstraction based on figural motifs (*Coal Separator in Komló*, 1960) in the course of the 1950s, argued that the boundary between realism and abstraction was actually an abstract construction, which he deduced from Marx's concept of reality:

An arbitrary categorization was developed with the tacit approval of both parties: today's artists are either experimental or realist ones. [...] It follows from what has been said above that one may choose to classify each artist as experimental or one may choose to classify them as realist. It follows, in turn, that each 'classification' is mistaken and overly subjective. There is no separate realist and experimental art.[22]

Whereas the attacks by the official art authorities simultaneously targeted modernist tendencies and neo-avant-garde artistic initiatives,[23] the gradual thaw of politics and cultural policy created an environment in which the rigid boundaries between abstraction and realism were beginning to blur.

Besides older and middle-aged artists in internal exile (such as Kassák and Gyarmathy, respectively), there was a number of young artists emerging in the early 1960s who could spend a period abroad (in Western Europe) and learn about contemporary trends in Western art thanks to the shift in cultural policy that gave the intelligentsia greater freedom. The Hungarian public sphere – press coverage and exhibitions – could still be controlled by application of art policy at this point, but the flow of information couldn't. Another way the young had access to information was through learning about the works of older Hungarian masters, particularly Dezső Korniss. He was the greatest influence on the abstract expressionist work of Endre Tót (fig. 5) between 1963 and 1968, Krisztián Frey's calligraphic works and Tamás Hencze's gesture painting with affinities to French tachism. Ilona Keserü was influenced by Ferenc Martyn at a young age and the traditions of Hungarian

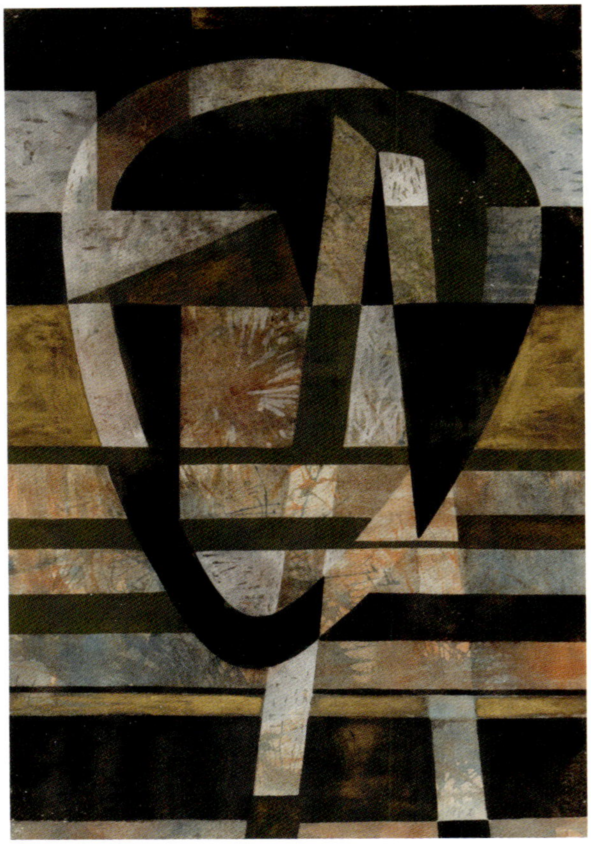

4

4. Ferenc Lantos, *Head*, 1961, gouache on paper, 43.5 × 29.5 cm, Janus Pannonius Múzeum, Pécs

5. Endre Tót, *Untitled (Bust)*, 1965, mixed technique, paper, 27.2, × 21 cm, Private collection

abstraction, as well as the formal repertoire of East and West European avant-garde (fig. 6). The first time Keserü saw abstract paintings – works by Tadeusz Kantor and Maria Jarema – at a public exhibition was in the early 1960s, when she visited Poland. Her own works still mixed abstract, semi-abstract and figural principles of image production. In 1962–63, she spent a year in Italy, where she was taken with the art of the Italian abstract painter Achille Perilli and that of the American Cy Twombly. When she returned home, her lyrical abstract works became more playful, and her wave motifs were created in a force field between gesture and geometric form.

The group later known as Zuglói kör (Zugló Circle) already existed in the late 1950s in Budapest as a self-study group (see also Flóra Barkóczi, 'Creative (Dis)Courses', pp. 95–109). Its core members included Sándor Molnár, Imre Bak (fig. 7), Pál Deim (fig. 8) and István Nádler. The circle, which continuously expanded in the early 1960s, explored ways to catch up with and connect to Western – primarily French – abstract art and forgotten Hungarian traditions. They organized debate nights, translated art theoretical texts from foreign languages and held studio visits. For instance, they visited Dezső Korniss and Tihamér Gyarmathy, members of the banned surrealist group Európai Iskola. Since the official art world refused to accept works by the artists in the circle – given their affinities to lyrical abstraction and particularly the works of Jean Bazaine – they began to present them in studio exhibitions in 1963.

The process of fermentation that began among the younger generation, possibly as a result of the thaw in cultural policy, seems to have occurred in parallel with the analogous process in official art policy. One of the central ideas of this thaw was the possibility of convergence between Eastern and Western approaches to realism, and the formation of a similar platform opposed to abstraction – which would entail an easing of restrictions by the Eastern side. From the vantage point of Eastern Europe in the early 1960s, it may have seemed that contemporary French and German artistic objectives, which included liberation from the influence of American abstract expressionism, might actually be compatible with socialist art's visions of the future.

5

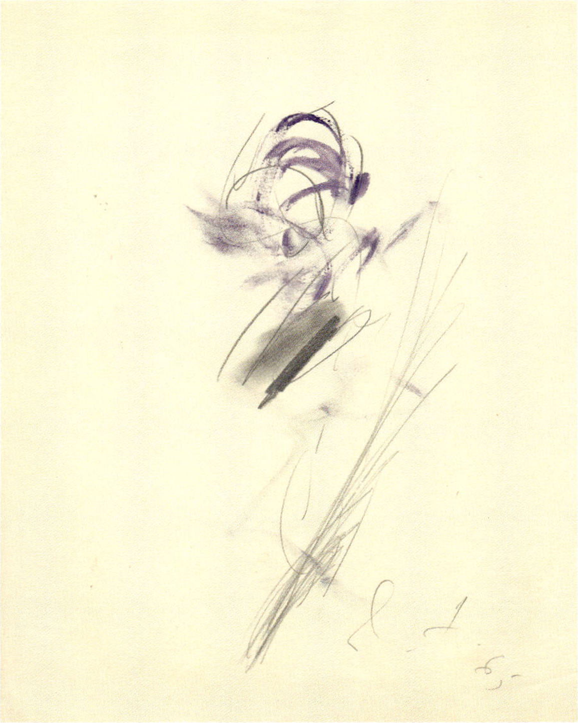

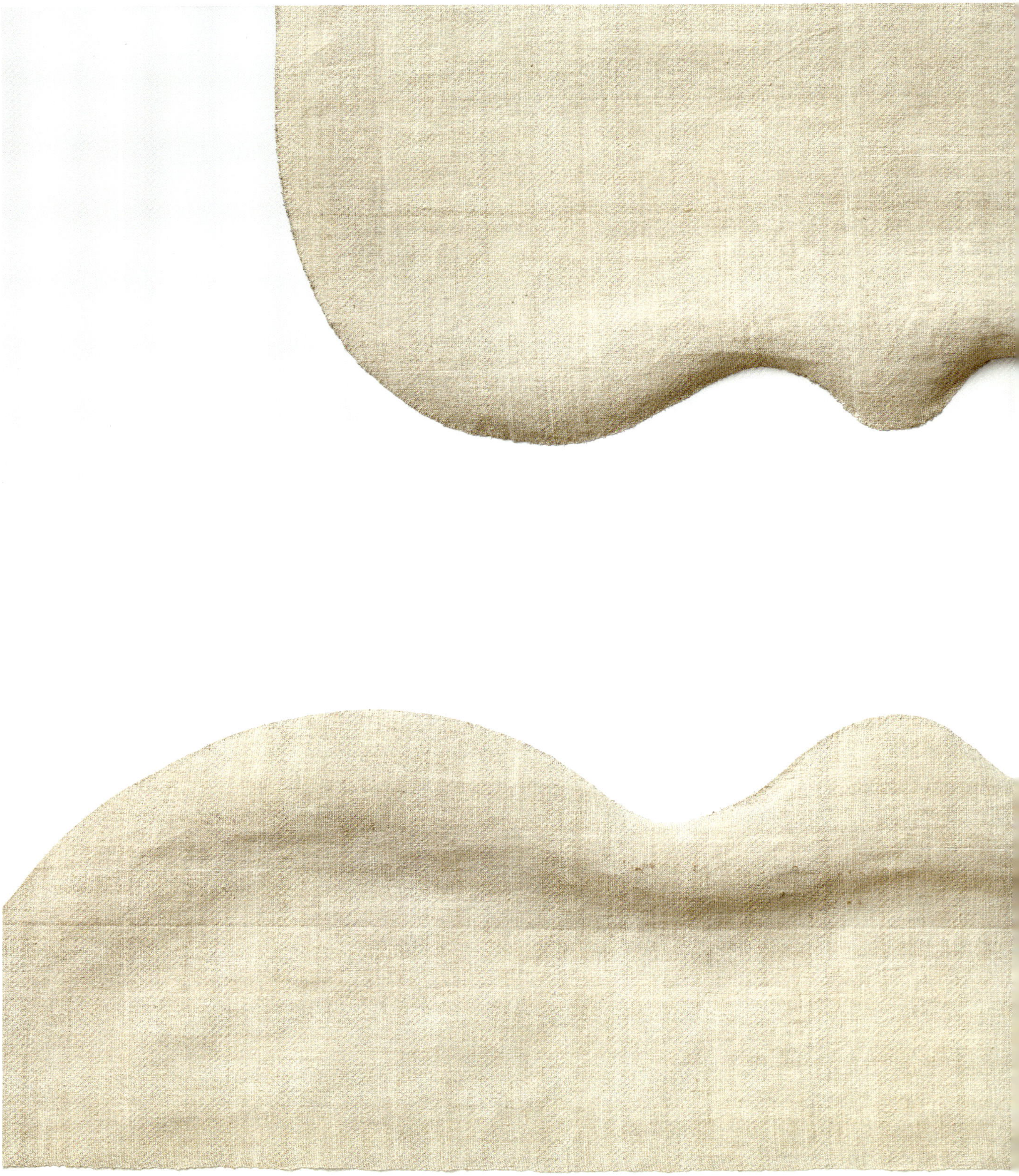

6

6. Ilona Keserü, *Approach II*, 1969, shaped canvas, 120 × 140 × 4 cm, Kolozsváry Collection, Győr

7. Imre Bak, *Stripes No. 1*, 1968, acrylic on canvas, 135.5 × 240 cm, Ludwig Múzeum – Kortárs Művészeti Múzeum, Budapest

8. Pál Deim, *Man and House*, 1969, oil on wood, 160 × 200 cm, Szépművészeti Múzeum – Magyar Nemzeti Galéria, Budapest

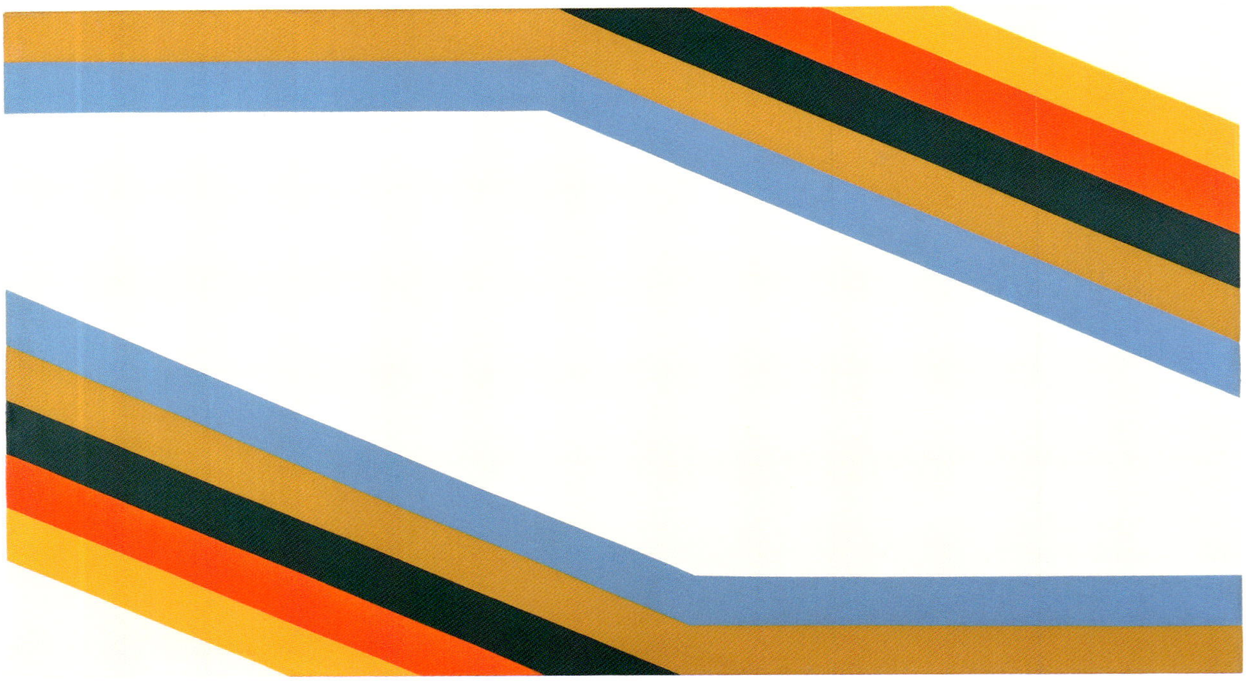

7

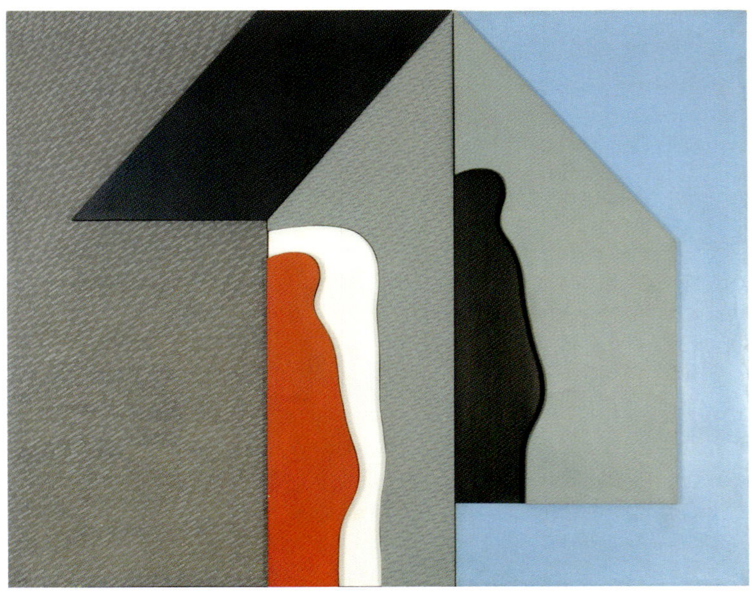

8

The ideological wall that had been built within Hungarian visual arts as a bulwark against abstraction after the 1956 revolution was about to fall in the mid-1960s. *Művészet* (Art), the official journal of the visual arts, still refused to publish reproductions of abstract works, and official state, county and local venues refused to exhibit the work of abstract artists, but the earlier rigidly negative and often sarcastic tone was disappearing. Even Nóra Aradi's volume *Absztrakt képzőművészet* (Abstract Visual Art), published in 1964, appears to be an attempt to modify her earlier rigid position rather than to set up a new line of defence.[24] Aradi tries to prove the superiority of modern realism over an 'obsolete' bourgeois art that reflects the 'contradictions of the imperialist period'. She justifies the discussion of the topic with the claim that thinking about the possible future of the visual arts requires one to study abstraction, which is popularized in the West as a type of ideological export and which 'exhibits and professes the morality of a rootless, unrestrained and irresponsible individual behaviour'. The shift in emphasis in the volume appears primarily in the assessment of the past. Aradi draws a firm line between the representatives of the early avant-garde 'seeking justice outside social reality' and their errant successors: in these terms, Piet Mondrian is a formalist dead end. Aradi thinks that abstract art, which consciously feeds social alienation, is incompatible with the art of socialist countries as a result of the past, and consequently it can only have a supplementary decorative architectural function today. The cold-war rhetoric remains when Aradi claims that 'the conflict of two social systems is also reflected in art', but the conclusion of the volume admits that the idea of convergence might be applicable to the visual arts, as 'We are on the verge of a new universality.' This envisioned outcome appears rather lopsided, however: it will be the rise of the socialist period of art history.

At the time the volume came out, in 1964, there was an enormous gap between the cultural projections of the official political party line and the actual artistic tendencies in Hungary, primarily the new initiatives of young artists. There was an unbridgeable distance between the works of Imre Bak, Pál Deim and Tamás Hencze in the mid-1960s and the official ideals of socialist art, which virtually only existed in theory. The evolution of Dóra Maurer's art illustrates this tendency well: the works she began to produce in the early 1960s with traditional graphic techniques such as copperplate etching, mezzotint and aquatint are characterized by organic forms and biomorphic motifs, which become increasingly abstract from the middle of the decade, while recognizable figures and identifiable forms disappear from the picture.

While abstract artists could begin to exhibit their work at smaller peripheral state exhibition venues from the middle of the decade, new voices were also appearing in Hungarian art: a number of artists, including sculptor György Jovánovics, began to employ pop-art elements. Jovánovics encountered the latest art trends first hand in the course of his studies in Vienna and Paris. Pop art, as a genre most distant from abstraction, was merely a liberating impulse for him that helped him reach a new understanding when representing humans (figs 9 and 10). Geometric patterns appeared on his plaster figures, and on the surface of his fragmentary or hollow figures, creating a playful passage between plane and space, figure and pattern, realism and abstraction. Consequently, Jovánovics's human figures supplanted the ideologically reinforced boundary between abstraction and figurativeness. Absurdly enough, the socialist realist principles of humanism could have been satisfied by the encounter between the allegedly anti-humanist abstract production of form and the figure infused with pop art's irony. In reality, of course, the representatives of official art policy were not enchanted by the works.

The ban on abstraction – a cornerstone of official Hungarian art policy – became obsolete by the middle of the 1960s. The changes in the art scene happened in parallel to the political opening up of the country in 1963, with the restoration of diplomatic relations with the West and greater freedom to travel, and preparations for the reform programme called the New Economic Mechanism, which began in 1968 and was fuelled by a desire to move away from the Soviet economic system. A consequence of these processes in terms of cultural policy

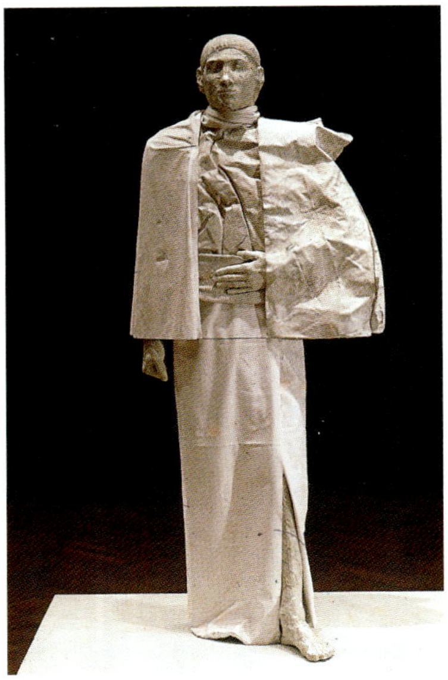

9

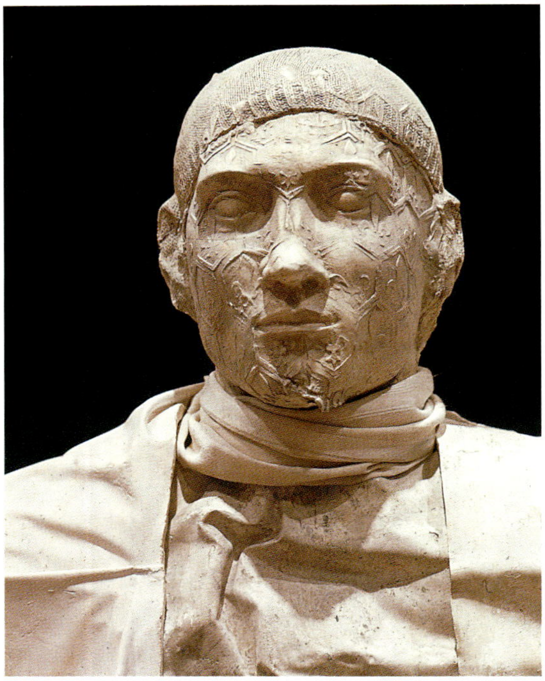

10

9. György Jovánovics, *Man*, 1968, plaster, textile, h. 180 cm, Szépművészeti Múzeum – Magyar Nemzeti Galéria, Budapest

10. György Jovánovics, *Man* (detail), 1968

11. Victor Vasarely in the parking lot of the Műcsarnok, Budapest, 1969

was an effort to lure back leftist émigré artists, primarily those, including abstract artists, who moved to France or Italy before the Second World War (see also Lóránt Bódi, 'Domesticated Modernism', pp. 179–89). The climax of this policy, which began in the mid-1960s, was Victor Vasarely's exhibition at Műcsarnok in 1969 (fig. 11).

Although abstraction and op art were the subjects of critical comments in *Művészet* just a year earlier, their justification evaporated by the end of the decade due to the broader context of the opening up in cultural policy. Western abstract art, which had been previously excommunicated, not only reached the Hungarian public through the works of foreign artists, but was also inescapably present as an integral part of Hungarian art. This was the case in the 'Iparterv' exhibitions, held in 1968 and 1969 (see Dávid Fehér, '(Dis) figuring Reality', pp. 137–59). The year 1968 also saw the publication of the volume *Modern magyar művészet* (Modern Art in Hungary) by Lajos Németh,[25] in which there is barely any trace of the boundaries that had generated such intense debate a few years before: surrealist and constructivist positions are no longer absent from the art historical treatment of the post-war decades.[26] From the early 1970s onwards, the concept of abstraction could appear in books, educational materials and even in the official journal *Művészet*, unaccompanied by the previous ideological negativity.

In a single decade, abstraction had run the course from official prohibition – which ranged from a denial of exhibition to the dissemination of anti-abstraction dogma in education – to being tolerated to the point that works could be seen in authorized exhibitions and publications, in however limited a form. The reasons for this process included the international political détente, the relative openness of Hungarian cultural policy and changes in the assessment of art historical styles and tendencies. As a result, the attitude of Hungarian art history to abstraction, both in its view of the past and vision of the future, changed significantly in the course of a decade. The concept of socialist realism was no longer a point of reference by the late 1960s, and the image of a Hungary hermetically sealed from the West in the field of art also vanished. At the same time, the issue of abstraction became almost completely marginalized, as official art kept finding newer enemies to fight; from the mid-1960s these were typically young neo-avant-garde artists whose work was linked to Western trends. They were given limited or no access to the public sphere, and a number of them were forced to leave the country in the early 1970s.

11

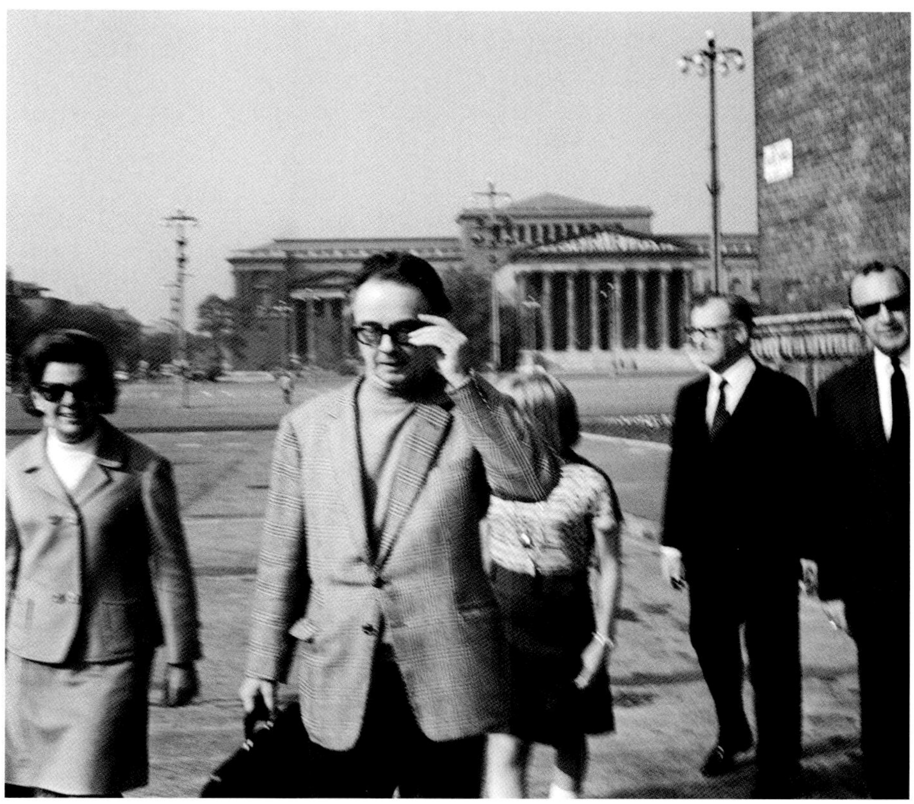

1 See David Caute, *The Dancer Defects: The Struggle for Cultural Supremacy During the Cold War*. Oxford: Oxford University Press, 2003.

2 György [Georg] Lukács, 'Hungarian Theories of Abstract Art', in Tyrus Miller (ed.), *The Culture of People's Democracy. Hungarian Essays on Literature, Art and Democratic Transition, 1945–1948*. Chicago: Haymarket Books, 2014, 224–40.

3 Richard Sheppard, 'Georg Lukács, Wilhelm Worringer and German Expressionism', *Journal of European Studies*, No. 25, 1995, 241–82.

4 The Elvont Művészek Csoportja (Group of Abstract Artists), which gathered representatives of abstract art, was formed under the intellectual guidance of Ernő Kállai, an art writer who had become a Central European authority in the interwar period. Although eight of the members still participated in the 'Salon des Réalités Nouvelles' in Paris in 1947, they never had another chance to show their works either abroad or in Hungary.

5 György Horváth, *A művészek bevonulása: A képzőművészet politikai irányításának és igazgatásának története 1945–1992* [The Entry of the Artists: A History of the Political Management and Control of Visual Art 1945–1992]. Budapest: Corvina, 2015.

6 Art historian Nóra Aradi (1924–2001) was one of the most important ideologues of the visual arts sector of official art policy from the mid-1950s to the mid-1960s, holding a variety of positions.

7 Nóra Aradi, 'A művészi szabadságról' [On Artistic Freedom], *Műterem*, Vol. 1, No. 1, 1958, 3.

8 Endre Murányi-Kovács, 'Az absztraktok csődje a Velencei Biennálén' [The Fiasco of the Abstracts at the Venice Biennale], *Élet és Irodalom*, Vol. 2, No. 26, 27 June 1958, 4–5.

9 Nóra Aradi, 'A Velencei Biennále néhány tanulsága' [A Few Lessons of the Venice Biennale], *Élet és Irodalom*, Vol. 2, No. 29, 18 July 1958, 11.

10 'The current value of abstract art from the perspective of society as a whole is virtually nil, or – should it be promoted to the masses – it could even be detrimental.' Máriusz Rabinovszky, 'Harc az absztrakt művészet körül' [The Battle Over Abstract Art], *Politika*, 22 May 1948. Republished in Máriusz Rabinovszky, *Két korszak határán: Válogatott művészeti írások* [At the Border of the Periods: Selected Art Writings]. Budapest: Corvina Kiadó, 1965, 141–43.

11 Lajos Vayer, 'Gondolatok a Biennále után' [Thoughts After the Biennale], *Műterem*, Vol. 1, No. 10, 1958, 14–19.

12 Nóra Aradi, 'Feladatokról' [On Tasks], *Műterem*, Vol. 1, No. 3, 1958, 3.

13 See Enikő Róka, 'A magyar pavilon Brüsszelben' [The Hungarian Pavilion in Brussels], in *Mutató nélkül: B. A. úr X-ben. Gróf Ferenc kiállítása a Kiscelli Múzeumban* [Without Index: Mr B. A. in X. Exhibition of Ferenc Gróf in Kiscelli Múzeum] (exhibition catalogue). Budapest: Fővárosi Képtár, 2016, 35–57.

14 See Vladimir Kemenov, 'Aspects of Two Cultures', in Charles Harrison (ed.), *Art in Theory, 1900–1990: An Anthology of Changing Ideas*. Oxford: Blackwell, 1992, 647–49. Kemenov's works appeared in nearly all socialist countries in the 1940s and 1950s. See, for instance: Vladimir Kemenov, *Decadența artei burgheze* [Decadent Bourgeois Art]. Bucharest: Editura Ziarului Scânteia, 1947; V. Kemenov and I. Grabar, *Harc a burzsoá művészet és művészetelmélet ellen* [Fight Against Bourgeois Art and Art Theory]. Budapest: Szikra, 1953; V. Kemenov, *Proti buržoasnímu umění a uměnovědě sborník statí* [Against Bourgeois Art and Its Theory]. Prague: Orbis, 1952.

15 The journal *Műterem*, which was launched in 1958 and survived for a year, reported on the exhibitions of the Salon Populiste in Paris and its Hungarian connections several times.

16 See Piotr Piotrowski, *In the Shadow of Yalta: Art and Avant-garde in Eastern Europe, 1945–1989*. London: Reaktion Books, 2009, 127.

17 *Ibid.*, 70.

18 Lajos Németh, 'Megjegyzések képzőművészetünk helyzetéről' [Notes on the State of Our Visual Art], *Új Írás*, Vol. 1, No. 8, 1961, 738–44.

19 The context for Lajos Németh's remark was the theoretical conclusions drawn in the Soviet Union from the 1956 Picasso exhibition in Moscow. See Caute, *The Dancer Defects*.

20 Dezső Korniss and Endre Bálint had a joint exhibition in the 't Oude Wevershuis Gallery in Amersfoort, 1958.

21 Gábor Ö. Pogány, 'A IX. Magyar Képzőművészeti Kiállítás' [The Ninth Magyar Képzőművészeti Kiállítás], *Művészet*, Vol. 2, No. 5, 1962, 3.
22 Ferenc Lantos, 'Fogalomtisztázás' [The Clarification of a Concept], *Jelenkor*, Vol. 6. No. 9, 1963, 837–42.
23 Sándor Hornyik, 'Veszélyes kiegészítések? Megjegyzések a magyar neoavantgárd elméletéhez' [Dangerous Supplements? Notes on the Theory of the Hungarian Neo-avant-garde], in Ágnes Berecz, Mária L. Molnár and Erzsébet Tatai (eds), *Nulla dies sine linea: Tanulmányok Passuth Krisztina hetvenedik születésnapjára* [Nulla dies sine linea: Studies for the Seventieth Birthday of Krisztina Passuth]. Budapest: Praesens, 2007, 171–77.
24 Nóra Aradi, *Absztrakt képzőművészet* [Abstract Visual Art]. Budapest: Kossuth Könyvkiadó, 1964.
25 Lajos Németh, *Modern magyar művészet*. Budapest: Corvina, 1968. An English-language edition was published in 1969.
26 On the scholarly literature of the era, see Gábor Andrási, 'Mérges gaz a művészet rónáján: Régi és új absztrakció Magyarországon 1957–1968' [Poisonous Weeds on the Meadow of Art: Old and New Abstraction in Hungary 1957–1968], *Ars Hungarica*, Vol. 37, No. 1, 2011.

1. Lajos Kassák's exhibition in the Galerie Denise René, Paris, 1960, Petőfi Irodalmi Múzeum – Kassák Múzeum, Budapest

1

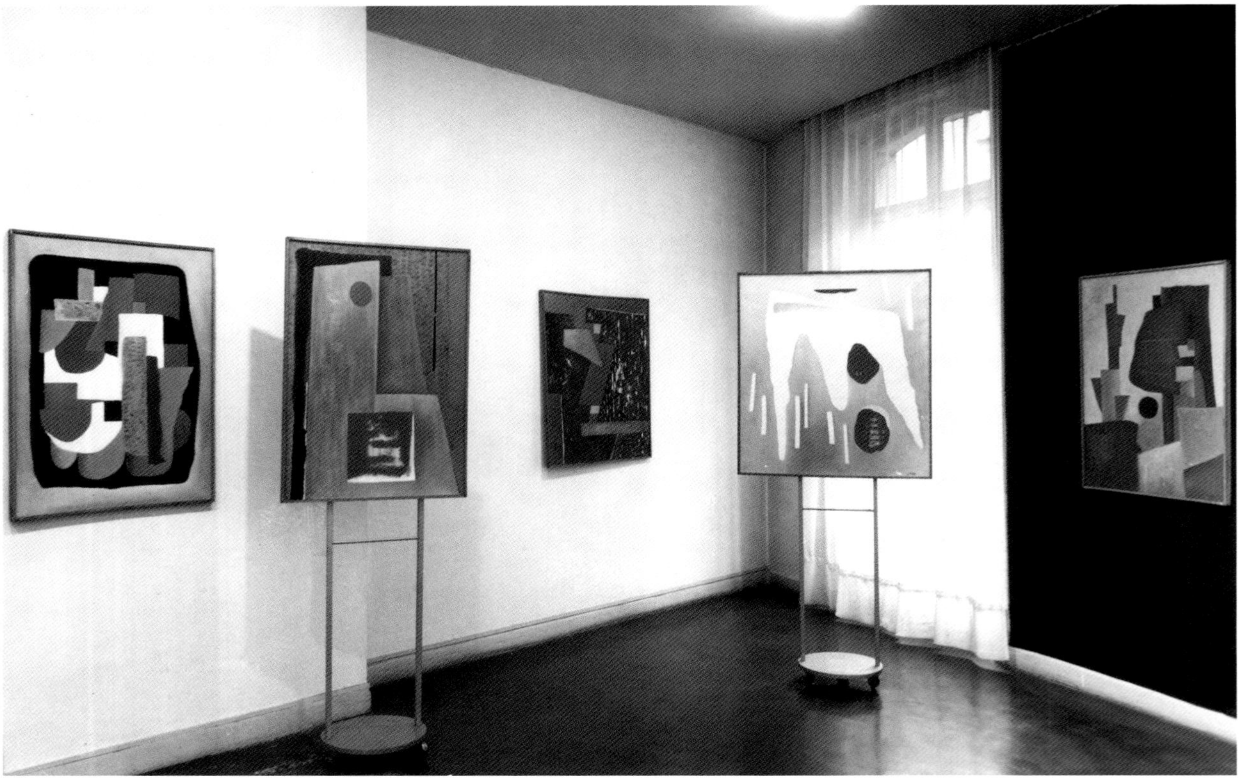

Lóránt Bódi

Domesticated Modernism

The Role of Western Émigré Artists in the Cultural Politics of the Kádár Era

Art and culture in general, alongside political, economic and military confrontation, had a rather complex role in the cold-war era. As a 'soft power'[1] – that is, having the ability to shape preferences and initiate change through appeal and attraction rather than physical or financial coercion – culture could be both a tacit tool for securing political interests and a device for positive national image-making. The János Kádár regime, established in the wake of the suppressed 1956 revolution, also recognized the role of culture in inculcating values. Cultural diplomacy became a significant component of the cultural politics of the era, with the establishment paying careful attention to the principles of selecting foreign artists to exhibit in Hungary and Hungarian artists fit for official 'exportation'. These interrelated cultural practices, as well as the changing role of visual art, the modernization of culture, and the changing assessment and significance of abstraction (the nonfigurative), are all relevant to the discussion of the exemplary cases of two Hungarian-born visual artists, sculptor Amerigo Tot (born Imre Tóth) and op-art master Victor Vasarely (born Győző Vásárhelyi).

After leaving Hungary in the 1930s, both artists joined international avant-garde movements, and their international careers began in the 1950s–60s. Their 'cultural repatriation'[2] and canonization in Hungary were an experiment in cultural politics in the 1960s, exemplifying rather spectacularly the Kádár regime's efforts to improve the country's image through representing émigrés both in Hungary and, at times, abroad through exhibitions, the founding of museums, state commissions and publications. This policy was meant to demonstrate – primarily to the West – the open, modern and progressive character of the cultural politics of the regime. Within the state apparatus, it was the Kulturális Kapcsolatok Intézete (Institute for Cultural Connections) that managed Hungarian cultural events abroad. Although its predecessor, the Kulturális Kapcsolatok Hivatala (Office for Cultural Connections), was established in 1949, under the regime of hardline Stalinist Mátyás Rákosi, it became a typical 'Kádárist' institution in its activities and roles, as the cultural isolationism of prior decades gave way to an opening in foreign relations in the 1960s. In this spirit, one of the key tasks of the institute was the organization of various foreign and domestic exhibitions (for both artists of Hungarian origin and foreigners), academic conferences, scholarships, trade shows and national promotional exhibitions (e.g. 'Hungarian Week').

The military suppression of the 1956 revolution and the establishment of the new political leadership had a number of social and political consequences. Approximately 200,000 people left Hungary between 23 October 1956 and 30 April 1957, most of them permanently. The United Nations General Assembly passed a resolution to suspend Hungary's UN membership, and a Special Committee on the Problem of Hungary was set up. Besides the demographic shock, 1956–57 also put Hungary into a state of international

2

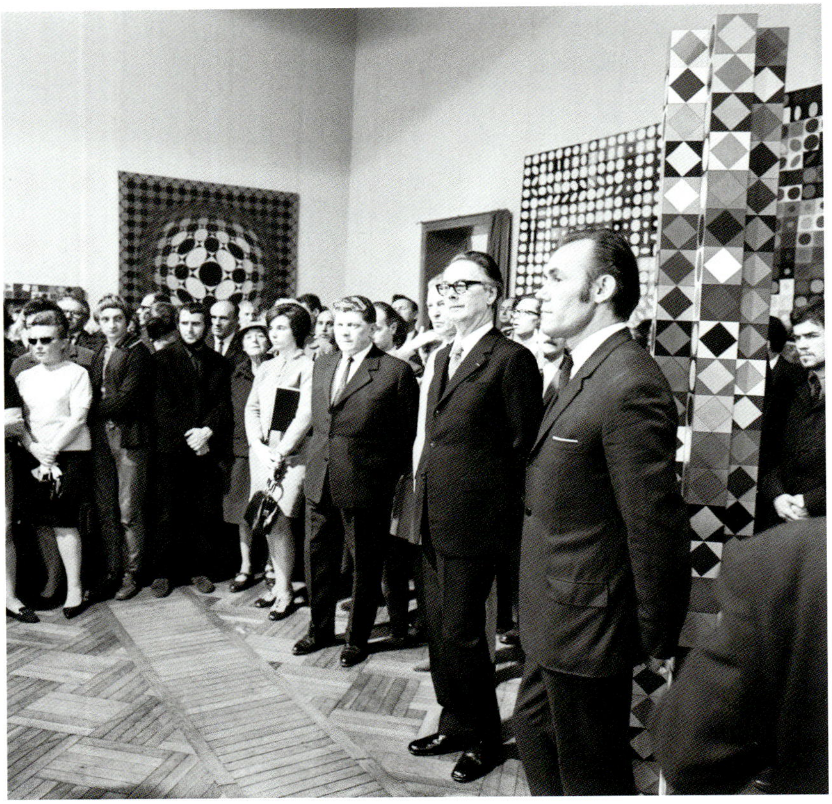

3

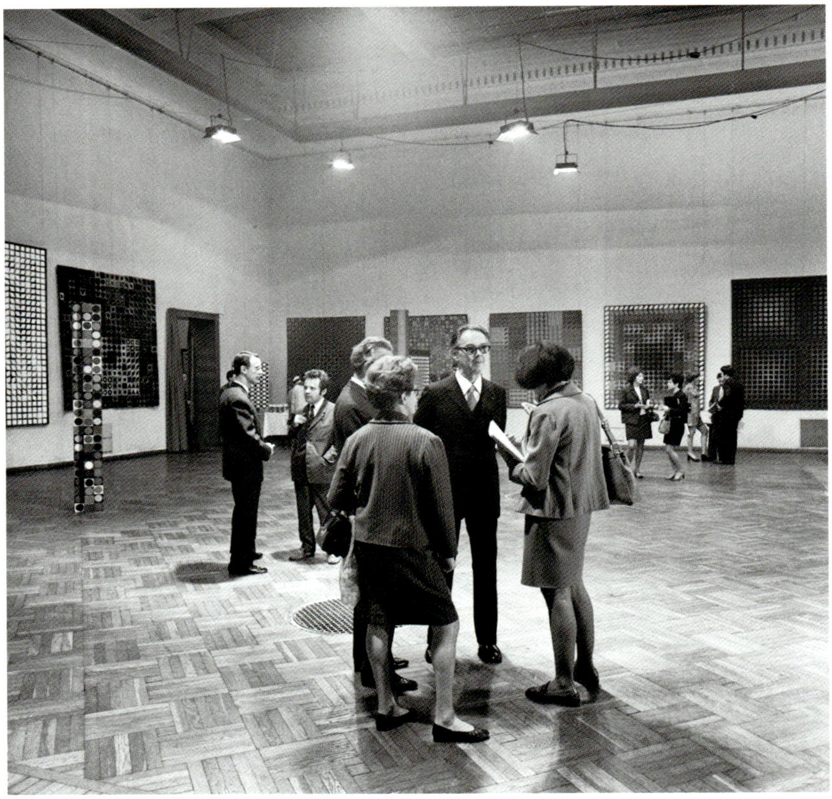

2 & 3. Victor Vasarely at the opening of his exhibition in the Műcsarnok, Budapest, 18 October 1969

isolation.[3] Hungary's diplomatic relations were limited to the countries of the Warsaw Pact, China and a few other countries with leftist leadership. In order to alleviate this severe isolation in foreign relations, the new political leadership began to use culture as a means of diplomacy. The Brussels World's Fair in 1958, organized in the early stages of the cold war, was a case in point. The new establishment led by Kádár wanted to use the fair, which the participating socialist countries also treated as a representative event, to stage an exhibition suggesting economic, social and cultural progression, thereby normalizing the image of the regime that had quashed the revolution.[4]

The exhibition organizers avoided, as much as possible, placing any socialist realist or 'dogmatic' works in key areas of the exhibition, and displayed only a single propaganda work, the sculpture *Smelter* by József Somogyi (p. 31, fig. 9), and even that in front of the pavilion. The axis of the visual arts exhibition was composed of works by symbolist painter Tivadar Csontváry Kosztka, who was presented in Brussels as a forerunner of modern Hungarian art. The self-contradictory workings of cultural politics are exemplified by the fact that the painting by László Moholy-Nagy on display at the central pavilion provoked a minor scandal among the Hungarian decision-makers, owing to the era's prevalent opposition to modernism and abstraction in the approach to art. At the same time, the pavilion building and the finished exhibition also radiated the vision of a new post-Stalinist modernizing era, even if political show trials and executions were in full progress in Hungary during the time of the Brussels expo.[5] The aim of the political powers-that-be was not just to show a positive image of Hungary to a foreign audience, but also to present the state to Hungarian society as culturally open and representing a modern mentality.

This ambition was fostered by the dual nature of the representation of power that characterized the regime after 1956. The political establishment began to regulate Western and Eastern cultural imports and exports on the basis of different principles. Hungary presented itself to the West as open to modernity, while the more conservative face of the regime was projected to the socialist bloc. One of the paradigmatic cases of this practice was the exhibition of work by the avant-garde author and artist Lajos Kassák (see also Edit Sasvári, 'Autonomy and Doublespeak', pp. 8–17, and Gábor Dobó and Merse Pál Szeredi, 'Hungarian Culture +/- Europe', pp. 39–57) at the Galerie Denise René in Paris in 1960 (artists belonging to the gallery included Alexander Calder, Hans Arp, Jean Tinguely, Nicolas Schöffer and Victor Vasarely).[6] Kassák was an uncomfortable, challenging figure for cultural politics as he defied attempts at integration due to his consistent leftist politics and modernist abstract art. In fact, the exhibition itself could only take place due to an 'error' in cultural policy, and the artist, whose passport application was refused, was not allowed to attend the opening in Paris. The exhibition made waves in cultural politics because shows by Kassák, either abroad or at home, were not officially supported by Hungary. György Aczél, a key figure in cultural policy during almost the entire Kádár era (1956–88), articulated the lesson of this case as a general principle of cultural politics: 'It is possible and even necessary to produce shirts for export only, because we need to export shirts and provide the best. But there are no separate cultures for export and for domestic use. Our culture cannot be different at home from what it is abroad.'[7]

Victor Vasarely mediated between Kassák and Denise René in order to make the exhibition happen.[8] The exhibition became the basis for the professional (master/disciple) relationship and friendship between the two. Vasarely may have sought a 'great predecessor' in Kassák, through whom he could associate his own art with the international history of the avant-garde. Exhibiting Kassák allowed the gallery to access and market East European material from the historical avant-garde, which may have also been an important consideration (fig. 1).

Those in charge of cultural politics insisted on dual politics even in the later decades of the Kádár era; even so, the reform initiatives of the 1960s made their mark on the selection of exhibited artists and works, as a memorandum written at the Művelődésügyi Minisztérium (Ministry of Culture) attests: 'Our exhibition policy and trade objectives are coordinated in accord with our principle of using identical principles of cultural politics for composing the materials for exhibitions at home and abroad; in other words, we refuse the use of dual cultural politics, while taking into account those differences of taste that we can accept without compromises in matters of principle.'[9] This was the beginning of a more flexible approach to exhibition management, which also took trade and financial considerations into account. Nevertheless, exhibition policy was far from unified until the cessation of Soviet influence and the political transition that began in 1989: the emphasis kept shifting between collaboration and confrontation. Though Hungary's cultural leadership wanted to present only particular artists abroad, there was still room for foreign partner institutions to request works by other artists, whom they knew through informal channels (fellowships, personal contact or exhibitions abroad). Neo-avant-garde artists, whose radical approach was at odds even with the more liberalized cultural policy, were at times prevented from exhibiting even when invited, but their works sometimes appeared at events arranged through bilateral collaboration, such as the Paris Youth Biennale in 1973, organized in the spirit of the neo-avant-garde. György Jovánovics, Gyula Pauer, Tamás Szentjóby and Péter Legéndy were exhibited there, and other participants included filmmakers Gábor Bódy and János Gulyás and contemporary composers László Sáry and Péter Eötvös.[10]

In addition to regulating which works could leave the country and what image a given exhibition projected about the political, social, economic and artistic conditions in Hungary, cultural diplomacy also regulated the domestic representation of contemporary culture, in a world multiply divided by the Iron Curtain, by determining which works could appear at home. It should also be noted that, with the exception of a short period after the Second World War, international 'modern' or contemporary works of art could reach Hungary only in very restricted ways until the mid-1960s. Both Hungarian artists and the public tended to encounter such works only in the form of reproductions, and were given no chance to experience the sensory qualities of the works directly.[11] There were, of course, other channels for learning about the world outside (journals, albums, copies, etc.), but the authorities could only accept one official image of culture.

A modernist experiment in culture

The gradually easing of isolation in foreign policy took a dramatic turn in the mid-1960s, and this opening occurred on several levels in culture.[12] The liveliest foreign policy and cultural relationships were formed with France, thanks to Charles de Gaulle's policy of opening to the East and Hungary's traditionally good relationship with the French Communist Party. The People's Republic of Hungary and the French Republic signed a cultural treaty on 18 June 1966 (replacing a 'memorandum of cultural exchange' accepted in 1961),[13] and the French-language magazine *Nouvelles Études Hongroises* was launched in Hungary in the same year. (It often included translated articles that had been published in the *New Hungarian Quarterly*, an English-language magazine edited by Iván Boldizsár, which had been in circulation since 1960.) From the mid-1960s onwards, a growing number of exhibitions presented foreign artists – primarily those of the classic avant-garde including Henry Moore, Fernand Léger, Pablo Picasso and Marc Chagall – in Budapest, but there were also a number of exhibitions of contemporary French art at the Műcsarnok (Kunsthalle), the most prestigious state exhibition venue of the era.[14]

The liberalization of the system in the early 1960s was probably increasingly apparent to the West, as former émigrés and their relatives offered their works to Hungarian cultural institutions increasingly often. Some of these offers were refused on political grounds or on the basis of quality, yet works by numerous artists who were unknown in their adopted countries were exhibited or acquired by museums in Hungary.[15] Some of those organizing the exhibitions may have been driven by personal or political interests. There was a sharp downturn in this practice in the late 1960s in order to prevent the exhibition of less significant artists who could not achieve popular success. The goal was to arrange exhibitions for Hungarian artists abroad not out of personal or political interests, but on the basis of a set of aesthetic criteria and a principle of quality. The cultural authorities gauged rather precisely which successful Hungarian-born artists were worth exhibiting. The idea of presenting Hungarian modernist artists living abroad first surfaced in the early

1960s, but it was not until 1967 that the notion of an exhibition – presenting Hungarian artists living in France – was considered jointly by the Művelődésügyi Minisztérium and the Kulturális Kapcsolatok Intézete on the initiative of Máté Major.[16] The cultural policy leadership asked Lucien Hervé (born László Elkán), living in Paris to assist, with arranging the exhibition. This original project was eventually realized with an expanded list of participants as 'XX. századi magyar származású művészek külföldön' (Artists of Hungarian Origins Abroad). Organized by Krisztina Passuth, the exhibition opened in 1970 and presented the work of prominent artists (Etienne Hajdú, Simon Hantaï, Zoltán Kemény, György Kepes, László Moholy-Nagy and Nicolas Schöffer among others), and included abstract art after its rejection in the early years of the decade. To avoid any direct political interpretation of the event, the exhibition was presented under the banner of the Magyarok Világszövetsége (World Federation of Hungarians), which was independent of the Party and the state. The organization of the exhibition was driven not just by the campaign to bolster a positive national image, but also by a conscious acquisition strategy: valuable 'modern' works of art, which otherwise would have to have been purchased for hard currency, were offered to the Szépművészeti Múzeum (Museum of Fine Arts) by the artists as gifts on the occasion of the exhibition. In response to the success of the exhibition, the Művelődésügyi Minisztérium issued an order to initiate a programme of other exhibitions of the work of émigré artists 'considered the most prominent abroad'. This programme was, in fact, partly realized over the next decade.

Amerigo Tot and Victor Vasarely were not the only artists whom the cultural political establishment tried to integrate: György Kepes,[17] first a member of Lajos Kassák's circle, then a student of Moholy-Nagy at the Bauhaus, and who was teaching at the Massachusetts Institute of Technology at the time, was another. There was also Nicolas Schöffer, known for his kinetic sculptures, who still mistrusted the regime (understandably in light of the tragic fate suffered by his family in the Holocaust) despite the fact that a museum, the Nicolas Schöffer gyűjtemény (Nicolas Schöffer Collection), was established in 1979 in the house in which he was born.[18] Unlike Kepes and Schöffer, Tot and Vasarely could enjoy the support of cultural politics in the form of a conscious building of a cult around them.

4

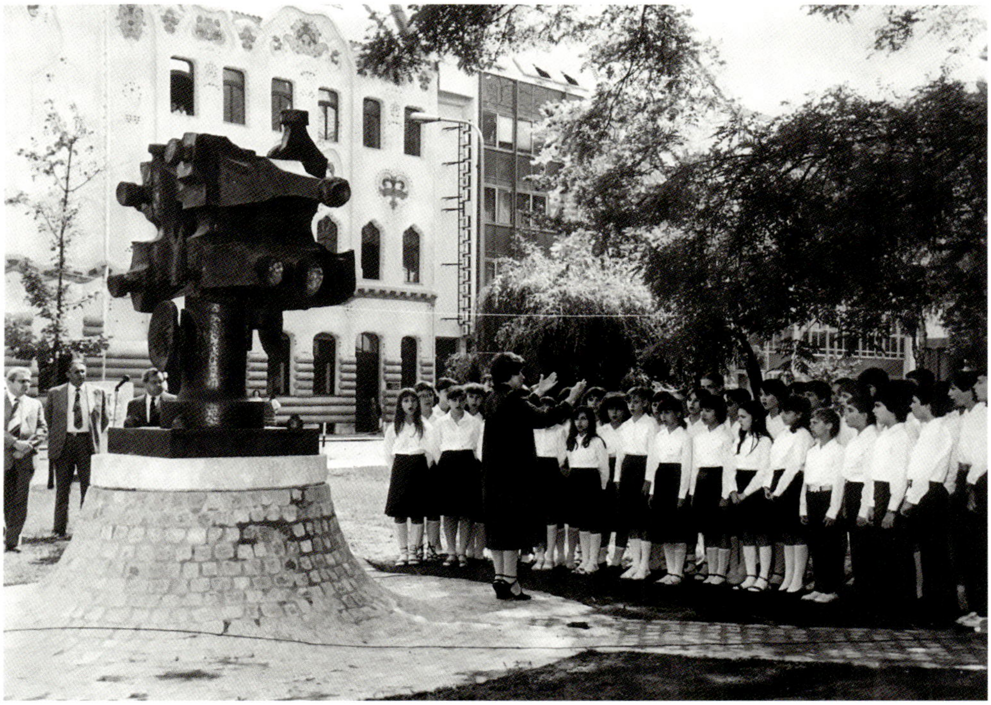

4. The inauguration of Amerigo Tot's sculpture *Microcosm in Macrocosm* in Kecskemét, 1984

The technocrat and the activist: the roles of Victor Vasarely and Amerigo Tot in cultural politics

The cultural repatriation of Vasarely[19] and Tot occurred in parallel over multiple phases,[20] starting in the late 1960s. Vasarely's first exhibition in Hungary was organized in the Janus Pannonius Múzeum in Pécs, his birthplace, in 1969. (Vasarely gifted to the museum a significant collection after the exhibition, and later gifts followed.) He subsequently had very successful retrospective shows at Műcsarnok as well (figs 2 and 3). The Magyar Iparművészeti Főiskola (Hungarian Academy of Applied Arts) conferred the title of honorary professor on Vasarely and Amerigo Tot in 1968, and the Magyar Képző- és Iparművészek Szövetsége (Association of Hungarian Artists) admitted both as members in 1969.

What may have driven Amerigo Tot's and Vasarely's reintegration? What impact on art in Hungary may have been expected by those who controlled cultural politics? Could such a modernist aesthetic turn be engineered in Hungarian art as well? Máté Major, one of the intermediaries between the émigré artists and the decision-makers in the cultural authorities, made a cautious statement on the occasion of Amerigo Tot's exhibition at Műcsarnok in 1969: he was hoping that Western modern art would generate a discourse rather than have a direct artistic effect (fig. 4).[21]

Both the daily press and cultural journals covered Vasarely's and Tot's art for a long time and contributed significantly to their high profile. Amerigo Tot's life, in particular was shrouded in legends concerning his antifascist past, and he consciously projected an air of mystery.[22] Both artists enjoyed what one can accurately describe as cult status.[23] In addition to their art, they also fostered a mythic role in the Hungarian public sphere: that of the émigré (dissident) who had once left the country and now returned triumphantly from the West. Their symbolic readmission was a message to other émigrés, indicating the softening of the regime. Visits by Hungarian émigrés or contact with them were now counted as politically less dangerous, even though the regime still eyed them with suspicion. On 25 December 1977, *Népszava*, which was effectively a trade union daily, devoted a long article to the number of the Hungarian émigrés, their breakdown by host country and their increasing willingness to return, presenting all of this as a success for the 'homeland'. The list of émigrés ended with the artists and scholars who had already returned, highlighting Tot and Vasarely. The article concluded:

But why has it recently become 'fashionable' to return or rather to bequeath to the homeland the treasures born of the homeland and inspired by a forced wandering in the world? Professors Szent-Györgyi and Selye, the world-famous artists Amerigo Tot and Vasarely, historians Borsányi and Dómján, and countless others, wish to replant oeuvres into this homeland. Because this homeland is now worthy enough to attract and hold one and to preserve enduring human values.[24]

Owing to the distinctive geopolitical status of the Eastern bloc, there was a significant wave of emigration by intellectuals from all countries of the region to politically and culturally more open countries in the middle of the twentieth century.[25] Hungary's political efforts to secure 'cultural repatriation' were not exceptional in the Eastern bloc. Romanian émigrés – such as Constantin Brancusi, Marcel Janco and Tristan Tzara – with links to Western progressive movements had an important role in national and cultural self-interpretation. Of these, the folk-inspired sculptures of Brancusi (1876–1957) made him the one who could simultaneously represent the essence of Romanian culture and cutting-edge modernism in the eyes of the regime: 'he is one of the national symbols in which Romanians have invested a great deal of emotional energy over the decades, and the artist has now come to be contextualized in explicitly nationalist situations that to a large extent have to do with the phenomenon of self-colonialization and protochronism'.[26] The cultural authorities began to rediscover Brancusi in the mid-1950s, 'transforming' him into the most important representative of socialist Romanian culture, whose 'repatriation' was emphatically framed as cultural nation-building (and they turned his birthplace into a museum, erected statues, mounted exhibitions and academic conferences, used his image on stamps, money, etc.).

Victor Vasarely

Victor Vasarely became a world-famous master of op art and kinetic art in the 1960s–70s. His image and his abstract art were also well-known in Hungary in this period (the Hungarian and French post offices jointly issued 4,480,000 stamps with Vasarely's work on them in 1979). He was a reference point even for discourses outside the sphere of art, ranging from studies in microelectronics to epistemology, and for the 'Colourful City' project, which was meant to break the greyness of the housing estates and was backed by the Ministry of Urban Development.

'Faith in progress', technological optimism and a revolutionary (future-oriented) and scientific attitude were all components of Vasarely's creative 'worldview' that could fit the vision state socialism developed for itself. The basic artistic practice of the multiplication of artworks could be regarded as exemplifying his non-elitist effort to have his works democratically displayed: his works were on the walls of 'dorm rooms' and, thanks to his 'plastic alphabet' could be seen in numerous (public and private) spaces. Vasarely's art seeped into the everyday through posters and postcards as well as public sculptures.[27] Kádár's cultural political establishment – enamoured by his projects such as the 'plastic alphabet' and 'planetary folklore'[28] and his abstract works with universal ambitions – found in Vasarely a suitable representative of modern, national and socialist non-figurative art (and even preferable to artists living in Hungary).

5

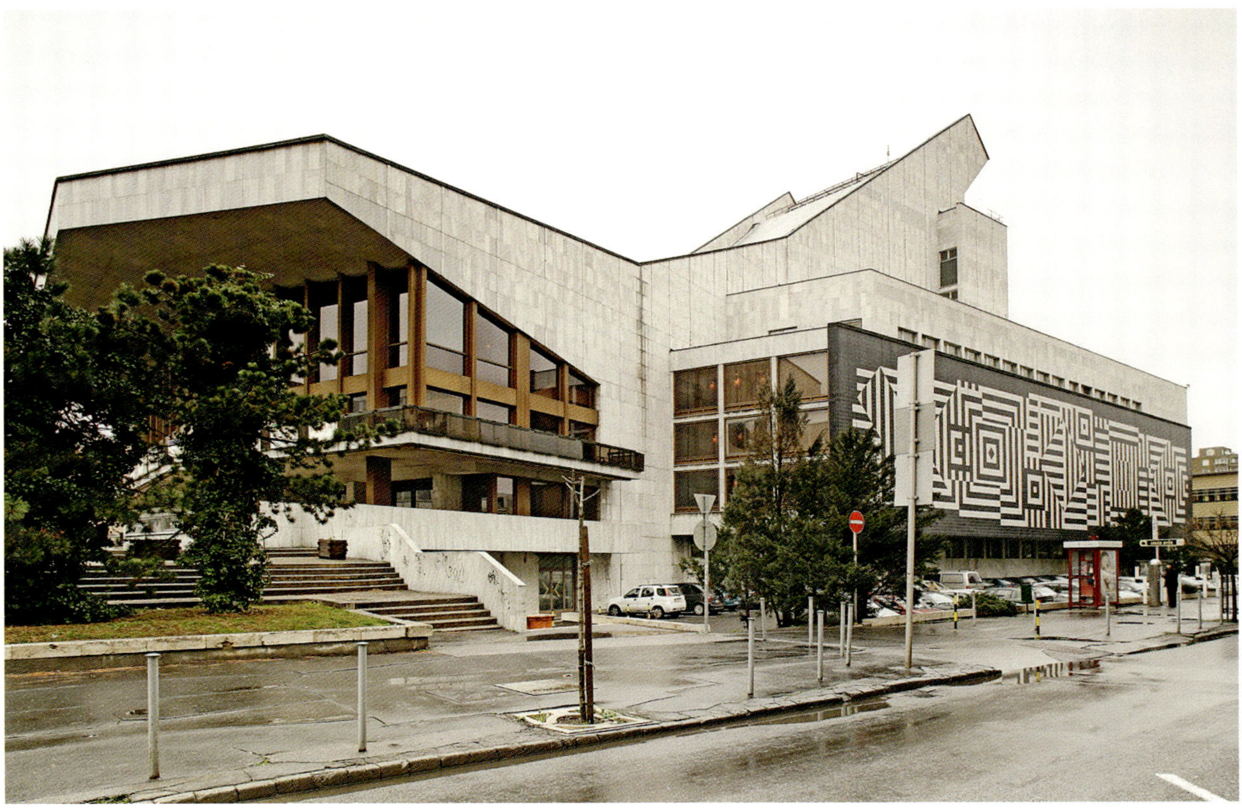

5. Victor Vasarely's work on the exterior of the National Theatre in Győr, 1978

Vasarely was engaged in the transformation of the large, urban scale through an 'aesthetics of the environment', the visual representation of a new kind of reality constructed through scholarly and technological innovation from the late 1960s onwards. His research and his ideas about his own work coincided with the interpretive framework determined by Hungary's cultural political establishment. He was commissioned to create several large-scale works in Hungary; the most outstanding being the ornamental decoration of the building of the Győri Nemzeti Színház (Győr National Theatre, fig. 5).

The idea of Vasarely having a dedicated museum in Hungary first appeared in the early 1970s, but György Aczél's intervention prevented it at the time.[29] When the museum was finally established in 1976, it opened in Pécs, Vasarely's birthplace, rather than in Budapest as desired by the artist. It opened simultaneously with his self-financed museum in Aix-en-Provence (his first museum opened in Gordes, France, in 1969). The Pécs museum was virtually next door to one devoted to the other major cultural 'discovery' of the Kádár era, Tivadar Csontváry Kosztka, which had opened three years earlier. There was a plan to develop Pécs into a southern centre of culture infused with a modernist spirit; the 'Museum Street' was complemented by the opening of the Amerigo Tot Múzeum in 1978. This implicit programme could be implemented thanks to significant support from Aczél, who was an MP for the Baranya county and Pécs district. It needs to be underscored that establishing the Vasarely Múzeum was fuelled by a political ambition to employ the notion of the homeland and the artist's past in order to help construct a sense of him belonging to the nation.[30]

Continuing his practice of donations, Vasarely gifted a collection of 400 works (including those of other artists) to the Szépművészeti Múzeum in 1982, with the openly declared aim of having them placed in yet another Vasarely museum. After a long period of hesitation, the political leadership finally decided to create a museum in Óbuda, away from the centre of Budapest, in the Baroque Zichy Palace (next to the Kassák Múzeum). It opened to the public in 1987.

Vasarely's canonization did not make him the principal representative of Hungarian culture abroad. The distinct official positions regarding two projected international exhibitions of his work is telling in this respect. The French cultural administration organized an exhibition of Vasarely's works in Portugal in 1980, which was acknowledged by the Hungarian embassy as a national success. The very same year, friendly socialist Cuba expressed an interest in organizing an exhibition of Vasarely works owned by the Hungarian state, but the Cuban request was denied. The proposal was rejected on the following grounds: 'sending a Vasarely exhibition abroad would be ill-advised, since it would not represent Hungarian art, and he does not even count as a Hungarian artist. We are planning to send a Hungarian ethnographic exhibition.' So, the policy when it came to foreign countries was far from unified, and the cultural identity that Hungary communicated to a Western country (such as Portugal) and a socialist country could be radically different. The response to Cuba may also reveal that the political strategy of embellishing the country's image abroad by engaging Hungarian-born participants of the international art scene may have been in decline by the beginning of the 1980s.

The political dynamic of the 1970s did not only entail the return and readmission of émigrés, but also another wave of emigration that arose due to the resurgence of repressive policies. A series of artists were leaving Hungary with their families: photorealist and pop-art painter László Lakner in 1974; Fluxus artist Szentjóby Tamás, who was sued by authorities over his participation in the Samizdat movement,[31] in 1975; and members of the neo-avant-garde *lakásszínház* (apartment theatre) of Dohány utca, Budapest, in 1976,[32] just as the Vasarely Múzeum of Pécs was opening. Then Endre Tót, known primarily for his conceptual and mail-art works, also decided to stay abroad after a German fellowship in 1978.

In light of these developments, what was the cultural path of Hungary in the 1960–70s? Sensing the changes in visual arts in the 1960s, both in the world and in Hungary (where the neo-avant-garde artists, who represented a new generation, emerged in the early 1960s), the cultural political establishment attempted to ease tensions by a cautious experiment in modernization, partly encouraged by recent reformist trends. The establishment gave Hungarian visual arts a new impetus by putting previously unseen classic avant-garde works on display, by showing the work of Hungarian artists who belonged to international trends – primarily neo-constructivism and lyrical abstraction – and by the 'cultural repatriation' of Vasarely. It did this, however, without getting embroiled in an ideological definition of the regime's concept of culture (i.e. how these policies were related to socialist realism and the tradition of realism, or the degree to which abstraction was approved).[33] At the same time, there was a tangible effort to create a national constructivist tradition along the axis running from Kassák, Moholy-Nagy and Sándor Bortnyik to the next generation of Victor Vasarely and Nicolas Schöffer.

This cautious modernism was belated, its context being a period in which the ideological mediating role of the visual arts had been transformed. In fact, the critique of modernism had been well underway by this time in Western art history and the history of ideas (the symbolic date being 1968). So, even though Vasarely and Tot did influence the emergence of certain artists and artist groups (e.g. János Fajó and the Pesti Műhely; see Flóra Barkóczi, 'Creative (Dis)Courses', pp. 95–109), neither could make a significant impact – not that they ever made this an objective – because the progressive and influential phases of their careers were over, and because of their respective artistic goals at the time. Nevertheless, László Maksay, a professor at the Magyar Képzőművészeti Főiskola (Hungarian Academy of Fine Arts), perceptively recognized the shift over the course of the 1960s, which turned abstract art and neo-constructivism into tools for the modern ornamental decoration of public institutions and spaces. The artists enumerated by him (Victor Vasarely, Nicolas Schöffer and Zoltán Kemény) could be integrated into Hungarian culture, albeit only through this decorative form.[34] This 'use' of their art actually suited the apolitical self-image of the Kádár era and its openness to modernism. Welcoming Hungarian émigrés back also signalled that one's return after an international career was worthwhile, since one would be accepted with understanding and appreciation at home. The powers-that-be implied that Hungary was finally in sync with the West, if only culturally, as if cultural progression had the same meaning within and outside the Eastern bloc.

1 Joseph S. Nye, *Soft Power*. New York: Public Affairs, 2004, 1–33.

2 Edit Sasvári, 'Cultural Repatriation as Political Strategy – Victor Vasarely and Kádár-Era Hungary', in Franciska Zólyom and Andreas Fogarasi, *Vasarely Go Home*. Leipzig and Zurich: Galerie für Zeitgenössische Kunst/Spector Books/Museum Haus Konstruktiv, 2014, 63–74.

3 Ferenc Gazdag, 'A kommunista típusú konszolidáció szovjet modellje és a magyar 1956; nemzetközi aspektusok' [The Soviet Model of Communist-type Consolidation and 1956 in Hungary: International Aspects], in Tibor Huszár and János Szabó (eds), *Restauráció vagy kiigazítás: A kádári represszió intézményesülése 1956–1962* [Restoration or Correction: The Institutionalization of Kádár's Repression 1956–1962]. Budapest: Zrínyi Kiadó, 1999.

4 Iván Boldizsár, 'Modern művészeti múzeumot' [The Need for a Modern Art Museum], *Művészet*, Vol. 14, No. 7, 1973, 5.

5 György Péteri, 'Transsystemic Fantasies: Counterrevolutionary Hungary at Brussels Expo '58', *Journal of Contemporary History*, Vol. 47, No. 1, 2012, 137–60.

6 The Paris gallery owned by Denise René (1913–2012) was one of the key exhibiting spaces for French and international geometric and lyrical abstraction.

7 Edit Sasvári, 'A mi kultúránk nem lehet más itthon, mint külföldön' [Our Culture Cannot be Different at Home from What it is Abroad], in Gábor Andrási (ed.), *'...fejünkből töröljük ki a regulákat': Kassák Lajos az író, képzőművész, szerkesztő és közszereplő, Tanulmányok* ['...erase regulations from our minds': Lajos Kassák, Writer, Artist, Editor and Public Figure, Studies]. Budapest: Petőfi Irodalmi Múzeum/Kassák Alapítvány, 2010.

8 Little is known about Vasarely's political-cultural plans in Hungary before the reform period. One of the available sources is a letter to Kassák: 'I am positive that socialist states can be persuaded to recognize the authenticity of abstract art. But it's high time we began this! The album will be the first step. I will start a debate series with the defenders of realism. Arguing will be long and hard, but they will have to admit that it is Kassák's work alone that has signalled and represented the path of development in Hungary. We must carefully prevent the wave of decadence that has flooded the world from spilling over there in its full intensity.' Petőfi Irodalmi Múzeum-Kassák Múzeum-Levelezés/1940/17. Imre Pán, Vasarely's co-author for *Izmusok története* [History of Isms] and later an émigré in Paris, tried to present Kassák's oeuvre in France before Vasarely took on the task. On one occasion, Pán offered his own quite significant collection of works by members of the Európai Iskola (European School) and various international artists to the Szépművészeti Múzeum in exchange for Kassák's reintegration in Hungary and exhibition abroad. The offer was rejected.

9 Magyar Nemzeti Levéltár/Kulturális Kapcsolatok Intézete, XIX-A-33-a/1132/15195/*Művészeti* külkereskedelmünk.

10 László Beke, 'Fiatalok Biennáléja Párizsban' [Paris Youth Biennale], *Művészet*, Vol. 15, No. 4, 1974, 40–41.

11 Sándor Radnóti, *Jöjj és láss! A modern művészetfogalom keletkezése Winckelmann és következmények* [Come and See! The Emergence of the Modern Concept of Art: Winckelmann and the Consequences]. Budapest: Atlantisz Kiadó, 2010.

12 Dr Csaba János Békés, 'Hungarian Foreign Policy in the Bipolar World, 1945–1991', *Foreign Policy Review*, Vol. 1, No. 1, 2011, 65–97.

13 Georges Diener, *A Francia Intézet Magyarországon 1947–1989, Francia–magyar kulturális kapcsolatok* [The French Institute in Hungary 1947–1989: French–Hungarian Bilateral Relationships]. Budapest: Magvető-L'Harmattan, 1990, 54.

14 Piotr Bernatowicz, 'Picasso Behind the Iron Curtain', in Jérôme Bazin, Pascal Dubourg Glatigny and Piotr Piotrowski (eds), *Art Beyond Borders*. Budapest: CEU Press, 2016, 151–65. The staging of the Budapest Picasso exhibition unambiguously indicated the changing climate in cultural politics. In one letter, György Aczél recommended purchasing Picasso graphic works for the Szépművészeti Múzeum in order to enlarge its modern collection and to patch its art historical 'holes'. This did not happen in the end because Daniel-Henry Kahnweiler – Picasso's one-time friend and collector – who participated in the exhibition gifted sixteen works to the Szépművészeti Múzeum. MNL, KKI- XIX-A-33-a/1121/15107/Picasso-kiállítás [Picasso exhibition].

15 The case of Frédéric Longuet's exhibition is particularly interesting, even though the Frenchman was not an émigré artist. Longuet, the great-grandson of Karl Marx, was exhibited at the Szépművészeti Múzeum, after several shows in the Soviet Union. Katalin Néray, on behalf of the Kulturális Kapcsolatok Intézete, recounted that the museum was only willing to purchase some of the exhibited works after prolonged institutional pressure, and the exhibition was stifled by a lack of professional and public interest.

16 Máté Major, one of the most important theorists on architecture in the state socialist period, was originally a member of the Hungarian section of the Congrès internationaux d'architecture moderne (CIAM, International Congress of Modern Architecture) founded by Le Corbusier. He returned from a Soviet prisoner-of-war camp after the Second World War and became involved

in socialist realist architecture and urbanization after 1945. In 1967, he initiated Új Építészet (New Architecture), a largely modern architectural programme that distanced itself from socialist realism. During the years of the New Economic Mechanism (1968–72, through which there was partial liberalization of the economy), architects articulated a need to renew modernism. At the same time, architects and theorists were already seeing folk art and folk architecture as potential sources of renewal. Cf. Tamás Scheibner, 'Building Empire through Self-Colonization: Literary Canons and Budapest as Sovietized Metropolis', in Dobrota Pucharová and Róbert Gáfrik (eds), *Postcolonial Europe? Essays on Post-Communist Literatures and Cultures*. Leiden and Boston: Brill, 2015, 221–23.

17 Although Kepes's artistic and theoretical activities were known in Hungary, his first solo show was held at Műcsarnok as late as 1976. His volume of essays *Közösségi művészet felé* [Towards a Communal Art] was published on that occasion, followed by *Látás nyelve* [Language of Vision] in 1979.

18 Spoken communication by Lajos Dargay, a student of Schöffer's and the first director of the museum.

19 It is worth noting that some artists openly disagreed with the support that Vasarely received. For example, at the opening of his solo exhibition at Műcsarnok in 1969 (see note 20), graphic artist János Major carried a small sign saying 'Vasarely Go Home'. See also Zólyom and Fogarasi, *Vasarely Go Home*, and Daniel Véri, *Major János (1934–2008): Monográfia és oeuvre-katalógus* [János Major (1934–2008): Monograph and Oeuvre Catalogue], doctoral dissertation. Budapest: ELTE, 2016, 24–29, 207.

20 It is no accident that the two artists' solo exhibitions at Műcsarnok in 1969 took place in close succession: 24 May to 28 June 1969 (Amerigo Tot), and 18 October to 16 November 1969 (Victor Vasarely).

21 Máté Major, 'Amerigo Tot kiállítása' [Exhibition of Amerigo Tot], *Élet és Irodalom*, Vol. 13, No. 23, 1969, 9.

22 Emese Kürti and József Mélyi (eds), *Amerigo Tot, párhuzamos konstrukciók* [Amerigo Tot, Parallel Constructions]. Budapest: Ludwig Múzeum/Kortárs Művészeti Múzeum, 2009.

23 Árpád Thiery, 'Vasarelyvel Magyarországon' [With Vasarely in Hungary], *Kortárs*, Vol. 18, No. 9, 1974, 1,451.

24 József Sztankay and Dénes Szüts, 'Megtalálni a hazát' [Finding the Homeland], *Népszava*, Vol. 105, No. 303, 25 December 1977, 4.

25 Tibor Frank, *Double-Exile: Migration of Jewish-Hungarian Professionals through Germany to the United States, 1919–1945*. Oxford: Peter Lang, 2009.

26 Alexander Croitoru, *Brancusi: An Afterlife*. Bucharest and Berlin: Salonul de proiecte/Archive Books, 2015, 54.

27 Julianna Gasparina, 'The Artist, the Futurologist, and the Technocrat', in Zólyom and Fogarasi, *Vasarely Go Home*, 51–63.

28 'Vasarely levele Rosta Endrének' [Vasarely's Letter to Endre Rosta], XIX-A-33-a/Propaganda Osztály/1132/15193/Victor Vasarely meghívása és kiállítása (1968) [The invitation and the exhibition of Victor Vasarely].

29 XIX-A-33-a/Propaganda Osztály/1159. doboz/Claire Vasarely kérése [Request of Claire Vasarely].

30 Cultural readmission and 'homecoming' were surrounded by numerous metaphors referring to the nation as a body and organism: 'replanting' was one of them.

31 Klara Kemp-Welch, *Antipolitics in Central European Art: Reticence as Dissidence under Post-Totalitarian Rule, 1956–1989*. London and New York: I. B. Tauris, 2013

32 Anna Koós, *Színházi történetek* [Stories from the Theatre]. Budapest: Akadémiai Kiadó, 2009, 140–50.

33 Edit Sasvári, 'Fából vaskarika, Marxista önmegvalósítás helyett kapitalista import – nemzeti alapon' [Squaring the Circle: Capitalist Imports Instead of Marxist Self-Realization – on a National Basis], in Kürti and Mélyi, *Amerigo Tot*, 25.

34 László Maksay, 'A Non-figuratív festészet helye – Hozzászólás a "Festészet Paradoxona" – című cikkhez' [The Place of Non-Figurative Painting – A Comment on the Article 'The Paradox of Painting'], *Művészet*, Vol. 12, No. 1, 1971, 40.

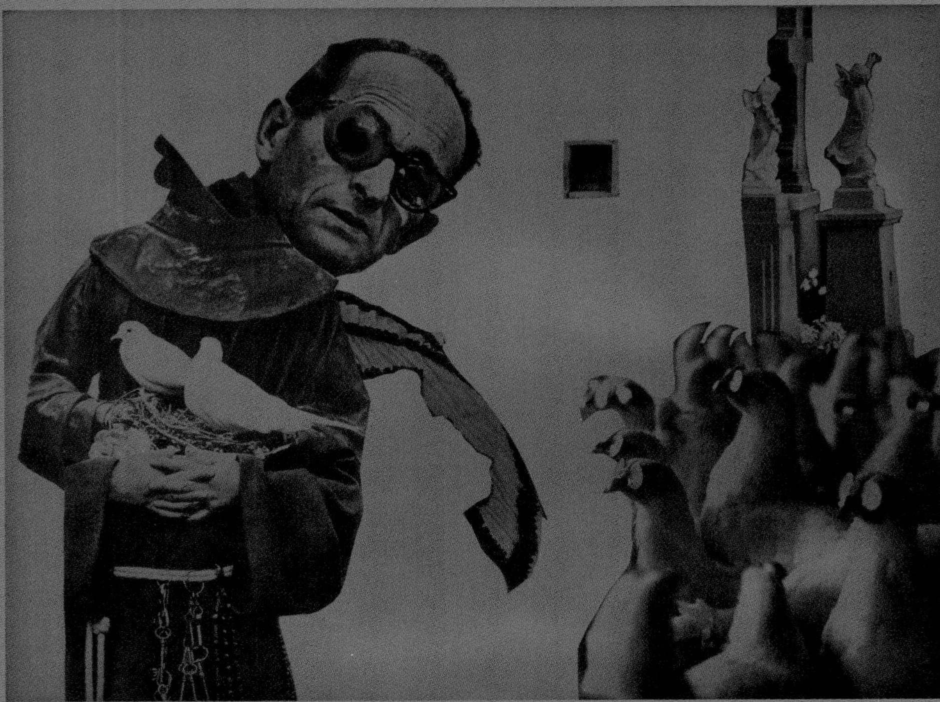

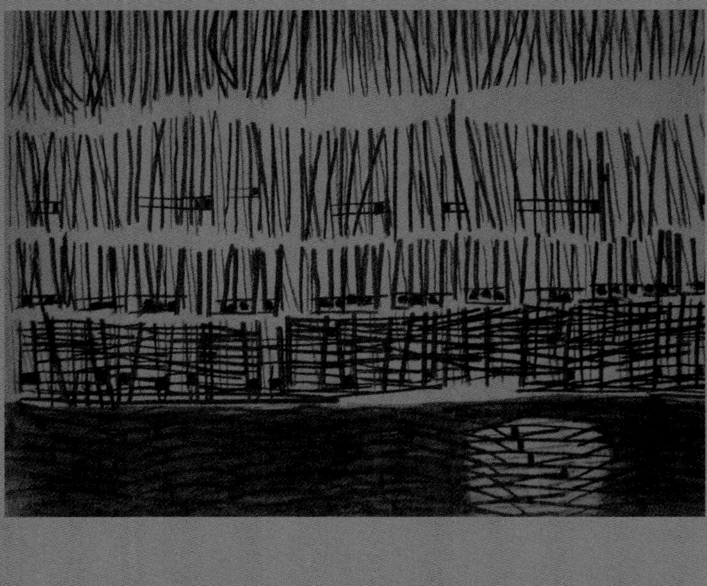

Disguises

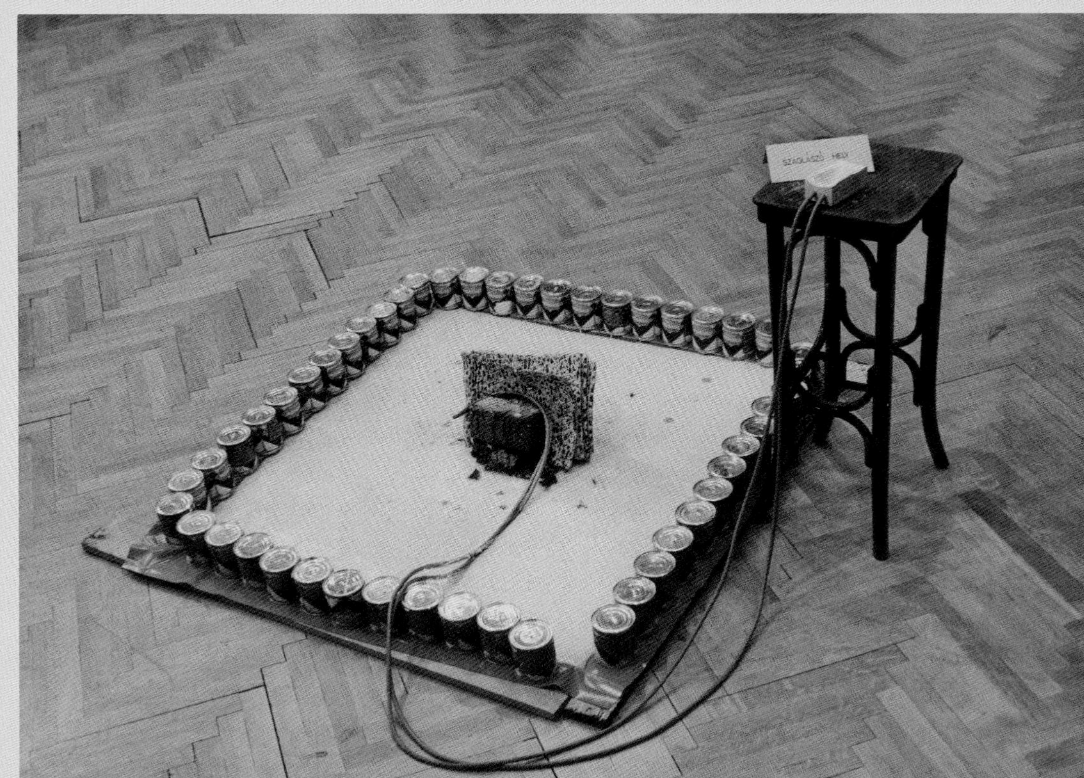

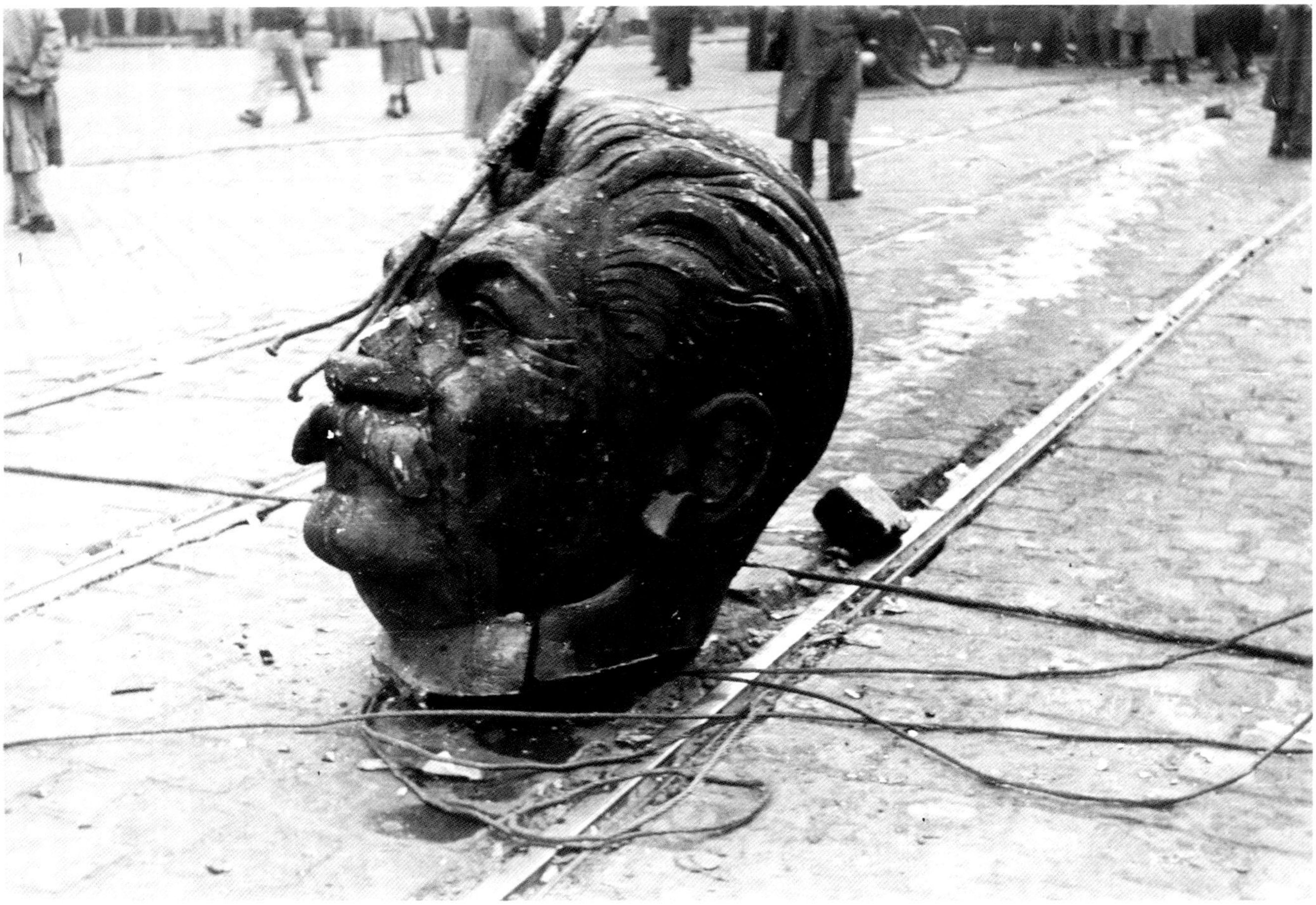

1

1. The remnants of Sándor Mikus's Stalin statue, Budapest, 1956

Taboo and Trauma: 1956

When it comes to art and 1956, one ought to begin with the best known and most influential art-related event: the toppling of the Stalin statue (see also Magdalena Radomska, 'Working in the Twice-mined Semantic Minefield', pp. 315–29). On the evening of 23 October, the day the revolution broke out, the 8-metre (26-ft) tall statue of Stalin on Budapest's Felvonulási tér (Felvonulási Square) was toppled by a crowd that was a hundred-thousand strong. The bulk of the statue (only Stalin's boots remained in place) was dragged to Blaha Lujza tér in the city centre, where, over a period of several days, it was hacked to pieces. This ecstatic event, a classic case of twentieth-century iconoclasm, meant the symbolic fall of the communist system. The significance of Stalin's statue was inherent in its destruction. American legal scholar Sanford Levinson considers the toppling of Stalin's statue in 1956 'the most permanent Hungarian contribution to political semiotics'.[1] The annihilation of the statue marked not only the fall of the political system, but also that of socialist realism, the dictatorially imposed style of the 1950s in Hungary. The dogmatic principles that controlled the arts could not be brought back after 1956 (fig. 1).

In the feverish days of the revolution, which lasted barely a fortnight from 23 October to 4 November 1956, artists considered ways of starting over and creating an artistic language that responded to the revolutionary situation. A sculpture design for a collective national monument commemorating the fallen heroes of the revolution, for example, meant to break with the traditions of sculptural monuments. Sculptors Béni Ferenczy, Tamás Vígh and Tibor Vilt wanted to express the national unity of the revolution by planting nineteen seedlings on top of mounds of earth brought from the nineteen counties of Hungary. The initiative stressed joint action, similar to the way in which money was collected for the families of the fallen (discussed below). This latter event was not infused with art historical significance until decades later, when it was subsequently linked to the work of Miklós Erdély, the iconic figure of the 1960s–70s avant-garde in Hungary.

Once the 1956 revolution was defeated, its ideas became the greatest taboo of the new regime and the memory of it as a popular, national uprising was wiped from the official record. Since János Kádár quashed the revolution with the help of the Soviet military, his power was based on Soviet intervention, and any reference to the revolution questioned the legitimacy of the existing regime. Kádár hypocritically claimed his own regime was 'revolutionary': his government, which was formed on 4 November 1956, would be called the Revolutionary Workers'-Peasants' Government of Hungary until 1973. One of the regime's most deceitful measures was perhaps its labelling of 1956 as a counterrevolution, which forced any reference to it into a negative context throughout the Kádár era.

Few artists dared to touch the topic of 1956 under the looming shadow of repression: such works could not be shown publicly and their authors could also expect to suffer repercussions and severe punishments. Keeping the memory of the crushed revolution alive called for various individual creative tactics, but the general public in Hungary had very limited access to the resulting works until after the political transition in 1989.

Post-1989 research has revealed that numerous representations of the events were, in fact, created even at the time of the revolution; these have been valued primarily for their documentary worth as records of the participants' first-hand experiences. After the fall of the revolution, quite a few artists attempted to process the trauma of 1956 or created works with allusive symbolism, if only in single works or series.[2]

Tactics and images

One of the most dramatic images of the 1956 revolution shows a half-naked man hung upside down. The photos of the mob justice after the siege of the Communist Party headquarters on Köztársaság tér became known worldwide thanks to *Life* and other Western magazines. The images of lynching victims were distillations of crowd cruelty and a desperate anti-communist fury.

János Major, one of the most original, transgressive figures of Hungarian visual art, created his early work *Hanged Man* (fig. 2) at the beginning of 1957 during his college studies. He recalled his experiences of lynching incidents seen in 1956, on which the work was based:

I saw two men hanged on Köztársaság tér – I lived close by, in Kun utca – one of them may have been János Asztalos, who had probably been assigned there to defend the party HQ. The other was behind the Erkel Theatre, on a square across from a school, a man hanging from a tree. It was a horrific sight, this half-naked man. His head was caked with dried blood, which made him unrecognizable. They may have already been dead, when they were hanged. It was a deeply shocking sight.[3]

Major made several sketches inspired by the impact of this experience, which resulted in his meticulously detailed copper engraving, small in size yet monumental in its effect. The monumentality is due to the vulnerable, dramatic pose of the corpse dominating the image space, which is accentuated by the desolate environment and the barrenness of the tree.

The human figure hanging upside down from a tree imprinted itself in general consciousness as the emblem of the lynched state-security officers, primarily due to contemporary press coverage and film footage. Major's representation of the violated and solitary hanging corpse was bound to be interpreted as a commemoration of the murdered communists. One of his

2

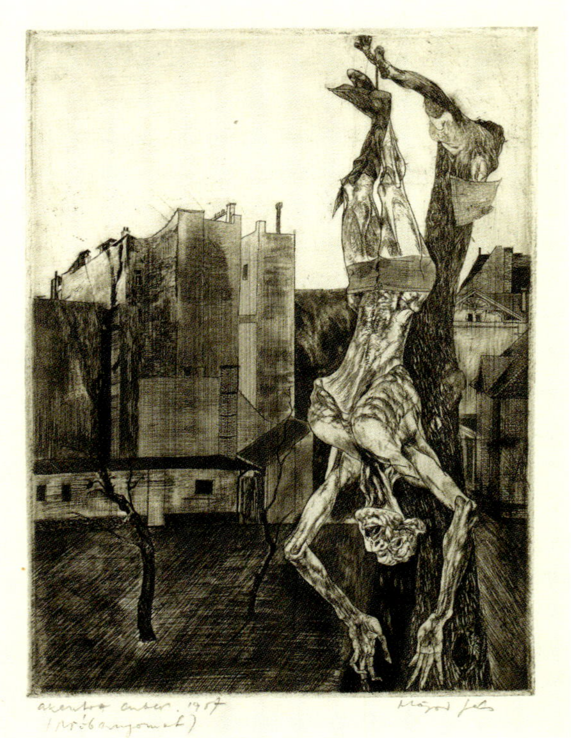

2. János Major, *Hanged Man*, 1957, etching, 23 × 17 cm, Private collection

friends' recollections suggest that 'he simply drew the horror without any further political agenda or ideology; his copper engraving was an articulation of the experience he had gone through there.'[4]

Interestingly, the work was subsequently put on display in several exhibitions that intended to commemorate the 'leftist martyrs' of the 1956 'counterrevolution', that is those fallen defending the communist regime. This happened first as early as 1959, but even the great survey exhibition 'Rejt/Jel/Képek '56 – A forradalom titkos művészete' (Hidden Symbols '56 – The Secret Art of the Revolution), which was held at the Magyar Nemzeti Múzeum (Hungarian National Museum) in 2016, included it among the representations of the 'counterrevolution'. The afterlife of Major's work is illustrative of the way representations with a somewhat distant view of things can be co-opted into a completely opposite view, and demonstrates the still powerful temptation to force works related to 1956 into political templates.

The events of Köztársaság tér and their photographic and visual art representations had a vital place in the memory politics of the Kádár regime. Köztársaság tér was 'the historiographic centre of the [political] restoration' after 1956: 'Köztársaság tér was meant to justify the reprisals, the ruthless retaliations, and the continued Soviet occupation.'[5] So, after crushing the revolution, Kádár's establishment chose Köztársaság tér, soaked in the blood of communist martyrs, to be the site of the official memorialization of 1956. Of all sites of the 'counterrevolution', this was best suited to ritualization. In 1957, the government decided to commemorate the 'heroic communist martyrs murdered by counterrevolutionaries' with a grand sculpture erected at this symbolic centre of state memory, but characteristically incorporated the announcement into a large workers' rally on the square, as if the government had merely responded to the workers' will. Viktor Kalló, a locksmith turned artist fresh out of the Magyar Képzőművészeti Főiskola (Hungarian Academy of Fine Arts), won the competition with his design. The colossus of a collapsing, dying worker – officially named *Monument to the Martyrs Who Fell for the Freedom of the Hungarian Workers* – was not completed until 1960 because of an extensive dispute about the sculpture.

The artist recalls:

The commissioners were satisfied. When we first tested the design in a life-size set, they wanted the sculpture to be ten metres tall, and I could barely talk them out of it. I designed it to be 2.6 metres tall and positioned it between the three poplars, where the atrocities had happened. The pain was still acute in our leaders at the time, and they wanted a monument as large as possible. We ended up bringing it down to five. But we had to move it to a different spot because of the size. It came to face the party HQ.[6]

This brutal and crude colossus vocally expressed the disjunction between official and everyday memory, the dichotomy of revolution and counterrevolution, and the gloomy atmosphere of the reprisal years. Even when political prisoners were released en masse in the 1963 amnesty, this thaw left the memory of the revolution a taboo and an unprocessed trauma. Though artists kept engaging with the topic, its artistic representations had to rely on hidden, allusive symbols, a sort of metalanguage. Hungarian society had learned this language since the 1950s, and many of the artists counted on people's ability to read between the lines. This was Béla Kondor's strategy, whose historical topics and traditional technique, which juxtaposed different temporal planes, symbols and motifs, were suited to ambiguous, parabolic representations. This gave him more opportunity to sneak current political references into his work.

Kondor, who graduated from the Graphics department of the Magyar Képzőművészeti Főiskola in the summer of 1956, had no direct experience of the revolution, which he nevertheless evoked in several works. His painting *Execution* was inspired, like Major's work above, by incidents of mob justice in 1956 and this work, once again like Major's, was also included in the 1959 exhibition remembering 1956 as a counterrevolution.

Kondor's large oil painting *The Angel of the Revolution* was a centrepiece of his first solo show, at the Fényes Adolf Terem (Adolf

Fényes Showroom) in 1960 (fig. 3). Four years after the revolution – while executions of those sentenced in 1956 were continuing – the mere use of the word 'revolution' was an act of courage. Many artists chose to make concealed references to 1956 through the theme of another revolution, the Hungarian communist revolution of 1919. Kondor's picture, dating from 1959 and commemorating the Commune or Hungarian Soviet Republic of 1919, represents an angel protecting its new-born baby against a reddish backdrop. The angel appears in Kondor's oeuvre in myriad forms, and he uses the possibilities inherent in the motif far beyond the traditions of Christian iconography, linking this component of his personal mythology to extreme meanings. The display of *The Angel of the Revolution* in 1960 – as emphasized in the memoirs of Kondor's friend Miklós Erdély – astonished many: 'The cause of astonishment was, of course, the contamination of communist and Catholic ideologies, because no one dared to think then and there – before the first general amnesty – that the angelic figure was actually a reference to the revolution of 1956 rather than 1919.'[7]

The graphic artist whose representations of the Hungarian revolution were especially influential and most often cited abroad was Lajos Szalay. Though Szalay was not restricted by Hungarian censorship, he did not have any first-hand experience of the Hungarian revolution or the subsequent reprisals, as he had moved to Paris in 1948 and then to Argentina, where he taught at the Academy of Fine Arts in Buenos Aires.

Szalay followed the Hungarian events of 1956 from Argentina – a country with a sizeable Hungarian immigrant community – with the help of radio broadcasts and newspapers. Despite a distance of thousands of miles, he recorded the drama of his homeland in a robust and evocative series of drawings. Instead of illustrating, he transformed the news into allegoric scenes often imbued with biblical or mythological allusions. He recalled: 'I tried to draw what I heard. I did not illustrate, but rather drew in the mood provoked by the radio. The drawings show the mood at the time. [...] I would listen to the radio and draw. The drawings are the graphic projection of how I was personally moved by the news on the radio.'[8] A compilation of these drawings and news items from free Hungarian radio broadcasts was published in the volume *SOS El drama de Hungria* in 1957, which the publisher sent to United Nations missions with the aim of influencing the organization's view on the Soviet intervention in Hungary and its ongoing situation.[9]

Szalay's drawings, reproduced in numbers and circulated among the Hungarian émigré press, showed the revolution in a classic narrative framework as the unequal fight between good and evil. This artistic interpretation fitted into the narrative of the cold war and global East–West conflict characteristic of the period. The Hungarian freedom fighters' memorial erected in Norwalk, Connecticut, in the United States in 1969 was, in fact, based on one of Szalay's drawings. The large bronze relief shows an unclothed horseman, holding a short Roman sword, about to trample on a male figure who has fallen to the ground. The hand of the latter rests on a harp, which not only symbolizes the conflict of barbarism and culture, but also refers to the significant role of poets and writers in the Hungarian wars of liberation. Szalay lived in New York from 1960 – after his relationship with the Hungarian immigrant community in Argentina had deteriorated due to his drawings about 1956 – until his return home in 1988.

By contrast, artists who experienced the revolution in Hungary were reduced to silence or suffered repression and censorship, which they tried to circumvent with indirect symbolism and doublespeak (see Edit Sasvári, 'Autonomy and Doublespeak', pp. 8–17). Reaching the public was not easy, as a date, symbol or shadow of a reference in a title was enough to make an artwork suspect in the eyes of the authorities or exhibition organizers.

Painter Endre Bálint, who was working in the spirit of École de Paris modernism instead of following the doctrine of socialist realism at the time, accepted positions in the new artists' organizations that hoped to renew artistic life during the revolution. Because of his conduct in 1956, Bálint decided to leave for Paris in the spring of 1957 and not to return until 1962.[10] Before he left, in late 1956, he painted the surrealist composition *Day of the Dead 1956* (fig. 4) as a reaction to the crushing of the revolution (see also Daniel Véri, 'The Holocaust and the Arts', pp. 209–27 for Bálint's work related to the Holocaust).

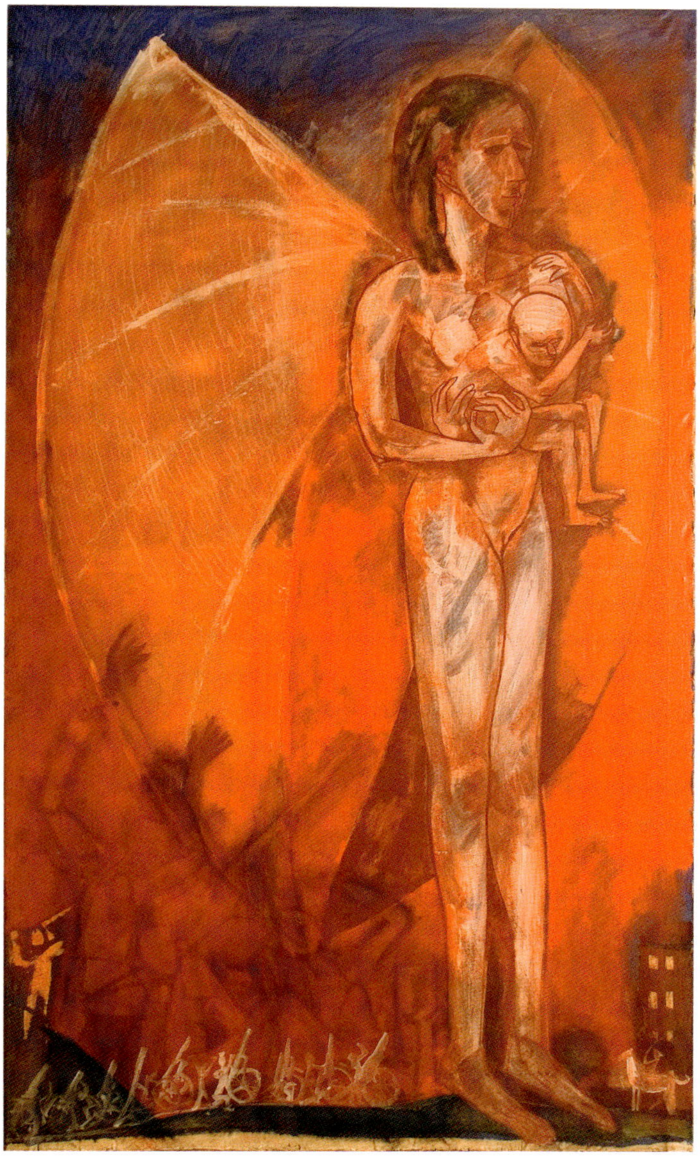

3

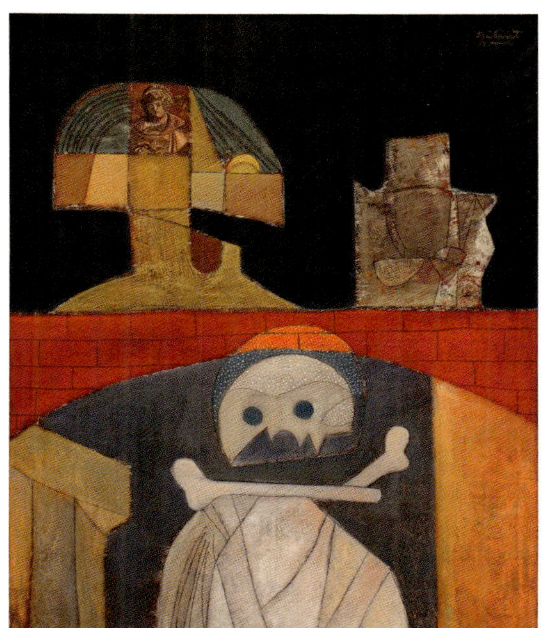

4

3. Béla Kondor, *The Angel of the Revolution*, 1959, oil on canvas, 200 × 110 cm, Petőfi Irodalmi Múzeum, Budapest

4. Endre Bálint, *Day of the Dead*, 1956, oil on canvas, 160 × 130 cm, Balassa Bálint Múzeum, Esztergom

The Művelődésügyi Minisztérium (Ministry of Culture) purchased the work as part of the policy of extensive state acquisition following the establishment of the Magyar Nemzeti Galéria (Hungarian National Gallery) in 1957. The work did not go to some new top-level state art institution, though: it entered the collection of a small provincial institution, the Balassa Bálint Múzeum (Bálint Balassa Museum) in Esztergom, which also acquired numerous other works by the abstract and surrealist artists of the Európai Iskola (European School), a post-war progressive group, the members of which were marginalized after 1948 (see Gábor Dobó and Merse Pál Szeredi, 'Hungarian Culture +/- Europe', pp. 39–57). One reason for the purchase of the work, besides its painterly qualities, may have been its somewhat elusive meaning. The date was routinely dropped from the title, thereby concealing the specific meaning of the work. Like many other artworks of the era, this one was infused retroactively with relevance to 1956: Bálint's principal motif in the painting, a skull and a cross made of bones, offered a visionary glimpse of later events, evoking a mythic component of the 1956 memorial cult: the burial of executed revolutionaries in unmarked graves, which led to 'grief without a grave'.

Tamás Lossonczy, who belonged to the circles of the Európai Iskola, secretly made a surrealist graphic series on 1956 that was never meant for publication, and worked on his grand painting *Great Purifying Storm* for years until finishing it in 1962 (pp. 167, fig. 3).[11] The work, which also commemorated 1956, was a grand synthesis of his political disappointments and aesthetic hopes and his whole oeuvre. Even though the painting evoking a biomorphic, microscopic world was abstract enough to conceal any explicit reference to 1956, it could not be exhibited until the late 1970s. Its innovation was primarily formal: its unusually large size and its conception were closer to Western abstract expressionism than to works of modern art in Hungary.

By the 1970s, the memory of 1956 had increasingly become a 'silent tradition', to use Péter György's phrase. 'Collective memory was restricted to the private sphere, and members of the new generation barely reflected on the revolution in their art.'[12] The younger generation rarely touched on the topic and even then did so very cautiously: painter Ádám Kéri had a diptych entitled *Revolution* on display at the exhibition of the Fiatal Képzőművészek Stúdiója (Young Artists' Studio) in 1972.[13] The first of the two parts shows a dirty white brick wall, while the second shows the same wall with the bloody bullet holes of machine-gun fire. The artist completed the series with a third part after the exhibition: it shows the wall whitewashed as a symbol of forgetting and the general hopelessness of the period. When Kéri had an opportunity to exhibit at the Műcsarnok (Kunsthalle), the chief state exhibiting institution, in 1974, he intended to show this triptych along with his works representing other bullet holes and evoking the 1848 revolution and war of independence. The exhibition was cancelled in the end because the allusion to the 1956 revolution would have been unmistakable.

Gyula Konkoly, one of the most important figures of the Hungarian neo-avant-garde generation in the 1960s (see also Dávid Fehér, '(Dis)figuring Reality', pp. 137–59), represented a far more radical approach in his oeuvre, which was also more in sync with a critical take on current political events and the international trends of contemporary art. His installation titled *Memorial* (fig. 5), which drew on conceptualism and pop art, was shown at the second 'Iparterv' exhibition, which opened on 24 October 1969.[14] The works shown at the 'Iparterv' exhibitions were usually experimenting with the latest trends of Western aesthetic modernism. Konkoly's installation consisted of a block of ice, forming a human figure, covered in medical gauze with some potassium permanganate sprinkled over it, which was all placed on a metal stand.[15] At the opening, the reddish liquid of the melting ice soaked through the gauze and dripped onto a plastic trough under the figure. Both the pool of 'blood' and the date of the opening were clear references to 1956. In the days around the anniversary of the revolution, state-security authorities were particularly alert to any suspicious signs in order to prevent unrest (at workplaces, even typewriters and other devices capable of reproducing material for distribution might be collected and locked up). *Memorial* was regarded as a provocative reference to the revolution so it was removed from the exhibition and destroyed after the

5. Gyula Konkoly, *Memorial*, 1969, ice, cotton, gauze, metal, potassium permanganate, perished

6. (overleaf) Miklós Erdély and others, *Unguarded Money* ('The purity of our revolution makes it possible for us to collect money in this way for the families of our fallen martyrs'), action, Budapest, 1956

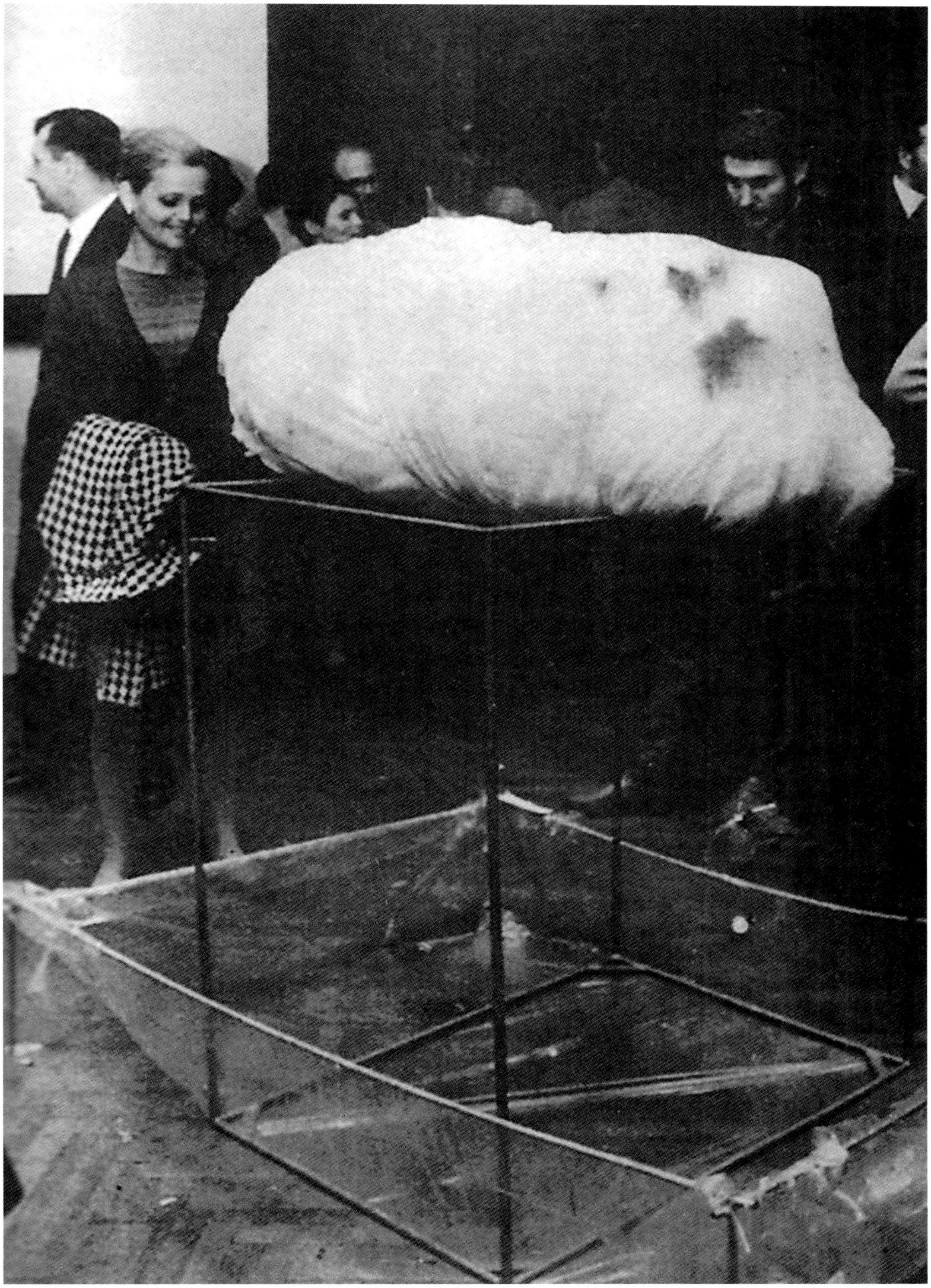

5

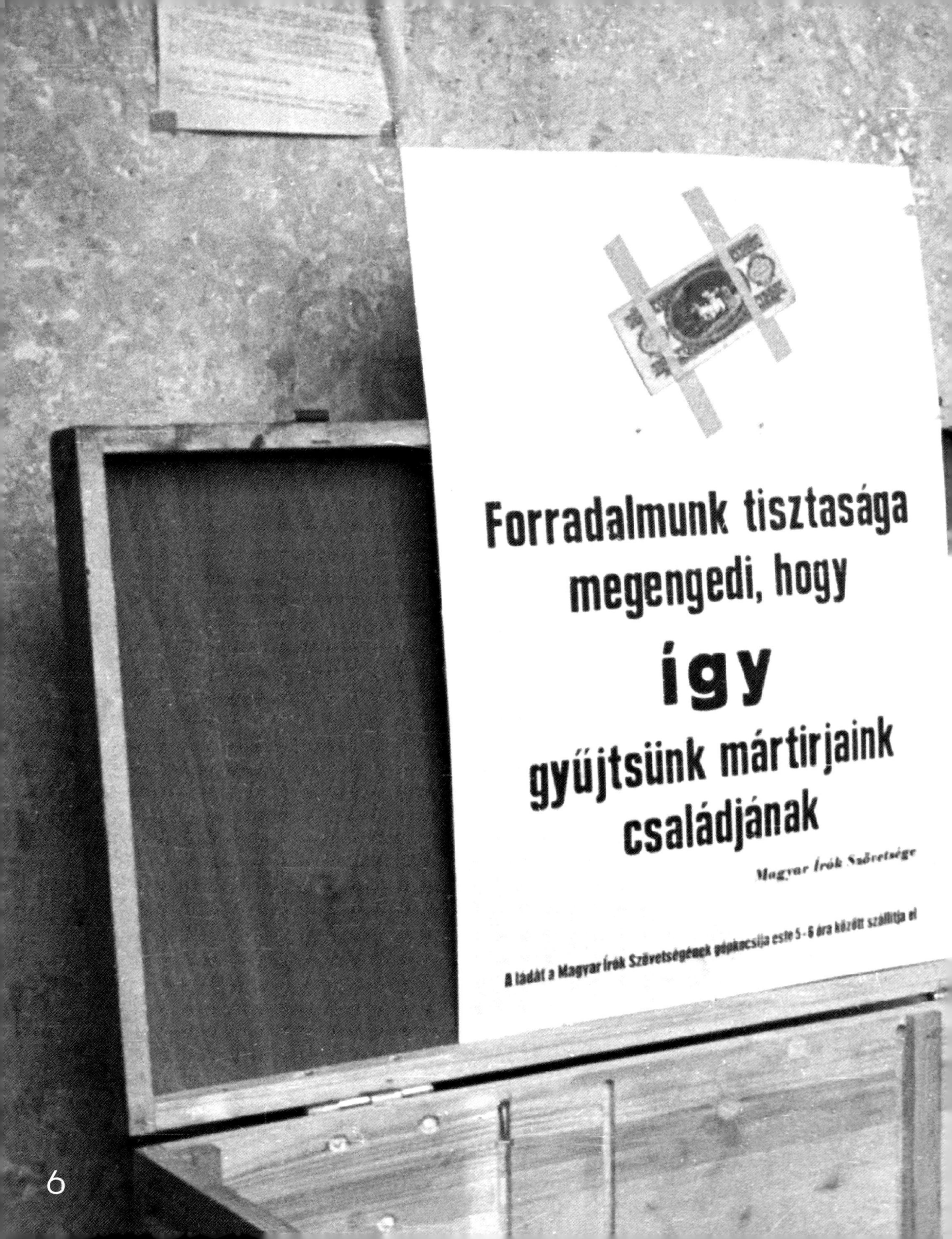
Forradalmunk tisztasága
megengedi, hogy
így
gyűjtsünk mártirjaink
családjának
Magyar Írók Szövetsége
A ládát a Magyar Írók Szövetségének gépkocsija este 5 - 6 óra között szállítja el

6

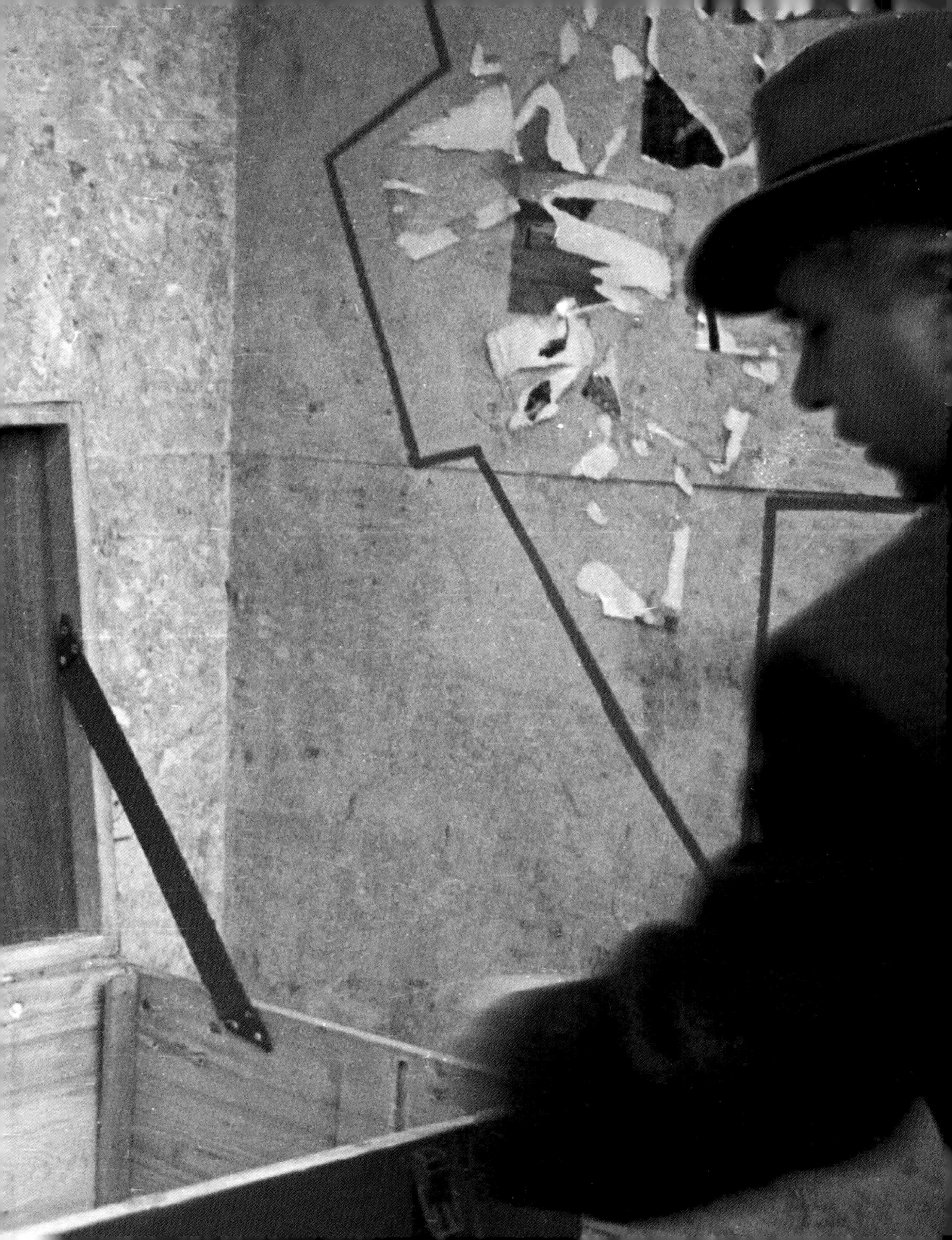

opening. Konkoly – like so many of the 'Iparterv generation' – emigrated to the West the following year. He lived in Paris until the early 1990s.

Konkoly's *Memorial* is one of those explicit political works – quite rare in Hungary – that simultaneously commemorate the tragedy of the Hungarian revolution and openly criticize the regime that turned that tragedy into a taboo.[16] The 1968 student protests in Paris and the events in Prague during the same year, when Czechoslovakia was invaded by Soviet forces to prevent liberal reforms, were also catalysts that reactivated the repressed memory of the revolution. The content and form of the resultant works were both radically open and tangible, which was in sync with the artistic intentions characterizing the region in the late 1960s. Konkoly's *Memorial* led Tony Godfrey to identify a direct critique of socialist and autonomous modernist art as the distinctive feature of Eastern European conceptual art.[17] Konkoly's work was a bold transgression even in a political sense. It would be decades before frank public views about 1956, either through art or in politics, would be possible in Hungary.

A revolutionary act

Thanks to the world press, documentary photography played a far greater role in preserving the memory of the 1956 Hungarian revolution than works of visual art could, with their limited ability to reach the public. An emblematic event that stands out in the visual archive of the revolution became known as *Unguarded Money* (fig. 6); until the 1980s, the fact that this event was linked to Miklós Erdély, a central figure of the Hungarian neo-avant-garde, remained largely unknown.

On 2–3 November 1956, while the revolution was still underway, activists from the Magyar Írók Szövetsége (Association of Hungarian Writers) placed boxes at six busy intersections in Budapest to collect money for the families of those who had been killed in the fighting. The collection boxes would remain in the street unguarded, which was an important aspect of the project. The posters that hung above the boxes confirmed this: 'The purity of our revolution makes it possible for us to collect money in this way for the families of our fallen martyrs.'

Miklós Erdély later revealed the act as his work, and in various international exhibitions and art historical surveys it has been identified as the first work in the history of Hungarian conceptual art. Clearly, the subtle implementation of the concept and the design and rigorous visual composition of the poster indicate that this was no spontaneous action. A banknote for 100 forints (the highest value available at the time) was affixed face down to each poster; consequently, instead of supplying symbolism through the portrait of Lajos Kossuth, the leader of the 1848 revolution, the notes showed *Fleeing the Approaching Storm*, a painting by Károly Lotz. Each note could be detached from the poster and taken. It is hard to tell if passers-by understood the subtlety of the design at the time; in any case, the action achieved its goal, as the amount collected – around 260,000 forints – was quite significant by the standards of the day. The organizers did not discriminate among the victims, so donations went to families of those fighting on both sides of the barricades.

Collections were taken in other countries, including Poland, to benefit the victims of the Hungarian revolution in 1956. What distinguishes the action in Budapest from these more traditionally executed collections is the unusual use of public space, the choice to leave the money unguarded, and the effort to make people aware of the latter. The text of the poster above the boxes summarizes the essence of the action by emphasizing the mode of collection with the word *így* ('like this') both in content and typography. Like this, that is leaving it unguarded, because the 'purity of our revolution' allows it. Erdély explained in an interview in 1983 that the collection was inspired by a news item on how goods behind broken shop windows were left undisturbed.[18] Tales of the untouched collection boxes and shop windows, as noble expressions of revolutionary morality, often appeared together in the news and in memoirs. Hannah Arendt also noted that 'shops and shop windows were not looted' during the 1956 revolution 'in a country with a great deal of poverty and hardship'.[19]

Money left unguarded in the street was not a novelty in itself, as this is the basis of any honour payment system.[20] But in Hungary in the 1950s, when money and goods were in short supply and people could vividly remember the greatest inflation in financial history (when valueless million-pengő notes were swept up in the streets of Budapest in 1946), attitudes to money could hardly be compared to those of a more stable society. This unusual mode of collection Erdély and his associates used was quite risky, as they had no way of knowing if the first 100-forint notes would instantly go missing. Value systems change instantaneously in a revolution when, supposedly, anarchy reigns, so the general reaction and the high level of solidarity were surprising. The money and goods left untouched in the boxes and shop windows were the result of a unique and unrepeatable state of grace. As a witness commented: as soon as the revolution was defeated, 'the shop windows were robbed right away after 4 November. Something snapped in the souls.'[21]

Social psychology explains the reaction to unguarded money and honour payment systems as something deeper than honesty: they work on the basis of mutuality and a respect for another's trust in oneself. There is no physical exchange of cash for goods or services in the case of the 1956 collection; the service rendered in exchange is symbolic and therefore too valuable to quantify: participants receive a communal experience of the revolutionary ethos. This message was more important than the collection itself. After the fall of the revolution, the Kádár regime considered the collection dangerous because its memory lived on and its impact was strengthened and prolonged by photographs.

The collection was recorded by numerous Hungarian photographers as well as renowned international press photographers, including Erich Lessing of Magnum and Stefan Moses. Film footage has also survived, for instance, in the documentary *Ungarn im Flammen* (Hungary in Flames, 1957) and the BBC programme *Cry Hungary* (1986). There may still be undiscovered recordings in Hungary, as many people hid their photos after the defeat of the revolution so that they couldn't be used as evidence against either the photographers themselves or others at the show trials. For example, Gyula Kinczler, an engineer who systematically photographed the streets of Budapest – including the collection action – during the revolution, wrapped up his negatives and nailed them to the bottom of a wardrobe, hiding them for almost five decades.

In the course of the reprisals, the collection led to one of a range of charges made against Gyula Fekete, a secretary of the Magyar Írók Szövetsége, in the so-called 'small writers' trial'. The aim of the trial was to punish the Magyar Írók Szövetsége, which played an important role in the revolution, and to lay the groundwork for a subsequent major trial, so there was no real interest in finding the actual initiators of the collection.

The trial documents confirm that the idea for the collection was proposed by young people who had been recruited on the recommendation of the Egyetemi Forradalmi Diákbizottság (University Revolutionary Student Committee), that is, from outside the Magyar Írók Szövetsége, on 31 October. Numerous delegations of all sorts approached the Magyar Írók Szövetsége during the revolution, proposing a variety of initiatives. Miklós Erdély's son, Dániel Erdély, recalls that a number of the participants were his father's friends and one-time members of a Jewish scout troop.[22] Two participants also confirm Miklós Erdély's role as the leader and initiator in the project. In 1996, architect and artist Tibor Gáyor, who was Erdély's friend and fellow student at the Műegyetem (University of Technology), wrote a detailed memorandum of the event.[23] This reveals that they needed a moral authority to legitimize the action, and this is how the Magyar Írók Szövetsége came to be involved.

The money-collection action was included in official histories of the Party state, where its meaning was distorted. It was described as a work of political propaganda used by 'certain revisionist groups' in order to 'whitewash the military' who sided with the revolutionaries. 'This was the most dangerous and the most detrimental of all,' wrote a historian loyal to the Party state in 1967, 'and a very important measure in the battle of deceiving the people in order to benefit the army and the counterrevolution.'[24]

One of the most notorious photos of the collection was included in a photo album published on the twenty-fifth anniversary of the 'liberation' (when Soviet forces took control of Hungary in 1945) with the caption 'the misleading poster of a collection organized by the Írószövetség (Magyar Írók Szövetsége) fantasizing about the purity of the revolution'.[25] The image was also included in the high-school history textbook introduced in 1982. Captioned 'the poster of the Írószövetség still fantasizes about the purity of the revolution', it was a counterpoint to a photo of the infamous lynching at Köztársaság tér. This pair of images represented 1956 for several generations of students until the political transition.[26] The editors of the textbook probably intuited correctly that the shocking experience of mob justice that cast a shadow over the revolution was instrumental in the shaping of the collection project. Tibor Gáyor recalls:

The sight of a supposed state security official hanged from a tree on the Körút near Aradi utca had a traumatic effect on me. I thought it was a disgrace to the revolution and it pushed me to search for some course of action that would conserve the experience of the admirable, the nation finding itself, finding a noble unity as opposed to the rise of vengeance.[27]

Commenting on this contrast, Colin Vernall remarks that there was a case when the use of money to make a public point in 1956 had the opposite meaning: when those defending the Party headquarters on Köztársaság tér were killed and had the money found in their pockets stuffed into their mouths in the course of the lynching.[28]

While the image of the collection box would appear in the Hungarian public sphere in an almost exclusively negative context from 1956 to the political transition, abroad it remained an important example of the purity of the revolution, retaining its original meaning and frequently appearing in émigré publications and anniversary celebrations. At home, the event continued to have at least some place in the country's collective memory, separate from the negative context provided by the textbooks. Ferenc Karinthy records it in his short novel *Budapest Autumn* (1982), where he discusses 1956 with an unusually courageous objectivity. It was the political transition that brought the real breakthrough. One of the later scenes in Géza Bereményi's film *Eldorado* (1988) features Monori, the 'vendor king' of the Teleki tér wholesale market, and his grandson passing a collection box of the Írószövetség in the bullet-riddled city. Monori throws a fistful of banknotes up in the air, telling the child: 'See? That's what it's worth. Nothing left but honour. Leave this place!'

Reinterpretations

The event was seen in a new light at the time of the political transition, when the historical narrative was recontextualized as art. The interview Miklós Erdély gave in 1983, identifying the 1956 collection as his artistic action *Unguarded Money*, was published in 1991.[29] Erdély's involvement had been known in a narrow professional circle; another central figure of the Hungarian neo-avant-garde, Tamás St Auby, for instance, claims that Erdély referred to the event as an artistic action as early as the 1960s. In the course of Erdély's canonization, Hungary's art scene related to the event and the work with a mixture of utter admiration – or in Tamás St Auby's terms, 'subservience'[30] – and scepticism.[31]

Unguarded Money first appears in Erdély's biography in 1980 ('1956: discovery of action as an art form – with Tibor Gáyor and others') in the exhibition catalogue of 'Künstler aus Ungarn' (Artists from Hungary) at the Wilhelmshaven Kunsthalle.[32] From that point on, the work is included as part of Erdély's oeuvre in each of his exhibitions, and a major art historical survey identifies it as the first Hungarian happening and a precursor of the Hungarian Fluxus movement.[33]

As part of Erdély's oeuvre, the collection project was shown in numerous major international exhibitions.[34] The international interest it generated can be explained by its connection it makes between the Hungarian revolution and its artistic representation. Erdély sensed what the artist's task was in the given situation, namely a revolution ('to recognize the new moral phenomenon' and 'to implement artistic thought in the given situation'). His entire oeuvre is suffused with this recognition. The 1956 action can be seen as remarkable and crystallizing the characteristics of the entire oeuvre – concurring with Péter György's assessment – because it is not only a candid proof of the general mood of the revolution, but also 'reveals that Erdély sensed the greatest challenge to neo-avant-garde art, namely the role of Money – and let's keep in mind the circumstances in which he did so.' One can find

> *everything that had ever fascinated Erdély: novelty, the artistic use of a given situation, direct participation in communication, or the experiment of direct actionism,* provocation, *the* gentle scandal, *the attack on the level of conventions and mentality, strong conceptualism and a powerful affinity with tautology and the absurd. Crossing genre boundaries or bringing external symbols and objects into the art scene are classic avant-garde traditions since Duchamp, and Erdély was perhaps their greatest master in Hungary.*[35]

The next time the uncommon use of money in a public space appears in Erdély's oeuvre is during his trip to Paris in 1963.[36] He proposed a street action in Paris, in which he would have sold money below nominal value in order to devalue both its purchase power and its symbolic significance. According to Géza Perneczky, one of the most influential art critics of the 1960s, who emigrated to Germany in 1970, this also exemplifies Erdély's characteristic tautological yet paradoxical conceptualist mindset: 'There should be less of anything of value, because its "symbolic value" can only grow below its value – in other words, only extinguished value is truly interesting.'[37]

Unguarded Money was originally created by the logic of artistic thinking, though not with artistic intent. It was not the collection action itself that was an avant-garde act, but Erdély's retrospective interpretation of it. Erdély, Gáyor and their fellow artists instinctively sensed that radical action in a public space, and the media recording and disseminating the action, formed an essential component of a modern revolution. It was in 1956 that Erdély recognized for the first time that 'art was not only for what it is used for – the functions of decoration, art collection and artworks', but could also serve as a force for creating communities, and for raising moral consciousness (in this case by collecting money based on trust) (see Flóra Barkóczi, 'Creative (Dis)Courses', pp. 95–109, for discussion of pedagogical aspects of Erdély's career).

In autumn 1956, in the euphoric days of growing liberty, 'everybody wanted to do something, something that had been lacking in art; they all wanted to make up for this lack.' Culturally and politically isolated from the world, 'we had no idea that happenings or actions even existed. It was in 1965 I think that I first heard from [conceptual artist László] Lakner that he had heard somewhere that [Tadeusz] Kantor and others had bricked up a wall in Poland,' recalled Erdély in 1983.[38] The art historical significance of Erdély's act was that it retroactively returned Hungarian art to the continuity of the avant-garde, which had been drastically disrupted in 1948 and only survived as an undercurrent during the four decades of communism and socialism.

1 Sanford Levinson, *Written in Stone: Public Monuments in Changing Societies*. Durham and London: Duke University Press, 1998, 12.
2 Thanks to György Sümegi's research and publications, several hundred works of this kind are known. György Sümegi, *Kép – Szó: Képzőművészek '56-ról* [Image – Word: Artists on '56]. Budapest: WordPolgART Könyvkiadó, 2004.
3 Sümegi, *Kép*, 146.
4 Quoted by Daniel Véri, *Major János (1934–2008). Monográfia és œuvre katalógus* [János Major (1934–2008): Monograph and œuvre catalogue], doctoral dissertation. Budapest: ELTE, 2016, 85. About the etching, see also Daniel Véri, "Leading the dead" – The World of János Major. Budapest, MKE, 2013, 8--11.
5 István Rév, 'A Terror Házának előképeiről' [On the Models of the House of Terror], *Élet és Irodalom*, Vol. 47, No. 10, 2003, 9.
6 Lajos Lóska, 'Egy művész ötven után: Beszélgetés Kalló Viktorral' [An Artist Fifty Years Later: Conversation with Viktor Kalló], *Művészet*, Vol. 21, No. 6, 1980, 25.
7 Sándor Hornyik, *Forradalmár, próféta, melós: Kondor Béla művészete* [Revolutionary, Prophet, Worker: The Art of Béla Kondor] (exhibition catalogue). Debrecen: MODEM, 2012.
8 Quoted in György Sümegi, 'Szalay Lajos műveinek a világa' [The World of Lajos Szalay's Works], *Forrás*, Vol. 41, No. 2, 2009, 65.
9 *SOS El drama de Hungria*, Buenos Aires, 1957. Hungarian edition: *SOS 1956: A magyar dráma* [SOS 1956: The Hungarian Drama]. Vác: Nalors Grafika, 1996.
10 It is a testimony to the fluidity of the state's art categories of 'prohibited, 'tolerated' and 'supported', and the malleability of protectionism in cultural policy, that according to the artist's monographer this Paris trip was proposed and arranged by Deputy Minister of Culture György Aczél, who had once been in the same orphanage as Bálint and who came to shape Hungarian cultural policy in his various positions from 1957 to 1982. Marianna Kolozsváry, *Bálint Endre: A nyolcadik templom* [Endre Bálint: The Eighth Temple]. Budapest: Magyar Nemzeti Galéria, 2014, 137.
11 On the series, see Tamás Lossonczy, *1956*. Budapest: Új Művészet Kiadó, 1995.
12 Péter György, *Néma hagyomány* [Silent Tradition]. Budapest: Magvető, 2000, 105.
13 The Fiatal Képzőművészek Stúdiója was founded in 1958 as a youth chapter of Magyar Népköztársaság Művészeti Alapja (Art Fund of the Hungarian People's Republic), the central organization of state patronage. Members could have their works displayed at annual collective exhibitions. See also Flóra Barkóczi, 'Creative (Dis)Courses', pp. 95–109.
14 Iparterv (Industrial Architecture Company) was a state architectural design company. The two 'Iparterv' exhibitions, arranged in its meeting hall in 1968 and 1969, presented a new generation who were mostly active in pop art and *art informel*, which was consistent with the international trends of the 1960s. See also Gábor Dobó and Merse Pál Szeredi, 'Hungarian Culture +/- Europe', pp. 39–57.
15 The work is also known as *October Monument* or *Bleeding Memorial* and was reconstructed in several forms by the artist in the 1990s.
16 Katalin Székely, 'Radikális jövőkép: Konkoly Gyula munkássága 1964-től 1973-ig' [Radical Image of Future: The Work of Gyula Konkoly, 1964–1973], in *Konkoly Gyula*. Budapest: St.art Galéria, 2008, 38.
17 Tony Godfrey, *Conceptual Art*. London: Phaidon, 1998, 267–69. Konkoly is the only Hungarian artist in Godfrey's book.
18 Miklós Peternák, 'Beszélgetés Erdély Miklóssal 1983 tavaszán' [Conversation with Miklós Erdély, Spring 1983], *Árgus*, Vol. 2, Nos 9–10, 1991, 77.
19 Hannah Arendt, *Die Ungarische Revolution und der Totalitäre Imperialismus*. Munich: Piper, 1958, n. p.; 'Totalitarian Imperialism: Reflections on the Hungarian Revolution', *Journal of Politics*, Vol. 20, No. 1, 1958, 5–43.
20 Honour payment systems spread in the late nineteenth century, particularly in the Netherlands and England, as variants of church donation boxes. Those living in smaller settlements could collect payment for their extra farm produce in unguarded boxes placed next to the goods. The success of this system is partly due to its ability to strengthen a sense of community. It became widespread especially in countries with a long tradition of democratic values (UK, Netherlands, Germany and Sweden).
21 György Sümegi, '1956 ismeretlen képeiből: Kinczler Gyula képei' [Unknown Images of 1956: Pictures by Gyula Kinzler], *Fotóművészet*, Vol. 28, Nos 1–2, 2005, 146.
22 Stated at the event 'Beszélgetés Erdély Miklós Őrizetlen pénz című művéről' [Discussing Miklós Erdély's Unguarded Money], organized at Műcsarnok in 2006. The transcript can be found in the archive of the Erdély Miklós Alapítvány (Miklós Erdély Foundation). Thanks to Annamária Szőke for facilitating access to the documents.
23 Tibor Gáyor, '1956-os személyes beszámoló' [A Personal Account of 1956], addressed to Regéczy-Nagy Lászlóhoz, President of Történelmi Igazságtétel Bizottsága (Committee for Historical Justice), 15 August 1996. Mimeographed typescript. Archive of the Erdély Miklós Alapítvány. For another version, see Gábor Sz. Szilágyi (ed.), *1956: Művészet emigrációban* [1956: Art in Emigration]. Szentendre: Pest Megyei Múzeumok Igazgatósága, 2006, 18–20.
24 János Molnár, *Ellenforradalom Magyarországon 1956-ban* [Counterrevolution in Hungary 1956]. Budapest: Akadémiai Kiadó, 1967, 192.

25 Péter Rényi and Ilona R. Sánta (eds), *A mi negyedszázadunk 1945–1970* [Our Quarter of a Century 1945–1970]. Budapest: Kossuth Könyvkiadó, 1970, 282–83.
26 Ágota Jóvérné Szirtes, *Történelem a gimnázium IV. osztálya számára: A legújabb kor története* [History for 4th grade, Secondary School: Modern History]. Budapest: Tankönyvkiadó Vállalat, 1982, 189. The textbook was in circulation until 1991. It was revised in 1989, when the post-1945 period was removed from the text.
27 Gáyor, '1956-os személyes beszámoló', 6.
28 Colin Vernall, 'Money No Object: Revolution and Revaluation in the Economics of Place and the Place of Economics in Art', http://www.gla.ac.uk/media/media_81279_en.pdf (17 May 2017).
29 Peternák, 'Beszélgetés Erdély Miklóssal 1983 tavaszán', 77.
30 Dénes Krusovszky, Marcel Szabó and Péter Urfi, 'Közegészségtelen töredékek (levélinterjú St. Auby Tamással)' [Public Un-Healthy Fragments (Letter Interview with Tamás St Auby)], *Puskin Utca*, Vol. 3, No. 10, 2009, 22. St Auby mentions András Müllner's interpretation as an example. See Mónika Dániel and András Müllner, 'Nyelvek karnevalizációja a neoavantgárd művészetben' [Carnivalization of Languages in Neo-avant-garde Art], in Mihály Szegedy-Maszák (ed.), *A magyar irodalom történetei 1920-tól napjainkig* [History of Hungarian Literature from 1920 to the Present]. Budapest: Gondolat Kiadó, 2007, 558–59.
31 An example of such reluctance is the large survey exhibition 'Codes/Signals/Images '56 – The Secret Art of the Revolution of 1956' at the Magyar Nemzeti Múzeum in 2016, where the event was captioned without any reference to Miklós Erdély: 'The collection of money was organized by Magyar Írók Szövetsége, although some art historians and visual artists consider this action the first work of conceptual art in Hungary.'
32 *Künstler aus Ungarn* (exhibition catalogue). Wilhelmshaven: Kunsthalle, 1980, 52.
33 László Beke, Eszter Gábor, Endre Prakfalvi, József Sisa and Julia Szabó, *Magyar művészet 1800-tól napjainkig* [Hungarian Art from 1800 to the Present]. Budapest: Corvina Kiadó, 2002, 338–39.
34 The exhibitions: 'Global Conceptualism – Points of Origin 1950s–1980s', New York: Queens Museum of Art, 1999; 'Samizdat: Alternative Kultur in Zentral- und Osteuropa 1956–1989', Berlin: Akademie der Künste, 2000; 'Periferic 8', Iasi, 2008; 'Promises of the Past', Paris: Centre Pompidou, 2010; 'Grafični Bienale', Ljubljana, 2011 (special prize); 'Kunst in Europa 1945–1968', Karlsruhe: ZKM, 2016.
35 Péter György, 'Erdély Miklós – a szelíd botrány művésze' [Miklós Erdély – Artist of Gentle Scandal], *Holmi*, Vol. 4, No. 8, 1992, 1172.
36 This action was never actually executed, as some mistakenly claim. It only existed in a literary form, as a suggestion included in the short story 'Anarchisták Párizsban' [Anarchists in Paris], published in issue 12 of *Magyar Műhely* in 1965. András Müllner writes, for example: 'when he got to Paris in 1964, he continued where he had left off in Budapest in 1956: he began to sell the franc below its nominal value, and the action had to be prohibited by the police to prevent artificial inflation'. Dániel and Müllner, 'Nyelvek karnevalizációja a neoavantgárd művészetben', 558.
37 Géza Perneczky, 'Erdély Miklós és müve, a dekonstruktív tautológia' [Miklós Erdély and His Work, A Deconstructive Tautology], in *Erdély Miklós (1928–1986)* (exhibition catalogue). Székesfehérvár: Csók István Képtár, István Király Múzeum, 1991, 16.
38 Peternák, 'Beszélgetés Erdély Miklóssal 1983 tavaszán', 77.

1. Agamemnon Makrisz, Model for the *Mauthausen Memorial*, 1960, 56 × 63 × 17 cm, lead, stone, Szépművészeti Múzeum – Magyar Nemzeti Galéria, Budapest

2. Rezső Berczeller, *Mauthausen*, 1958, terracotta, 9 × 29 × 10.7 cm, location unknown

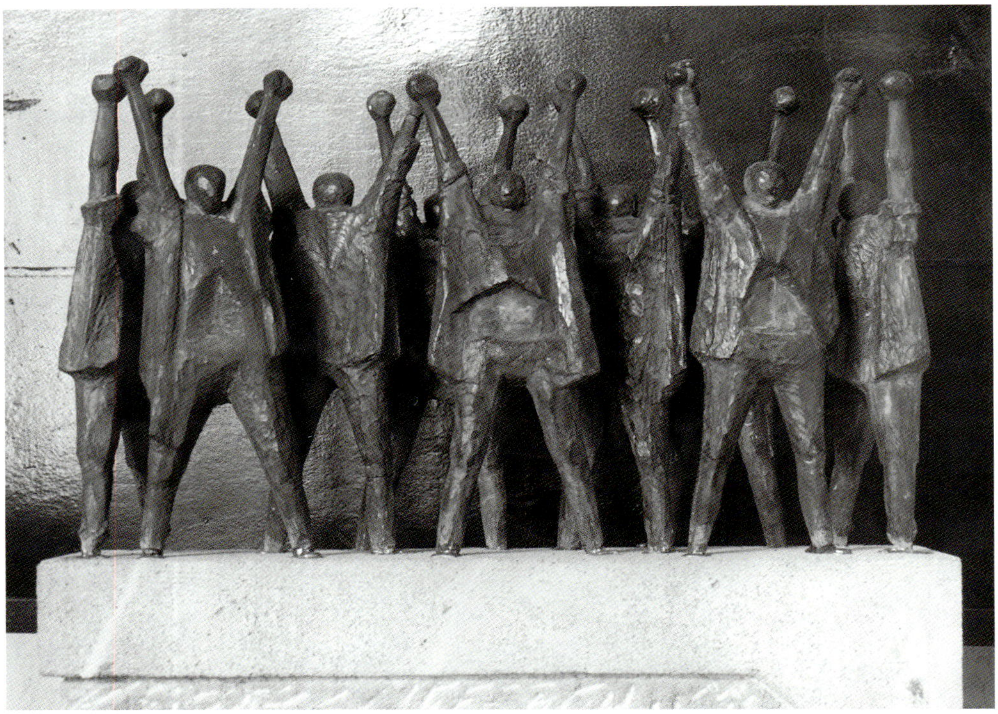

1

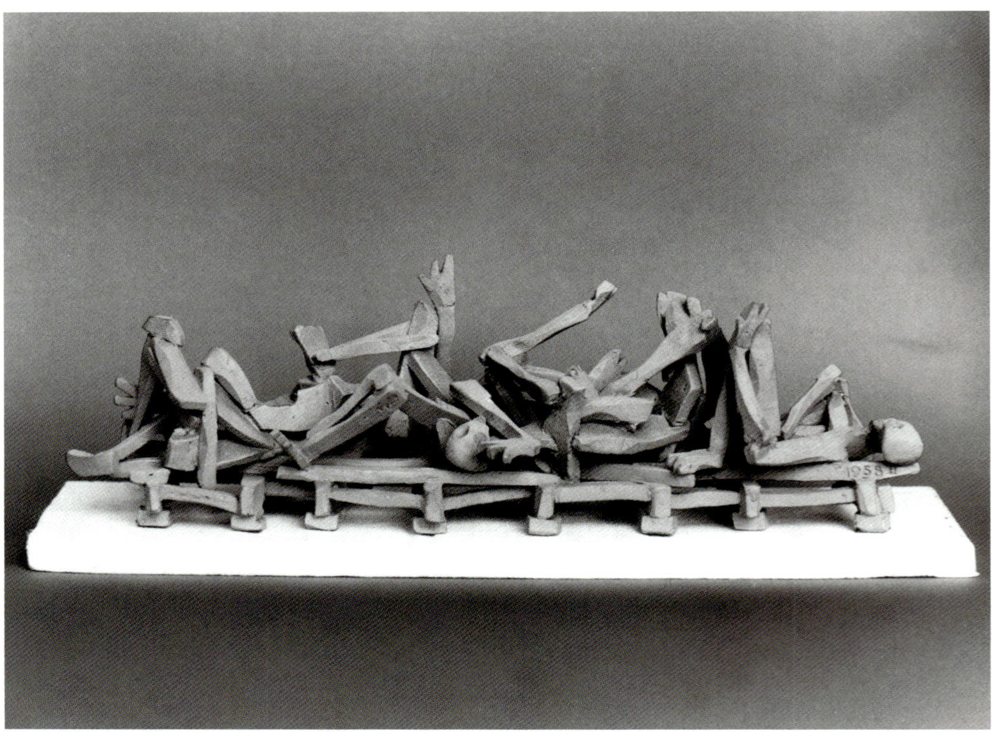

2

Daniel Véri

The Holocaust and the Arts

Paths and Crossroads

The Jewish population – or rather those defined as Jewish by law – of the Hungarian countryside were deported in 1944 under German supervision with the active and effective participation of the Hungarian government and authorities. Most of the adult men had been called up for 'labour service' for years, which meant unarmed forced labour under the supervision of the military. Many of them did not die as a consequence of the war itself, but were killed by armed Hungarian soldiers supervising Jewish labour groups. The Budapest Jewry was already confined to a ghetto when, following the suspension of the deportations, the Nyilaskeresztes Párt (Arrow-Cross Party) – the Hungarian national socialist party – seized power in October 1944, and committed a series of mass murders in the capital, primarily on the bank of the Danube. Many people went into hiding under assumed names with forged documents.[1]

Despite the manifold artistic reflections on the trauma of the Holocaust, art historical research has primarily focused on works produced during the war, in the camps and ghettos, and immediately after the war, as well as on works created after 1989. By contrast, the corpus of works produced between the communist takeover in the late 1940s and the political transition in the late 1980s have received less attention. The fullest regional art historical study of this period so far is *In the Shadow of Yalta* by Piotr Piotrowski. Despite the author's sensitivity to historical and political contexts, as a result of the book's narrative, focusing on stylistic developments and trends, the topic of the Holocaust was virtually absent.[2] East-Central Europe's first attempt at addressing this issue in art historical terms was the exhibition 'Polish Art and the Holocaust' held in 2013.[3] This can be considered an exception since exhibitions related to the Holocaust organized from the 1990s onwards in East-Central Europe or displaying material from the region usually focused on contemporary artistic reflections.

Artworks relevant to the context of Holocaust memory in Hungary between the late 1950s and the 1970s can be divided into two distinct groups: those initiated by the artist and those commissioned by the state. This distinction is not merely one of funding, but rather concerns fundamental interpretive differences. The commissioned works served the official politics of memory, positioning the Shoah primarily in the framework of the anti-fascist struggle. In this narrative, the emphasis shifted from the victims to the struggle and to the communist state power appropriating it by positioning itself as its central force. By contrast, the works artists produced on their own initiative commemorate the victims and raise the question of the perpetrators' responsibility instead of focusing on the anti-fascist struggle. Most of those who would revisit the theme of the Holocaust repeatedly during the decades of socialism were first-generation Holocaust survivors. For them, the tragedy of the Holocaust was not a distant, abstract historical and cultural reference, but a primal experience; the works were therefore driven by the traumas and losses endured by the artists, their families and friends. Whether they were adults, youths or children in 1944, their memories of the Holocaust would surface in their works.

Margit Anna and Endre Bálint belonged to the generation that survived the Holocaust as adults. Anna had to go into hiding in 1944; her husband, Imre Ámos, an outstanding Hungarian painter, was murdered while working as a forced labourer. Bálint was also on labour service; his wife was hiding with their son; while his brother-in-law, the renowned literary historian, Antal Szerb, also on labour service, was murdered by his guards.[4] The younger generation included Lili Ország, who fled to Budapest after narrowly escaping deportation and went into hiding with false papers, and Miklós Erdély, who was also on labour service and lost a brother and two half-brothers in the Holocaust.[5] Further artists were children at the time of the Shoah. János Major's father disappeared on the Eastern front in 1943 while on labour service; the artist himself, still a child, hid with false papers in Budapest.[6] György Kemény was also a child when an unexpected air-raid saved him from being shot into the Danube, literally, by the Arrow-Cross.[7]

Memory politics: victors vs victims

The history of the Hungarian memorial at the Mauthausen concentration camp illustrates the difference between the official and private memory of the Holocaust, thereby also characterizing the communist politics of memory. The invitation-only design competition, announced in 1959, was won by Agamemnon Makrisz, a sculptor of Greek origin who had a stellar career in Hungary (fig. 1). While Rezső Berczeller was not invited to the competition, his sculpture *Mauthausen* (1958, fig. 2) was probably influenced by news of the planned memorial. Makrisz's sculpture was selected because the jury found that 'its main virtue is that it is not pessimistic, it expresses the positive traits of the fight against fascism'.[8] Indeed, the nine solid figures stand back to back, raising their arms and fists to the sky, forming a powerful and dynamic composition. The figures recall strong, protesting workers rather than prisoners at a concentration camp. By contrast, Berczeller's never realized plan struck a far more personal and tragic tone: an unidentifiable mass of bodies is seen in a haphazard pile on a pedestal recalling a wooden bunk, but also evoking the rhythm of rails and railway sleepers.[9] Instead of celebrating the victors of the anti-fascist struggle, his sculpture pays respect to the victims of the Holocaust. A memorial comparable to Berczeller's design is the state-commissioned *Memorial of the Yugoslav Victims* in Mauthausen (commissioned: 1957, erected 1958) by Nandor Glid, a Yugoslav sculptor of Hungarian origin.[10] The composition, reduced to basic geometric forms, shows a disorderly pile of bodies with arms raised high as a cry for help.[11] When comparing Makrisz's and Glid's memorials, the difference between the Hungarian and Yugoslav memory politics is striking. While the Hungarian commissioners wanted to see militant anti-fascism, the Yugoslavs were 'satisfied' with suffering victims. The difference in the expectations of memory politics is even more remarkable if one considers the history of the two countries: there was virtually no armed resistance against the Nazis and the Arrow-Cross in Hungary – the polar opposite of the activities of Yugoslav partisans. Yet, out of the two communist states it was Hungary that had a symbol of the fight against fascism cast in bronze.

Mauthausen, as part of Hungary's historical self-representation in the socialist era, makes evident the attempt to overcompensate or – to put it more harshly – falsify history. It also exemplifies how the communist authorities in Hungary instrumentalized the memory of the Shoah. The Jewish victims of the Holocaust were stylized into martyrs of the anti-fascist struggle, with the communists cast as the struggle's heroes both in the past and present. There was little room within this self-legitimizing narrative for the fact that the victims were Jews.

The memory of the Roma Holocaust

Historical research ignored the Roma victims for a long time, and *Porajmos*, the term for the Roma Holocaust, did not exist until the 1990s.[12] If one also takes into account the poor social conditions endured by much of the Roma population and the widespread prejudice and discrimination they suffered, it is hardly surprising that there is a scarcity of works of visual art dealing with the topic. Nevertheless, plans for a memorial to the victims of the Roma Holocaust in Hungary were made by 1974,

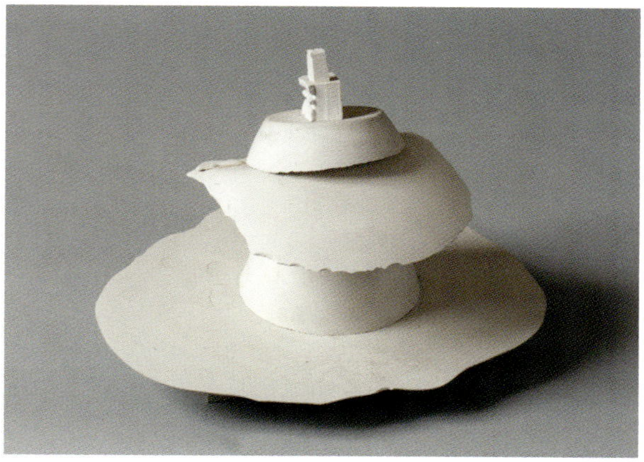

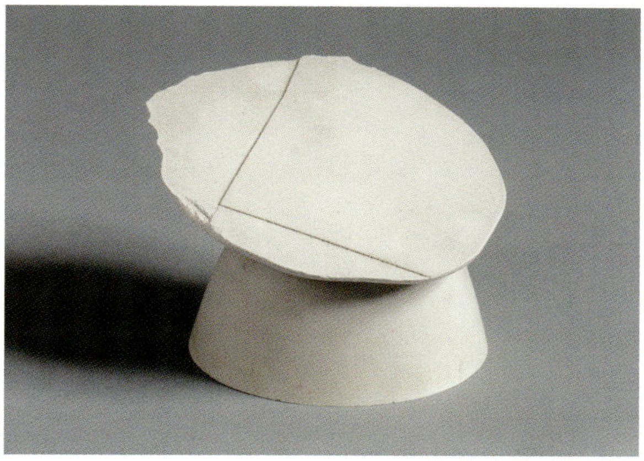

3

quite early even by international standards. The sculptor was György Jovánovics, an outstanding Hungarian neo-avant-garde artist (fig. 3). The memorial was intended to serve as a reminder of the crimes committed by Hungarians against Hungarians shortly before the end of the Second World War. In the first days of February 1945, Arrow-Cross members and gendarmes gathered together the local Roma on the outskirts of Várpalota, where they were forced to dig a pit: 118 people were shot on the site and further 5 were executed in the main square of the town.[13]

Roma intellectuals proposed setting up a memorial in Várpalota in 1974, a plan supported even by the leadership of the ruling Hungarian Socialist Workers' Party.[14] However, as soon as the project reached the lower – county – level, local authorities rejected the plan with the shameful explanation that the victims – women, men and children – were common criminals. The memorial was never built, even though its objective and content would have been novel and, judging by its plaster models, even innovative in its abstracted form and style compared to the traditional figurative memorials of the period.

To our knowledge, there were no further artworks dealing with the Roma Holocaust in Hungary in the 1970s. In 1983, however, Tamás Péli, who graduated from the State Academy of Fine Arts in Amsterdam, created a large painting – 42 sq. m (452 sq. ft) in size – for a children's home in a castle in Tiszadob, a remote corner of Hungary.[15] The painting depicts the history of the Hungarian Roma, and includes an enormous eagle – the symbol of Nazi Germany – with a representation of the Roma Holocaust under its extended wings. The work, which is exceptionally significant in terms of Roma identity and the Holocaust, has been languishing disassembled in storage since the renovation of the castle. The fate of *Porajmos*-related works, either planned or produced, illustrates the substantial obstacles that stand in the way of the memorialization of the Roma Holocaust.

3. György Jovánovics, *Plan for the Roma Holocaust Memorial I–II*, 1974, plaster, Private collection

Commemorating the victims

As outlined above, the public memory of the Holocaust in the field of memorial sculpture was constructed and controlled by official memory politics. Nevertheless, the topic began to surface in more individual forms in the late 1950s, particularly among painters who addressed the tragedy of the Holocaust through a veiled surrealist symbolism. The most prominent of these artists were Endre Bálint and Lili Ország. Bálint's early works address the well-known locations and tools of the genocide. His distinctive Holocaust iconography includes the cattle-wagons used for deportations, the entrance to the concentration camp and the crematorium: his works commemorate the victims indirectly, through evoking the events and thus prompting remembrance. This kind of Holocaust iconography can be considered the most widespread type of representation, which would appear in various styles and forms over different periods. These motifs appear overtly in Bálint's *Auschwitz Dawn* (1958, fig. 4); the tall chimney of the building in the centre of the image is a crematorium, the figure of the mummy to the left refers to the victims and grief. This easily identifiable, figurative representation gives way to a more

4

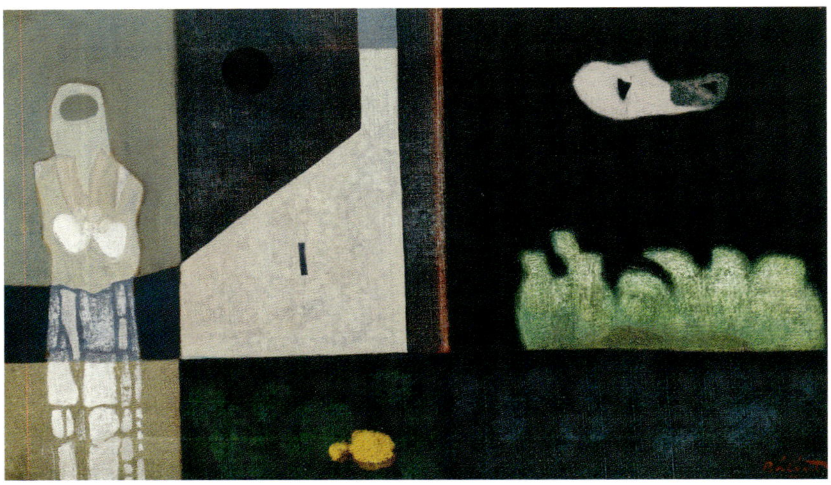

4. Endre Bálint, *Auschwitz Dawn*, 1958, oil on canvas, 32 × 55.5 cm, Private collection

5. Lili Ország, *Requiem on Seven Panels, in Memory of Perished Cities and People*, 1963, oil on fibreboard, 7 panels, 125 × 60 cm each, Kiscelli Múzeum – Fővárosi Képtár, Budapest

5

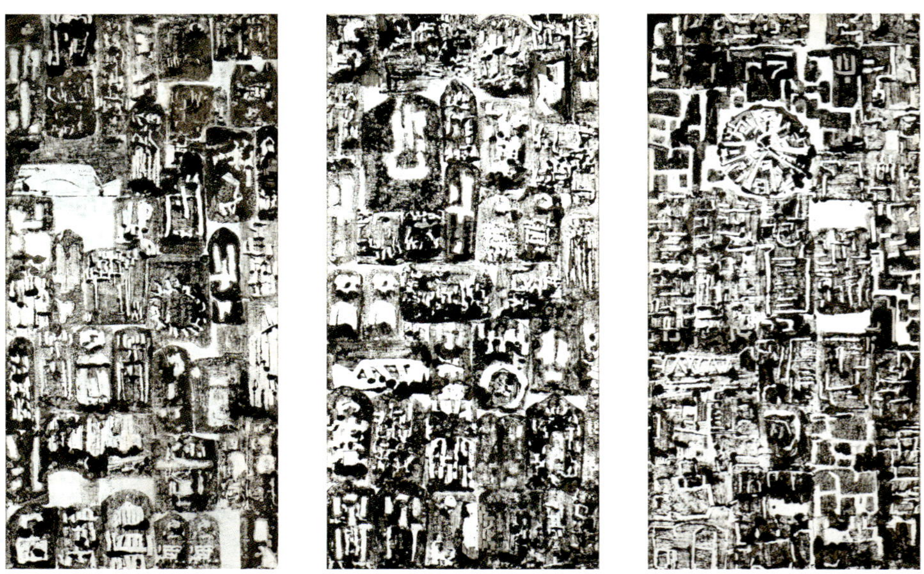

abstract, surrealist treatment of the subject in Bálint's works in the 1960s, where the only Holocaust reference tends to be the title (*Crematorium*, 1965, and *Arbeit macht frei* [Work Sets You Free], 1966).

Contrarily, Lili Ország's emphasis lay not on the locations and tools, that is the material reality of genocide, but rather on its victims and their commemoration (see also Hedvig Turai, 'Limited Access to Greatness', pp. 251–69, for a discussion of Ország and Margit Anna). Her series, *Requiem on Seven Panels, in Memory of Perished Cities and People* (1963) consists of seven paintings: *I. Interior of a Cathedral*; *II. Writing on the Wall*; *III. Cemetery in Ur and Hiroshima*; *IV. Martyrs*; *V. The Dead City*; *VI. After Devastation*; *VII. Requiem* (fig. 5).[16] The title of the central painting is key to the interpretation of the work: the term martyr was an unequivocal reference to the Holocaust in the given Hungarian context. This was the prevailing expression at the (often merely symbolic) graves of the victims and 'martyr memorial services' of the Jewish communities after the Second World War. This term, used primarily in the context of Christianity, might have spread because it referred to innocent victims murdered for their faith. It has, however, vanished from Hungarian usage since then, and 'victim' (*áldozat*) has replaced it in general use.

Ország discusses the Holocaust in a historical context, placing it in the middle of the composition after human catastrophes of antiquity (Ur) and the contemporary period (Hiroshima). Consequently, the early version of the title, given at the time of its production – *Great White Wall* – can be interpreted as a reference to the Holocaust as *tabula rasa*, a break in the history of human civilization. Panels following the centrally positioned Holocaust include *After Devastation* and the concluding *Requiem*, which features the menorah, a seven-branched candelabrum, symbolizing hope.[17] Lili Ország's series integrates the Shoah into a general historical narrative: it commemorates the victims, and the composition, leading from past to present, urges the viewer to remember.

Iconic images and personal histories

A number of works of the period evoked the Holocaust far more directly than the abstract visual symbolism of Bálint's and Ország's discussed works. They are based on well-known iconic historical photographs that enable the viewer to identify the subject of the work. (Such photos were also used by the Polish artists Alina Szapocznikow and Jonasz Stern.) However, most of them also allude to personal stories related to the Shoah, so the documentary photograph representing the macro-perspective of history facilitates the understanding of the private micro-historical approach to the

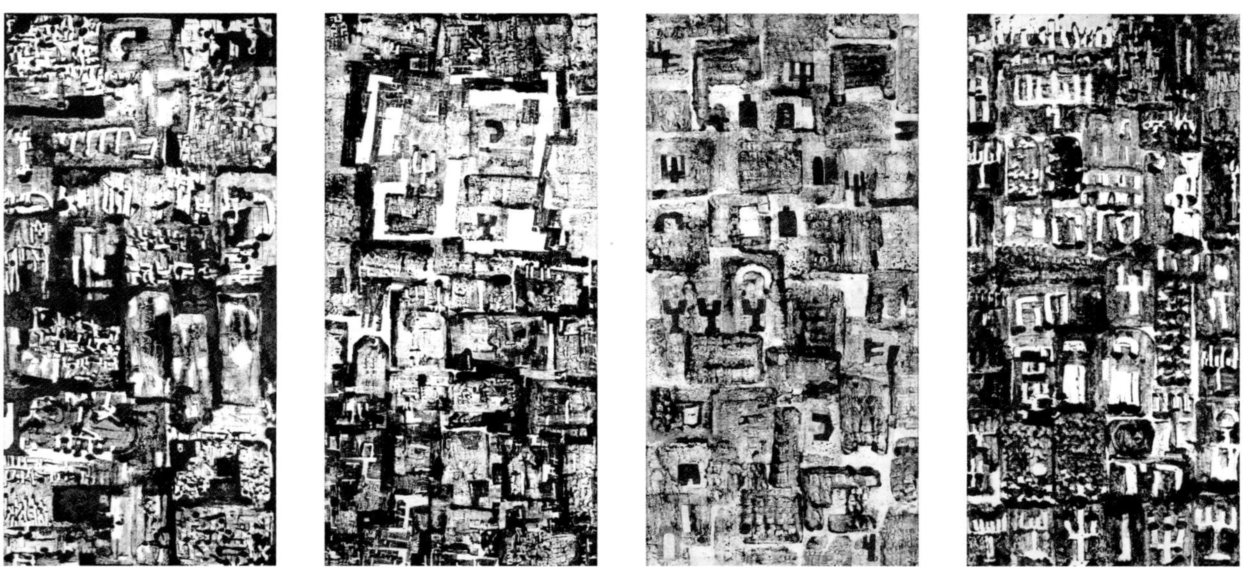

Holocaust. The original Hungarian title of Endre Bálint's *Cattle-Wagon-lit* (1968, fig. 6) was *Marhawagon-lit*, which is mordantly coined from '*marhavagon*' (cattle wagon) and '*wagon-lit*' (sleeping car), evoking with black humour the rail carriages used for deportation. The title links the work organically to the Holocaust iconography mentioned above. Bálint glued the image of two skin-and-bone men – concentration-camp prisoners – to the middle of the three-part painting. The two figures are mirror images positioned in the manner of playing cards.[18] By contrast to the familiar documentary photos, the photograph affixed to the right side of the painting evokes a personal tragedy: it is a portrait of the artist's brother-in-law, Antal Szerb, who was killed on labour service.[19]

György Kemény's *Self-Portrait as a Child* (1968, fig. 7) also combines a historical document and a personal story. The figure of the young boy accurately follows Kemény's photo taken in 1940; the pop-art influences, the cheerful, vivid colours and the form reminiscent of comics evoke a carefree childhood. At the top right of the image, we can see memories of holidays by Lake Balaton: the boy and his father lying on a deck at the lake, with a glass of raspberry soda – Kemény's childhood favourite – positioned alongside, highlighted in a way reminiscent of advertisements and pop art's interest in consumer society.[20]

By contrast, the mood captured in the left-hand side of the image is far from carefree despite the attractive colour scheme. An arrow leads from the boy's coat to the figure of Mickey Mouse on fire. One might think that the cartoon character is merely a pop-culture reference, but it actually refers to Kemény's own life story.[21] His father used forged documents in 1944 and found shelter in a protected house, while Kemény's mother was in the Pest ghetto, and Kemény was placed by his father in a Jewish orphanage he hoped would offer more security. The Arrow-Cross showed up at the orphanage and took the children and their young teacher, who had read to them from Kemény's Mickey Mouse book every evening. The teacher was shot by Arrow-Cross members the next day, and the children were marched to the Danube bank to be shot. The Arrow-Cross members ran away due to a sudden Soviet artillery (*katyusha*) attack, and Kemény was spared as a result. Based on this story, Mickey Mouse on fire symbolizes not only the lost children's book, but also the murder of the teacher who read from it, Kemény's fate and, more broadly, the Shoah as a whole. Many viewers of the painting, however, would be unaware of the artist's life story. Therefore, decoding the work is aided by the top left of the picture, where the artist painted a sketchy, but easily recognizable image of a world-famous photograph taken during the liquidation of the Warsaw ghetto.[22] As a familiar symbol of the Shoah, the iconic documentary photograph draws attention to Kemény's own story.

The painting as a whole and the incorporated photograph feature similar motifs: the girl in the photograph is parallel to the boy wearing a coat. The Warsaw photograph is inserted only as a quote; the coat, however, is made of real fabric and wooden buttons, which does not merely evoke the one-time little boy, but presents him by breaking into the third dimension, which helps his personal story move, even burst, from the past into the present, into the viewer's space.

Perpetrators

Another group of works features, rather than documentary photographs of specific events of the Holocaust, the representation of – or at least an allusion to – the perpetrators, typically the main culprits. The earliest such work is László Lakner's painting *Seamstresses Listen to Hitler's Speech* (1960, p. 141, fig. 4).[23] The precursor to the work is a photograph taken in 1937, which was published in a magazine in 1960. The peculiarity of the painting is that Hitler is only referred to in the title, but does not appear in the picture. The specific theme of the work is, in fact, the impact of the absent suggestive speaker on those present. Instead of the invisible perpetrator, we can see a group of passive bystanders or accomplices. Significantly, Lakner published the work in 1974 with the title *The Ilse Kochs of the Future Listen to Hitler's Speech on the Loudspeaker*.[24] He may have heard about Koch, the wife of the Nazi commandant of Buchenwald concentration camp, having lampshades made out of the tattooed skin

6. Endre Bálint, *Cattle-Wagon-lit*, 1968, mixed media, wood, 53 × 110 cm, Private collection

7. György Kemény, *Self-Portrait as a Child*, 1968, Wallkyd resin and mixed media on fibreboard, 140 × 100 × 8 cm, Private collection

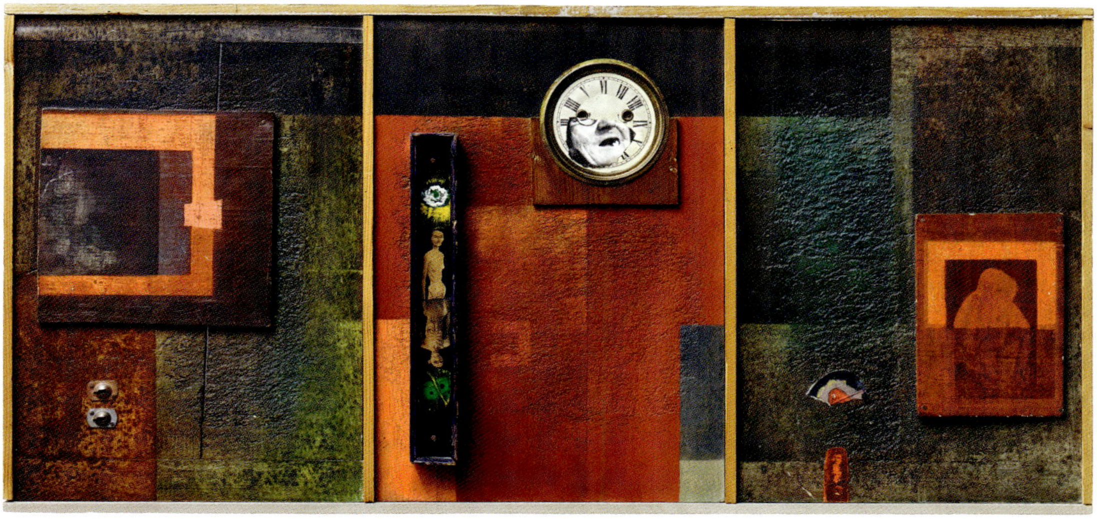

6

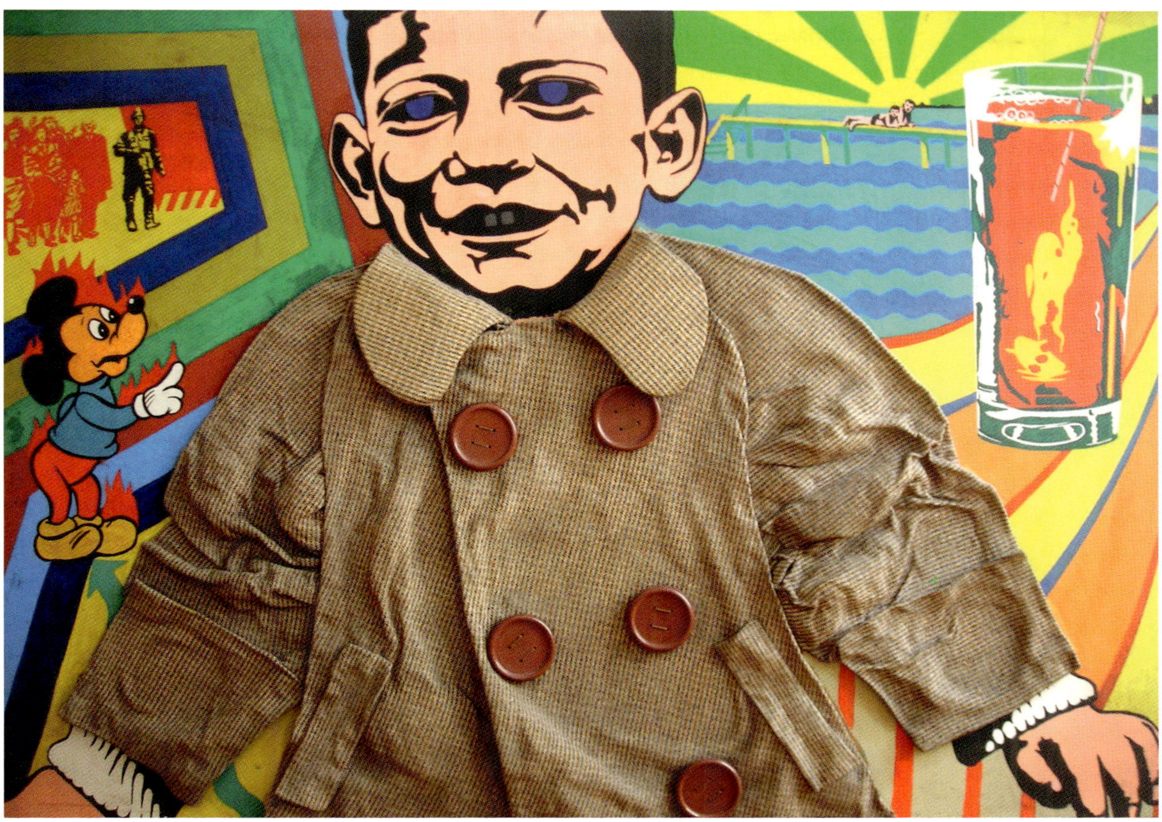

7

8

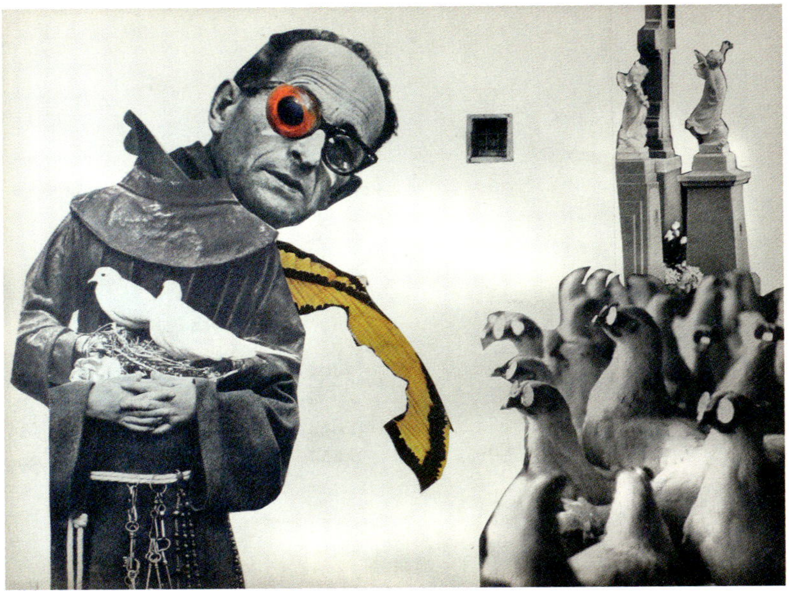

9

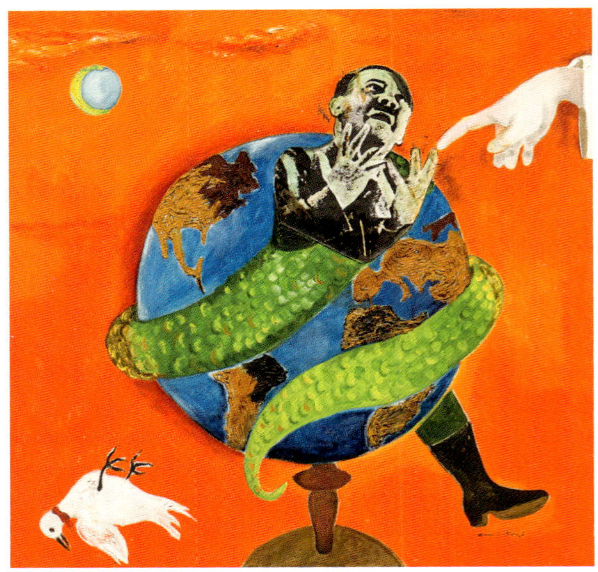

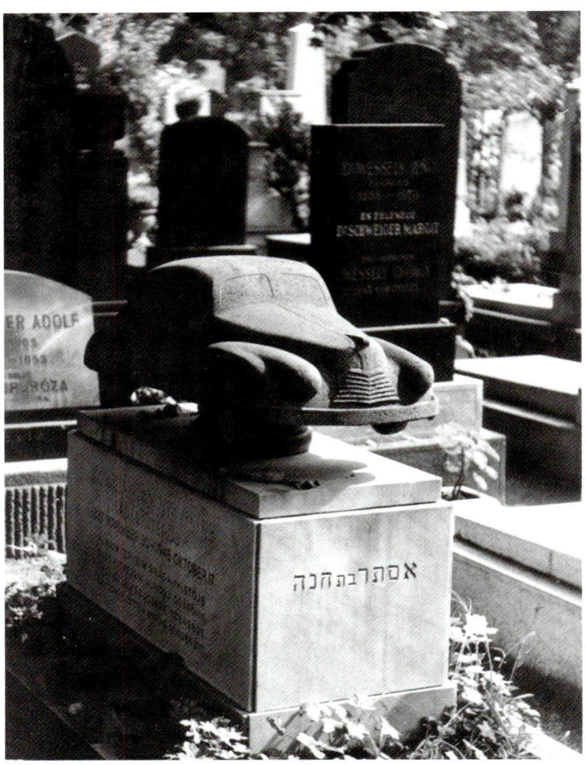

10

8. Endre Bálint, *Mr Eichmann, or of the dead, good or – bad!*, 1962, photomontage, 50 × 65 cm, Vintage Galéria, Budapest

9. Margit Anna, *Millions for One*, 1977, oil on canvas, photo, 92 × 92 cm, Ferenczy Múzeumi Centrum, Szentendre

10. János Major, *Tomb with a Car (...ER ADOLF)*, before 1972, photo, 24 × 18 cm, Private collection

11. (overleaf) János Major, *The Yid Is Washing Himself*, 1967, iron etching, 42 × 26.2 cm, Private collection

of prisoners before he painted the picture; if so, the seamstresses depicted in the painting can no longer be considered innocent outsiders and observers, but rather appear as potential perpetrators. The fact that the women in the original photograph are not seamstresses also confirms this interpretation; the fictional profession given in the title should be considered a device to remind the viewer of Ilse Koch's crimes by association.[25]

Adolf Eichmann, the Nazi officer tasked with administering the Holocaust, is the protagonist of Endre Bálint's photomontage *Mr Eichmann, or of the dead, good or – bad!* (1962, fig. 8). Eichmann was responsible for organizing the deportation of Hungarian Jews; at the end of the war, he escaped to Austria and then Argentina, where he was caught in 1960 before being brought to justice in Israel. Bálint came across a portrait of Eichmann in *Life* magazine during his stay in Paris.[26] The title – an ironic twist on the saying '*De mortuis nihil nisi bonum*' (Of the dead, nothing unless good) – makes it clear that the montage was made after Eichmann's execution in 1962. In line with the title, the representation is similarly satirical, as if showing how the war criminal would have to be seen if the Latin saying were to be observed. Eichmann stands in a monk's robe, holding a bird's nest in his arms. Two white doves proclaim his innocence; they evoke associations of the good shepherd and the dove of peace. This message is also affirmed by the winged angel statues in the Christian cemetery on the right and the wings growing out of the man's shoulders. The title and the biting satire of the representation point to the unforgivable nature of the crimes. Bálint's work added a new colour to artistic interpretations of the Holocaust; given its critical approach and satirical tone, it is comparable only to later works, especially those of János Major.

Margit Anna's painting *Millions for One* (1977, fig. 9) also contains a photo of a perpetrator: the snake circling the globe – Lucifer, the tempter of Paradise – bears Hitler's face.[27] The work, which is part of Margit Anna's biblically inspired *Creation* series, paraphrases Michelangelo's fresco in the Sistine Chapel, except it is the dictator and not Adam who is brought to life by God's right hand.[28] The falling dove in the lower part of the picture alludes to the victims, and Hitler's boots are about to trample on the signature of the artist, whose husband was killed as a forced labourer. Like Lili Ország's *Requiem*, Margit Anna also integrated the theme of the Holocaust into a broader context, though – unlike Ország – she used a biblical rather than a historical reference.

János Major's photograph *Tomb with a Car (...ER ADOLF)* (before 1972, fig. 10) is a good example of a mode of expression that called for reading between the lines, something that characterized both the artist and the Hungarian context of the time. Despite the unusual funeral monument in the shape of a car, the Hebrew script and the tombstones make it clear that we are in a Jewish cemetery. Yet, the primary message of the work is not related to the curiosity at its centre; rather, the interest lies at the far left of the photograph, where the composition and cropping of the image shows the inscription '...ER ADOLF' on a tombstone. Contemporaries of Major have confirmed that the artist intended to allude to the inscription 'Hitler Adolf', absurdly suggesting that the grave of the Nazi dictator had been found in the Jewish cemetery in Budapest.[29] For if Eichmann could flee to South America, who is to say Hitler could not have lived in Budapest after the war?

Jewish body, anti-Semitic gaze

Another work by Major takes a more radical approach to the problem of perpetrators, focusing on their way of seeing rather than their person. The interior of a bathroom is depicted in his iron etching *The Yid Is Washing Himself* (1967, fig. 11), complete with Major's merciless self-caricature recalling a cloven-hoofed devil: the man appears to be deformed, his praying-mantis-like figure with a grinning face is not unlike an anti-Semitic caricature. In particular, the cartoonish exaggeration of Jewish features evokes images from the Nazi propaganda paper, *Der Stürmer*, while the praying-mantis-like figure refers to the Nazis' use of language to identify Jews with vermin. Major's figure also recalls Gregor Samsa, the protagonist of Franz Kafka's *Metamorphosis* (1915): he is similarly transformed in a private space – a bathroom instead of a bedroom –

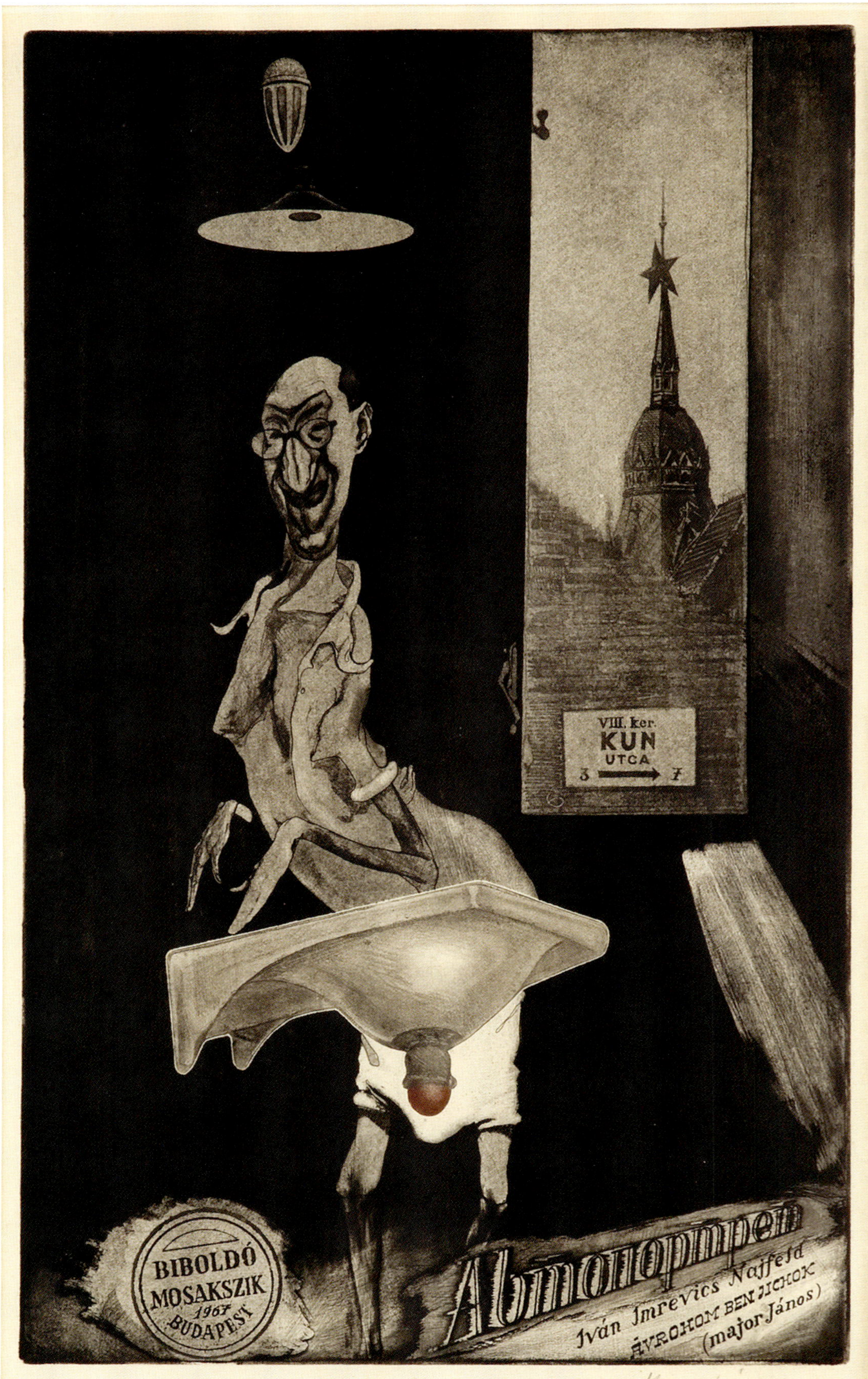
VIII. ker.
KUN
UTCA
3 7
BIBOLDÓ
MOSAKSZIK
1967
BUDAPEST
Iván Imrevics Najfeld
ÁVROHOM BEN JICHOK
(major János)
Major János

into an insect-like creature in a surreal way. The siphon of the sink, which partly conceals the man's body, may be mistaken for his genitals: the obscene detail clarifies the Jewish origins of the artist.

The title, date and location of the work are arranged in the form of a seal in the bottom-left corner of the image. On the right-hand side, the genre of the self-portrait is indicated by '*Avtoportret*' – using the *lingua franca* of the Eastern bloc dominated by the Soviet Union – with a triple signature below. The Russian variant of Major's name ('Iván Imrevics Najfeld') alludes to his father, Imre Neufeld, murdered on labour service, thereby also evoking the Shoah, whereas his Hebrew name printed in Latin script imitating the Hebrew font ('Ávrohom ben Jichok') stresses his Jewish identity. The view through the window refers to the Hungary of the time, indicating the artist's place of residence through the street sign ('Kun utca') and the tower of the fire station in Kun street with an oversized red star on top, reminiscent of the Hungarian Parliament building.

The anti-Semitic perspective visualized by Major on *The Yid Is Washing Himself* is not merely a historical quotation: besides evoking Nazism, it expresses a critical view of contemporary society and politics. By representing himself in the distorting mirror of anti-Semitism, the artist provokes the viewers, forcing them to take a stand against historical and contemporary anti-Semitism. This extreme satire, however, was not understood by all: in fact, representatives of the state authorities mistook the Jewish artist's anti-anti-Semitic work for anti-Semitic incitement and he was hence issued a warning by the police for including the work in a catalogue published without a permit.[30]

The subversive power of *The Yid Is Washing Himself* is derived from the fact that the artist projects anti-Semitic iconography on himself, thereby inverting its original meaning. This artistic focus on the perpetrators and their point of view is unparalleled in its radicalness in the art of the era.[31] Major visualized an anti-Semitic modus of representation used by the Nazi press: rather than depicting events of the Holocaust, involving his person and body allowed him to express an anti-anti-Semitic message based on the shared historical experience of the Holocaust: 'if I represent myself the way an anti-Semitic caricature would represent me [...], this must provoke greater astonishment in any well-meaning viewer than painting people standing in line for the gas chamber'.[32] Therefore his work could also be considered a critique of the approach identified above as Holocaust iconography.

Historical parallels: the Bible and the Tiszaeszlár blood libel

In visual art, the subject of the Holocaust often appeared indirectly, through motifs borrowed from history and culture. Artists used episodes of the more distant past as parables in order to speak of recent events and the present. The Holocaust did not appear explicitly in Margit Anna's oeuvre until quite late, in the second half of the 1970s, when she turned to biblical stories. The two sources appear together in a number of her works, as in *Millions for One* (1977) mentioned above. Her painting *The Creator Is Resting* (1977, fig. 12) depicts God as a simple mortal, wearing a prayer shawl and phylacteries, resting with his creatures – the first human couple – before him. The yellow star on God's shoulder adds another layer, aside from the biblical reference: such a symbol was used to mark the Jewish population during the Holocaust in preparation for confinement in the ghettos and deportation.

References to the Old and New Testaments, Judaism, the Holocaust and Anna's personal life are interwoven at multiple instances in another painting of hers, *Is This the Promised Land?* (1976, fig. 13). The Creator, sitting on a throne in the centre of the composition with the Globe under his feet, evokes the standard iconographical form of Christ enthroned. The two lions by his side are borrowed from ornaments on Torah shields, the metal plates protecting the Torah scroll, which contains the five books of Moses. The biblical motif is accompanied by a Holocaust reference: the flames surrounding the composition emerge from the chimney of a crematorium with a scroll that reads '*Arbeit macht frei*'. The third, personal layer of the painting is indicated by photographs glued onto it: the figures include the painter Imre Ámos, the artist's murdered husband; her father beside the throne; her mother in the bottom-right corner; her elder son next to the globe; and finally herself in the bottom-left corner engulfed by flames no doubt representing painful memories.[33] The sun and moon appear in the top corners of the painting – in a position reminiscent of medieval representations of the crucifixion – while the figure of a musician in the moon is a reference to the musical *Fiddler on the Roof*.

Besides the familiar biblical allusions, another frequently referenced story, prominent specifically in a Hungarian context, was the blood libel of Tiszaeszlár. In 1882, Jews were accused of murdering a Christian peasant girl called Eszter Solymosi and allegedly taking her blood in order to make the Passover matzo. Since an anti-Semitic officer was in charge of the investigation, the case went to trial in 1883, where all the defendants were cleared of the charges. Numerous artists were inspired by the case, which was world-famous in its time, and particularly by the story of Móric Scharf, a coerced and later brainwashed boy, who offered false testimony against the accused, including his father. The etching *In Memoriam Móric Scharf* (1966) by János Major is inspired by the story of the blood libel while evoking Nazi Germany and the Holocaust.[34] In the 1970s, Margit Anna painted portraits of both the son offering false witness against his parents and the alleged (actually drowned) victim.[35] Miklós Erdély's film entitled *Version* (1979, fig. 14) evokes – besides the rehearsal of the false testimony – two further temporal layers: the show trials of the Stalinist Rákosi era in Hungary (1948–53, namely the trial of former minister of the interior László Rajk in 1949) and the Holocaust.[36] Jewish artists began to address the late nineteenth-century blood libel after the Second World War. Judging by their works, it is evident that the story of Tiszaeszlár was used primarily as a legitimate way to express or formulate messages about the recent past and the present. In fact, the majority of these works evoked the Holocaust, whereas the earlier anti-Semitic episode served as a historical parable.

12

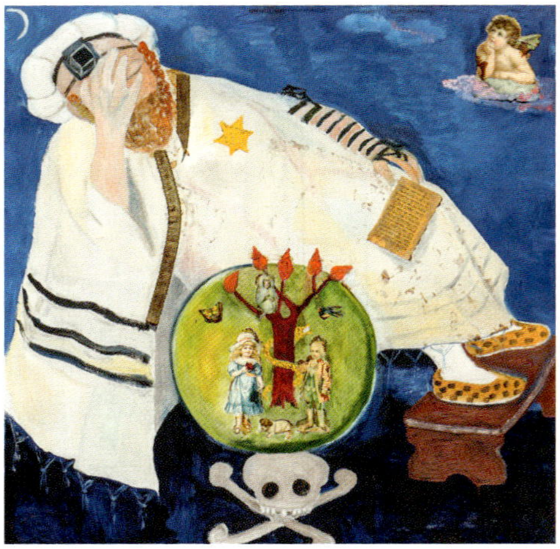

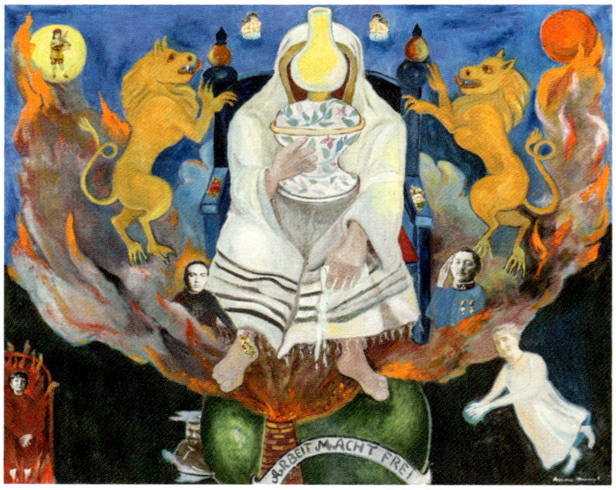

13

12. Margit Anna, *The Creator Is Resting* (*Creation* series), 1977, oil on canvas, collage, 92 × 92 cm, Ferenczy Múzeumi Centrum, Szentendre

13. Margit Anna, *Is This the Promised Land?*, 1976, oil on canvas, collage, 101 × 123 cm, Ferenczy Múzeumi Centrum, Szentendre

14. Miklós Erdély, *Version*, 1979–81, 16 mm film, 54', Magyar Nemzeti Filmarchivum, Budapest

15. Miklós Erdély, *The Pool of Gentleness*, 1970, environment in the 'R' exhibition, Budapest, perished

Contemporary politics: the Six-Day War

The Arab–Israeli Six-Day War (1967) was an important event for Hungarian Jewry. The overwhelming Israeli victory filled many with pride; the founding of the Jewish state and the success of its military became a positive affirmation of Jewish identity after the recent negative experience of the Holocaust. Although Hungary, following the pro-Arab Soviet Union, terminated diplomatic relations with Israel after the war, an anti-Semitic ('anti-Zionist') campaign comparable in extent to other countries of the Eastern bloc did not develop.[37]

After her trip to Israel in 1966, Lili Ország was preparing for an exhibition that was due to open in Székesfehérvár the following year. The authorities attempted to ban the exhibition due to the recent Six-Day War, feeling uneasy about titles referring to Israel and Jewish history. However, they wished to avoid open interference, particularly in writing, and the potential for a subsequent scandal. Ultimately, both the exhibition and the catalogue were realized, thanks to the perseverance of Péter Kovács, the organizer of the exhibition. A few titles had to be modified, however, and names referring to locations in present-day Israel or its prehistory (e.g. Jerusalem, Jericho, Negev and the Wailing Wall) were removed.[38]

The topic of the Six-Day War, often in combination with motifs directly or indirectly referring to the Holocaust, was addressed by a number of artists. For instance, János Major's etching *The Aggressor Is Being Unveiled* (1967) also refers to the blood libel of Tiszaeszlár, while his *Associations* (1967) is connected to contemporary anti-Semitism. Subsequently, Miklós Erdély created his installation *The Pool of Gentleness* (fig. 15) for the 'R' exhibition in 1970. A blue plastic pool was surrounded by forty-nine cans of Soviet condensed milk, with sheets of matzo among blocks of yeast in the middle.[39] Erdély punctured the cans at the opening, making the milk flow into the pool. Meanwhile, water was dripping on the installation from a can hung above. A sign stating 'THERE WILL BE GAS HERE!' (Hungarian slang for there will be trouble) was placed near the installation. Two red medical pipes led from the pool to a plaster cast of the artist's nose positioned on a small

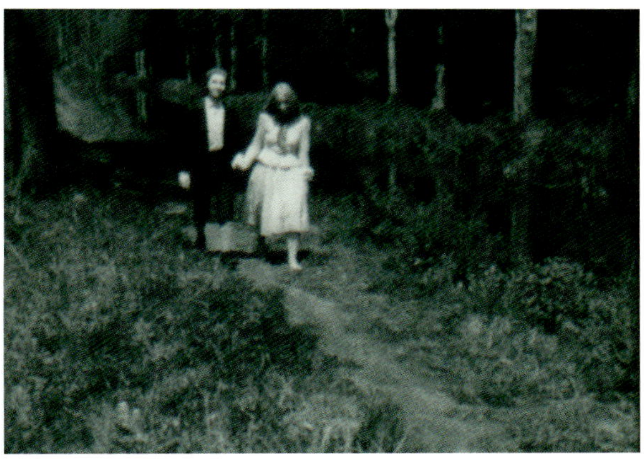

14

15

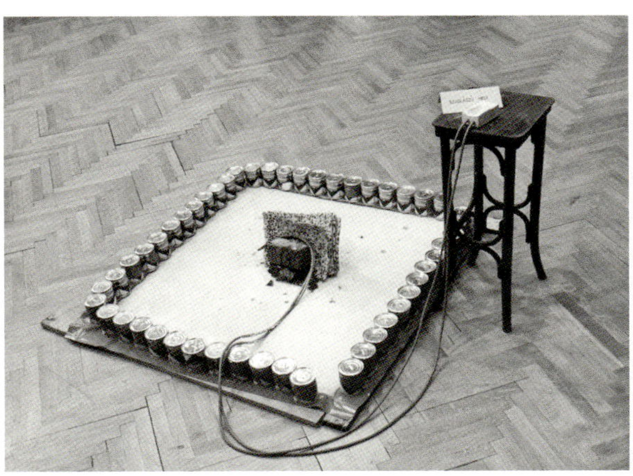

16. György Kemény, *I Am György Kemény...*, first prize at the international poster competition '30th Anniversary of Victory', Warsaw, 1975, poster, Magyar Zsidó Múzeum, Budapest

17. László Lakner, *Citation Piece (Paul Celan)*, 1971, serigraph, 74.5 × 52 cm, Private collection

16

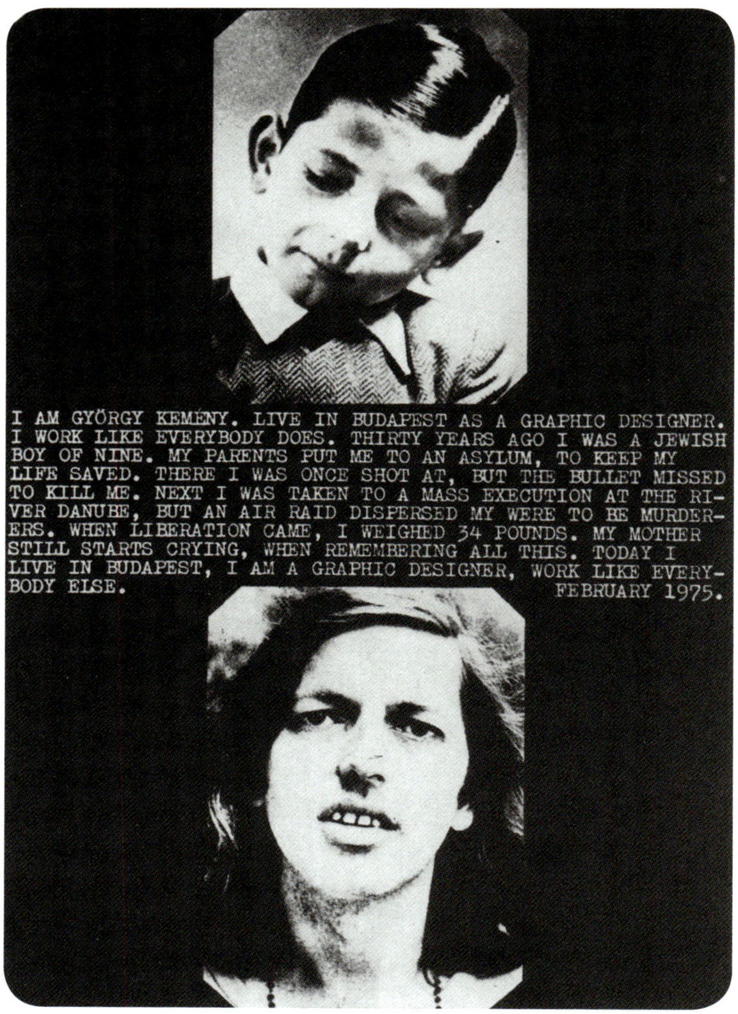

17

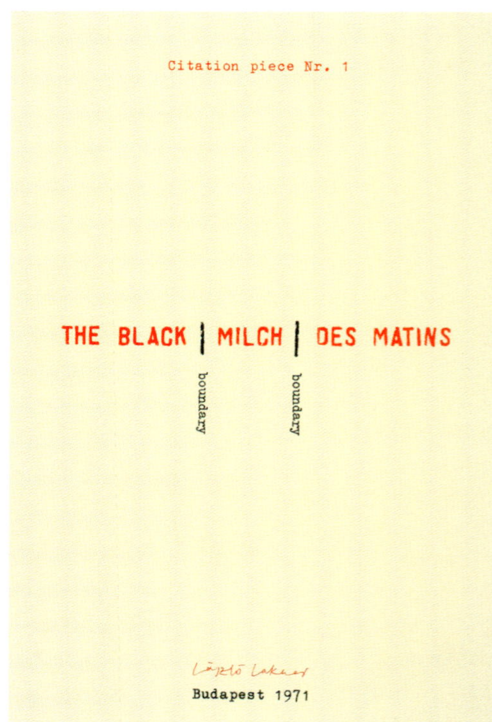

table, complete with a sign: 'SMELLING PLACE'. The milk and the yeast began to ferment, emitting a presumably unpleasant odour referenced in the inscription.

Erdély later commented on the installation in a 1983 interview: 'it was meant as a tribute to Kádár [...] For this was the time when an anti-Semitic wave began in the Soviet Union, and Kádár blocked this right at the border. This is why I called it the "Pool of Gentleness".'[40] Considering the period before 1970, this anti-Semitic wave could only have been the 'anti-Zionist' campaign that occurred in most of the Eastern bloc following the Six-Day War, as a result of which most of the Polish Jews who had survived the Holocaust left their country. János Kádár, General Secretary of the Hungarian Socialist Workers' Party, voiced the Party's agreement with the Soviet Union's anti-Israeli position. Nonetheless, he also made it clear – in a way unparalleled in the region – that Hungarians of Jewish origin are understandably sensitive about the Six-Day War: 'It is understandable that someone's political position may be confused when they have a sibling or relative living in the country that is committing the aggression.'[41]

The Pool of Gentleness can be interpreted as follows: Hungarian Jews are symbolized by the matzo, non-Jewish Hungarians by the yeast missing from the former, and the two materials in combination refer to the two groups living side by side. The milk flowing from the Soviet cans into the pool of gentleness – the Carpathian Basin – represents the anti-Semitic wave originating in the Soviet Union, obstructed by the blocks of yeast – symbolically Hungary and Kádár – flanking the matzo. The term 'gas' in the sign refers not only to the chemical reaction, but to newly emerging problems (due to the slang meaning), while also evoking the gas chambers and thereby the Holocaust. As outsiders, visitors to the exhibition were invited to perceive – smell – the problems arising from historical and contemporary anti-Semitism and from the difference between the Soviet and Hungarian positions. Erdély's complex installation reacts to a contemporary historical event and its political context by simultaneously thematizing the Holocaust in a public space through an accessible reference.

Conceptual art: textual references

Works produced after the conceptual turn of Hungarian art in the late 1960s have already been mentioned in connection to specific thematic approaches. These works were not only novel in formal terms; the new modes of expression were also coupled with a more openly critical approach. Besides photography and objects, artists often produced text-centred works. The topics discussed here were addressed in a conceptual manner in the first half of the 1970s most often by János Major and Miklós Erdély, and to a lesser extent by György Kemény and László Lakner.

György Kemény won first prize with his work *I Am György Kemény...* (fig. 16) at the international poster competition organized in Warsaw in 1975 to mark the thirtieth anniversary of the victory over fascism.[42] The poster had the following text typed in English in between a childhood photo of the artist and a current one:

I am György Kemény. Live in Budapest as a graphic designer. I work like everybody does. Thirty years ago I was a Jewish boy of nine. My parents put me to an asylum, to keep my life saved. There I was once shot at, but the bullet missed to kill me. Next I was taken to a mass execution at the river Danube, but an air raid dispersed my were to be murderers. When liberation came, I weighed 34 pounds. My mother still starts crying, when remembering all this. Today I live in Budapest, I am a graphic designer, work like everybody else. February 1975.

This circularly structured text is shockingly objective, as Kemény recounts how he was nearly murdered as a child on two occasions as if these were ordinary events. The unemotional character of the sentences is made all the more emphatic by the recollection of his mother's emotional reaction as a counterpoint to his own. The narrator's distance and neutral tone are analogous to Imre Kertész's novel *Faithlessness*, originally published in 1975 (Kertész was awarded the Nobel Prize in Literature in 2002).[43]

László Lakner's *Citation Piece (Paul Celan)* from 1971 has a literary context as well (fig. 17). The artist split '*Schwarze Milch der*

Frühe' (Black milk of morning), the opening of a major piece of Holocaust literature, Paul Celan's poem 'Todesfuge' (Death Fugue), into three parts and translated the fragments into English and French besides the German original: 'THE BLACK | MILCH | DES MATINS'. He also emphasized the separation of the individual parts with the inscription 'boundary'. By borrowing the iconic opening sentence (which is also a powerful image), Lakner unambiguously evokes the Holocaust for the educated viewer, although his work also reflects an interest in linguistics. The linguistic diversity may refer to the universal experience of the Holocaust and to its global memory, which was only emerging at the time.[44] The work can also be related to another quotation piece from 1971, which splits the Austrian philosopher Ludwig Wittgenstein's dictum 'Whereof one cannot speak, thereof one must be silent' into multilingual sections (see also Klara Kemp-Welch, 'Soft-spoken Encounters', pp. 273–89, including fig. 6).[45] If one examines this in the context of Theodor W. Adorno's famous statement that 'to write poetry after Auschwitz is barbaric' (often misquoted as 'it is impossible to write poetry after Auschwitz'), one returns to the questions raised in Celan's poem: the absence of speech about the Holocaust and the difficulty of utterance. Although Lakner was not a Holocaust survivor he was clearly engaged with the Shoah, which he addressed in a number of works, the first being *Seamstresses Listen to Hitler's Speech*. He returned to Celan a number of times after *Citation Piece*. Furthermore, he created a work commemorating Miklós Radnóti, the renowned Hungarian poet who was killed during the Shoah: literature is an important context for nearly all of Lakner's works on the Holocaust.[46]

Conclusion

From the late 1950s onwards, the topic of the Holocaust had a significant reception in Hungarian art. Besides the artists discussed here, who returned to the subject several times, others also touched upon the topic in singular works. Additionally, there were state commissions, but it seems that the independently produced works and the commissioned ones resulted in developments unfolding in parallel, mostly disconnected from one another. This was due to the fact that the non-commissioned artists' perspective was typically very different from that of official memory politics, which focused on the anti-fascist struggle and thereby instrumentalized the memory of the Holocaust, as exemplified here by the Mauthausen case study.

The examples analysed here also shed light on differences in approach between periods and generations. Artists of the older generation, still temporally close to the traumatic experiences, adopted a surrealist, symbolic approach from the late 1950s; the primary objective of their works was the commemoration of the victims. Accordingly, they employed a Holocaust iconography referring to the locations and tools of the genocide, and symbols alluding to the victims and their memory. By contrast, a more open representation and a critical approach became prevalent in the mid-1960s, and particularly at the end of the decade; besides remembering, identifying those responsible for the Holocaust and the reasons behind it gained importance, which were frequently connected to present-day problems, such as contemporary anti-Semitism. This tendency was partly due to the fresh approach of the younger generation emerging at this time, but also influenced by the conceptual turn of the late 1960s, which brought new forms of expression. For example, the inclusion of texts helped foster a new, more open tone. It is also important to consider, besides the generational differences, the artists' personalities, e.g. the works of Endre Bálint and János Major have significant affinities due to their satirical tone despite any differences in generation or genre.

The 1960s and 1970s were characterized not only by the coexistence of generations and styles but also by a kind of thematic plurality in the works. In a number of cases the theme of the Holocaust surfaced in connection with further topics, thus visualizing different time periods simultaneously. The two possible perspectives on the Holocaust – social and individual – often appeared together, most notably in the works based on well-known documentary photographs but also recounting personal stories. These simultaneously reflect two tendencies that characterize further works as well: the generalization of the experiences of the Holocaust and personalization through emphasizing aspects of the event related to individuals or families.

A number of works link the Holocaust and the Nazi era to contemporary anti-Semitism and to events such as the Six-Day War. These works represent the Holocaust as part of a broader narrative of anti-Semitism running from the past to the present. Another important characteristic of the period was the indirect articulation of messages that were nevertheless quite accessible to contemporaries. Such works leave it to the viewer to complement and interpret the visual representation by 'reading between the lines'. A characteristic example of this elliptical mode of expression is János Major's photograph of a gravestone marked '...ER ADOLF', referencing Hitler. The use of biblical and historical allusions also belongs to this tendency. In these cases, the remote event is not used primarily to illustrate something about itself, but as a reference to the Holocaust: for instance, works dealing with the late nineteenth-century blood-libel case of Tiszaeszlár do not simply present an interesting historical episode, but use it as a parable to address the Holocaust and issues from the artists' own era.

A significant number of the works discussed here were shown to a Hungarian and (primarily in the case of conceptual works) international audience at the time of their production or a few years later. Even so, the public display of works was restricted: the works of neo-avant-garde artists, for example, often reached only a narrow subcultural audience, regardless of their topic. Despite occasional, temporary access to most of these works, no broad public discourse about the Shoah emerged during this period, and this lack of discourse was not exclusively the result of the socialist system in Hungary. In fact, such a discourse would have been anachronistic as it would have occurred before the memory of the Holocaust became globalized and the term Holocaust was widely established. The works discussed here are exceptionally significant for the very reason that (in time and in critical attitude) they were ahead of the prevailing social discourse, or – as seen in the case of the Roma Holocaust – even ahead of scholarly research on the subject.

1 See Randolph L. Braham, *The Politics of Genocide: The Holocaust in Hungary*. New York: Columbia University Press, 2016. The author is indebted to Ágnes Fazakas for offering substantial help in revising the translation of the following text. He would also like to acknowledge the support of an Ernő Kállai Fellowship in art history and art criticism (funded by the Ministry of Human Resources) during the revision of the Hungarian and English versions.

2 The topic of the Holocaust only surfaces in Piotrowski's book in relation to László Fehér's works in the 1980s, even though four of the artists discussed here in detail are included in the book. Piotr Piotrowski, *In the Shadow of Yalta: Art and the Avant-garde in Eastern Europe, 1945–1989*. London: Reaktion Books, 2009, 408.

3 Marta Budkowska (ed.), *Sztuka polska wobec Holokaustu/Polish Art and the Holocaust*. Warsaw: Jewish Historical Institute, 2013. Several works discussed in the following pages were presented at the 2014 exhibition 'Holocaust and the Arts: Hungarian Stories (1945–1989)' organized by the author at the Hungarian Institute in Paris.

4 Hedvig Turai, *Anna Margit*. Budapest: Szemimpex, 2002, 65; József Román, *Bálint Endre*. Budapest: Képzőművészeti Alap, 1980, 50, 53.

5 Katalin S. Nagy, *Ország Lili*. Budapest: Arthis, 1993, 9; Dániel Erdély, '"Mi kis" életünk' ['Our Little' Lives], *Árgus*, Vol. 2, No. 5, 1991, 100.

6 Cf. Daniel Véri, *'Leading the Dead' – The World of János Major*. Budapest: MKE, 2013; Daniel Véri, 'Major János (1934–2008). Monográfia és œuvre katalógus' [János Major (1934–2008): Monograph and Oeuvre Catalogue], doctoral dissertation. Budapest: ELTE, 2016, 60.

7 György Kemény, 'Cím nélkül' [Untitled], in László Böröcz (ed.), *Waldsee, 1944*. Budapest: 2B, 2005, n.p. Victims of the firing squads were positioned so that their bodies would fall backwards into the river.

8 László Kertész, 'Mauthauseni magyar emlékmű' [Hungarian Mauthausen Memorial], in Ildikó Nagy (ed.), *Kortárs művészet. Szoborpályázatok 1950–2000* [Contemporary Art: Sculpture Contests 1950–2000]. Budapest: Képző- és Iparművészeti Lektorátus, 2006, 45.

9 It is interpreted as a bunk in László Beke, 'Berczeller Rudolf szobrászata' [The Sculptures of Rudolf Berczeller], *Ars Hungarica*, Vol. 11, No. 2, 1985, 208.

10 Irina Subotić, *Nandor Glid*. Belgrade: Fondacija Vujičić kolekcija, 2012, 93.

11 Glid's later work, *Dachau, International Memorial, 1933–1945*, depicting bodies caught up in barbed wire, is a further development of this composition. His design was selected by the jury in 1965, and the memorial was erected in 1968. Subotić, *Nandor Glid*, 97–99.

12 For more detail, see Anna Lujza Szász, 'Memory Emancipated: Exploring the Memory of the Nazi Genocide of Roma in Hungary', doctoral dissertation. Budapest: ELTE, 2015. The concept was created by Ian Hancock. Szász, *Memory Emancipated*, 134.

13 See József Harmat, *Roma holokauszt a Grábler-tónál. A székesfehérvári és várpalotai cigányok tömeges kivégzése Várpalotán 1945-ben* [Roma Holocaust by the Grabler Lake: Mass Executions of the Roma of Székesfehérvár and Várpalota in 1945]. Várpalota and Veszprém: MNL VML, 2015.

14 János Bársony, 'A Pharrajimos utóélete Magyarországon' [The Afterlife of the Porajmos in Hungary], in János Bársony and Ágnes Daróczi (eds), *Pharrajimos* [Porajmos]. Budapest: L'Harmattan, 2004, 32–33.

15 Szász, *Memory Emancipated*, 54–57. A similarly significant work, though in a different genre, is the documentary film *Forgotten Dead* by József Lojkó Lakatos, primarily based on survivor testimony and historical narrative but also including certain elements of fiction. Despite all the interventions from censors during both pre-production and the shoot, the film was made in 1981. Szász, *Memory Emancipated*, 119–26.

16 The work was created in connection with a prospective (though ultimately never realized) commission for a privately owned former chapel. Consequently, the series needs to be envisioned in an octagonal space closed on three of its sides, rather than on a single plane, and divided into a triptych consisting of panels I–II, III–V and VI–VII. The original title of the work was *Great White Wall*; the later title – approved by Ország – was given by one of her most important collectors, István Rácz, who catalogued her oeuvre. Mária Árvai, 'Ország Lili: Rekviem' [Lili Ország: Requiem], *Művészettörténeti Értesítő*, Vol. 53, No. 2, 2014, 363, 365.

17 For the interpretation of the menorah, see S. Nagy, *Ország Lili*, 79; Árvai, 'Ország Lili', 365.

18 Interpretation of the form as playing cards: Ede Tarbay, 'Bálint Endre – a biblikus' [Endre Bálint – the Biblical], *Vigília*, Vol. 49, No. 1, 1982, 73.

19 Identification of the figure: Marianna Kolozsváry, 'Bálint Endre: Marhavagon-lit, 1968' [Endre Bálint: Cattle-Wagon-lit, 1968], in *Kieselbach Galéria aukciós katalógus* [Kieselbach Gallery Auction Catalogue] (2014), http://www.kieselbach.hu/alkotas/marhavagon-lit-1431 (2 August 2017).

20 Raspberry soda is mentioned in Kemény's email published in Dávid Fehér, 'KEMÉNY/POP. Kemény György és a pop-art' [KEMÉNY/POP: György Kemény and Pop Art], *Artmagazin*, Vol. 14, No. 6, 2016, 36–37. On the painting, see Dávid Fehér, 'Where Is the Light? Transformations of Pop Art in Hungary', in Darsie Alexander and Bartholomew Ryan (eds), *International Pop*. Minneapolis: Walker Art Center, 2015, 142.

21 Kemény, 'Cím nélkül'.

22 See Yad Vashem Photo Archives 2807/114. János Major used another photograph taken here (a boy with raised hands) in one of his works; see Véri, *Major János*, 190–91.

23 See Dávid Fehér, *Lakner László. Varrólányok Hitler beszédét hallgatják/Seamstresses Listen to Hitler's Speech*. Budapest: Szépművészeti Múzeum, 2011; Dávid Fehér, '(Dis)figuring Reality', pp. 137–59.

24 *Opus International*, No. 49, 1974, 111. See Fehér, *Lakner László*, 15.

25 I wish to thank Dávid Fehér for sharing this information about the photograph with me.

26 Gjon Mili, *Nazi War Criminal Adolf Eichmann in His Cell at Djalameh Jail*, 1961, The LIFE Picture Collection, 92930924.

27 For the broader context of the work, see Turai, *Anna Margit*, 125–47.

28 The Michelangelo parallel is noted in Turai, *Anna Margit*, 105.

29 Sándor Bacskai, 'Beszélgetés Baranyay András képzőművésszel' [Conversation with András Baranyay], *Fotóművészet*, Vol. 47, Nos 3–4, 2004; László Beke interviewed by the author, 2009.

30 Ferenc Gál, *Az ellenség tanulmányozása. Ideiglenes jegyzet a Rendőrtiszti Főiskola számára* [Studying the Enemy. Provisory Textbook for the Police Academy]. Budapest: BM, 1972. From the Historical Archives of the Hungarian State Security, ÁSZTL–ÁB 370 – courtesy of Edit Sasvári. ÁBTL 3.1.7. T-9481/4, '*Összetartók* csoportdosszié' [Solidary Team, group folder], Vol. 4, 267.

31 In this respect, only Major's *Self-Portrait* (1969), is comparable. On later works with a similar approach, see Norman L. Kleeblatt (ed.), *Mirroring Evil. Nazi Imagery/Recent Art*. New York: The Jewish Museum–Rutgers University Press, 2002.

32 János Major, '*Tisztelt Rosta Endre elvtárs!' kezdetű levél kétoldalas piszkozata* [Two-Page Draft of a Letter Beginning with 'Dear Comrade Rosta'], 1970–71, 1.

33 For the identification of the depicted figures, see Turai, *Anna Margit*, 107.

34 Véri, *'Leading the Dead'*, 14–29.

35 On these and other works addressing the Tiszaeszlár case, see Daniel Véri, 'A tiszaeszlári vérvád zenei feldolgozásai' [Musical Adaptations of the Tiszaeszlár Blood Libel], *Múlt és Jövő*, Vol. 17, No. 2, 2014, 23–36.

36 Cf. 'Krónika' [Chronicle], in Miklós Erdély, *A filmről* [On Film], compiled by Miklós Peternák. Budapest: Balassi/BAE Tartóshullám/Intermedia, 1995, 250.

37 Véri, 'Major János', 142–50.

38 Véri, 'Major János', 148; Mária Árvai, 'Ország Lili első magyarországi gyűjteményes kiállítása, 1967. Székesfehérvár' [Lili Ország's First Retrospective Exhibition in Hungary, 1967. Székesfehérvár], *Múlt és Jövő*, Vol. 19, No. 4, 2016, 86–95.

39 The description is based upon photographs, as well as Miklós Peternák, 'Beszélgetés Erdély Miklóssal, 1983 tavaszán' [Conversation with Miklós Erdély, Spring 1983], *Árgus*, No. 5, 1991, 80. The reconstruction of the exhibition: Eszter Greskovics, 'Az "R"-kiállítás' [The 'R' Exhibition], 1970, thesis. Budapest: ELTE, 2012.

40 Peternák, Beszélgetés Erdély Miklóssal, 1983 tavaszán, 80. Erdély also puts Kádár (beside his wife) in one of his action photos: *Two People Who Have Had a Decisive Influence on My Life*, 1972 (p. 240, fig. 9).

41 The speech was published in *Népszabadság* (2 February 1967, 4) and nearly all the daily papers.

42 Kemény shared the first prize with Shigeo Fukuda. S. Mason, '30th Anniversary of Victory, Warsaw. An International Poster Competition', *Graphis*, No. 178, 1975, 212–13; Jozef Mroszczak (ed.), *Plakat/Poster/плакат/L'affiche*. Warsaw: Krajowa Agencja Wydawnicza, 1977; Véri, *'Leading the Dead'*, 55–56.

43 The parallel with Kertész was highlighted at the 2014 exhibition 'Holocaust and the Arts' and in Fehér, 'KEMÉNY/POP', 37.

44 On the universality of the Holocaust and the diversity of languages: János Brendel, 'Hommage à Celan' [Homage to Celan], in Thomas Hirsch and Katalin Néray (eds), *Lakner László: Metamorphosis*. Budapest: Ludwig Múzeum, 2004, 71.

45 *Citation Piece (Ludwig Wittgenstein)*, 1972. The quotation is Proposition 7 of Wittgenstein's *Tractatus Logico-Philosophicus*. See Dávid Fehér, *Lakner László*. Budapest: HUNGART, 2016, 22–23.

46 Theo Buck, *Bildersprache. Celan-Motive bei László Lakner und Anselm Kiefer* [Imagery: Celan Motifs by László Lakner and Anselm Kiefer]. Aachen: Rimbaud, 1993; Brendel, 'Hommage à Celan', 71–75; Fehér, *Lakner László*, 25–26.

1. Tibor Hajas – János Vető, *Lou Reed Total*, 1979, silver gelatine print, 29.8 × 21 cm, Ludwig Múzeum – Kortárs Művészeti Múzeum, Budapest

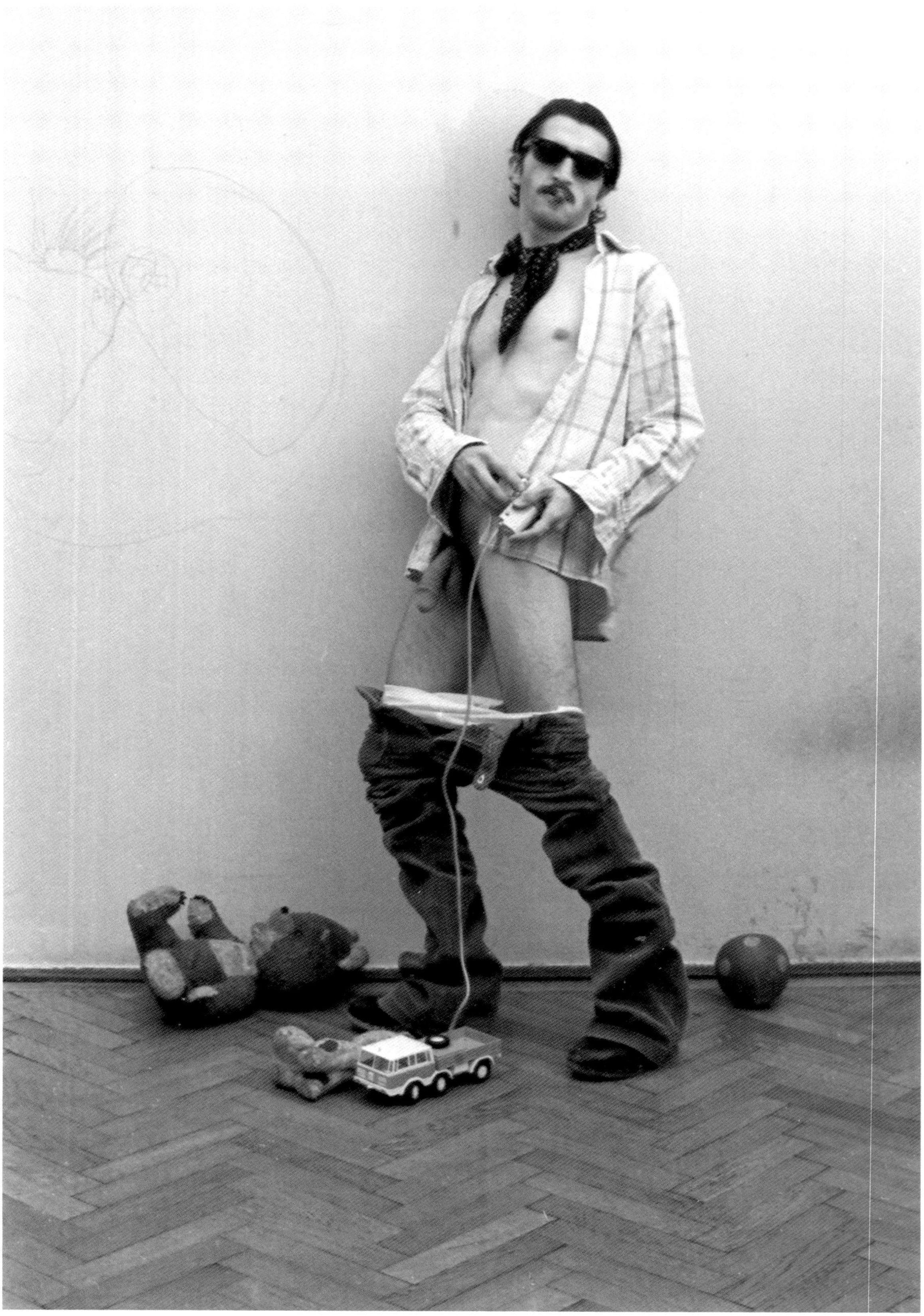

1

Edit András

Out of Private Public Opinion into Shared Personal Opinion

The Public, the Private and the Political

The title of this essay comes from Tibor Hajas's work *Made in Hungary I–II* (1975), a graffito on a wall in a public space, saying, 'We hereby declare this wall nonexistent. It is an unfounded forgery.'[1] The documentary photograph was signed by representatives of the era's alternative culture. The document's handwritten heading designates the action as 'Out of private public opinion into shared personal opinion.' The document was posted in three locations around Budapest as a kind of manifesto.

It is this muddled, 'upside-down' nature of public/private relations in socialist Hungary in the 1970s, articulated so cunningly by Hajas, that my essay examines in a two-fold argument. Firstly, it will show that the basic concept of public space (open and accessible to all) and its meaning (an arena of discursive interaction, which can be critical of the state and which is distinct from it),[2] as well as the private sphere (secured by rights), relevant for modern Western societies, are not applicable to the conditions of socialism. Secondly, the essay argues that the Western assertion of the total division and sharply opposed character of the Soviet-type spheres ('passive, victimized societies and victorious, omnipotent and relentlessly oppressive party-state') does not hold true.[3] In agreement with the statement that agency is lost in such discourses of totalitarianism, the essay aims to restore the agency of the artist, which was implemented through imaginary transgressions of public space and therefore infiltrated politics in the socialist era.[4] The nature of socialist private space from the perspective of the artists will be scrutinized as well. Furthermore, the relevance of the Western feminist claim that the 'personal is political' will be weighed against the claim of artist-agents operating in different conditions behind the Iron Curtain. The essay will use selected neo-avant-garde works and artistic strategies to explore the validity and misconceptions, differences and specificities of the dichotomies, including their gender connotations.

The private public opinion of the artist

The division of the social world into public and private is never an innocent analytical exercise; it often carries powerful and normative implications about what is hidden or withdrawn and what is visible and openly accessible, what concerns the collective and what is relegated to partial private life. This raises the question: under whose authority do the public and private realms operate? And, consequently, who is entitled to participate and who is excluded?[5]

In a broad sense, the public/private distinction in modern culture demarcates the private realm of personal life (the realm of domesticity and intimacy) from the public realm (social and/or civil society). It corresponds to the distinction between political/non-political as well. In the Western sense, private does not only connote a particular interest as opposed to the common, communal, non-partial interest, but 'also indicates privacy, a right-shielded realm of personal life experienced in the household'.[6]

Since official discourse and practice were monopolized by the party-state in the Soviet satellite countries, subjecting all manner of autonomous, socially visible forms of critical political discourse to strict control, they had different formulae for public and private polarization from those of modern Western societies. Party-state domination meant monopolization of the public sphere; thus, no publicly available space remained for political life outside of the official discourse, from which an autonomous civil or political society could emerge.

Comparing the Western and Eastern meanings of these concepts and practices, Marc Garcelon states that 'under communism, one simply cannot speak of either in terms of normatively recognized pursuit of legitimate civil interests...or in terms of an institutionally secured realm of personal life...social dependency under communism effectively prevented the institutionalization of secure spaces for an autonomous personal life'.[7] As for social and political life, he asserts that the communist ideological project was a 'community without participation'.[8] The absence of a public realm that has institutional frameworks for participation led to the 'enforced passivity and depoliticization' of the population.[9] In the case of the Soviet Union, he argues for the domestic space as a 'subversive source of social autonomy', which formed as a 'reservoir' of unofficial values, traditions and beliefs that persisted as 'latent symbolic resources'.[10]

The case of socialist Hungary was somewhat different with respect to both public and private realms. The status quo was based on a broad social consensus between the state and society. 'Society must accept the group of those exercising power and their tools for legitimization, respect political taboos, and agree to take part in public life regulated by the state through officially controlled institutions... as a consequence of this or as a compensation for that the private life (and paradoxically the public life as well) became apolitical.'[11] József Havasréti argues for the phenomenon of an 'alternative public sphere', which he conceives as a mixture of a type of public sphere and certain elements of private life, a zone where the most important element of the social consensus in Hungary – the absence of politics – could be ignored. Elsewhere, he describes this peculiar formation as 'making the private sphere public' by means of creating institutions of an alternative public space, enlisting in this category different circles, like the Petrigalla salon, the Zugló Circle, the Halász theatre and György Galántai's Balatonboglári Kápolnaműterem (Balatonboglár Chapel Studio) (see also Júlia Perczel, 'The Art Sphere as a Grey Zone', pp. 59–75, and Flóra Barkóczi, 'Creative (Dis)Courses', pp. 95–109).[12]

I wish to focus on individual artistic practices and introduce those that created a space beyond the rigid dichotomy by cutting across and blurring the binary opposition of public and private realms. The artworks analysed here reversed the public and the private or confused the 'sacred' distinction between them that constituted the backbone of the socialist society. The creation of various imaginary alternative spaces counteracted exclusion from public space and public politics, and served as a substitute both for personal involvement in public life and for the politics lost in personal life.

In the spatial conception of power, power is equated with the public sphere, a traditionally masculine space. However, public space was not available for those who were not involved in the common delusion of communism, least of all for those who operated or were accused of operating outside the state-controlled dream machine. In his analysis, Piotr Piotrowski closely examines artworks that undermine the traditional hierarchy of power within the context of gender in socialist Eastern Europe.[13] He analyses the strategies applied by the Romanian conceptual artist Ion Grigorescu, who feminized his body in private space to undermine the socialist political authority. In his work *Delivery* (1977), the phallus appears to be contingent and unstable in the course of its degradation. Piotrowski states, 'This destabilization of gender difference is fundamentally subversive in character, by revealing the conventional character of the legitimacy of any power; it suggests the possibility of its overturn.'[14] In his observation, male body art mostly confirmed the conventional male roles, instead of becoming an instrument of critique.

I wish to challenge this view in my analysis of Hajas's infamous 'private' photo, *Lou*

Reed Total (1979, fig. 1), which has never been included as part of his professional oeuvre, and when it was first published in 2005, it was within the framework of hyper-masculinity as a manifestation of male power.[15] The background of the half-naked self-portrait is contradictory; it is a pronounced private space, generally assigned to women and, by the socialist definition, a depoliticized space. It informs us about the absence of the public presence of the artist: he is excluded from the core expression of masculinity as is traditionally associated with public space and power. The space shown in the photograph has a peculiar position even within the category of private spaces: it belongs to a child, a male child, signified by the typical boy's toys dispersed about the room. In this context, the adult man playing with a toy machine refers to the infantilized nature of masculinity within the socialist scenario and not the mechanized nature of male sexuality.[16] As Susan Buck-Morss points out: 'In his parental role, Stalin as father is motherly more than punitive, nurturing rather than disciplinary. The Soviet family drama is pre-Oedipal. It is for not loving the mother/leader that the child is punished, which makes the psychic transition of adulthood impossible.'[17] Although the description refers to the Stalinist Soviet Union, that understanding of the relationship between the state and its subjects applies to socialist Hungary as well.

Within the dynamics of reality and fantasy, the child's room represents the world of fairy-tales and fiction. Thus, by means of exposing male genitalia in the children's room, the whole scene is transformed into the realm of imagination. As the large, exposed penis stands for the desired masculinity, the message is that the privileges connected to its symbolical equivalent, the phallus, are available only to the imagination. This imaginary 'private' masculinity compensates for the lack of masculinity (and power) constructed in the socialist public space.

The private sphere in socialism is regarded as a space that is free from political pressure,[18] but this can't be taken at face value. For the artist, not even the private space – 'the room' – can provide security and shelter; there is no way out of his nightmares, there is no escape from total surveillance and the system of control if he is put on the surveillance list. Hajas cries out his anxiety in a heart-breaking poem entitled 'Counterpoint' in which he compares his room (in a manner of denial which accentuates the comparison) to solitary confinement, a gas chamber, an abattoir, a cage, death row, a quarantine room and a trap. Private space, in principle, is where the socialist subject can withdraw and regenerate. However, Hajas envisions his room, his private space, as 'a last refuge' that is in flames, from where 'the cry of death cannot be heard, and the corpse can't be identified'.[19]

At the age of nineteen, Hajas was sent to prison for fourteen months, from 23 October 1965 until Christmas 1966. The charge was incitement against the state; that is, breaking the consensus. In 1979, a year before his tragic death at the age of thirty-four, and in the very year of making *Lou Reed Total*, pictures of unpredictable terror were surfacing in his mind in the form of flashbacks (see also Emese Kürti, 'Poetry in Action', pp. 291–313).

In *Discipline and Punish*, Foucault's seminal book about the prison system, he states that:

the body being in most cases the only property accessible...in our societies, the systems of punishment are to be situated in a certain 'political economy' of the body: even if they do not make use of violent or bloody punishment, even when they use 'lenient' methods involving confinement or correction, it is always the body that is at issue – the body and its forces, their utility and their docility, their distribution and their submission.[20]

He meticulously describes the whole technology and mechanism of power over the body in the rites of punishment. In this construction, the body is an object and target of power and not the least bit the bearer of power. Phantoms of imagination are the outgrowths that counterbalance total defencelessness. Being dispossessed and controlled traditionally gives way to extreme displays of lost masculinity. In this context, exaggerated hyper-masculinity substitutes for the one that was stolen. The display of the penis in prison signifies the bare, physical, 'untamed' masculinity deviated from its transformation into its transcendental equivalent the phallus, and its symbolical meaning as the privileged site of power.

This is why in Hajas's photo the penis is not hidden, but in fact unabashedly exposed. This corresponds to the notion that the penis works best as a signifier of power when it is veiled.[21] Foucault connects a panoptic quality to the exercise of power, insisting that 'the prison, the place where the penalty is carried out, is also the place of observation of punished individuals'.[22]

As for Hajas, the site of his freedom, as he noted in different texts, consisted of no more than his own body and the medium of the photo. However, his much-desired freedom is sufficient only for playing with children's toys and his own penis, a male body part stable only in its symbolic, phallic transformation, but unpredictable in his physicality. Considering the children's room as the site of a father–son relationship, the only munitions he can provide to his offspring are the lack of freedom, lack of power and the inability to enter into adulthood.

In his interpretation, the family is pushed into the private sphere, which does not function as a safe haven, a secure place for intimacy, but rather as an institution of repression, rejection, exclusion and marginalization, resembling the institution of punishment, the main force of the power of normalization. The room as a micro-universe might also act as a symbol of the country, correlating with the mechanism of the prison, while the experience of freedom is fully delusional. In this regard, neither private space nor the body gives release, except in the realm of imagination.

The withdrawal from public life to one's 'personal micro-universe', a general strategy in the 1970s, was not a voluntary choice for those attracted to the same sex. While criticizing the exclusive psychoanalytical approach to social identity for neglecting its discursive character, Nancy Fraser identifies the public sphere as a locus of identity reconstruction. She argues that public space is a vital arena for the formation and enactment of social identity. Furthermore, she emphasizes that in order to participate in public discourse, members of the public should be able to speak 'in [their] own voice'.[23] In Hungary, 'the lack of private space and the surveillance of public spaces and private lives, along with legally institutionalized

2

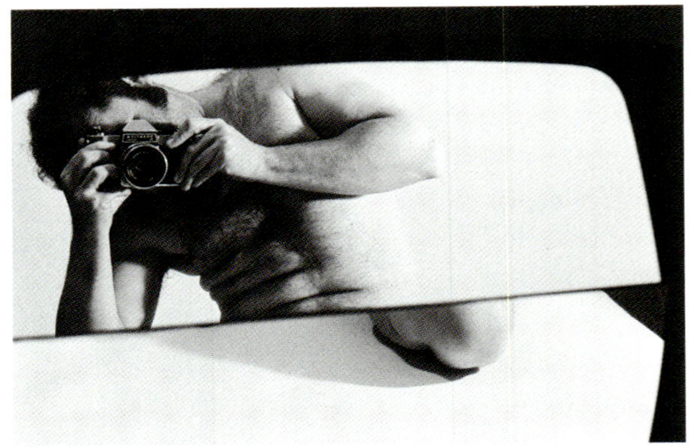

3

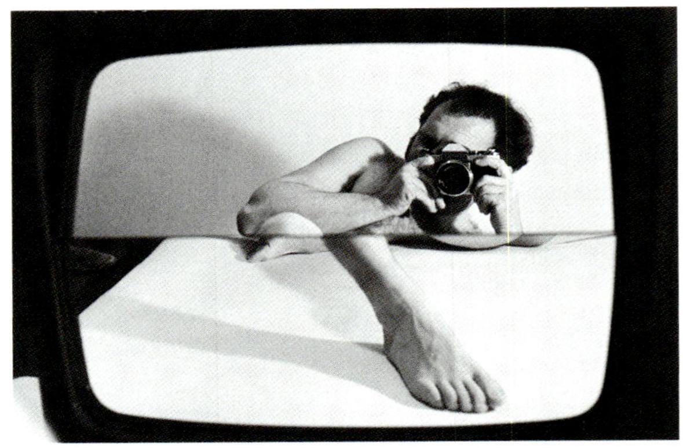

2 & 3. Károly Halász, *Pseudo Video*, 1975, silver gelatine print, each 18 × 24 cm, Vintage Galéria, Budapest

4 & 5. Károly Halász, *Private Broadcast*, 1974, silver gelatine print, each 18 × 24 cm, Vintage Galéria, Budapest

stigmatization of homosexuality, constituted serious burdens', so homosexual practices were relegated to the 'publicly unnoticeable sphere of privacy'.[24] Károly Halász, an artist from the Pécsi Műhely (Pécs Workshop) who has never come out publicly, struggled to keep his gay identity secret and lived in the shadows, inside his private chamber. His art is inseparable from his life's experiences, much of which revolved around his identity as a gay man within the context of socialist control and was about his desire to speak up and break out of the cell of his closeted identity (see also Katalin Székely, 'The Influx of Images', pp. 331–55).

Officially sanctioned public life in Hungary was built on a system of taboos, which covered negative discussion of the role of the Soviet Union, the interpretation of the 1956 revolution, poverty, Jewishness, nationalism and the concept of the nation, and socialist cultural norms.[25] Homosexuality was obviously a taboo, but one that failed to register with most writers of the period as sensational; it is seldom even mentioned. In his *Pseudo Video* series (1975, figs 2 and 3), Halász clashes with the tacit agreement to be excluded from the public sphere and invades public media through his own 'broadcast', a political act in itself given the total state control of broadcasting. In a speech in 1960, János Kádár considered the messages delivered by daily newspapers and radio broadcasts as directly influencing social life and 'having repercussion on the political fight'.[26] During the 1960s, at a time of booming consumerism in Hungary,[27] television broadcasting was no doubt the most powerful medium in this regard, and it served as the most important forum in the public sphere. Halász rejected the status quo and the division between public and private. In his work, he uses the symbol of public media, an empty TV box, as his own living space, his own 'closet' from which he observes the outside world. The act of monitoring and the direction of the public gaze was turned back on itself through his act. However, he can't help interiorizing the public view against which he rebels; it forms part of his self-image like a straitjacket, as seen in another photo series, *Private Broadcast* (1974–75, figs 4 and 5).[28]

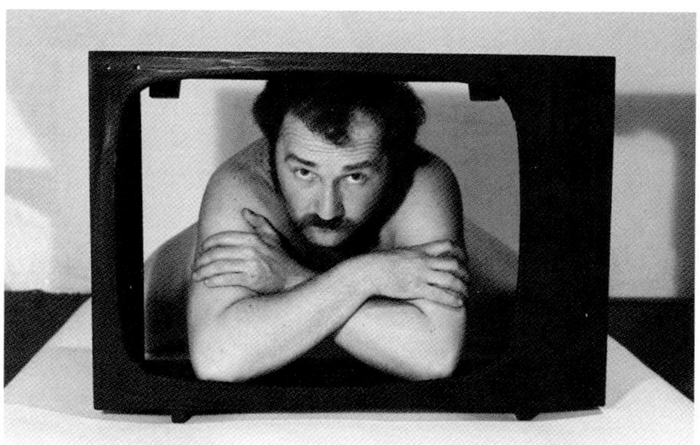
4

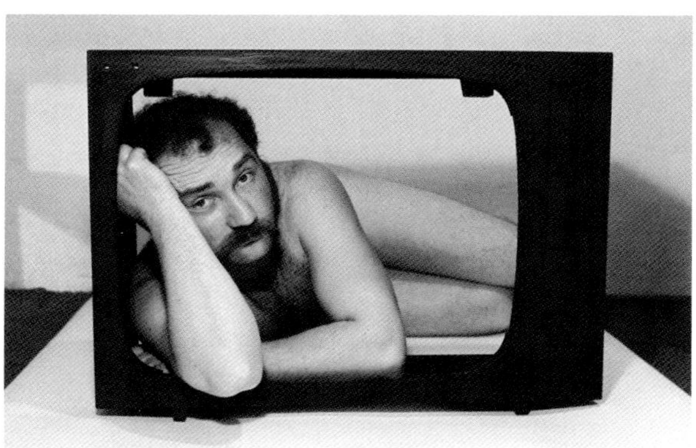
5

The title of the latter refers to a notion that is an oxymoron in a socialist country. It documents his actions of huddling up in various poses inside an empty TV box that frames his existence, confirming Fraser's assumption. The TV set, in accordance with the mythologizing and sacralizing character of contemporary neo-avant-garde discourse, was compared to an altar.[29] His action, however, is far from being sacred or elevated. He is trying hard to fit into the frame, but his naked body bulges out here and there. The disturbing uneasiness of the photos comes from a feeling of the insecurity and vulnerability of the body being publicly exposed in ungraceful poses. The awkward mismatch with the public image of the body was detected at the time and the work was interpreted as a 'Chaplin-like action, meaning that the artist cannot take anything for impossible once he needs to tell something'.[30]

Halász kept alluding in interviews to what he needed to say, or at least to his troubled feelings. In a private letter, he defined his own art as a 'cry from a dark room'.[31] In another case his cry for help was even more literal, the word 'Help' being written on the floor in front of his self-portrait. It was defined later as a 'naively political text', while his one-man show in the television was conceived as a 'one-man revolution against his own practice of watching television'.[32] Halász's verbal statements related to his art and life, as in 'the feeling being closed in' or the unspecified 'everyday regular insults' that occupied his mind, did not resonate in the reviews written about his works.[33] His art was perceived consistently, even retrospectively, as a constructivist or conceptualist practice in which 'he uses his own body to construct endless variations in living geometry'.[34] Some obscure, enigmatic references in connection to his works popped up from time to time in the discourse, like his *High Stands* (1972) interpreted as a hidden place for hunters where 'they silently wait for their prey' or as a 'threatening anti-utopia, if not the...lived-through reality'.[35] However, the nature of this 'lived-through reality' was shyly ignored. In spite of the hints that he repeatedly provided, what he was trying to say was not talked about or elaborated on further, as, willingly or not, art criticism shared the taboo of homosexuality, strengthened by the discipline's own assumption that an artist's identity has nothing to do with his art.

Nevertheless, the photos are readable from the perspective of queerness and are also quite telling with regard to the public image of gay men at the time. The huddled bodies in his *Private Broadcast* series lack self-confidence; they are deviant, distorted, grotesque bodies resembling acts from nineteenth-century freak shows, which were popular entertainment at that time.

After the Stonewall riot in New York in 1969, which inverted the stereotype of meek, limp-wristed, effeminate gay men into a positive image of strength, the 1970s gave rise to a cult of gay men identifying themselves through masculine stereotypes. This change in the public image of gay men, along with the queer visual code popularized by Hal Fischer's photos entitled *Gay Semiotics*,[36] was widely disseminated in Western countries but did not pass through the Iron Curtain; neither did identity politics, the gay liberation movement, nor the theoretical implications of the issue, let alone gay pride.

The public image of a gay man in socialist Hungary in the 1970s and the self-image of the artist correspond to the attitude of the pre-Stonewall era, when homosexuality was regarded internationally as a pathology to be cured; a gay man was imagined as a woman trapped in a male body, and such 'imitation women' were consequently meant to spend their lives in the shadows, on the margins. In the case of *Pseudo Video*, the penis – equated with power, dominance and public space in its symbolic equivalent, the phallus – is hidden in all the photos. What we can see, and what Halász communicates about himself through the media, is the pain of sexual repression through bodily distortion, the shame over the lack of a penis, and thus the lack of privileged masculinity, and, most of all, over the fact that his body is (or imagined to be) truncated and castrated: namely, it is a feminized body.

According to sociologist Judit Takács, despite the fact that homosexuality was declared a biological phenomenon, a pathology, and as such was decriminalized in Hungary in 1961, it could still be considered a 'perversion against nature conducted in a scandalous manner' and would be sufficient cause for police action against the 'abnormality', punishable by up to three years of imprisonment. 'Thus, the long tradition of specialized state surveillance on homosexuality could continue also after 1961, as the compilation of "homosexual inventories" providing information on potential blackmail victims...has been part of regular police work, especially in urban areas, since the 1920s.'[37] On one of the *Pseudo Video* images, the grids behind which he is confined naked could be associated with prison bars. The distress saturating his verbal statements, as well as his cries for help in many different forms, could be taken as fear of physical imprisonment when even the mental prison he was locked in seemed almost unbearable for him. On the other hand, he empowered himself by creating a counter-language and a parallel discursive channel for his own broadcast, through which he was able to reduce the anxiety level of his subjugation and disadvantage in the official public sphere. Fraser recognizes and names alternative discursive spaces, which are generally occupied by subordinate social groups such as women, people of colour, gay people, etc., as 'subaltern counterpublics'.[38] Within the conditions of socialism, this type of space was not created by a supportive community, but was part of the artistic strategy of an individual agent, who failed to conform to the hegemonic notion of masculinity at a time when there was no space for in-between categories and who was also a misfit in the gender-blind local neo-avant-garde discourse.

The political is the personal

The general feminist understanding of the public/private dichotomy is that 'the separation of the private domestic life of women from the public world of men has been constitutive of patriarchal-liberalism from its origins, since the mid-nineteenth century'.[39] The hierarchical nature and the gender connotations of the public/private division both in concept and practice are emphasized. 'At a conceptual level, the distinction is bound up with a distinction between history and nature that constructs the private sphere as having a timelessness associated with nature and reproductive cyclical time which supposedly disconnects it from politics.'[40] The recent feminist critique of the rigid separation of the public and private realms (echoed in the separation of nature/culture, and personal/political) connects the lines of opposition to liberal patriarchy. The meaning of the powerful slogan 'the personal is political', aiming to bridge the two distant realms, is that if personal factors are structured by public factors (by laws, the welfare system, the sexual division of labour, etc.) then 'personal problems can be solved only through political means and political action'.[41] Despite the heavy criticism of the slogan from various positions, it has remained very powerful and influential.[42] On top of that, it drove female artistic practices in the 1970s in the West (and, later on, in Eastern Europe), prompting artists to involve their personal lives or personal issues in their artistic practices as a way to politicize their art.[43]

As this attitude proved to be decisive for the first and second generations of feminist artists in Western countries, it became a normative standard by which the output of other art scenes was to be measured, and the socialist Eastern bloc region, with its vastly different conditions, came off badly. This is not surprising as the concept was derived from Western liberal experience, and applied without taking into consideration the distinctive social-political framework. I believe that discovering traces of feminist concepts or patches of gender consciousness in the East does not really help to restore the balance. I would rather argue in favour of applying concepts that resonate with the distinctive social and political nature of the local experience. I suggest, therefore, that the slogan 'the personal is political' is useless behind the Iron Curtain as it does not apply; in fact, the opposite, 'the political is the personal', is appropriate, and instead of applying specifically to women, it is applicable to both men and women under socialist conditions.

Instead of declaring that the personal is in itself political, the works analysed here appropriate and internalize politics, turning it into intimate private property, or smuggle the political into art in an era when the public was infantilized and excluded from politics; even when the public was involved in politics, the politics were pre-digested and pre-packaged. Artists still found ways to invade the terrain they were warned off and commented on it by creating spaces in which to formulate their political opinions.

Festive holidays, ceremonial parades and symbolic politics were inseparable companions to the godless religion of communism. If independent political and public life was in short supply in the existing socialist party-states, carefully orchestrated mass celebrations tried to maintain the illusion of collective cohesion in a community politically and ideologically loyal to the leaders. These rituals were supposed to display strength and order, as in military parades, or provide a carnivalesque image of freedom and generate euphoria through marching and singing together surrounded by flags and ribbons, as in May Day parades. Attendance was obligatory and organized meticulously through workplaces. Dóra Maurer's *May-Day Private March on Artificial Ground* (1971, fig. 6) is a kind of 'privatization' of the public celebration, the direct opposite of the official one. This 'parade' took place in an isolated, claustrophobic private space and resembled the monotonous physical exercise one might undertake for survival in a solitary cell. This is not a triumphal march towards the bright future, but effectively a standstill, a circular movement circling back on itself again and again, which could be taken as a symbolic comment on the country's ideology. The reference to 'artificial ground' in the work's title suggests that the official, mandatory march, outside on the streets, is the 'natural' one, or that the artist, in a declaration made privately, regards the whole celebration as fabricated and built on artificial ground. In Havasréti's typology, the work and its reference to the 'artificial' could be linked to the phenomenon of 'substitution by necessity',[44] a kind of puritanical, do-it-yourself, low-tech aesthetic,[45] an outcome of the shortage economy and central distribution of resources that impacted especially those artists who were put into the category of 'tolerated' and 'prohibited' art (see Júlia Perczel, 'The Art Sphere as a Grey Zone', pp. 59–75). 'In the circles of politically or culturally excluded in opposition to the dominant norms, the "do it yourself" genres and practices, characteristic of the activity of western subcultures and countercultural groups, were taken over.'[46]

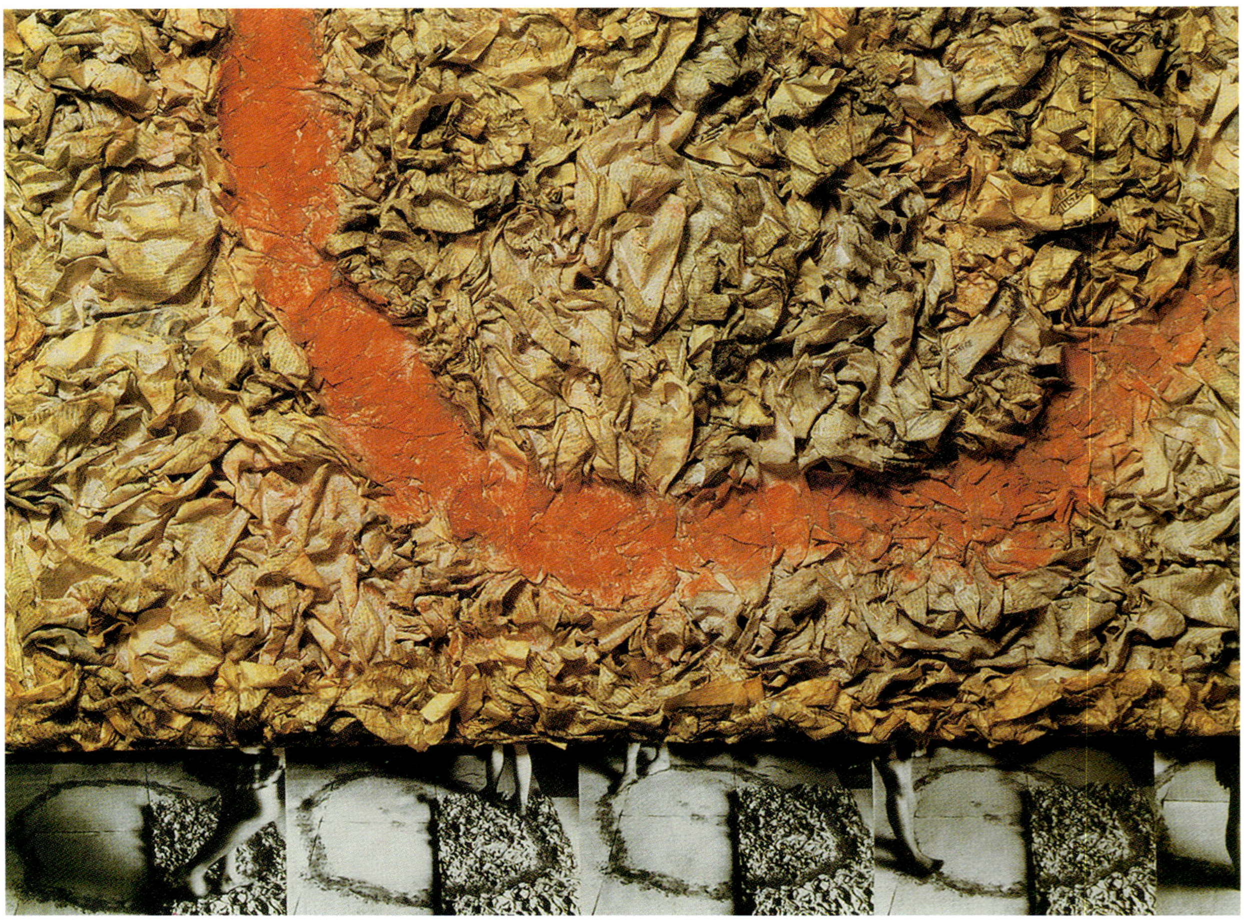

6

6. Dóra Maurer, *V's Private May-Day March on Artificial Ground*, 1971, fibreboard, paper maché, powdered paint, cold glue, trash, photo, pedotypia, 69 × 88 cm, Szépművészeti Múzeum – Magyar Nemzeti Galéria, Budapest

7. Dóra Maurer, *What Can One Do With a Paving Stone?*, 1971, black and white photos mounted on cardboard, 80 × 70 cm, Private collection

7

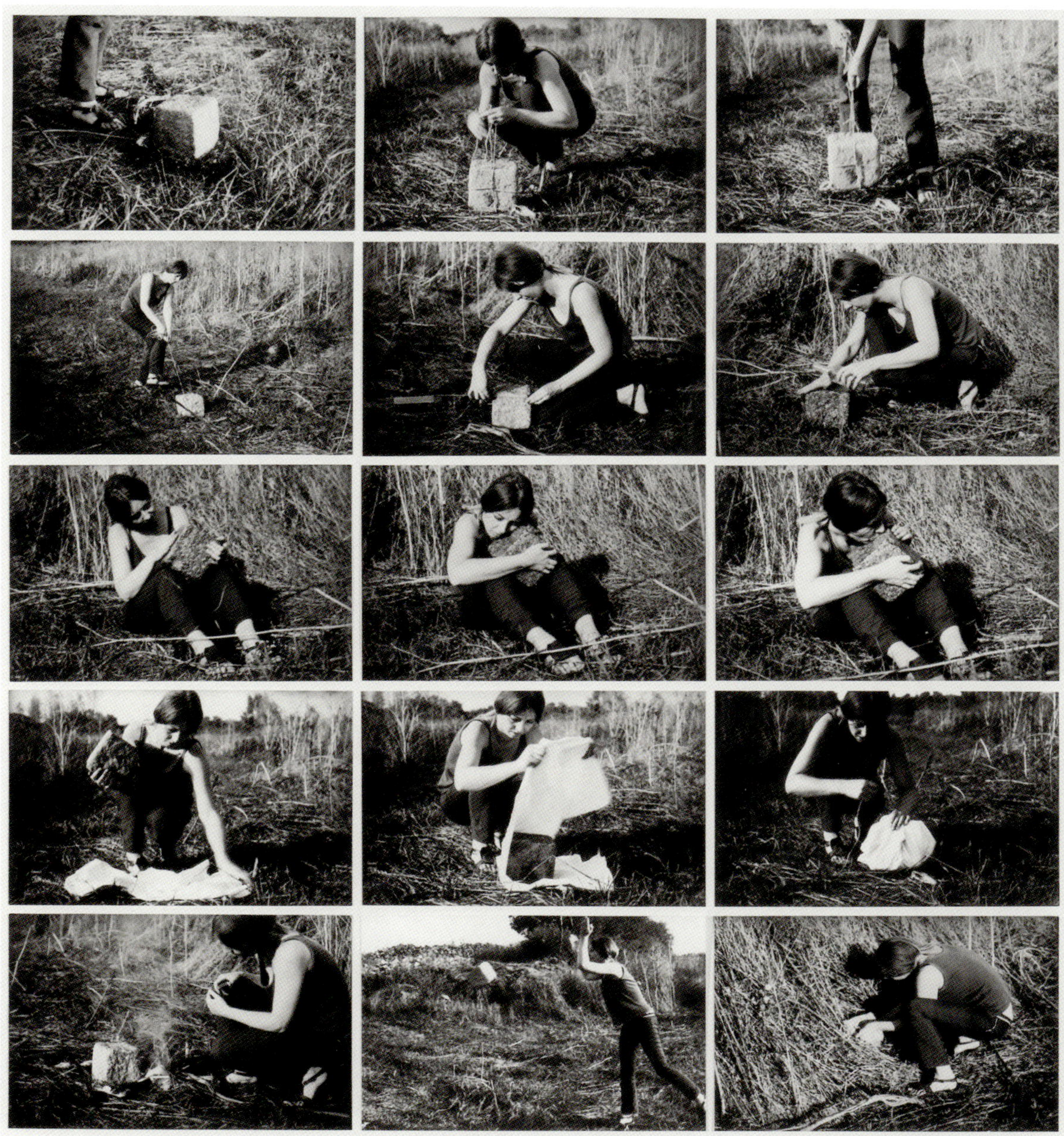

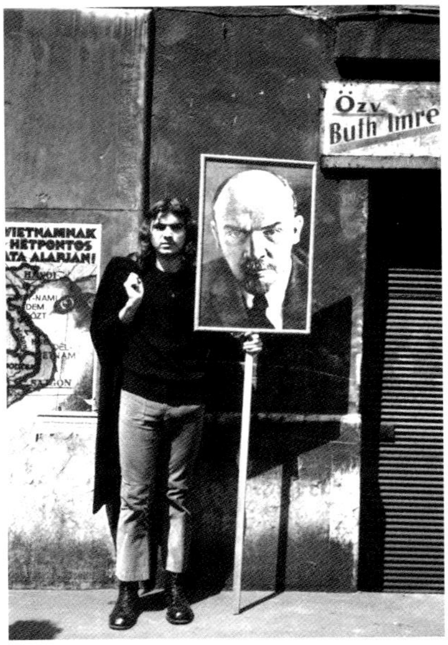

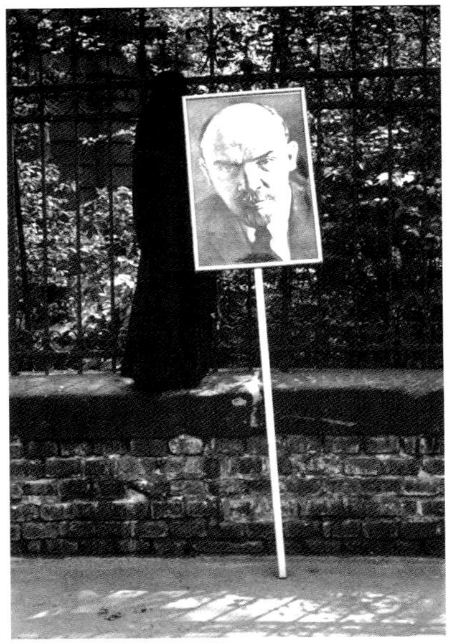
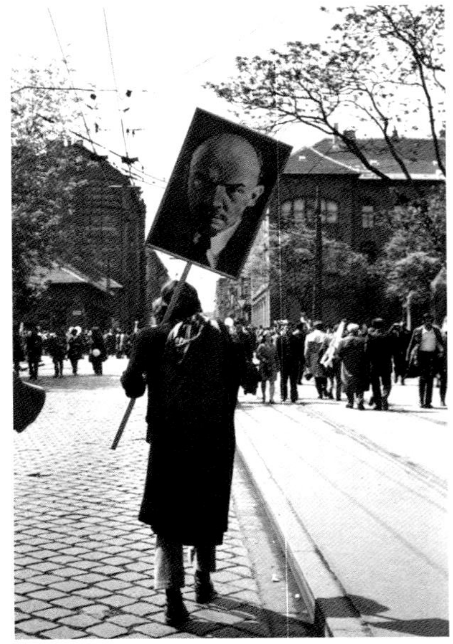
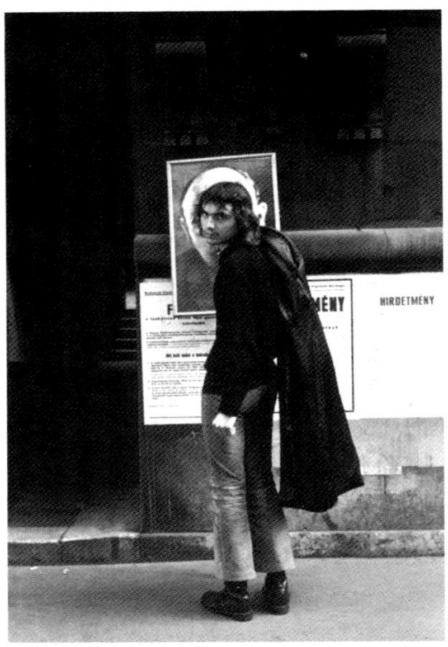

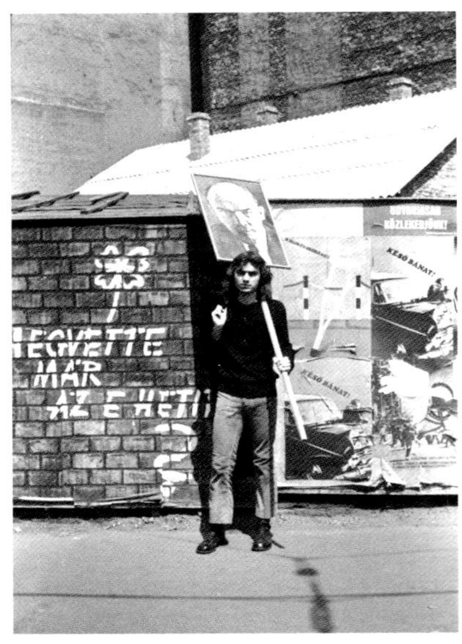
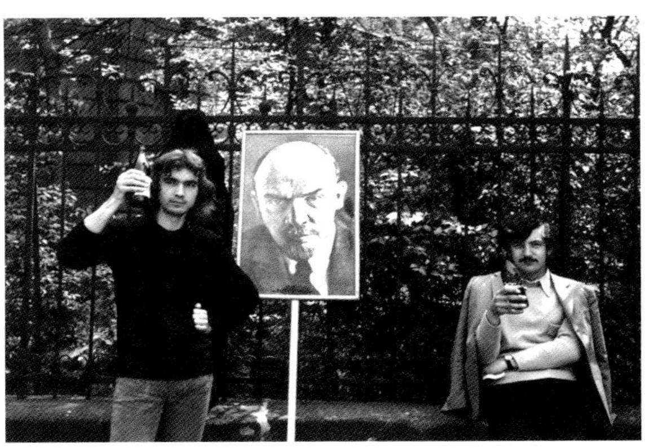

8

8. Bálint Szombathy, *Lenin in Budapest* (street action), 1972, performance documentation, 13 pieces, each 40 × 30 cm, Ludwig Múzeum – Kortárs Művészeti Múzeum, Budapest

In a documented action, *What Can One Do With a Paving Stone?* (1971, fig. 7), Dóra Maurer entitles herself to speak about history and politics through 'privatizing' the interpretation of history monopolized in Hungary by official history writing, the backbone of which was the well-entrenched system of taboos. The most important and 'sacred' taboo was the attempt to understand and define the historical significance of the quelled 1956 revolution against the Stalinist state; the subject was truly untouchable until the collapse of the socialist system in 1989. Being able to question the uprising's designation as a counterrevolution, as stipulated by the regime and echoed in history writing, signalled the very end of an era. The cobblestone, a local signifier of the 1956 revolution, is treated by Maurer as a close family member with whom she is in an intimate love–hate relationship; she sometimes wishes to get rid of it, and on another day to hug and embrace it, like a child. She does not treat politics as something out there, but as part of the private realm.

The leaders of the Russian Revolution and symbols of the legitimacy of the Soviet political system were unquestionable cornerstones of the Hungarian socialist regime, and were to be taken seriously. Bálint Szombathy, a minority Hungarian artist in Vojvodina, Yugoslavia, joined the end of a May Day parade in Budapest, when the crowd and the enthusiasm were both dissipating, and documented his performance in the photo series *Lenin in Budapest* (1972, fig. 8).

In Soviet socialist culture, heroes are the triumphant embodiments of collective identity and represent the sacred in the mundane world. Their exceptionalism comes from embodying the charisma of the group and is based on the belief of the followers, so they are very fragile constructions. Distance is constitutive of heroism.[47] Communist heroes are in abundance in socialist mass celebrations, but distance is emphasized by the enormous size of their portraits raised high above the heads of the ordinary people. Szombathy breaks the unwritten rules when he carries a pole with a placard showing Lenin's head, much like those carried by the marchers, but as if he were just hanging out with his buddy; they drink together, rest together and enjoy each other's company. Both the artist's personal body and the substitute for the leader exist in the same ordinary world in which the hero loses his distinctive value and is deflated. The exceptional hero does not just lose his aura in this performance, but the silhouette of his covered bald head serves as a radiant nimbus around the artist's head. In this configuration, it is the artist and not the fallen political leader whose activity is 'sanctioned'. The hero who is supposed to lead the masses finds himself alone, isolated, forgotten, or marching in the opposite direction, turning his back on the people. The untouchable hero, the symbol of the regime, is demystified and commercialized next to the slogan of the lottery advertisement 'Have you bought your weekly yet?' The artist blurs the boundaries between public and private and between art and propaganda. Compared to the local art scene, Szombathy's defiance and clear irony lie in his position as an outsider, mocking the bizarre political scenery elsewhere.

Local artists employed different, less direct, but more ambiguous and puzzling artistic strategies. Endre Tót was also flirting with the political symbols of the regime, but he opted for a subtler approach than straightforward criticism or irony. In an insightful essay, Klara Kemp-Welch identifies Tót's 'espousal of zero and his humorous parodies of the culture of optimism' as the 'two central pillars' of his conceptualism.[48] If the 'culture of optimism' was the bottom-line of the ideology when it came to everyday life in the barracks – the Soviet satellites – the Hungarian model was a flawed one, haunted by the spectre of 1956, a defeated fight for freedom, the memory of which can't be underestimated. It is clearly one of the underlying messages of Miklós Erdély's *Two People Who Have Had a Decisive Influence on My Life* (1972, fig. 9), a double portrait of János Kádár, the leader of the country rewarded for collaborating with the Soviets in the defeat of the revolution, and the artist's wife, Zsuzsa Szenes, also an artist (see also Júlia Perczel, 'The Art Sphere as a Grey Zone', pp. 59–75, on Erdély and Tót). The photo could also be regarded as a visual manifesto of the subverted nature of the public/private, communicating that politics filtered through all barriers and moved into people's personal lives as unwanted bedfellows. Tót focuses

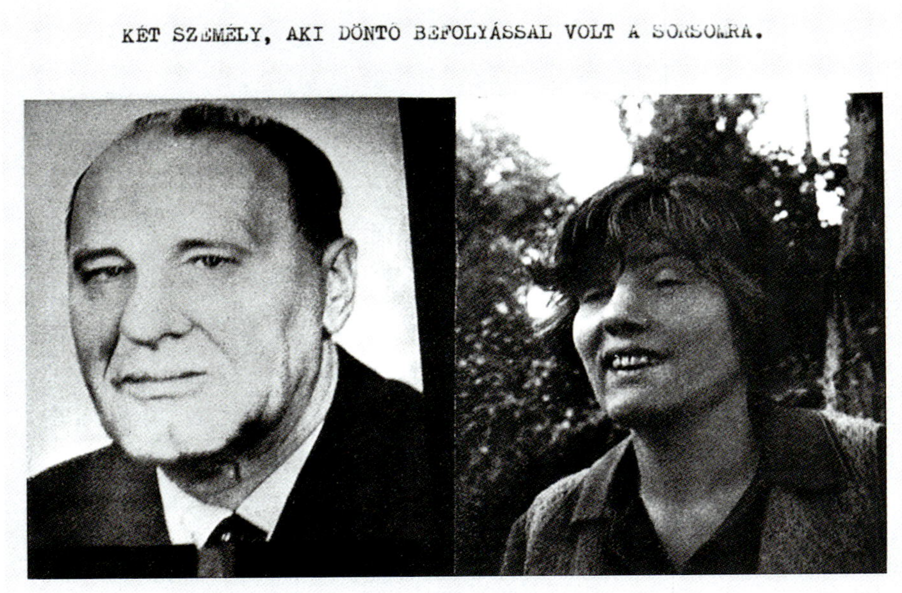

9

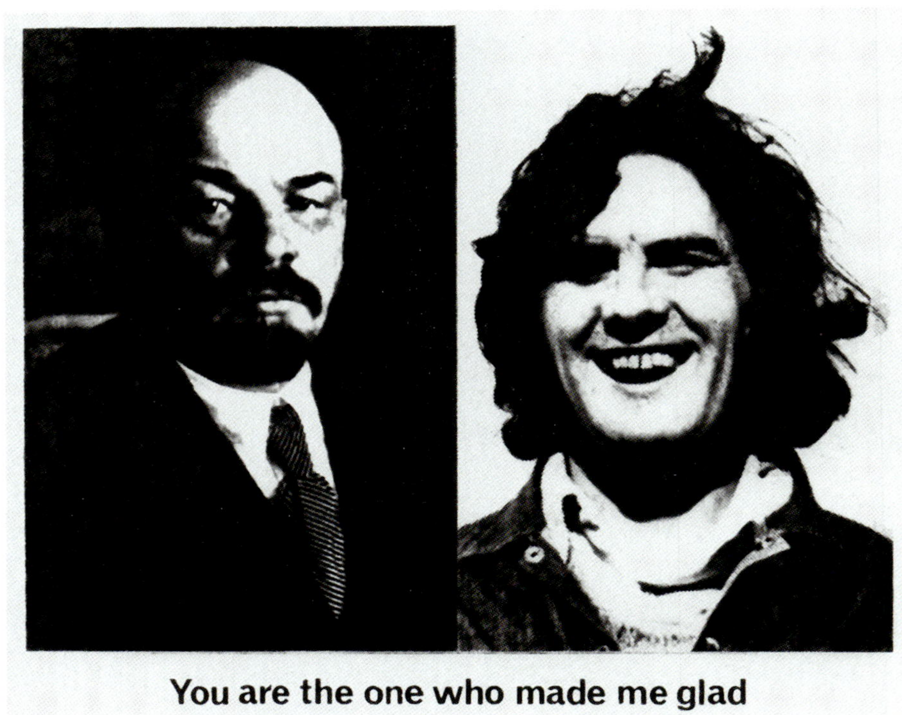

10

9. Miklós Erdély, *Two People Who Have Had a Decisive Influence on My Life*, 1972, Published in: László Beke and Urs Graf, 'Junge Kunst in Ungarn' [Young Art in Hungary], *Werk*, Vol. 59, No. 10, 1972, p. 592.

10. Endre Tót, *You Are The One Who Made Me Glad*, 1973–75, silver gelatine print, 20 × 30 cm, Private collection

11. Endre Tót, *I am glad if I can stand next to you*, 1973–75, silver gelatine print, 12 × 9 cm, acb Galéria, Budapest

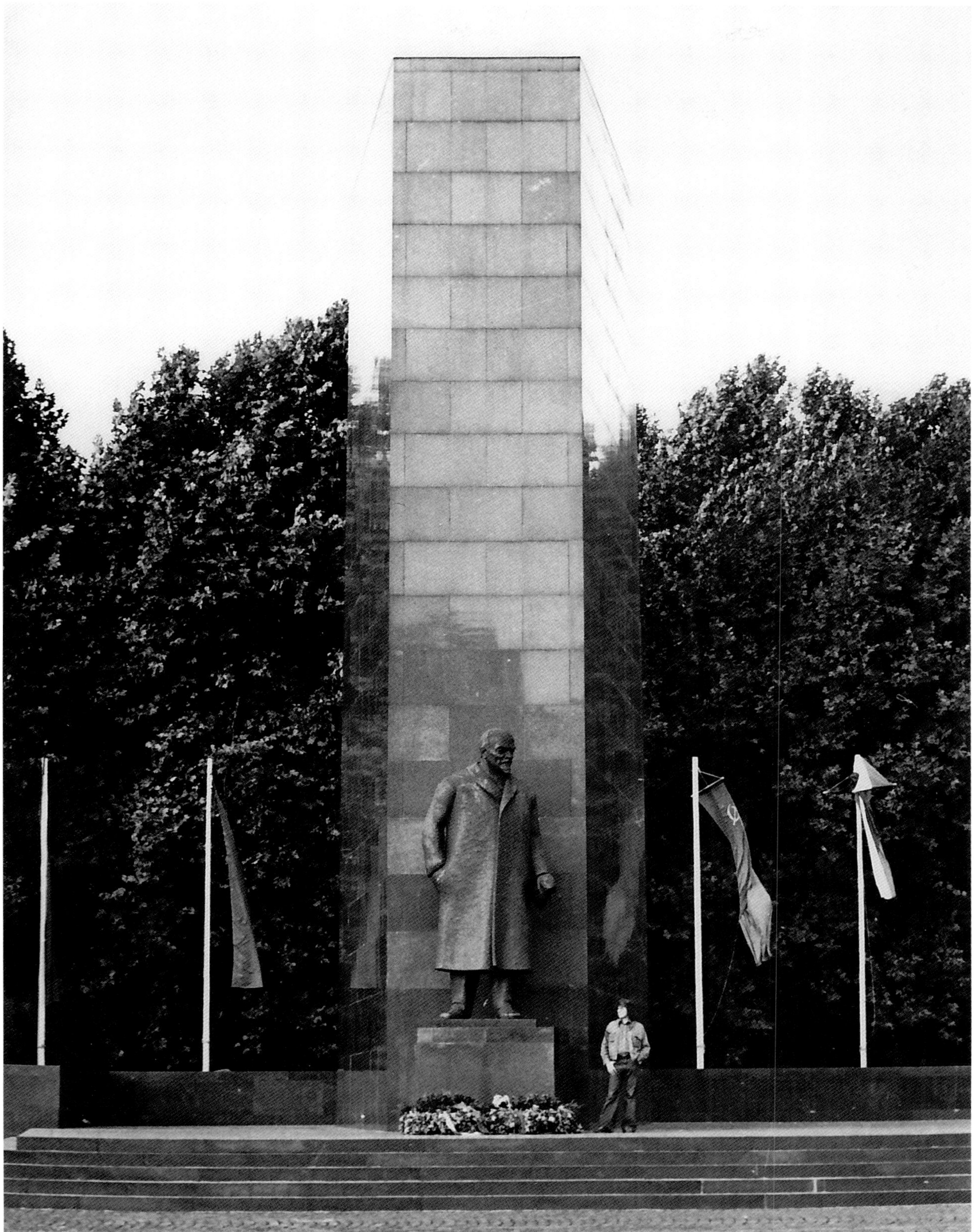

11

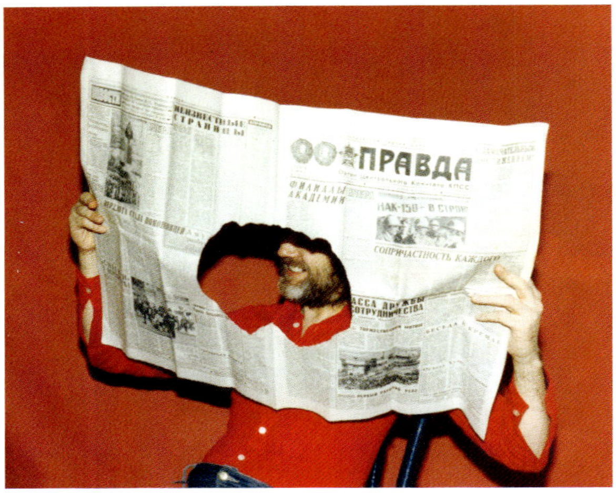

12

more on ideology, when he pairs himself with Lenin, and pursues the strategy of over-identification with the aroused enthusiasm. When he confronts his fresh happy face with Lenin's deadly serious, worn-out face, he portrays the attitude expected of him. While Erdély leaves it open whether the influence on him is negative or positive, and does not reveal the priorities between the two, Tót (over) identifies his private persona with politics, taking it to the extreme and thereby giving his works a hint of irony (fig. 10). This 'unconditional identification' with the father-figure justifies the idea of an overcommitted citizen blindly following the leaders, which exposes the infantilized nature of the public under socialist conditions. Although public space was no longer saturated by the cult of personality after 1956 and a more moderate era started with the political thaw, the symbolic signposts of the ideology were still needed by the state.[49]

Tót's *I am glad if I can stand next to you* (1973–75, fig. 11), in which the informal 'you' is Lenin, implicitly refers to Stalin as well: Lenin's monument was placed close to the spot where Stalin's enormous statue stood before it was demolished during the turbulent events of 1956 (see also Géza Boros, 'Taboo and Trauma: 1956', pp. 193–207). The zeros, a signature element of Tót's conceptual works, did not merely refer to the 'elimination of language barriers' or his 'sweet nothings', 'meaningless nonsense' and 'existential urgency to convey an unconveyable message', as poetically phrased by Kemp-Welch, but are literal manifestations of the other cornerstone of ideology, the complete erasure of the past with all its memories, which was especially embraced by the post-1956 Kádár regime.[50] The site where Tót 'encountered' Lenin is not a neutral space; it is historically loaded.

In *I am glad if I can gaze at something nice* (1973–75, fig. 13), Tót faces the five-pointed star adorning the Ministry of Foreign Affairs building. He symbolically turns his back on the building's past, and identifies with its present. Thus, all the references to the current state of affairs are at the same time references to the erased history, and emptied memory.

Compared to this political act, it might be relevant that his renegade action, *I am glad if I can read a newspaper* (1971–75, fig. 12), in which he smiles through a large hole in the middle of a local Hungarian (or Soviet) newspaper, is 'an ironic armchair re-enactment, calling into question the relationship between artistic and political action'.[51] However, as an artistic method, it specifies the neuralgic point of a regime that was legitimized by the defeat of the 1956 revolution: the national flag with a hole in the middle was the symbol of the revolution, as the socialist state symbol was cut out of the flag. He asks the viewer to remember what the Kádár regime tried to forget and make the population forget: the central lie upon which the regime was built. After a long period of total denial, this 'flashback' made visible, and thus addressed, the collective unconscious in which the memory of 1956 was deeply suppressed.

Like Tót's work, Sándor Pinczehelyi's self-portrait, *Sickle and Hammer* (1973, fig. 14), features the face of the artist seen through a hole. However, he is completely stuck in the hole, which is surrounded by socialist symbols, raising disturbing doubts as to whether he identifies with the hole-tearing act or with the violent tools (i.e. the socialist symbols) that frame the hole. Thus, the question is whether he is referring to the revolution through its symbol, the hole, or to the post-revolutionary years of consolidation interpreted by socialist ideology. The tools, rather than being 'outdated and ridiculous',[52] as they might be viewed from today's perspective, are inseparably melted and burned into his body, which also demonstrates an over-identification, a critical method employed to approach the official discourse. Ales Erjavec interprets this strategy as 'the use of mimicry, of conscious and complete identification of the secondary discourse with the ideological discourse, thus paradoxically revealing the inconsistencies of the latter, the void in its purportedly impregnable discursive armour, and especially its ideological nature.'[53] Thus, the work is understood as commenting on the 'secondary discourse' (i.e. the neo-avant-garde), and as such is conceived as demonstrating a kind of self-critical, self-reflective attitude, which has actually never been part of the Hungarian neo-avant-garde. It rather comments on the official discourse at a time when the official culture slowly began to lose its power, but still insisted on some of its taboos.

In socialist countries life was oversaturated by politics; public space was occupied by the official politics of the state, while private space was suspect from the perspective of the communist ethos of collectivity. The separation between private and public realms occurred along the line of (political) power rather than by a traditional gender division. Hence, the alienation from politics and the public sphere equally applied to men and women. This situation subverted, or at least jumbled, the gender roles so neatly described in the Western canon.

Zsuzsa Szenes's art practice and the phenomenon of the Velemi Textilművészeti Alkotóműhely (Velem Workshop for Textile Art) were seemingly in complete parity with the Pattern and Decoration art movement of female and feminist artists of the 1970s in California, who used soft materials, textiles and traditionally female handicraft methods like weaving and embroidery as part of 'women's empowerment'.[54] By contrast, however, Velem was not nurtured by an exclusive female self-consciousness, nor by the desire to empower female craft, which traditionally had a submissive, low position in the hierarchy of genres. Textile art, as an insignificant terrain, fell into the blindspot of the all-encompassing monitoring system of the cultural-political authorities in Hungary, and was converted into an outlet, an escape route for those not conforming to official ideas. It functioned as a substitute public space for freedom, and was equally available to men and women, even though the roles within the artform were divided along gender lines;

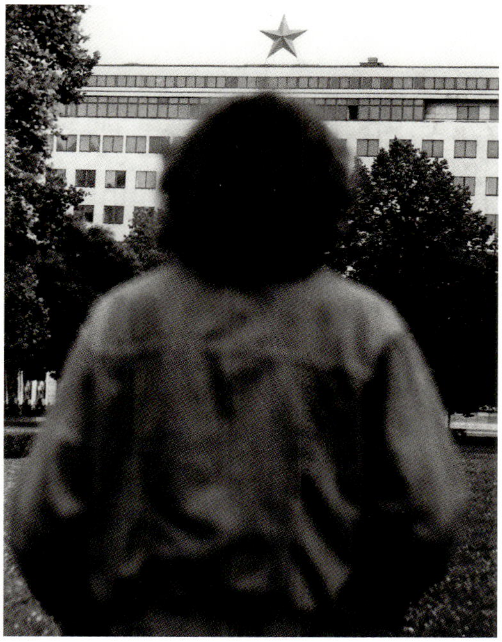

13

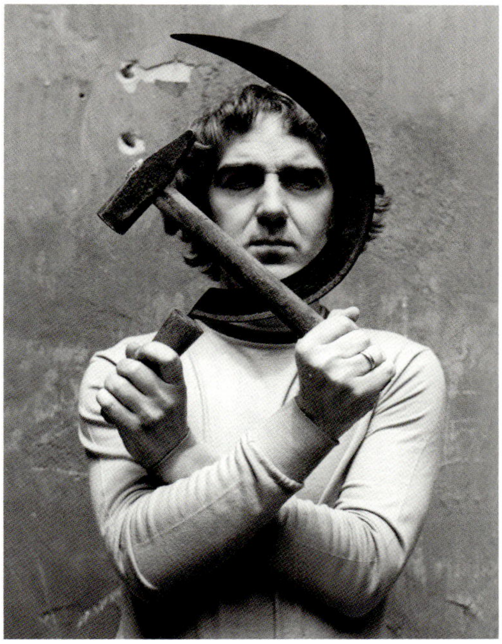

14

12. Endre Tót, *I am glad if I can read a newspaper*, 1971–75, silver gelatine print, Private collection

13. Endre Tót, *I am glad if I can gaze at something nice*, 1973–75, silver gelatine print, 30 × 20 cm, acb Galéria, Budapest

14. Sándor Pinczehelyi, *Sickle and Hammer*, 1973, silver gelatine print, 60 × 50 cm, Ludwig Múzeum – Kortárs Művészeti Múzeum, Budapest

producers were mostly women artists and critics were mostly male art historians.

Zsuzsa Szenes, wife of the 'head' and 'guru' of the Hungarian neo-avant-garde, Miklós Erdély, was one of the most prominent figures of what was referred to as the 'textile revolution'. Her 'emblematic works' *What Used to Be a Commodity is Decoration Today* (1975, fig. 15) and *Against the Cold in General* (1978, fig. 16), transformed violent or military objects into harmless 'decoration' with the techniques of embroidery and weaving. Szenes domesticated, tamed and feminized objects with heavily masculine connotations. Her private act deactivated a whole range of war paraphernalia. Taking the procedure literally, she put the empty slogans of the era's socialist peace movement into practice, so much so that contemporary critics considered a transformed gas mask to be an 'obvious allegory of peace'.[55] *Against the Cold in General* was called a 'direct anthem of peace but without commonplaces'[56] in complete convergence with the repertoire of terminology of the time when socialist countries advocated themselves as flagships of the peace movement.

The transformed objects, however, carried a more complex message. In terms of social and political meaning, the method, transformation and consequent neutralization of the symbols of the given world order indicate the transformability of the system itself. In terms of cultural meaning, the process reveals the restorative, healing potential of art, a notion that became the underlying idea of the memory discourse decades later. Although contemporary understanding detects the power of art over reality,[57] and that even horror can be done away through an artistic attitude,[58] when it comes to the gender regime, the good old stereotypes run the show. In fellow artist Gábor Attalai's interpretation – expressed in a sensual language spiced with sexual allusion – the all-resistant, tough masculine military object is 'disabled by the touch of an embroidering woman's hand and becomes fallible through the contrast created by this act'.[59] However, the final verdict is that the action is 'feminine and too naive'.[60]

Szenes's *Cell* (1977, fig. 17) provides a more nuanced commentary on real life, and its perception, behind the Iron Curtain, as well as

15

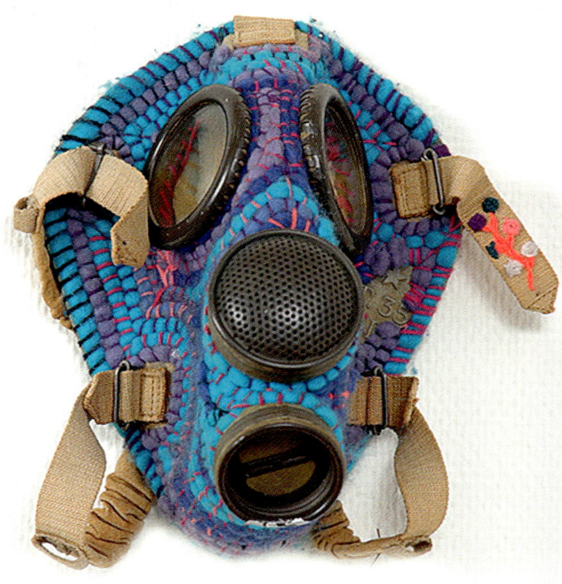

15. Zsuzsa Szenes, *What Used to Be a Commodity is Decoration Today (Gas mask)*, 1975, mixed media, 18 × 15 × 15 cm, Savaria Múzeum – Szombathelyi Képtár, Szombathely

16. Zsuzsa Szenes, *Against the Cold in General*, 1978, knitted wool, wood, 220 × 60 × 60 cm, Savaria Múzeum – Szombathelyi Képtár, Szombathely

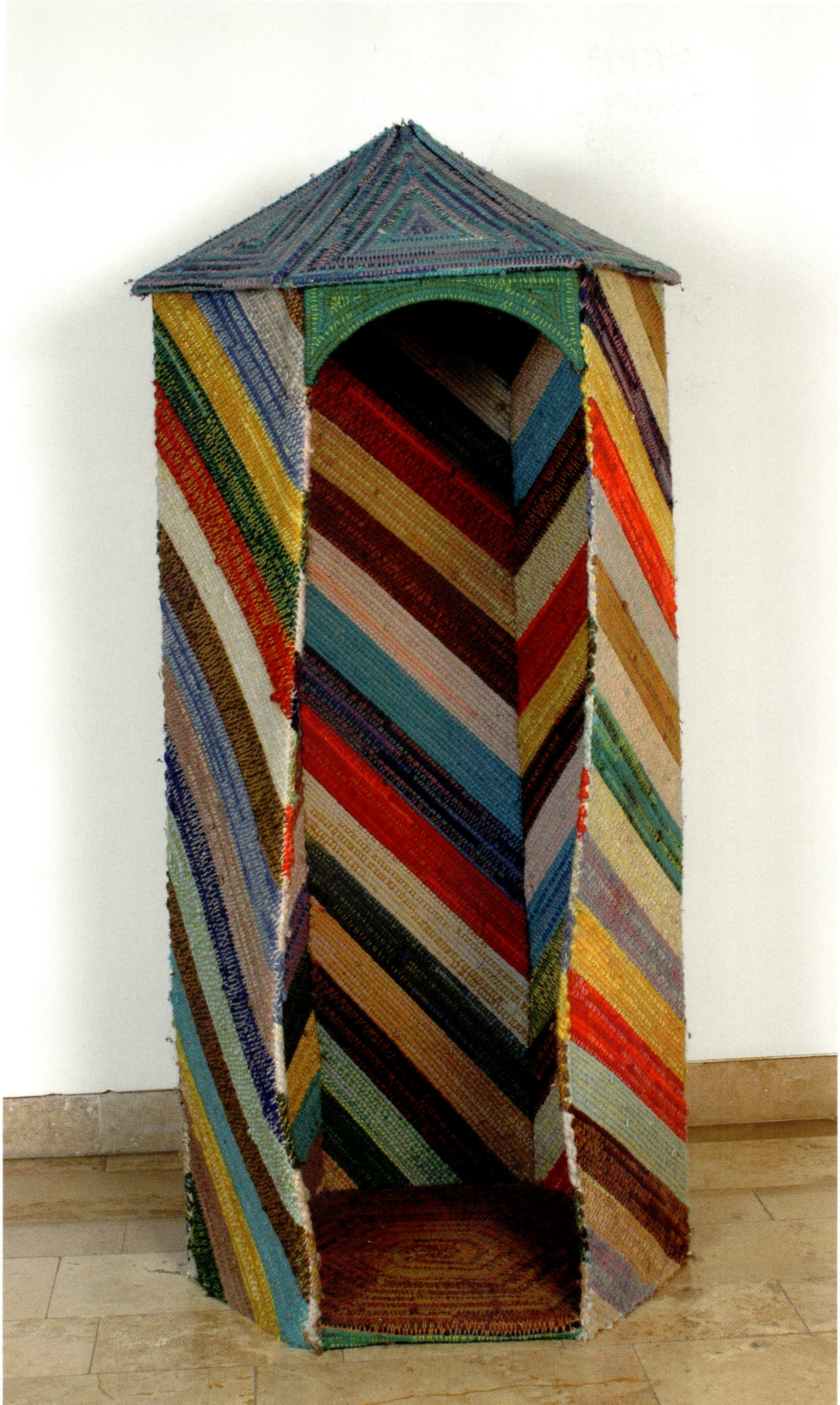

16

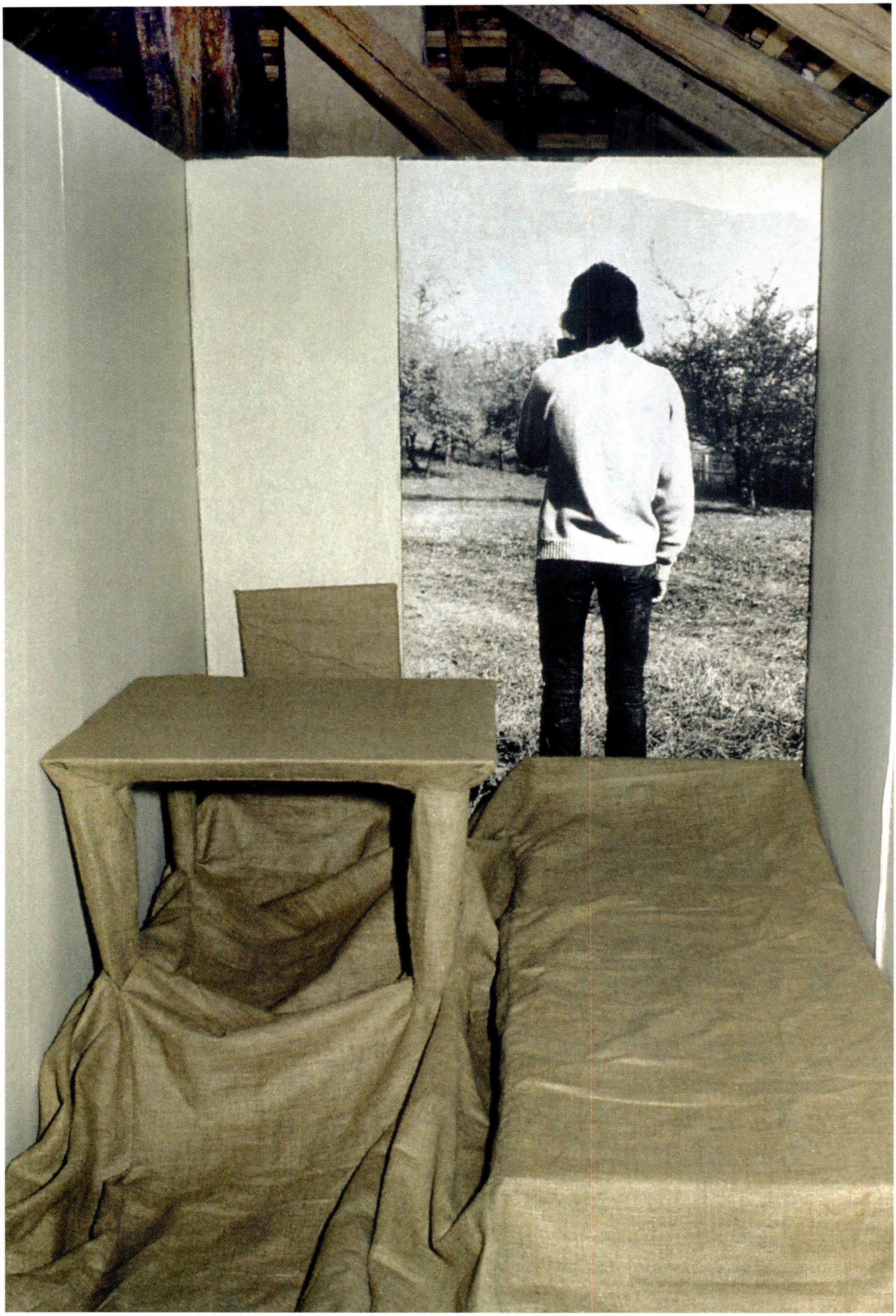

on illusions and fantasies. Éva Forgács offers illuminating and still valid insights about the contemporary perception of private and public in the 1970s:

Zsuzsa Szenes cut a cell-like interior out of the space in the attic of the Velem workshop. It holds a table, a chair and a couch, all covered with a coarse burlap cover...there is a nearly life-size...photograph of a young man in a pullover, standing with his back to us, seen in a garden with trees at a distance...The young man in the picture is just as free as the objects are captives in the room. The discord between inside and outside is stirred up by the equally laconic trademarks of narrowness and spaciousness... we can look into the cell we are out of, while he [the young man] is looking out at the nature he stands in...The covering material falsifies without lies, as it plainly indicates the objects but also ties them up within a given context forever, putting an end to their free and independent life...The black and white photo is an illusion in the real interior, a distant dream, a fictitious window on the closed cell. The cell is the absence of everything the picture recalls. Zsuzsa Szenes's interior is a concise plastic-optical-spatial allegory of false existence in the last analysis.[61]

Conclusion

Like the post-colonial theorists who argue that subaltern subjects are able to challenge the power and discourse of colonialism, feminist political scholar Nancy Fraser suggests the notion of 'subaltern counterpublics', public spaces where marginal groups are able to articulate their needs, constructing them in opposition to the dominant or legitimate uses of these spaces.[62]

As a possible subcategory under the umbrella term 'subaltern counterpublics', the strategy employed by the socially conscious artists behind the Iron Curtain could be what I call 'imaginary transgression'. The strategy was supposed to restore, at least in the imagination, the human and artistic agency seemingly lost in 'existing socialism'. This created room for participation and retained the emancipatory possibility of public space. It also secured an escape route from daily oppression and submission, as well as an alternative formation of public/private relations, both of them malfunctioning under socialism.

17. Zsuzsa Szenes, *Cell*, 1977, plywood, burlap, wood, photo, mixed media, 200 × 160 × 215 cm, 7 pieces, Savaria Múzeum – Szombathelyi Képtár, Szombathely

1 Tibor Hajas, *Made in Hungary I–II*, 1975, paper, silver print, ink, 70 × 100 cm (27 ½ × 39 ⅜ in) each. Photo: Júlia Veres, László Najmányi. Property of Vintage Gallery, Budapest.
2 See Jürgen Habermas, *The Structural Transformation of the Public Sphere: An Inquiry into a Category of Bourgeois Society*. Cambridge: MIT Press, 1991.
3 György Péteri, 'Introduction', *Contemporary European History*, special issue on 'Patronage, Personal Networks and the Party-state: Everyday Life in the Cultural Sphere in Communist Russia and East-Central Europe', Vol. II, No. 1, February 2002, 1.
4 *Ibid.*
5 See Jeff Weintraub, 'The Theory and Politics of the Public/Private Distinction', in Jeff Weintraub and Krishan Kumar (eds), *Public and Private in Thought and Practice: Perspectives on a Grand Dichotomy*. Chicago and London: University of Chicago Press, 1997, 1–42.
6 Marc Garcelon, 'The Shadow of the Leviathan: Public and Private in Communist and Post-Communist Society', in Weintraub and Kumar, *Public and Private in Thought and Practice*, 323–24.
7 József Havasréti, *Alternatív regiszterek: A kulturális ellenállás formái a magyar neoavantgárdban* [Alternative Registers: Forms of Cultural Opposition in the Hungarian Neo-avant-garde]. Budapest: Typotex, 2006, 323–24.
8 *Ibid.*, 322.
9 *Ibid.*, 324.
10 *Ibid.*, 326.
11 *Ibid.*, 89.
12 *Ibid.*, 97–100.
13 Piotr Piotrowski, *In the Shadow of Yalta: Art and the Avant-garde in Eastern Europe*. London: Reaktion Books, 2009, 341–87.
14 *Ibid.*, 384.
15 János Sturcz, *A heroikus ego lebontása: A művész teste mint metafora a magyar művészetben a nyolcvanas évek közepétől napjainkig* [The Deconstruction of the Heroic Ego: The Artist's Body as a Metaphor in Hungarian Art from the Mid-80s to the Present]. Budapest: Magyar Képzőművészeti Egyetem, 2005.
16 *Ibid.*, 58.
17 Susan Buck-Morss, *Dreamworld and Catastrophe: The Passing of Mass Utopia in East and West*. Cambridge and London: MIT Press, 2002, 197.
18 Havasréti, *Alternatív regiszterek*, 96.
19 Tibor Hajas, *Szövegek* [Texts], compiled by Éva F. Almási. Budapest: Enciklopédia kiadó, 2005, 233.
20 Michel Foucault, *Discipline and Punish: The Birth of the Prison*, trans. Alan Sheridan. London: Penguin, 1991, 25.
21 Ernst van Alphen, 'Strategies of Identification', in Norman Bryson, Michael Ann Holly and Keith Moxey (eds), *Visual Culture: Images and Interpretations*. Hanover and London: Wesleyan University Press, 1994, 260–71.
22 Foucault, *Discipline and Punish*, 249.
23 Nancy Fraser, 'Rethinking the Public Sphere: A Contribution to the Critique of Actually Existing Democracy', *Social Text*, Nos 25–26, 1990, 68–69.
24 Judit Takács, 'Disciplining Gender and (Homo)sexuality in State-socialist Hungary in the 1970s'. *European Review of History – Revue européenne d'histoire*, Vol. 22, No. 1, 2015, 170.
25 Havasréti, *Alternatív regiszterek*, 83.
26 Cited in Havasréti, *Alternatív regiszterek*, 81.
27 Edit András, 'From the Coffee Grinder to the Sputnik: The Culture of Objects and Woman in the Service of Ideology', *Acta Historiae Artium*, special issue on 'The Long Sixties' edited by Edit András and Hedvig Turai, Vol. 56, No. 1, 2015, 297–306.
28 The title of the series has had various English translations, such as *Private Viewing*; *Private Transmission*; I stick to *Private Broadcast*.
29 Géza Perneczky, 'Halász Károly és a kofferbe csomagolt konstruktivizmus' [Károly Halász and Constructivism Packed in a Suitcase], in *Halász Károly: Privát adás, 1967–1993* [Károly Halász: Private Broadcast, 1967–1993]. Budapest: Balassi Kiadó, 1995, 7.
30 *Halász Károly* (exhibition catalogue). Introductory text by Júlia Szabó, trans. Éva Forgács. Székesfehérvár: István Király Múzeum, 1982, 4–5.
31 Cited by Géza Perneczky, in Sándor Pincehelyi (ed.), *Hopp Halász Károly*. Pécs: Pécsi Galéria és Vizuális Művészeti Műhely, 2011, 44.
32 Katalin Aknai, *Halász Károly: Privát adás/Fotómunkák, 1971–79* [Károly Halász: Private Transmissions/Photoworks, 1971–79], trans. Zsolt Kozma. Budapest: Vintage Galéria, 2010, 9.
33 Éva Körner, 'The Absurd as Concept', in *Josep Kosuth* (exhibition catalogue, Venice Biennale, Hungarian Pavilion). Budapest: Műcsarnok, 1993, 188.
34 Aknai, *Halász Károly*, 9.
35 Dávid Fehér, '"Cry from a Dark Room": Remarks upon the Conceptual Works and Actions of Károly Halász', in Pincehelyi, *Hopp Halász Károly*, 67.
36 Hal Fischer, *Gay Semiotics: A Photographic Study of Visual Coding among Homosexual Men*. Los Angeles: Cherry and Martin, 1977.
37 Takács, 'Disciplining Gender', 170.
38 Fraser, 'Rethinking the Public Sphere', 67.
39 Carole Pateman, *The Disorder of Women: Democracy, Feminism and Political Theory*. Stanford: Stanford University Press, 1989, 132.
40 Valeria Bryson, *Gender and the Politics of Time: Feminist Theory and Contemporary Debates*. Bristol: Policy Press, 2007, 67.
41 Pateman, *The Disorder of Women*, 131.
42 Pateman, *The Disorder of Women*, 131–34.

43 Carol Hanisch, 'The Personal is Political', in *Notes from the Second Year: Women's Liberation*, 1970. Republished in Barbara A. Crow (ed.), *Radical Feminism: A Documentary Reader*. New York: New York University Press, 2000, 113.
44 Havasréti, *Alternatív regiszterek*, 143.
45 Havasréti, *Alternatív regiszterek*, 151.
46 Havasréti, *Alternatív regiszterek*, 143.
47 See Bernhard Giesen, *Triumph and Trauma*. Boulder and London: Paradigm, 2004, 17.
48 Klara Kemp-Welch, *Antipolitics in Central European Art*. London and New York: I. B. Tauris, 2014, 150.
49 Kemp-Welch, *Antipolitics*, 160.
50 Kemp-Welch, *Antipolitics*, 152.
51 Kemp-Welch, *Antipolitics*, 163.
52 *Ibid.*
53 Ales Erjavec (ed.), *Postmodernism and the Postsocialist Condition: Politicised Art under Late Socialism*. Berkeley: University of California Press, 2003, 10.
54 See Norma Broude and Mary D. Garrard, *Power of Feminist Art: The American Movement of the 1970s, History and Impact*. New York: Harry N. Abrams, 1996.
55 János Frank, *Az eleven textil: Új magyar textilművészet – térbeliség – tárgyak* [Living Textile: New Hungarian Textile Art/Spatiality/Objects]. Budapest: Corvina Könyvkiadó, 1980, 107.
56 *Ibid.*
57 Márta Kovalovszky, 'good if you don't have to become a grown...', in *Szenes Zsuzsa 1931–2001* (exhibition catalogue). Budapest: Budapest Galéria Kiállítóháza, 2003, 14.
58 Gábor Attalai, cited in Kovalovszky, 'good if you don't', 18.
59 *Ibid.*
60 *Ibid.*, 14.
61 Éva Forgács, 'Cell', in *Velemi Textilművészeti Alkotóműhely* [Velem Workshop for Textile Art]. Velem: Velemi Textilművészeti Alkotóműhely, 1977, 70–71.
62 Linda McDowell, *Gender, Identity and Space: Understanding Feminist Geographies*. Cambridge: Polity Press and Minneapolis: University of Minnesota Press, 1999, 151. McDowell refers to Fraser, 'Rethinking the Public Sphere'.

1

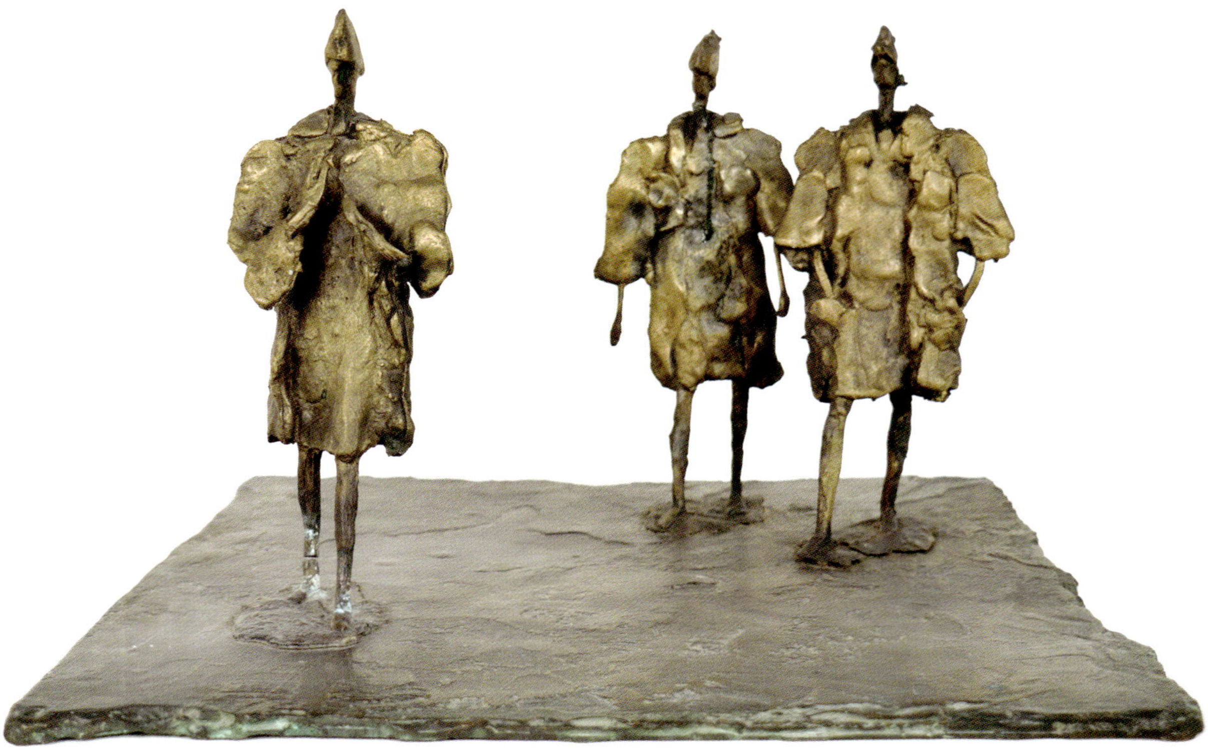

1. Erzsébet Schaár, *Women in Fur*, 1964, bronze, 32 × 20 cm, Szent István Király Múzeum, Székesfehérvár

Hedvig Turai

Limited Access to Greatness

The Position of Women Artists

The four female artists Erzsébet Schaár, Margit Anna, Júlia Vajda and Lili Ország were all born in the first decades of the twentieth century but were still active in the 1960s and 1970s. They were of Jewish descent, and were labelled Jewish during the years of discrimination and persecution in the 1930s and 1940s. With one exception, they were intimately connected to their male-artist partners, so they were 'significant others'. These women artists cannot be called invisible or unknown, and yet there is some insecurity in terms of their acknowledgment, appreciation and position in accepted twentieth-century Hungarian art history. They do not need to be written into Hungarian art, but their position needs to be rewritten.

They were never considered as 'great' as their male contemporaries, in conformity with the myth of the great artist, which is always connected to the male. They belonged to the 'second line' of Hungarian art, both in the (changing) official canon and the canon that was set up by the artists, art historians and critics of the neo-avant-garde. They belonged to neither of the two fully and, yet, also a little to both. Due to the quality of their work as progressive modern artists in the 1930s and 1940s, and due to their relationships and connections – their 'network' – they always enjoyed a certain degree of respect even in the era after the Second World War and during the 1960s and 1970s. However, they never made it to the 'first line'. It begs the question whether this has anything to do with their gender or their Jewishness, or whether they simply were not as 'good' as their male contemporaries.

There are different ways in which we can examine the role gender played in the work and evaluation of these women artists. In terms of their output, we can examine their topics and how they approached them; we can detect mostly suppressed, unintended, unconscious elements that still speak about their gender; we can explore how femininity and the female body, including their own, are represented by them and how they represent themselves; and we can consider what they explicitly say about their own work in interviews and letters. In terms of reception, we can examine what art historians and critics wrote about them, how they discussed their works, what linguistic metaphors they used in their interpretation of the work of women artists, what fellow artists said about them and their work, and how the female body, the body of the women artists, is present in the discourse, if sometimes only as what art historian Edit András calls a Freudian slip of the tongue.[1]

We also need to explore the silence around gender.[2] To approach their work from a gendered point of view was not yet a tool that art historians or artists used in Hungary at the time (and even today) on the assumption that there was no need for it. But as art historian Mara Traumane says in connection with Latvian art history: 'This position comes from researchers, not from the art scene itself.'[3] Critical discourse and reception are parts of the institutional system, and gendered power relations are inscribed in the discourse. The structural sexism of most academic disciplines contributes actively to the creation and perpetuation of a gender hierarchy. 'What we can learn about the world and its peoples is ideologically patterned in conformity with the social order within which it is produced,' as Griselda Pollock puts it.[4]

In the context of Hungary, this social order is further complicated and 'doublespeak' (see Edit Sasvári, 'Autonomy and Doublespeak', pp. 8–17) has an additional dimension when we examine the position of women under socialism. The Soviet model of 'gender equality' was adopted in Hungary, as well as in other socialist countries. In terms of rhetoric, equality in the workplace and in all walks of life was a basic slogan of socialism. It was indeed more than a slogan, as childcare institutions such as nurseries, for example, were introduced to free women for work. Yet, as has been elaborated by sociologists, this equality meant a double burden on women, and inequality still characterized women's access to professional careers.[5] We can grasp this gender inequality in the field of art as well, in the supported, tolerated and banned categories of artworks.

In Hungary, after the end of the Second World War and the short-lived Európai Iskola (European School; see Gábor Dobó and Merse Pál Szeredi, 'Hungarian Culture +/- Europe', pp. 39–57), modern art was something for which many artists, both male and female, strove – if they believed in artistic freedom and ideology-free, up-to-date art in a Western sense – in the 1960s and 1970s. So, the ideals of modernism should be added to this picture, as modernism also stood for the great artist-individual, and the myth that art is pure and above the everyday realm in which the particularities of race, ethnicity and gender are experienced.

'It is an awful condition for a woman to be a sculptor'

So said Erzsébet Schaár in an interview conducted in 1967, and she added, 'It might be no longer than the last ten years that I have been able to call myself a sculptor.'[6] This is a rare confession by an artist who talked about her work almost exclusively in abstract terms, and characterized her artistic approach as the exploration of spatial relations: the connection of space and human beings (see also Magdalena Radomska, 'Working in the Twice-mined Semantic Minefield', pp. 315–29). Schaár's assertion supports the view that there was a gender hierarchy within art, and sculpture was one of the least feminized fields. Sculpture was the territory of male artists in the main, and it was even more difficult to get into this 'male club' than the one for painting. The 'last ten years' refer to the time since Erzsébet Schaár had been accepted into the 'official' hall of art and had received some degree of acknowledgment. It is implicit that she did not question the set values of art, the canon; rather, she wanted to make it into the canon. Eventually, she would belong to the modernist, universalist, apparently genderless canon after years of work. Schaár did not want to be considered a woman artist, 'just an artist'. This is a well-known pattern and, in the 1960s and 1970s, a common attitude among female artists, who were yet to adopt gender consciousness.

Erzsébet Schaár started as a portrait sculptor; she was a 'wonder kid', accepted by the Magyar Képzőművészeti Főiskola (Hungarian Academy of Fine Arts) at the age of sixteen. She did not, however, complete her academic studies, as is shown by her academic files. In her art-academy study file for 1926, we can find a box that reads 'Religion: Israelite'.[7] Later in her career, her Jewish origin is hardly if ever mentioned in

2. Erzsébet Schaár, *Chairs/ Story of a Relationship*, 1969–72, bronze, 13 pieces, 10–15 cm each, Szent István Király Múzeum, Székesfehérvár

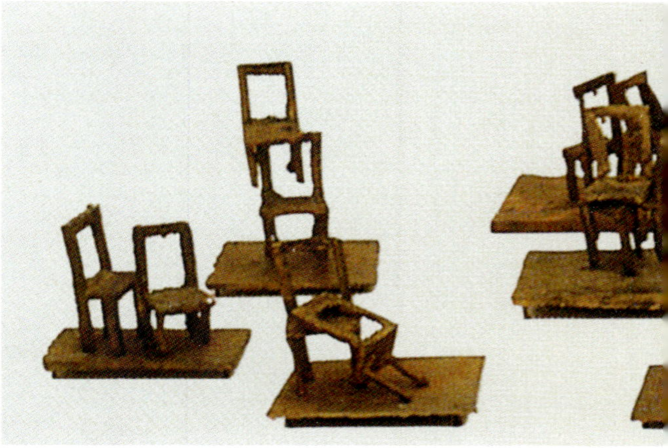

art historical texts and review articles. In 1935, she married the sculptor Tibor Vilt, and having a non-Jewish husband, she probably was exempted for a time from the ever-stricter anti-Jewish laws; by 1944, however, she had to go into hiding. Aided by the connections of her husband, who deserted from the army, she went to a Catholic cloister in Miskolc, within Hungary, where Margit Slachta, a nun and politician, was shielding Jews.[8] Schaár pretended to be a novice called Erzsi Wilt, the 'sister' of Tibor Wilt.[9]

After she returned to the family home in Budafok, Budapest, at the end of the war, her sister committed suicide.[10] What caused the suicide is still something of a secret, although art historians have referred to the event in coded language and her son alluded to it in a short story.[11] The tragic family event was connected to the war, to the labelling of Erzsébet Schaár as a Jew and the fact that she was in hiding; a romantic relationship may have developed between her husband and her sister. Schaár's art can be understood in light of the trauma of survival. She not only endured the trauma of the war and persecution, but she also carried feelings of guilt about her survival. The Budafok family home remained an artistic topic throughout her life; it was a ghost house that kept haunting her. The house and the uncanny figures within it have always been the subjects of art historical interpretations of her work, but exclusively in an abstract, universal sense and in language that denies this imagery of any particularity of reference (fig. 2).

After the Second World War, a group of artists who strove to establish modern European art in Hungary founded the Európai Iskola. Many of these artists had been forced into exile or pushed to the margins by the conservative art system of the Horthy regime (1920–44), and had been persecuted because of their views or Jewish descent. Tibor Vilt joined, as did Margit Anna, but not Erzsébet Schaár. This is not only a sign that she simply did not like to join groups or follow any group mentality, but also of artistic intent. It may be that she was not as 'modern' or avant-garde, in the sense of either formal innovations or radical political ideas, as the Európai Iskola artists. She did not work much during the hardest years of the Hungarian version of Stalinism – the Rákosi era (1949–56) – which saved her from being artistically corrupted by the demand for artists to adhere to socialist realism.

There was a turning point in her style during the 1960s when she began to create elongated, Giacometti-like figures. One of the wittiest art historians and critics of the time, Géza Perneczky called her works 'Tanagra figures from Váci street'.[12] This was a very sharp simile

2

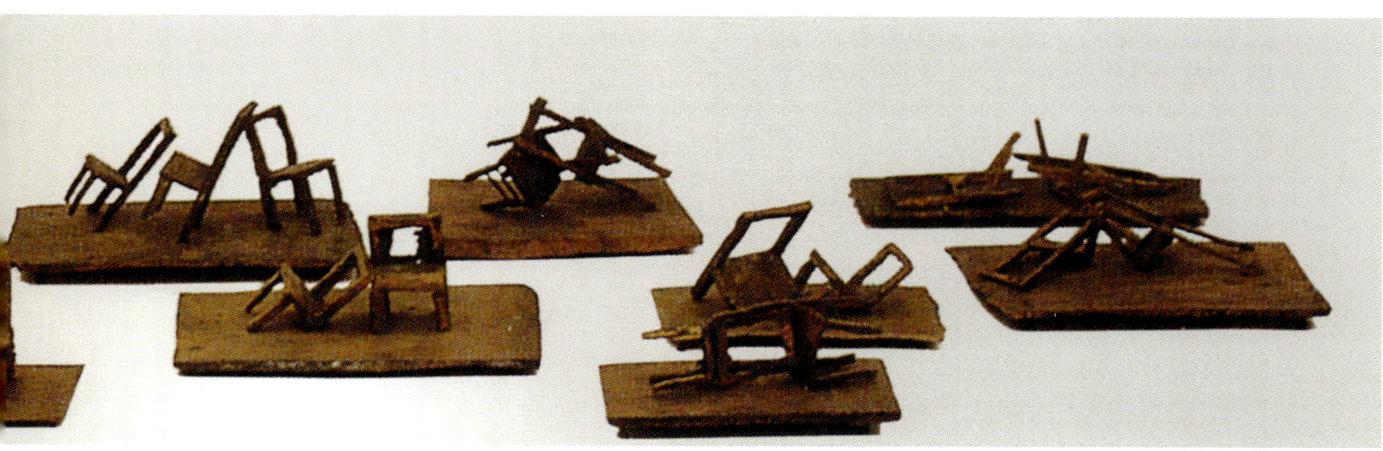

that connected Schaár's small terracotta figurines to the Tanagra figurines of classical Greece, while the reference to Váci street, in downtown Budapest, associated her with modern urban life, thus giving her works both respect and an aura of contemporariness. Perneczky, an admired and open-minded art critic, wrote in a way that helped to make sense of allegedly difficult modern and contemporary art. His interpretative gesture helped foster understanding and acknowledgment of Schaár, who was already in her fifties by then. Perneczky's piece was published after an exhibition in Székesfehérvár in 1966, curated by the art historian couple Péter Kovacs and Márta Kovalovszky. The text on Schaár can be compared with a piece on Tibor Vilt, and begins by explaining how independent she is from her husband, while stating that it is difficult to write about the wife of a sculptor who herself is a sculptor. Perneczky says that one cannot help but compare the two of them, but it is important to underscore that the wife is not following or copying her husband: she is even one step ahead of him. Nevertheless, in the text on Tibor Vilt there is no word about Erzsébet Schaár, and no mention of a suspicion that Vilt might have followed his wife: in the case of a male artist, his marital relationship is not something that needs explanation.

In a later text, Perneczky evokes his memories of Schaár, and his characterization here is important for us in the context of examining how gender biases work. Perneczky writes that, for a while, the art scene did not really consider her anything but the wife of Tibor Vilt, who modelled portrait sculptures like other women make flower bouquets or cook or have dinner parties. A turning point came much later in her career, he continues, when she was probably afraid of aging and began to be interested in other things as well.[13] It is strange to look back at this, he says. He mentions, in a later text, Schaár's final exhibition, 'Street' (1974), which Perneczky considered to be one of the most important exhibitions of the time, as belonging to the 'Neoclassical Branch of the Neoavant-garde'.[14] This resonates with Lajos Németh's account, according to which Erzsébet Schaár really found herself and her style when she began to use plaster casts of human faces and hands while the trunk of the body was simply a styrofoam block.[15] With these body blocks, Erzsébet Schaár, probably in an unconscious way, avoided displaying the female nude, one of the major topics of traditional sculpture. She had also avoided displaying the female nude in her earlier pieces, such as *Women in Fur* (1964, fig. 1).

Schaár generally worked at a small scale in bronze or at a larger scale using less long-lasting materials. Critics often commented on this, saying that she should be given the opportunity to make large-scale pieces in lasting materials as her works are monumental in their spirit; her bronzes were referred to as small-scale monuments.[16] Monuments of what, however, was not ever made clear. The adjective 'monumental' often refers to war, persecution, pain and suffering, and, implicitly, also to monuments and memorials of the war. Lajos Németh was one of the art historians who mentioned that she survived fascism, the years of persecution, then Stalinist authoritarianism. These traumas were the basis of an art full of anxiety, and she found the relevant form to show these feelings.[17]

3

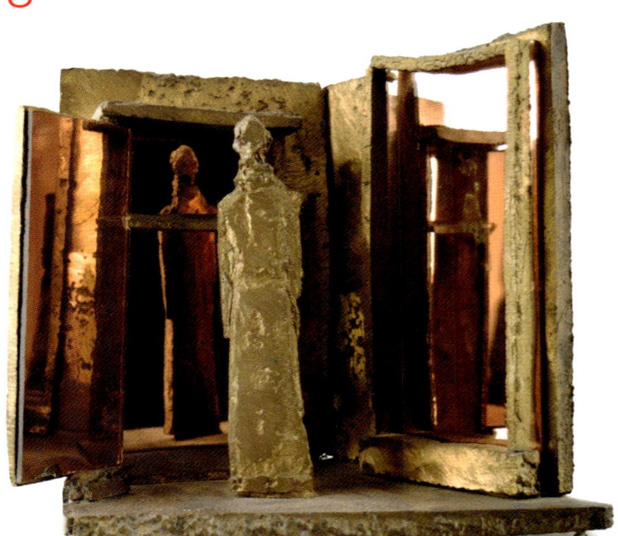

Art historians often single out one experience in particular as crucial to an understanding of Schaár small-scale plastic pieces and her installations. After returning home from an exhibition abroad in the early 1960s, she describes her experience in the Budafok house:

I opened the windows and the doors. They stood firmly, as if they cut the air, as if the air had been a solid mass. I was looking at the three doors opening to three adjacent rooms. Each opened to different directions. And I was standing there in the middle, as if I were a small point in space, and the three edges of the three doors, each in different directions.[18]

Although it is sometimes noted that she had come home from abroad and wanted to clean the house, this reference is either omitted or framed differently, in a more elevated way. Instead of being a 'cleaning housewife', she had a universal, metaphysical experience of space, which was an immediate inspiration for her art (fig. 3).

There were two aspects of her life that were not mentioned in the contemporary discourse: that she was a woman and that she was persecuted as somebody labelled Jewish. One was not considered important, while the other was shrouded in silence. Yet among her works there are many explicitly 'feminine' topics (*Women in Fur*; *Miniskirt/Legs*, fig. 4; *Hooligan Girl*; *At the Cosmetician*; *The Castle of Bluebird*), and the majority of her figures are women. Open and public discourse on Jewishness and what later became known as the Holocaust was severely limited. The anxiety and suffering that could be clearly felt in her works were only euphemistically connected to the persecution of Jews; typically, the connection is made to more generic victims of fascism. Her own Jewishness was hardly ever explicitly stated in the discussion of her work; it is a poem, entitled 'Auschwitz' and dedicated to Erzsébet Schaár by the poet János Pilinszky, that is probably the most open reference to her descent.

She herself avoided discussing personal influences, withholding any clue to a particular interpretation. Her personality and character, however, surfaced in critical, interpretative

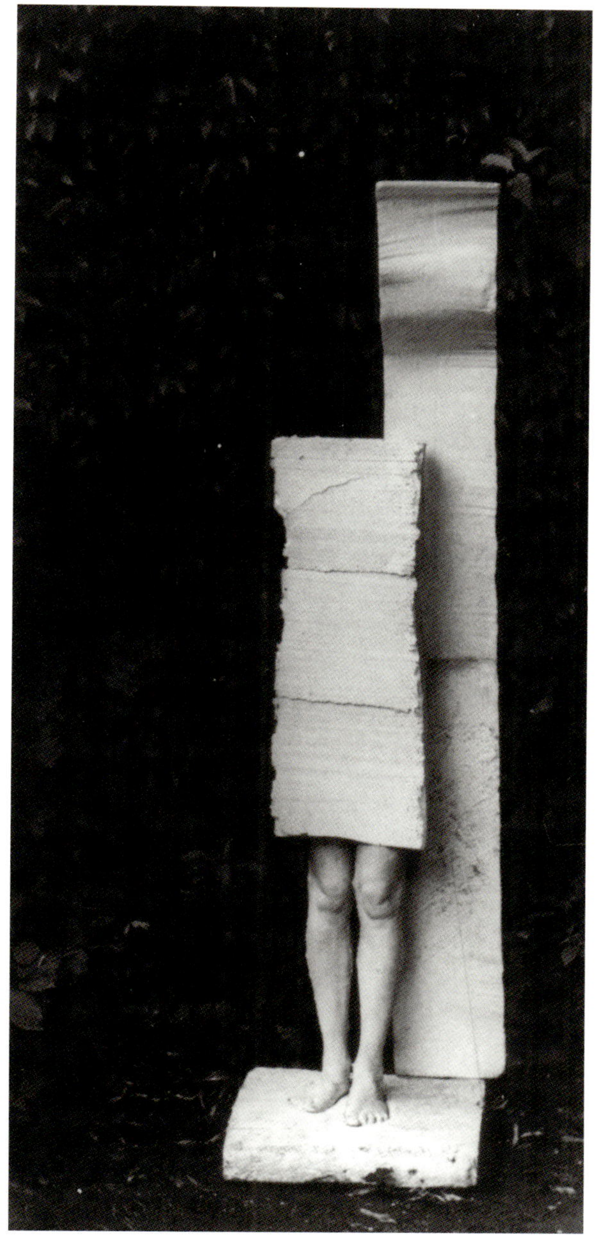

4

3. Erzsébet Schaár, *Between Two Mirrors*, 1972, bronze, glass, 17 × 17 × 25 cm, Szent István Király Múzeum, Székesfehérvár

4. Erzsébet Schaár, *Miniskirt/Legs*, 1969, polyurethane foam, plaster, h. 243 cm, perished

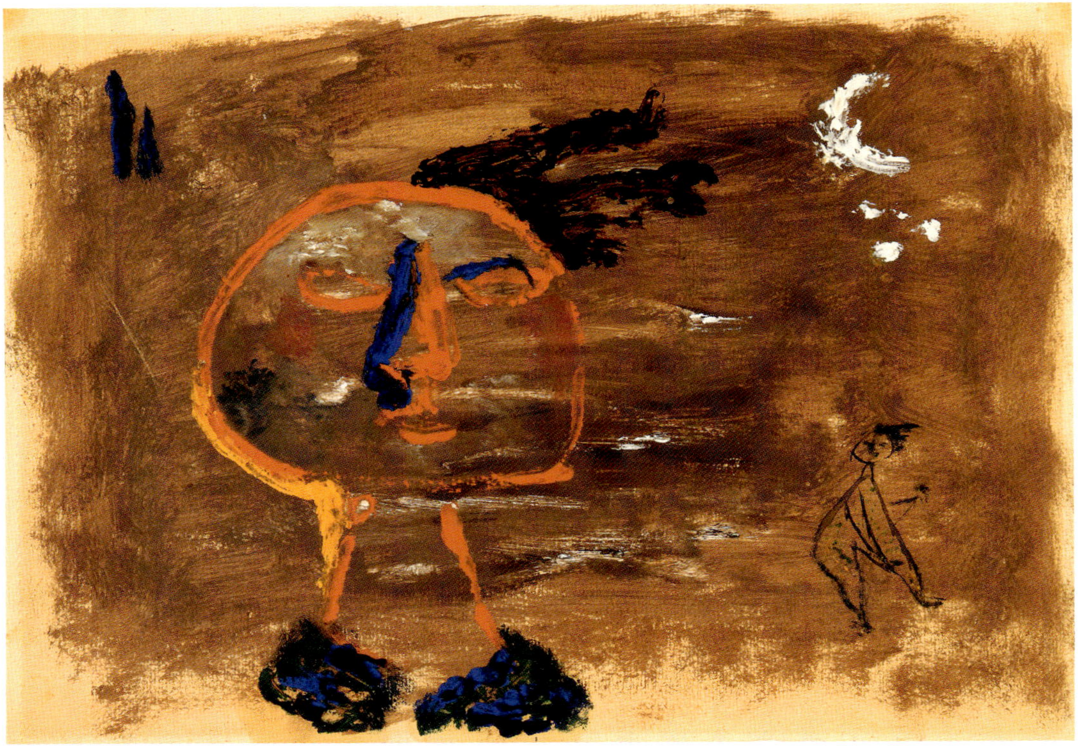

5

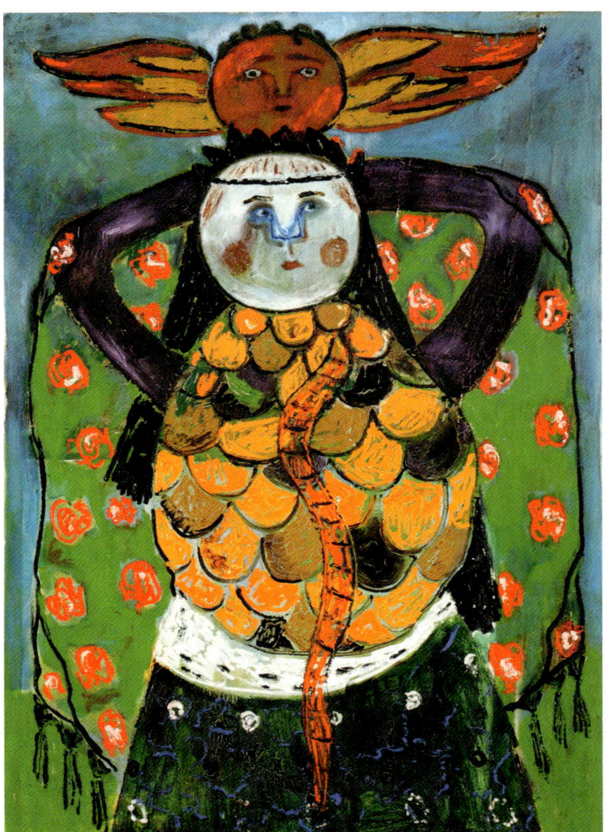

6

5. Margit Anna, *Solitude*, 1948, oil on paper, 25 × 35.5 cm, Kiscelli Múzeum – Fővárosi Képtár, Budapest

6. Margit Anna, *The Painter and Her Muse*, 1969, oil on canvas, 100 × 70 cm, Kiscelli Múzeum – Fővárosi Képtár, Budapest

texts. Lajos Németh wrote about her 'witch-like' character, her mesmerizing sensitivity. He characterized her as somebody who wanted to learn and know everything, who wanted to get information about everything what was going on in the art world but rarely moved from her house. He says that she protected her sculptures like a tiger protects her cubs. She managed with female tricks and cuteness to be loved; this small, thin woman was a dominating figure.[19] Within such interpretations of her character, certain aspects of Erzsébet Schaár's art remained hidden, or were even erased from the discourse of art history.[20]

'A painter is not a Jewish woman'

Margit Anna's life and work reflect many of the issues of twentieth-century Hungarian art (see also Daniel Véri, 'The Holocaust and the Arts', pp. 209–27, for information on Margit Anna and Lili Ország, discussed later in the essay).[21] In the 1930s and 1940s she, like many artists, worked in poverty; many such artists had Jewish roots and did not receive proper training or exhibition opportunities. Her master was her husband, the painter Imre Ámos, who gained a proper art education; she was often considered a follower or an epigone of him. For a short period after 1945, as a representative of interwar progressive art, opportunities opened up for her, while in the 1950s and 1960s she stood in opposition to the obligatory socialist realism, the cultural tool of the state. She believed in the autonomy of art, independent of and beyond political ties, and wanted to be a part of universal art. In the Európai Iskola (1945–48), she was among like-minded artists and became one of the emblematic figures of the group.

Her husband's disappearance in the war (for a while, she knew nothing certain about his death in Ohrdurf concentration camp in Germany) left her in a state of expectation of his return, eventually disappointed (fig. 5). The experience of the war appears indirectly, or sublimated, in her works. In this period, from 1945 to 1948, she deals more with the nature of human beings, and the trials of history in general, rather than with the sufferings of the Jews in particular. Critics at the time placed Margit Anna among the best representatives of Hungarian art during its revitalization after the war. 'They suppose that was my best style, the Európai Iskola style...' she said in a later interview.[22] We may read some irony into this remark, some reservations and opposition to the judgments of art historians and critics, with their labels and classifications. The fact that a work or a period is judged to be of high quality is inseparable from whether it fitted into the main current of Hungarian art of the time.

The fact that in her works of this period Anna presents 'universal human suffering' rather than specific Jewish subjects – the horrors of the war that she experienced, her hiding as a Jew, her husband's fate as a victim of the Holocaust – can be partially explained by the post-war political-historical situation and by her life as an artist. For some years following 1945, the situation sustained hopes that modern art would be rehabilitated, that nobody would be discriminated against on grounds of race, ethnic origin or sex, that no groups would be marginalized. Aesthetic freedom and the acceptance of modernism and other 'isms' promised the end of prejudice and submission.[23] The war she had lived through, the difficulty in representing her pain, the need to start everything from scratch, the opportunity to join with others, all helped put differences, and the representation of these differences, into the background. In this situation, artists turned to abstract human values in the spirit of the universality of modernism. Later, between 1948 and 1968 she was busy with raising her two sons from her second marriage, and with trying to make ends meet. As she wrote in a private letter:

Do you know how I work? I go to the ceramics studio at 11 o'clock to do hourly paid work for 9–11 hours a day, I get up at 6.30, I go shopping, while the food is cooking I paint, rushing to check that it doesn't burn, and in the evening, I collapse into bed to gather strength for the next day. On holidays I clean, wash and iron. I get my experiences on the tram and at the market. Do you think I could paint large-scale pictures in these circumstances?[24]

The graceful female forms of the 1940s are gradually transformed to awkward, clumsy figures, puppets, threatening females, often mythological female characters, aged women, witches. *Red Rebecca II* (1979, fig. 7), inspired by a Hungarian ballad, is the very embodiment of female malevolence. The bird-like, ominous figure, wearing a red scarf and flying above the fields, is an old woman, a witch-like creature. The powers of seduction are gone. Feminine beauty has been replaced. The power of the old woman, according to social stereotypes, lies instead in her wickedness, in her ability to destroy, in contrast to the wise old man. *Lilith* (1967, fig. 8) is presented as a mythological figure, with legs ending in claws, standing on the crescent moon above the world, a female devil standing before the night sky. Margit Anna invests herself with contradictory characteristics and takes the risk of identifying herself with the social stereotypes surrounding old women, old hags.

In the late 1960s and early 1970s her memories and losses – and with them Jewishness and the Holocaust – came more and more to the fore in her art. This also meant resisting silence. As Imre Kertész notes, 'The proletarian dictatorship was displeased at the mention of the Holocaust; and since they were displeased, they almost invariably silenced such voices, or forced them to utter conformist euphemisms.'[25] However, Anna did not conform to this silencing, and nor did she allow herself to be directed. In relation to a later exhibition (in 1984), she said: 'I had an exhibition in Geneva, Switzerland, where twelve pictures were sold in three minutes…But which ones do you think were sold? Those with a Jewish theme. So the exhibition organiser told me to paint pictures with Jewish themes, and he would sell them all. I told him that I do not paint pictures with Jewish themes to commission, only if it comes from my heart. Only if I feel that I have to paint it.'[26]

In the 1970s, Margit Anna was one of the artists 'tolerated', not really supported, but certainly not prohibited either by the official art world. She could have a few exhibitions; she did not produce openly political works in opposition to the socialist system, nor did she follow any avant-garde tradition. She went against the grain of 'progressive' art; when abstraction began to be tolerated, she painted figurative narrative pictures; just when folk art was held up as a 'pure source' of authentic art, she turned to popular, 'low' culture, the impure, non-authentic, consumerist 'folk art': the kitsch decorativeness of a touristic peasant style.

7

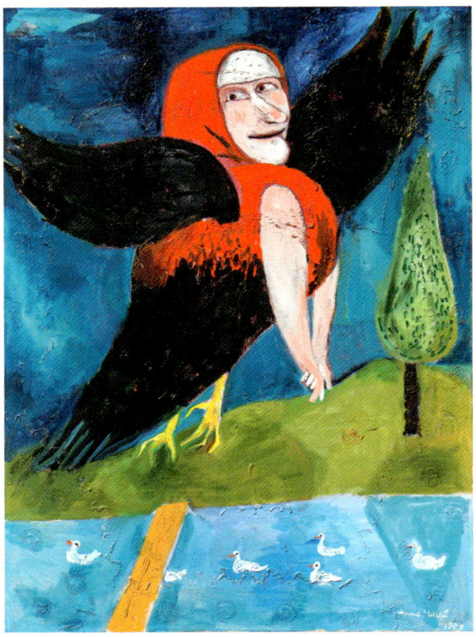

8

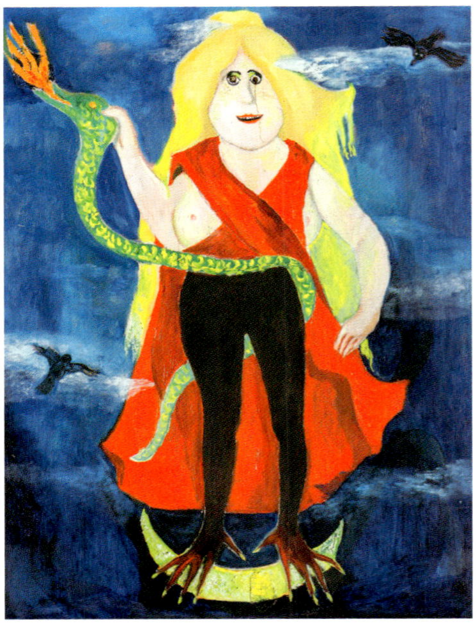

7. Margit Anna, *Red Rebbeca II*, 1979, oil on canvas, 92 × 72 cm, Ferenczy Múzeumi Centrum, Szentendre

8. Margit Anna, *Lilith*, 1967, oil on canvas, application, 82 × 62 cm, Ferenczy Múzeumi Centrum, Szentendre

Her identity as a Jew and as a woman made her a double 'other'. However, it was not as a Jewish woman that she wished to be judged, but as an artist. Yet at the end of the 1970s she released her repressed trauma and let herself come to terms with it, painting more and more pictures that openly dealt with the persecution and suffering of Jews. Still, in 1978, when the Jewish themes appeared with elemental strength in the pictures shown at her solo exhibition in the Műcsarnok (Kunsthalle), the majority of critics wrote euphemistically, in a somewhat coded way, about the war and the atrocities she suffered: 'Margit Anna's thematic cramp is beginning to heal...a disturbingly concrete world of experience is appearing, one which she tried to escape from for thirty years by dressing it up as a puppet.'[27] By the time she was in her sixties and taking account of her life, she was granted a certain level of acknowledgment.

Margit Anna did not accept the taboos of official cultural policy, but this did not make her more acceptable to alternative neo-avant-garde circles either. She did not want to be categorized as the representative of some kind of subculture, either as woman or as Jewish, rather than as an artist. When she started to speak of the grievances she had suffered as a Jew, she already had the success of her first solo exhibition behind her, held in 1968 in the Ernst Museum, and the public and elements of the art world alike accepted her. The content and the narrative nature of her work grew stronger in the 1970s. Her ageing, her sense of approaching death and her feeling that 'nothing matters any more' allowed her to explore the issues that she, as an elderly Jewish female artist and the widow of a Holocaust victim, faced.

Except for the short period following the Second World War when she was part of the Európai Iskola, Anna was embedded neither in the official culture nor in the neo-avant-garde. Her evaluation and position in the art world was never really fixed or safe. Her work was emerging in a no-man's-land: her narrativity, her talking pictures with clear messages, her attraction to low culture, kitsch and explicitly Jewish topics were subjects of criticism from both sides, and many found her non-compromising personality uncomfortable.

'It is a blessing and a curse'

The life of Júlia Vajda (born Richter) was defined by the fact that she was the wife and widow of Lajos Vajda (also see Gábor Dobó and Merse Pál Szeredi, 'Hungarian Culture +/- Europe', pp. 39–57). He was a posthumous member of the Európai Iskola, whose artistic legacy was the base on which the desired new Hungarian modern art could be built. During the 1930s, the Vajdas lived in poverty; Júlia sewed to make some money for both of them. Lajos Vajda was called up for forced labour service under the military, and he died in 1941 as a consequence of pulmonary disease that, due to his weak physical state, he suffered. After the death of her husband, Júlia Vajda carried on as an artist, participating in exhibitions. As she said, 'Lajos Vajda directed me towards constructive structures but as the expressive element is very strong in me, I have been combining the two ever since' (figs 9 and 11).[28]

The work of Júlia Vajda does not follow a linear order or evolution of style that can be connected to certain creative periods; she was experimenting with different styles sometimes at the same time. According to artist and friend Endre Bálint, the commonplace was repulsive to her, and she risked jumping into the unknown rather than saying what had already been said either by somebody else or herself. The frequent changes, Bálint said, were due to an ethical stand, as if she were afraid of repetition or watering down her own work.[29] This condemnation of repetition and obsessive search for new artistic expressions tells us more about Bálint and the ideals he represented – the value system of twentieth-century Hungarian art – than about Júlia Vajda herself. The frequent changes are rather signs of searching for her own voice, her own place, and her relation to the artistic heritage of Lajos Vajda, which for her was both a blessing and a curse, as one critic said.[30]

Júlia Vajda belonged to the community of 1 Rottenbiller utca (street) – a state-owned, administratively allocated apartment which was a metonymy of a creative community, a circle of artists and a family, an island of intellectual freedom, and an everyday place of living.[31] The apartment was the home of Endre Bálint, his wife, who was the sister of

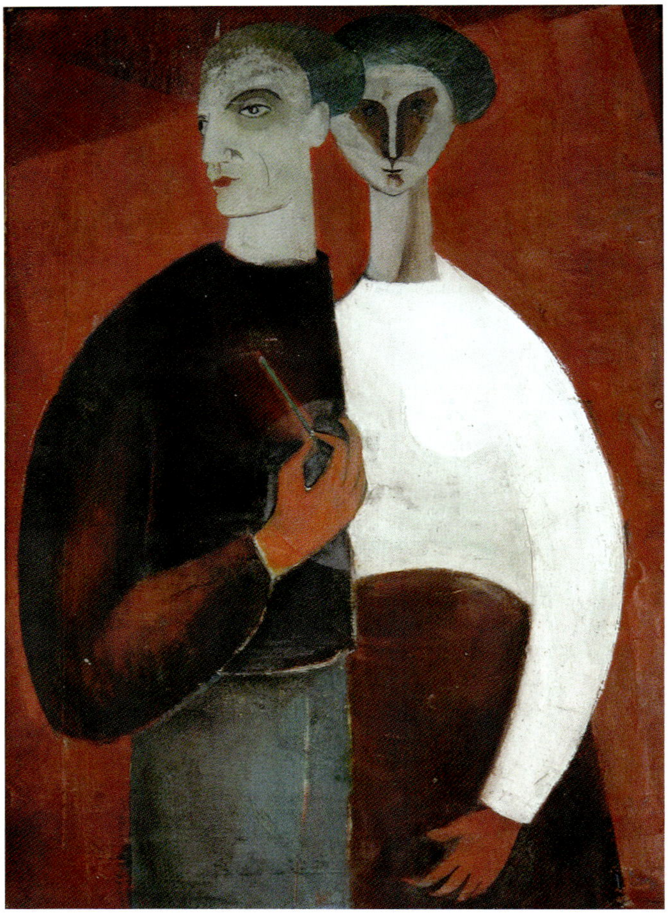

9

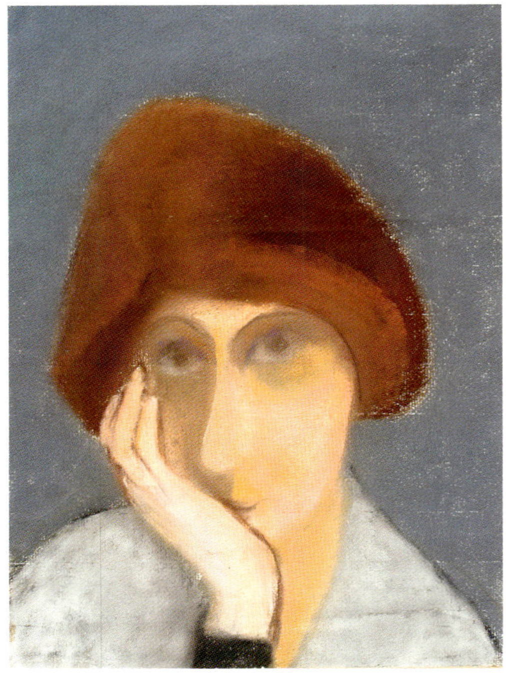

10

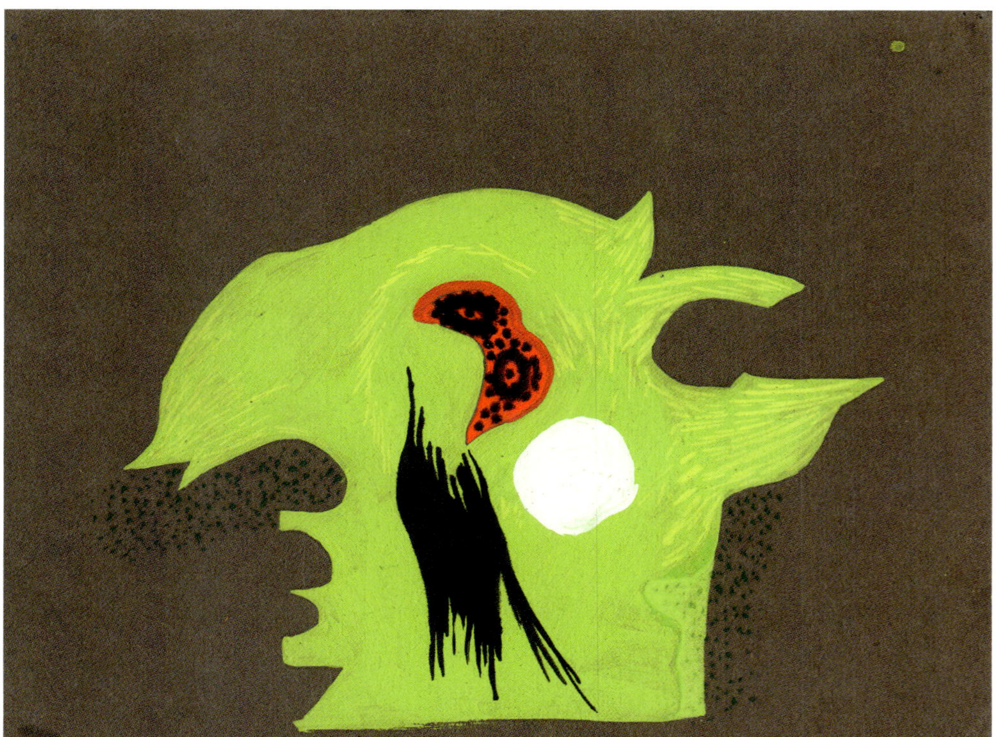

11

9. Júlia Vajda, *Double Portrait (Self-Portrait with Lajos Vajda)*, 1942, oil on fibreboard, 49 × 34.5 cm, Private collection

10. Júlia Vajda, *Self-Portrait*, 1953, chalk, paper, 44 × 35 cm, Private collection

11. Júlia Vajda, *Green Flame, Red Mask*, 1948, tempera, cardboard, 17.5 × 12.5 cm, Private collection

12. Júlia Vajda, *Self-Portraits Without a Mirror*, 1945, paper, pencil, 2 pieces, 18.5 × 13.5 cm each, Private collection

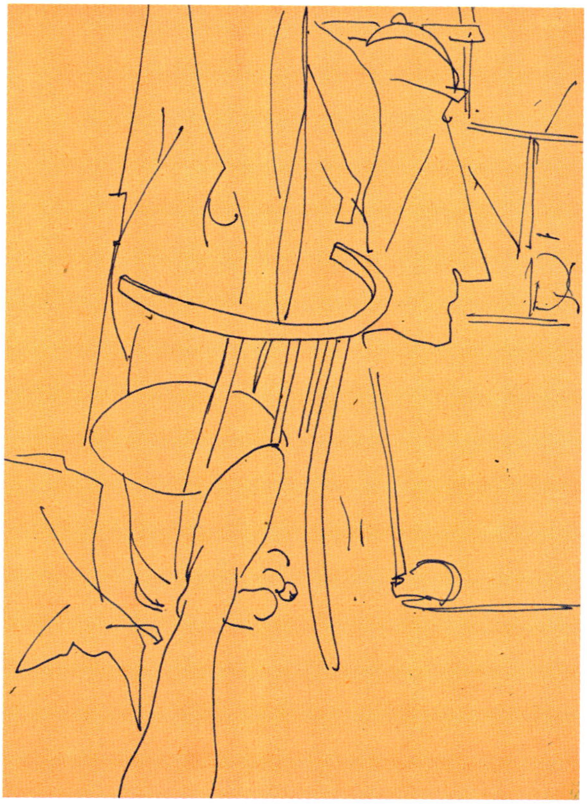

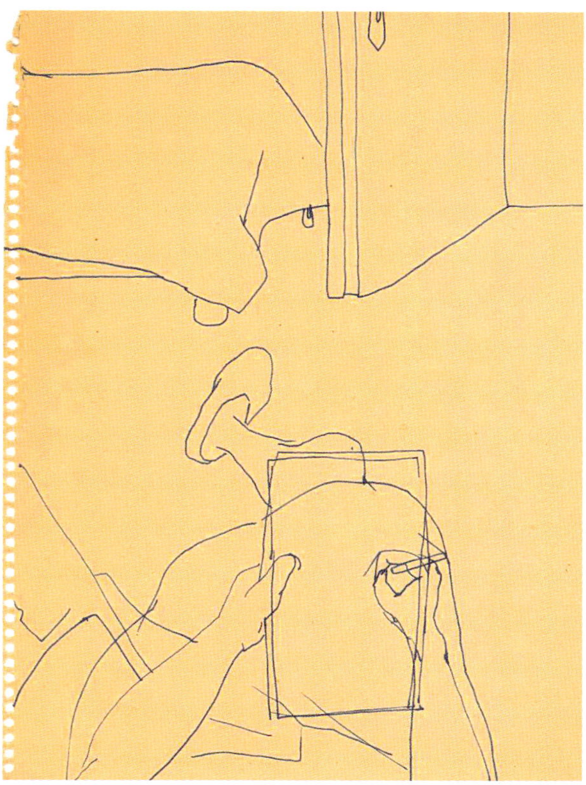

12

Júlia Vajda, and their son, as well as Júlia herself, her second husband (the sculptor József Jakovits), their twin children and other people, as there were always visitors, friends and fellow artists in the apartment. It is not easy to establish who lived with whom in the apartment, and for how long, and hearsay, gossip and personal accounts have played an important role in this. For a time, nobody could even locate where Júlia either worked or slept in the cramped apartment.[32] Nevertheless, she guarded the artistic heritage of her late husband; his works were kept in a foldable bed.

Friends and colleagues knew about her work but she was basically known as the guardian of the Lajos Vajda oeuvre. This is what filled her life, even during and after her second marriage. Although she could show some of her works in group exhibitions, she did not have a solo show until 1974, at the age of sixty-one; this was followed by another, not long before her death in 1982. Thus, her major exhibition opportunities only came at a mature age, as an 'old woman', and in a sense, her work has still not been acknowledged appropriately: she still does not have a place in the canonized art history of Hungary. When critics did approach her work, rarely did they forget about her late husband. Nor did she. She tied herself to the heritage of Lajos Vajda and kept his name throughout her life.

As Endre Bálint said in 1976, Júlia Vajda withdrew behind her works; those who wanted to get to know her had to do so exclusively through her art. From the beginning of her career and through the 1950s, she painted and drew several self-portraits – non-idealizing, meditating images of herself (fig. 10). Some of her self-portraits were done without a mirror (fig. 12) and without the head, as if the viewer took the position of the artist looking down on to her own body. Through her self-portraits she was looking for her place as an artist, consciously or not, portraying herself not as an object but as a subject. She also withdrew herself from being on display. She did not examine how she was seen but how she saw herself. She chose self-expression without self-representation within the expected, recognizable framework, in order to remain invisible. The only works that later received attention of art historians and critics in the

1940s and 1950s were those that could be classified as part of progressive trends, i.e. the works she exhibited within the Európai Iskola and the Elvont Művészek Csoportja (Group of Abstract Artists). Her early abstract compositions were often characterized as a continuation and rethinking of Lajos Vajda's later works, his artistic heritage, and, as such, were praised. Later, she used geometric abstraction as another device through which she could withdraw herself from her work (figs 13–15).

Among the women artists discussed here, she was the closest to the neo-avant-garde circles, the younger generation of artists. Through her family relations, she was well informed about the activities of the members of Péter Halász's theatre (Endre Bálint's son, István Bálint, was involved). She also exhibited her abstract works with those of József Jakovits and René Kelemen in the Balatonboglári Kápolnaműterem (the Balatonboglár Chapel Studio of György Galántai) in 1973 (see Maja Fowkes and Reuben Fowkes, 'Liberty Controlled', pp. 77–93, and Klara Kemp-Welch, 'Soft-spoken Encounters', pp. 273–89). When the Balatonboglár Chapel and György Galántai were attacked in the official daily *Népszabadság* because of allegedly being obscene, hostile to socialist ideas and imitative of Western art trends and happenings, she wrote a letter to the editor-in-chief of the paper in defence of the artistic work in the chapel. The letter did not receive any answer or publicity.[33]

Due to her circumstances living as a female artist widow and 'treasurer' of the heritage of her late husband, her own artistic work struggling with the articulation of her own voice remained lesser known. She had only a few exhibitions, received few critical appraisals, and remained invisible behind the name 'Vajda'.

An enigmatic ancient Egyptian beauty

Both Júlia Vajda and Lili Ország, who was the youngest of the four painters discussed here, produced abstract works of art after their initial figurative works. The question 'how abstraction functions as a representation of gender difference [...] and more specifically of the differently gendered body, which modernist criticism has signally failed to acknowledge'[34] should be raised in connection with both of them. For them, abstraction, i.e. non-representational practice, was an option to avoid associations with their femininity. They, like Erzsébet Schaár and Margit Anna as well as several other women artists of the time, believed in the universal idea of the artist-genius without any adjective. However, great artist-geniuses 'happened to be' males.

As a young girl during the years between 1938 and 1945, Ország experienced the stigma of being a Jew, the walls of the ghetto, persecution. She hid with the aid of fake documents and survived the war, but her father died. She lived with the trauma of her experiences, and the trauma of survival itself. When she gradually shifted from figurative work to a type of abstract art, where figurative elements often could be identified in a recurrent pattern, she said that earlier she painted walls but now the surface of the painting had become the wall itself.[35] She painted letters and signs as well and repeated them, thus building a surface that seemed to have volume and layers. Her painterly motifs included Hebrew letters or letter-like elements and ruins. In an interview, she said that she built herself into and among the stones of her walls so that she could dream with them and hear what they had to say. 'What I say through these stones, I cannot tell, I hope they talk for themselves.'[36]

She travelled within the Eastern bloc relatively often, as travel restrictions were not so strict among the socialist countries. She was also able to visit Western countries, carefully ensuring that she followed all the legal requirements determined by the Hungarian authorities and getting invitation letters, foreign currency, etc. Her journeys were, for her, time travel: when she visited churches in Bulgaria, the ruins of Pompeii or the lands of Israel (fig. 16), she descended into the past. Her paintings evoked Jewish mythology and history. Towards the end of her life, she created a series of paintings of labyrinths in which printed electric circuit designs were added to the motifs of past cultures. The present and the past are part of the labyrinth, implying that we need to find our way in the course of our lives (fig. 17).[37]

13. Júlia Vajda, *Articulation in Five*, 1964, charcoal, paper, 49 × 63 cm, Private collection

14. Júlia Vajda, *Glass Window I*, 1973, oil on plywood, 60 × 33 cm, Private collection

15. Júlia Vajda, *Red Painting I*, 1975, oil on canvas, 55 × 55 cm, Private collection

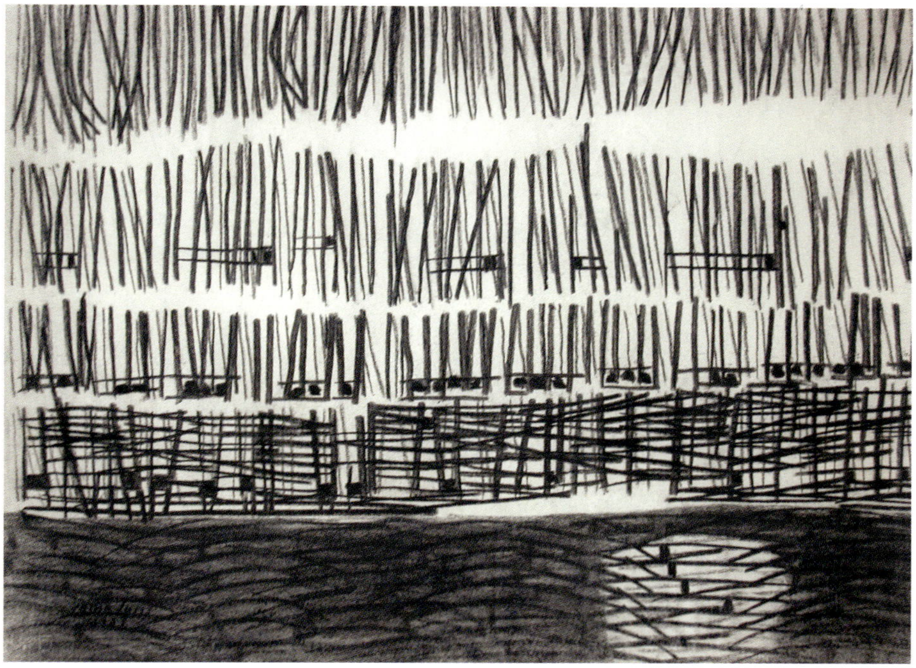

13

14

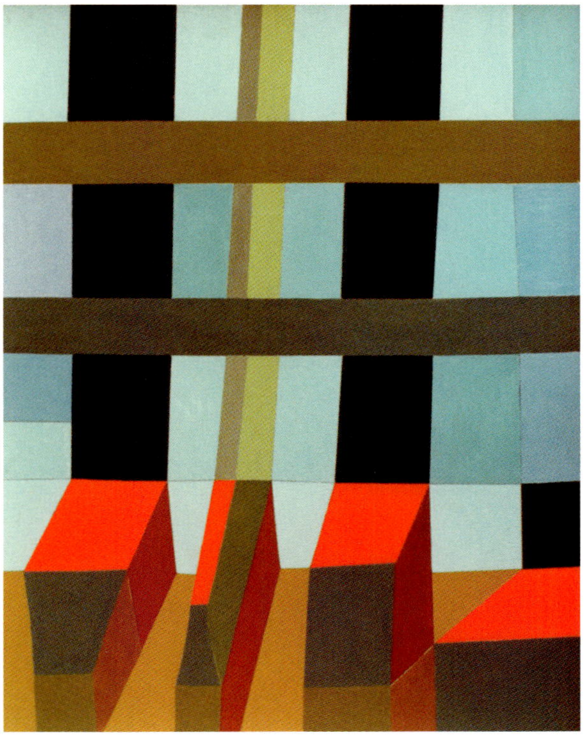

15

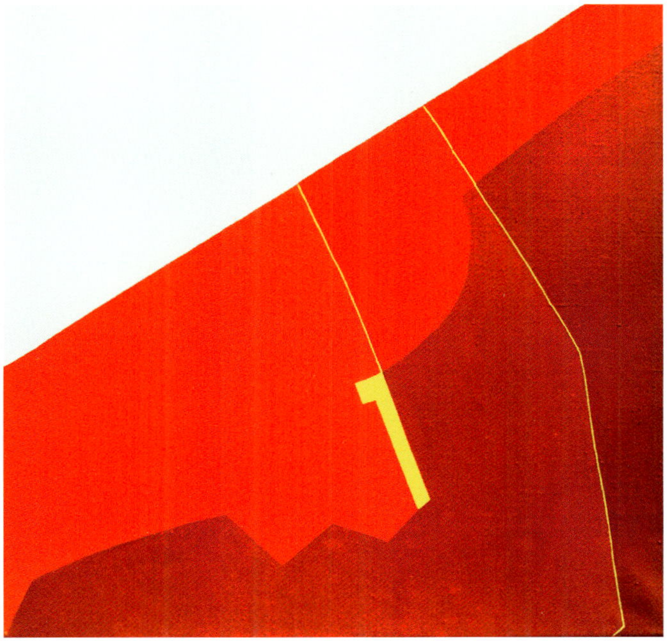

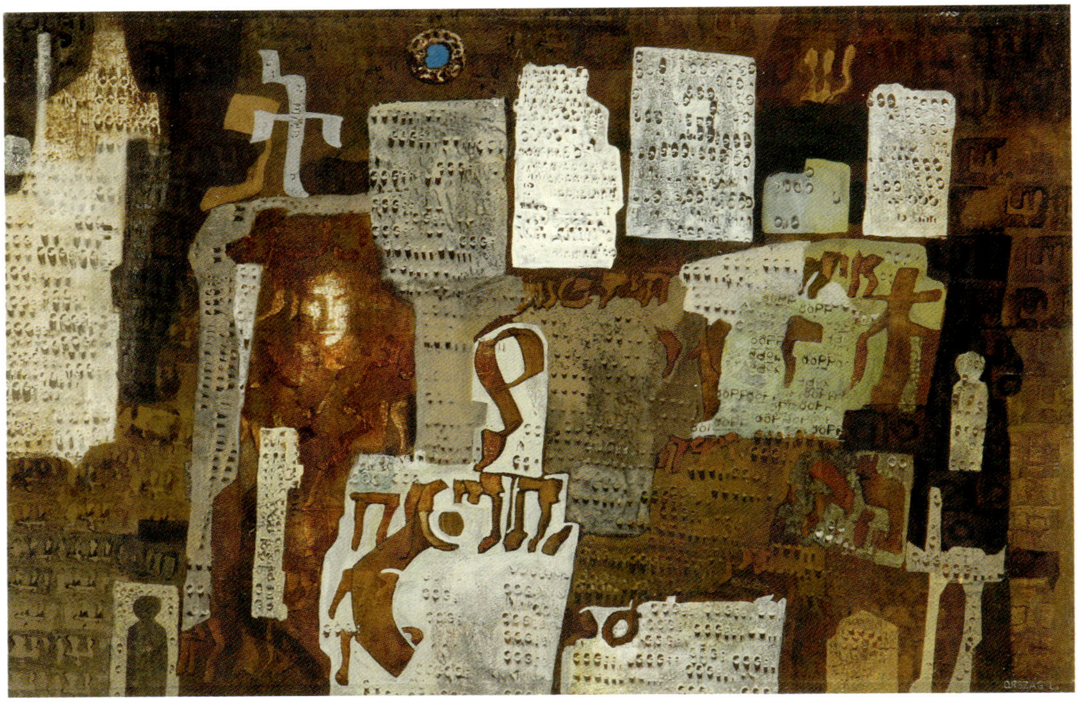

16

17

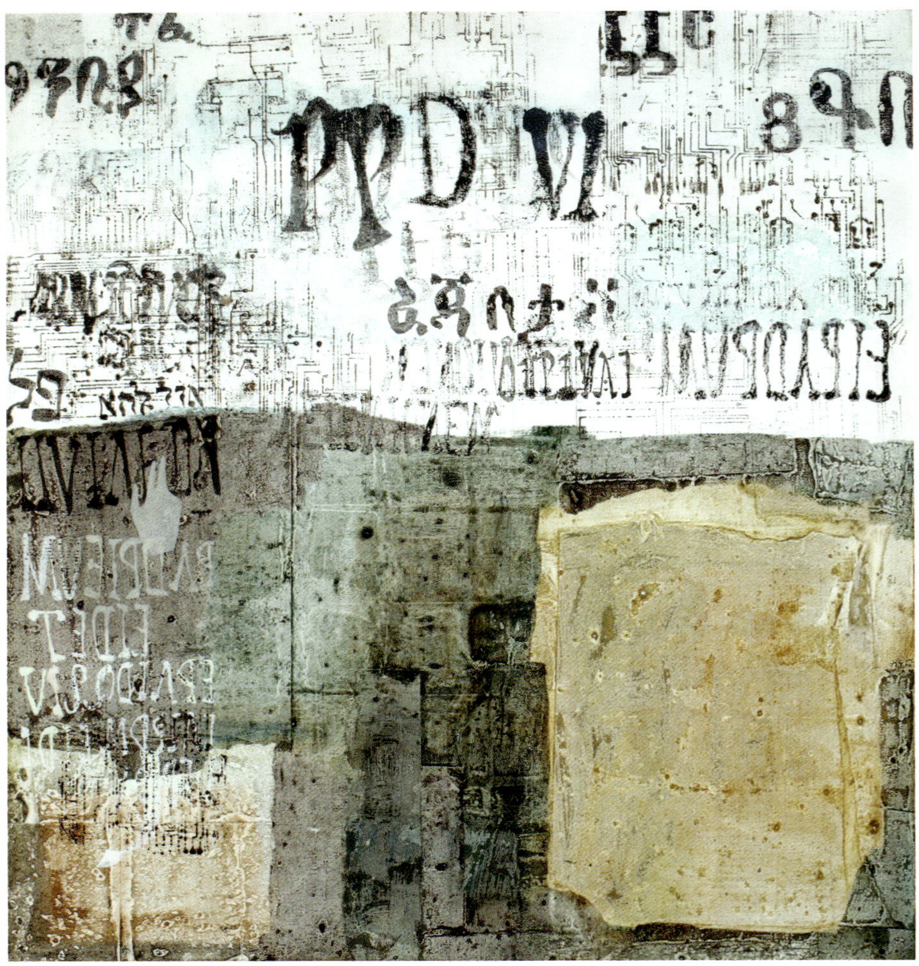

16. Lili Ország, *Vision (Jewish Cemetery in Prague)*, 1968, oil on paper, 42 × 61.5 cm, Kiscelli Múzeum – Fővárosi Képtár, Budapest

17. Lili Ország, *Wall of Pompeii*, 1968, oil on fibreboard, 70 × 63 cm, Rómer Flóris Művészeti és Történeti Múzeum – Vasilescu Collection, Győr

Struggling with how to analyse and interpret her works, critics, art historians and friends wrote about her work in an almost poetic, elevated, associative style. Her biography always played an important role in investing meaning into these paintings, including her Jewishness, anxiety and early life in the ghetto in Ungvár (now known as Uzhhorod, Ukraine). Lajos Németh calls her method 'spiritual archaeology',[38] while Katalin Néray says that Lili Ország's archaization refers to a deeper identification but without specifying this identity.[39] He says that her signs and squirming letters are not just calligraphy or decorative signs; they also evoke the 'pain of birth'. Her art cannot be classified into any particular style, according to Németh: 'her art is difficult to embed into Hungarian tradition'.[40] Her style is individual, and 'ancient experiences are embodied in them'.[41] She approaches ancient mythical pasts through her emotions.[42]

Ország herself felt that she had a particular capacity to sense the past of humankind; she looks 'down' on it from the height of the twentieth century, and the ruined ancient cities seen from above hauntingly recall the aerial view of war-destroyed cities. This is the topic of a major work, *Requiem on Seven Panels, in Memory of Perished People and Cities* (1963, pp. 212–13, fig. 5). With a change of viewpoint and scale, she uses a contemporary printed electric circuit as a pattern to print the surface of the picture, which 'fits to the remnants of ancient East, antique and medieval civilizations in an obvious way'.[43]

Except for her early self-portraits, Ország did not represent herself, her own body, in her pictures. Yet we know that she was a beautiful woman. We know this from the many photographs reproduced of her, and art historians, friends and various written pieces about her mention that she was beautiful, very feminine, an enigmatic ancient Egyptian beauty;[44] a friend even writes about her 'tragic', Jewish look.[45] Her body is missing from her works, but it is written into the texts of others. This is a rather common phenomenon when it comes to women artists: we also know that Erzsébet Schaár was a fragile, small lady who had a suggestive personality.[46] Rosemary Betterton analyses how a woman's body figures in her work or outside of her work, in the art or in the texts.[47] Descriptions of Lili Ország identify her as possessing a special, strange beauty. Adjectives like ancient, Egyptian, enigmatic, evoke not only her femininity but also her otherness, her being different. At the same time, she and her art remained too special, too particular, to allow her access to the allegedly universal hall of great artists of the time in socialist Hungary.

Her deteriorating walls and Jewish letters evidently signalled her personal experiences, the ruined synagogues that were left empty, the missing Jews. Their specific titles also drew attention to a gap, a hole in the continuity of history. These references to the specific Jewish past, and inescapably to the Holocaust, raised interest in her art and opened up the way for an exhibition in Israel in 1966 (fig. 18). A year later, socialist Hungary would only allow the exhibition of these images without their specific titles; instead of direct references, they had to be universalized as remembering the war or fascism, or as ancient ruins. This was right after the Six-Day War, and Ország had to pay that price in order to have her first solo exhibition in Hungary.[48]

Her enigmatic look and beauty – even if this really was an honest appreciation or admiration – made a metaphor out of her: she herself became the embodiment of Jewish history. Not only was her body missing from her paintings, but it was also a sign that she always remained other, different and not qualified to stand among the modernist 'great artists' as a marked, Jewish woman artist.

Conclusion

The women artists discussed here dealt with their own femininity and their own female identity in different ways. When they created abstract works of art where their femininity was not displayed, it was the discourse connected to their art that talked about their femininity. There was no escape; what could not be found in the work itself was made up in the discourse.[49]

It was not only the Holocaust that was a traumatic experience and memory: for them, survival itself was traumatic, as Cathy Caruth has discussed in other contexts.[50] Erzsébet Schaár could never free herself from something that we know only from informal comments: the death of her sister. Júlia Vajda, whose priority was her husband's art and wellbeing, survived him; when he was alive, she was never sure if she could do enough for him while they were enduring poor living conditions, without money.[51] After his death, she worked not only for 'Art' but also for his heritage, to somehow make up for her own guilty feelings, throughout her life. Both Júlia Vajda and Margit Anna worked for their husband's memory, investing time and finances to set up museums in their honour, and seeking proper acknowledgment and a position for them in art history, home and abroad. Lili Ország survived many members of her family; she escaped from the ghetto but the walls of the ghetto remained with her.

The four artists followed different artistic strategies. Erzsébet Schaár aimed to sublimate her experiences and created a universal experience of suffering and death. Lili Ország carefully avoided anything that could be connected to her femininity in her art. Júlia Vajda withdrew herself, her personality, from her work. Margit Anna dealt with herself, with her life story, pain and Jewish themes at a time when openly talking about Jewishness was not well received. They paid different prices for the art career they chose. Erzsébet Schaár was accepted into the canon of Hungarian art, but her life story, her femininity, her experiences as a Jewish woman were cut off, silenced. Júlia Vajda withdrew herself so successfully that she and her work are hardly visible even today. In the case of Margit Anna, the shadow of kitsch, the biggest enemy of modern art, was often cast onto her late work, and there is only one period in her art – her Európai Iskola work – that is unquestionably accepted. No matter how carefully Lili Ország avoided personal issues in her art, she is regularly evoked as

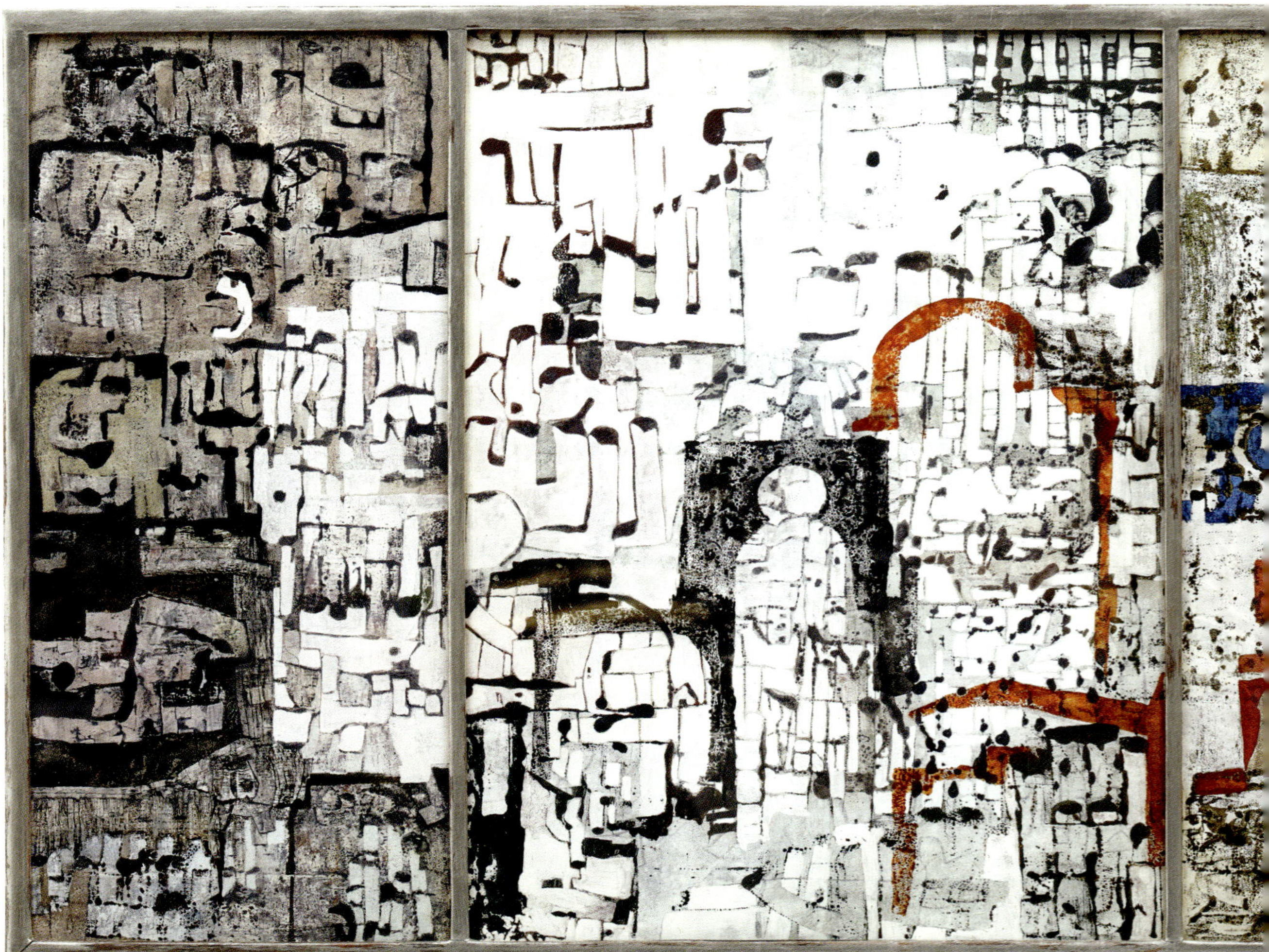

a beautiful, mysterious, exotic female beauty. Some of these artists' capabilities were often connected to witch-like capacities: intuitions that only women can have. All of them received appreciation and exhibition opportunities late in life, towards the end. They were seen 'as significant artists only in old age'.[52] They 'enjoyed' most of the advantages of being a woman artist; as the feminist art-action group Guerrilla Girls have perceived, these 'benefits' include the fact that 'your career might pick up after you're eighty'. However, none of them would live long enough to reach eighty.

Socialism helped to make women artists invisible as women. Both the official and oppositional sides of the art world expelled the relevance of gender and other particular identities. Gender and other particular identities were not constitutive elements of modernism, the aim of which was to rise above particularities and beyond localities in the name of universal truth. Within the marginalized group of artists, women were further marginalized. Although they were acknowledged, respected members of artists' circles, these women artists could not be in the 'first line' of great artists unless they were not considered women.

No doubt, a gendered approach to understanding their work would not have been welcomed by the artists themselves. The discourse that focuses on how these women artists found their strategies and how the issue of gender played a role in their position, consciously or unconsciously, was not part of the discourse of art criticism, be it official, semi-official or non-official. But the works of art themselves and the discourse around them allow such an approach; we can see the traces and elements that were connected to their creators' position as women in the art world.

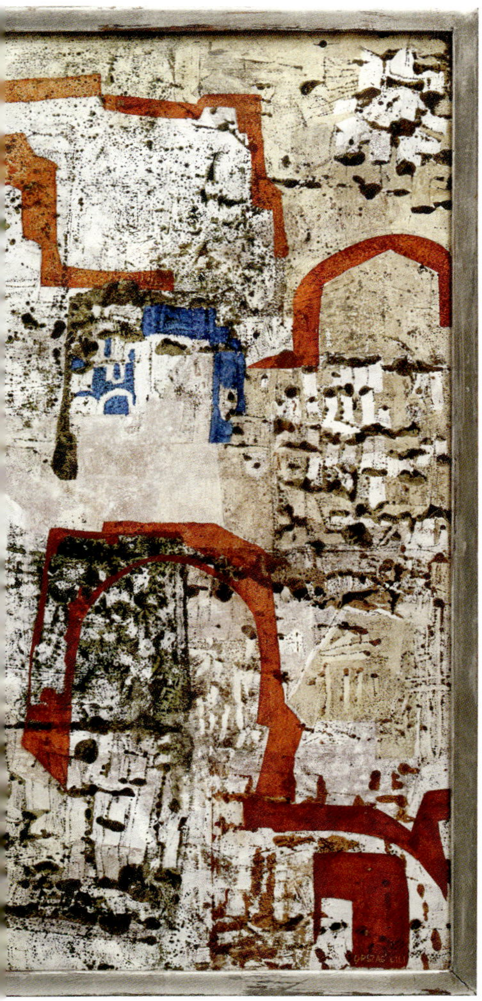

18

18. Lili Ország, *Walls of Jerusalem*, 1962, oil on fibreboard, 60 × 111 cm, Private collection

1 Verbal remark.
2 Jan Matohona, 'Dispositives of Silence: Gender, Feminism and Czech Literature between 1948 and 1989', in Hana Havelkova and Libora Oates-Indruchová (eds), *The Politics of Gender Culture under State Socialism*. London and New York: Routledge, 2014, 162–87.
3 Mara Traumane, 'Discussion, Writing and Translating Art from the Former Eastern Europe: The Relationship between Post-communist and Post-colonial', in Ieva Astahovska (ed.), *Recuperating the Invisible Past*. Riga: Latvian Centre for Contemporary Art, 2012, 165.
4 Griselda Pollock, *Vision and Difference*. London and New York: Routledge, 1988, 1.
5 Maria Adamson and Erika Kispeter, 'Gender and Professional Work in Russia and Hungary', in Catherine Baker (ed.), *Gender in Twentieth-century Eastern Europe and the USSR*. London: Palgrave Macmillan, 2017, 214–27.
6 János Frank, *Szóra bírt műterme*k [Studios Speak]. Budapest: Magvető Kiadó, 1975, 111–14.
7 I thank art historian Ildikó Nagy for this information. See the archive of Magyar Képzőművészeti Főiskola beiratkozási lapjai, 11/a Vol. 118, 1925–26, 2nd semester.
8 In 1985, Margit Slachta was posthumously awarded the honorific title 'Righteous among the Nations' by the state of Israel and has a tree dedicated to her at Yad Vashem, the Holocaust memorial.
9 The spelling of the name Vilt is the 'artistic' version of the original name, Wilt. Ilona Mona, *Slachta Margit*. Budapest: Corvina Kiadó, 1997, 159.
10 I am grateful to the late Pál Wilt, the artist's son, for talking to me.
11 Irit Rogoff, 'Gossip as Testimony: A Postmodern Signature', in Griselda Pollock (ed.), *Generations and Geographies in the Visual Arts*. London and New York: Routledge, 1996, 58–65; Pál Wilt, 'A költözködés' [The Moving], *Mindennap más* [Everyday Something Different]. Budapest: Magvető, 1969, 381–84. I thank Ildikó Nagy for calling my attention to the short story.
12 Géza Perneczky, 'A váci utcai tanagrák mestre' [Master of the Tanagra Figures from Váci Street], in *Tanulmányút a Pávakertbe* [Study Tour to Peacock Garden]. Budapest: Magvető Könyvkiadó, 1969, 320–24.
13 Géza Perneczky, '"és az itteni Aczél elvtárs?" Schaár Erzsi és a kölni Stapelrecht' ['And the local comrade Aczél?' Erzsi Schaár and the Storage Right of Cologne], *Jelenkor*, Vol. 59, No. 11, 2016, 1195.
14 Géza Perneczky on Erzsébet Schaár, in Dóra Hegyi, Sándor Hornyik and Zsuzsa László (eds), *Parallel Chronologies: 'Other' Revolutionary Traditions: How Art Becomes Public. An Exhibition in Newspaper Format*. Budapest: Tranzit Hungary Public Benefit Association, 2011, 38. See http://tranzit.org/exhibitionarchive/tag/schaar-erzsebet (4 August 2017).
15 Lajos Németh, *'Szigetet és mentőövet': Életinterjú 1986* ['Island and Lifebelt': Life Interview 1986]. Edited by László Beke, Katalin Németh, Gábor Pataki and Árpád Timár. Budapest: Magyar Tudományos Akadémia/Bölcsészettudományi Kutatóközpont/Művészettörténeti Intézet/Mission Art Galéria, 2017, 258.
16 Pierre Emmanuel, 'Preface', in László Beke, *Erzsébet Schaár*. Budapest: Corvina, 1973, 6.
17 Lajos Németh, 'Schaár Erzsébetről' [On Erzsébet Schaár], *Jelenkor*, Vol. 20, No. 8, 1977, 684.
18 The artist quoted in Beke, *Erzsébet Schaár*, 19.
19 Németh, 'Schaár Erzsébetről', 684.
20 Hedvig Turai, 'Intersection of Erasures in Hungarian Art History: Erzsébet Schaár', in Andrea Pető, Louise Hecht and Karolina Krasuska (eds), *Women and the Holocaust: New Perspectives and Challenges*. Warsaw: Instytut Badan Literackich PAN, 2015, 145–60.
21 The Margit Anna quote that forms the heading of this section is from Sándor Kabán, interview with Margit Anna, 24 April 1986. Hungarian National Gallery Archives, 22722/1987, 31.
22 'Conversation with Margit Anna. Interviewer: Péter Szabó', in Ildikó Nagy (ed.), *A hatvanas évek. Új törekvések a magyar képzőművészetben* [The Sixties: New Strivings in Hungarian Art] (exhibition catalogue). Budapest: Képzőművészeti Kiadó, Hungarian National Gallery, Ludwig Museum, 1991, 85.
23 Griselda Pollock, 'Inscriptions in the Feminine', in M. Catherine de Zegher (ed.), *Inside the Visible: An Elliptical Traverse of Twentieth Century Art in, of, and from the Feminine* (exhibition catalogue). Boston, Kortrijk and London: Institute of Contemporary Art/Kanaal Art Foundation/MIT Press, 1996, 68.
24 Undated letter, no envelope. Property of Gábor Mezei.
25 Imre Kertész, *A holocaust mint kultúra* [The Holocaust as Culture]. Budapest: Századvég Kiadó, 1993, 41.
26 Kabán, interview, 36–37.
27 Julianna P. Szűcs, 'A mai Anna Margit' [Margit Anna Today], *Népszabadság*, 10 March 1978.
28 Frank, *Szóra bírt műtermek*, 195.
29 Endre Bálint, 'Vajda Júlia képeiről' [About the Pictures of Júlia Vajda], in *Sorsomról van szó* [It Is My Fate]. Budapest: Magvető Könyvkiadó, 1987, 178–79.
30 Júlianna P. Szűcs, 'Vajda Júlia gyűjteményes kiállítása a Műcsarnokban' [Júlia Vajda's Exhibition in Műcsarnok], *Népszabadság*, 13 March 1981, 7.
31 Gyula Kozák, *A szabadság kicsiny szigete: Művészsorsok a 20. században: Bálint Endre, Jakovits József, Vajda Júlia* [Little Island of Freedom: Artists' Fate in the 20th Century: Endre Bálint, József Jakovits, Júlia Vajda]. Budapest: Balassi Kiadó, 2016.

32 I am grateful to Vera Jakovits and Gyula Kozák for our conversations; see also Kozák, *A szabadság kicsiny szigete*, 260.
33 Published in Kozák, *A szabadság kicsiny szigete*, 276.
34 Rosemary Betterton, *An Intimate Distance: Women, Artists, and the Body*. London: Routledge, 1996, 79.
35 Iván Rozgonyi, 'Beszélgetés Ország Lili festőművésszel' [Conversation with Painter Lili Ország], in Katalin S. Nagy, *Ország Lili*. Budapest: Arthis Alapítvány, n.d., 134.
36 'A múlt birodalma (Ország Lili festőművész, 1964)' [The Realm of Past (Painter Lili Ország, 1964)], in Iván Rozgonyi, *Párbeszég müvekkel: Interjúk 1955–1981* [Dialogue with Works of Art: Interviews 1955–1981]. Budapest: MTA, Művészettörténeti Kutató Csoport, 1988, 206.
37 Katalin Néray, 'A fal mint a közép-európai lét metaforája: Ország Lili pécsi kiállításához' [Wall as a Metaphor of Central European Existence: To Lili Ország's Exhibition in Pécs], in *Ország Lili müvei a Vasilescu gyüjteményben* [Lili Ország's Works in the Vasilescu Collection] (exhibition catalogue). Pécs: Művészetek Háza, 1993, 18.
38 Lajos Németh, *Ország Lili*. Budapest: Képzőművészeti Alap Kiadóvállalata, 1974, 8.
39 Néray, 'A fal mint a közép-európai lét metaforája', 18.
40 Németh, *Ország Lili*, 10.
41 Németh, *Ország Lili*, 12.
42 Németh, *Ország Lili*, 8.
43 Quoted by Néray, 'A fal mint a közép-európai lét metaforája', 18.
44 S. Nagy, *Ország Lili*, 14; Mrs. Lajos Kassák, 'Találkozásaim Ország Lilivel' [My Meetings with Lili Ország], *Életünk*, Vol. 18, No. 11, 1981, 980–81.
45 Paolo Santarcangeli, 'Ország Lili', *Életünk*, Vol. 16, No. 11, 1979, 684.
46 Németh, 'Schaár Erzsébetről', 683.
47 Betterton, *An Intimate Distance*, 86–91.
48 Péter Kovács, 'Emlékezés Ország Lili székesfehérvári kiállításaira' [Remembering Lili Ország's Exhibitions in Székesfehérvár], in *Ország Lili müvei a Vasilescu gyüjteményben*, 14.
49 Betterton, *An Intimate Distance*, 79–91.
50 Cathy Caruth, *Unclaimed Experience: Trauma, Narrative, and History*. Baltimore: Johns Hopkins University Press, 1996.
51 Kozák, *A szabadság kicsiny szigete*, 292.
52 Griselda Pollock, 'Old Bones and Cocktail Dresses: Louise Bourgeois and the Question of Age', *Oxford Art Journal*, Vol. 22, No. 2, 1999, 94.

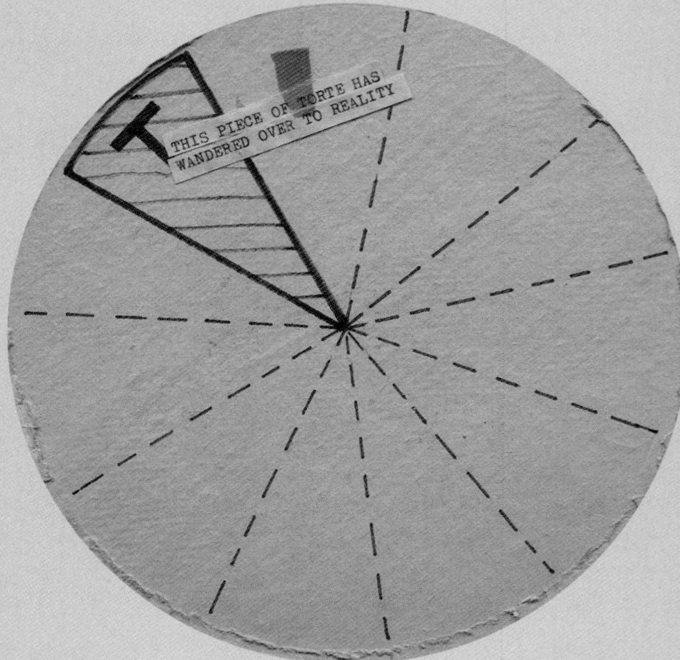
THIS PIECE OF TORTE HAS
WANDERED OVER TO REALITY

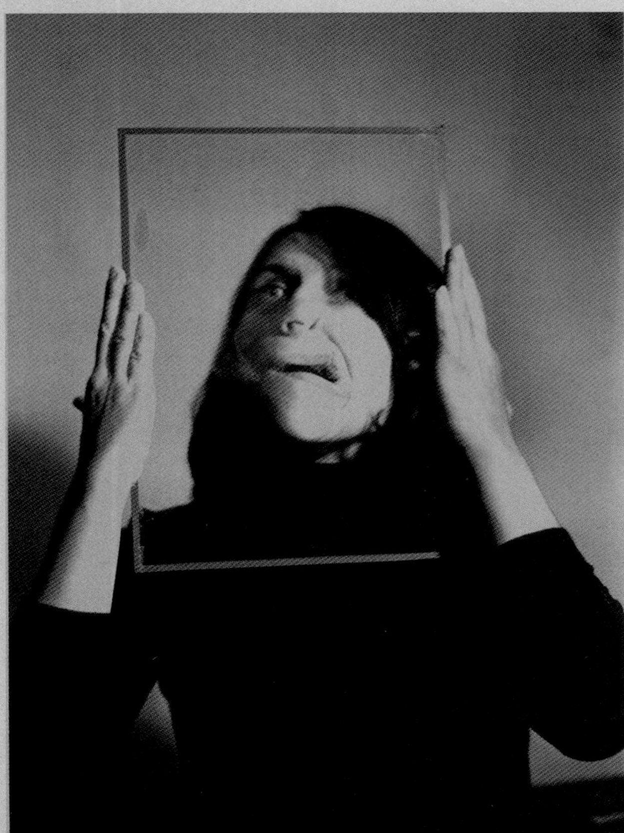

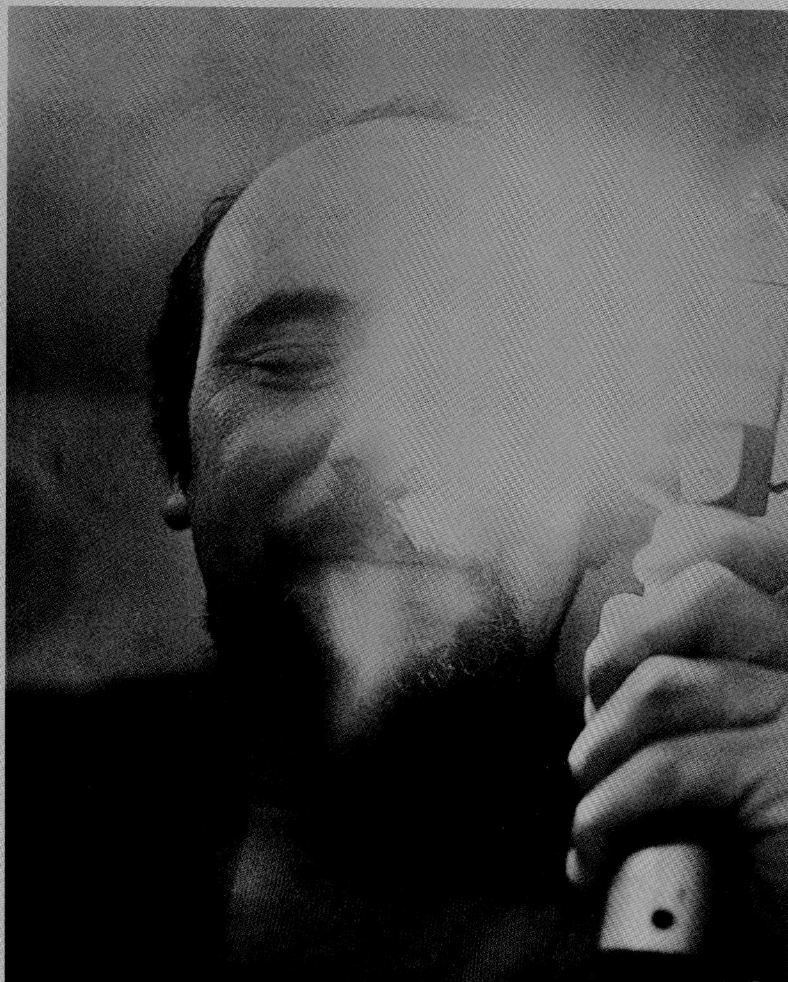

Speech Acts

1

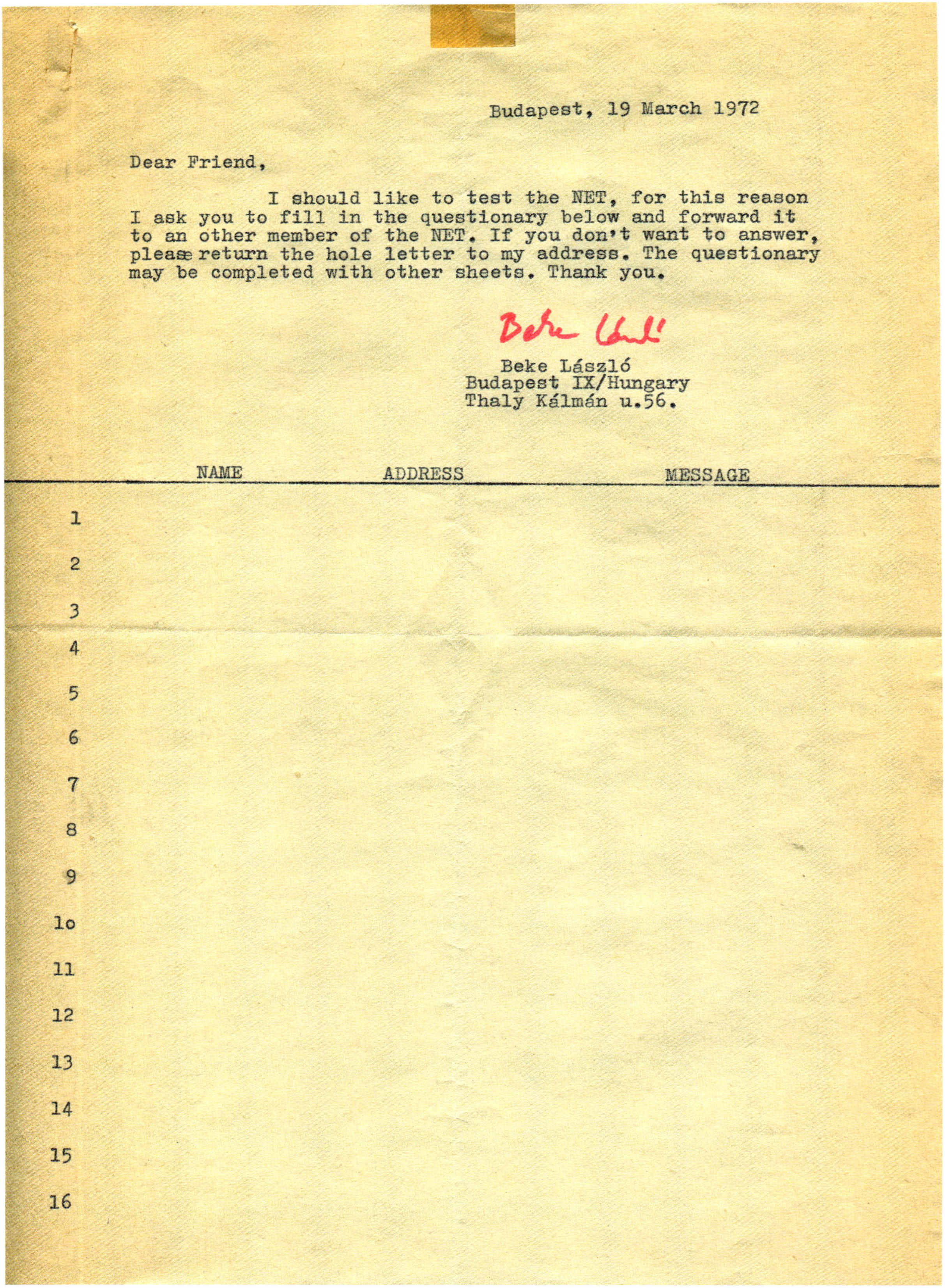

Budapest, 19 March 1972

Dear Friend,

I should like to test the NET, for this reason I ask you to fill in the questionary below and forward it to an other member of the NET. If you don't want to answer, please return the hole letter to my address. The questionary may be completed with other sheets. Thank you.

Beke László
Budapest IX/Hungary
Thaly Kálmán u.56.

NAME	ADDRESS	MESSAGE

1
2
3
4
5
6
7
8
9
1o
11
12
13
14
15
16

1. László Beke's letter to Jarosław Kozłowski, 19 March 1972, typing on paper, 29.7 × 21 cm, Private collection

Soft-spoken Encounters

International Exchanges and the Hungarian 'Underground'

In the spring of 1972, Béla Hap and Árpád Ajtony launched a samizdat magazine entitled *EXPRESSZIÓ*.[1] Dóra Maurer recalled the 'snowball effect' of its production: 'According to the rules, the new editor had to take one-third of the content of the examples that had reached her/him from the previous issue, but above and beyond this, the new issue could be compiled at everyone's own discretion.'[2] The February 1973 issue of the magazine, produced by Maurer, included a key theoretical essay with the title 'Soft-Spoken Hungarian Underground Manifesto'. 'What is the underground?' asked Hap. He replied: it is a 'cultural "movement" which neither supports nor attacks the establishment but is rather outside of it', for, as he reasoned, 'if it attacked the establishment, it would be acknowledging its existence. If it were a true organized movement, it would be playing the games of the superficial world.'[3]

Hap's theorization of a programmatically *weak* position, 'soft-spoken' rather than loud and clear – operational rather than oppositional – was shared by alternative artistic circles across the Soviet bloc in the 1960s and early 1970s. Elsewhere, I have aligned such an approach with the idea of 'self-organization' developed by Central European dissidents in the 1970s and 1980s – in particular with the idea of 'antipolitics' proposed by György Konrád in 1984.[4] Here, I am specifically interested in thinking about how different sorts of artistic encounters related to Konrád's question, 'How can we strengthen the horizontal human relationships of civil society against the vertical human relationships of military society?'[5] I want to argue that the most important function of the underground was to bring people together within a new creative framework.

Hap explained that the bonds between those associated with the underground were 'those of friendship' and that the underground was based on a 'one artist to another' principle – addressed to 'everyone who has a positive interest in it'.[6] There are clear parallels here with the Polish NET project, distributed to a mailing list of some 350 recipients worldwide in 1971–72 (see also Júlia Perczel's 'The Art Sphere as a Grey Zone', pp. 59–75, and Flóra Barkóczi, 'Creative (Dis)Courses', pp. 95–109). Its authors, Jarosław Kozłowski and Andrzej Kostołowski, devised a conceptual proposal that would be 'open and uncommercial', noting that 'points of the NET' could be 'private homes, studios and any other places, where art propositions are articulated'. What mattered was that 'propositions are presented to persons interested in them' and that 'points of the NET are in contact among themselves and exchange concepts, propositions, projects and other forms of articulation'.[7]

One of the early respondents to NET was the Hungarian art historian László Beke. He contributed a spin-off proposal, asking recipients to each fill out a questionnaire with their name and address, and to add a message of their own before forwarding the letter to another recipient on the mailing list; the project would end when one person decided they didn't want to add their name, in which case they were asked to return the information gathered to Beke in Budapest (fig. 1).[8] Designed to test the efficacy of NET, the piece also highlighted the extent to which the entire operation was a voluntary one that relied on cooperation and trust. Another Hungarian respondent to the NET call was the conceptualist László Lakner, who sent in an invitation to eat a slice of paper torte (a variation on the theme 'Let them eat cake!'), explaining that in this way the proposal on paper would cross over into the realm of 'reality' (fig. 2).[9] In the accompanying set of typed instructions, participants were urged either to photograph themselves eating the torte, to hang the torte on the wall or, in the event that they did not wish to do either, to give it 'to an ex-convict'. For his part, the artist János Urban, who had left Budapest in 1956 and eventually settled in Lausanne, Switzerland, sent in a poetic proposal for a small portable light source that could be carried anywhere in the world, would not require any wiring system and would shine for twelve years (fig. 3). Like NET itself, these sorts of proposals tended to be collaborative in spirit and were connected to the sharing of experiences or the production of wider possibilities for exchange, whether actual or symbolic.

In August 1971, Beke had initiated a project entitled 'Imagination', proposing that 'the WORK = the DOCUMENTATION OF AN IDEA' (see also Maja Fowkes and Reuben Fowkes, 'Liberty Controlled', pp. 77–93) and inviting a selection of Hungarian artists to send him work directly so that he could put together an overview of the 'current state of a few tendencies in Hungarian art' as a way 'to find a solution to the well known difficulties of exhibiting, publishing etc.'[10] He later noted that the collection of works on paper received in response to his call had reflected a moment in which 'traditional painting, sculpture, and graphic arts were gradually replaced by a new system of media that could record light, witty, and provocative thoughts: typed texts, photos, montages, drafts, audio tapes', all of which 'represented intellectual freedom, rather than material values'.[11] 'Imagination' was conceived of as an exhibition, one that while 'only realised in thought' could nevertheless be 'accurately documented'.[12] Beke also noted that the works

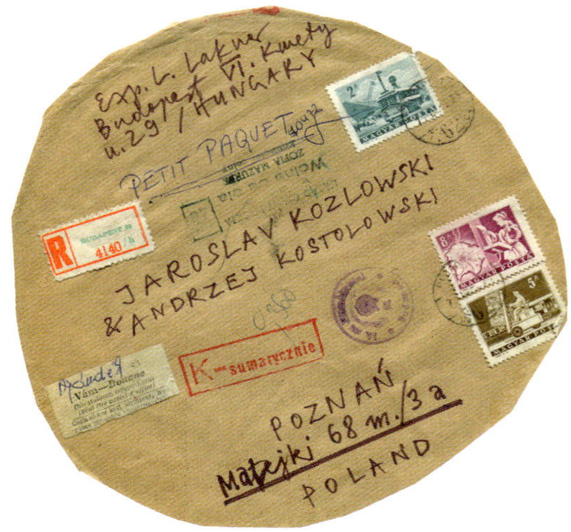

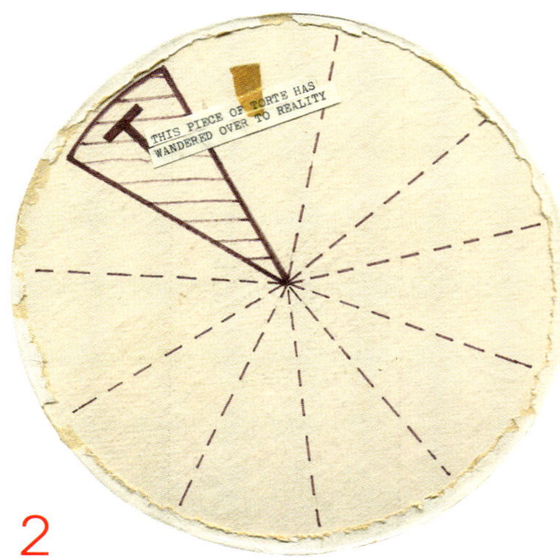

2

2. László Lakner, *This Piece of Torte Has Wandered Over to Reality*, 1972, paper, pen, typing, diameter 18.5 cm, Private collection

3. János Urbán, *Pocket Sculpture with Light*, 1971, silver gelatine print, 8.6 × 6.9 cm, Private collection

4. Tamás Hencze, *Underground (project)*, 1971, paper, pencil, each 12.7 × 7.6 cm, Private collection

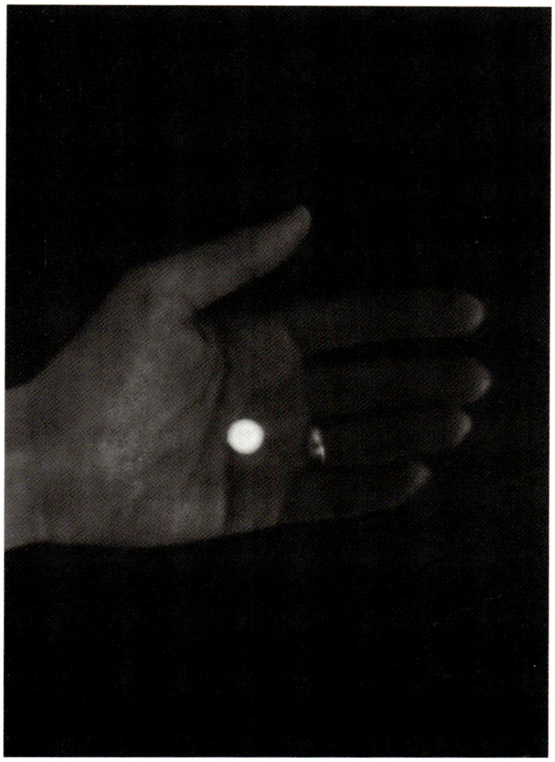

3

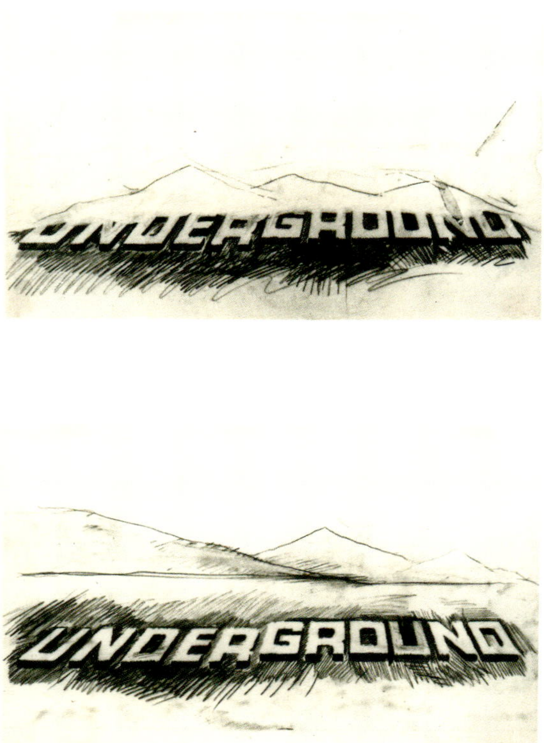

4

received (from thirty-one artists) had for the most part been 'unrealisable' at the time, 'given political constraints'.[13]

With hindsight, it is clear that such a project chimed with observations made in the United States by Lucy Lippard and others concerning the liberating potential of what she and Robert Chandler had called, in 1968, the 'dematerialization of art' – the idea that 'unfettered by object status, Conceptual artists were free to let their imaginations run rampant'.[14] Indeed, as the Hungarian émigré artist, critic and encyclopaedic art historian Géza Perneczky would later remark, the shift towards more ephemeral and process-oriented work either side of the Iron Curtain should not be treated as entirely dissimilar in motivation. He noted that once artists from Eastern Europe visited Western Europe, 'they could contrast the disadvantages of institutionalised and monopolistic modernism there with the drawbacks of the autocratic, conservative cultural policy in their homeland. The difference they found was miniscule at best.'[15] Having taken the step of emigrating from Budapest to Cologne in 1970, Perneczky's assessment of the cultural situation of the underground was far from optimistic: 'The best artists of Eastern Europe resembled the shipwrecked who make desperate attempts to contact the outside world with their bottled messages,' he later claimed.[16] On the other hand, he also noted that this isolation had served as the 'main engine' for the birth of an alternative artistic network in the region.[17] Irrespective of whether or not one agrees that the umbrella term 'global conceptualism' – as proposed by the influential 1999 exhibition of the same name at Queens Museum of Art, New York – is the most useful rubric for bringing disparate practices together, there is a strong case for claiming that an 'underground' network was forged among alternative artists in the 1970s.[18]

Tamás Hencze's response to Beke's call for 'Imagination' visualized a reply to Hap's question, 'What is the underground?' His *Underground (project)* (fig. 4), delivered in textual form with a series of sketches, was a plan that could be 'constructed in any part of the world on whatever scale is preferred. The recommended size is "as monumental as possible." This can be achieved through a great

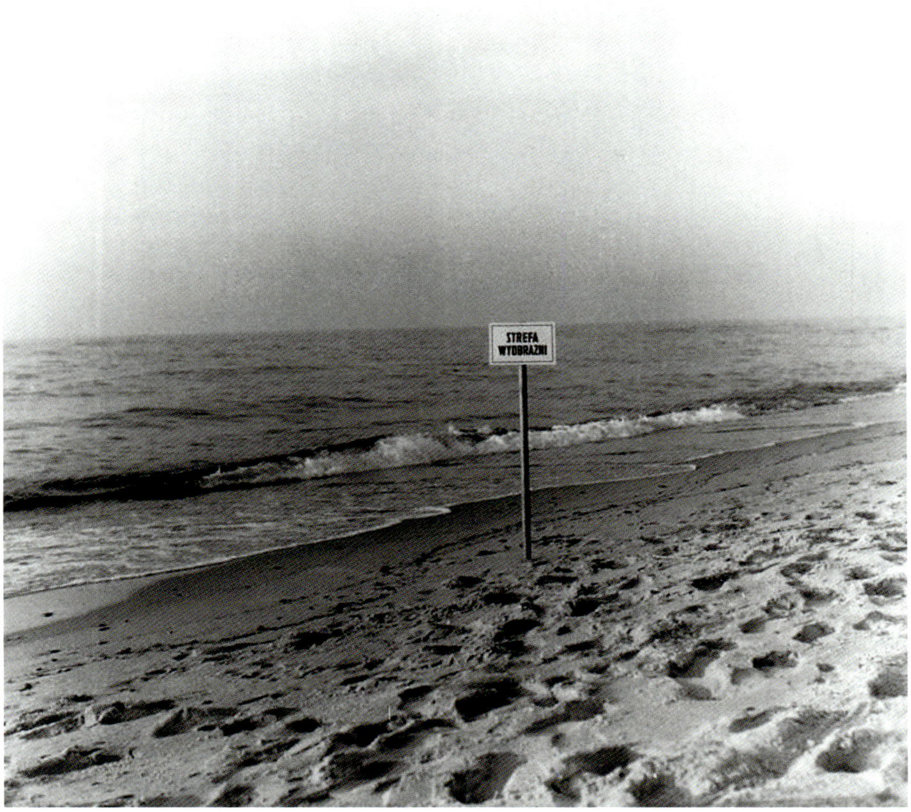

5

5. Jarosław Kozłowski, *Imagination Zone*, Osieki (action series), silver gelatine print, 21 pieces, each 18 × 18 cm, Private collection

amount of earthwork until the ground surface takes on the shape of UNDERGROUND Size: 1:10, 1:100, 1:1000, 1:10000, 1:100000'. Beke commented on the multiple layers of meaning so successfully mobilized by Hencze's piece that it was clear that these plans were not just a 'simple joke' revolving around the irony of a textual proposition assuming monumental proportions while paradoxically still retaining its status as text, but that in addition to meaning 'under the ground' Hencze's use of the term *underground* also referred to 'a form of behaviour'. The project staged an interpretative collision by imagining and representing the materialization of an immaterial concept above-ground, yielding, as Beke rightly argues, the possibility of a 'paradoxical situation when the whole globe becomes underground'.[19] This situation was also highlighted by the 'Imagination' project itself in so far as it was designed to serve as a forum within which such flights of the imagination could be realized – making the passage from idea to material, if only in paper form. Kozłowski had drawn attention to the same potential for creative liberation when he installed a large number of placards reading 'Imagination Zone' around Osieki during the landmark *plein-air* meetings held there in 1970 (fig. 5), drawing attention to the multiple possibilities for crossing over between imagination and reality. It was a dichotomy that the idea of the 'underground' undid at every stage.

Beke wrote to Kozłowski about his initiatives, including a 'World Archive of Ideas' and an 'international exhibition of mails in my and my friends' ownership'.[20] His project for a 'World-Famous World Archive of Ideas, Concepts, Projects etc.' of 1972 was designed to operate on a voluntary, collaborative basis. Beke recalled that 'at the end of the 60s I had a vision that all these countries had to unify or join the radical avant-gardist artists'.[21] Like 'Imagination', which he had collated in the form of some forty folders, this project was also presented in A4 format, as a ring binder with a black cover with proposals in plastic covers punched with holes. He would make 'a regular show each month of another artist with the same black ring-binder', turning the small room where he lived with his family into a gallery to which he would invite one or two people at a time to see the project (he estimates having shown the piece to a circle of around eighty or ninety people in this way), recalling the irony of the space being so cramped while the activities being presented were worldwide. If the hyperbolically named 'World-Famous World Archive' had begun life as a 'trendy manifesto', it was also a form of advertisement: more like an appeal on Beke's part to 'send me materials from all over the world'.[22] The black folder eventually became something of a 'fetishist object', he recollects, despite its 'very primitive' format. Beke recalled that, later, the project was condensed into the form of a portable book of some eighty pages, which could be presented in different locations, for example in 1974 in Zagreb on the occasion of an Association Internationale des Critiques d'Art (AICA, International Association of Art Critics) congress there.

If Beke's Budapest-based initiative represented an extra-institutional materialization of a dematerialized underground exhibition, there were also a small number of group shows of Hungarian art involving artists associated with the underground. These were invariably facilitated either by émigré artists or foreigners. The remarkable exhibition of six Hungarian artists at Galeria Foksal in Warsaw in May 1972 was the last in a series of shows developed by Poznań-based Hungarian émigré János Brendel (whom Piotr Piotrowski has referred to as an unofficial 'ambassador of Hungarian culture' in the period),[23] following on from a touring exhibition under the title 'Wystawa grupy artystów węgierskich' (Exhibition of a Group of Hungarian Artists) at the state-run Biuro Wystaw Artystycznych (BWA, Bureau of Artistic Exhibitions) in Poznań, Łódź, Sopot, Szczecin and Koszalin, beginning in 1970. When a version of the exhibition was shown in Warsaw, however, it was rather different in character for it involved fewer, and arguably more radical, artists and artworks.

The 1972 group show of artists from Budapest remains anomalous not only in the Foksal's history, but also in the history of unofficial art in Central Europe at this time: there were very few unofficially organized group shows of artists from the Soviet satellites in neighbouring satellite countries. Although one-man shows and pairings of artists were common at the Foksal, and the gallery (which operated under the auspices of a state-funded artistic organization) had a lively international programme, this was entirely Western-oriented: no further artists from Soviet bloc countries found their way into the gallery's programme over the course of the remainder of the 1970s (see also Maja Fowkes and Reuben Fowkes, 'Liberty Controlled', pp. 77–93).

The exhibition opened on 27 May 1972, with contributions from Miklós Erdély, Tamás Szentjóby (his name in this exhibition was given as either St Jouby or St Jauby), György Jovánovics, László Lakner, Gyula Pauer and Endre Tót.[24] A catalogue was also produced in the form of a folder containing an introductory statement by Brendel and a set of loose-leaf sheets with each participating artist's name and year of birth and one or two reproductions of works (only in some cases coinciding with pieces included in the exhibition itself).[25] In his introduction, Brendel made a point of noting that the artists whose work was being presented 'do not constitute any consolidate[d] group, nor are they a representation of the Hungarian art'. It seems likely that this was a way of trying to avoid problems with the authorities: proposing that the artists were merely individuals, rather than individuals who were in some way connected to one another, or individuals purporting to 'represent' the nation in any way. However, he also goes on to stress that their work has been shaped by 'definite conditions' and that they have all been 'vitally active in Budapest for a few years', though 'not extensively displayed'. Reading between the lines, it is clear that Brendel is alluding to the cultural politics, if not also the wider politics, of life in the country he had himself chosen to leave behind. It is also clear that he knows how to use the particular tone of the press release, with its characteristic lack of specificity, to make certain allusions to context, without exceeding an art-world remit. He confines himself to writing in a sort of code, legible to all concerned, explaining that artists' conceptual pursuits were directed 'at once towards the purest centres and towards the fringes which they claim for themselves, giving them specific meanings and using them to their advantage'. Arguably, the fringes to which he refers are synonymous with the space occupied by the underground, and his observation that the artists whose work he has selected have found a way to give them 'specific meanings' is an invitation to the reader to participate in the creative process of decoding them.

The intimate space of the gallery was activated in a range of interesting ways, exceeding the installation of propositions and documents on the walls with the addition of elements suspended from the ceiling and a range of floor pieces. Archival photographs show that, rather than wall labels, titles were written directly onto the walls, accompanied by a range of arrows and drawn rectangular outlines; a series of modernist, square, white stools with the words LIVING ARCHIVES, usually in the adjoining room where the archives are held, were deployed in versatile ways as plinths and performance props. One bore stacks of envelopes and a rubber stamp, left over from Endre Tót's stamping performance at the opening (and positioned beneath a wall full of stamped or typed sheets of zeros hung on the wall above); another stool was home to reproduced stacks of Pauer's *Marx–Lenin* piece, consisting of copies of an official photograph of a bust of Marx from Karl-Marx-Stadt on the one hand, and further blank pieces of card with matching Lenin-shaped holes cut out of it, such that one could superimpose the shape of Lenin over the portrait to Marx to reveal a hidden portrait of Lenin in the Marx statue. With his 'Soviet-made' representation of Marx, Pauer called into question the possibility of there being any 'original' Marx to return to, contributing his own tautological take to intellectual debates about the 'reformability of socialism'.[26] On another stool, there was a record player with what Beke has called Lakner's 'phonetic drawing', *Tuk Tuk*, above which a medical cross-section of the throat purports to offer information on the particular qualities of the sound. As Beke recollects, 'if you repeat continuously the word TukTuk, you observe an unconscious voice in between'.[27]

Lakner also showed one of his 'citation pieces', a variation on the last line on Wittgenstein's *Tractatus Logico-Philosophicus*: Whereof one cannot speak, thereof one must be silent' (see also Daniel Véri, 'The Holocaust and the Arts', pp. 209–27). He broke up the sentence into five distinct parts and presented each in a different European language (English, French, German, Hungarian and Polish), so that it became 'Whereof | Il n'est pas possible de | Sprechen | arról | trzeba milczeć' (fig. 6). Far from presenting the phrase in the form of a seamless Central European-oriented Esperanto, Lakner printed vertical dividing lines to demarcate divisions between each phrase, dryly labelling each of these a 'border' ('*granica*' in Polish, is also the term used to denote the borders between nations), thus presenting both the linguistic and the geopolitical isolation of each part of the sentence from the others. It goes without saying that in order to make sense of the whole, one visually has to traverse the borders, conceptually echoing Wittgenstein's tautological point that if something cannot be spoken of then it will necessarily be passed over in silence. In the context of an unofficial Hungarian exhibition in Poland, the necessarily international message to be deciphered clearly acquired further meanings, not least because of the impediments to free movement across European borders in the period.

His card in the exhibition folder showed a second citation piece by Lakner, this time one taken from the Hungarian Marxist philosopher Georg Lukács's essay 'Aesthetic Culture', dated 1913, in which he declared that 'The Form is: the maximum effort in the given possibilities of a given situation.' As the photograph in the folder revealed, rather than being mounted on a wall, the artists' unframed board with the citation written on it was casually propped up against some metal fencing, potentially drawing attention to the limitations of the 'given situation' in question and presenting the debate on aesthetics and politics as being as relevant as ever to that 'given situation'. Given that Lukács was no hero of the Hungarian underground, Lakner's courage in recalling the theoretical openness of his early, pre-revolutionary writings was all the more remarkable.

Pauer's contribution took the form of a selection of *Pseudo* pieces and two copies of his *Pseudo Manifesto*: a flat sheet meticulously airbrushed to look like nonchalant photocopies of crumpled surfaces. The manifesto (translated into Polish for the occasion) was a theory of objects deliberately provoking false ideas, passing by way of minimal and op art to explain that 'PSEUDO sculpture is an imitation of sculpture. PSEUDO sculpture says nothing about sculpture, but about its situation.' In addition to the works on paper, there was a three-dimensional post-minimalist pseudo piece: a rectangular form (Beke recalls that it was pink) with the illusion of a crumpled flat surface airbrushed onto the sides, further complicating matters (in similar ways to Hencze's *Underground (project)*, discussed above) by creating the illusion of three dimensions represented by a two-dimensional form, but actually on a three-dimensional object (fig. 7). Hanging from threads suspended from the ceiling nearby were three sheets of white card with strips of coloured paper just the right width to be held up to one's face to serve as glasses. These formed part of an installation Pauer called *Pseudo voting* whereby the artist had created a visual relay of exchanges between the terms 'yes' and 'no' according to whether one looked through a red filter or not, such that 'yes' became 'no' and vice-versa.[28] That the distorting filter happened to be a red one would doubtless not have been lost on the audience. (See Maja Fowkes and Reuben Fowkes, 'Liberty Controlled', pp. 77–93, for further discussion of the *Pseudo* project.)

The most complex piece was undoubtedly Erdély's photomontage, *Moral Algebra – Solidarity Action*. One element of this consisted of a hard-hitting and complex montage of text and image featuring a French press photograph of a 'Cambodian head hunter' and demonstrating by way of charts and statements that 'according to the logic of massacre, if everybody kills two people, all of humankind can be exterminated in thirty-two moves, considering that a person cannot be killed twice'.[29] As Annamária Szőke has argued, the project rejected 'inhumanity, murder and all forms of warfare'.[30] Another part of the project consisted of a play on the words 'Everybody, Everywhere' on sheets of paper in different languages, echoing Lakner's variation on the Wittgenstein quote. Szentjóby proposes that the piece itself was made by everyone everywhere at the same time, and it is clear that there were a number of

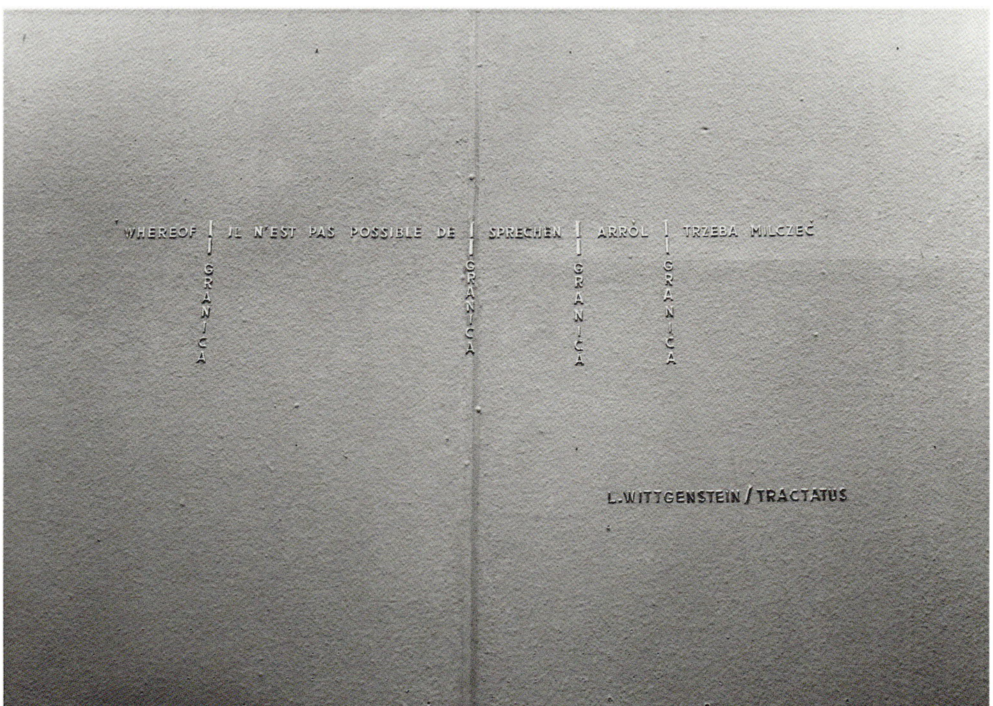

6

6. László Lakner, *Citation Piece (Ludwig Wittgenstein)*, 1972, installation in Galeria Foksal, Warsaw

contributions collaged together as part of the text and photo-board devoted to this theme; Beke notes that his own letter to Erdély on the topic included thirteen different language versions.[31] Individual pages of the exhibition folder were also marked with one of two possible bullet-pointed annotations (in Polish):

- everyone-everywhere-simultaneously
- while others

The annotations designate Tamás Szentjóby/ St Jouby's and Pauer's contributions as fitting in the 'everyone-everywhere-simultaneously' category and Lakner's and Jovánovics's as 'while others'. Assuming that the pages in the catalogue were intended to be housed in alphabetical order, as listed on the title page, Endre Tót's page, which was given over entirely to an assortment of his characteristically empty but expressive zeros, would have been last; it was also the only one to stand alone, without any annotation defining it as either simultaneous or other. Tót's zeros return the spectator elegantly to the theme of silence raised in the first instance by Lakner's Wittgenstein citation, in a gesture of self-censorship.

Szentjóby recollects: 'Since my request for a passport was refused even to Poland (!), I decided to ask the I Ching: WHAT SHOULD I SHOW AT FOKSAL?, make a photo-documentation about the divisions of the sticks (with red flag on them, but black and white photos) and to exhibit the photos and the answer.' The answer he received from the ancient Chinese text, in response to the arrangement of the divination sticks he had cast, served only to confirm his situation: 'AT THIS TIME OF THE YEAR, THE KING DOES NOT TRAVEL.' So, he had his friends bring the result with them to Warsaw for the exhibition where it was installed as a series of photographs of the arrangement of the fallen sticks and texts, on the left, as one entered the gallery space (fig. 7).[32] He also sent instructions for a second interactive piece, relating to censorship mechanisms, with the title *Action Object (the visitor of the exhibition can do what the secret-police does occasionally with letters)*. Its components were 'an official, white, A/3, sealed, postal adhesive envelope' with 'a piece of paper' in it and a 'ready-made stick cut long ways in two parts'. The instructions ran as follows:

place the sticks into the open end of the envelope, shake the paper into the split of the sticks without opening the envelope, roll up the paper on the sticks, pull out the sticks with the paper through the hole at the end of the envelope, read the text aloud written on it: 'NEVER TALK ONE-TO-ONE' (Mahatma Gandhi), roll up the paper on the sticks, replace it in the envelope through the hole at the end of the envelope.[33]

Like Pauer's *Pseudo voting* piece, Szentjóby's invitation to the public was a form of role play: in one case, visitors were encouraged to play at being active citizens, in the other, they were given insight into the bizarre means by which the state surveyed its citizens' private activities, in order to be issued with an eerie warning. The St Jouby card in the exhibition folder, though, consisted of a series of images of his iconic *Portable Trench for Three*, first exhibited at the 'Iparterv' exhibition of 1969 (see also Gábor Dobó and Merse Pál Szeredi, 'Hungarian Culture +/- Europe', pp. 39–57, including fig. 13). The piece notably resisted any clear narrative interpretation while evidently raising a range of troubling spectres with its fragile frame – awkwardly balanced above ground, though of course meant to be dug in *underground*. As such, it introduced another interesting variation on the underground theme, this time in combination with a readymade strategy whereby the artist made something designed to be practical and then installed it in a situation where its only value became conceptual or aesthetic, invoking issues of the front line, the rear-guard, issues around attack and defence, visibility and invisibility, and, perhaps above all, the exposure to danger. These ideas were portable only in dematerialized form because, of course, the fragile trench made of wood, aluminium, gauze, sulphur and cane had not been brought to Warsaw, only photographs.

One of the characteristics that united the selection of works made by Brendel and the artists themselves for the Warsaw audience of this sophisticated gallery space was the degree to which the works transgressed a tautological form of art about art. Irrespective of their often sleek, pared down form, they all point outwards to the surrounding situation, which each of them invites us to re-examine

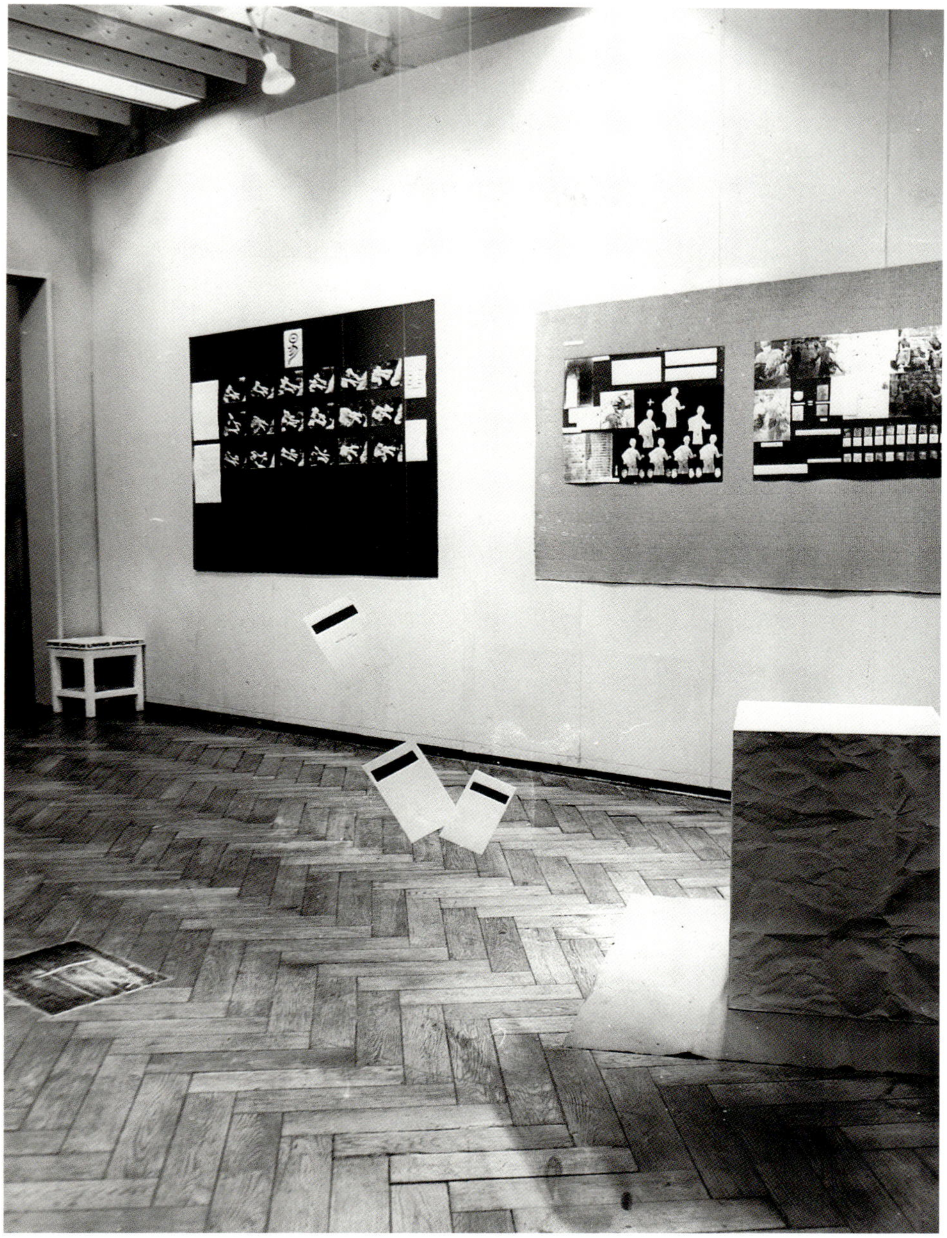

7

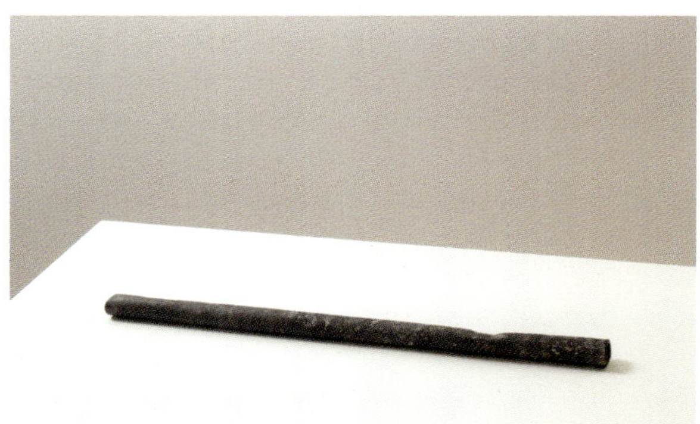

8

7. Hungarian artists' exhibition at Galeria Foksal, Warsaw. Exhibition view showing (from left) Tamás Szentjóby's *I Ching*, Miklós Erdély's *Moral Algebra – Solidarity Action* (detail) and Gyula Pauer's *Pseudo works*, 1972

8. Tamás Szentjóby, *A New Unit of Measurement*, 1965/2012, lead, approx. 3 × 60 cm, Ludwig Múzeum – Kortárs Müvészeti Múzeum, Budapest

in the light of their particular proposal. From a contemporary perspective, it seems extraordinary that the Foksal dared show such powerful works abounding in political overtones, albeit none of them entirely explicit – ranging from an apparent over-identification with activities of a bureaucratic nature (Tót) to the spurious nature of the voting procedures (Pauer) to the denunciation of the global catastrophe of the Cambodian proxy war (Erdély). If the show risked being all the more polemical in view of the coincidence that Richard Nixon would visit the city just a few days after its opening and the fact that security services must have been on high alert, then this presumably served only to demonstrate the lack of overlap between political circles, the circle of regular attendees at the Foksal openings and the public at large.

In his manifesto, Hap had explained that the underground 'does not ban its followers from addressing political themes, since, as a general rule, it neither forbids nor commands, and the emergence of such themes are always the private affair of the respective artist'.[34] The emphasis is strategically placed on individual over collective responsibility, and he insists that underground art is ultimately art that is 'unidentifiable, defies analysis, remains an outsider, and which cannot be appraised and corrupted'. The idea of the 'underground' as separate from official life and from 'the establishment', then, was in part devised as a defence against the awareness of an entropic tendency towards corruption, with all the moral overtones this entailed (staged so drastically in Erdély's *Moral Algebra*), not least because under state socialism, the state was the sole employer and to be unemployed was illegal. Any discussion of the underground therefore inevitably has to confront the moral dichotomies of the day. Hap's manifesto mobilized the idea of private life as a form of defence against what I am tempted to call moral entropy. This was not pure idealism on his part but also a reflection of the operational pragmatism entailed in sustaining an underground that could deliver international cultural encounters.

The Foksal show had been organized on a 'personal' basis, through private invitations to artists. Wiesław Borowski, the founder of the gallery, recalled: 'in fact I'm not really sure how the Hungarian thing was arranged [...] everything was under cover and unofficial or it would never have been allowed'. He noted that the gallery had been in a unique position:

The Czechs and everyone were envious of the possibilities and relative freedom we had in Poland at that time, that we could organise exhibitions [....] They had much tighter restrictions and control there. All the same, we were not allowed to have any exhibitions with them here [....] They [the authorities] wanted to promote a new Poland, free and international, with a happening art scene, but certainly to make impossible the development of any cooperation among artists from the Eastern bloc, to prevent any larger-scale organizations developing that might be potentially subversive.[35]

Different countries were more or less closed at different points in the 1970s, but in almost all cases there was some degree of unofficial cultural exchange among likeminded people internationally.

Piotrowski has argued that the Galeria Foksal had secured its relative autonomy in part by focusing on propagating 'art's right to be concerned solely with itself' and notes that this could be seen as constituting 'a political campaign' of sorts, in hindsight.[36] But he is also at pains to point out that artists' commitment to autonomy in Poland was encouraged by the state, potentially lobotomizing artistic life by co-opting it so as to secure the artistic community's passivity and conformity. Artists' emphasis on personal and stylistic freedom, he contends, established a dangerous precedent, which the authorities exploited, stifling impulses to opposition by appearing to offer freedom of expression. He speculates that there were undoubtedly many artists in Poland, working in what he calls 'so-called independent galleries' (which received financial subventions from the state), who 'simply did not ask themselves whether or to what extent their freedom was controlled and limited' and, in failing to do so, acted in complicity with the 'the pseudo-liberal cultural politics of the Ideological State Apparatus'.[37] If Poland acquired a reputation as the most open of the countries of the Soviet bloc in cultural terms, then this may also have been a measure of the success with which the state bought off critique by encouraging a veneer of autonomy in artistic matters. For Piotrowski, this amounted to the promotion of a 'spirit of opportunism' among artists who espoused modernism and could thereby 'conveniently' adopt the position that 'modernist autonomous art was not supposed to be politically engaged'.[38] This is important to note in so far as it reflects the moral complexities of the situation, and it is worth pointing out that the Hungarian exhibition was one of the most radical shows to be held at the Foksal in terms of addressing the 'given situation'. But if there was a degree of complicity in the gallery's focus on cultivating Western over Eastern contacts, this was also part of a consciously devised programme whose founders were not unaware of what that meant in political terms. Though Borowski recalls at times 'leading the authorities by the nose' in terms of the profile of the gallery, the Hungarian exhibition's radicalism was unique.[39]

In Hungary, the authorities' open hostility to what György Galántai has called artists' 'passive resistance to the aesthetic demands of "socialist realism" [...] treated as political resistance by the regime', resulted in 'initially apolitical artists' grouping together, and step by step became more politicized'.[40] The authorities' surveillance of members of the unofficial art scene by collaborators integrated into their social circle did not achieve its fragmentation. There was reportedly a sense of unity in opposition. The politicization of the nascent Hungarian underground art scene was cemented by the invasion of Czechoslovakia by Warsaw Pact forces in August 1968 and the poignancy, in its wake, of some of the contributions to the 'Iparterv' exhibition of 1969. Alongside a range of pop- and neo-constructivist-oriented works, the independently organized exhibition had (before its forced closure) included Szentjóby's *New Unit of Measurement* (fig. 8) and Gyula Konkoly's *Memorial* (p. 199, fig. 5), both exemplary of the underground position later sketched by Hap in that they incited political subtexts but flatly refused to confirm alluding to them.

After this, diverse strands of the art scene in Budapest came together. György Galántai recalls that artists began to operate 'as a culture or a movement-type network', coalescing around the once derelict Roman Catholic chapel in the village of Balatonboglár, at Lake Balaton, which he had succeeded in leasing in 1968 (see also Maja Fowkes and Reuben Fowkes, 'Liberty Controlled', pp. 77–93).[41] Over the course of 1970–73, Balatonboglári Kápolnaműterem (The Balatonboglár Chapel Studio of György Galántai) held self-organized exhibitions by artists some eight to twelve times per year – their organization delegated to artists grouped according to their interests. A large sign visible from the village appeared on the chapel in 1971, and visitors were able to use a stencil Galántai had made to decorate T-shirts, further advertising the venue. Gyula Pauer sometimes provided guided tours of the exhibitions, and explained to locals that the most important factors were the 'attitude, intellectual disposition and behaviour, which characterize our community and hold us together'.[42]

While there was some delay before an underground Czechoslovak–Hungarian declaration of friendship materialized, the fact that it did at all remains remarkable in the circumstances, and no doubt explains the iconic status of the images taken on the occasion. On 26 August 1972, Balatonboglár was the site of a legendary meeting between Hungarian and Czechoslovak artists almost exactly four years after the Soviet invasion of Czechoslovakia. The meeting happened at the instigation of László Beke, who later recalled that he 'had always been irritated by the fact that Slovaks and Hungarians have seemed to hate one another for 150 years', observing that 'whenever we take a closer look at things, we can co-operate in really productive ways'.[43] Having come across a photograph of Warsaw Pact troops playing tug-of-war after marching into Czechoslovakia in a special issue of the periodical *Pages*, he had the idea of turning the event into a *tableau vivant*, using his international networks to invite eleven experimental artists from Czechoslovakia to meet their Hungarian counterparts at Balatonboglár (fig. 9). Among the Czechoslovak participants were Péter Bartoš, Stano Filko, Rudolf Sikora, Jiří Valoch, Jiří Kocman and Petr Štembera. Hungarians present included Hap himself, as well as Miklós Erdély, Gyula Pauer, Tamás Szentjóby, Endre Tót and others.

The tug-of-war entailed everyone lining up to grab the magazine containing the original image, and pulling. It was exemplary of Beke's later definition of what he calls the 'Eastern European variant' of conceptual art as 'flexible and elastic, ironic, humorous and ambiguous, nonprofessional, communicable, always ready to become a social activity of a group of young people or even an alternative movement [...] most likely an expression of utopian notions of social organisation [...] intrinsically critical of statist regulation.'[44] While Beke admitted that it had been a 'naïve event' in some respects, it yielded extraordinary historical photographs, and an 'action board' documenting individual handshakes of solidarity and forgiveness between the Czechoslovak and Hungarian participants (fig. 10). Pauer observed: 'we symbolically made peace with each other, at a time when our political system was still in conflict with Czechoslovakia. We made peace, and that's what was important.'[45] As Magdalena Radomska has argued, the project ironically 'realized in practice the slogan justifying the Warsaw Pact invasion, namely fraternal support'.[46] The following day the artists drew up a list of a hundred words that sounded similar in Czech, Slovak and Hungarian. By the end of the following summer, the Balatonboglár Chapel Studio was closed on the pretext of a breach in construction law, and boarded up by a team of military policemen.[47]

Thereafter, the central node in the Hungarian underground shifted to the Budapest Fiatal Művészek Klubja (FMK, Young Artists' Club; see also Maja Fowkes and Reuben Fowkes, 'Liberty Controlled', pp. 77–93).[48] Beke's commitment to a Hungarian–Czechoslovak exchange continued when he worked there as a volunteer in the years 1973–76.[49] Júlia Klaniczay recalls that, at the time, it was the only available space for young artists to meet and organize events: 'there was a regular exhibition programme also, so artists could apply to do personal shows, and also if someone had an idea for a programme ... The art director of the club was always a colleague, and you could discuss it so there was not an official application.' Despite this intimacy, the club was large, and an opening might bring in hundreds of guests: 'any member could take in a visitor within him or her'. Unlike other

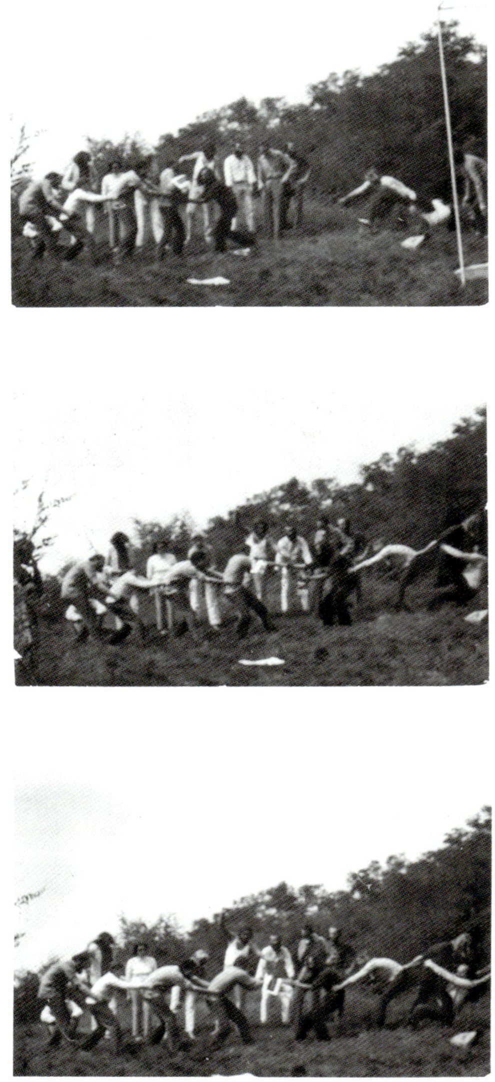

9

9. Meeting of Czech, Slovak and Hungarian artists in Balatonboglár (Tug of War), 1972, Balatonboglár

10. Meeting of Czech, Slovak and Hungarian artists in Balatonboglár. Tableau of László Beke's *Handshaking Action*, 1972, photos mounted on cardboard, 53.5 × 39.7 cm, 1972, Ludwig Múzeum – Kortárs Művészeti Múzeum, Budapest

11. Jan Mlčoch, *Zig – zag – wiggle – waggle*, action, Prague – Budapest, 27–28 February 1975. 'I kept a handful of earthworms on my body in a special bandage. They lived in earth taken from a greenhouse and I gave them water using a syringe. Despite my utmost care, they did not survive the transfer to Budapest.'

10

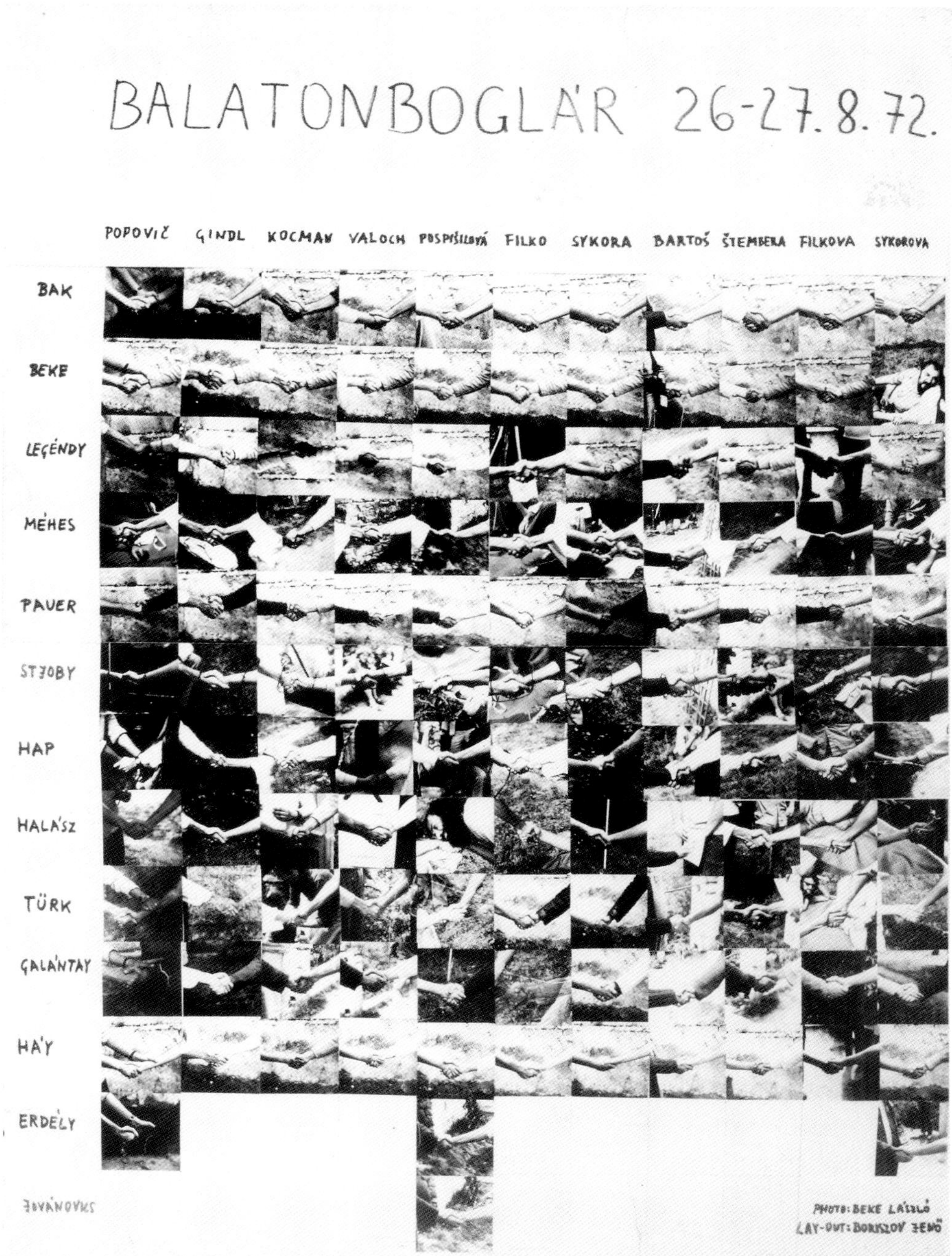
BALATONBOGLÁR 26-27.8.72.
POPOVIČ
GINDL
KOCMAN
VALOCH
POSPÍŠILOVÁ
FILKO
SYKORA
BARTOŠ
ŠTEMBERA
FILKOVA
SYKOROVA
BAK
BEKE
LEGÉNDY
MÉHES
PAUER
SZOBY
HAP
HALÁSZ
TÜRK
GALÁNTAY
HAÝ
ERDÉLY
JOVÁNOVICS
PHOTO: BEKE LÁSZLÓ
LAY-OUT: BORKSZOV JENŐ

11

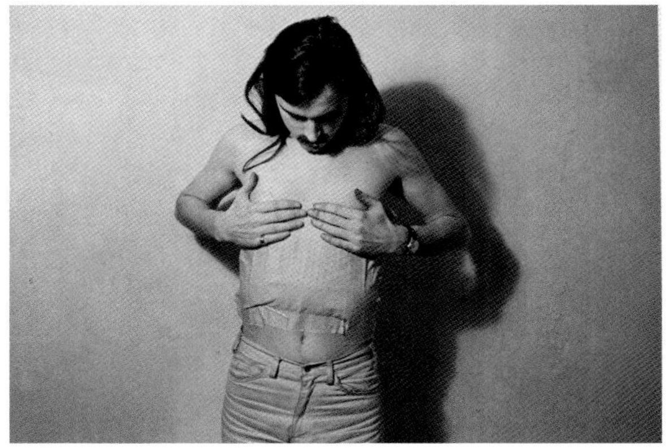

university clubs, which also had events, the FMK 'had a restaurant and a bar and there was a performance room for lecture screenings and so on and there were two exhibition spaces'.[50]

One of the most important exhibitions organized by Beke at the FMK, at least from the point of view of international encounters among underground artists, was an exhibition of work by the Czech performance trio Petr Štembera, Karel Miler and Jan Mlčoch, in 1973. Beke recalls that such events were tolerated up until a new wave of restrictions in 1976, on condition that attendance was limited. Štembera performed a version of his piece *Narcissus No. 1*.[51] Tamás Szentjóby remembers the event and says that Štembera 'must have been the first foreign neo-avant-garde artist invited to Budapest: he ate or burned, "sacrificed", the fragments of his own body – nails, hair, earwax, urine, etc. It was a significant act, almost like an initiation ... We were just standing there, watching the whole operation with enormous empathy and tacit agreement – we felt one with the flow of history.'[52] The first incarnation of *Narcissus No. 1*, performed the previous year, was subtitled as follows: 'After looking at my portrait (photograph) on an improvised "altar" lit by candles, my assistant took some blood from my vein with a syringe. This I mixed with my urine, hair and nails which I had cut off. I then drank this potion, again my eyes fixed on the "altar".' Jan Mlčoch arrived in town with earthworms strapped to his chest in a layer of earth – effectively smuggling live cargo across the Czechoslovak–Hungarian border without being apprehended by police. Despite the earthworms being given water by way of a syringe during the trip, when Mlčoch unwrapped the bandage upon arrival at the FMK, it transpired that the creatures had not survived their ordeal (fig. 11). The American artist Tom Marioni recalls that, on meeting Mlčoch in Prague, having been told the story of the worms by Gábor Attalai in Budapest, the Czech artist had simply 'laughed, and said that the Hungarians are very politically oriented, and they would see the work as being full of intrigue and mystery. As far as he was concerned, the work was about his relationship with the worms.'[53] Rivalling Mlčoch's deadpan attitude to his art, Miler arrived in Budapest with a bag full of stones, which he then swallowed. The stones he exhibited at FMK a few days later were these same stones, but after they had passed through his digestive system.[54]

Mlčoch's attitude to the meaning of his piece ultimately returns us to the central question of Hap's manifesto – the issue is whether Mlčoch was simply involved in a personal affair with his collection of worms, or whether this can legitimately be taken to have meant something more political. Arguably it is as clear a case as any of the personal being political. If the softly spoken position of the 'underground' proposed by Hap (and intellectually parodied in Lakner's internationalization of Wittgenstein's conclusion of the *Tractatus*, among others) was always bound to be vulnerable to accusations of idealism, then by the mid-1970s, many members of this underground had themselves been forced to conclude that maintaining such a creative position might not remain indefinitely tenable. Towards the end of the 1970s, for instance, Prague performance artists decided that their activities no longer carried the same freight and that the language of performance no longer had its former power to produce the sorts of 'horizontal relationships' that I want to argue were the hallmark of the collective underground project, internationally.

The idea of the 'underground' that once linked artistic and political concerns – and insisted on a symbolic and conceptual separation from official life and from 'the establishment' – was an essential mode of defence against moral entropy under a system that nobody imagined would end during their lifetime. While, as Ksenya Gurshtein has proposed, 'taking assumptions articulated by Cold War era dissident writers as the foundation for the analysis of the state socialist cultural situation risks redrawing in the present the ideological lines and moral dichotomies of the period', rather than interrogating such positions as 'historical artefacts in their own right',[55] one might equally maintain that the myriad contradictions that surface in the biographies and the evolution of dissident political thinkers make them their own best critics. The invidiousness of the moral entropy with which Hungarian artists had to wrestle for decades was brilliantly satirized in Miklós Haraszti's *The Aesthetics of Censorship*, devoted to understanding the compromises of a cultural life lived within the framework of what he calls the 'velvet prison'.[56] Haraszti's narrator announces that 'traditional censorship presupposes the inherent opposition of creators and censors; the new censorship strives to eliminate this antagonism. The artist and the censor – the two faces of official culture – diligently and cheerfully cultivate the gardens of art together.'[57] He explains: 'progressive censorship does not demand from us the vision of the perfect society, or even evidence of ideological fealty, but rather the proof of sincere participation'.[58] Clearly, a refusal to participate in the dissemination of official ideology in cultural form was central to the underground project. The difficulty of pursuing such a position long-term had already been dissected and discussed by György Konrád and Iván Szelényi in their secret study of the role of the intelligentsia in socialism, *Intellectuals on the Road to Class Power*, over the course of 1973–74. When their manuscript was discovered and confiscated (though another copy had been successfully smuggled abroad and was to be published), the pair were accused of writing a book that could 'serve as the programme of a counterrevolution', imprisoned, issued with a Prosecutor's Warning banning them from publishing the text, and offered the option of emigrating. After a few years abroad, Konrád returned to Hungary, opting for what came to be known as 'internal emigration': a life circumscribed by surveillance and professional and personal limitation, lived on the margins.[59] The authors of *Intellectuals on the Road to Class Power* had noted that while socialism had failed to deliver a classless society or to improve the lot of workers in any substantial sense, 'the differences between intellectuals and bureaucrats' were 'gradually disappearing': the intelligentsia was effectively ensuring that 'the system functioned effectively by refraining from calling the power hierarchy into question, while perceiving itself as an abused victim and thereby absolving itself of responsibility'.[60] In view of this, there can be no doubt, I think, that Hungarian underground artists were also acutely aware of the degree to which 'communism is a system whose power is sustained not by the police alone'.[61]

1 The magazine survived for five issues, circulated and produced over the course of a year, before a report on it was filed by an informant. The first issue, edited by Hap, included several Czechoslovak contributions. Amy Brouillette, 'Remapping Samizdat: Underground Publishing and the Hungarian Avant-garde, 1966–1975', unpublished MA thesis, Central European University, Budapest, 2009, 65.

2 Dóra Maurer, 'SUMUS', in Dóra Maurer (ed.), *Maurer, Gáyor. Párhuzamos életmüvek / Parallele Lebenswerke / Parallel Oeuvres* (exhibition catalogue). Győr: Városi Müvészeti Múzeum, 2002, 141.

3 Béla Hap, 'Soft-spoken Hungarian Underground Manifesto', *EXPRESSZIÓ*, February 1973. Unpublished English translation by Krisztina Sarkady-Hart of György Galántai, 'Hogyan tudott a müvészet az életben elkezdődni? Adalékok a boglári történethez' [How Art Could Begin as Life? Supplement to the Boglár Story], in Júlia Klaniczay and Edit Sasvári (eds), *Törvénytelen avantgárd: Galántai György balatonboglári kápolnamüterme 1970–1973* [Illegal Avant-garde: The Chapel Studio of György Galántai in Balatonboglár 1970–1973]. Budapest: Artpool, 2003.

4 Klara Kemp-Welch, *Antipolitics in Central European Art: Reticence as Dissidence under Post-Totalitarian Rule 1956–1989*. London: I. B. Tauris, 2014.

5 György Konrád, *Antipolitics: An Essay*, trans. Richard E. Allen. San Diego, New York and London: Harcourt Brace Jovanovich, 1984. I interrogate this in full in my forthcoming monograph *Networking the Bloc* (2018).

6 Hap, 'Soft-spoken Hungarian Underground Manifesto'.

7 Jarosław Kozłowski and Andrzej Kostołowski, NET, 1971.

8 László Beke, proposal dated 19 March 1972. Kozłowski archive.

9 Letter dated 1 March 1972.

10 László Beke, 'On Imagination' typescript from *As Little Johnny Imagines, Letter to My Friends*, 1972. Reproduced and translated in Dóra Hegyi, Zsuzsa László and Eszter Szakács (eds), *Imagination/Idea: The Beginning of Hungarian Conceptual Art – The László Beke Collection 1971*. Budapest: tranzit.hu, 2014, 17.

11 'Prolog', in Hegyi, László and Szakács, *Imagination/Idea*, 3.

12 *Ibid.*, 5.

13 László Beke, 'Conceptual Tendencies in Eastern European Art', in J. Ferver, L. Camnitzer and R. Weiss (eds), *Global Conceptualism: Points of Origin 1950s–1980s*. New York: Queens Museum of Art, 1999, 43.

14 Lucy Lippard, 'Escape Attempts', first printed in Ann Goldstein and Ann Rorimer (eds), *Reconsidering the Object of Art*. Los Angeles: The Museum of Contemporary Art; Cambridge and London: MIT Press, 1995, reproduced in Lucy Lippard, *Six Years: The Dematerialization of the Art Object from 1966 to 1972*. Berkeley, Los Angeles: University of California Press, 1995, vii.

15 Géza Perneczky, *The Magazine Network: The Trends of Alternative Art in the Light of Their Periodicals 1968–1988*. Cologne: Soft Geometry, 1993, 53.

16 *Ibid.*

17 *Ibid.*, 13.

18 Criticism of such an approach for the most part hinges on opposition to the idea of taking Anglo-American conceptual art as a basic starting point and tacking other global developments on to this within the framework of its expansion to an 'ism'. Walter Mignolo's calls to decolonize language, for instance, can clearly be mobilized to make the case for this as an unacceptable starting point.

19 Hegyi, László and Szakács, *Imagination/Idea* , 19.

20 László Beke, letter to Kozłowski, not dated (*c.* 1973), Kozłowski archive.

21 Author's interview with László Beke, Budapest, 18 April 2014.

22 *Ibid.*

23 Piotr Piotrowski, 'Nationalizing Modernism: Exhibitions of Hungarian and Czechoslovakian Avant-garde in Warsaw', in Jérôme Bazin, Pascal Dubourg Glatigny and Piotr Piotrowski (eds), *Art Beyond Borders: Artistic Exchange in Communist Europe (1945–1989)*. Budapest: Central European University Press, 2016, 209–25.

24 See also Magdalena Radomska, *Polityka kierunkow neoawangardy wegierskiej (1966–1980)* [The Politics of the Hungarian Neo-avant-garde Movements (1966–1980)]. Kraków: Uniwersytas, 2013; Kemp-Welch, *Antipolitics*.

25 That Miklós Erdély is listed under Miklós rather than his family name, unlike all the other artists, is intriguing in so far as it must either mean that Brendel was not involved in overseeing the catalogue, or that Erdély's identity was deliberately obfuscated in the documentation by playing with the Hungarian convention of putting surnames before forenames.

26 Author's interview with Miklós Haraszti, Budapest, November 2003.

27 Author's email correspondence with László Beke, 2 July 2017.

28 *Ibid.*

29 Annamária Szőke, 'Miklós Erdély: Moral Algebra – Solidarity Action (1972). A case-study', trans. Zsuzsanna Szegedy-Maszák. Transcript of 'Vivid [Radical] Memory' workshop, Stuttgart, 2007. Available online at http://www.vividradicalmemory.org/htm/workshop/stu_essays/szoke.pdf (6 August 2017).

30 Szőke, 'Miklós Erdély: Moral Algebra', 7.

31 Author's email correspondence with László Beke, 2 July 2017.

32 Author's email correspondence with Tamás Szentjóby, 31 June 2017.

33 Author's email correspondence with Tamás Szentjóby, 5 July 2017.

34 Hap, 'Soft-spoken Hungarian Underground Manifesto'.

35 Author's interview with Wiesław Borowski in Warsaw, April 2004.

36 Piotr Piotrowski, *Art and Democracy in Post-Communist Europe*. London: Reaktion, 2012, 82.
37 *Ibid.*, 87.
38 *Ibid.*
39 Author's interview with Wiesław Borowski in Warsaw, April 2004.
40 Galántai, 'Hogyan tudott a művészet az életben elkezdődni?'.
41 *Ibid.*
42 *Ibid.*
43 Interview with László Beke. Originally printed in Klaniczay and Sasvári, *Törvénytelen avantgárd*, 141, reproduced and translated in Dóra Hegyi, Sándor Hornyik and Zsuzsa László (eds), *Parallel Chronologies: 'Other' Revolutionary Traditions: How Art Becomes Public. An Exhibition in Newspaper Format*. Budapest: Tranzit Hungary Public Benefit Association, 2011, 33.
44 Beke, 'Conceptual Tendencies', 42.
45 Interview with Gyula Pauer, 1998. Originally printed in Klaniczay and Sasvári, *Törvénytelen avantgárd*, 142.
46 Radomska, 'Correcting the Czech(oslovakian) Error', in Bazin, Glatigny and Piotrowski, *Art Beyond Borders*, p. 376.
47 Galántai, 'Hogyan tudott a művészet az életben elkezdődni?'.
48 The club is the focus of an interview-based monograph by Tamás Szentjóby under the pseudonym: Tamás St Turba, *FIKA (Fiatal Művészek Klubja)/BOGEY (The Young Artists' Club), An interview with Tamás St Auby*, trans. Katalin Orbán. Budapest: Ludwig Museum, 2006.
49 Author's interview with László Beke, Budapest, 18 April 2014.
50 Author's interview with Júlia Klaniczay, Budapest, 26 May 2016.
51 First performed in Prague, 28 December 1974.
52 St Turba, *FIKA*, 30.
53 Tom Marioni, *Vision 2*. San Francisco: Crown Press Point, 1976, 12.
54 Beke, personal communication with Gergely Kovaks, 9 August 2017.
55 Ksenya Gurshtein, 'Dissecting Dissent and its Discontents,' *ArtMargins*, Vol. 5, No. 1, 2016, 96–107.
56 *The Aesthetics of Censorship* was first published in French as *L'Artiste d'Etat* in 1983, then in English as *The Velvet Prison* and only in 1986 in Hungarian samizdat as *A cenzúra esztétikája*.
57 Miklós Haraszti, *The Velvet Prison: Artists Under State Socialism*, trans. Katalin and Stephen Landesmann. London: Tauris & Co, 1988, 7.
58 *Ibid.*, 79.
59 György Konrád, foreword to Haraszti, *The Velvet Prison*, xii.
60 György Konrád, *A Guest in My Own Country*. New York: Other Press, 2007, 265.
61 Konrád, foreword to Haraszti, *The Velvet Prison*, xiii.

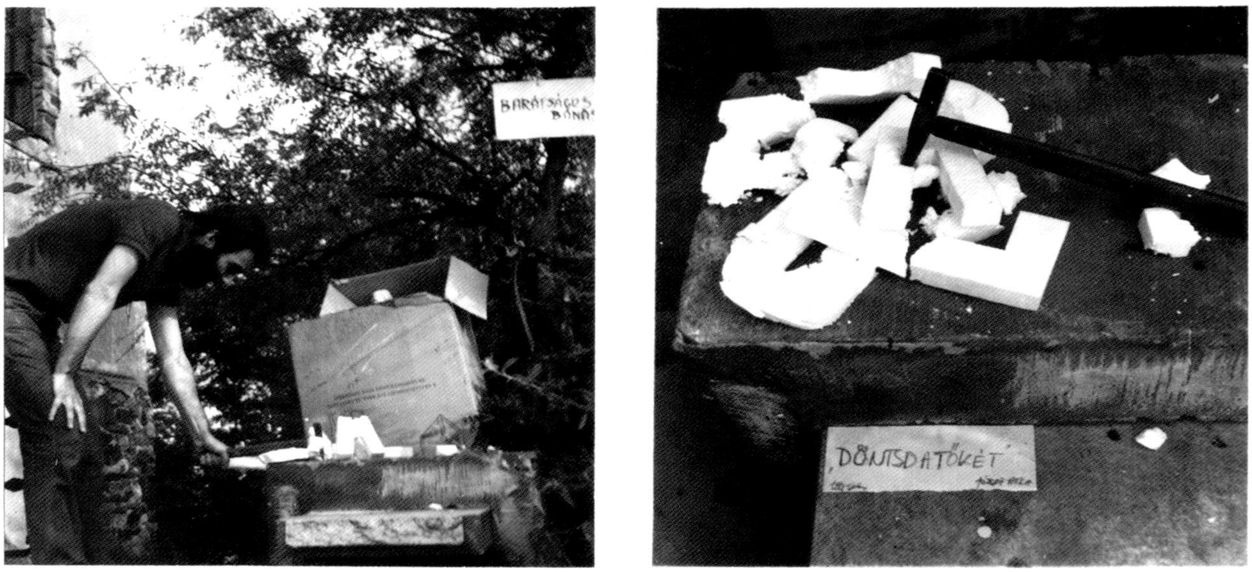

1

1. Gábor Tóth, *Smash Capital!*, 1973, action documentation, photos taken at the Balatonboglár Chapel Studio of György Galántai, silver gelatine print, 15 × 32 cm, Private collection

Emese Kürti

Poetry in Action

Language as a Performative Medium in the Hungarian Neo-avant-garde

A photograph, famous in Hungarian cultural history, shows Attila József, an emblematic figure of Hungarian poetry, imitating felling a tree with a broad swing. The young communist poet's freshly banned 1931 volume *Döntsd a tőkét* (the title of which can be translated as 'Smash Capital!' but can also mean 'Chop at the roots') was tied to a tree trunk by his friends, when they were out hiking together. The poet, in posing for the photo, realized the spontaneous performativity of poetry and action, promising, as it were, the actionism of the 1960s ahead of its time.

Forty years later, in 1973, the artist Gábor Tóth evoked this historical event in György Galántai's Balatonboglári Kápolnaműterem (the Balatonboglár Chapel Studio of György Galántai), an emblematic venue of the Hungarian neo-avant-garde (see Maja Fowkes and Reuben Fowkes, 'Liberty Controlled', pp. 77–93, and Klara Kemp-Welch, 'Soft-spoken Encounters', pp. 273–89). This action, entitled *Smash Capital!* (fig. 1), was performed during 'TEXTS', an international exhibition of concrete and visual poetry co-organized with Dóra Maurer, and it entailed him smashing styrofoam letters with a hammer. The title referred to Attila József's poem – well-known to the point of a cliché in Hungarian intellectual life – while also ironically commenting on the anti-capitalistic content of the poem, given the context of socialism.

Attila József became a celebrated proletarian poet of the Kádár regime after the quashed 1956 Hungarian revolution. Although he was one of the greatest figures of twentieth-century progressive poetry in Hungary, the appropriation of his Marxism by the socialist regime made him a problematic figure for later modernist generations of poets. As for the apolitical layers of his poetry, their extreme subjectiveness also irritated the neo-avant-garde poets of the 1960s, who favoured an elimination of the lyrical subject. The mid-1960s neo-avant-garde turn in Hungarian literature rejected classic poetry and the central role of the lyrical subject, and returned instead to the linguistic-visual heritage of the historical avant-garde.[1] So Gábor Tóth's work not only aimed to rethink leftist ideology, but also relied on what J. L. Austin's speech-act theory defines as the performative, or a performative utterance. Austin deconstructs the traditional dichotomy of words and actions and calls attention to speech acts as actions. Gábor Tóth's action interrogated the performative of *Smash Capital!* – the self-evident, symmetrical relationship between action and language – when he turned objectified signs (letters) into the objects of a semiotic action.[2]

Kristine Stiles defines actionism as a new form of communication that emerged in the 1960s and strengthened the role of perception and experience in the public space in which the artist intervenes.[3] The event unfolding in time and space became a new, independent medium of action concurrently with the linguistic turn, which art historians have largely attributed to the activities of John Cage in New York due to the musical genealogy of Fluxus. The late 1950s saw an increasing prominence of language in the visual arts, as printed, painted or vocalized words permeated visual art practice and were closely intertwined with poetry and experimental music.[4] The brief textual scores for Fluxus events could be interpreted as autonomous texts, as practical instructions for actions, but also as objects. The concept of intermedia originated from Dick Higgins[5] and the intellectual circles of Fluxus, and spread to the international art scene, including countries behind the Iron Curtain, where East European artists often independently reached the same conclusions as their Western counterparts.

One can also examine Hungarian actionism in terms of its symbiotic relationship with poetry. Literature and a critical approach to language played an important part in the neo-avant-garde oeuvres taking shape in the 1960s. As will be shown below, linguistic experimentation was not merely a launching pad for actionist practice by the neo-avant-garde authors who employed the dialectic, inter-relationist approach of intermedia; in fact, they operated simultaneously in the spheres of several mediums (visual art, theatre and literature). This new approach in the first visual actions emerged in tandem with the neo-avant-garde turn in literature, and the mutual interest between the two helped alleviate the prior isolation of the mediums. Hungarian actionism can be described as expanded poetry, a linguistic performative transpiring in time and space, in which – in the spirit of Jacques Derrida's interpretation – 'gesture and speech have not yet been separated by the logic of representation'.[6]

Given the traditionally literature-centric culture of Hungary and the reality of socialist cultural politics at the time, any initiative that was a critical renewal of language was inescapably politicized. As art historian György Széphelyi wrote about his brother, the poet and performer Tibor Hajas, the most authentic expression of his actionism was his 'refusal to speak the same language as the powers-that-be'.[7] While one should not ignore the historical context of this sentence after the demise of the socialist state and political transition of 1989, the intention of ignoring dominant discourses and the creation of a parallel construct (culture, language and a system of institutions) was one of the crucial aspects of the neo-avant-garde in the 1960s and 1970s. The case studies that follow present such parallel strategies and positions aiming at autonomy.

The performative turn of art occurred in Hungary – like in other art scenes of the region – in the mid-1960s, concurrently with the emergence of new mediums critiquing the traditional concept of the art object. The first happening (*The Lunch. In memoriam Batu Khan*, fig. 2) was organized by Gábor Altorjay

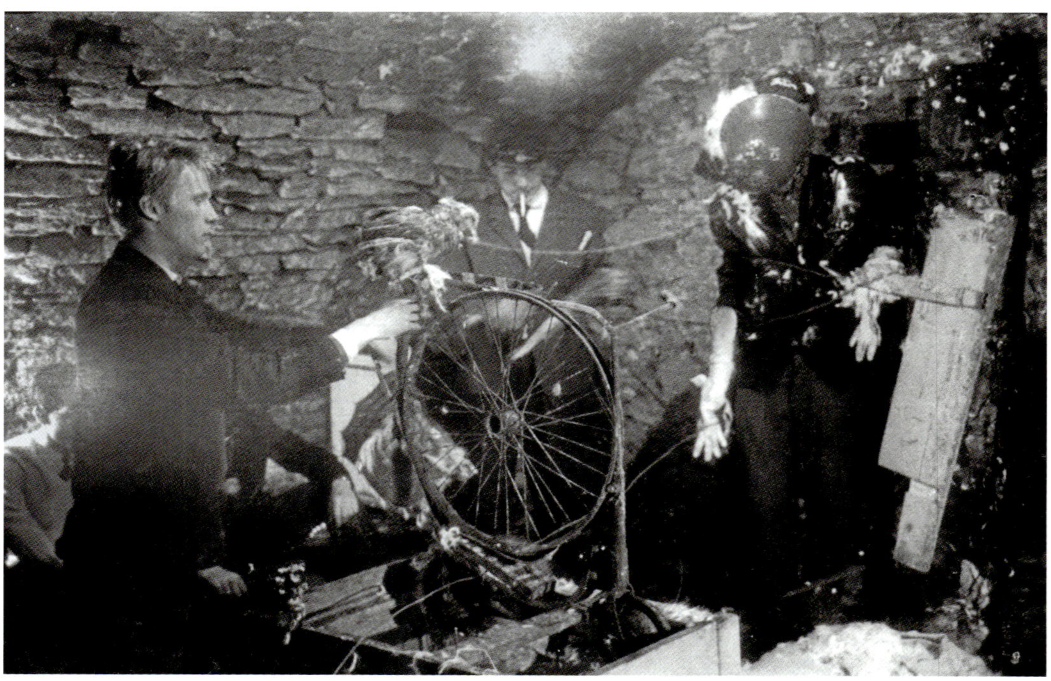

2

2. Gábor Altorjay – Tamás Szentjóby, *The Lunch. In memoriam Batu Khan* (happening), 1966, private house, Budapest

and Tamás Szentjóby in June 1966 in the cellar of a private house in Budapest.[8] The venue ironically reflected the 'underground' nature of the event outside the system of art institutions; Altorjay and Szentjóby used a series of random objects to execute the destruction that was the core of the happening, and the randomness generated surreal associations. Szentjóby, the underground poet, was typing on a typewriter near the entrance, while buried hip-deep in the ground, then Polish composer Krzysztof Penderecki's piece on the apocalyptic theme of Hiroshima was played, and the happening began with the consumption of a dish called paprika potatoes. The happening led to an increasingly brutal and chaotic series of events, including vomiting and throwing plaster on the wall and the participants, whom were all tied together with different objects in the cellar. The devices of the happening and its narrative partly built on audience reaction were clearly opposed to traditional art, but the conception of *The Lunch* can also be derived from an expanded concept of poetry. As Szentjóby said, 'everything is poetry to begin with', so the emergence of a happening does not amount to some kind of poetry-to-action turn; rather it is poetry that pours forth in the direction of the happening, environment and action, and even further towards concrete poetry, object, music and film.[9]

The turn or shift in Szentjóby's oeuvre – after his traditionally structured mystical poetry written until the mid-1960s – resulted from a reassessment of the linguistic and visual functions of poetry. Traditional poetry writing, based on linguistic meaning and therefore confined to the local linguistic boundaries of Hungarian interpretation, was replaced by the visual focus of contemporary avant-garde poetry.[10] The picture-poems he created after the mid-1960s were montages of texts, visual components, found texts and drawings of disparate quality; these were parts of an experimental art in which action was a central component. Picture-poems, poem-pictures and poem-objects aim at actively engaging the reader. At times, the legibility of a text needs to be restored by the viewer's intervention, such as smoothing the sheet of paper. At other times, it is the crumpling of the paper that marks traditional and discursively intact texts as invalid and privileges the processual approach of the neo-avant-garde. So, language does not merely convey the poetic, but also – intermedially – visuality and intervention (fig. 3).

Szentjóby's expanded notion of poetry resonates with Allan Kaprow's theory of the happening, which defines the happening as an expanded environment, the mediums being 'the passive and active sides of a single coin'.[11] Kaprow identified six criteria of the happening, the first of which was the breaking of the boundary between life and art, and he also stressed the simplicity of the happening, its distance from theatre and its affinity with collage. His examples of music were taken from the twentieth-century and contemporary avant-garde, with reference to Arnold Schönberg's and John Cage's approach to music.[12] The first Hungarian happenings also followed the intellectual 'polymorphous' (a term used by George Maciunas) actionism of the New York school with its origins in music. Altorjay's and Szentjóby's inquiry was directed towards experimental music – set against the dominance of modernist abstract painting – which was identical with the logic of the international trends: it was the rejection of the medium of painting that led them to organizing the happening. They participated in the important Polish contemporary music festival, Warszawska Jesień (Warsaw Autumn), in 1964 and 1965, where they attended performances and events by Cornelius Cardew, David Tudor and John Cage, among others.[13] Yet, they actually learned about the existence of happening as a contemporary genre indirectly, from a Hungarian account. A derisive article in the official Hungarian press gave some examples and defined the happening as a decadent symptom of 'American imperialism'.[14] Given the negative tone of the article, the first happening was motivated by a species of cold-war defiance; in the polarized world political situation, this expressed an unequivocal commitment to contemporary American art, which was labelled 'foreign', 'cosmopolitan' and 'imperialist' in the official rhetoric (fig. 4).

This alliance with the Western neo-avant-garde distinguishes the cultural identity of Hungarian actionism from happening practices elsewhere in the region. Stano Filko and Alex Mlynárčik of Bratislava appropriated

3. Tamás Szentjóby, *To read* (action), headquarters of Iparterv (Ipari Épülettervező Vállalat/Industrial Buildings Consulting Co.), Budapest, 1968

4. Tamás Szentjóby, *Harakiri*, 1967, typed text, paper, 3 pieces, 29.7 × 21 cm, Szépművészeti Múzeum – Magyar Nemzeti Galéria, Budapest

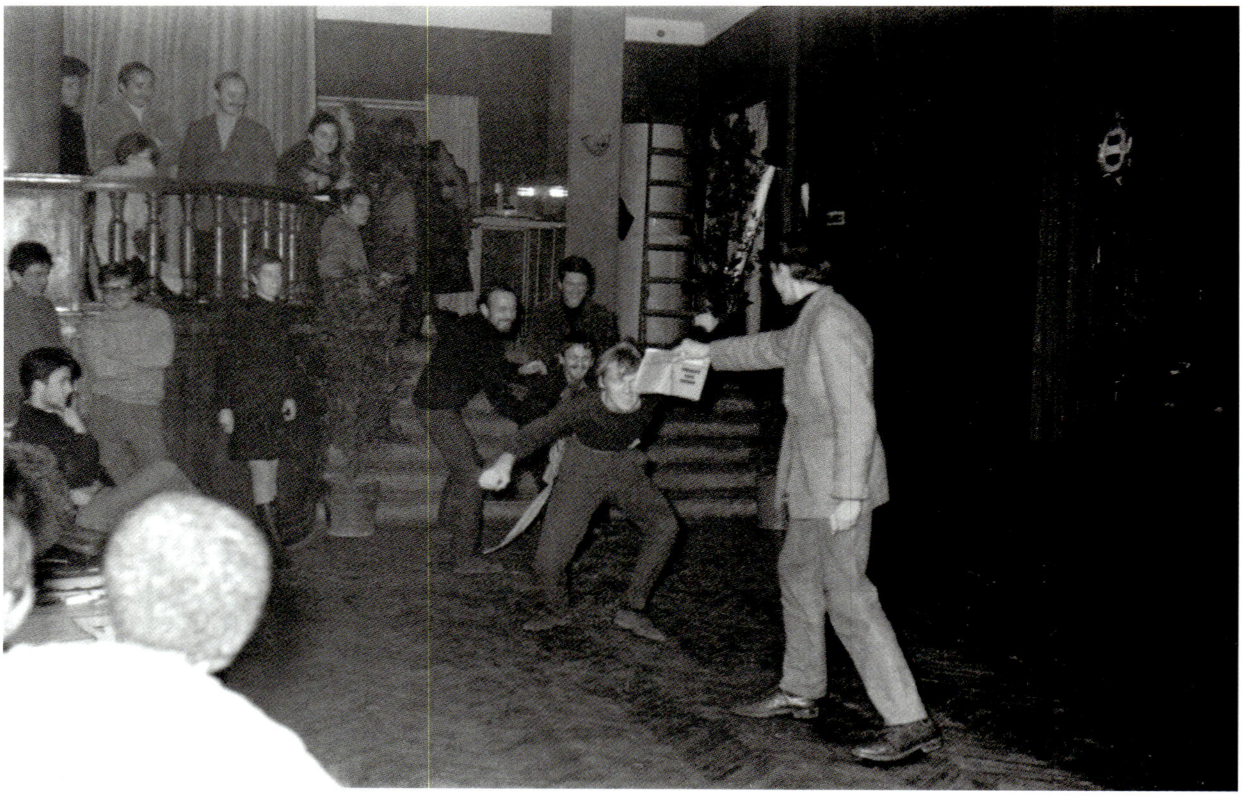

3

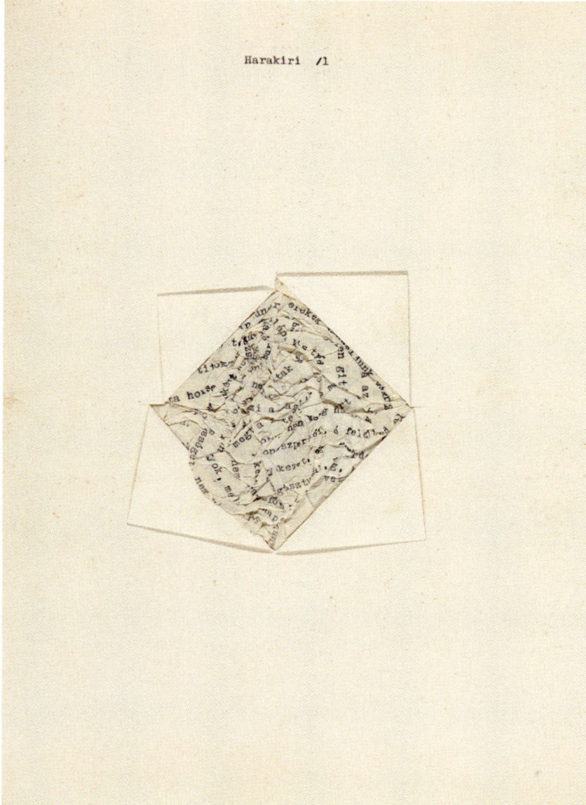
Harakiri /1

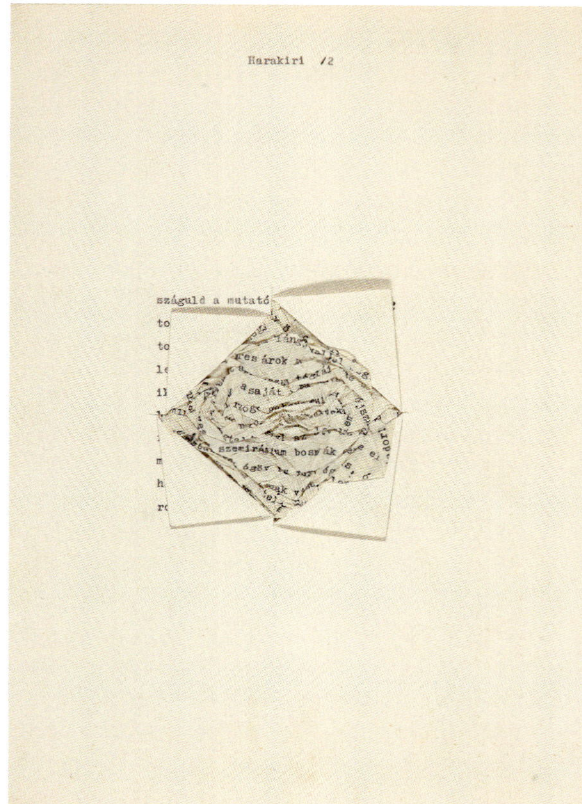
Harakiri /2
száguld a mutató

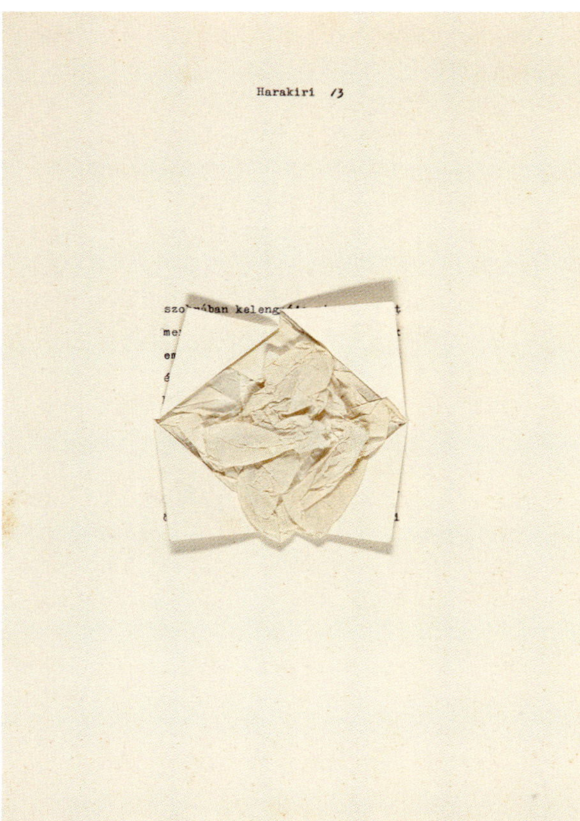
Harakiri /3

the image of the crowd mobilized for political purposes; their manifesto and action plan *Happsoc I* (1965) was coined from the words 'Happening', 'society' and 'socialism'. In Claire Bishop's words, Filko and Mlynárčik's ethnographic interpretation of the spectacle of state parades re-coded the event as a kind of 'sociological happening'.[15] The Slovakian Július Koller, who composed a manifesto of *Anti-Happening* in 1965, distanced himself from the spirit of the American happening even more radically. Koller considered the happening to be no more than a theatrical, popular Western fad that tore through the Bratislava art scene, and he used bureaucratic language to parody his fashionable contemporaries.[16] The future doyen of 'East European Fluxus', the Czech Milán Knizák was perhaps best positioned to meet Kaprow's criteria thanks to his extensive contacts with the American avant-garde, though he sometimes proved even more radical.[17]

The first Hungarian happening was based on the model of Kaprow's happenings both in construction and in its motifs,[18] as it transpired as an escalating nonverbal montage, including the abuse of the audience, concluding in the participants' ecstasy. All of this happened intuitively, however, without any prior direct experience of a happening. The first encounter of Hungarian actionists with an actual happening was in Poland in 1967, when they participated in Tadeusz Kantor's *Panoramic Sea Happening* and met one of the most significant contemporary artists of the region.[19]

By this time, Altorjay's and Szentjóby's approach to the new genre was theoretical in nature, and they were helped by one of the important sourcebooks of the period, *Happenings, Fluxus, Pop Art, Nouveau Réalisme: Eine Dokumentation*, which included texts by Joseph Beuys, Wolf Vostell and Allan Kaprow among others.[20] Both of them analysed the relationship between the happening and other mediums. Influenced most of all by Kantor at that time, Altorjay was intrigued by the relationship between the happening and theatre, and he planned to write a book on the topic. Szentjóby, however, defined the happening as a critical genre and the most avant-garde medium, which transcended the aesthetic dimensions of art and could influence the workings of reality:

A parallel situation: on the one hand, an elimination of the status quo, on the other the initiation of a new history at the same time, in the same place: on a parallel course. In parallel with the way art wanted it to no avail. Compared to the happening-ecstasy, art is imperceptible. Compared to the self-aesthetics of an action, art is unaesthetic. This is why the happening is non-art-art.[21]

Gábor Altorjay emigrated to West Germany in 1967 – partly to escape police harassment due to his participation in happenings – and joined Wolf Vostell's circle. Altorjay's activities in Germany grew organically out of his practice in Hungarian Fluxus, including his conscious representation of 'Eastern actionism'. He was eager to promote Hungarian actionism in the 'West' and planned to publish anthologies that were to include writings and works by Szentjóby and Miklós Erdély along with those of contemporary German artists. One of his first moves was to realize Miklós Erdély's object *Newspaper Cake* (1967) in Stuttgart and to invite Erdély to Nuremberg, where they performed a joint action (*Building a Wall*, 1968).

Influenced by the New Left and the local communities of German activism shaping the revolutionary events of 1968, Altorjay began to create more radical, political and often participatory works. One of the important spaces for this activity was the art collective and commune Kombinat 1 in Cologne, founded by Mauricio Kagel, Wolf Vostell and others; Altorjay joined them in 1968 and participated in several joint actions there. They made and reproduced cheap objects, multiples in the spirit of Fluxus as a critique of the art market, but also to ensure a broader access to art. Altorjay's objects and actions frequently reflected on topics of current political events and were based on the symbols of the cold-war superpowers, such as kvass (the Slavic fermented drink made from rye bread), Coca-Cola and flags. His environmental works – which were linked to collective action series that were institutional critiques, such as the *Fünf Tage Rennen* (Five Days of Racing) organized in opposition to the Cologne Fair – have affinities with those of Vostell (fig. 5).

Tamás Szentjóby created his own intermedial programme *Parallel Course/Study Track* in the late 1960s and realized a

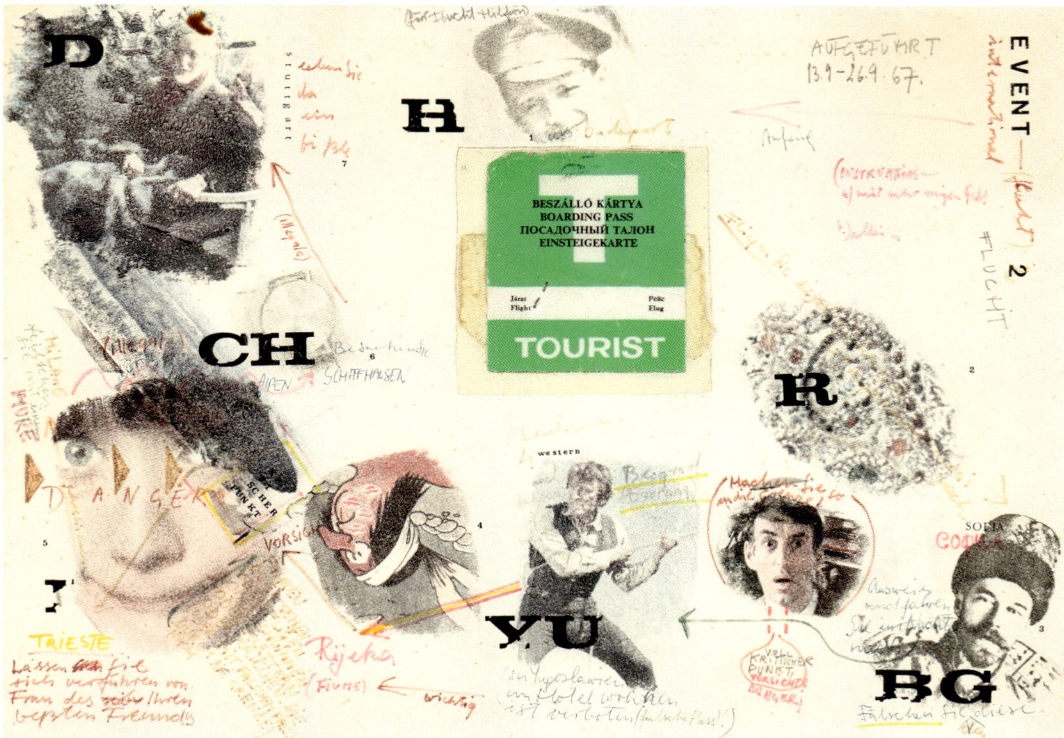

5

5. Gábor Altorjay, *My Path to Freedom*, 1967, collage, frottage, mixed media, 29.5 × 41.5 cm, Private collection

number of objects, visual poems and actions in this framework (see also Flóra Barkóczi, 'Creative (Dis)Courses', pp. 95–109). *Parallel Course* focused on the concept of 'change' as a species of pedagogical programme of alternative art, analogous to Joseph Beuys's open university courses and Robert Filliou's alternative art pedagogy. It was around 1968 that Szentjóby gradually shifted from the neutral intellectual model of Fluxus events to a growing interest in political topics, the events of the contemporary 'Western' New Left, human rights issues, and classic leftist subjects like labour and strikes. He organized actions jointly with Miklós Erdély and László Méhes in 1968 to accompany the 'Iparterv' exhibition, the first major group event of the Hungarian neo-avant-garde (see also Gábor Dobó and Merse Pál Szeredi, 'Hungarian Culture +/- Europe', pp. 39–57, for more information on the 'Iparterv' exhibitions).[22]

Szentjóby held two actions that powerfully involved the audience: the text-based *Distance*, amplified by a tape recorder, and an 'action reading'.[23] The script of the latter states that Szentjóby tied straps around his waist and handed the end of the straps to some participants. Another performer held a book in front of Szentjóby and he read aloud from it. The book was held farther and farther from him, and its legibility was determined by the other performer and the audience members holding the straps. After a few minutes of strenuous effort, Szentjóby knocked the book out of his performing partner's hand. The event can be interpreted more generally as a commentary on free will or as a critique of access to information in the cold-war environment. It is worth noting, however, that the volume in question was the selected works of quantum physicist Werner Heisenberg, published in 1967. Recalling the action in 1983,

Miklós Erdély, who based the majority of his own works on elements of contemporary natural science, said Szentjóby tended to reject the methods of natural science as 'incomprehensible'.[24] Given this, the action can also be interpreted as a critique of the scientific rhetoric and mindset that dominated cold-war discourses.

Miklós Erdély performed three text-based actions in connection with the 'Iparterv' exhibition. It took Erdély fifteen years' experience as a poet to realize the limits of language; inspired by the exactitude of twentieth-century scientific thought, he called this 'categorical poetry'. 'The confusion of consciousness can occur via the confusion of language. [...] The poet's task is to loosen the restrictions of language to make room for the new,' he said in conversation.[25] The 'Iparterv' actions involved readings of fragmented texts combining avant-garde language with scientific topics in a montage-like structure. The text of the action *Dirac in Front of the Cinema Box Office* (figs 6 and 7), which was composed in advance, reflected the concepts and spatio-temporal views of the contemporary scientific worldview based on quantum physics. The dialogic text was recited by Erdély, Miklós Urbán, Tamás Cseh and Tamás Szentjóby standing in single file. Whoever uttered a sentence took a step forward, so they slowly moved towards the exit. However, a large sign and an arrow pointing in the direction opposite to their movement indicated 'the direction of truth flow'. Using quantum physicist Paul Dirac's hole theory about the creation of the positron, Erdély focused on the paradoxical incompatibility of everyday and scientific thought. Yet the juxtaposition of the recited text, the sign and the movement of the participants also implied that the world was composed of matter and anti-matter together, and its structure was constantly changing according to the logic of quantum physics.

Tamás Szentjóby's happening *UFO* was held on 1 May 1968, the International Workers' Day and the most important holiday of the socialist system.[26] Szentjóby had been corresponding with Katalin Ladik, one of the most significant authors of Hungarian avant-garde poetry in Yugoslavia, for a year by this time. Ladik attracted a great deal of attention in literary life with her erotic, surreal poems on topics unusual for women authors at the time. The *UFO* happening was the occasion of their first meeting in person. Upon her arrival in Budapest, Katalin Ladik received a letter via the concierge of her hotel. The letter included a series of instructions for their meeting the following day: Szentjóby informed her that a man with a dog would be waiting for her in front of the hotel and that she was to sit in his car.

The car took Ladik to the bank of the Danube in Szentendre, a small town nearby, where she found a human body wrapped in aluminium foil. A bit further off, a man unclothed from the waist up – Miklós Erdély – was flagellating himself. Ladik knew what she was supposed to do without any instruction and slowly unwrapped the body. It was Szentjóby, who sat up and opened a can of fish, which he proceeded to share with Ladik, before they returned to the city.

Katalin Ladik said her participation in the *UFO* happening was formative for her own later performance practice. Her relationship with the neo-avant-garde in Hungary and the happening realized jointly with Szentjóby inspired her to explore new forms that gave her creative work a new perspective and shifted it towards performativity. Even her first volume, *The Ballad of the Silver Bicycle* (1968), went beyond a simple printed book by including an audio record supplement, and the role of sound kept rising in importance later on. She interpreted her body as an instrument, and sounded her unique vocal technique in an archaic-folkloristic register, which resulted in a radically new, feminine version of contemporary phonic poetry.

The manuscript for Ladik's *UFO Party* (1969) refers back to the happening experience shared with Szentjóby, and the enlarging or shrinking of the font size in the text evokes the physical dimensions of the flow of sounds. As Hendrik Folkerts remarked, this score could itself be interpreted as concrete poetry and 'demonstrates the search for a visual language to denote the asemantic use of the artist's voice in a highly ceremonial environment'.[27]

Katalin Ladik burst onto the Hungarian cultural scene with her first performance. She appeared in 1970 in a joint performance with Jenő Balaskó, a well-known figure of Hungarian neo-avant-garde poetry previously

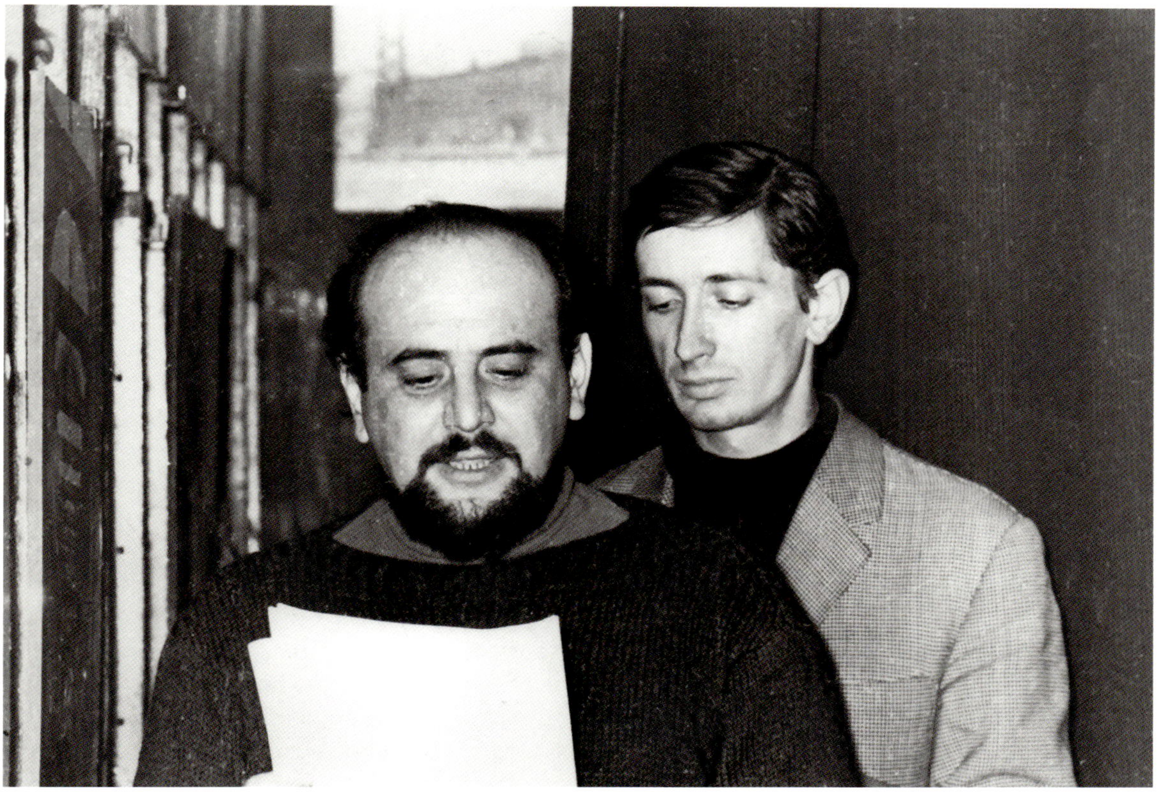

6

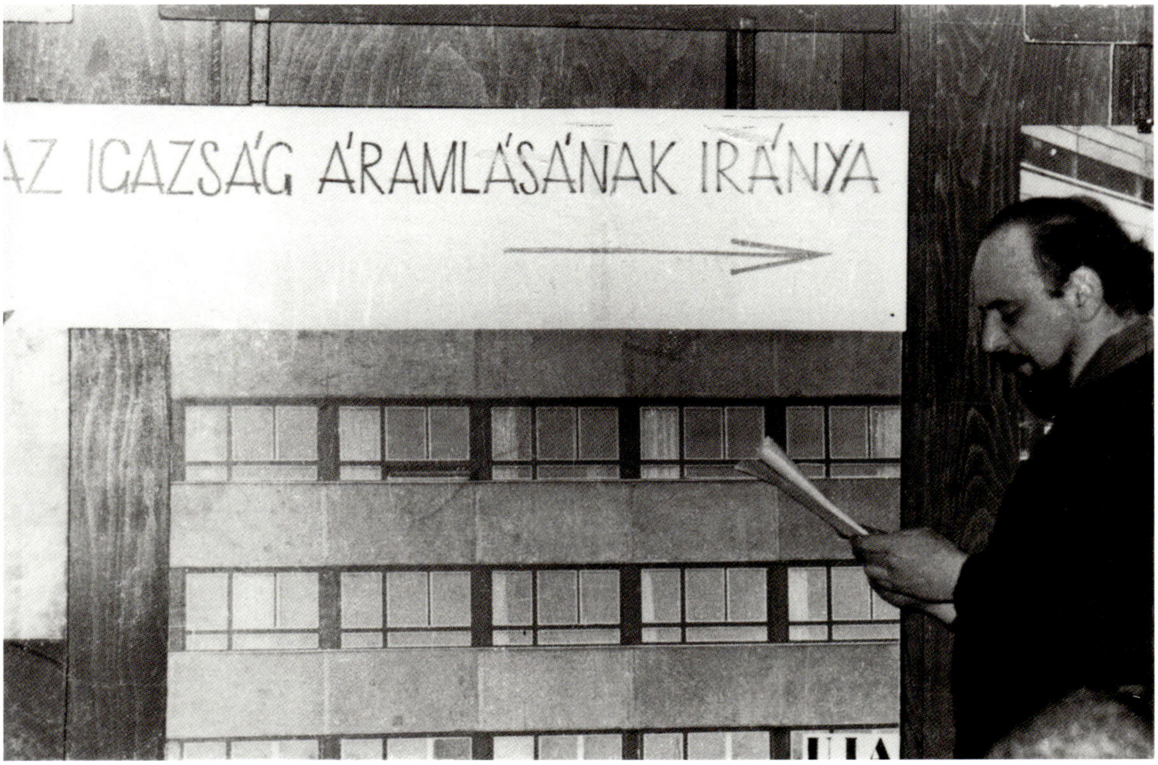

7

6 & 7. Miklós Erdély, *Three Quarks for King Marke (Dirac in Front of the Cinema Box Office)*, performance in the headquarters of the Iparterv (Ipari Épülettervező Vállalat/Industrial Buildings Consulting Co.), Budapest, 29 November 1968

imprisoned for his involvement in the 1956 revolution. The event took place at the József Attila Művelődési Központ, a cultural centre in Budapest typical of the underground venues of the period. According to the script, Ladik read her poetry in a distinct recitativo style she had developed, then left the stage for a few minutes. She returned to the darkened room with a candle and performed a shamanistic, ritual 'voco-visual' performance that utterly shocked the audience (fig. 8). This mode of poetic performance was unimaginable in Hungary before Ladik's appearance, and particularly in the case of a female performer; in fact, Katalin Ladik's phonic performance was unique even by international standards. François Dufrêne, who participated in phonic poetry events with Ladik several times in the 1970s, thought performers should have 'a voice that varies in intensity from the natural tone to the most irritating artifice'.[28] The erotic effect of the bearskin barely covering Ladik's body, the folkloristic instruments, the broad range of her guttural sounds, the ecstatic effect of her performance style that dissolved into pure phonic poetry, her wheezing and screams – these were all very distant from the modernist poetry prevailing in the period. Moreover, art and performance spaces that were used as part of the official representation of culture in Hungary were dominated by doses of highly controlled popular culture, while the youth subculture was regulated by the rules of macho sexuality interpreted as a space of freedom. Given this, the condemnation of public nudity became a common ground for participants of both the official and unofficial scenes. Ladik's branding as the 'naked poetess' deflected public discourse from the critical edge of her performance that positioned her in opposition to a masculine environment. Furthermore, the interpretive focus on the body deflected attention from the other mediums of her art, even though the Ladik phenomenon, which took shape in the 1970s, was unique due to its medial connection between body art and phonic poetry, the movement of linguistic experimentation into spatiality, and the reinterpretation of musicality.

8

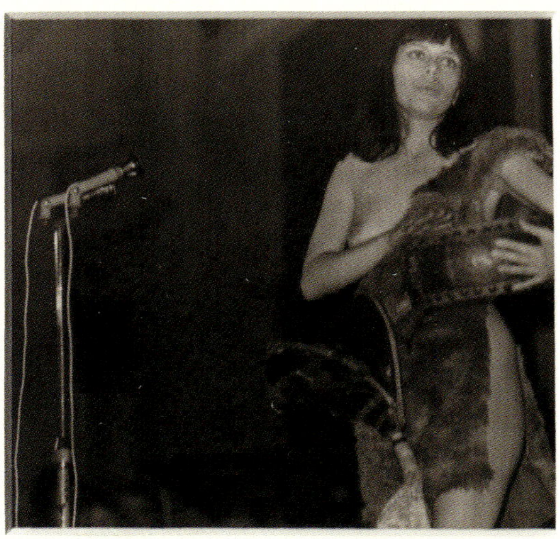

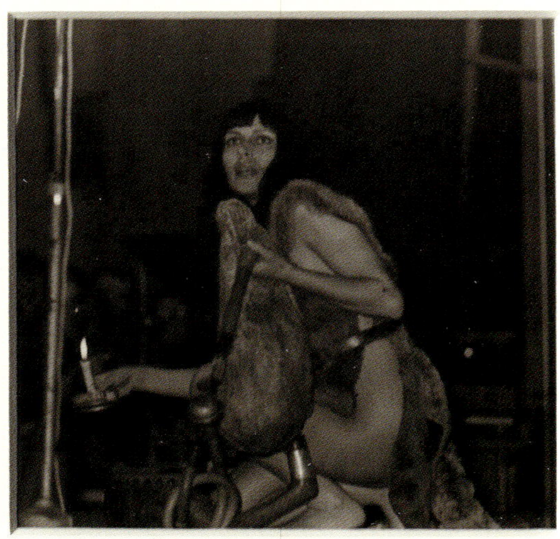

8. Joint performance by Katalin Ladik and Jenő Balaskó at their poetry reading, 1970, silver gelatine print, each 9 × 9 cm, acb Galéria, Budapest

9. Katalin Ladik, *Phonopoetica: Phonetic Interpretation of Visual Poetry* (vinyl disc & cover), 1976, audio recording, 33', acb Galéria, Budapest

10. (overleaf) Katalin Ladik, *Poemim*, 1978/2016, silver gelatine print, 9 pieces, each 40 × 30 cm, acb Galéria, Budapest

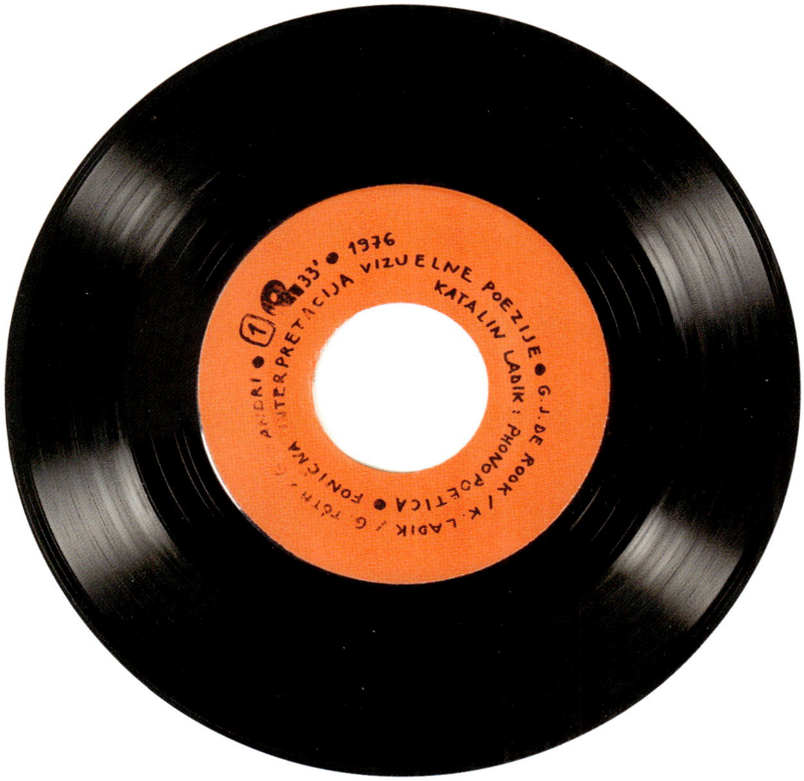

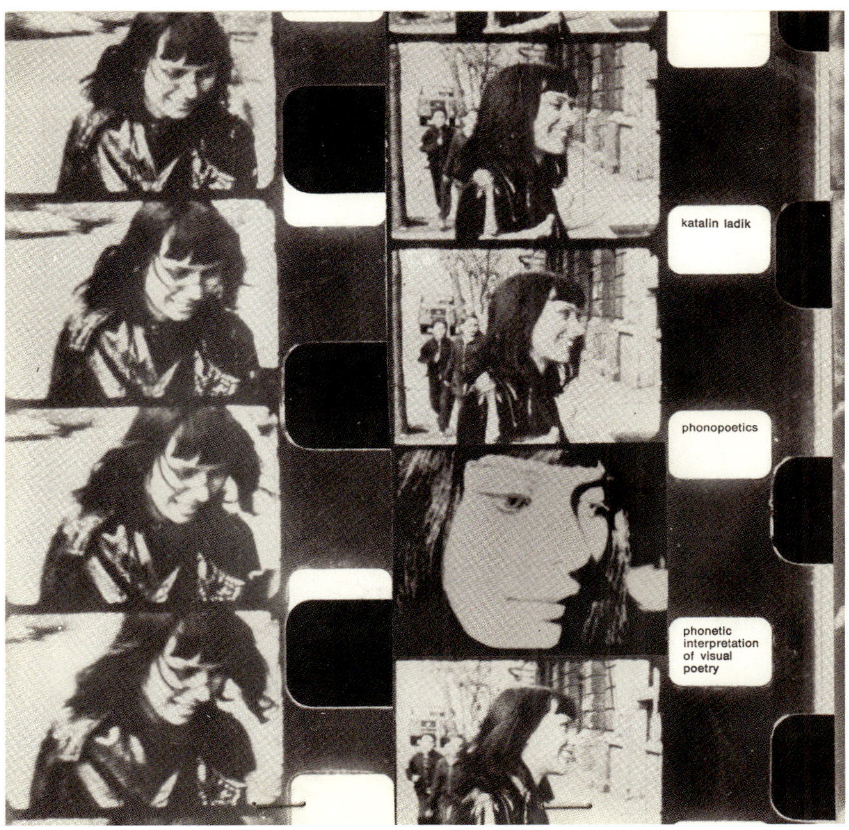

9

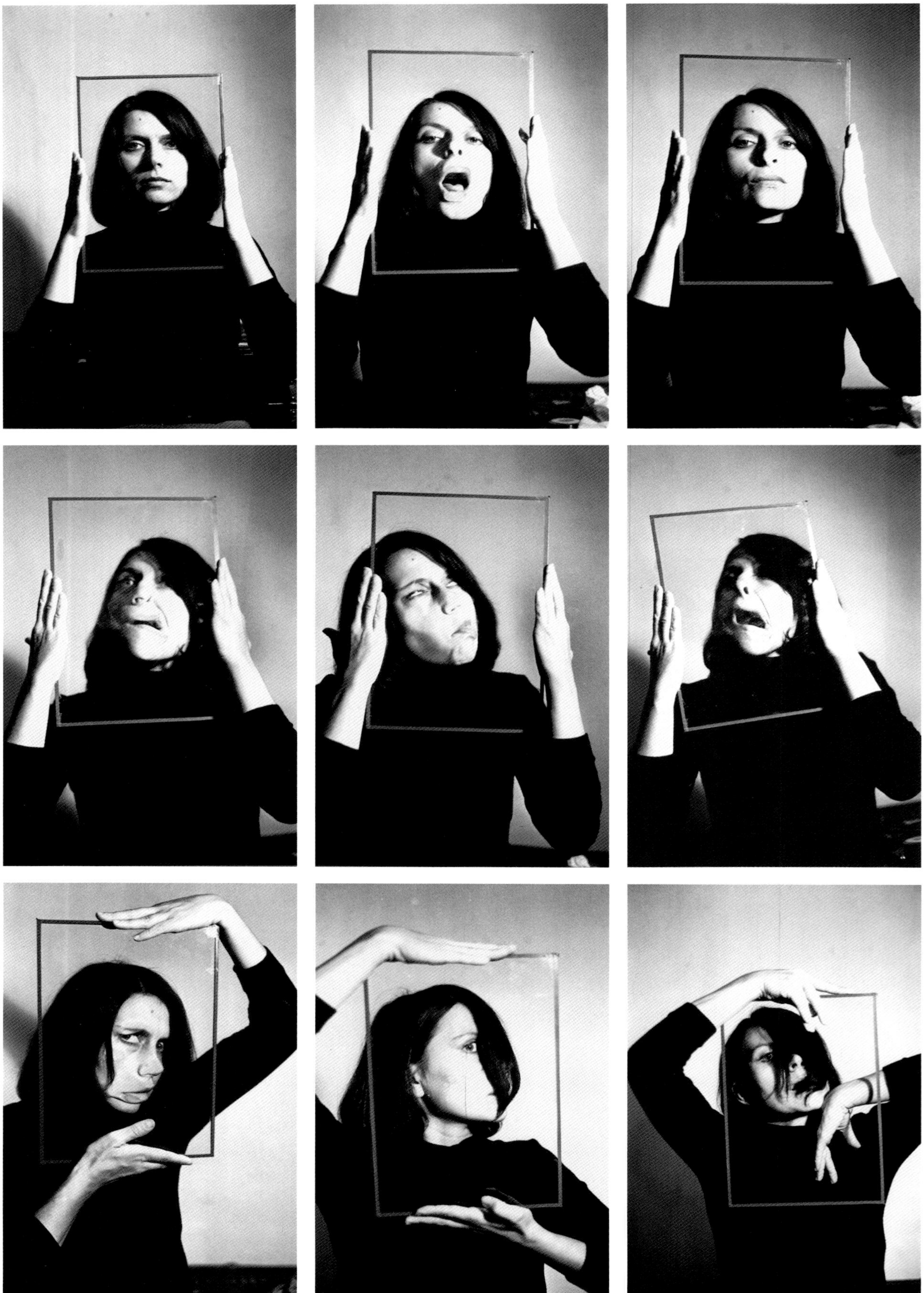

Secret service agents were among those in attendance at her first performance, since the genre of the happening became criminalized in Hungary after the first such event in 1966. Happenings were targeted by the police as suspicious and alien to the system; Gábor Altorjay and Tamás Szentjóby were interrogated several times after organizing their happening and were put under surveillance afterwards. The state press could be expected to target Ladik's reading as well; their attack on her highlighted the motif of nudity, which ran afoul of the regime's prudish standards. Ladik's reception in official terms shows a broader regional consensual unity in this respect: a similar performance and a similar reasoning led to her expulsion from the Party in Yugoslavia.

Despite these attacks, Katalin Ladik was not only a busy actress from the early 1970s onwards and continued her activities as poet and performer, but she became a star in the Yugoslav media and was increasingly accepted in Hungary by the 1980s. The second half of the 1970s brought Ladik a measure of international fame, the breakthrough being her record *Phonopoetica: Phonetic Interpretation of Visual Poetry* in 1976 (fig. 9). This included her characteristic phonic interpretations of contemporary poets like Bálint Szombathy, Gábor Tóth and Franci Zagoričnik. Bob Cobbing, a central figure of British experimental poetry, discovered Ladik for himself, and she soon became a prominent figure in the genre and a regular participant of international festivals of phonic poetry. Avant-garde artists both in Hungary and Yugoslavia could benefit from Ladik's international integration, since she played an important role in the international circulation of manuscripts, artworks and publications between 'East' and 'West'.

Katalin Ladik was primarily known on the international scene as a phonic poet and performer; her works – like those of other East-Central European women artists – represented a female position independent of the discourses and theoretical framework of contemporary 'Western' feminism. The 'classic' feminist position is absent from Hungarian art in this sense, as Beáta Hock has noted in connection to Dóra Maurer, Orsolya Drozdik, Judit Kele and Katalin Ladik.[29] Ladik's earlier actionism and her trademark genre of para-ritual musical performance gave way to a more conceptual approach in the mid-1970s. In her photo performance *Poemim* (1978, fig. 10), she used her face as a medium, brutally distorting it with a sheet of glass. Ladik's revision of the conventional visual representations of beauty is comparable to Ana Mendieta's series (*Untitled – Glass on Body Imprints*, 1972/1997) employing a surprisingly similar iconography, inspired by Mexican symbols and rituals.[30] By contrast to Mendieta (who died in 1985 at the age of thirty-six), Ladik's extreme perspective remained within the territory of poetry instead of striving to exploit the possibilities of endangering the body.

The reinterpretation of the linguistic from the aspect of the visual was realized in Ladik's oeuvre not only in performances, but also in visual objects, collages and scores that could be interpreted (i.e. sung) performatively. The genre of visual poetry was prominent in the work of an artists' group involved in the New Art Practice of the Yugoslav neo-avant-garde. Ladik joined the group, Bosch+Bosch, in 1973. A linguistic-textual orientation characterized all the group members, though in different forms: Slavko Matković was engaged in experimental poetry, Attila Csernik focused on visual semiotics and body art, while Bálint Szombathy did visual research in the semiotics of poetry and urban space.[31] The group's work also extended to problems of landscape intervention, land art, project art and mail art. Bálint Szombathy states in their Zagreb statement in 1978 that none of them accepted American or British conceptual art as a model to emulate, though they all worked within the same conceptual matrix.[32]

Szombathy and Matković co-founded the group in Subotica in 1969. They were confronted with the problem of being on the periphery and emphasized their critique of the medium of painting, as they searched for the possibilities of progressive art in a small town with Hungarian cultural traditions, and was marginal even within Yugoslavia. Besides some international contemporaries (primarily Fluxus artists and Joseph Beuys), a crucial influence in this respect was Lajos Kassák, a prominent figure of the Hungarian classic avant-garde forced into political and cultural exile for most of his life (see also

Gábor Dobó and Merse Pál Szeredi, 'Hungarian Culture +/- Europe', pp. 39–57). Szombathy's early experimental poems reinterpreted the tradition of Kassák's constructivism, but the adaptation of the historical model was not limited to aesthetic conclusions. The activities of Szombathy and the Bosch+Bosch group revived the spirit of the leftist movement and its critique operating with the latest visual apparatus in the Vojvodina region of Yugoslavia. In fact, Kassák's rediscovery by the Hungarian neo-avant-garde occurred in no small part due to their mediation through inter-regional relations and pieces in the journal *Új Symposion*.

Új Symposion, which was published in Novi Sad, Vojvodina, functioned as a key site of cultural transfer; Bálint Szombathy became its visual arts editor in 1971. Besides Lajos Kassák and theorist Georg Lukács, the journal published other intellectuals of the Hungarian scene, particularly illegal and semi-legal contemporary authors, such as Miklós Erdély, Tibor Hajas, Gábor Altorjay and Tamás Szentjóby. While the internationality of concrete and visual poetry was due to its supranational character, the problem of the locality of languages and the cultural position of the Hungarian linguistic minority were profound issues in regional literature. Both as author and editor, Szombathy tried to make up for the lack of progressive art criticism in Hungarian and frequently stepped in to provide a critical interpretation of experimental poetry (increasingly popular in the 1970s) and conceptual tendencies.[33]

Szombathy's own poetic activity was related to current linguistic theories, particularly to semiotics; he gradually departed from the two-dimensional limitations of paper, which he indicated by attributing a spatial sense to letter spacing and subsequently by creating relationships different from the original textual logic (*Nontextualité series*, 1972, fig. 11). His semiotic research extended to non-literary linguistic forms within his distinct practice of appropriation, which admittedly demoted aesthetic concerns: 'My works became increasingly determined by the theoretical-plus-practical reflections which ultimately led to the insight that we could pronounce as poetry (art) anything we found to be poetry

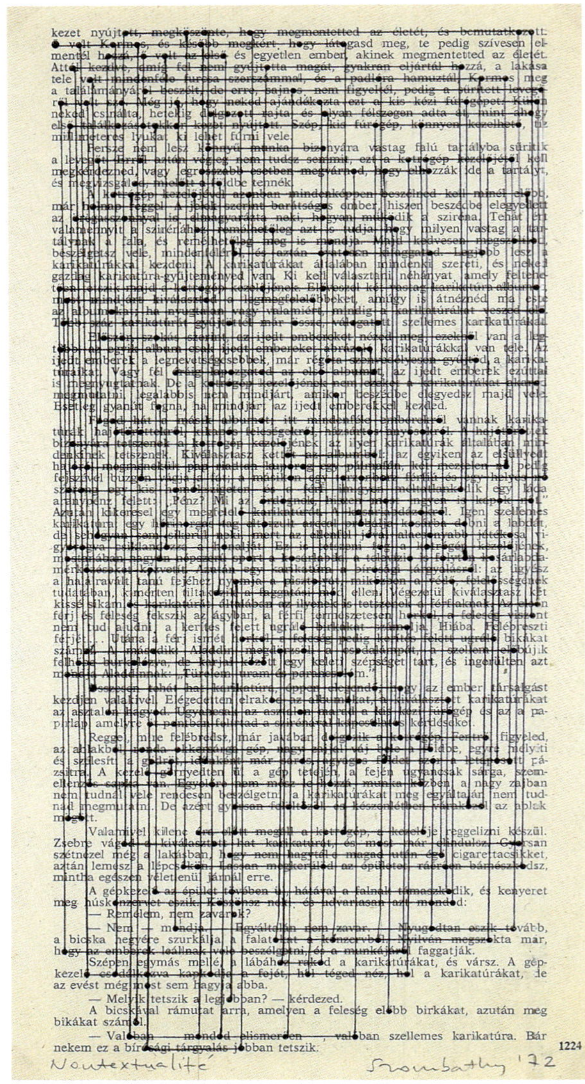

11

11. Bálint Szombathy, *Nontextualité series*, 1972, paper, pen, typed text, 28.5 × 14.7 cm, Szépművészeti Múzeum – Magyar Nemzeti Galéria, Budapest

12. (overleaf) Bálint Szombathy, *Bauhaus*, 1971, photo performance, Novi Sad, 8 pieces, 40 × 30 cm each, Private collection

(art), that is, whatever we individually accepted as poetry (art).'[34] Szombathy interpreted the visual relations of found poetry, image and sign by treating the built urban environment as a readymade and by interventions in urban space. His semiotic research was founded on the observation of spontaneously created linguistic systems and on the notion that the origin of languages can be traced back to the human environment and to a broad sphere of human activity.[35]

In an emblematic series on the semiotics of urban space, Szombathy contrasted the aesthetics of poverty in the attic of his house in Novi Sad to the social and aesthetic modernism of the Bauhaus. His photo action *Bauhaus* (1971, fig. 12), performed for the first time in Balatonboglár, mixes its references to the classic avant-garde with the spirit of Fluxus, eliminating the boundaries of art and life. The artist appears in various spaces while conveying the fragility of personal existence; as Nebojša Milenković remarks, he becomes a participant and neutral observer of his own action while examining the linguistic codes of the medium used.[36] Identifying the locations of the scenes is aided by the portrait of Josip Broz Tito, the Yugoslav President and head of the League of Communists, generally dominating public space.

Bálint Szombathy first visited Hungary to discuss plans for an exhibition of Lajos Kassák's work in Novi Sad and that was when he realized that the representation of power in Hungary was quite different in style from Yugoslavia. The cult of personality came to an end in Hungary as a result of the de-Stalinization process after 1953, and the portraits of the leaders of the Party disappeared from public space. János Kádár, who defeated the 1956 revolution with Soviet assistance, presented himself as a humble and Spartan leader. This situation gave rise to Szombathy's *Lenin in Budapest* (1972, p. 238, fig. 8), in which he carried a placard with a portrait of the icon of the Soviet revolution along a predetermined route in the streets and public spaces of Budapest. The framework for this 'linguistic play presented as an intimate spectacle'[37] was the public space of political representation, where the artist's body became a politicized medium of provocation, much like in the Bauhaus series.

Confronting various relevant symbols and situations, Szombathy's increasingly politicized actions followed the crisis of multi-ethnic Yugoslavia and its eventual disintegration in the 1990s. The artist was not merely subjected to the changing historical conditions, but emerged as a subject whose existence as a conscious entity was based on reflection. This attitude, which can be traced back to the avant-garde spirit of the 1920s, was quite different from the characteristic use of the body in Hungarian actionism. Tibor Hajas, for instance, used his physical presence to dissociate himself from the contemporary social context and to have an existential sense of being that was universal enough to deny the determining effect of any political structure (see also Edit András, 'Out of Private Public Opinion into Shared Personal Opinion', pp. 229–49, and Katalin Székely, 'The Influx of Images', pp. 331–55). Hajas, whose entire oeuvre was based on experiencing the nearness of death and who realized increasingly risky performances, often endangering his own life, eventually died in a car crash in 1980. The enduring myth around him was fed partly by his charismatic personality and partly by the accident which left his oeuvre unfinished. This oeuvre – an actionist attempt at denying socialist reality that was retrospectively made even more dramatic by its tragic end – has proven quite difficult to integrate into the genealogies of the contemporary avant-garde.

Hajas's denial of the social context must have been mainly, though perhaps not exclusively, motivated by the trauma of an early conflict with political power. The Kádár regime, consolidating itself in the early 1960s, launched an attack on the unconventional lifestyle of youths, demonizing 'thugs' in 'gangs'.[38] Tibor Hajas became a target as the author of the allegedly anti-Semitic poem 'Fascist Comrades', through which he became involved in a case criminalizing juveniles. The trial, which drew enormous media attention, ended with a two-year prison sentence for Hajas, never reflected directly in his pieces. His main media were the body and texts, or rather the performative body and text as the primary media of his creative identity.[39] His texts aimed at the autonomous sphere of a politically neutral existentialism and often alluded to ancient Eastern philosophies and

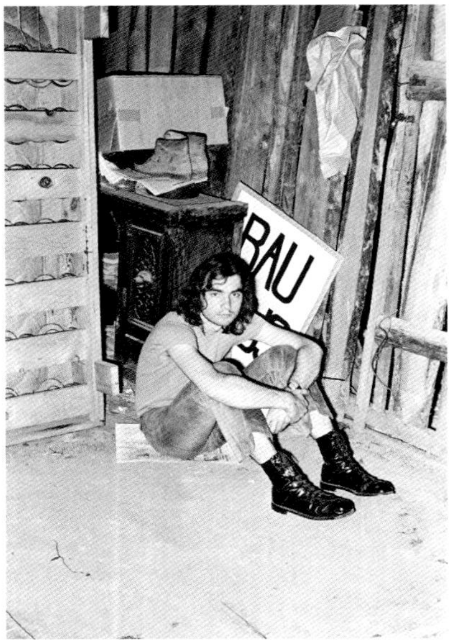
BAU

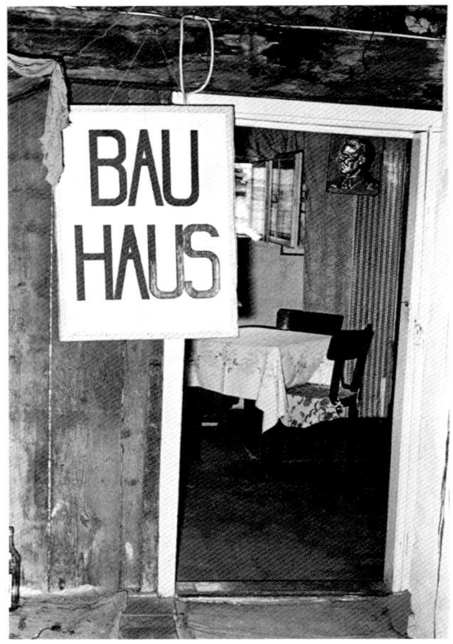
BAU
HAUS

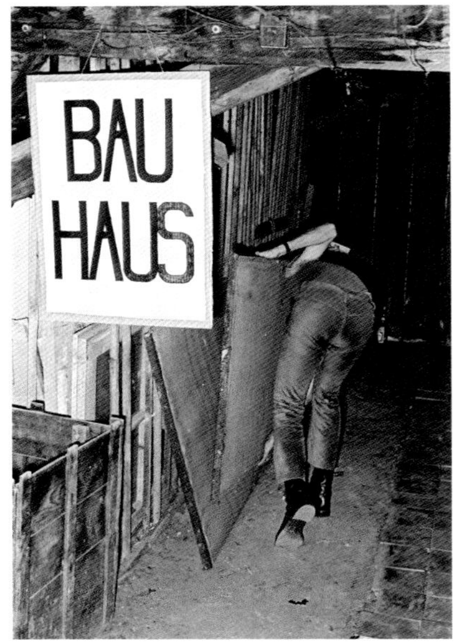
BAU
HAUS

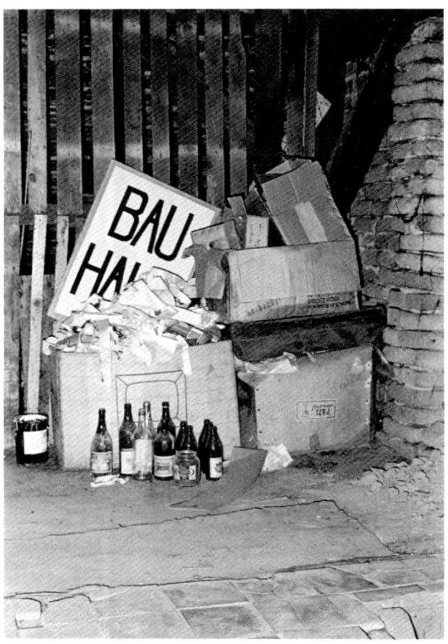
BAU

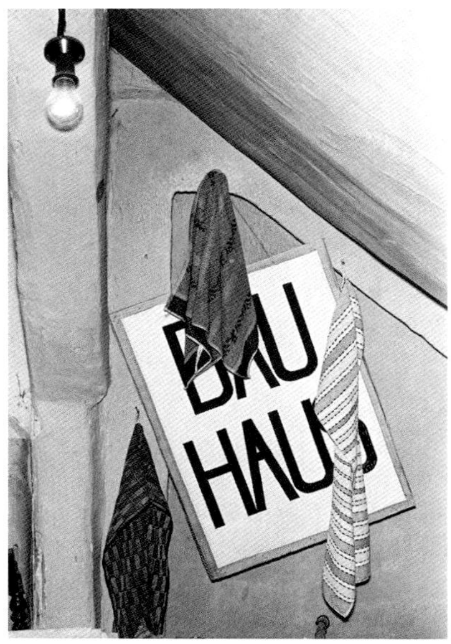

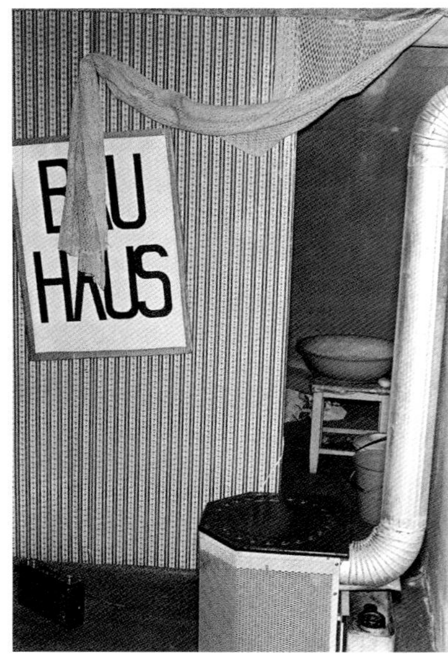
HAUS

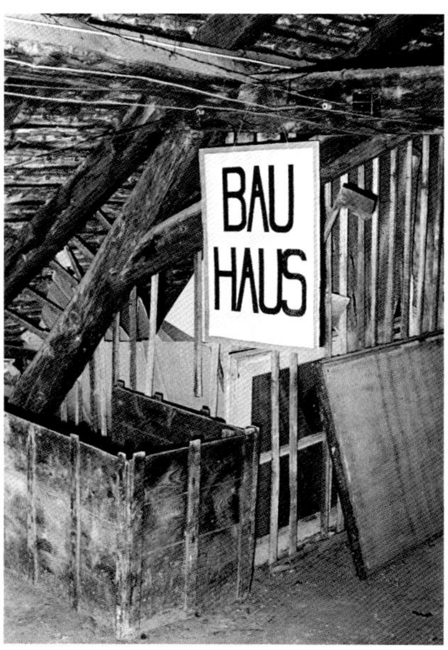
BAU
HAUS

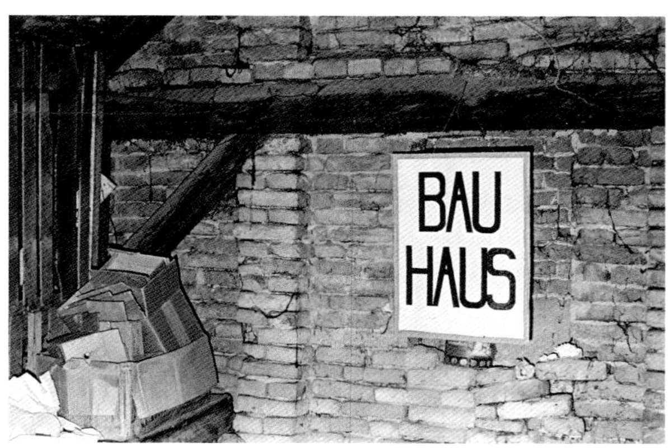
BAU
HAUS

to extraordinary experiences of being in Tibetan Buddhism (the Tibetan Book of the Dead). That said, the naked bodies of Hajas and his contemporaries (Czech Petr Štembera and Romanian Ion Grigorescu) had a destabilizing social and cultural effect, and a political meaning, in the conservative milieu of socialist society.[40]

Photo actions, photo sequences and performances were exceptionally important components of actionism in Hajas's oeuvre. He made the former in close collaboration with photographer János Vető; their first joint action involved public poetry writing at a pop concert in January 1976 (fig. 14). It is as if they moved the typing poet – the motif of the first happening – into a broader social context, indicating the increasingly expansive spaces opening to actionism in Budapest in the 1970s. Hajas faced the audience and occupied a corner of the stage with his typewriter. The normally intimate character of writing was enriched with a public layer of meaning, and the socio-cultural terrain of actionism increasingly merged with the mechanisms of representation characteristic of pop music and youth subculture. Tamás Szentjóby had laid the groundwork for this, in a sense, in the early 1970s, as he began to use the intermissions of pop concerts for his somewhat camouflaged actions, having no access to other public spaces for the purpose. All this was possible partly because actionism had close ties to underground music, especially to the band KEX headed by poet János Baksa-Soós. In Hajas's case, the weight of authorial presence shifted the emphasis from the text – inaccessible to the audience at the moment of its creation – to the action, the process of creation. In the conceptual understanding of Hajas and Vető, the photograph of the event was identical to the action not only in a philosophical but also in an intermedial sense.[41]

Compared to this minimalist event popularizing writing and held before an audience, the photo actions by Hajas and Vető had a completely different degree of intimacy, excluding the public and held for the camera only. Hajas wrote notes and scripts for all his actions and (in his own term) pre-performances, which consistently use the third person from a completely external position in the tone of Fluxus, and numerous sources confirm his self-identification as a poet, and yet his actionist practice employed the body as a medium substituted for poetry.[42] It is the medium of the body that constructs the poetics of the visual in an incredibly rich and layered system, where the body is both signifying icon, the means of representation, the vulnerable subject of interventions, and an object of exposure, self-torture and destruction (*Flesh Painting I–III*, 1978, fig. 13). The conceptual twist in the Hajas–Vető works is that the torture of the image is also the torture of the body in the intermedial relationship of action and image (*Surface Torturing*, 1978). Magnesium catching fire and burning the face, wounds inflicted on the represented body and burned areas on the image surface show the concurrent destruction and gradual elimination of body and image.[43]

Tibor Hajas's oeuvre, which literature has interpreted in a sphere of the sacred due to his Eastern mystical sources and in a sphere of destruction and the rejection of art characteristic of Viennese actionism,[44] entailed the increasingly radical questioning of bodily existence through its metaphysical solitude and the struggle of a humble subject nevertheless speaking with the voice of authority. The motif of losing consciousness during his performances – first accidentally, then in an increasingly intentional and ritualized manner – and the rising level of risks taken became tests of the spirit's liberation from physical restrictions. According to Hajas's main source, the texts of the Tibetan Book of the Dead, total freedom can be reached through the path leading to death and the state of death, which resists ingrained habits and is therefore the only state that can allow learning the true nature of the human being. Not even those closest to Hajas could follow his entire oeuvre due to the intensifying radicalism of the performances, the raising of the stakes and the shattering experience of near-death states. This impossibility to follow also applied to the literary part of the oeuvre, since Hajas's 'pseudo-libertine and transgressive mode of writing' has confined his texts to a solitary ghetto, which contemporary interpretations have not succeeded in opening to this day.[45]

Hajas's last performance, *Wake* (1980, fig. 15), can be interpreted as the concluding

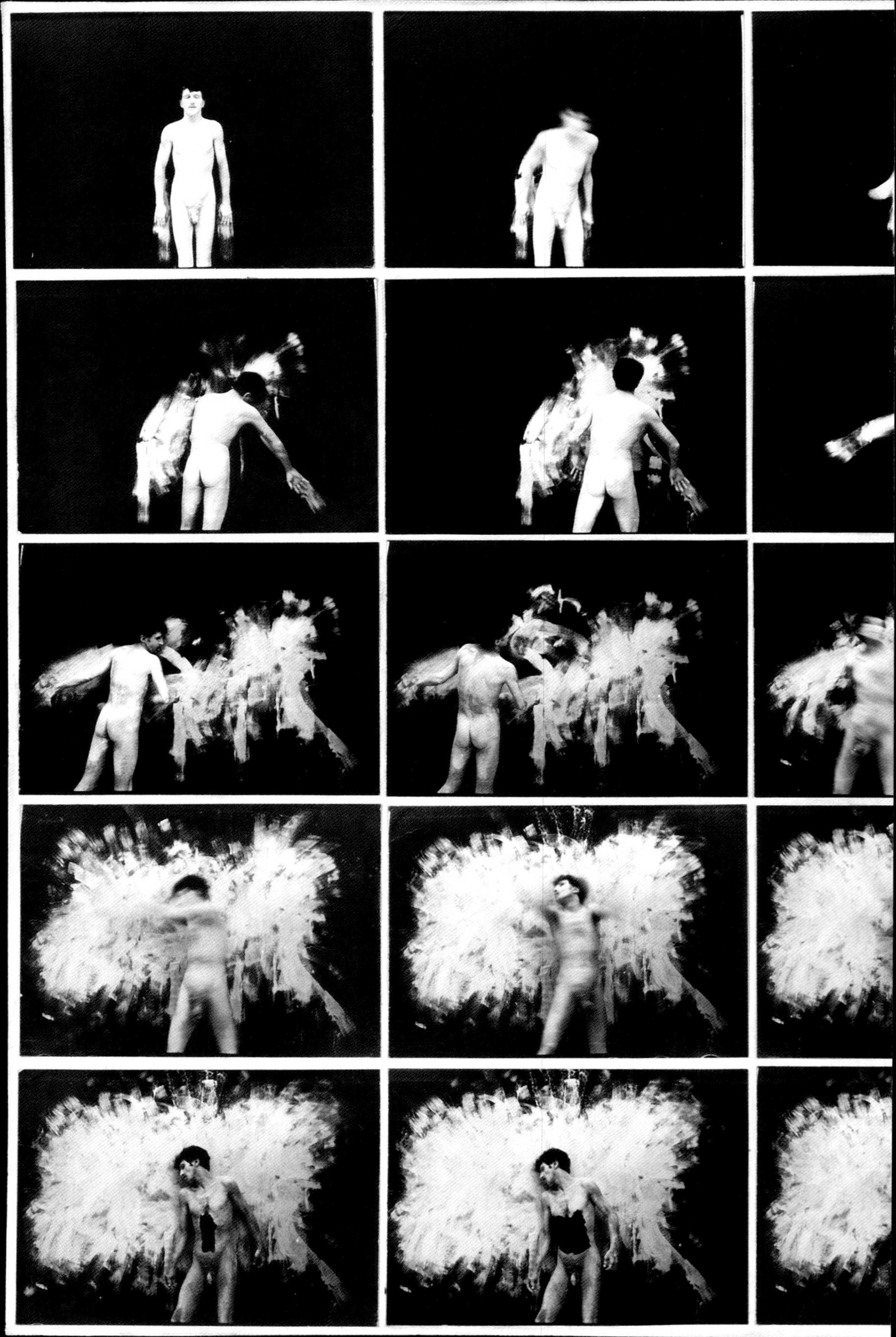

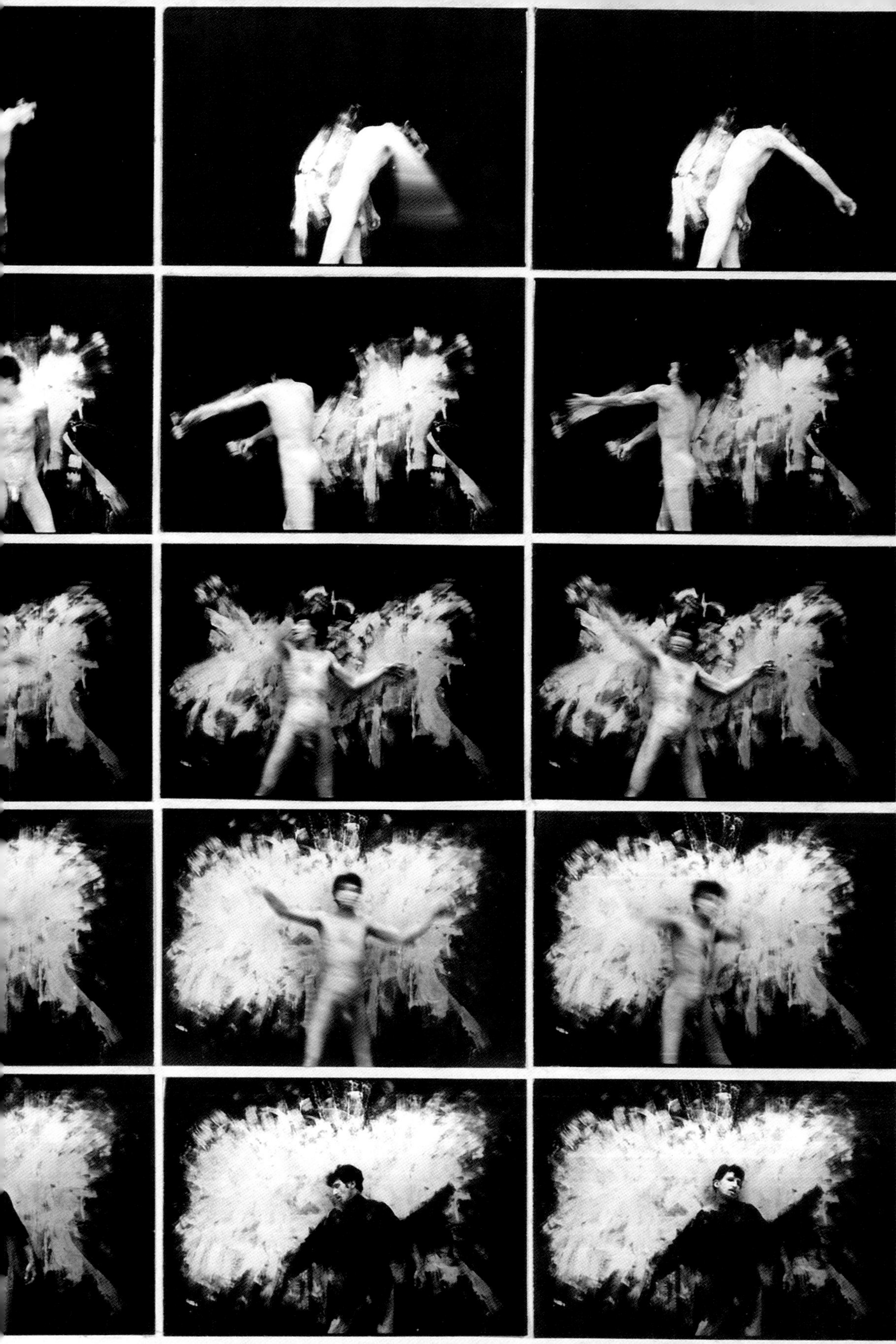

13. (previous pages) Tibor Hajas, *Flesh Painting IV*, 1978, silver gelatine prints mounted on fibreboard (Photo: János Vetö), 20 pieces, 80 × 100 cm, Ludwig Múzeum – Kortárs Müvészeti Múzeum, Budapest

14. Tibor Hajas, *Poem writing*, 1976, action (Photo: János Vető), Budapest, Private collection

15. Tibor Hajas, *Wake*, performance in the Bercsényi Kollégium in Budapest, 18 May 1980, silver gelatine print (Photo: Tibor Zátonyi), 18 × 24,2 cm, NA Collection, Budapest

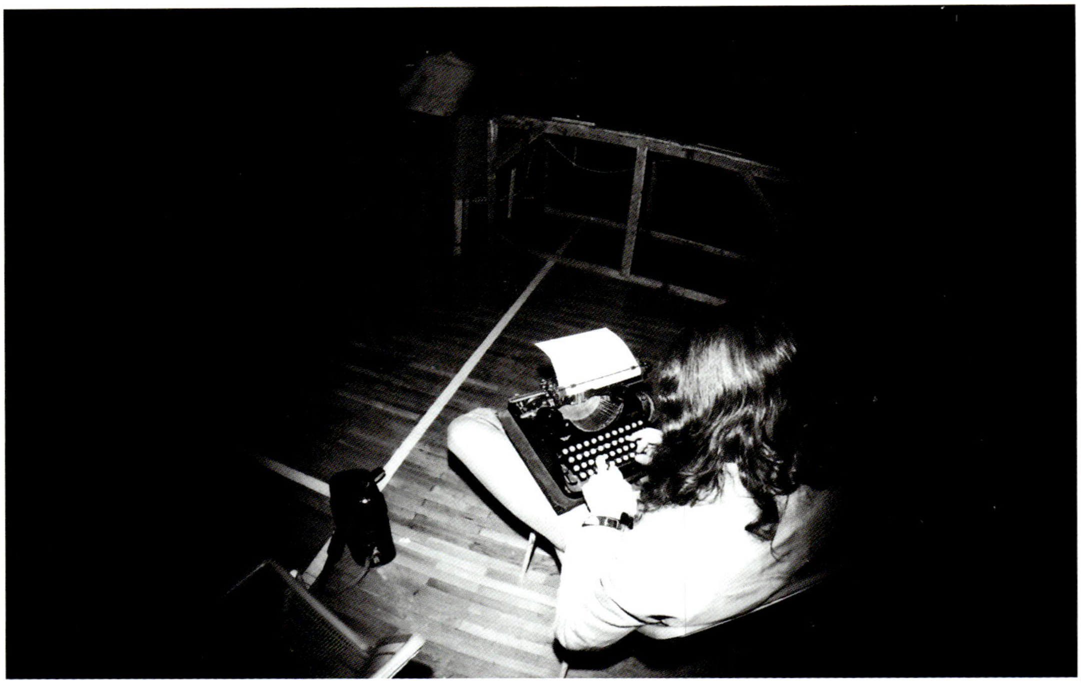

14

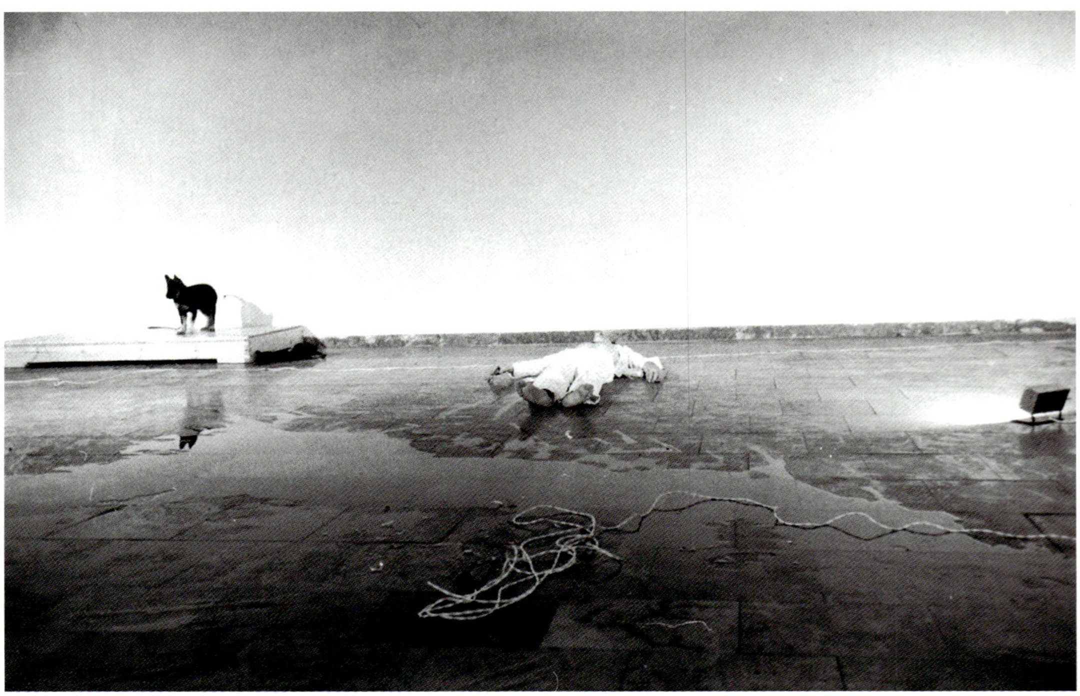

15

event of Hungarian actionism. The event was staged in a carefully constructed but bare space, using the effects of light and shadow, where the shocking minimalism of the view was organized by a text extending to the smallest details. After pouring a bucket of water on the stone floor, the blindfolded performer threw a long cord with a 200-watt lightbulb hanging on its end into the puddle.[46] His assistants (János Vető and István Csömöri) wore scrubs and intravenously administered a fast-working sleep medication that suspended his life functions. Then they proceeded to drag the unconscious body of Hajas back and forth to mop up the floor. (In fact, János Vető disobeyed Hajas's order and, unknown to him, disconnected the electric current from the water.) Meanwhile, a German shepherd puppy, which had grown an enormous shadow, kept yelping on the stage, and Hajas's own voice was played on a tape recorder. The text traces Hajas's unapproachability and self-confidence back to the original vulnerability and ephemerality of existence, addressing an unknown entity presumed to be a partner and himself as pure consciousness relieved of the body. 'I am invulnerable. I am invulnerable due to a total awareness of my fragility. I am invulnerable enough to be able to fall silent; I dare to fall asleep. I dare to go dark in the midst of the light of glowing lamps, alone – and I can stand the world staying on...undamaged, untouched, without a master...'.[47] The motionless body was left on the stage at the end, and Hajas was brought back to consciousness when the audience had left.

Although Hajas's death in 1980 symbolically closes the history of Hungarian actionism in the 1960s–70s, and its former participants all reacted to the postmodern turn and the expansion of painting, though in different ways, language-based actionism did not disappear entirely from Hungarian visual art. The desire to rediscover and reinterpret historical precursors has opened new collaborative, participatory and intermedial chapters in actionism in the practice of later generations.

1 János Bányai, 'Diszkontinuitás és versbeszéd: Az Új Symposion homályos útja a neoavantgárd és posztmodern felé' [Discontinuity and Poetic Discourse: The Murky Path of the Új Symposion toward the Neo-avant-garde and Postmodernism], in Pál Deréky and András Müllner (eds), *Né/ma? Tanulmányok a magyar neoavantgárd köréből* [Mute? Studies on the Hungarian Neo-avant-garde]. Budapest: Ráció Kiadó, 2004. http://www.tankonyvtar.hu/hu/tartalom/tkt/ne-ma-ne-ma/ch03.html (21 June 2017).

2 J. L. Austin, *How to do Things with Words. The William James Lectures delivered at Harvard University in 1955.* Oxford: Oxford University Press, 1962, 6.

3 Kristine Stiles, 'Uncorrupted Joy: International Art Actions', in Russell Ferguson (ed.), *Out of Actions: Between Performance and the Object, 1949–1979* (exhibition catalogue). New York and London: Thames & Hudson, 1998, 227–329, especially 231.

4 Liz Kotz, *Words to be looked at: Language in 1960s Art.* Cambridge and London: MIT Press, 2007.

5 Dick Higgins, 'Statement on Intermedia' (1966), in Wolf Vostell (ed.), *Dé-coll/age (décollage) No. 6*. New York and Frankfurt: Typos Verlag and Something Else Press, 1967.

6 Jacques Derrida, 'The Theatre of Cruelty', in *Writing and Difference*, trans. Alan Bass. Chicago: University of Chicago Press, 1978, 240.

7 Miklós Szalai, '"A semmi egében utak fehéren…" Beke Lászlóval és Széphelyi F. Györggyel Hajas Tiborról beszélget Szalai Miklós' ['White Paths in the Sky of Nothingness…' Miklós Szalai in Conversation with László Beke and György F. Széphelyi about Tibor Hajas], *Orpheus Irodalmi Folyóirat*, Vol. 3, No. 10, 1992, 75–88, especially 81.

8 Tamás St Turba and Zsuzsa László (eds), *Az ebéd (In memoriam Batu Kán)* [The Lunch (In memoriam Batu Khan)]. Budapest: Tranzit Hungary Közhasznú Egyesület, 2011.

9 St Turba and László, *Az ebéd*, 51.

10 Emmet Williams (ed.), *Anthology of Concrete Poetry*. New York, Villefranche and Frankfurt: Something Else Press, 1967.

11 Emese Kürti, 'A szabadság anti-esztétikája: Az első magyarországi happening' [The Anti-Aesthetic of Freedom: The First Hungarian Happening], *Exindex*, 2015, http://exindex.hu/index.php?l=hu&page=3&id=967 (22 April 2017).

12 Allan Kaprow, 'Excerpts from Assemblages, Environments & Happenings', in Mariellen R. Sandford (ed.), *Happenings and Other Acts*. New York: Routledge, 1995, 197–205.

13 Emese Kürti, 'Generations in Experiment: The Cage-effect in the Early Sixties of Hungary', in Katalin Székely (ed.), *John Cage behind the Iron Curtain.* Budapest: Ludwig Museum/Museum of Contemporary Art, 2013, 134–51.

14 Mária Ember, 'Happening és antihappening' [Happening and Antihappening], *Film Színház Muzsika*, Vol. 10, No. 19, 13 May 1966, 18.

15 Claire Bishop, *Artificial Hells: Participatory Art and the Politics of Spectatorship*. London and New York: Verso, 2012, 142.

16 Klara Kemp-Welch, *Antipolitics in Central-European Art: Reticence as Dissidence under Post-totalitarian Rule, 1956–1989.* London: I. B. Tauris, 2013, 64.

17 Pavlína Morganová, *Czech Action Art: Happenings, Actions, Events, Land Art, Body Art and Performance Art behind the Iron Curtain.* Prague: Charles University/Karolinum Press, 2014, 64.

18 Judith F. Rodenbeck, *Radical Prototypes: Allan Kaprow and the Invention of Happenings*. Cambridge: MIT Press, 2011.

19 IPUT (Tamás St Auby), 'Fluxus – Art – Life – Politics', in Petra Stegmann (ed.), *Fluxus Networks in Central Eastern Europe*. Berlin: Künstlerhaus Bethanien, 2007, 108.

20 Jürgen Becker and Wolf Vostell (eds), *Happenings, Fluxus, Pop Art, Nouveau Réalisme: Eine Dokumentation*. Hamburg: Rowohlt Verlag, 1965. Szentjóby would perform the Fluxus scores included in this volume in 1969 at the first Fluxus concert in Budapest.

21 Tamás Szentjóby, 'A happeningről (részletek) (1966–2010)' [On Happening (excerpts) (1966–2010)], in St Turba and László, *Az ebéd*, 45–46.

22 '3 Quarks for King Marke! Miklós Erdély: Clips, Dirac in Front of the Box Office, Conjectures. Tamás Szentjóby: Film, Distance. László Méhes: Images, Just to Say an Example'. 29 November 1968.

23 Dóra Hegyi, Sándor Hornyik and Zsuzsa László (eds), *Parallel Chronologies: 'Other' Revolutionary Traditions: How Art becomes Public. An Exhibition in Newspaper Format*. Budapest: Tranzit Hungary Public Benefit Association, 2011, 21.

24 Miklós Peternák, 'Beszélgetés Erdély Miklóssal, 1983 tavaszán' [A Conversation with Miklós Erdély in the Spring of 1983], *Árgus*, Vol. 2, No. 5, 1991, 79.

25 '*Új misztika felé: Sebők Zoltán beszélgetése Erdély Miklóssal*' [Towards a New Mysticism: Zoltán Sebők in Conversation with Miklós Erdély], *Híd*, Vol. 46, No. 3, 1982, 375.

26 Tamás St Auby/Miklós Erdély: 'UFO (tryst). Happening / without invited public / 1st of May 1968, Szentendre. Participants: Katalin Ladik, Tamás Szentjóby, Miklós Erdély, Györgyi Szalay, István Dárday, Antal Dúl, Miklós Urbán, Roger Benichou, topical doormen, ad hoc car mechanics, Joyce (the dog)'.

27 Hendrik Folkerts, 'Keeping Score: Notation, Embodiment, and Liveness', documenta 14. http://www.documenta14.de/en/south/464_keeping_score_notation_embodiment_and_liveness (16 October 2016).

28 François Dufrêne, 'Prodrome', *Ion* (1952). Paris: Jean-Paul Rocher, 1999, 196.

29 Beáta Hock, ‘Women Artists’ Trajectories and Networks’, in Jérôme Bazin, Pascal Dubourg Glatigny and Piotr Piotrowski (eds), *Art beyond Borders: Artistic Exchange in Communist Europe (1945–1989)*. Budapest and New York: CEU Press, 2016.
30 Gabriele Schor, *Feminist Avant-garde. Art of the 1970s: The Sammlung Verbund Collection, Vienna, Munich, London*. New York: Prestel, 2016.
31 Besides Szombathy and Matković, another founding member was László Szalma. László Kerekes joined Bosch+Bosch in 1971, Attila Csernik and Katalin Ladik in 1973, Vukov Ante in 1975, and the group dissolved in 1976. Emese Kürti, *Transregional Discourses: The Bosch+Bosch in the Yugoslav and the Hungarian Avant-garde*. Budapest: acb ResearchLab, 2016.
32 Bálint Szombathy, ‘Landmarks in the Work of the Group Bosch+Bosch’, in Marijan Susovski (ed.), *The New Art Practice in Yugoslavia 1966–1978*. Zagreb: Gallery of Contemporary Art, 1978, 51.
33 Bálint Szombathy, ‘A konkrét költészet útjai’ [The Paths of Concrete Poetry] (1977), http://www.artpool.hu/Poetry/konkret/konkret.html (22 April 2017).
34 Quoted by Nebojša Milenković, *Szombathy Art*. Novi Sad: Muzej Savremene likovne umetnosti Novi Sad, 2005, 11.
35 Szombathy, ‘Landmarks’, 52.
36 Nebojša Milenković, ‘A történelmi bőség mint művészeti alapanyag’ [Historical Plenty as Raw Material for Art], in Bálint Szombathy, *YU RETORIKA: Válogatás negyvenöt év munkáiból* [YU RHETORIC: Selections from the Work of Forty-Five Years]. Újvidék: Forum Könyvkiadó, 2014, 30.
37 *Ibid.*, 31.
38 Sándor Horváth, *Kádár gyermekei: Ifjúsági lázadás a hatvanas években* [Kádár’s Children: Youth Revolt in the Sixties]. Budapest: Nyitott könyvműhely, 2009.
39 Tibor Hajas, *Szövegek* [Texts], compiled by Éva F. Almási. Budapest: Enciklopédia kiadó, 2005.
40 Piotr Piotrowski, ‘Male Artist’s Body: National Identity vs Identity Politics’, in Bojana Pejić (ed.), *Gender Check. A Reader: Art and Theory in Eastern Europe*. Cologne: Verlag der Buchhandlung Walther König, 2010, 127–36, especially 127.
41 ‘I need to interfere with reality for the sake of the picture,’ says János Vető. ‘I hate “stolen moments”. The camera doesn’t spy. It must make its subject engaged. Photography is action.’ See Tibor Hajas, ‘Töredékek az “Új Fotó”-ról Vető János munkáinak ürügyén’ [Fragments about ‘New Photo’ on the Occasion of János Vető’s Works], *Mozgó Világ*, Vol. 3, No. 1, 1977, 68–70.
42 Szalai, ‘A semmi egében utak fehéren…’, 79.
43 Károly Szűcs, ‘Test és kép: Hajas Tibor kiállítása’ [Body and Image: The Exhibition of Tibor Hajas], *Balkon*, Vol. 13, No. 6, 2005. http://www.balkon.hu/archiv/balkon05_06/02szucs.html (2 November 2016).
44 Márió Z. Nemes, ‘Hajas Tibor kettős teste: a destruktív body-art és egy szakrális diskurzus’ [Tibor Hajas’s Dual Body: Destructive Body Art and Sacral Discourse], *Prae: irodalmi folyóirat*, Vol. 8, No. 1, 2006, 21–29.
45 Márió Z. Nemes, ‘Mutagén Gólem – Nemes Z. Márió Hajas Tiborról’ [Mutagenetic Golem – Márió Z. Nemes on Tibor Hajas], *Litera*, 16 May 2014. http://www.litera.hu/hirek/mutagen-golem-nemes-z-mario-hajas-tiborrol (2 November 2016).
46 Communication by János Vető.
47 Tibor Hajas, ‘Virrasztás’ [Wake], in Hajas, *Szövegek*, 355.

1. Erzsébet Schaár, *In Front of and Behind the Wall*, 1968, aluminium, bronze, h. 214 cm, Szent István Király Múzeum, Székesfehérvár

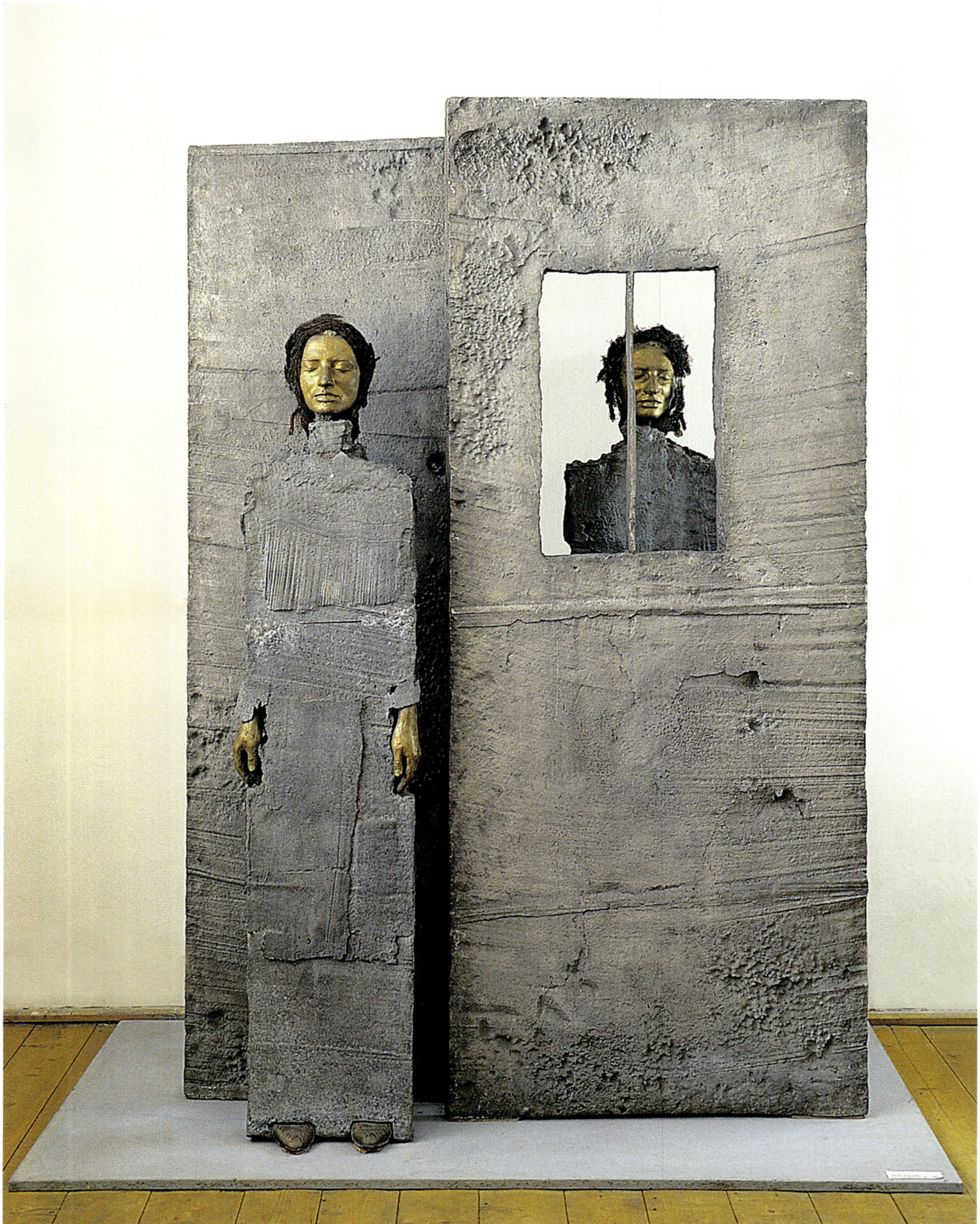

1

Magdalena Radomska

Working in the Twice-mined Semantic Minefield

The Politics of Hungarian Neo-avant-garde Movements

Savak [the Iranian secret police] had a good ear for all allusions. One scorching afternoon an old man with a bad heart turned up at the bus stop and gasped, 'It's so oppressive you can't catch your breath.' 'So it is,' the Savak agent replied immediately, edging closer to the winded stranger. 'It's getting more and more oppressive and people are fighting for air.' 'Too true,' replied the naive old man, clapping his hand over his heart, 'such heavy air, so oppressive.' Immediately the Savak agent barked, 'Now you'll have a chance to regain your strength,' and marched him off.

The other people at the bus stop had been listening in dread, for they had sensed from the beginning that the feeble elderly man was committing an unpardonable error by saying 'oppressive' to a stranger.

Experience had taught them to avoid uttering such terms as oppressiveness, darkness, burden, abyss, collapse, quagmire, putrefaction, cage, bars, chain, gag, truncheon, boot, claptrap, screw, pocket, paw, madness, and expressions like lie down, lie flat, spreadeagle, fall on your face, wither away, gotten flabby, go blind, go deaf, wallow in it, something's out of kilter, something's wrong, all screwed up, something's got to give – because all of them, these nouns, verbs, adjectives, and pronouns, could hide allusions to the Shah's regime, and thus formed a semantic minefield where you could get blown to bits with one slip of the tongue. — Ryszard Kapuściński, *Shah of Shahs*[1]

The art of the neo-avant-garde can be best described as a case of the 'Asiatic mode of production' in the history of Hungarian art. The concept of the Asiatic mode of production, one of few non-operational and inexpedient Marxist categories, became for the eminent Polish philosopher Leszek Kołakowski a tool in his criticism of the Marxist philosophy of history. The concept first appeared, as Kołakowski claims, in several articles and letters written by Karl Marx in 1853 and in his *Grundrisse der Kritik der Politischen Ökonomie* (Fundamentals of Political Economy Criticism).[2] The Asiatic mode of production was an exceptional form of economy in China, India and several Muslim countries, characterized by the fact that

private ownership of land was almost unknown, as geographical and climactic conditions called for an irrigation system that could only be provided by a centralized administration. Hence the special autonomous role of the despotic state apparatus, on which the economy largely depended; commerce developed to a very small extent, towns did not exist as centres of trade and industry, and there was scarcely any native bourgeoisie. The traditional village communities lived on through the ages in social and technical stagnation. The gradual dissolution of these communities and of the state of despotism was due to European capitalism rather than internal causes.[3]

The concept, which according to Kołakowski would suffice to question the foundations of historical materialism, such as the primary role of productive forces, the uniformity of human evolution and, ultimately, the inevitability of progress, was banned in Stalin's time.[4] We may only guess at why it happened only then. Perhaps Marx's own intellectual honesty would not let him pass over the discovery, although it did not stop him from drawing radical conclusions from his reasoning, which resulted in the theoretical approach to history, one of the most influential in humanist thought.

The art of the Hungarian neo-avant-garde may serve as a *causus* of the Asiatic mode of production because an analysis of its visual aspect makes one question the pertinence of the categories offered by the contemporary discourse of the history of art. It is characterized by a clear connection to the language and analytical categories of Western Europe, as is perfectly visible in the fundamental texts of Hungarian art history of the period. An important element of the discourse of the history of Hungarian art of the 1970s is a mechanism that can be defined most precisely as 'chase-escape'. The first part of the combination – the chase – is present in twentieth-century Hungarian art as a variety of the aspiration to 'catch up',[5] 'put time, derailed in 1949, back on its track',[6] and match 'the pace'[7] of developments in the mainstream of Western art expressed by the creators of every avant-garde tendency. However, the second part – the escape[8] – seems to clarify in a particular way the idea of the 'chase' conducted by neo-avant-garde artists, forming an unbreakable bond. This category reverberates in the majority of these texts as a reflection of the idea that the art of the Hungarian neo-avant-garde, highly political in character, was political only out of necessity. It was political because it employed Western language, which was then perceived as the language of opposition against the dominating movement of socialist realism and the realistic tendencies supported by the authorities.

An analysis of the language of the Hungarian neo-avant-garde contradicts this view. The art created in the years from 1966 to 1980 was not oppositional art in a sense that is clear from the discourse. It did not shun political language – quite the contrary. Both the ideology and the philosophy of Marxism, as well as the visual memory of the images of propaganda, created a background that was appreciated by the artists. In order to redefine this background in their works, they had to master the language of ideology, which they treated not dogmatically but rather as a tool, revealing that the ideology was a language phenomenon limited by its own notional categories rather than a universal and omnipotent model of reality. The Marxist background supplied the artists of the neo-avant-garde with relativism and a fundamental distrust towards universalist languages. As a result, they treated the '-isms' of Western provenance in an unorthodox manner, mostly as tools for their work; they were languages that they spoke for a time only to abandon them in favour of other languages. In Hungary, various '-isms' enjoyed the status of language rather than movements. The approach towards the art of the Hungarian neo-avant-garde through the stylistic notional system accepted like readymade, the particular orientation of this art towards catching up with the Western discourse – perceived as 'organic' – is merely a characteristic of the language of Hungarian art history, characterized by a clearly visible yearning for the Western European language. Instead of creating a context-oriented discourse that would reflect the visual complexity of this art, Hungarian art history attempted to squeeze its visuality into the existing discourse of the West, which was quite oppressive and simplifying for this art.

As a result, imprecise terms – such as 'Iparterv' – were coined, the use of which ran parallel to the strategy of appropriating as many Western conceptual categories as possible. They were important tools of oppression, resulting in the invalidation of both the Western terminology and the Hungarian works of art they were being used to describe, the meaning of which often ran contrary to the terminology. Consequently, there is a need to analyse the language of Hungarian art history in order to clarify its determinants, and to add necessary caveats to its fundamental concepts.

A striking example of a discourse that was almost absent in the history of Hungarian art but nonetheless forms a vital element of the visuality of the Hungarian neo-avant-garde was body discourse in the form of a politically active language that would allow an in-depth interpretation of the problem of the entanglement of the body in the structure of power. The underestimation or, perhaps, absence of this discourse in critical writings may be the result of the fact that elementary works of art and phenomena related to the body were either appropriated by the categories within which the discourse of the Hungarian art history operated – so the works/phenomena could not defend their true status – or they were rejected and overlooked.

Consequently, the politics of the Hungarian neo-avant-garde movements were generated by the following two factors. On the one hand, they were shaped by the contemporary discourse of art history – aimed at the Western notional categories. On the other hand, they were the language of art directed at politics, of which a semantic minefield was the creative sphere. The preoccupation of the artists with the political language – the concepts of wall, cage, cobblestone, as well as the intellectual engagement in events such as the military intervention in Czechoslovakia in 1968 – results in the fact that analyses of their works reveal an extremely self-conscious language and categories that the language of Hungarian art history – based on the primacy of artistic movements – fails to deal with successfully. This 'semantic minefield' was the subject of the artists' interest; however, from the point of view of a scholar, it seems mined twice – not only by the categories of Marxist ideology but also by Western notional categories. Therefore, it is possible to write about the art of the Hungarian neo-avant-garde exclusively on the basis of the twice-mined semantic minefield. The authors must watch their every step. Their work is like the work of a sapper – they must not merely avoid the mines but blow them up adroitly; the mastery is in not laying new mines.

The use of the language of geometrical or non-geometrical abstraction to describe a body of art can be seen as a necessary result of rejecting the tendency in Western art to refer only to the names of artistic movements (pop art, conceptual art, etc). It was a particularly crucial tendency, through which Hungarian art history built a bridge between the neo-avant-garde tendencies and the Hungarian tradition of the old avant-garde – a formation seen as the one that for a short time managed to bring Hungarian art back to its 'organic' mainstream. Reconciling the language created by the abstractionists with the self-conscious language of those artists whose works were characterized by high degree of politicization seems an important research objective. So is answering the question whether their involvement in the language of abstraction was connected with their belief in the universal language of structure. Finally, it is important to establish analytical categories appropriate for an analysis of the works and the characteristics of the language.

The concept of censorship, particularly among the categories of this semantic minefield, is a crucial problem here. It defines precisely the mechanism of complex interrelations between the neo-avant-garde and the communist authorities; it describes the sphere in which the revaluation of the language of ideology took place through revealing the linguistic character of censorship, which – as a language – proved powerless in relation to the language of Hungarian art.

The categories of Western origin that feature in the discourse seem – just as Marxism – a strategy of power; a language self-validating to such a degree that while using the language it is impossible to contradict it. Its universalist tendencies result in a situation when, although it is contrary to the Marxist ideology, it cannot be used successfully to defeat the ideological language; it does not form an alternative as it characterized, by similarly strong orientation, a tendency towards naturalization and the drive towards omnipotence.

It is not my aim to take works of art outside the discourse of art history, as that is impossible. Rather, I have attempted to seek the essence of the phenomenon, indicate the fractures and – thanks to analyses – raise the status of individual works of art and discover the categories that were part of them in the moment of their creation. In attempting to grasp the meanings generated by those works of art characterized by a high dependency on language, one should rely not on 'clarification' but on 'translation'.

Wall and cage

In 1991, Géza Perneczky wrote of the discourse created by one of the most influential art critics:

[László] Beke presents the Hungarian development of the 1960s as if it had been an organic part of the contemporary international scene and guides the reader to look for a possibly complete and varied manifestations of all the various -isms and modern endeavours typical of the period, here in Hungary too, which he happens to be visiting. So that he gets the impression of being in a small Western European country or one of the states of the USA, with a fairly cosmopolitan taste in the arts.[9]

However, even such a direct criticism as that found in Perneczky's text does not result in a critical attitude towards the very notional categories of -isms. Perneczky's research strategy is, instead, an arbitrary word formation aiming at 'coupling [the movements] with the most important local names'.[10] Perneczky characterizes his critical background as follows: 'I was [...] a member of that lucky group in Hungary which started their working lives in the Khrushchev years. We turned our backs more or less openly on Marxist dogma and the language and terminology of our criticism was fairly similar to that being used in the West. We felt we had escaped the Marxist cliché.'[11]

A discourse focused on adapting concepts of Western art history to the visuality of Hungarian art seems doomed to failure. Although the language thus created with its universalist pretences may be applied universally, its apparent adequacy becomes a function of its utopia. Oddly, the paradox on which the discourse is founded becomes more visible the greater the erudition of the scholars, the better the strategy of text and the more convincing the argument. The same notional categories both legitimize and exclude Hungarian art as an avant-garde art. Euphemisms rooted in the concepts of 'synchronization', 'attempt' and 'reference' rewrite the categories into 'delay', 'catching up', 'imitating' and 'following', and, consequently, place them in opposition to the contemporary avant-garde criteria.

The traditional criteria of the avant-garde, which may be simply defined as a rebellion with a name,[12] are originality, novelty and an uncompromising nature, which are possible to maintain when the political and cultural situation, out of which the Hungarian neo-avant-garde grew, is the point of reference. Consequently, the adjective 'Hungarian' is used in critical literature not as a specification of the art movements but rather as a justification for the use of these terms. It points to the dimension in which the avant-garde may be perceived as such, specifying the territory where the art was avant-garde, and consequently granting to Hungarian art the status of the 'Hungarian variant' – a dialect. The use of this language as the language of art and about art leads to a paradoxical situation that results in the reduction of the meaning of original works of art to the meaning of Western works of art, which are the only ones that deserve the status of originality.

In an attempt to prove that the artists moved within a 'universal' artistic space regardless of the Berlin Wall, the collective author formulating this point of view reveals themselves to be a participant in the culture not of Western but specifically East-Central Europe. The more one talks about 'an attempt at synchronization', which the artists undertook 'regardless of the Wall', the more clearly one situates them outside the Wall, consequently weakening the status of the Hungarian neo-avant-garde, making it even more parochial.

While the discourse of Hungarian art history was created 'regardless of the Wall', the works of art and art definitions created in Hungary not only took it into account but thematized it. The artists purposefully entered the semantic minefield, one of the central notional categories of which was the Wall.

The Berlin Wall as de Saussure's piece of paper

The Wall as the content and, at the same time, the subject of art appears in the works of the Hungarian artist Endre Tót. In the series 'I am glad if...' (see also Edit András, 'Out of Private Public Opinion into Shared Personal Opinion', pp. 229–49), the artist, departing largely from the accepted grammatical form, creates a work of art the title and matter of which is a sentence, *Ich würde mich freuen wenn ich etwas an die andere Seite der Maurer schreiben dürfte* (I would be glad if I could write something on the other side of the wall), written in German directly on the Berlin Wall. The artist makes the matter of the border the matter of his creative activity, placing himself within the matter. The inscription occupies the whole surface, the side of the wall; regardless of the absence of distance between the inscription and the clean surface of the wall, the inscription is only on one side, while the text refers to the signified, the other side of the wall, which remains outside the border. Even if the width of the wall equalled one mathematical point, its two surfaces would remain distant from one another. As long as the wall exists, everything that is created close to its boundary, on its surface, must refer to the other side. At the same time, everything that takes the other side for the signified must situate itself within the border zone, and consequently in the semantic minefield. The two sides of the wall remain as far away from each other as possible and, at the same time, they are inextricably linked like the signified and the signifier of Ferdinand de Saussure's piece of paper, that could be cut in any way, except the one which would separate its two sides.

The artist – although he sees the dependency brought about by political conditions – incorporates the Wall into his art, partly liberating himself from it. He creates an independent work of art as it is conscious of its own determinants.

In Front of and Behind the Wall

The sculpture *In Front of and Behind the Wall* (1968, fig. 1) by Erzsébet Schaár seems to present emphatically the complexity of the relationship presented in the title. Schaár, due to her age, is extremely seldom counted among the artists of the neo-avant-garde (see also Hedvig Turai, 'Limited Access to Greatness', pp. 251–69).[13] However, if we accept her radicalism as the criterion, she certainly is a member of the group.

We see a wall and two figures, one of whom is located in the space that is 'behind' and the other 'in front of' the wall from the point of view of a spectator. The women are almost identical; their heads are on the same level; consequently, their position relative to the wall is the only difference. The woman behind the wall is seen by the spectator through a prison window with a single bar, which cuts the figure into two. The woman standing in front of the wall, with her back towards it, has only empty space in front of her, and yet the spectator sees her against the wall. The wall itself was constructed so that both figures are separated and contact is impossible; their location on the two different sides is reflected in the vertical division of the surface of the wall in such a way that the women are each located in a sectioned-off space. The woman located in front of the wall is at the same time located within the very wall. Except for the head, hands and tips of shoes, her body is cut out within the wall in the shape of a human figure. The body of the woman behind the wall is cut out within the wall in the same manner. As a result, although there is an area 'in front of' and 'behind' the wall, there is nothing 'outside' the wall: there is no external point of reference, no external position. The wall imprisons both sides although they are not both imprisoned behind it. The viewers are the only ones who can move. They can choose on which side of the wall to stand, change sides or even stand along the line of the wall, in the middle, thus, in an impartial position.

However, even a mobile spectator cannot liberate either of the figures. There is no point of view that would place either of the women in an open space, located without the wall in the background. Across the wall from the side allotted to the spectators by the artist, they would see the whole figure of the woman who is hidden by the wall, but this view would also be partial, deprived of knowledge of the existence of the figure on the other side of the wall. It would be a view from the point of view of a prisoner. It would be the same if one places oneself at a different standpoint: one would only see the profile of one of the women visible against the background of the wall. The spectator thus, when moving to see more, realizes that that one can merely change the perspective, and the initial point of view against which he rebelled when he began this exercise was actually the most comfortable in terms of seeing the content. He comprehends the pointlessness of the exercise itself, as by moving in order to obtain as complex a picture as possible, he was entangled in one point of view only and he was able to assume only one position at a time. Even if he continued the journey around the installation in order to gain a processual perception, then the only thing he would really gain would be relativity. The spectator cannot eliminate the wall visually even for a moment.

The incessant changes and mutual relativization of 'in front of' and 'behind' stress the powerful status of the wall, as if adding new layers of plaster. Furthermore, the spectator himself becomes aware of the fact that he is caught in the trap of being at once 'in front of' and 'behind' the wall. Once he moves from his original spot, he loses the certainty of which of the two positions becomes him. He realizes that his own hopeless journey was not the quest for meaning but the meaning of the work of art.

The work does not content itself with the relativization of 'in front of' and 'behind' but rather states their conditions. 'Behind' (the position of communist Europe) equals the position facing the wall when, as one wants to move forwards, one always hits the wall. 'In front of' (the position of Western Europe) is the opposite – with one's back towards the wall. It is not an obstacle but functions rather as an unnoticed support. One can move ahead without meeting the obstacle, actually unaware of its existence. One cannot move from this point in just one direction, however; there are so many directions available that they make one believe in the existence of a plethora of possibilities.

The message of Schaár's work seems to equate to each of the discourses that claims universality in the presence of the Wall. It allows us to interpret as unconscious the discourse of Hungarian art history dismissive of the Wall, but it also seems crucial to the discussion of the imitative character of the art created in East-Central Europe, indicating its potentially greater self-awareness, which has been increased by the awareness of the existence of the Wall.

Telegram across the border of censorship

The works of Endre Tót are the clearest proof of how important was the awareness of the existence of the Wall to the Hungarian neo-avant-garde. Tót is an artist who – although he seems to operate with a most universal language – actually creates a language comprehensible on two levels, intentionally giving a misleading sense of satisfaction within the order of the universal perception.

In 1972, as part of a series of mail-art works sent to the West via Yugoslavia, Endre Tót created a telegram. Its content, deemed banal by the critics,[14] was 'I am writing to you because you are there and I am here.' Its elements, the two geographical points expressed by 'there' and 'here', are not the only important parts of the message – the despatch – there is also the boundary that separates them, the boundary of censorship. The geographical border that is chosen as the crossing point for the telegram is also the boundary across which, as Alfred Fischer points out, it was easiest to send something when one wanted to avoid censorship.[15] The text of the telegram was constructed in such a way that, at the same time, it does not carry any message but transmits an essence. It exhibits the function of telegram, seemingly without conveying any content, and yet it is a message sent across the geographical boundary of censorship, the Wall. It points to the very fact of the existence of two sides, the division into 'here' and 'there'.

In emphasizing the basic division of the 'here' of the sender and the 'there' of the recipient, Tót's work is far from being merely a tautological understanding of mail art. It is inseparable from its political context and

2

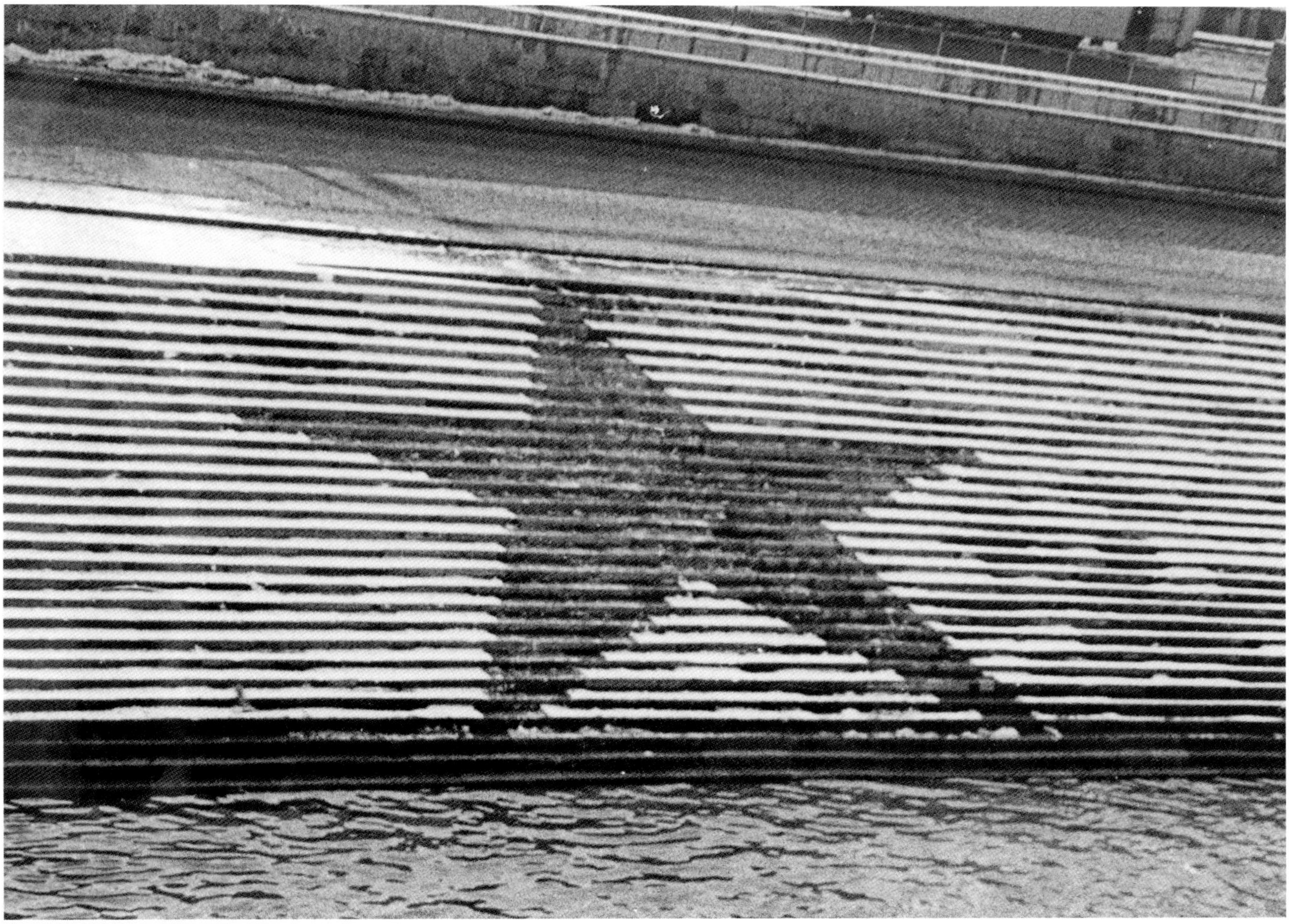

2. Gábor Attalai, *Negative Star*, 1970–71, silver gelatine print, 20.2 × 27.5 cm, Vintage Galéria, Budapest

3

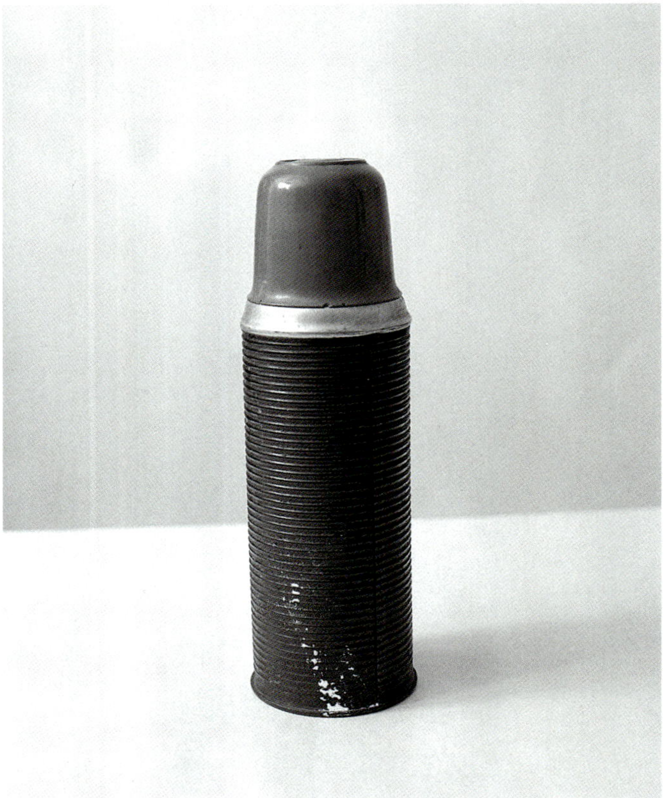

4

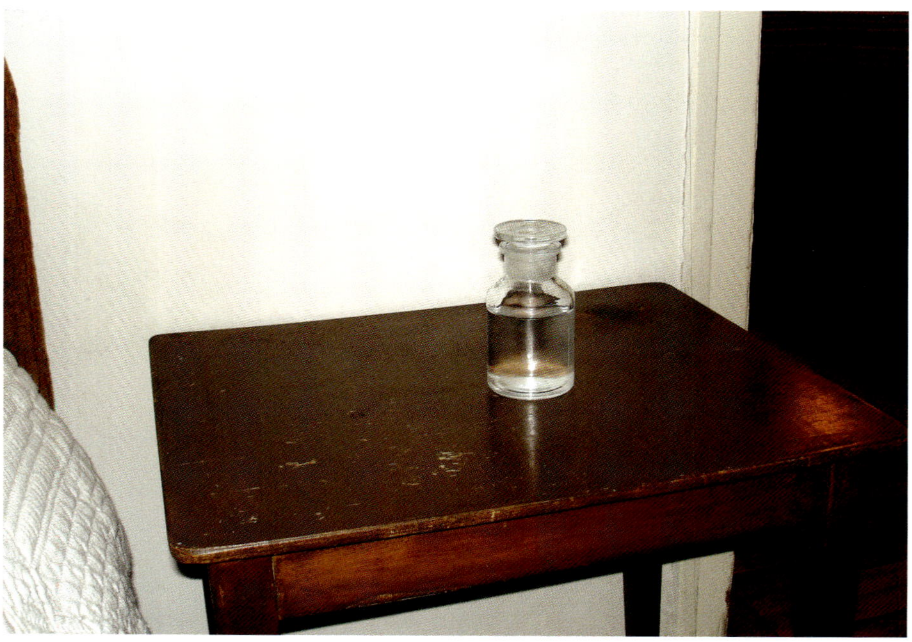

3. Miklós Erdély, *Last Year's Snow*, 1970, readymade: vacuum flask, d. 9 cm, h. 25.5 cm, Péter Sáránszki Collection, Budapest

4. Tamás Szentjóby, *Cooling Water*, 1965, glass, warm water (if the water cools down, it should be replaced with warm water), Private collection

5. Dóra Maurer, *Looking for Dózsa*, 1972, pencil, paper, cardboard, action-graphic, 60 × 110 cm, Janus Pannonius Múzeum, Pécs

directly formulates information about the existence of the sides, and, consequently, about the Wall itself. Sent to Western Europe, it is a request from the artist for Western art to take the position indicated to the spectator in the work of Erzsébet Schaár and to turn – in its space defined as 'in front of the wall' – towards the Wall. However, the message of the telegram remains unintelligible for the external receiver as it is formulated in Hungarian.

The communist freezer

One of the most important terminological fields that located the art of the neo-avant-garde in the semantic minefield was connected to the political thaw. The thaw had a particular course in Hungary, due to the complex processes which resulted from János Kádár's politics after the quelling of the 1956 Hungarian uprising. Kádár attempted to combine 'inevitable communist progress' with the liberalization propagated by his government. The thaw began in 1963 and developed fully – as Bogdan Góralczyk claims – from 1968 to 1972,[16] in the period when the more economically liberal New Economic Mechanism was introduced. The idea of the thaw was regulated by the 'communist freezer', through which political, social, cultural and economic liberalization could be frozen solid. This paradoxical dual mechanism is present in the phrase coined by Miklós Haraszti – 'the velvet prison' – and in the visual language of István Harasztÿ's work, *Cage* (1972, p. 67, fig. 6) As a result of a series of governmental decisions, mostly for propaganda value, the reforms were halted because – if they continued – they would inevitably result in the collapse of the system. The process was 'frozen', in the language of propaganda that on the one hand propagated the progress essentially linked to the political system, and on the other hand discouraged any activity. Various Hungarian artists active in the 1968–72 period, when the propaganda was the most active, created works of art using

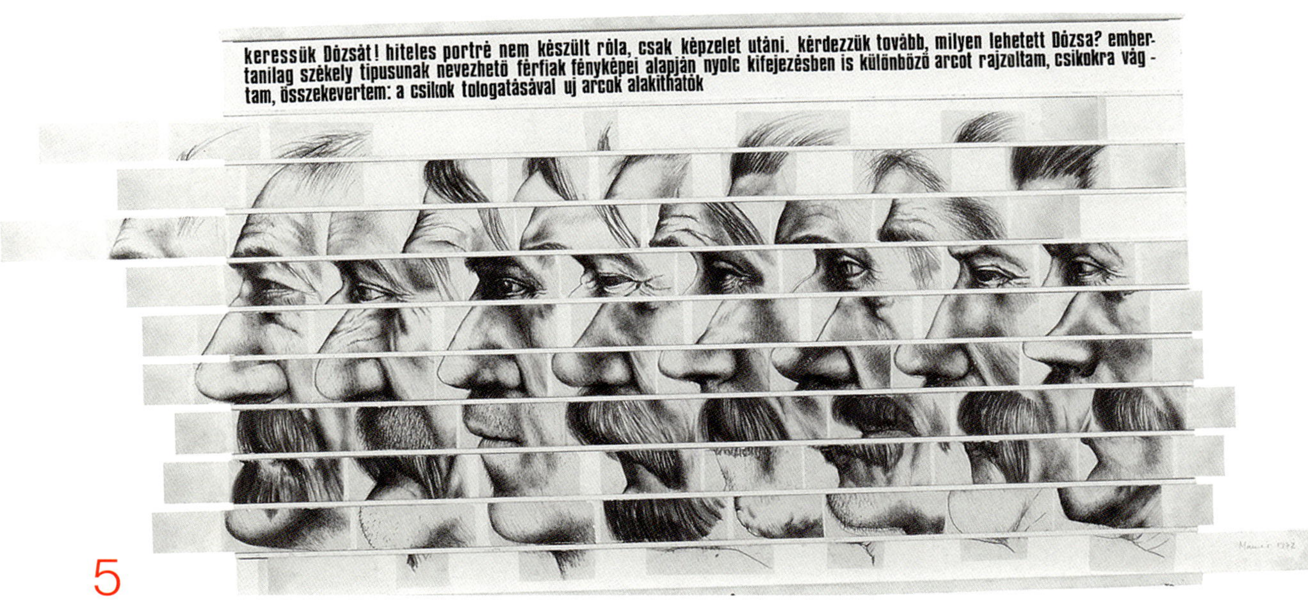

5

water in various states of matter, successfully recording the nature of this complex political and propaganda thaw/freeze mechanism as if they were not subject to it themselves.

Gábor Attalai's *Negative Star* (1970–71, fig. 2), which uses the motif of the five-pointed star, is an interesting work that has a place alongside better-known works such as *Last Year's Snow* by Miklós Erdély and *Cooling Water* by Tamás Szentjóby (figs 3 and 4). The artist's five-pointed star draws its meaning – according to János Sturcz – from the temporary aspect of continuance or, rather, impermanence.[17] Made of snow, the star's existence is limited to a single season and its decomposition seems proper according to the law of nature. Although the work can be understand universally on the level of its visual language, its crucial meaning can be arrived at only through the local context and the Hungarian language. From the point of view of a spectator from outside this linguistic system, the potentiality of colour does not exist. One automatically negates the lack of colour, as expressing it would be merely stating the obvious. However, in the Hungarian context, the star exists in relation to the 'original' Soviet one, and seems deprived of its red colour. Further, a spectator from the Hungarian linguistic system knows that snow may be red. The phrase '*majd ha piros hó esik*' ('when it snows red') means 'never' in Hungarian. Although red snow does not exist, it does exist in the Hungarian language, which is not only the language of a prospective spectator but foremost the language of the artist.

Looking for Dózsa, Finding Stalin

Dóra Maurer's *Looking for Dózsa* (1972, fig. 5) is an important work of art which so far has been the subject of rather general analyses in Hungarian art history, although it is impossible to ignore its political message. Beke's statement that 'Maurer had never been a politicizing artist' seems to influence heavily its reception, although one should note that the art historian actually lists it as one of three political works by this artist.[18] However, Beke makes only a rather enigmatic remark that she employs the method of transposition used to create an identikit picture.[19] This work, exhibited in Pécs, is representative of the Hungarian neo-avant-garde and is mentioned in every scholarly study on Maurer.

The work is an interactive installation and consists of ten vertical cardboard strips over which the following text is placed:

Let's look for Dózsa! No authentic portraits are left to us, only fictive ones [such as the well-known painting by Gyula Derkovits]. Let's go and ask: What could Dózsa be like? I drew eight faces with different expressions after photographs of the anthropologically Transylvanian type of man. Then I cut them into strips and mixed them, by moving the strips new faces can be produced.[20]

Maurer later shot a film showing her work in use (see also Katalin Székely, 'The Influx of Images', pp. 331–55). The discrepancy between what the critical studies (it is important to note that they were written mostly after the political transition in 1989) include and what the visual aspect of the work supplies when one moves its structure – usually limited in photographs and catalogues to a single elementary rectangle – is undoubtedly the greatest surprise which awaits a 'reader' of Hungarian art history. It is impossible to find in the critical studies anything beyond a mere description of the work. However, when the structure is moved, it reveals a visual aspect that one cannot miss or, ironically, pass over. Almost every profile that appears when the strips are arranged shows – in a way which leaves no doubt – the face of Josef Stalin. The left profile reminds one of the most emphatic and the best-known images in Hungarian historical visual memory: the severed head of Stalin's monument cast aside among tramway lines in a street of burning Budapest during the 1956 uprising (p. 192, fig. 1).[21] It is quite telling that, before it was dismantled by the insurgents, the monument – the destruction of which Reuben Fowkes called one of 'the most dramatic examples of popular iconoclasm in the twentieth century'[22] – had been located in Felvonulási tér (Felvonulási Square). It was the only monument to Stalin in the city, 25 meters (82 ft) high in total, and the focal point of all state celebrations from 1951, when it was raised to commemorate Stalin's seventieth birthday, onwards.[23]

6

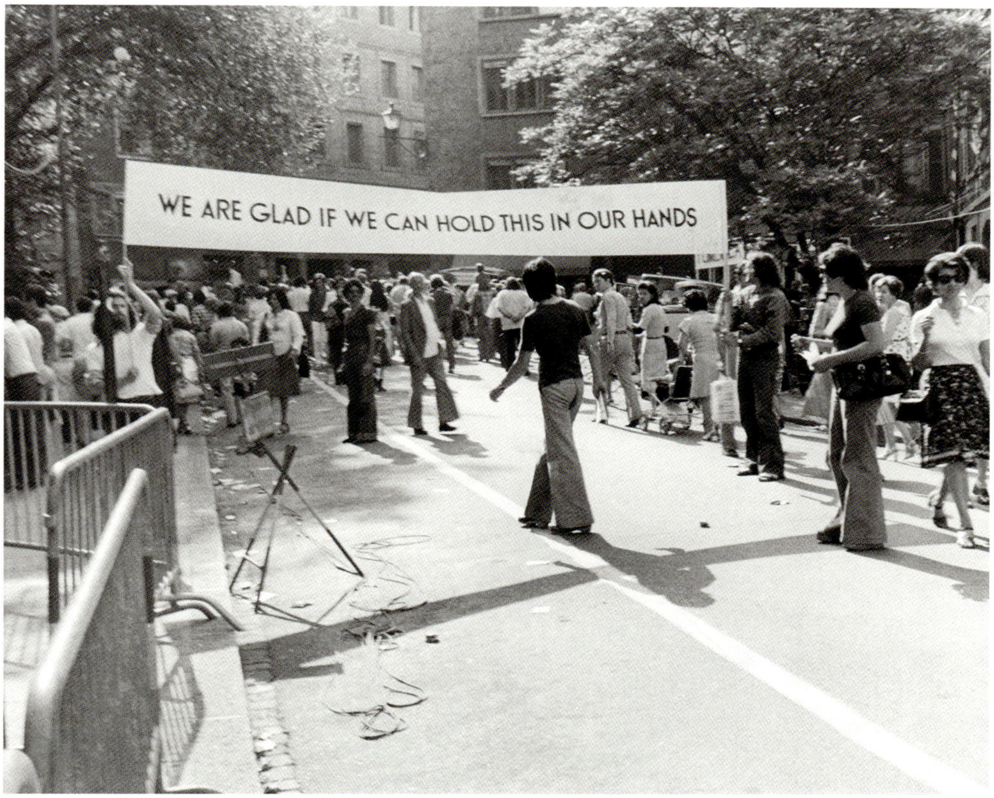

7

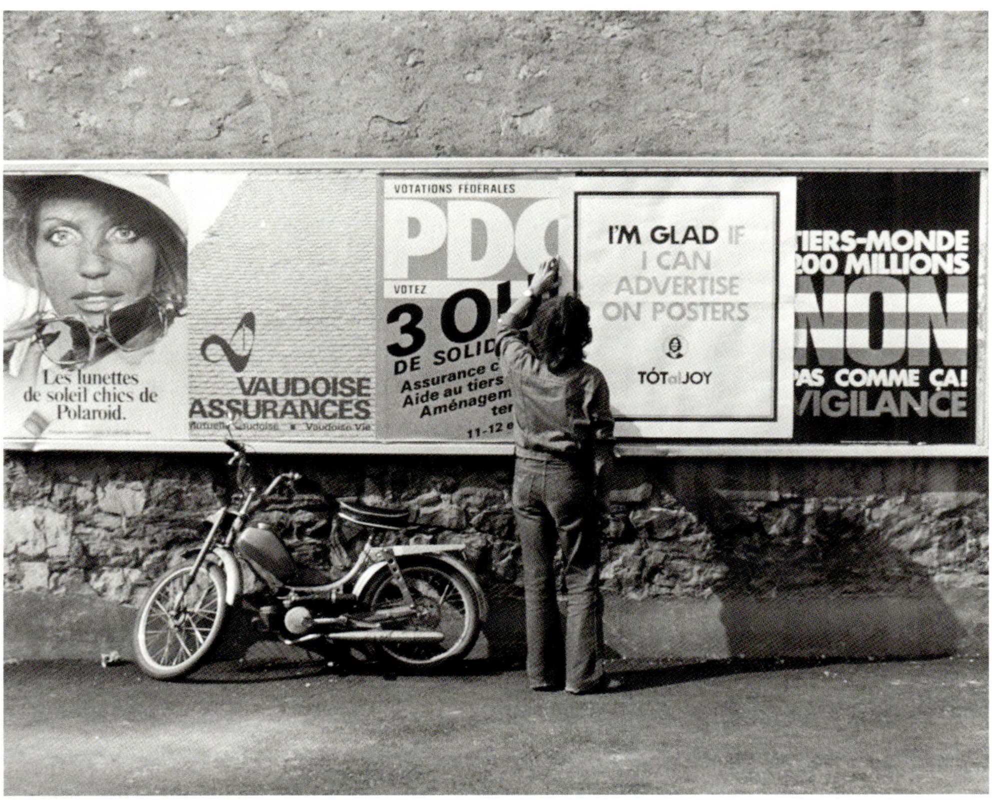

6 & 7. Endre Tót, *TÓTalJOYS*, Geneva, street action series, 1976 (1970–79), silver gelatine prints, each 50 × 62 cm, acb Galéria, Budapest

The cardboard strips can be rearranged to transform the work into a portrait of György Dózsa, an action that is not without meaning. Dózsa was a highly controversial figure – a criminal and a martyr – who in 1514 led a peasant uprising in Hungary, which turned into a bloody war against landowners; mostly due to his Transylvanian roots, his image was used cunningly in Romanian communist propaganda. Beke's comparison of the work to the creation of an identikit picture gains new meaning, as the piece reaches back into the historical memory of the nation. Linking the form of an identikit portrait of a criminal who is considered in history a mass murderer and the portrait of Stalin was especially radical. What is expressed in Maurer's work in an unusually clear manner has been left unsaid in Hungarian art history, which all too often departed from the visual aspect of works of art and their political context, concentrating instead on the universal discourse.

The joy of language

The limitations of applying Western discourse and the English language as decisive elements in the interpretation of works by Hungarian artists are most clearly visible in the analysis of Endre Tót's watchword. The watchword uniting all his actions – the identifying stamp of Endre Tót – is *TÓTalJOYS*. The use of English makes the first impression on the viewer: the receiver knows the language of the watchword even before he notices the pun proposed by the artist. It is only in the process of reading the watchword that the receiver realizes the difference in the identification of the language and its comprehension, which, according to de Saussure, starts at the moment when individual words can be distinguished and comprehended from the flow of speech.[24] Distinguishing the meaning proves a tedious task here. The first part is doubtlessly the name of the artist, and it connects visually with the third part, as they are both written in capital letters. The third part of the watchword is without any doubt an English word: 'JOYS'. The combination of the two words seems to make the message clear. The receiver can easily guess that the watchword refers to the 'joys' of the artist. However, the words that would have sufficed to get this message across were not enough for the artist: we notice the connecting lowercase letters. The reader inclined to read this text as written in English automatically assumes that the second word is 'all', indicating the amount of the artist's joys. However, when we look more closely at the lowercase letters, we notice that one 'l' is missing in the word 'all'. The receiver, in a desperate attempt to make the words make sense in English, connects the mutilated 'al' to the word 'TÓT' that precedes it and, ignoring the accent in 'ó', obtains a message satisfying the most demanding receivers – the watchword 'total joys'. The message remains almost the same, as 'total' and 'all' are almost synonymous.

'Total joys', enriched with the hidden name of the subject, seems to exhaust the meanings of the message. The artist's watchword constructed in English seems to support a language utopia; however, the watchword is actually a sophisticated subversion, constructed in a way in which it could find faithful followers without attracting suspicion. The discovery of the artist's ploy requires from the receiver a critical attitude. There is a third logical combination that allows us to deal with the problematic element of the watchword – 'al'. It does not, however, belong to the logic of English, the language initially used by the receiver as a skeleton key to decode the message. The 'al' part should be attached to the third element of the watchword. The prefix '*al*' is used in Hungarian to express subordination, thus the total joys turn out to be 'sub-joys'. As the prefix '*al*' is connected to an English word, one must also consider its other, less often encountered uses, and we arrive then at 'pseudo-joys' (from the way that '*al*' is pronounced in Hungarian).

This reading alters the meaning of the whole series of works by the artist entitled *I am glad if* ... When we deal only with inferior joys, the superior joy becomes the signifier for all the works. One does not probably need a clarification in the form of a portrait of Lenin entitled *You are the one who made me glad* (1973–75, p. 240, fig. 10) juxtaposed with the laughing face of the artist to make the political message of this work unambiguous. 'Sub-joys', making and holding a banner (fig. 6), or making an announcement through a poster (fig. 7), aim at but never reach the sum that would mean the signified 'true' joy. After the fall of communism, the 'joyful' artistic output of Endre Tót suddenly stopped. It was not yet another avant-garde gesture but an artist's block that happened when he lost an important point of reference for his creative activity.

One of Tamás Szentjóby's works created in 1972, as a part of the series 'Be Forbidden', was a straight line signed 'deadline'. The artist's gesture incorporated the official category of 'forbidden' art and made it the basic criterion of art. In doing this, he expressed his awareness that the same criterion that determined the death of art – enforcing its absence in the delicate political sphere – was responsible for the birth of what now, with the perspective of time, may be seen as the particular quality of the Hungarian neo-avant-garde art within the European context.

The Hungarian history of art presents the purposeful activities of artists not only in a direct manner – by stating their purpose (joining the sphere of Western art) but also by indicating the obstacles (avoiding censorship). The existence of an obstacle constitutes that the path is leading somewhere. On the contrary, István Örkény – in the book *The Toth Family* (original title: *Tóték*) – introduces the theoretical concept of a walk, a path taken in a pointless manner, back and forth, by the major and the head of the family.[25] The author changes the situation by placing on the road the shadow of a transformer lit up by the light from the window of a local prostitute, which signals that she has no customers at the moment. The major, who leads the walk, jumps over the shadow, which he apparently thinks is a ditch, and Mr Tót follows his example. They pass the 'obstacle' several times during their walk back and forth until the light goes out and there is no longer a shadow. The major, 'watching the surface attentively', lets Mr Tót go first. The episode, funny as it may be, is not funny in a natural manner. The awkwardness of Tót's position is not the result of the major's presence, the absence of the shadow or the major's mistake: it results from his own earlier activity – his own leaps. The jumping activity, which he saw as conditionally necessary, now seems to him to involve a decision conditioning other decisions, its meaning shaped by the new context.

If we agree that the political situation and censorship were for Hungarian artists merely obstacles stopping them from creating art such as that made by artists from Western Europe, Hungarian art would be in serious trouble. Once the 'major' lets the art go first, the political necessities seem artistic choices. Once entangled in the trap of 'necessity', Tót jumps across the place where the shadow of the transformer once was; with this decision, he continuously avoids making a decision. The works of Hungarian artists confronted with the artistic criterion can meet it without any doubt. This ability, just like Tót's indolence, must be a consequence of the artists' primary consciousness – perceiving the situation, context and code not as natural but as conventional. From this point of view, censorship and the Marxist background emerge as important elements of their work, and they were appreciated by the artists.

The artists themselves answered the question of how to create art while powerful structures appropriated the semantic field. The art created in the discussed period in Hungary was not an oppositional art in the sense that it went against the official current, which is a position different from that proposed by Hungarian art history. The works of the period are characterized by their high artistic level brought about by the fact that the strength of neo-avant-garde artists lay not so much in their opposition as in their lateral position.

The concept of the politics of Hungarian neo-avant-garde movements is constructed in such a way as to make it the generator of ideas and intellectual constructs necessary for an analysis of the phenomenon. Thus, the politics of the movements may be interpreted as a collection of strategies connected to the direction taken by Hungarian neo-avant-garde art. The neo-avant-garde (understood as the product of Hungarian art history) accepted out of necessity its link to the movements determined by the discourse and, quite literally, ascribed component works and phenomena to it. The politics of this discourse was – paradoxically – political neutrality understood in a particular manner, i.e. the belief in a universalist language, understood as an opposition to the structures of power that bound reality and the language of art. The language of art actually was not, and could not be, an opposition against the language of power based on similar principles.

The politics of the Hungarian neo-avant-garde, understood as a group of artists, consisted in the reformulation of the way of perceiving reality within which the existing ideology appeared as a strategy of power, and the language of Western art – perceived as organic – as a tool of liberation. The key issue of the reformulation of these categories, clear in the works of the neo-avant-garde artists, was the recognition of the linguistic dimension in the strategy of power, and the strategy of power in the seemingly neutral language. The politics of the artists was a politics of a gaze that was not blind to the political context of the reality, which treated this context as a language. Consequently, the field of activity for neo-avant-garde artists was a politically oriented semantic minefield. They neither followed nor objected to any of the strongly directed discourses or movements that were driving towards omnipotence (the discourse of the official power, the discourse of Western art). Instead, they were moving Hungarian art from its discursive limitations to the aforementioned minefield, which generates meanings that are rooted in the context of the creation of their artworks, and which requires vigilant translation, rather than clarification, so as to free them from the power of seemingly omnipotent discourses.

1 Ryszard Kapuściński, *Shah of Shahs.* London, Melbourne and New York: Quartet Books, 1985, 44. In the English translation (by William L. Brand and Katarzyna Mroczkowska-Brand), the original phrase in Polish, '*semantyczne pole minowe*', is rendered, somewhat imprecisely, as 'connotative minefield' rather than 'semantic minefield'.
2 Leszek Kołakowski, *Main Currents of Marxism: Its Rise, Growth, and Dissolution*, trans. P. S. Falla. Oxford: Clarendon Press, 1978, 349.
3 *Ibid.*, 350.
4 *Ibid.*
5 Lajos Németh, 'Introduction to Contemporary Hungarian Art', *Modern and Contemporary Hungarian Art, Bulletin 1985–1990*, 1991. http://www.c3.hu/ican.artnet.org/ican/text8dc1.html?id_text=90 (7 August 2017).
6 Márta Kovalovszky, 'Twice Fifteen', in Gyula Fülöp (ed.), *Bak Imre 1965–1999: Kétszer tizenöt/Twice Fifteen.* Székesfehérvár: Szent István Király Múzeum, 1999, 13.
7 Ottó Mezei, 'A szürenon és kisugárzása' [Surenon and Its Influence], in Lajos Lóska (ed.), *Hommage á Szürenon.* Budapest: Mester Nyomda, 1997, n.p.
8 Géza Perneczky, 'Art in the Sixties: New Trends in Hungarian Art', *New Hungarian Quarterly*, Spring 1991, No. 122, 119.
9 Perneczky, 'Art in the Sixties', 120.
10 *Ibid.*
11 *Ibid.*, 119.
12 Nikosz Hadjinicolaou, 'Sur ideologue de l'avant-gardisme', *Historie et Critique des Art*, No. 6, 1978, 76, quoted by Andrzej Turowski, 'Granice Awangardy' [Avant-garde Borders], in Urszuli Czartoryska (ed.), *Wybory i ryzyka awangardy: Studia z teorii awangardy.* Warsaw: Państwowe Wydawnictwo Naukowe, 30.
13 Péter Kovács wrote about her that she was not a revolutionary and was in no way connected with any avant-garde movement. Péter Kovács, 'About Erzsébet Schaár Again', in István Halas (ed.), *Schaár Erzsébet.* Budapest and Székesfehérvár: Szent István Király Múzeum/N&N Galéria, 2003, 9.
14 Alfred M. Fischer, 'Absent and Still Present: An Introduction to the Work of Endre Tót', in *Tót Endre: Who' s Afraid of Nothing? Absent Pictures* (exhibition catalogue), Cologne: Ludwig Museum, 1999, 17.
15 *Ibid.*
16 Bogdan Góralczyk, *Węgierski Pakiet.* Warsaw: Studio Wydawnicze Familia, 2000, 34.
17 János Sturcz, 'Naturally...in Hungary: The Use of Natural Materials, Energies and Venues in Hungarian Art From 1970 to This Day', in Anna Bálványos and Johanna Bárd (eds), *Természetesen: Természet és Müvészet Közép-Európában/Naturally: Nature and Art in Central Europe.* Budapest: Ernst Múzeum, 1994, 171.
18 László Beke, 'Objective Tenderness', in Dieter Ronte and László Beke (eds), *Dóra Maurer: Arbeiten/Munkák/Works 1970–1993.* Budapest: Present Time Foundation, 1994, 101.
19 *Ibid.*
20 Sándor Pinczehelyi (ed.), *Maurer Dóra: Filmek/Films 1973–83.* Pécs: Pécsi Galéria, 1983, 4.
21 The monument was destroyed on 23 October 1956.
22 Reuben Fowkes, 'Public Sculpture and Hungarian Revolution of 1956', *Inferno*, March 2003. See http://www.ungarn1956.de/node/95 (6 May 2007).
23 The actual birthday was two years earlier, in 1949, when the competition for the construction of the monument was announced. See Fowkes, 'Public Sculpture and Hungarian Revolution of 1956'.
24 Ferdinand de Saussure, *Course in General Linguistics.* New York: Philosophical Library, 1959, 103–104.
25 István Örkény, *The Toth Family*, translated by Clara Gyorgyey, in *The Flower Show and The Tóth Family.* New York: A New Directions Book, 1982, 126–29.

1. Endre Bálint, *I Have a Mind to Impart that My Mind Is in Parts*, 1958, photomontage, 50 × 70 cm, Szépmüvészeti Múzeum – Magyar Nemzeti Galéria, Budapest

1

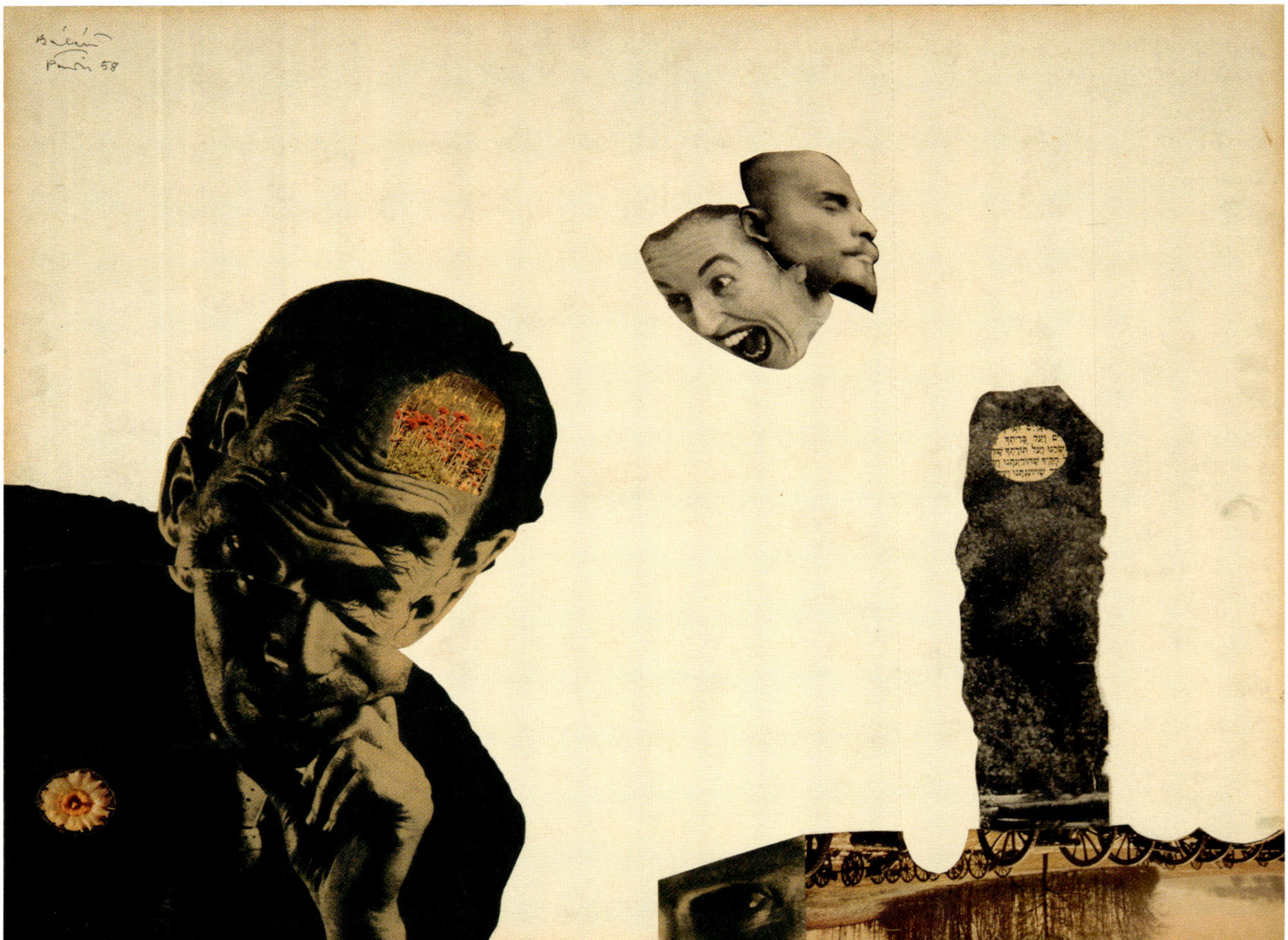

Katalin Székely

The Influx of Images

Photo, Experimental Film and Video Art in the Hungarian Neo-avant-garde

Any clever technical devices that are capable of transmitting information will instantly lead to the creation of a new branch of art. — Miklós Erdély[1]

By the late 1960s, Marshall McLuhan, the Canadian philosopher of media theory, had conquered the Hungarian cultural scene: everybody quoted and debated him, though hardly anyone had actually read him. Although even his critics acknowledged his influence, McLuhan's 'global village' seemed alarming to the devotees of the 'socialist world revolution': a world shrinking as a result of developing technologies of electronic communication allowed everyone – including those failing to proclaim the victory of the communist world order – to be simultaneously informed about every event. The American Moon landing was broadcast to millions of TV viewers on both sides of the Iron Curtain. As Miklós Haraszti, a member of Hungary's democratic opposition before the political transition in 1989, said in the 1990s: the US Moon landing was a strike against the socialist countries' 'communication monopoly'.

The Americans reached into the family with this broadcast and overwrote the interpretive power of agitprop on our own screens. [...] In fact, the Americans brought together the community promised by communism: humankind itself. When all nations and all people see and feel the same thing, gratefully astounded, that's what used to be called a miracle. Suddenly, both offers of the Soviet lifestyle caved in: the old hard promise of the Soviets leading the world and the newer softer promise of catching up with it.[2]

As the 1960s drew to an end, people in Central and Eastern Europe knew not only that the space race had been lost by the Soviet Union to the United States, but the crushing of the Czechoslovakian reforms after the Prague Spring of 1968 also made it clear that the Soviets would not hesitate to defend their control of 'friendly socialist countries' by military means.

In Hungary, as elsewhere, mass communication became the most important means of political control and influence in the 1960s. Since mass media reached the majority of people, political attention shifted from elite culture to pop culture. In some respects, this had a liberating effect on the visual arts, where new media began to appear in the 1960s, and the medium as such became the centre of attention in no small part thanks to McLuhan. Medium-consciousness and types of works reflecting on the local socio-political environment can also be traced back to the rise of mass media.

At the same time, the art practices that consciously reflected on the new media of visual art (photo, film, and video) were closely intertwined with the appearance of conceptual art in Hungary from the late 1960s onwards. Photo, film and video employed a new concept of art, which made an impact not so much as a mode of mechanically documenting reality, but rather as means of critiquing and understanding reality. Just as images poured from the West into the tightly controlled channels of mass media and questioned the image of reality promoted by the political authorities, the images of the new technical media destabilized thinking about art and its framing of socio-political consensus.

The medial turn that transpired in the spirit of McLuhan became especially significant in East-Central European countries, including Hungary, where the traditional genres of visual art operated within ideologically regulated frameworks. Photo, experimental film and video were less exposed to the state-managed and controlled art infrastructure than painting and sculpture because – unlike genres of 'grand art' – they were beyond the horizons of cultural politics. Neo-avant-garde artists experimenting with new media could not hope for large public exposure at state exhibition venues; they were shown in smaller provincial museums, cultural centres in Budapest districts and the countryside, and at youth clubs. A number of alternative venues completely evaded state control in Hungary, just like in other East-Central European countries. This is how György Galántai's studio, the most important site of neo-avant-garde art in Hungary, could operate in an unused chapel in Balatonboglár for four summers from 1970 until it was closed by the authorities in 1973 (see Maja Fowkes and Reuben Fowkes, 'Liberty Controlled', pp. 77–93, and Klara Kemp-Welch, 'Soft-spoken Encounters', pp. 273–89).[3]

The photo as a medium of visual art

The new media of visual art were not published in the mainstream cultural and art journals either: in fact, it was not *Művészet* (Art), the sole art journal in Hungary, but *Fotóművészet* (Photo Art) that published an article surveying these new media with international examples, including works by Michael Snow, Jan Dibbets, Jochen Gerz and Joseph Beuys. This was also where the first excerpt from McLuhan's *Understanding Media* (1964) appeared in Hungarian. A staunch supporter of modernist art photography, the editorial team of *Fotóművészet* was far more open to the progressive photography of the era and to Hungarian and international conceptual art than the conservative *Művészet*, which, in those years, used to be the main propagator and defender of socialist realism. *Fotóművészet* published the first text by art historian László Beke – one of the main theorists and organizers of the Hungarian neo-avant-garde – that discussed the new image-making practices of Hungarian visual art, particularly the use of photography, in light of Western trends (the happening, land art and conceptual art). Beke's study, which was one of the significant early theoretical texts of Hungarian conceptual art, included Hungarian hyperrealist painting as well, arguing that 'new realist' paintings based on photos were similar to conceptual photo works in probing the question of the representability of the view, the mechanical representation of 'reality' in visual art.[4]

The problem of representing reality was a recurrent topic in the official art discourse. No such questions could arise in relation to photography. A photo was traditionally meant to document progress and everyday life in socialism. It was only the subject of the photo that could prove problematic (for instance, the taboo topics of poverty or sexuality). These new works described by Beke, however, disrupted the consensus of the documentary – basically descriptive and realist – approach to photography. They probed the relationship between reality and the image, and explored the function of photography as a medium. Can photography document reality and what is the 'reality' it documents? What are the new possibilities a photographic approach offers for learning about 'reality'? What kind of new 'visual reality' is produced by such images?

Photography became the most important medium of the Hungarian neo-avant-garde in the late 1960s. The first review of these achievements was the group exhibition 'Exposition. Photo/Art' organized by László Beke and Dóra Maurer in 1976.[5] Held in the small town of Hatvan, a place marginal to cultural politicians, the show was the first attempt in

Hungary to present the use of photography in visual art, and primarily displayed conceptual works besides avant-garde precursors. In her study 'Reinventing the Medium', Rosalind Krauss points out that as photography became emancipated as high art (accepted by the museum, scholarship and art market), it also turned into a theoretical object in the 1960s and 1970s and successfully subverted the conventions of thinking about art. Krauss claims that conceptual art played a unique part in this process, since photography allowed artists to depart from traditional art practice while remaining within the sphere of visuality, and they could also bring structural (semantic and syntactic) relations between photo and text into play (captions).[6]

Krauss's analysis of 'conceptual art', however, does not match the 'conceptual' practice of Hungarian or East-Central European artists. It was not matters of content (representation) or form (dematerialization) that presented the significant differences, but rather the fact that East-Central European conceptual art was more powerfully influenced by its political and economic environment. Within the narrow confines of art production in the region, conceptual art was perhaps most capable of intellectually and materially expanding creative work and creating opportunities of contact with international art and artists: these works could be mailed without a permit or be packed in a suitcase and find their way to international exhibitions, anthologies, journals or even socialist countries more liberal than Hungary (especially Poland and the former Yugoslavia).

The 1960s was a crucial decade in Hungarian art photography as well. Artists emerging in this period – especially György Lőrinczy, Csaba Koncz and László Haris – had broken with the descriptive, realist forms of photography in the mid-1960s. Their innovative abstract photos influenced the use of photos in visual art: their 'objectless' photos pointed the way to turning the very medium of photography into the subject of photographs. This was also when the first major art historical surveys of the avant-garde of the interwar period were published and helped (re)discover photography as a genre of art. Endre Bálint, who employed photomontages in his own work, wrote a study about László Moholy-Nagy, Lajos Kassák and Lajos Vajda, internationally famous pre-war artists of the photomontage genre. He found parallels between their works and those of his contemporaries (e.g. Dezső Korniss) or younger colleagues (e.g. Lili Ország).[7] These works, which often reflected on social issues and veered towards the absurd (for instance, Bálint's *I Have a Mind to Impart that My Mind Is in Parts*, made in Paris in 1958, fig. 1), were only rarely presented to a broader public.

Miklós Erdély, one of the most prominent figures of the Hungarian neo-avant-garde, lauded one of the rare exhibitions of Bálint's montages in a review.[8] Erdély, who became one of the most influential artists of the era due not only to his art, but also to his theoretical texts and art pedagogical practice, writes about the changed status of photography (its elevation into the sphere of 'grand art') and considers photomontage a truly democratic genre that does not require special equipment or even significant expertise, as 'montage reveals mental intelligence almost immaterially'.[9]

Besides his study on art film, 'Hunger for Montage' (1966),[10] and his films, poems and sonic works, Erdély's numerous photo works indicate his attraction to the genre of montage. Yet montage is not merely a technique in his oeuvre; it's also a framework for his scholarly theoretical research. Erdély constructed his art theory also as a kind of montage, combining current topics and discoveries of science and the humanities with pseudoscientific theories, while he aimed to narrow or even to close the gap between scientific and artistic thought.[11] Thanks to montage, as interpreted by Erdély, art was capable of showing the complexity and inner contradictions of human thought. In fact, Erdély points to the fragility of our knowledge and concepts by exhibiting these contradictions, by juxtaposing conflicting statements. In the first piece of his montage series *Oath* (1970, fig. 2), a quotation by Erwin Schrödinger on the wave-particle duality of light is projected on Erdély's chest, as he raises his hand in an oath. The sentences on the paradoxes of scientific discovery and the finitude of human perception are linked with the infinite vistas of artistic perception in Erdély's work: just as devices of formal logic fall short of comprehending the great scientific theories of the twentieth century (quantum

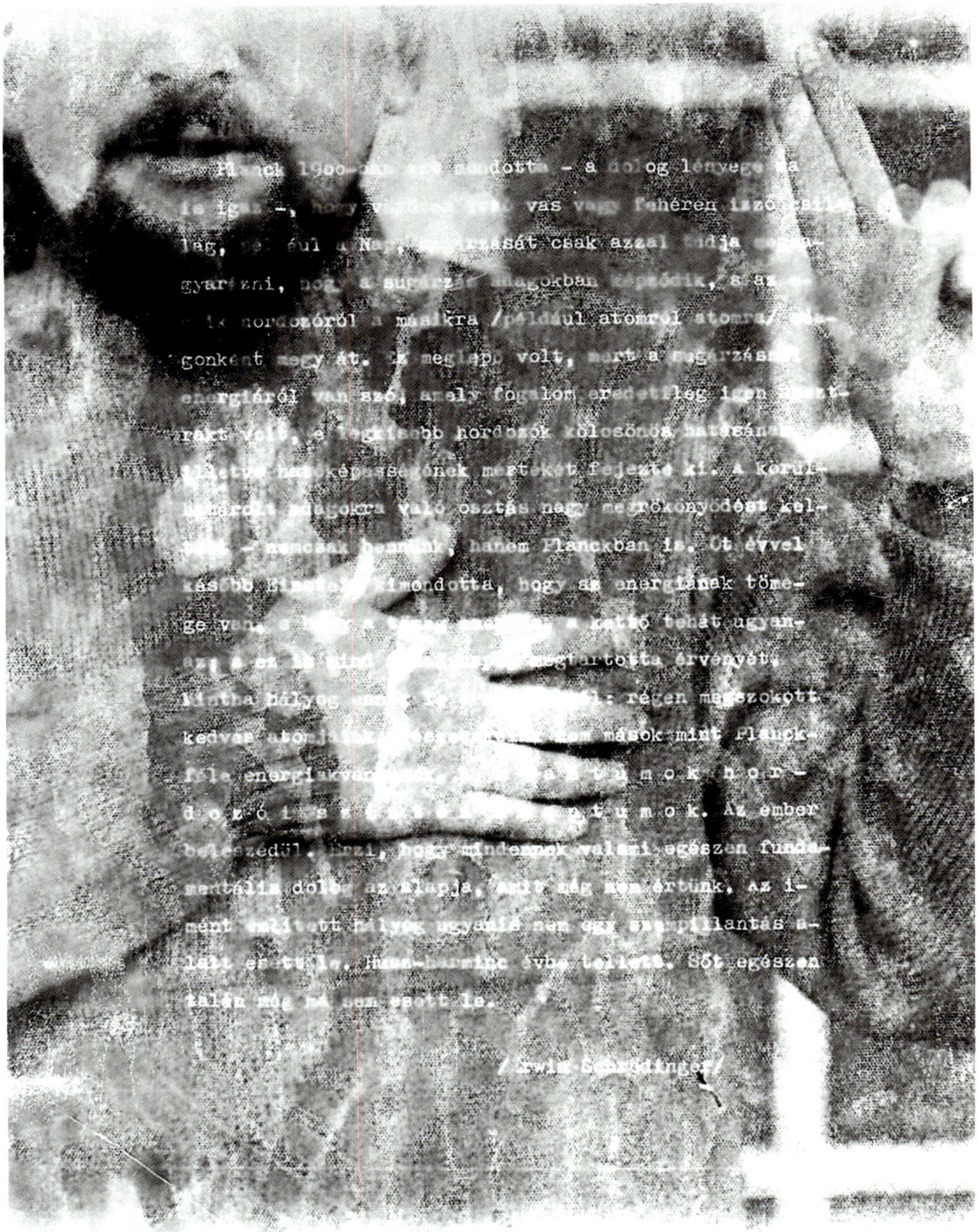

2

2. Miklós Erdély, *Oath (1.)*, 1970, photomontage, silver gelatine print, 29.5 × 21 cm, Péter Sáránszki Collection

theory and the theory of relativity), one cannot rely solely on one's sight when encountering works of art. Images always mean something else – this insight of Magritte's (*The Treachery of Images*), that is, the paradoxical logic of representation, is the subject of Erdély's photo *No Photographs!* (1974, fig. 3), which inescapably reads as a critique of the images of power and of mass media manipulation in a repressive political system.

The Moebius metaphor, which is closely linked to montage theory, is central to Erdély's oeuvre. His five-part work *Time Travel* (*Time Moebius*, fig. 4) in 1975–76 takes on the paradox of the Moebius cartoon strip (the beginning equals the end, life equals death and existence equals non-existence): time circles in on itself in a montage of the Erdélys' family photos from different eras, which photography can separate into tangible moments. The Moebius problem also appears in Erdély's films, and the tension of existence and non-existence in the infinite loop of time is a subject of the photo documentation of Erdély's actions too. The 'extinguishing of meaning', another central tenet of Erdély's writings, plays an important role in one of his actions in 1969. Erdély's facial features are obliterated by the light of the flash he is holding in his hand in *Self-Illumination (Light Eats up Man)* (fig. 5), which exists in several versions. The ontological/spiritual associations of light ('Let There Be Light!') are connected to the power aspects of the technical medium here: the flash evokes an interrogation light aimed at the artist by himself.

The flash as a device for annihilating the artist – even physically – is exceptionally important in Tibor Hajas's oeuvre as well: both in his performances and his photo tableaus with János Vető (see also Emese Kürti, 'Poetry in Action', pp. 291–313, and Edit András, 'Out of Private Public Opinion into Shared Personal Opinion', pp. 229–49).[12] Just as light can be both a creative and a destructive force, the photograph can also record and question reality. Hajas's series *Restorations* (1976, fig. 6) is a conceptual montage modelling his photo-theoretical ideas ('the photograph: a quotation from reality'). When objects (a twenty-forint coin, a book by Huxley and a cigar) are juxtaposed with their photographs, Hajas examines the relationship between reality and its depiction, between object reality and image reality. Hajas, who initially wanted to become a poet, did not take many photos (like Erdély), nevertheless he discussed photography extensively in his writings. He explains in 'The Photo as a Medium of Visual Art':

> *Photography is a natural environment and civilizational milieu for the 'new photo', this culture has been so thoroughly saturated by the images of film, television, video recorders, and the press [...], and these have become such foundations for our attitudes that the new photo can break its alliance with art photography and visual art alike; its trends and achievements speak – though on different levels – on behalf of the entire civilization that has made this medium one of the foundations of its forms of communication.*[13]

Hajas thought photography was one of the most effective means of publicizing ideas. His work *To the Streets with Your Message I–II* (1975, fig. 7) consists of two photo tableaus, each documenting one of Hajas's actions. The private message written by Hajas in chalk reaches its addressee by involving the broadest public (i.e. through public space) in *A Letter to My Friend in Paris*. In the tableau *Living Comics*, he uses montage to place a private conversation in public space, employing speech bubbles appearing from the artist's mouth as he walks in the street. As if critiquing the private communication channels and their close monitoring by the authorities (bugged telephone lines and violations of mail privacy), Hajas's 'stationery' for his private message is public space, which was appropriated by state power for the transmission of its own messages at the time.

Numerous East-Central European artists' works entail such a contrast between propaganda-ridden public space and personal private space. In the photo series *1 May 1975* (1975) by Mladen Stilinović of Zagreb, the artist places his confession of love next to the shop windows decorated for the state holiday. Such works offer a critique of politics that banishes private expressions from public space while also oppressively controlling individual lives in the era.

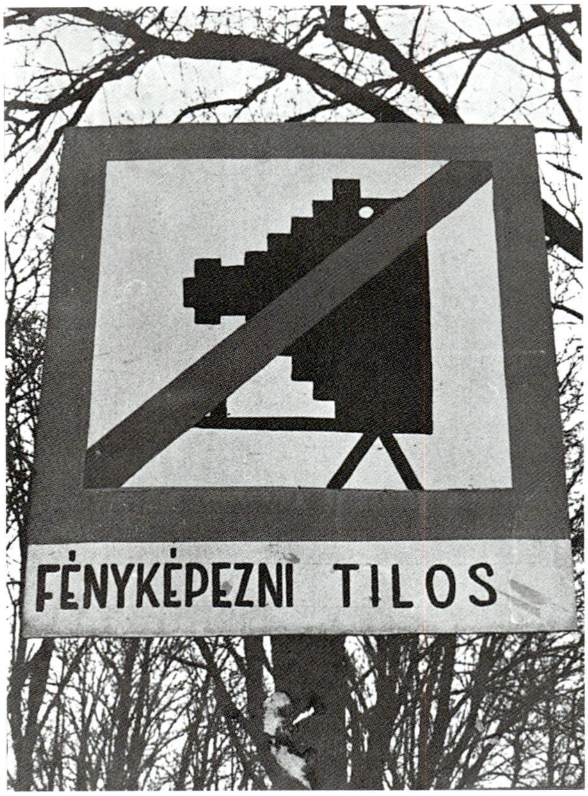

3

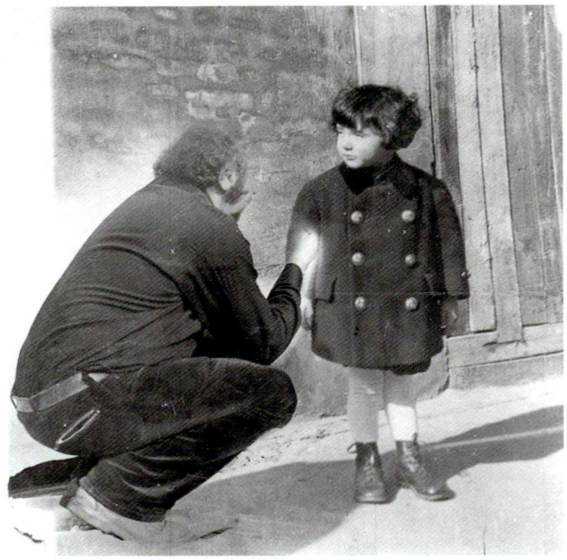

4

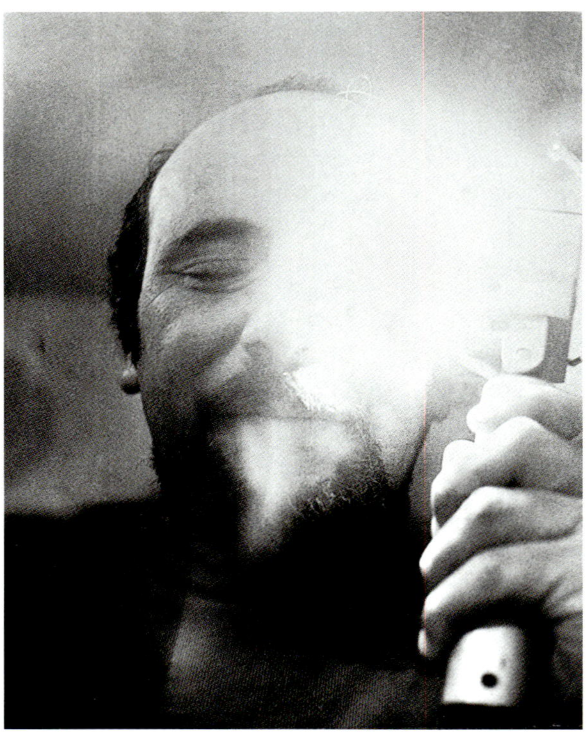

5

3. Miklós Erdély, *No Photographs!*, 1974 (Photo by Gizella Rákóczy), silver gelatine print, Forte Dokubrom Copy Paper, 29.5 × 21 cm, Miklós Erdély Estate

4. Miklós Erdély, *Time Travel II*, 1975, photomontage on fibreboard, 48 × 49 × 5 cm, Szent István Király Múzeum, Székesfehérvár

5. Miklós Erdély, *Self-Illumination (Light Eats up Man)*, 1970 (Photo by Gyula Zaránd), silver gelatine print, Forte Dokubrom Copy Paper, 29.5 × 21 cm, Spengler–Somlói Collection

6. Tibor Hajas, *Restorations 2. Restored Money*, 1976, money, completed with a photograph, 45.8 × 33 × 1.6 cm, Ludwig Múzeum – Kortárs Művészeti Múzeum, Budapest

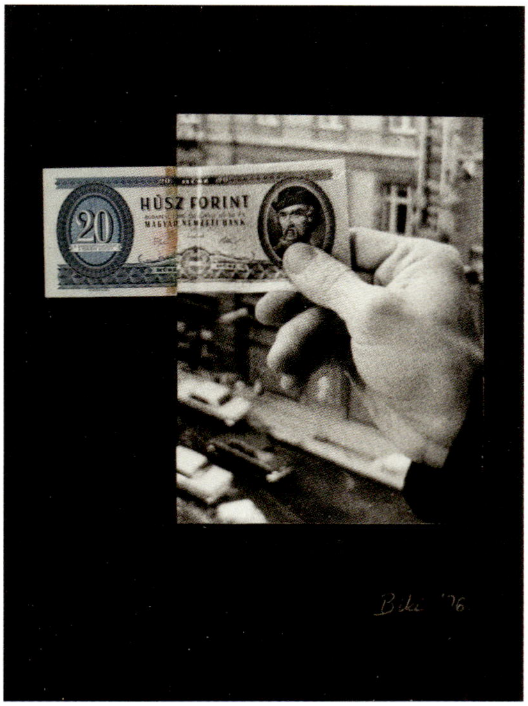

6

'The basic themes of the "new photo": the camera, the medium itself, and the language of the medium; looking as a pure intellectual activity', writes Hajas.[14] The photograph as a device of understanding the laws of seeing was something that fascinated György Jovánovics as well. He began to take photos in the early 1970s as an offshoot of his sculptural work, saying he was interested in 'making sculptures with a camera'.[15] It was in the mid-1960s that he began to make his sculptures nearly exclusively of plaster: like photographs, his moulds were based on the principle of the mechanical reproduction of reality. The plaster mould (for instance, the motif of drapery used frequently by Jovánovics) preserves the original form as an imprint of reality, while also questioning it. As the light falling on the work keeps redrawing and rearranging the view (it is hard to tell if one sees a two or three-dimensional object), so do conventional borderlines disappear in Jovánovics's art between sculpture and architecture or sculpture and photography. One of the notions running through his entire oeuvre is the search for the 'complete image', and this appears in his sculptures based on the principle of the camera obscura (*The First Camera Obscura*, 1970). The notion of the 'complete image' is inherited from Moholy-Nagy; what fascinated Jovánovics, like Moholy-Nagy before him, is photography's ability to expand the dimensions of seeing rather than its naturalistic ability to capture the visible perfectly. Similar to Moholy-Nagy's light sculptures, Jovánovics's works do not simply employ light to represent reality, but to shape it, to create its form. His series of 'conceptual comics' *Liza Wiathruck: HOLOS GRAPHOS* (1976, fig. 8) is, in the artist's words, a 'blind manifesto on sight', an 'organic photomontage', which is not produced through tricks of photo technique (or scissors and glue): it is reality itself that montages itself together into a single exposable image.[16] The work includes Jovánovics's sculptural themes (mask, drapery, the window frame) in a palimpsest of narrative layers. The series of photographs, which also includes a long text, mixes inside and outside, reality and its record in images composed through multiple reflections and superimpositions. Liza Wiathruck, the female protagonist of his comics and the artist's 'magic alter ego' (who would also be embodied in sculpture in 1980), is called a 'holograph' or a 'light sculpture' by Jovánovics. The work reinterprets the Pygmalion myth of the statue coming to

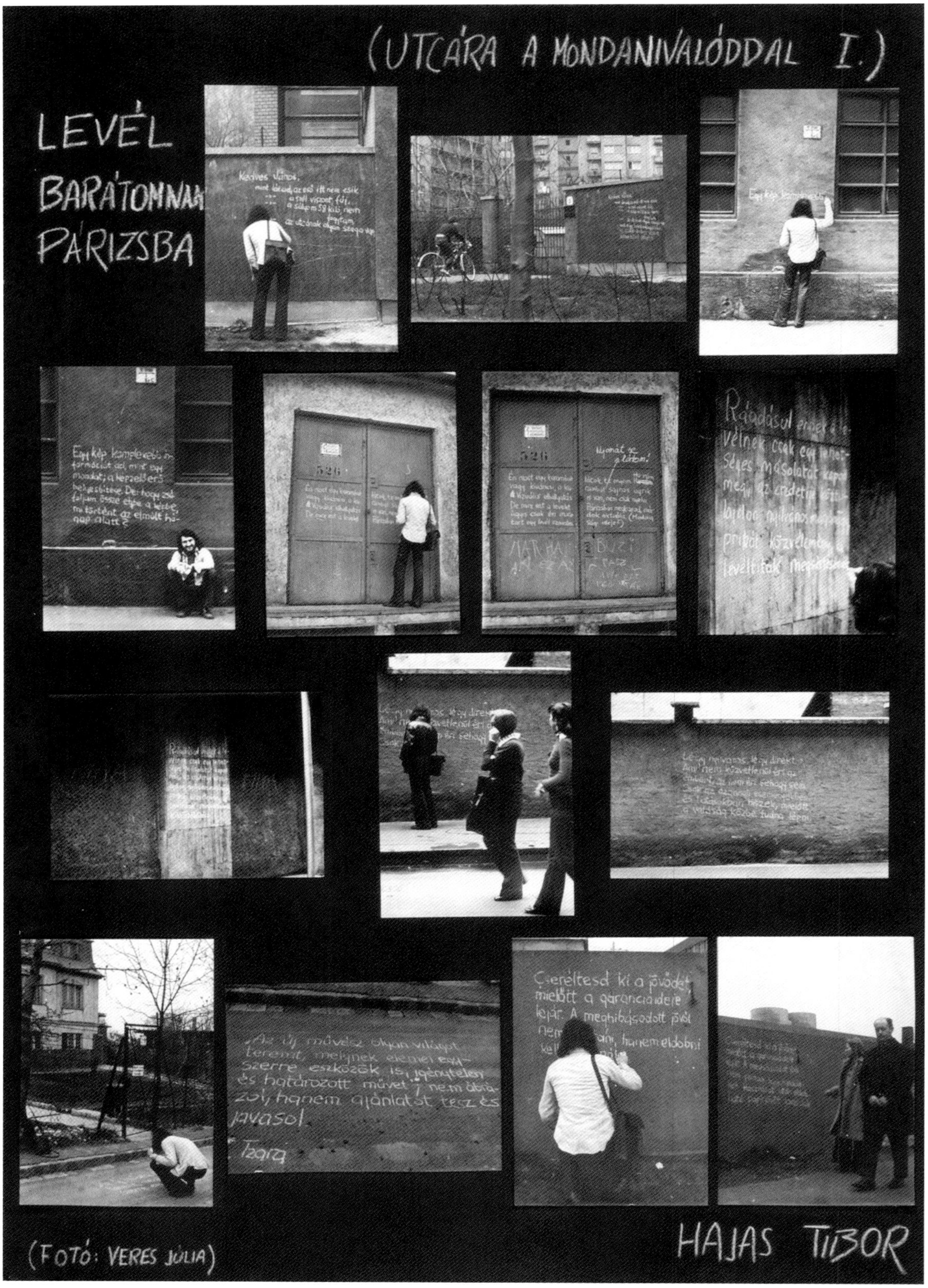
(UTCÁRA A MONDANIVALÓDDAL I.)
LEVÉL
BARÁTOMNAK
PÁRIZSBA
(FOTÓ: VERES JÚLIA)
HAJAS TIBOR

7

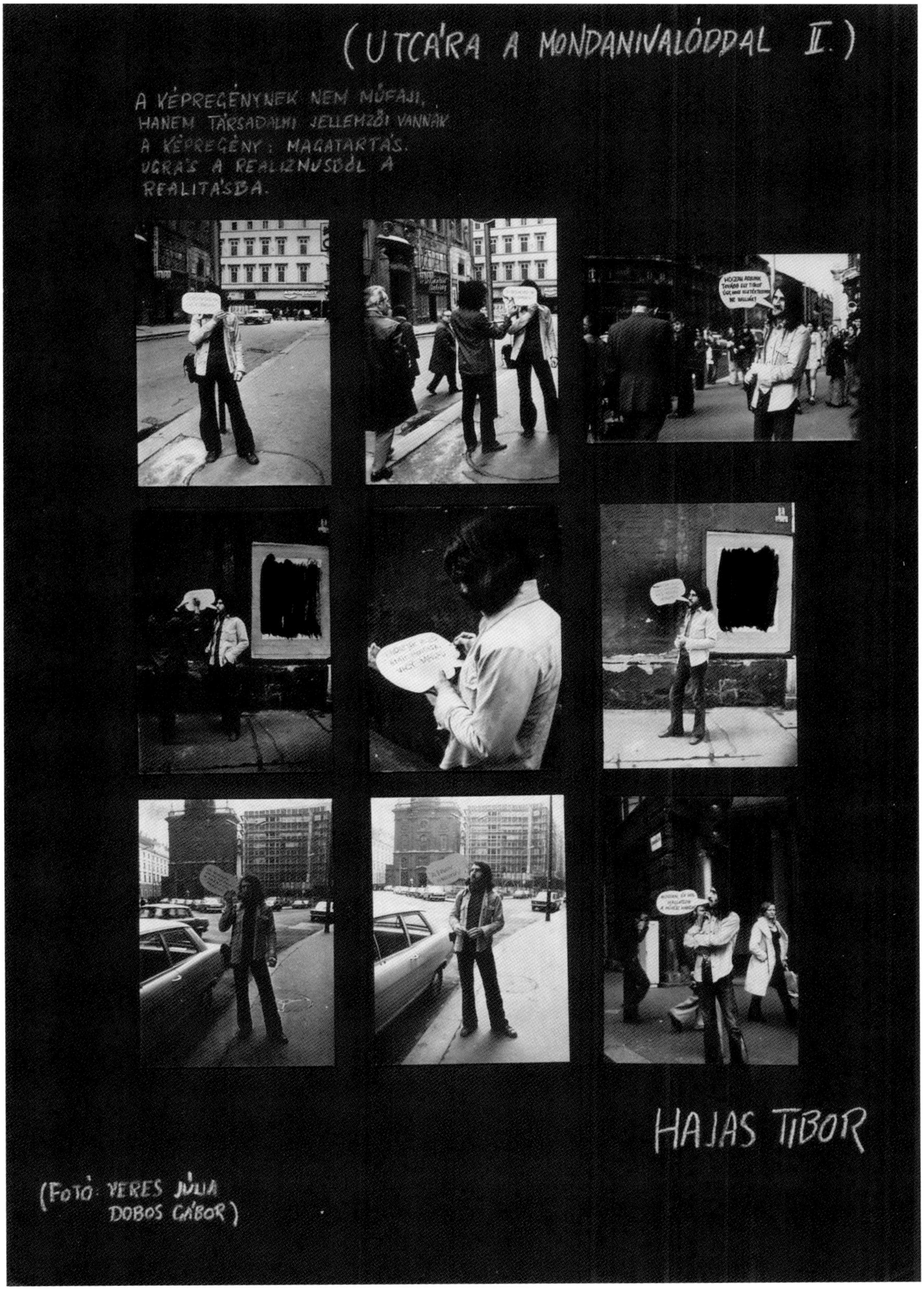

7. Tibor Hajas, *To the Streets with Your Message I–II*, 1975, white chalk, photographs mounted on black cardboard (Photo: Gábor Dobos and Júlia Veres), 2 panels, 100.3 × 70.2 cm each, Ludwig Múzeum – Kortárs Művészeti Múzeum, Budapest

life to probe ontological and art theoretical questions, while evoking the erotic registers of the original myth. Liza's story (the mysterious female character is under surveillance, then she falls in love and becomes pregnant) is connected to visual perception or, in Jovánovics's terms, 'image surveillance', and insight offered by seeing with closed eyes. Jovánovics poses questions about the image and one's relation to it: how does seeing aid understanding? How is reality produced through sight and is what we can see reality? 'Image surveillance' was interpreted by socialist cultural politics not only as a device for expanding vision, but also as a dangerous, subversive message. In 1977, the exhibition at the Fiatal Művészek Klubja (Young Artists' Club) in which the work was to be displayed was banned before opening.

Inspirations and models inherited from Moholy-Nagy and members of earlier avant-garde generations like György Kepes and Tihamér Gyarmathy were an important resource for neo-avant-garde artists experimenting with technical media. Yet, the photogram, this popular genre of 'new photo', was not simply a salute to avant-garde forerunners. Within the limited possibilities of the underground scene, it was also advantageous that the photogram only required cheap Dokubrom paper and not even a camera or a negative stock. Objects were directly placed on photosensitive material, and their shadows 'drew' the image, the imprint of reality. Dóra Maurer says that 'making a photogram is actually the use of simple devices to provoke the laws of reality so that they present themselves in countless variations'.[17] Maurer's career began with copperplate etchings influenced by surnaturalism. Her first experiments also involved this medium, as in *Throwing the Plate from Very High* (1970). In the case of both graphic plates and 'light-drawn images', Maurer was fascinated by the issue of leaving a trace: for instance, her photogram series *Sluices* (1977–80, fig. 9) explores how the movement of dust or liquid can be represented, or what trace a material leaves on photosensitive paper when it encounters obstacles to its motion.

Maurer was highly regarded in the symbolic order of a male-dominated cultural life not only for her works, but also her art organizing and art pedagogical activities.[18] She organized a number of exhibitions – she co-curated 'Expozíció' – while 'Kreativitási gyakorlatok' (Creativity Exercises), her joint art pedagogical programme with Miklós Erdély, and her later courses had an elemental effect on numerous young artists (see also Flóra Barkóczi, 'Creative (Dis)Courses', pp. 95–109). It was in the early 1970s that her attention turned to nature actions and serial works modelling mathematical sequences. This structuralist mindset also appears in her paintings and graphic works, which were produced in parallel to her conceptual works and in close connection to them. These examine the complex mathematical relations of basic geometric forms (squares, rectangles). Movement is a central notion in her whole oeuvre: it is present in her painting, graphic works, photos and experimental films alike. She builds minimal movements into sequences, as in the photo series *Reversible and Interchangeable Phases of Motion* (1972–75, fig. 10), where she arranges the snapshots of these minute movements (a figure standing, then sitting down in a chair, a hand raising a stone). Images follow each other in a constantly changing order, suggesting new narratives and possible interpretations. With Maurer, movement is often linked to perception itself: in her photos modelling eye movements, the distinct angles of the two eyes' perspectives (*Right Eye – Left Eye Double Object Photos 1–2*, 1973) evoke stereoscopic images, early experiments in the history of photography.

The camera also plays an important part in Maurer's works. It 'draws', feels the space, interacts and communicates (*Photo-Interaction for Two Cameras*, 1977, with Zoltán Lábas). Like her geometric abstract paintings, Mauer's photo series *Seven Twists* (1977–78, fig. 11) also shows the movement of forms shifted relative to each other. The self-portrait appearing in infinite reflection is not just formal play, but one of the most emblematic images of the artist's use of photography: for Maurer, photography is a means to model and understand, classify and rearrange reality.

However, the primary function of photography in conceptual art was a documentary one: visualizing ideas or

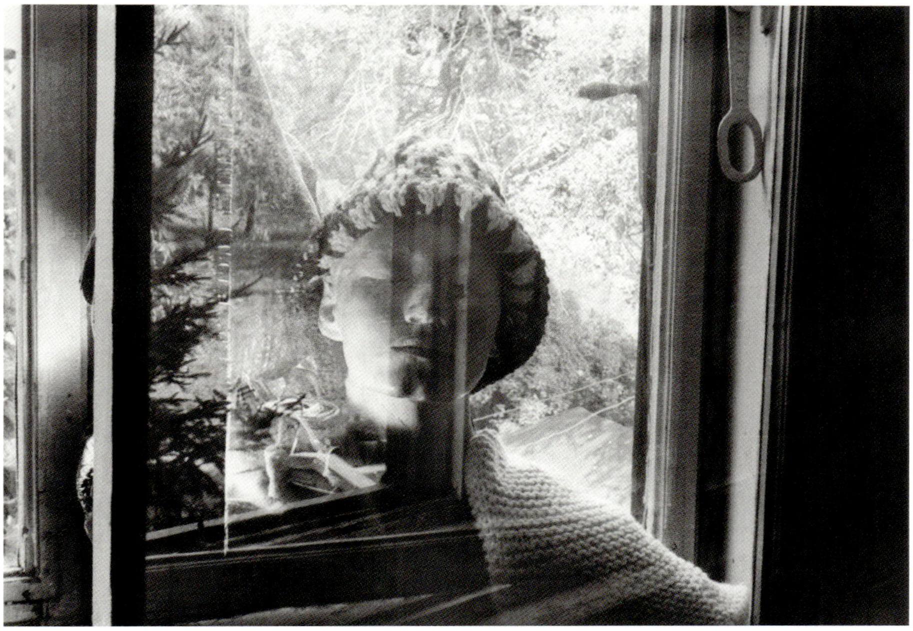

8

8. György Jovánovics, *Drummond-light, Liza Wiathruck: HOLOS GRAPHOS 19*, 1976, silver gelatine print, 70 × 100 cm, Szépművészeti Múzeum – Magyar Nemzeti Galéria, Budapest

9. Dóra Maurer, *Sluices I–II*, 1980, photogram, 2 pieces, 48 × 43 cm each, Vintage Galéria, Budapest

9

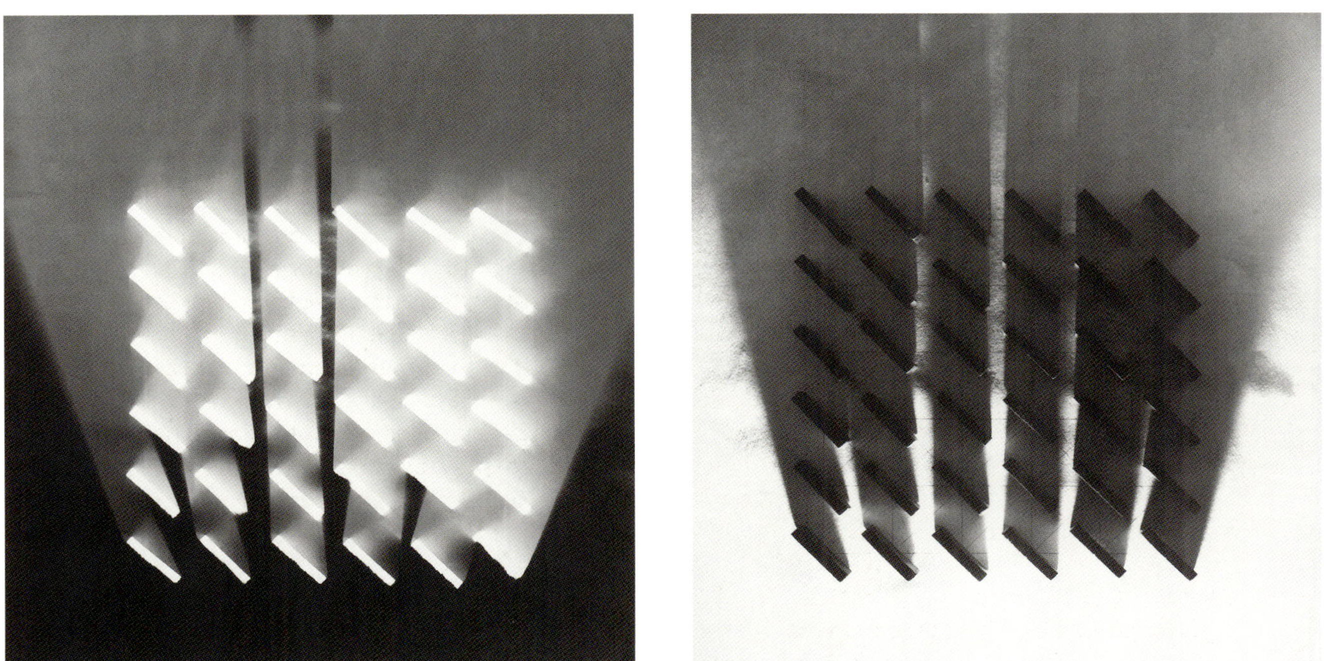

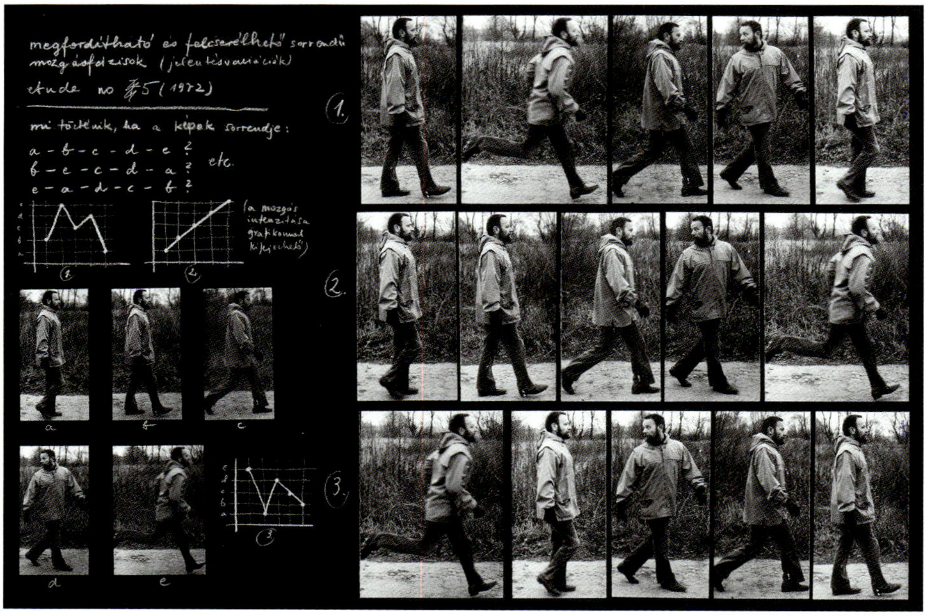

10

10. Dóra Maurer, *Reversible and Interchangeable Phases of Motion*, etude No. 5, 1972, white pencil, photos mounted on cardboard, 70 × 100 cm, Ludwig Múzeum – Kortárs Művészeti Múzeum, Budapest

11. Dóra Maurer, *Seven Twists I–VI*, 1977–78, photo, 6 pieces, 20 × 20 cm each, Tate Modern, London

11

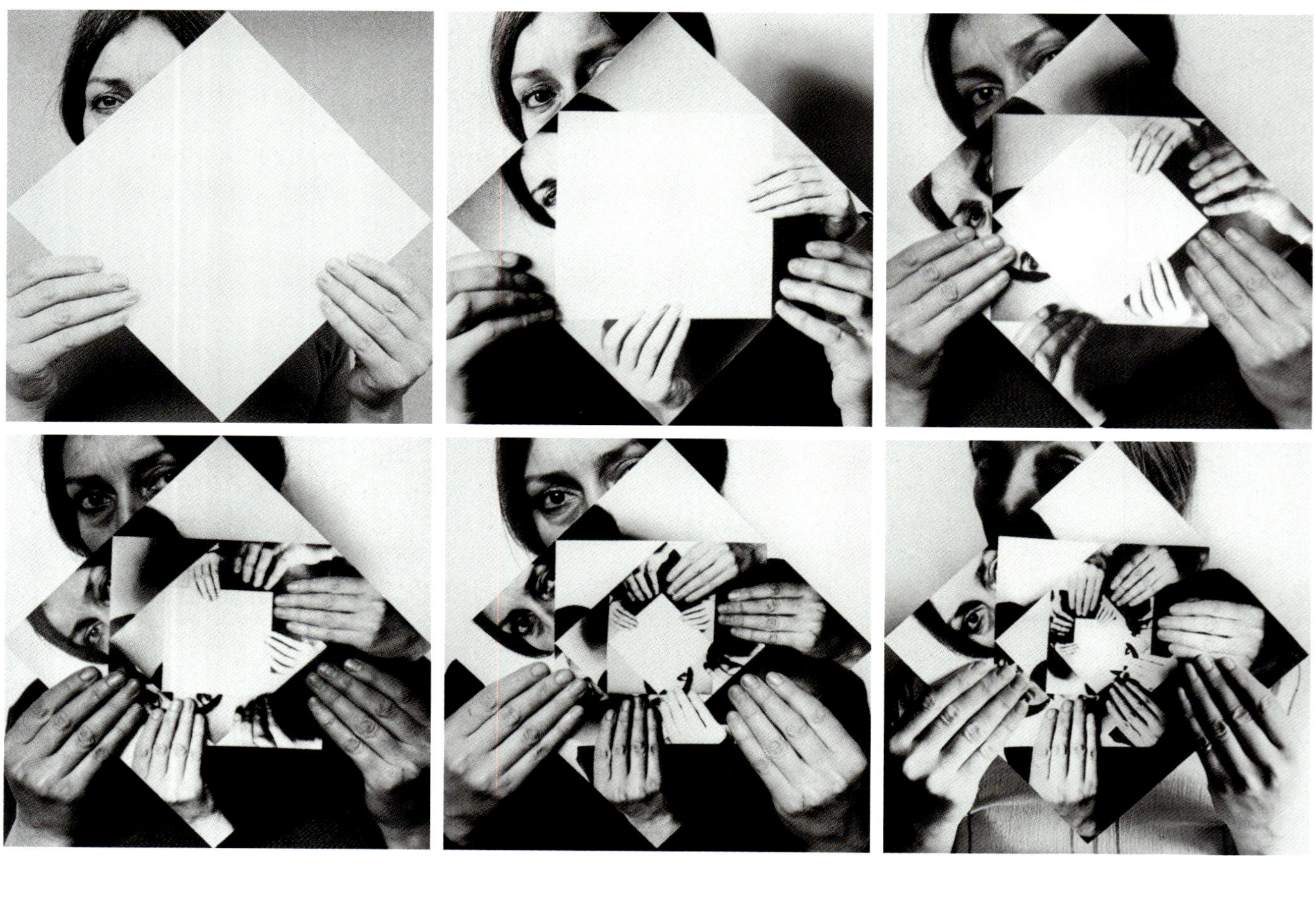

recording events. Members of the Pécsi Műhely (Pécs Workshop) – Ferenc Ficzek, Károly Halász, Károly Kismányoki, Sándor Pinczehelyi and Kálmán Szíjártó – used photo documentation as pioneering artists of Hungarian land art (see also Flóra Barkóczi, 'Creative (Dis)Courses', pp. 95–109).[19] Compared to the neo-avant-garde artists mentioned above – especially Hajas and Erdély – the Pécsi Műhely had a privileged position: their infrastructure (e.g. the studio or the cameras documenting their actions) was funded by local state institutions, they could organize exhibitions and publish catalogues, and the (no less state-controlled) local media – for instance, the newly established Pécs Television – was genial in its treatment of the artists who occasionally produced quite politically charged works (see, for instance, Pinczehelyi's *Sickle and Hammer* self-portrait series, 1973, p. 243).

Besides his joint land-art actions with the Pécsi Műhely, Károly Halász also conducted light and photo experiments as homage to the art of László Moholy-Nagy. One of his central subjects was television, the most important mass medium of the day. As a critique of the regimes' use of state television for manipulation, Halász created objects out of empty TV sets, then began to manipulate the TV broadcast (see also Edit András, 'Out of Private Public Opinion into Shared Personal Opinion', pp. 229–49). His *Modulated Television* series (1972–73, fig. 12) appropriated television broadcasts (cultural programmes, soccer games or the state television's programme on current events). The geometric patterns, which were drawn on transparent foil and placed on the screen, overwrote the images transmitted through the mass medium, removing them from the official political-aesthetic context. The same gesture of appropriation appears in the series *Private Broadcast* (1974–75, p. 233, figs 4 and 5), where Halász literally takes ownership of television. For Halász, television is simultaneously a tool of manipulation by state power and a window on the world – a window where he can also appear, looking out. For Halász is the protagonist of his own 'private broadcast': he is crouching in the box, he is looking and being looked at, watching and being watched. The problem of watching and being watched, with all its political connotations, appears in the series *Pseudo Video* (1975, p. 232, figs 2 and 3) as well, where the artist photographing himself is participant, cameraman and viewer of his own 'private broadcast'. The work imitates the video technique quite prevalent in Western European art in the period, its title reflecting on the humble technical resources of Eastern European artists. Halász's relationship to television is both intimate and critical: we watch TV because it transmits information from the world outside, but it watches and controls us too (see his outdoor action in 1973: '*Watch the TV*' – '*The TV Watches Us*'). In comparison to a more closely monitored Budapest scene, Pécs was a more open milieu, as attested by the broadcast of Halász's performance *Private Broadcast* in 1975 (fig. 13) by Pécs Television.

Experiments in film language

Whereas the Pécs Workshop could receive some support thanks to the openness of those in charge of local cultural institutions and media, Balázs Béla Stúdió, the workshop of Hungarian experimental film, had regular state support and funding. The establishment of the studio was an initiative of young filmmakers in 1959 and became an official institution in 1961. The BBS enjoyed a degree of freedom unprecedented in the period: members could make their films without any obligation to screen them publicly, which allowed young directors to experiment without compromise. At the same time, the BBS was an excellent tool for cultural politics: young artists were corralled and monitored as they worked and their films reached a limited public. The primary objective of the BBS was to allow young directors, recently graduated from the Színház- és Filmművészeti Főiskola (Theatre and Film Academy), to prepare for their feature films; yet, from the very start, numerous films made here departed from the conventional language of state-film productions.

The pattern of duality in Hungary's cultural politics – a doublespeak whereby there was strict control at home while trying to appear liberal in the eyes of the West – is evident in the fact that the most progressive and critical works of the period were made in

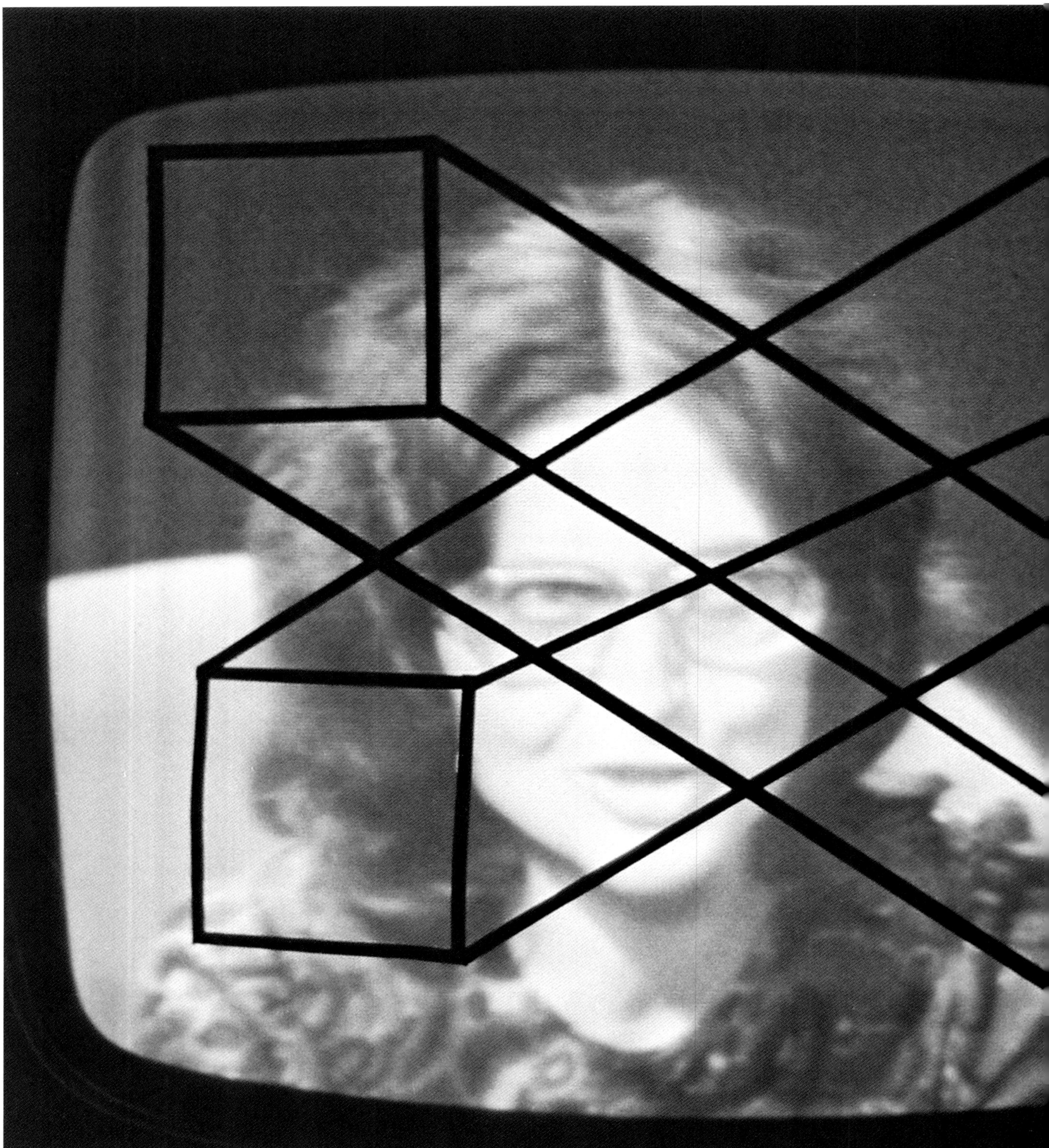

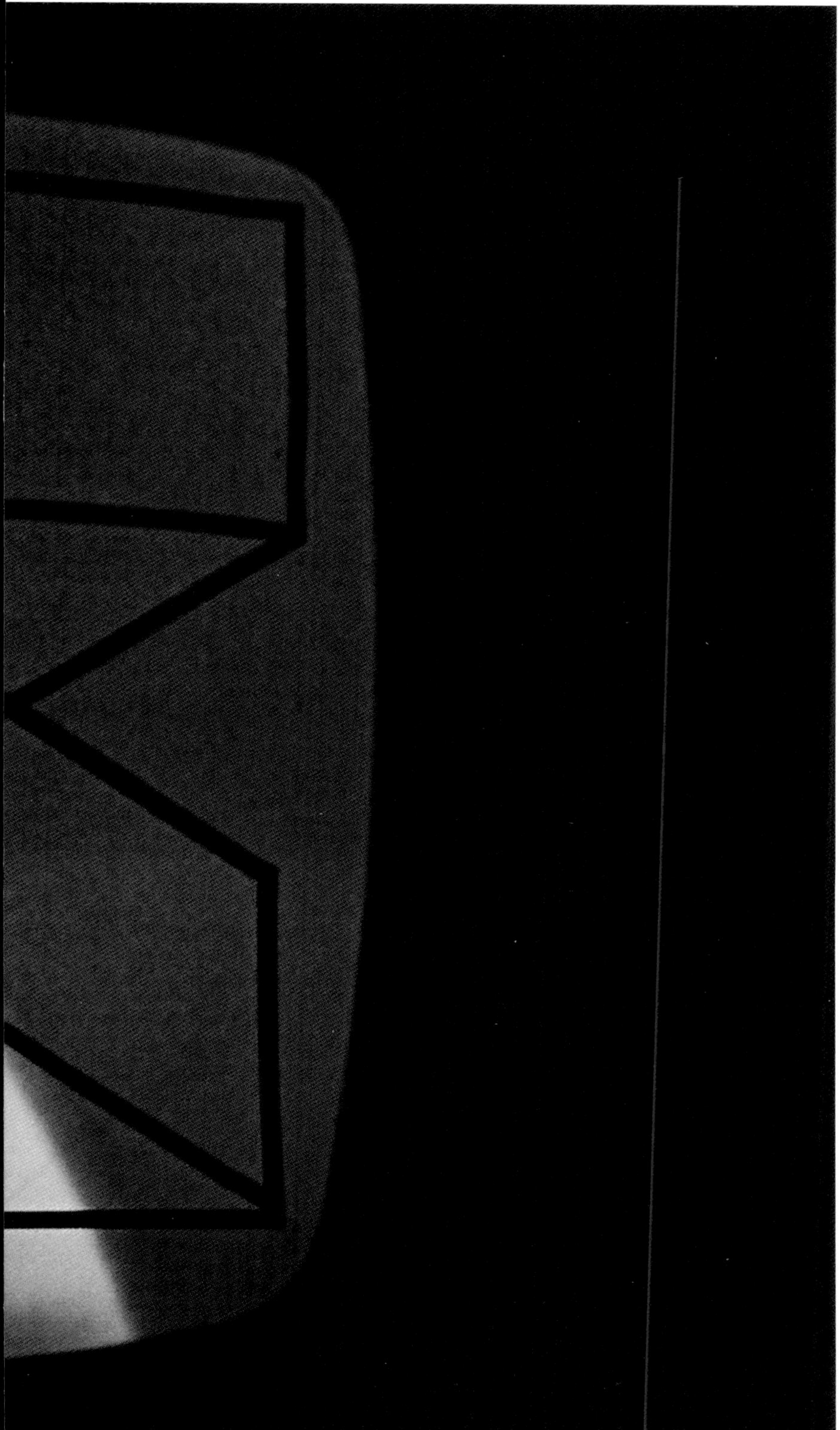

12. Károly Halász, *Modulated Television XIV*, 1972–73, silver gelatine print, 18 × 24 cm, Vintage Galéria, Budapest

this state-supported filmmaking workshop. These could only be viewed by a very small circle (if they were not banned, that is), but several were screened at large international (Western) exhibitions and festivals, where Hungarian artists participated.[20] Continuous and freely applied state subvention made the BBS an object of envy even among filmmakers of other East European countries, where experimental art was far more tolerated by the cultural political establishment. A comparable institution in Poland was the Warsztat Formy Filmowej (Film Form Workshop) between 1970 and 1977, formed by Jozef Robakowski, Ryszard Wasko, Wojciech Bruszewski and Pawel Kwiek as a section of the scientific society of the State Film, Television and Theatre School in Łódz.[21] In the former Yugoslavia, visual art and experimental films could be made in the framework of 'amateur' film clubs. These workshops tended to operate in youth centres, which were the main playing field of experimental visual art.[22]

Balázs Béla Stúdió was not the only place, however, where experimental films were made in Hungary. Numerous works were made independently outside the state studio system. A photogram animation (of which only fragments remain) by Tihamér Gyarmathy, a member of Európai Iskola (European School), had been made in an earlier era (between 1948 and 1952), when private persons were not officially allowed to own a camera in Hungary. The amateur movement also gave rise to important experimental films from the early 1960s on, but artist György Kemény, known for his pop-art posters, also made films (*Reverse Lunch*, 1969) in the context of amateur film with privately owned (or borrowed) 16 or 8 mm cameras, and so did László Lakner (*Flesh*, 1968), who was also making pop-art works at the time.

Miklós Erdély also began to use film in visual art outside the studio. His approach to film was influenced primarily by the Russian avant-garde (especially Eisenstein's montage theory), and he also relied on the then prominent semiotic-linguistic theories. Erdély discusses film as a language, a medium communicating meanings, in his text 'Hunger for Montage'.[23] At the same time, he strove to create 'cognitive' films, which were not merely experimental in nature, but aimed to change the viewer's thinking. This is why Eisenstein's 'intellectual montage' was such a central motif in Erdély's first films, montaged at home from 'editing scraps', from 'television trash', which are only known from later reconstructions.[24] His action in the Balatonboglár Chapel in 1972 (*Moebius Screening*) was similarly based on previously recorded footage (television newsreels showing the handshakes of heads of state). Later films, in which he managed to transfer his film language and theory into practice, would be made in the Balázs Béla Stúdió: *Partita* (1974, fig. 14), which was banned

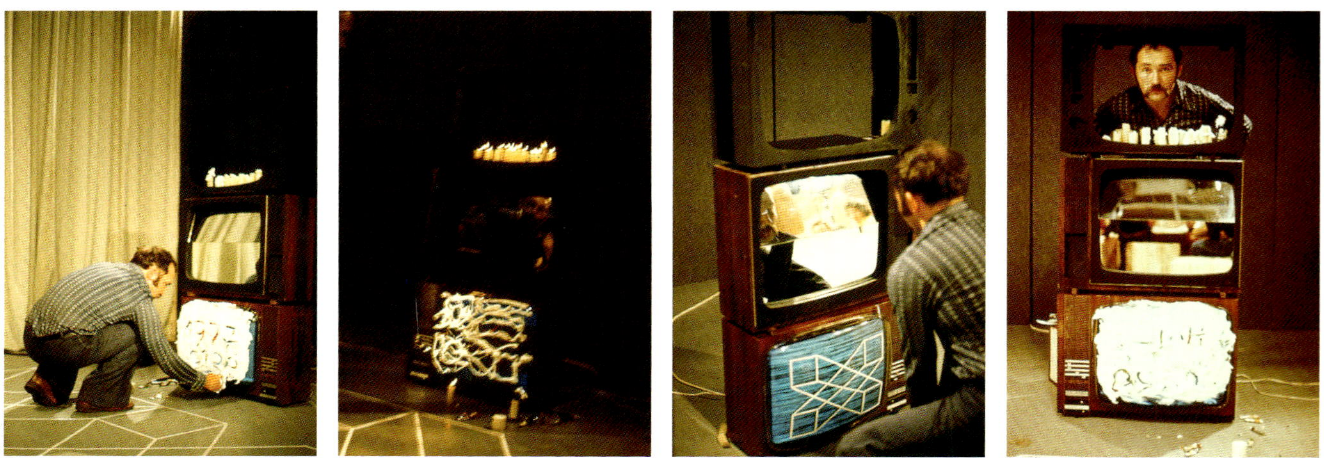

13

13. Károly Halász, *Private Broadcast* in the Pécs studio of MTV, 1975, performance documentation, dimensions variable

for a long time; *Version* (1979), which was based on the blood-libel case of Tiszaeszlár (see Daniel Véri, 'The Holocaust and the Arts', pp. 209–27); and *Dream Copies* (1977, fig. 15). The last one took a fragment by Heraclitus as its starting point: 'The waking have one world in common, sleepers have each a private world of his own.' Erdély presents these interior, self-enclosed worlds: the protagonists try to reconstruct their dreams, making them transmissible, tangible and real. Yet, dream reconstructions are doomed to failure, since they transpire in the illusory world of film: neither dreams nor film can have a direct relation to reality. The characters of the film discourse with projected images instead of each other; in fact, they even step out of the image, exposing the illusion. Erdély uses shots re-recorded on the compound table and twisted, in which he exploits the superimposition of temporal planes; in other words, he uses devices of film language to foreground the illusory nature of the medium.

There were others besides Erdély who engaged in semiotically informed film theoretical research. Gábor Bódy, one of the most influential film directors of the 1970s–80s, also developed his film theory under the influence of recent linguistic theories. As a member of the BBS board, he assigned film-language experiments as the main programme of the studio,[25] which in turn became the most important experimental film workshop in the country (and the wider region) from the 1970s onwards. Bódy thought film was a 'form of thought' and he aimed to overwrite 'retinal' habits and schemes of thought. His theory dealt extensively with electronic images and the reception of images, and he thought film was a mediated reality, where filmic and photographic images simultaneously bore the traces of reality and of the medium. Both making and understanding films, he argued, called for a specific kind of thinking, so his programme paid a great deal of attention to reception (his educational film, *Film School*, was made in this spirit in 1976). The task of experimental film was to expand the boundaries of the medium and perception, Bódy claimed, which could best be realized with extra-filmic devices, with artists who were already actively trying to renew their own field (visual art, theatre or music). Bódy launched the BBS 'Film Language Series' in 1973, followed by the K/3 (Kinematografikus Kísérleti Központ vagy Közművelődési Komplex Kutatások, Centre for Cinematographic Experiments or Complex Researches in Public Culture) group in 1976, inviting the most outstanding figures of progressive visual art, music and theatre to participate in the latter. Besides Erdély, experimental films were made by Dóra Maurer, Tamás Szentjóby, Tibor Hajas, members of Hungarian experimental music workshop Új Zenei Stúdió (New Music Studio), 180-as Csoport (Group 180) and neo-avant-garde theatre groups (Kassák Színház [Kassák Theatre], Kovács István Stúdió [István Kovács Studio]).

The focus of both Bódy's film theory and his films is the method he calls a 'second gaze', where manipulation and sequential repetitions in post-production create meanings in film language based on structuralist and semiotic considerations. This was the method he used in making the feature film *American Torso* (or *American Postcard*, 1975, fig. 16), his diploma film (also made at the BBS) for the Színház- és Filmművészeti Főiskola, which left his professors bewildered. They only accepted Bódy's film once it had won a number of prizes (including the Grand Prize at the 25th Internationale Filmwoche Mannheim). The film evokes the history of émigrés leaving Hungary after the 1848 revolution and war of independence and subsequently fighting in the American Civil War. The past is evoked not only on the level of the plot, but also in film language. He manipulated the traditionally recorded footage in post-production by re-recording on the compound table, editing, masking and distorting the soundtrack, which eventually had the effect of making it look like archival amateur footage from the time in question. At the same time, the seemingly documentary images overwrote the official historical narrative: they replaced obvious heroism with vulnerable heroes, great battles with internal struggles, and grand narratives with episodic story fragments.[26]

Although it was the experimental feature films that made Bódy internationally famous and a highly respected artist in Hungary (besides *American Torso*, he made the monumental *Narcissus and Psyche*, 1981, and *The Dog's Night Song*, 1983), the impact made by his short films (e.g. *Four Bagatelles*, 1975, fig. 17) and theoretical writings is just as significant.[27] The latter has affinities with the work of Polish filmmaker Zbigniew Rybczyński; though the two never met, their ideas about images and film show remarkable similarities.

Dóra Maurer's film *Looking for Dózsa* (1973) – much like *American Torso* – exposed the constructed nature of official historical narratives. Maurer's films that foregrounded camera movements and questioned the objectivity of film (such as *Relative Swings*, 1973) were made concurrently with her photo works in the early 1970s. *Looking for Dózsa* is based on the image composition method familiar from her abstract, geometric serial works of visual art – the image is separated into sequences and individual components are shifted away from each other – but it is far more politicized in tone. As in a graphic work a year earlier (see Magdalena Radomska, 'Working in the Twice-mined Semantic Minefield', pp. 315–29, including fig. 5), Maurer once again produces an 'authentic' portrait of György Dózsa, the leader of a sixteenth-century peasant revolt, who was glorified by the regime as a forerunner of the current workers' and peasant's government: since no depictions of Dózsa survived from the folk hero's own time, she created a Dózsa portrait series composed of strips from multiple portraits that could be moved relative to each other. The portrait of Dózsa depicted as a model and heroic forerunner is composed from the details of ordinary people's faces, and the resulting fictive representation is no less authentic than the official propaganda image of the same person.

Besides experimental films, documentaries also played a major role in the BBS from the early 1970s onwards. In fact, the documentaries tended to be shown to a much broader audience than the experimental films. The screenings were accompanied by public discussion sessions, where various relevant social issues were debated, in Budapest and country towns. The 'experimental documentaries' of the BBS were based on thorough sociological research and brought social problems that were denied by the regime (such as poverty, the situation of the Roma, the conduct of local potentates, etc.) into public discourse. The issue of the critical

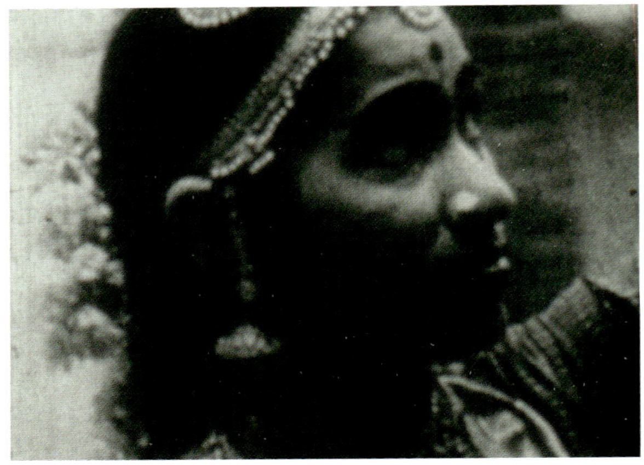

14

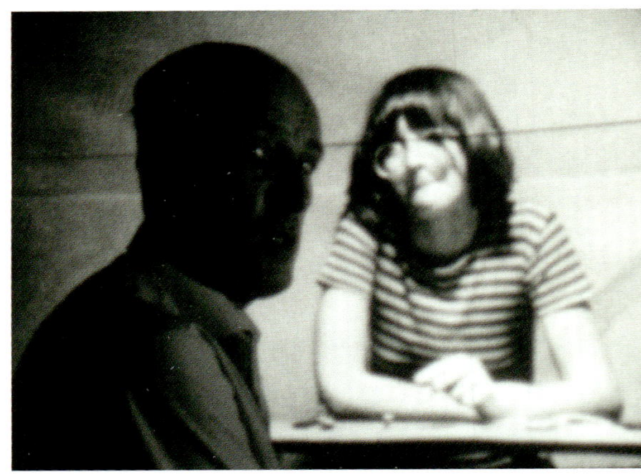

15

14. Miklós Erdély, *Partita*, 1974, 16 mm film, 34', Magyar Nemzeti Filmarchívum, Budapest

15. Miklós Erdély, *Dream Copies*, 1977, 16 mm film, 93', Magyar Nemzeti Filmarchívum, Budapest

16. Gábor Bódy, *American Torso*, 1975, 35 mm film, 91', Magyar Nemzeti Filmarchívum, Budapest

17. Photo showing the making of Gábor Bódy's short film *Four Bagatelles* (1975), Magyar Nemzeti Filmarchívum, Budapest

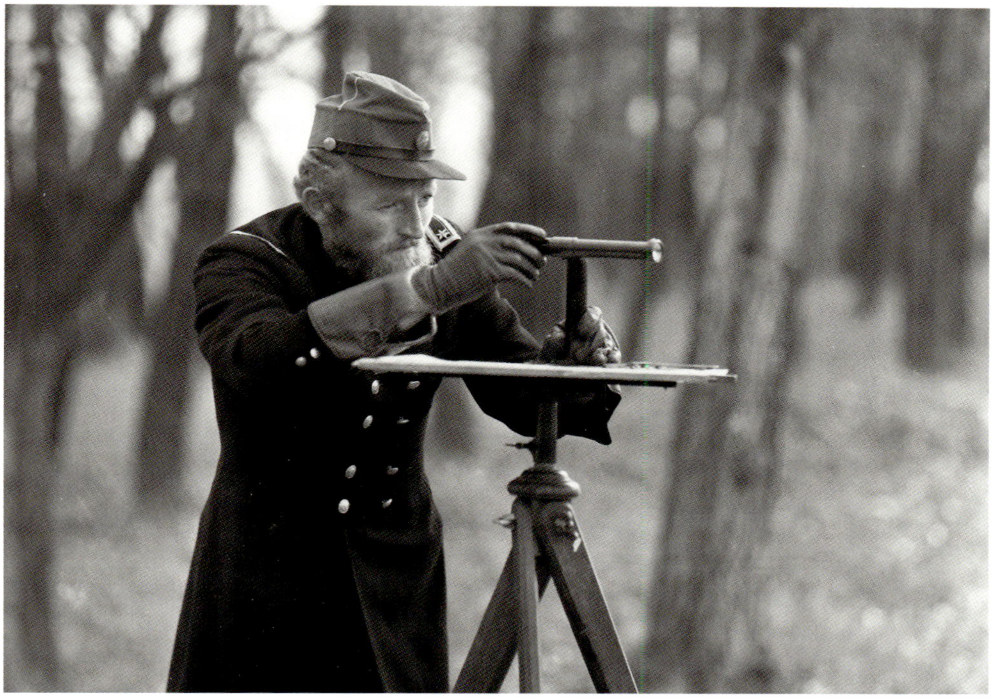

16

17

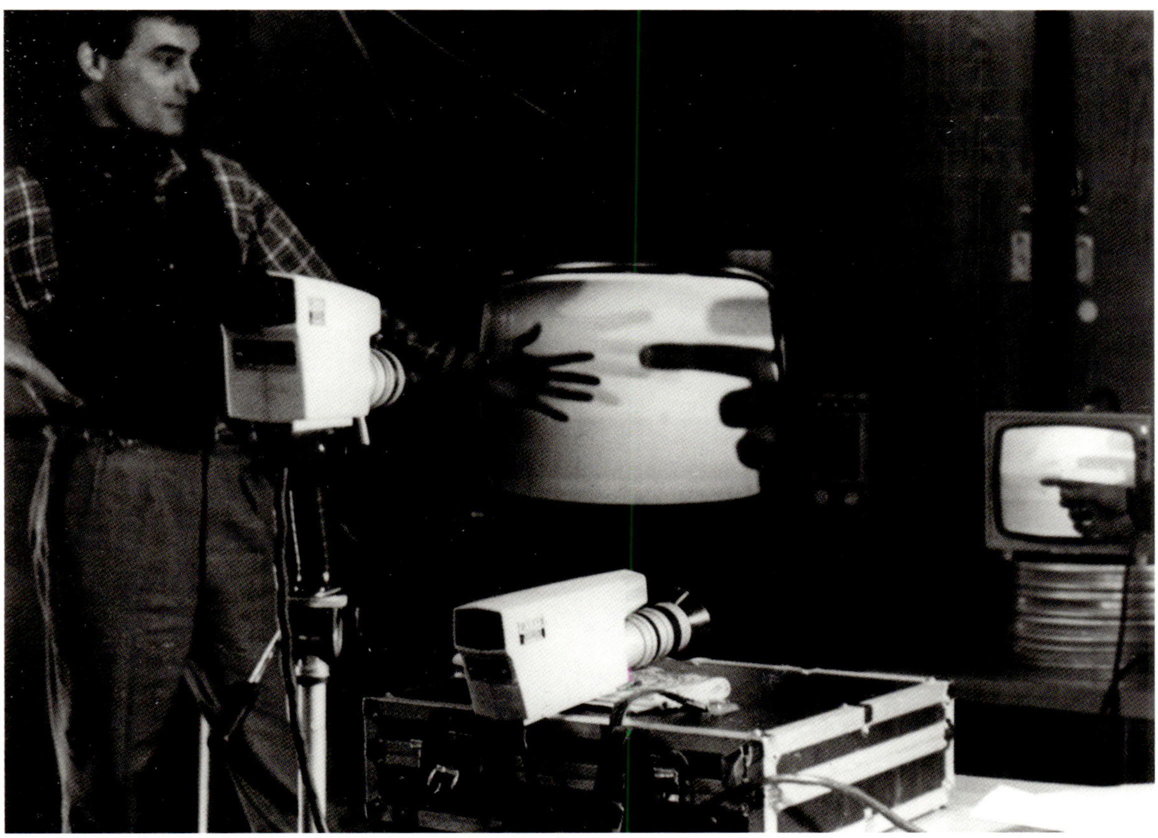

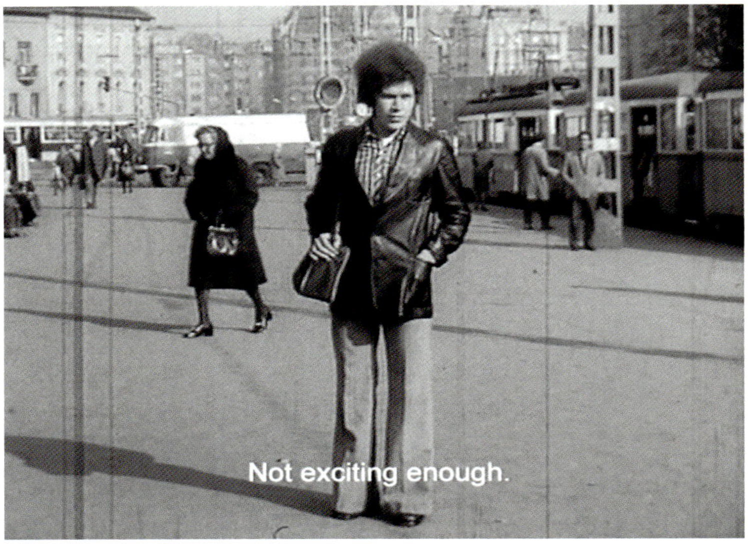

18

18. Tibor Hajas, *Self-Fashion Show*, 1976, 35 mm film, 14' 20", Magyar Nemzeti Filmarchívum, Budapest

19. Tibor Hajas, *Jewels of the Night*, 1978, photo reconstruction of the film (Photo: János Vető), originally video AKAI VTR-5, 19' 19", Ludwig Múzeum – Kortárs Művészeti Múzeum, Budapest

representation of reality was an important topic in the experimental film section as well, and numerous works made in the 'Film Language Series' and by the K/3 group were frowned upon by the regime.

Tamás Szentjóby's film *Centaur*, for example, proved exceptionally subversive in political terms. The film, which was made in 1973–75, includes image sequences of people labouring to build socialism (female workers in a box factory and in the fields, engineers, etc.) in the manner of newsreel and television newscast propaganda. Yet the dialogue is often dissonant with the images, the film's witty and occasionally grotesque expressions and philosophical depth radically questioning the image of socialist society propagated through the state-controlled channels of communication.[28] Although the film was banned in 1975 before its completion, it remained a highly cited legendary film of the neo-avant-garde.[29]

While most BBS films were routinely shown at major international exhibitions and screenings, *Centaur*, Erdély's similarly banned *Partita* and Tibor Hajas's *Self-Fashion Show* were dropped from BBS programmes abroad, as demanded by high-level authorities. The characters of the short film *Self-Fashion Show* (1976, fig. 18) are randomly chosen passersby at Moszkva tér, one of Budapest's busiest spots, who awkwardly try to fulfil the tasks heard in the film (e.g. 'Try to find the most flattering pose'). Segments with and without sound alternate in the film; the image and soundtracks diverge; the streetscape behind the passersby is increasingly replaced with a neutral black drapery; the characters are cut off from the crowd, the busy throng of Moszkva tér. Hajas exposes the filmmakers' manipulation, thereby questioning the verisimilitude of documentaries: 'We won't distort your sentences. We won't recontextualize your gestures. We don't want others to learn the lessons of your fate as we see fit.'[30] In his *Self-Fashion Show*, Hajas critically presents how vulnerable and easily manipulated ordinary people are, but also reflects on his own responsibility, the manipulation by the artist and the medium.

The beginnings of video art

The techniques of manipulation described by Hajas are most familiar from the practice of mass media, the role of which became a central concern in the 1970s–80s in East-Central Europe as well. Video art, the birth of which entailed the democratization of a technological process, recognized and even contributed to this change. Artists appropriated the industrial technology originally developed for television as well as the television screens originally reserved for television broadcasts. The advantages and democratizing potential of video had been

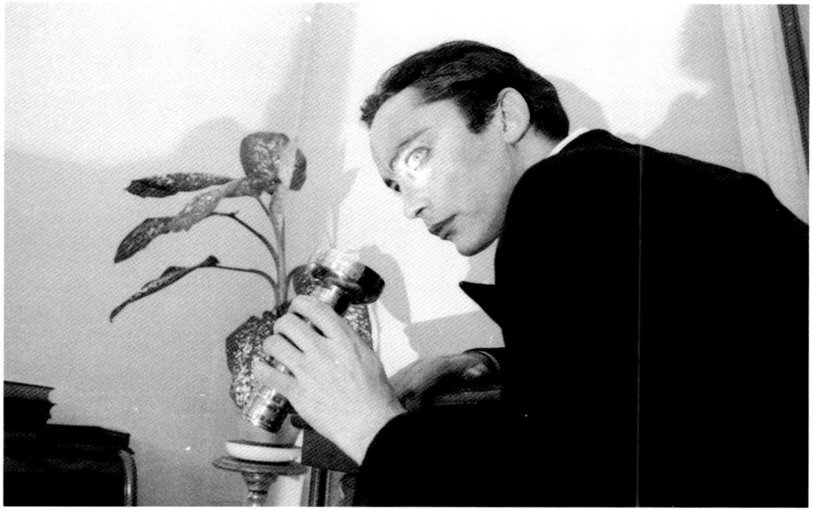

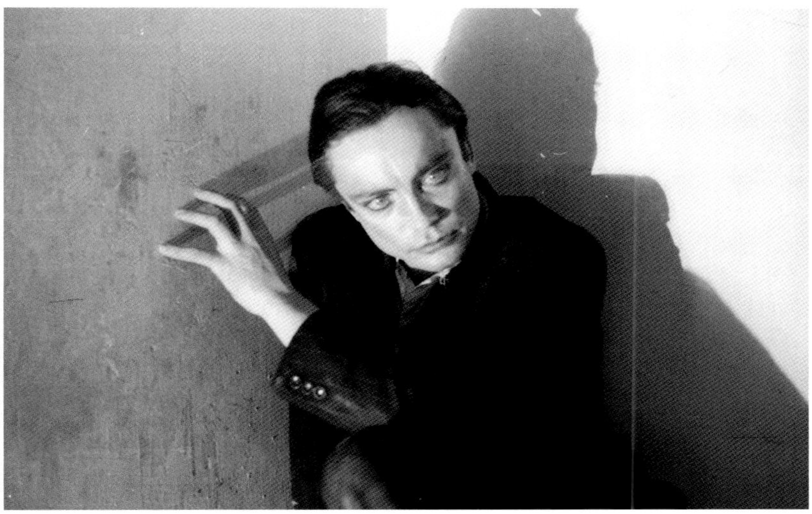

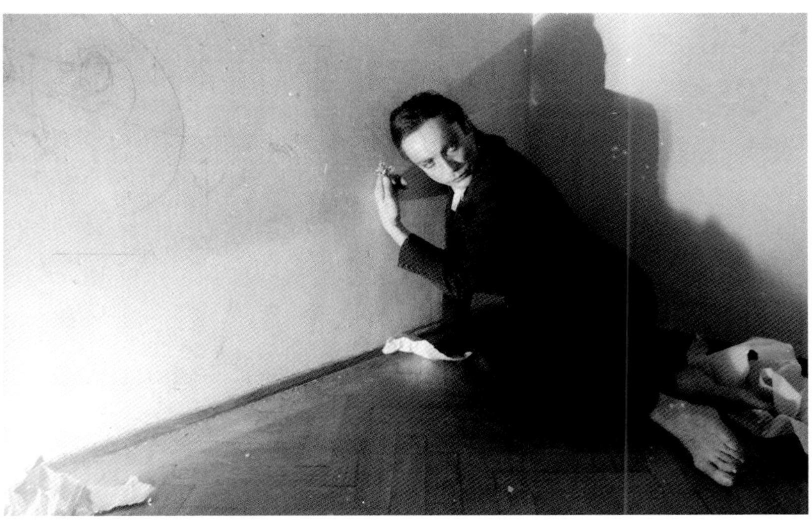

19

frequently discussed since the early 1970s – even in official venues – but it was actually very difficult to access a video camera in Hungary (just like in the other socialist countries). As Tibor Hajas remarked: 'the democratic character of video is a phantasm'.[31] When this technology, which was declared to be simple and cheap in Hungary, was exalted as a medium of visual art at the Kassel documenta in 1977, Sanja Iveković and Dalibor Martinis[32] in the former Yugoslavia and the artists of Warsztat Formy Filmowej (e.g. Józef Robakowski) in Poland had barely begun to discover this new medium.[33]

Video art began in Hungary with the final part of Gábor Bódy's film *Four Bagatelles*, entitled 'Infinite Mirror-Tube'.[34] *Four Bagatelles*, made within the framework of the 'Film Language Series', is actually a four-part educational film, in which Bódy presented characteristic techniques of film as a medium (camera movement, masking, etc.). Bódy set up two closed-circuit video installations for shooting 'Infinite Mirror-Tube' (so the video work was preserved on the 35-mm film). Bódy thought video permitted the extension of all prior cinematographic experimentation; for unlike film, video could simultaneously record and transmit images, allowing one to see dynamic, transforming processes (meanings) rather than finalized images (signs). Bódy understood video as a 'creative thinking device' and valued it for the freedom and intimacy of communication. *INFERMENTAL*, the international journal of video art established by Bódy, which appeared from 1982 to 1990 for a total of ten issues, hoped to build on this unique possibility of communication that avoids the hierarchy of centralized media control.[35]

The new medium of video created a new language and a distinct set of devices. In 1977 Dóra Maurer invited Austrian media artist and theorist Peter Weibel to hold a video presentation at the Ganz-MÁVAG Művelődési Ház (Ganz-MÁVAG Culture House). This was the first time the general public could see video works (by the Austrian artist Valie Export among others) in Budapest. No Hungarian works could be shown at this point: video technology was still inaccessible and artists would usually make their works on foreign trips (mostly to the West). Károly Halász, for instance, recorded his video performance *Transition – An Indian in Amsterdam* (1978) at Videoheads Studio, which belonged to De Appel centre for contemporary art, in Amsterdam. Halász was now able to realize his earlier *Pseudo Video* actually in the medium of video. In *Transition*, he tries to familiarize himself with video like a savage encountering civilization: he wants to possess the TV set with all his senses, magically paints his own face on the screen, and dances around the set. Halász ironically adopts the role of the uncivilized savage, who lives far from Western society, has no knowledge of the development of technologies of mass communication and can therefore use the medium more freely. However, the disco dance concluding the video performance ('Video disco') is no real liberation, but rather an attempt to escape into a world of fantasy where even an 'Indian' is free to create works of video art.

It became increasingly easier to get a video camera in the late 1970s: numerous video works were made in the workshops of university film clubs and cultural centres, though few of them survive (data disappears from video tapes relatively soon – in ten to fifteen years). The handful of exceptions include Tibor Hajas and János Vető's video film *Jewels of the Night* (1978, fig. 19), featuring the German actor Udo Kier who happened to be shooting a film in Hungary at the time (playing the male protagonist in Bódy's *Narcissus and Psyche*). The video is a phantasmagorical vision of the ghosts, demons and stifling beauties of the night. Hajas draws on the expressiveness of 1920s avant-garde film to create his own stylized dream world, while presenting the mirages of night with a nearly sensuous directness.

The late 1970s saw the establishment of a separate video section in the BBS, and the now truly democratic medium became part of official mass communication in the 1980s: experimental video works were also made in the experimental workshops of MAFILM (Hungarian Film Production Company) and Hungarian Television. A rising number of households had video recorders, which had grave consequences for television controlled by the party-state in East-Central Europe. During various opposition actions in the late 1980s, the video samizdat *Fekete Doboz*

(Black Box) produced by BBS members broke the news monopoly of state news channels and made a significant contribution to the disintegration of the state socialist regime in Hungary. The images of various actions by the democratic opposition and of protests drawing increasingly large crowds reached viewers thanks to the new medium of video, bypassing state television channels.

The genre of the computer film appeared in Hungary alongside video and almost concurrently with it. The first Hungarian computer film, also made by Bódy, was *Psychocosmoses* (1976, fig. 20); due to the still rudimentary technology this was recorded on film (just like 'Infinite Mirror-Tube') because the punchcard-based computers worked with a raster display incapable of real-time imaging at that point.[36] Yet, despite its simple computer graphics and rudimentary program language, *Psychocosmoses* was the herald of a new era – an era in which images flowed freely through electronic information channels throughout the globe, as McLuhan had predicted.

20

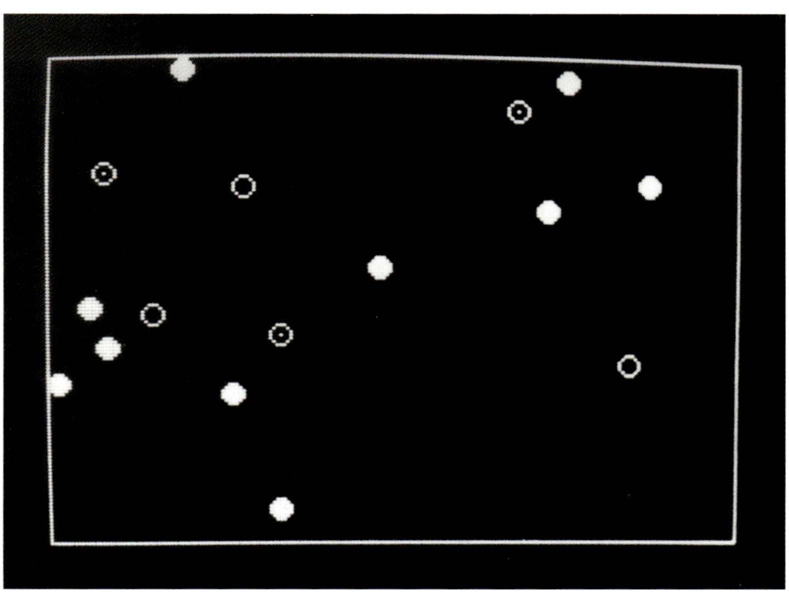

20. Gábor Bódy, *Psychocosmoses*, 1976, 35 mm film, 13', Magyar Nemzeti Filmarchívum, Budapest

1 Miklós Erdély, 'Egy mesterség és mestere: Bálint Endre fotómontázs-kiállítása' [A Craft and Its Master: An Exhibition of Photomontages by Endre Bálint], *Fotóművészet*, Vol. 10, No. 2, 1967, 25–28. Republished in Miklós Erdély, *Művészeti* írások [On Art], compiled by Miklós Peternák. Budapest: Képzőművészeti Kiadó, 1991, 86–92.

2 Miklós Haraszti, '1969 – Az évek meccse' [1969 – Match of the Years], *Beszélő*, Vol. 11, No. 12, 1997. http://www.c3.hu/scripta/beszelo/97/12/1969.htm (November 2016).

3 Júlia Klaniczay and Edit Sasvári (eds), *Törvénytelen avantgárd. Galántai György balatonboglári kápolnaműterme, 1970–1973* [Illegal Avant-garde: The Balatonboglár Chapel Studio of György Galántai, 1970–1973]. Budapest: Artpool-Balassi, 2003.

4 László Beke, 'Fotó-látás, fotóhasználat az új magyar művészetben' [Photographic Seeing and Photo Use in New Hungarian Art], *Fotóművészet*, Vol. 15, No. 3, 1972, 18–24.

5 Flóra Barkóczi (ed.), *Expozíció – fotó/művészet – 1976/2017/ Exposition – Photo/Art – 1976/2017* (exhibition catalogue). Budapest: Vintage Galéria, 2017.

6 Rosalind Krauss, 'Reinventing the Medium', *Critical Inquiry*, Vol. 25, No. 2, 1999, 289–305.

7 Endre Bálint, 'A fotómontázs néhány magyar képzőművész munkásságában' [Photomontage in the Work of Some Hungarian Artists], *Fényképművészeti Tájékoztató*, Nos 2–3, 1965, 74–90.

8 Annamária Szőke (ed.), *Miklós Erdély* (exhibition catalogue). Vienna and Budapest: Georg Kargl Fine Arts, Kisterem/tranzit.hu/ Miklós Erdély Foundation, 2014.

9 Erdély, 'Egy mesterség és mestere'.

10 Miklós Erdély, 'Montázs-éhség' [Hunger for Montage], *Valóság*, Vol. 9, No. 4, 1966, 100–106.

11 Annamária Szőke, 'Die Gegenwart der Zukunft: ein Rätsel. Wissenschaft innerhalb der Kunst im Werk von Miklós Erdély' [The Present of the Future: A Mystery. Science within Art in the Work of Miklós Erdély], *Acta Historiae Artium*, Vol. 39, Nos 1–4, 1997, 197–221.

12 Vera Baksa-Soós (ed.), *Kényszerleszállás – Hajas Tibor retrospektív kiállítása (1946–1980)/Emergency Landing – Tibor Hajas Retrospective Exhibition (1946–1980)*. Budapest: Ludwig Múzeum, 2005, n.p.

13 Tibor Hajas, 'A fotó mint képzőművészeti medium' [The Photo as a Medium of Visual Art] (1976), in Tamás Papp (ed.), *Jelenlét*, Vols 14–15, Nos 1–2, 1989, 115–16.

14 Tibor Hajas, *Szövegek* [Texts], compiled by Éva F. Almási. Budapest: Enciklopédia kiadó, 2005, 292–93.

15 Zoltán Hafner (ed.), *Jovánovics*. Budapest: Corvina, 2004.

16 György Jovánovics, *Liza Wiathruck: HOLOS GRAPHOS – Képregény/Ein Bild Werk/ Comics*. Pécs: Jelenkor, 1999.

17 Dóra Maurer, *Fényelvtan – A fotogramról* [Photogrammar: On the Photogram]. Kecskemét and Budapest: Magyar Fotográfiai Múzeum/Balassi, 2001, 41–65.

18 Anna Bványos (ed.), *Maurer Dóra*. Budapest: Ludwig Múzeum/ Kortárs Művészeti Múzeum, 2008, 9.

19 Maja Fowkes, 'Abstract Elements in the Industrial Environment: The Land Art of the Hungarian Group Pécs Workshop', in *The Green Bloc: Neo-avant-garde Art and Ecology under Socialism*. Budapest: CEU Press, 2015, 23–64.

20 Lívia Páldi, 'Other Voices, Other Rooms – Attempt(s) at Reconstruction: 50 Years of the Balázs Béla Stúdió', in Georg Schöllhammer and Ruben Areyvshatyan (eds), *Sweet Sixties*. Berlin: Sternberg Press, 2013, 198–208.

21 Łukasz Ronduda and Florian Zeyfang (eds), *1, 2,...Avant-Gardes. Film/Art between Experiment and Archive*. Warsaw, Berlin and New York: Center for Contemporary Art/ Ujazdowski Castle/Sternberg Press, 2007.

22 Bojana Piškur and Tamara Soban (eds), *This is All Film: Experimental Film in Yugoslavia, 1951–1991* (exhibition catalogue). Ljubljana: Moderna Galerija, 2010.

23 Erdély, 'Montázs-éhség'.

24 Miklós Peternák, 'Rejtett paraméterek: Erdély Miklós elveszett filmjei' [Hidden Parameters: Miklós Erdély's Lost Films], *Filmvilág*, Vol. 44, No. 8, 2001, 44–46. Erdély obtained recycled scraps of film in this period as an editor for Hungarian Television.

25 András Bálint Kovács, 'Gábor Bódy: A Precursor of the Digital Age', in Anikó Imre (ed.), *East European Cinemas*. New York and London: Routledge, 2005, 151–64, and László Beke and Miklós Peternák (eds), *Bódy Gábor 1946–1985: Életmübemutató/Gábor Bódy 1946–1985: A Presentation of His Work* (exhibition catalogue). Budapest: Mücsarnok, 1987.

26 Sonja Simonyi, 'Second Looks: Archival Aesthetics and Historical Representation in *American Postcard (1975)*', *Studies in Eastern European Cinema*, Vol. 7, No. 1, 2016, 66–81.

27 Bódy was in a very privileged position, which was only partly due to his talent, as he was later revealed to have been an informant of the Belügyminisztérium (Ministry of Interior Affairs) with the code name 'Pesti'. While this does not detract from the value of his films and writings, it is an unprocessed and insufficiently discussed factor that casts a shadow over his whole oeuvre.

28 Klara Kemp-Welch, *Antipolitics in Central European Art*. London and New York: I. B. Tauris, 2014, 101–140.

29 The restoration of the copy and the reconstruction of the film did not take place until 2009, when the curatorial group WHW (What, How and for Whom) of Zagreb brought it to the 11th Istanbul Biennial.

30 Tibor Hajas, János Vető and Gábor Dobos, 'Öndivatbemutató' [Self-Fashion Show], in Hajas, *Szövegek*, 192.

31 Tibor Hajas, 'A katódsugárzás szépsége' [The Beauty of Cathode Radiation], in Hajas, *Szövegek*, 306–307.

32 Barbara Borčić, 'Video Art from Conceptualism to Postmodernism', in Dubravka Djurić and Miško Šuvaković (eds), *Impossible Histories: Historical Avant-gardes, Neo-avant-gardes, and Post-avant-gardes in Yugoslavia, 1918–1991*. London and Cambridge: MIT Press, 2003, 490–520.

33 Ryszard W. Kluszczyński, 'Video Art in Poland', in Edit András (ed.), *Transitland: Video Art from Central and Eastern Europe*. Budapest: Ludwig Múzeum, 2009, 149–55.

34 Bódy shot 'Infinite Mirror-Tube' in 1973. (*Four Bagatelles* combined works made more or less independently of each other between 1972 and 1975.)

35 http://www.infermental.de.

36 Márton Orosz, 'Magyarok a komputerművészet korai történetében/Hungarians in the Early History of Computer Art', in Judit Borus (ed.), *Magyar művészek és a számítógép/Hungarian Artists and the Computer*. Budapest: Szépművészeti Múzeum/Vasarely Múzeum, 2016, 16–53, 22 ff.

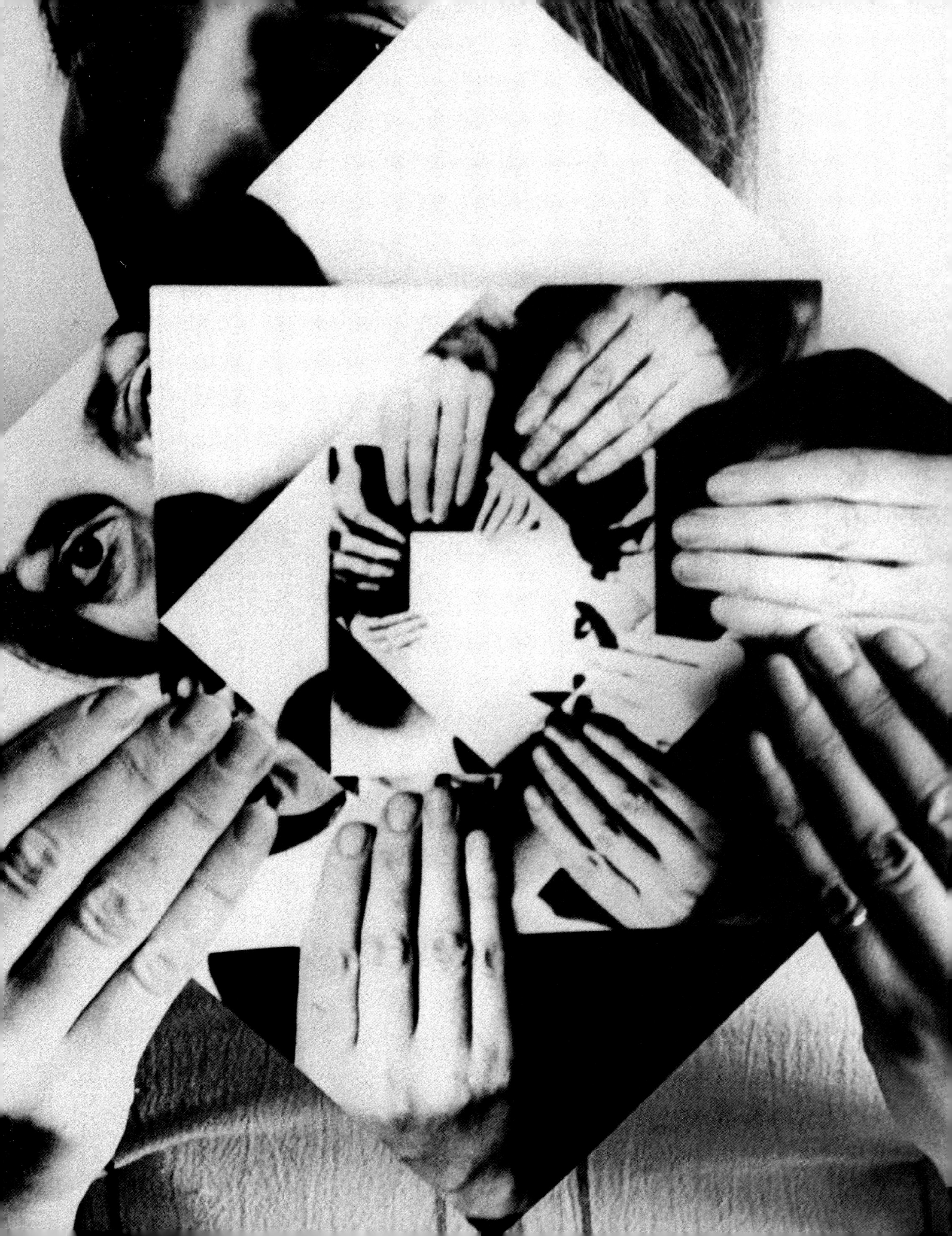

Biographies

Key
Elvont Művészek Csoportja – Group of Abstract Artists

Galántai György Balatonboglári Kápolnaműterme – Balatonboglár Chapel Studio of György Galántai

Eötvös Loránd Tudomány Egyetem (ELTE) – Eötvös Loránd University, Budapest

Európai Iskola – European School

Gresham kör – Gresham Circle of artists

Magyar Iparművészeti Főiskola – Hungarian Academy of Applied Arts, Budapest

Magyar Képzőművészeti Főiskola – Hungarian Academy of Fine Arts, Budapest

Magyar Színház- és Filmművészeti Főiskola – Hungarian Theatre and Film Academy, Budapest

Magyar Szocialista Munkáspárt (MSZMP) – Hungarian Socialist Workers' Party

Magyar Dolgozók Pártja (MDP) – Hungarian Workers' Party

Magyar Tudományos Akadémia (MTA) – Hungarian Academy of Sciences

Műcsarnok – Kunsthalle Budapest

Pécsi Műhely – Pécs Workshop, artist group

Pesti Műhely – Budapest Workshop, artist group

Zuglói kör – Zugló Circle of artists

ALTORJAI, Sándor (1933, Maklár – 1979, Szigliget), visual artist
After obtaining his diploma in pharmaceutics, he studied painting at the Magyar Képzőművészeti Főiskola from 1958 until 1963. Initially he painted surnaturalist compositions and made a living by painting pictures in a style he characterized as 'homecraft abstraction' for sale by the state-owned Képcsarnok Vállalat (Art Gallery Company). In 1965, he became acquainted with Miklós Erdély, many of whose radio plays and films feature him as a character (*Hidden Parameters*, 1968; *Version*, 1980). In 1967, his enormous pop art-style collage (*Let Me Sink Upwards*) was voted out of the 1967 annual exhibition of the Fiatal Képzőművészek Stúdiója (Young Artists' Studio). His 'Gyagyaist' (*gyagya* = idle) pictures were made using a dripping technique mixed with surnaturalism, and were exhibited at his first and only solo show in 1971; they earned him critical denunciation and political attacks. In the 1970s, in addition to collage he incorporated transfer prints of photos and newspaper cut-outs into his works. He also came up with new amorphous creatures (toddlographs). In 1979, he made large montages from slices of his former works and designed his posthumous exhibition along with an invitation to his 'exhibition and funeral'.

ALTORJAY, Gábor (1946, Budapest), Fluxus artist
Between 1965 and 1967, he studied theology in Budapest and worked as a tour guide in Poland. Between 1963 and 1966, he and Tamás Szentjóby established and ran the Buta Költők Társasága (Dumb Poet's Circle). In 1966 he edited a manuscript journal (*Laura*), which comprised of five, single-copy issues, and organized the first Hungarian happening with Szentjóby. He made 'anti-art' objects (*Chess-Preserve*, *Short Circuit Instrument*, *Uncomfortable*) and collages on the borderline of art and literature. In 1967, he emigrated to Germany. In 1968, he joined the Kombinat 1 commune and exhibition space funded by Wolf Vostell and signed the manifesto against documenta, Kassel. While still in Hungary, he had translated the texts of a number of Fluxus artworks. In 1969, he issued a box containing his Fluxus works (*Kurzschlussobjekt*) and created the Electroshock Automat, which combined socialist phraseology and capitalist consumption, meant for use by the masses who voluntarily submitted themselves to control. He has been making experimental films since the 1980s and lives in Berlin.

ANNA, Margit (1913, Borota – 1991, Budapest), painter
She studied at János Vaszary's private school, the so-called Új Művészeti Iskola (New School of Art). There, she met painter Imre Ámos, whom she married in 1935. Her early works were conceived in close correlation to Ámos's art, but the most important theme of her oeuvre, the self-portrait, was already present. Her female figures are virtual role-play; she is the dancer, the muse, the painter, the prostitute or the orphan. Between 1938 and 1941 the couple spent the summers in Szentendre in the company of Lajos Vajda, Júlia Vajda and Dezső Korniss. Her post-impressionism of the 1930s gained contour and became expressive and surrealist during the Second World War and her husband's time in labour service; her figures became puppets at the mercy of fate. She was one of the founding members of the Európai Iskola. After 1948, she did not get an opportunity to exhibit for twenty years. Her art is full of grotesque, black humour as well as motifs of popular imagery.

ATTALAI, Gábor (1934, Budapest – 2011, Budapest), textile artist, conceptual artist
He completed his studies at the Magyar Iparművészeti Főiskola in 1958, and began to create wall and textile or felt compositions in space, revisiting traditional techniques. He was one of the initiators of the Hungarian so-called spatial textile movement. From the second half of the 1960s to the mid-1970s, he was active in several genres. He created land-art works that were rich in political references (*Negative Star*, 1970–71), body-art works, conceptual actions, as well as 'private performances' (*Stuffed Nostrils*) and documentation of simple, everyday acts (*Scratching*). He also created artist's books (*TIME BOOK*, 1973). Klaus Groh, in his 1972 survey of Eastern European art, labelled Attalai's activity 'L-P-C art' (connecting land art, project art and

conceptual art). Attalai participated in the international mail-art movement, and placed 'transfer paintings' in the neighbourhoods of museums abroad. In his readymade series started in 1974, which echoed Duchamp, he covered different objects with red paint. From the mid-1980s he gradually withdrew from the public art scene. He also produced a significant body of work as an art writer.

BAK, Imre (1939, Budapest), painter
From 1958 until 1964, he studied painting at the Magyar Képzőművészeti Főiskola. From the mid-1960s, he began making geometrical compositions with stripes (*Stripes*, 1968), aligning himself with American minimalism and hard-edge painting while also making use of Hungarian folk motifs. In 1968 and 1969, he took part in the 'Iparterv' exhibitions. In 1973, in collaboration with János Fajó and István Nádler, he founded the Pesti Műhely, a group of creative artists who aimed to popularize art. In the first half of the 1970s, he made conceptual works in order to rethink and systematically analyse his approach as a painter, and after evaluating the results, he returned to painting. In the 1980s, his geometrical systems, in which shapes coalesced into symbols, became increasingly complex. In 1986, his work was exhibited at the Hungarian Pavilion of the Venice Biennale together with Ákos Birkás, Károly Kelemen and István Nádler. In 1988, he was awarded the Munkácsy Prize. Between 1987 and 1992, he taught at the Magyar Iparművészeti Főiskola.

BÁLINT, Endre (1914, Budapest – 1986, Budapest), graphic artist, painter
From 1930 until 1934, he studied advertising design at the Budapesti Iparművészeti Iskola (Budapest School of Arts and Crafts), and in 1934 he travelled to Paris. In 1935, he studied at János Vaszary's private school and met Lajos Vajda, who was a great influence. In 1936, he began working together with Vajda and Dezső Korniss in Szentendre. He was forced into labour service during the Second World War. In 1945, he was one of the founding members of the Európai Iskola. In 1947, he took part in the second International Surrealist Exhibition in Paris. Following his return, he was banned from exhibiting until the mid-1960s. Influenced by Vajda's transparent montage method in the mid-1950s, he created surrealist visions incorporating personal motifs (elements of the so-called 'Bálint-dictionary', the horse-head trade sign and mummy-like Swabian women). These motifs also appeared in his works (including *Jerusalem Bible*, 1959) between 1957 and 1961, his Paris period, and are a defining trait of his entire subsequent oeuvre. From the 1950s, he also made photomontages, which became an inspiration for artists of the Hungarian neo-avant-garde.

BARCSAY, Jenő (1900, Cătina, Romania – 1988, Budapest), painter, graphic artist
From 1919 until 1924, he studied at the Magyar Képzőművészeti Főiskola. In 1926, he travelled on a state grant to Paris, where he was greatly impressed by the compositions of Modigliani, Matisse and Braque, and later, in 1929, by the art of Cézanne and van Gogh. In 1929, he became a member of the Szentendrei Festők Társasága (Szentendre Painters' Society) and started painting landscapes from high vantage points as well as icon-like figures with closed contours and golden backgrounds in the style of Lajos Vajda. Based on Kassák's '*képarchitektúra*' (picture architecture) in the 1930s, he developed a Hungarian version of constructivism (with strict structural elements and landscape associations). His works feature both nonfigurative forms and depictions of figures. Between 1945 and 1947, he took part in the exhibitions of the Európai Iskola, and in 1945 he became a professor of anatomy and perspective studies at the Magyar Képzőművészeti Főiskola; in 1953, he completed his book *Anatomy for the Artist*, which was translated into several languages. In the 1960s, he made monumental mosaics and tapestries for public spaces. In 1964, he was exhibited in the Hungarian Pavilion at the Venice Biennale. In 1978, a permanent exhibition of his works opened in Szentendre, and was later turned into the Barcsay Múzeum.

BERCZELLER, Rezső (1912, Trsztena, Slovakia – 1992, Budapest), painter, sculptor
In 1931–32, he studied painting at the Magyar Képzőművészeti Főiskola, but he was more interested in sculpture. His first works were small-size sculptures and portraits, from which he developed his characteristic themes in the 1950s–1960s, interpreting people en masse (marchers, fighters, dancers, etc.) as constructs, machines or convoluted monsters. He was influenced by historical artforms; he was intrigued by Egyptian sculpture, Pre-Columbian culture, Indian art, the painting and sculpture of Matthias Grünewald, and medieval triptych altarpieces. He made his first large-format works out of wood; today, *The Impaled* (1968–69) is exhibited at the Middelheimmuseum in Antwerp. He experimented with unusual materials as well as traditional ones; in the 1980s, he created the *Cripples* series, for which he also made vast charcoal sketches, out of zinc mesh. He showed keen interest in physical anguish (hanged, executed people, women giving birth, people with physical disabilities), disasters and visions of the Apocalypse.

BERNÁTH, Aurél (1895, Marcali – 1982, Budapest), painter
From 1915, he studied at the Nagybányai Művésztelep (Nagybánya Artists' Colony) before he was drafted for military service. After his demobilization in 1918, he did not continue his studies but instead contacted Lajos Kassák and the Hungarian activists. He moved to Vienna in 1921 and published his expressive symbolist album *Graphik*. Between 1923 and 1926, he lived in Berlin; in 1923 and 1924, he exhibited at Galerie Der Sturm. In 1927, he moved back to Hungary and painted *Riviera*, his first important painting in a renewed style; besides a lyrical approach and an unusual colour scheme, his works from this period are characterized by a meditative, philosophical attitude. The formal and aesthetic principles of his naturalist post-avant-garde painting made him the leading figure of the Gresham kör from the 1930s. In 1945, he was appointed professor at the Magyar Képzőművészeti Főiskola. Between 1948 and 1949, he edited the journal

Magyar Művészet (Hungarian Art); his writings challenge conservative naturalism and nonfigurative art. From the late 1950s onwards, he was among the most influential Hungarian artists, and also a member of the Művészeti Tanács (Art Council of the Ministry of Culture). From the 1960s, he made a number of monumental murals.

BIRKÁS, Ákos (1941, Budapest), painter
From 1959 until 1964, he studied painting at the Magyar Képzőművészeti Főiskola, then taught at the Képző- és Iparművészeti Szakközépiskola (Secondary School of Fine and Applied Arts) in Budapest until 1984. His early works featured portraiture, and his portraits (*K. F. series*, 1977), photographs and films from the 1970s incorporated the problems of the picture within a picture, frame, mirroring and duplication. In the mid-1980s, he conceived the abstract oval 'Head' that he would paint onto double boards, playing with asymmetry and symmetry. In 1986, he was exhibited in the Hungarian pavilion at the Venice Biennale. He received a Herder scholarship in 1989, and one from DAAD (Deutscher Akademischer Austauschdienst/German Academic Exchange Service) in 1995. He lived in Vienna between 1986 and 1990, and in Berlin between 1991 and 2003. Following his retrospective exhibition in 1996 at the Museum des 20. Jahrhunderts in Vienna, he returned to Hungary in the early 2000s and radically broke with the oval format. Initially, he painted split 'realist' portraits, then 'narrative' pieces with political content. His works often feature art historical and philosophical references, and rely on current photographs from the media. He had major shows in 2006 at the Göttingen Kunstverein and in 2014 at the MODEM in Debrecen.

BÓDY, Gábor (1946, Budapest – 1985, Budapest), film director, video artist
From 1964 until 1971, he studied philosophy and history at the ELTE, then from 1971 until 1975 he studied film and television directing at the Színház- és Filmművészeti Főiskola. In 1971, he became a member of the Balázs Béla Stúdió (BBS), where, in 1973, he organized its first experimental film project: the 'Film Language Series'. His films were awarded several prizes. He received the Grand Prize for best new filmmaker at the 25th Mannheim Film Festival for his diploma work (*American Torso*) in 1976. In the same year, he was awarded the Hungarian Film Critics Prize for best first film. In 1981, he was awarded the Bronze Leopard at the Locarno Festival for *Narcissus and Psyche*. His feature film from 1983, *Dog's Night Song*, was the first Hungarian example of the postmodern 'New Sensibility' and became an underground hit. In 1980 he founded the international video magazine *INFERMENTAL*, which was published until 1991. In 1982, he received a DAAD scholarship, and he taught at the German Film and Television Academy in Berlin in 1982–83. His final videos laid the foundations of new media genres.

CSERNUS, Tibor (1927, Kondoros – 2017, Paris), painter, graphic artist
From 1946 until 1953 he studied painting in Aurél Bernáth's class at the Magyar Képzőművészeti Főiskola; he received the Munkácsy Prize in 1952. He started out painting landscapes (*Déli Train Station*, 1953), followed by portraits (*The Three Lectors*, 1955) in the footsteps of Aurél Bernáth and French modernism. When he visited Paris in 1957, Simon Hantaï introduced him to automatist calligraphy and the surrealist technique of décollage. Inspired by this, he developed a trendsetting style often called surnaturalism or magic realism, which made use of the imaging principles of tachism and surrealism while being fundamentally figurative and realist (*Lehel Square Market*, 1962; *Reeds*, 1964). He illustrated books in both Paris and Budapest. Despite his successful activity as a graphic artist, he was not given the opportunity to have a solo exhibition in Hungary. He moved to Paris in 1964, joined the movement La Figuration Narrative, and then turned to photorealism; his works from the 1980s onwards were fusions of the visual topoi of Baroque painting, surnaturalism, hyperrealism and academic realism.

DEIM, Pál (1932, Szentendre – 2016, Szentendre), painter, graphic artist, sculptor
From 1958 until 1963, he studied painting and graphic art at the Magyar Képzőművészeti Főiskola. On a trip to Moscow and Leningrad in 1960, he became familiar with the classics of modern art (Picasso, Matisse), and during his sojourn in Brussels and Paris in 1967 he became acquainted with contemporary art (Appel, Bacon, Giacometti, Vasarely, Ben Nicholson). Between 1963 and 1968, he was an active member of the Zuglói kör. His art was an organic continuation of Szentendre's painting traditions (Lajos Vajda, Jenő Barcsay) and its subjects, such as alleys, Baroque stone crosses, crucifixes, tin crosses. By the mid-1960s, he had developed his own style and distinctive imagery: an organic figure – a human-shaped doll – wedged between the two panels of a divided two-dimensional image. Towards the end of the decade, the figure or its shadow extended beyond the plane; in 1971, he began making painted wood and bronze sculptures. His works are characterized by the contrast of constructivist structure and transcendent philosophical content.

DOMANOVSZKY, Endre (1907, Budapest – 1974, Budapest), painter
From 1926 until 1932, he studied at the Magyar Képzőművészeti Főiskola and from 1931 he was a professor at the Magyar Iparművészeti Főiskola. His early works are characterized by expressionism and neo-classicism; the composition and rendering of space in his works was designed according to strict rules (*The Resurrection of Jairus' Daughter*, 1929). In the 1930s, he experimented with a new genre, designing tapestries which were then woven by his wife. In 1936, one of his tapestries was featured at the Venice Biennale and, in 1937, he received the Diplôme d'honneur for his tapestry at the Paris Expo. In the 1940s his neo-classical, archaic style was replaced with a more expressive and decorative patchwork-like composition. From 1945, he led an upholstery weaving workshop at the Magyar Képzőművészeti Főiskola; from 1949 he taught painting; and from 1956 he was the rector of the academy. In the 1950s he successfully adapted

his former style to the expectations of socialist realism, as a result of which he was commissioned to create monumental panel paintings, frescoes and sgraffiti for public spaces. He designed a large panel painted on aluminium board for the 1958 Brussels World's Fair and he was featured at the Venice Biennale. He was the president of the Magyar Képző- és Iparművészek Szövetsége (Association of Hungarian Artists) between 1963 and 1966.

ERDÉLY, Miklós (1928, Budapest – 1986, Budapest), architect, visual artist, film director, writer
He studied sculpture at the Magyar Képzőművészeti Főiskola in 1946–47, and then moved on to study architecture at the Budapesti Műszaki Egyetem (Budapest University of Technology) from 1947 until 1951. He was a conceptual artist, he was intrigued by new possibilities for art as well as by the relationship between natural sciences and art. His apartment housed a number of events (action readings, film screenings, text actions) by artists, and he also took part in events at György Galántai's Balatonboglári Kápolnaműterem. In 1974, he received the Kassák Prize for his poetry and writing. From 1975, he led an art workshop called 'Kreativitási gyakorlatok' (Creativity Exercises) together with Dóra Maurer during its first year. In 1977, he established the FAFEJ (Fantasy-developing Exercises) and in 1978 the INDIGO (Interdisciplinary Thinking) workshop. At the Balázs Béla Stúdió (BBS), he made a number of feature films including *Version* (1979), addressing anti-Semitism in Hungary, which was banned. His films were based on his own linguistically and psychologically inspired theory of montage.

FAJÓ, János (1937, Orosháza), painter
From 1956 until 1961, he studied decorative painting at the Magyar Iparművészeti Főiskola. He developed a unique style by the second half of the 1960s, influenced by op art, minimal art and new geometrical approaches to art, as well as the constructivist approach. His intellectual master was Lajos Kassák and, in 1965, Fajó organized an exhibition of his works at the Fiatal Művészek Klubja (Young Artists' Club). The compositional principle behind his paintings is reduction, based on reducing natural forms to basic geometrical shapes and the variation of these reductive elements. Coupled with the basic colours and their variations, the exact system of forms in his works yields a harmonic world of form and colour and a clean system of proportions. Contrary to the impersonal, modelling approach of minimal art, sensuality plays a fundamental role in his works. Multiplication is also an important feature in his creative method. In 1973, he was a founding member of the Pesti Műhely, which aimed to popularize modern art. Between 1976 and 1988, he was the head of the Józsefvárosi Galéria.

FEHÉR, László (1953, Székesfehérvár), painter
From 1971 until 1976, he studied painting at the Magyar Képzőművészeti Főiskola. In the mid-1970s, he made photorealist paintings; his often black and white hyperrealist works, which focus on the bleakness of metropolitan life, the repressive climate of a dictatorship, the questions of personal and collective memory, and issues of Jewish identity. In the early 1980s he started to create expressionistic paintings, which became saturated with colour. From the beginnings, the artist often uses old family photographs as prototypes, giving them a mystical transcendence. In 1988, he reduced his rich colours to just three (black, white and yellow) in a large series of painting; in these works, abstract surfaces are populated by monumental architectural elements and black and white figures, often marked by a single outline. In the early 2000s after a long period of creating black and white pictures, he returned to photorealistic painting, depicting various themes (large-scale portraits, everyday scenes, homeless people). He participated at the Venice Biennale in 1980 and 1990. His solo exhibitions were shown, among others, at the Barbican Centre, London (1989), the Museum Moderner Kunst Stiftung Ludwig, Vienna (1997), the Ludwig Museum, Budapest (2007), and at the Musée d'art moderne, Saint-Étienne (2011).

FREY, Krisztián (1929, Budapest – 1997, Zurich), painter
He was a self-taught artist who experimented with a number of styles. In 1958, he painted his first grey picture, which grew into a series by the mid-1960s, augmented by textual elements and characters. In 1964, he went to Germany and, in 1967, to Italy on study trips; he was influenced by abstract expressionism. He made so-called 'script' experiments wherein trickling paint was coupled with calligraphic renderings and dynamic linear fractures projecting the artist's state of mind. He applied everyday objects (slips, shoes) onto the surface of paintings (*All Vanishable Is Only a Comparison*, 1969). In 1968 and 1969, he took part in the 'Iparterv' exhibitions. In 1970, he emigrated to Zurich and, from 1974, he studied music history, then mathematics and programming. His so-called stochastic pictures from the early 1980s examine the law of random numbers and its application. In the 1990s, he defined his works as algebraic art.

GALÁNTAI, György (1941, Bikács), sculptor, graphic artist, art organizer
Having graduated from the department of painting at the Magyar Képzőművészeti Főiskola in 1967, he began experimenting with various techniques and genres; he made graphics combining montage and photogram, sculpture from scrap materials, politically charged 're-functioned' objects, sound sculptures, performances and video installations. Between 1970 and 1973, he ran the Balatonboglári Kápolnaműterem, organizing modernist and neo-avant-garde exhibitions in his own studio. The studio was shut down by the authorities in 1973 and his artistic activity was undermined. In 1983, he received the Kassák Prize. From the late 1960s, he was in close contact with the international Fluxus movement and the mail artists; in order to preserve these marginal genres and archive Hungarian underground events, in 1979 he founded the Artpool Archive, and edited the samizdat *AL* (*Artpool Letter*), an alternative art magazine, between 1983 and 1985. He considers his activity as an organizer a form of artistic expression.

GYARMATHY, Tihamér (1915, Pécs – 2005, Budapest), painter
From 1933, he studied at the Magyar Képzőművészeti Főiskola. Between 1937 and 1939, he took study trips across Western Europe; he became acquainted with Piet Mondrian, André Breton, Jean Arp and Max Bill. In 1945, he joined the Európai Iskola and in 1946 the Elvont Művészek Csoportja, which advocated nonfigurative art. His surreal, nonfigurative works from the early 1940s transcended into an unusual style of biomorphic abstraction, named '*bioromantika*' (bioromanticism) by Ernő Kállai; the imaginary conceptual space is filled with symbols and organic systems sectioned by geometric figures. In 1948, he retreated into 'internal exile', and worked in physical and later technical jobs for more than two decades. Besides his small abstract/surrealist paintings, he also made photograms and films in the early 1950s. In the 1960s, his painterly system of symbols composed of geometric and organic elements was associated with research into 'the hidden face of nature' (Ernő Kállai's expression): the structures of the micro- and macro-world.

GYÉMÁNT, László (1935, Budapest), painter
From 1957 until 1963, he studied painting at the Magyar Képzőművészeti Főiskola. He became one of the surnaturalists associated with Tibor Csernus. At first, he was inspired by Csernus's style, then from the mid-1960s he veered towards pop art and his magic realist paintings were crammed with a montage-like conglomeration of text, fragments and objects. Towards the late 1960s, his paintings became less crowded and the compositions started focusing on single figures; his portrait-like works often feature American jazz musicians. His exhibition in 1968 was banned on the opening day. In 1970, he moved to London and resettled in Vienna in 1973, opening a private drawing school. In 1982, he returned to Hungary and founded the Óbudai Művészeti Iskola (Óbuda School of Arts) in 1987. Since the 1990s, he has been painting large canvases based on his own photographs modified with chemicals. He refers to these works, using his own name (*gyémánt* = diamond) as Diamondography.

HAJAS, Tibor (1946, Budapest – 1980, Szeged), performer, artist
In 1964–65, he studied English at the ELTE. He was arrested for, allegedly, possession of fascist symbols and was sentenced to two years in prison. From 1967, he published poems in weekly magazines and anthologies. He started practising visual and conceptual art in 1969. He documented his street actions on photographs (*To the Streets with Your Message I–II*, 1975); later his interest turned towards photography, then film and video as a medium (*Self-Fashion Show*, 1976). From 1976 he gave introductory presentations to film screenings at the Ganz-MÁVAG Művelődési Ház (Ganz-MÁVAG Culture House). From 1978, he held ritual-like performances using his own body as a medium. Influenced by Viennese actionism and later by Tibetan philosophies, he pushed himself to the brink of death by enduring extreme physical and psychological strain (*Expiation*, 1978; *Wake*, 1980). He carried out photo performances with the aid of János Vető (*Flesh Painting*, 1978; *Emergency Landing*, 1979). Since his death, his works have been represented at a number of group exhibitions, most recently in the Central Pavilion of the 2017 Venice Biennale.

HALÁSZ, Károly (1946, Paks – 2016, Paks), painter, graphic artist
From 1961 until 1965, he studied decorative painting at the Pécsi Művészeti Gimnázium (Pécs Secondary School of Arts). He organized a number of exhibitions in fine and decorative arts throughout the 1960s–70s. He was a founding member of the Pécsi Műhely. From 1974 until 1979, he worked as a graphic designer and exhibition organizer at the Janus Pannonius Múzeum of Pécs; in 1980, he founded the Paksi Vizuális Kísérleti Művésztelep (Artist Colony for Visual Experiments in Paks). He was an experimental artist, engaged in structures constructed by optical motion and building constructivist spaces in the early 1970s, as well as conceptual land- and body-art works, installations, performances and photo series operating with axonometric geometrical elements (*Modulated Television*). He exhibited at the Balatonboglári Kápolnaműterem and in 1979 he participated in the 'Works and Words' exhibition at De Appel in Amsterdam. In 1990, he was given a scholarship by the Collegium Hungaricum in Rome. In 1991, he founded the Paksi Képtár, of which he was director until 2006.

HALÁSZ, Péter (1943, Budapest – 2006, New York), avant-garde writer, theatre director, actor
Between 1962 and 1969 he was a member of the Universitas theatre company and, after the dispersal of the company, he founded his own theatre named Kassák Ház Stúdió (Kassák House Studio). In 1971, they participated at the World Theatre Festival in Nancy. In 1972 their show *Murder in the Skanzen* was banned and their licence was revoked; the company continued its activity as an apartment theatre in Budapest. Their imposing performances – continuously under surveillance by the secret service – deconstructed the border between life and art. They held performances at the Balatonboglári Kápolnaműterem and participated at a theatre festival in Wrocław without permission, for which their passports were revoked. Following their emigration (1976), the members continued operating as Squat Theater; first in Western Europe then in New York. In 1991, Halász returned to Hungary where he directed plays at several theatres. Before his death, he arranged his own funeral at Műcsarnok, where he listened to his friends' eulogies while lying in a coffin.

HARASZTŸ, István (1934, Pestszentimre), sculptor
From 1951 until 1953, he studied engine fitting and later smithery. Between 1967 and 1989, he worked as an interior architect at the South Pest Catering Company. From 1960 until 1970 he was a junior member of the Dési Huber Képzőművészeti Kör (Dési Huber Art Circle). Since his first mobile sculpture in 1967, his kinetic works have been characterized by a deeply political and ironically subversive approach (*Six-twenty Express*, *Fig Pitter*, 1970). His most important works from the 1970s include *Cage* (1972), modelling captivity and faux-freedom, and

Steel Smile (1972), a safe that imparts laughter instead of money, referring to György Aczél, the cultural despot of Hungary, with a pun on his name (*aczél* = steel). The light playfulness of his metal pendulums, steel ball structures and Plexiglas mobile sculptures is offset by the witty irony of their titles. He calls his conceptual works 'play art', wherein the beauty arising from the technical possibilities always bears some not-so-hidden social critique. In 1975, he received the Kassák Prize; in 1984, he was awarded a DAAD scholarship.

HENCZE, Tamás (1938, Szekszárd – 2018, Budapest), painter
After graduating as a decorator at the Kirakatrendező Iskola (School of Shop-window Design) in 1960, he worked in advertising design. He combined his early gesture painting with tachism, and by the mid-1960s he was using a spray gun and a rubber roller to apply spots with blurry edges in a grid structure. In 1965, he became acquainted with painter Dezső Korniss, whom he considered his master. In 1968, he was featured in the 'Iparterv' exhibition with his op-art style paintings. In the early 1970s, he made conceptual land-art works and actions (*Fire Pictures*, 1974) and later returned to painting. By the late 1970s, he had an established style: he used rubber rollers and masks to paint, achieving illusory spatiality in the process. He uses reduced forms and colours. His means of expression include vertical cylindrical forms, monochrome colours and repetitive rhythm, serving visual perception instead of narrativity in the spirit of the abstraction of Malevich.

HINCZ, Gyula (1904, Budapest – 1986, Budapest), painter, graphic artist, applied artist
He graduated from the Magyar Képzőművészeti Főiskola in 1929. Owing to his exceptional technical knowledge and adaptive talent, his art was influenced by very diverse tendencies. During his study trip to Paris in 1926, he became inspired by Gauguin, Picasso and surrealism. His trip to Berlin in 1928 was decisive for him; *Der Sturm* familiarized him with expressionism, cubism, futurism, constructivism and dada. In 1929, he had a joint exhibition with László Moholy-Nagy at Der Sturm Gallery. The abstract style of his still-lifes, rife with post-cubist and classical motifs, conveys a nostalgic dream world. He called his biomorphic, abstract compositions 'amoebaism'. His oeuvre spans a broad palette: he made collages, stage designs, graphics, book illustrations, calligraphic works after his journey to the Far East in 1947–48, socialist realist art in the 1950s, then monumental tapestries. Between 1949 and 1963, he taught at the Magyar Képzőművészeti Főiskola and, between 1958 and 1963, he was the director of the Magyar Iparművészeti Főiskola.

JOVÁNOVICS, György (1939, Budapest), sculptor
From 1957 until 1960, he studied sculpture at the Magyar Képzőművészeti Főiskola, then philosophy at the ELTE; he attended the Akademie der Bildenden Künste (Academy of Fine Arts) in Vienna in 1964 and the École nationale supérieure des Beaux-Arts in Paris in 1965, and in 1971 he received a scholarship from the Museum Folkwang in Essen. He exhibited at the 'Iparterv' exhibitions and the Balatonboglári Kápolnaműterem. In the 1960s, he became interested in the relationship between minimally plastic sculptural surfaces and light along with methods of mapping. Made almost exclusively out of plaster, his works are not merely reliefs or sculptures, but rather installations. His early torsos and human figures were inspired partly by existentialism and partly by classical humanism (*Detail of the Great Gilles*, 1967; *Lying Man*, 1969), and were followed by the exploration of the philosophical and medial problems of the relationship of reality and its representation. He also made a conceptual 'comic' based on his own photo series (*Liza Wiathruck*, 1974). Between 1980 and 1983, he was on a DAAD scholarship in Berlin; in 1988, he received a Philip Morris Grant. In 1991, he was appointed professor at the Magyar Képzőművészeti Főiskola. In 1995, he represented Hungary at the Venice Biennale.

KASSÁK, Lajos (1887, Érsekújvár [now Nové Zámky, Slovakia] – 1967, Budapest), writer, poet, editor
A self-educated man, he journeyed across Western Europe on foot in 1909. He launched the journal *A Tett* (The Action) in 1915 and, after it was banned, the activist journal *MA* (Today), which was closely connected to *Die Aktion* and *Der Sturm* in Berlin. Between 1916 and 1919, *MA*'s editorial office hosted a number of exhibitions. After the fall of the short-lived communist Magyarországi Tanácsköztársaság (Hungarian Republic of Councils) in 1919, he fled to Vienna and re-launched *MA*. In the 1920s, he developed theories related to socially engaged activism and '*képarchitektúra*' (picture architecture), while also making aquarelles, collages and printed graphics. Between 1924 and 1933, the journal *Nyugat* (West) published his autobiography, *Egy ember élete* (A Man's Life). After his return to Hungary in 1926, he established the journals *Dokumentum* (Document, 1926–27) and later *Munka* (Work, 1928), which was banned in 1939. After 1945, he returned to literature and edited the journals *Alkotás* (Creation) and *Kortárs* (Contemporary) in 1947–49, but he never found common ground with József Révai's communist cultural policy and was expelled from the Party in 1953. From the late 1950s, his works were exhibited in several Western European exhibitions, but in Hungary he was not rehabilitated until his death in 1967. A museum dedicated to his work opened in 1976 in Budapest.

KEMÉNY, György (1936, Budapest), graphic artist, designer
He was a student of graphic artist Pál Gábor before studying serigraphy at the Magyar Képzőművészeti Főiskola in 1956–61. In 1963, he travelled to Paris and became greatly influenced by pop art and the works of Warhol, Wesselmann and Lichtenstein. By the late 1960s, he was one of the most important graphic artists in Hungary and his street posters became widely known. His poster *New Bathing Suits* was vandalized and labelled by the socialist media as 'imperialist porn'. In 1971, he made a giant pop-art secco in the apartment of the opposition politician Ferenc Kőszeg. In 1973, he designed the cover of the record

An Imaginary Report on an American Rock Festival. His installations, posters and production designs are characterized by a conceptual approach based on a montage technique coupled with a grotesque, ironic tone. Shock and playfulness are dominant traits in his work. In the 1960s, his vivid graphic style and strong contours were influenced by pop art; he integrated aspects of Western consumer society and pop into Hungarian commercial advertising.

KERÉNYI, Jenő (1908, Budapest – 1975, Budapest), sculptor
From 1930 until 1937, he studied at the Magyar Képzőművészeti Főiskola. In 1937, he was on a scholarship at the Collegium Hungaricum in Rome; he was greatly influenced by Etruscan art as well as Auguste Rodin's and Antoine Bourdelle's sculpture. His art was figural with classical inspirations, made of stone and bronze, as well as aluminium from the 1950s. His signature style – dramatic expressiveness and powerful multifigure compositions – had already emerged in his early period. His favourite sculptural subjects include mother-and-child and the female form, but he also made works commissioned by the state (*Partisan Memorial*, 1948; *Ostapenko*, 1951). In 1958, he won the Grand Prix at the Brussels World's Fair with *Dancers*, a sculpture made in collaboration with József Somogyi, and in 1960 he was one of the representatives of Hungary at the Venice Biennale. Towards the end of his career, he turned to biblical themes; these works are characterized by a vibrant formal order and ragged surface treatment.

KESERÜ, Ilona (1933, Pécs), painter
From 1952 until 1958, she studied painting at the Magyar Képzőművészeti Főiskola. In 1962–63, she visited Rome on a study trip; her brisk calligraphic work gradually shifted towards gesture painting. In 1967, she saw the heart-shaped tombstones of the cemetery in Balatonudvari, and implemented them as the central motif of her painting. Around 1969, her art became infused with plasticity (bulging canvases and the application of fabrics). Her raw unpainted works were gradually pervaded by rainbow colours in geometrical arrangements, followed by supplementary grades of neutral skin colour. From the 1980s, she was intrigued by the optical problem of afterimages that appear on the retina of the closed eye. She participated in the 'Iparterv' exhibitions and was a member of the Pesti Műhely (1975–79). In 1980, she was one of the representatives of Hungary at the Venice Biennale. In 1986, she was a guest lecturer at the École nationale supérieure d'arts in Cergy-Pontoise, France. Since 1995, she has been head of the Doctor of Liberal Arts programme in painting at the Institute of Visual Arts at the University of Pécs.

KONDOR, Béla (1931, Pestszentlőrinc – 1972, Budapest), painter, graphic artist, poet
From 1950 until 1956, he studied painting and then graphic arts at the Magyar Képzőművészeti Főiskol. His diploma work, a series of copper etchings entitled *Scenes from the Times of György Dózsa* (1956), was considered anachronistic by the conservative board of professors, but some art historians celebrated him as the reformer of socialist realism. Although he was at home in a number of genres (woodcut, etching, drypoint, lithography, monotype, paper etching, photography, poetry as well as organ music), his style, which drew on masters such as William Blake and Albrecht Dürer, and his particular vision were not in line with any of the official or unofficial artistic tendencies of the 1960s. His works were often rejected by official juries, but he was admired by young graphic artists. His art is characterized by the reinterpretation of universal symbols. Recurring elements of his unusual iconography include motifs of a human-Christ and human-angel, flight and soaring (aeroplane constructs made of sticks), featured in apocalyptic visions. His work was exhibited at the Tokyo International Biennial of Graphic Art in 1965 and at the Hungarian Pavilion of the Venice Biennale in 1968.

KONKOLY, Gyula (1941, Budapest), artist
From 1959 until 1964, he studied painting at the Magyar Képzőművészeti Főiskola. As one of the leading figures of the Hungarian neo-avant-garde, he first made surnaturalist works (*The Academy of Fine Arts Visited by the Muse*, 1964) and then pop art, including painting and applied objects (*Softened Egg, A Rose Speaks More Pleasantly*, 1968). His conceptual and politically loaded works include a man-size block of ice wrapped in cotton wool and gauze, bleeding potassium permanganate, exhibited at the 1969 'Iparterv' exhibition, and *Five Identical Persons Apply Here* (1970). In 1970, he had the first solo exhibition of conceptual art in Hungary. In the same year, he emigrated to France. In 1972, he published a manifesto on the death of the neo-avant-garde. In the 1980s, he returned to painting, and in 1991 he moved back to Hungary. Between 1992 and 1995 he taught at the University of Pécs.

KORNISS, Dezső (1908, Bistrița, Romania – 1984, Budapest), painter
From 1925 until 1929, he studied at the Magyar Képzőművészeti Főiskola. Between 1928 and 1930, he was a member of the Új progresszív művészek (New Progressive Artists) group, and in 1930–31 he participated in the Munka kör (Work Circle) of Lajos Kassák. From 1935, he and Lajos Vajda collected folk art and architectural motifs in the town of Szentendre, which bore the marks of Hungarian, German and Serbian culture alike, and used them in their painting. Influenced by Béla Bartók's approach to music, their goal was to lay the foundations of a new Central and Eastern European art by integrating influences from both the West and East. Korniss was one of the founding members of the Európai Iskola. He simultaneously made constructivist-figurative paintings composed of pure spots of colour (*Cricket Wedding*, 1949) and works of an expressive surrealist character (*Illumination*, 1945–62). From the late 1950s, he made calligraphic pictures influenced by French tachism and, following a brief conceptual period, in the 1970s he began making

geometric abstract paintings using elements from Hungarian folk culture (including a haircloth-robe motif).

LADIK, Katalin (1942, Novi Sad, Serbia), poet, performer, actress
She is a performing artist who is equally active in the fields of literature, art and theatre. She composes poetry, sound poetry, visual poetry, experimental music, sound plays and gesture poems. She uses her own body and voice as her media in her performances. In the 1970s, she was a member of the Bosch+Bosch group, participated in a number of happenings and actions, and joined the mail-art movement. In 1978, her visual poetry and collages were featured at the Venice Biennale. From 1977 until 1992, she was an actress at the Theatre of Novi Sad and had leading roles in a number of TV films. Her poems were published in international anthologies. In the 1980s, she performed with Boris Kovač's band, among others. In 1991, she received the Kassák Prize and in 2001 the Attila József Prize. In 2016, she was awarded the LennonOno Grant for Peace by Yoko Ono. In 2017, her works were exhibited in documenta 14, Kassel. She lives in Budapest.

LAKNER, László (1936, Budapest), painter, graphic artist
Between 1954 and 1960, he studied painting at the Magyar Képzőművészeti Főiskola. Following his diploma work, he was drawn towards the surnaturalism associated with Tibor Csernus. His study trip in Italy in 1963–64 was followed by a series of pop art paintings and, around 1968, conceptualism and hyperrealism appeared in his art simultaneously. In 1968, he spent a month in Germany and Switzerland on a scholarship from the Museum Folkwang, Essen. He took part in the 'Iparterv' exhibitions. Of his conceptual works from around 1970 (book works, protest poems, citations, signature series, actions, photo and film concepts), his screen print *My Georg Lukacs-book* was presented at the 1972 Venice Biennale, where he was also exhibited in 1976 and 1990 at the Central Pavilion. His photorealistic, full-body nude self-portrait from 1970 was acquired by the Uffizi Gallery in Florence. In 1974, he received a DAAD scholarship. Since 1974, he has been based in Germany. In 1977, he received the German Critics' Award and was exhibited at documenta in Kassel.

LANTOS, Ferenc (1929, Pécs – 2014, Balatonberény), painter, graphic artist, art educator
He graduated as a painter and teacher at the Magyar Képzőművészeti Főiskola in 1964. He founded the fine arts class at the Pécsi Művészeti Gimnázium (Pécs Secondary School of Arts) in 1959 and the Pécsi Műhely in 1968. His career as a painter started in the 1950s with socialist realism. Later, he turned to geometrical structures and colour compositions offered by landscape painting. In the late 1960s, he worked with grid structures and mathematical laws in accordance with the serial, combinatorial and systematic approach of international geometric art; from the 1970s, he delved into the optical effects of horizontal parallel lines. Many of his works can be interpreted as musical structures or visual poetry. His works were motivated by autonomy and the ideal of pure art, the existence of images as autonomous reality. From 1994, he taught at the University of Pécs.

LOSSONCZY, Tamás (1904, Budapest – 2009, Budapest), painter
After his legal studies, he attended the Magyar Képzőművészeti Főiskola from 1923 until 1926, and then travelled to Paris and Amsterdam. In the late 1920s, he created organic-constructivist spatial structures, but then gave up his art practice for years. He began painting again in 1939: on the one hand, his canvases were populated by shapes that aroused organic associations, in the spirit of Ernő Kállai's bioromanticism; and on the other hand, he experimented with reforming abstraction. He was a member of the Európai Iskola and the Elvont Művészek Csoportja from 1946 until 1948. The pinnacle of his artistic career was between 1945 and 1948; he conceived an ethereal system of motifs with cosmic and biological associations, based on simple geometric shapes (triangles, circles). He made a few socialist realist works in the early 1950s, and then gave up art until 1956. After 1956, he spent years painting his monumental abstract work entitled *Great Purifying Storm* (completed in 1962), a monument to the 1956 revolution in Hungary. He was permitted to exhibit his nonfigurative art only from the 1970s.

MAJOR, János (1934, Budapest – 2008, Budapest), graphic artist
He was one of the most original but least easily classifiable figures of Hungarian neo-avant-garde art. He began his career as a graphic artist. One of his most important works is the engraving *In Memoriam of Móric Scharf* (1966). As a graphical equivalent of scraping layers of paint, it was not only a technical innovation, but also a rather provocative, taboo-breaking representation of problems arising from his Jewish identity. His work was readily labelled as pornography – for which he was often harassed by the police. His self-ironic and grotesque approach is also apparent in his photographs of tombstones and text-based conceptual works from the early 1970s. He destroyed most of his works in the mid-1970s. From 1976, he worked at the Budapesti Történeti Múzeum (Budapest History Museum) as an archaeological graphic artist. In the late 1980s, he made a comic book loaded with erotic references and several graphics of tombs. In the 2000s, he made his so-called 'chess problem composition' pictures, based on illusionary perspective.

MAKRISZ, Agamemnon (1913, Patra, Greece – 1993, Athens), sculptor
From 1933 until 1938, he studied at the Athens Academy of Fine Arts. In the Second World War, he took part in the Greek resistance movement and fought in the Greek Civil War. In 1945, he received a three-year scholarship from the French government and stayed in Paris; after being elected as Greece's representative in the World Peace Council, he was expelled from the country by the French government. From 1950 until the late 1980s, he lived in Hungary. His early portraits are characterized by a fusion of classical Greek tradition and modern sculptural tendencies, and from the mid-1950s his work has a formal diversity that couples cubist solutions with a plastic expression of the environment. He was a well-known figure of the political and the arts scene alike; he initiated the founding of the Derkovits scholarship

(1955), a state support scheme for young artists, and as a government commissioner he organized the 'Tavaszi Tárlat' (Spring Exhibition) of 1957. His public works (including *Mauthausen Memorial*, 1964) are characterized by anthropomorphic and expressive monumentality.

MARTYN, Ferenc (1899, Kaposvár – 1986, Pécs), sculptor, painter
In 1918–19 and 1923–24, he studied at the Magyar Képzőművészeti Főiskola. Between 1926 and 1940, he worked in Paris, joining the surrealists at first and from 1930 as a member of the Abstraction-Création group. By 1939, he had developed his painterly universe, based on a depiction of movement and three-dimensional space in two dimensions and an abstracted, sublimated rendering of reality. Returning to Hungary, he continued painting along the same lines. During the war, he protested against violence with his series of drawings, *Monsters of Fascism*. He was a member of the Európai Iskola. He did not exhibit his abstract paintings until 1969; he made drawings on natural and figural themes and drew two-dimensional geometrical structures, as well as literary illustrations. His colours and formal language draw greatly on music. He was among the first experimental modern Hungarian sculptors; he also made fine ceramics, plates and vases at the Pécs Porcelain Factory.

MAURER, Dóra (1937, Budapest), painter
From 1955 until 1961, she studied painting and graphic art at the Magyar Képzőművészeti Főiskola. Following her early surnaturalist copper engravings, she made collages using the motif of masking, and later turned to analytical yet sensuously rendered seriality influenced by conceptual art (*Quantity Tables*, *Reversible and Interchangeable Phases of Motion*, *Shifts*, 1972). In the 1980s, she explored the relation of the flat surface and the spatial illusion of two-dimensional formations (*Quasi-Pictures*) and later the 'metaphorical colours' produced by modulating standard colours with light (*Relative Quasi-Pictures*). In 1970, she founded the SUMUS group with Tibor Gáyor, in order to help the flow of information between the Hungarian and the Western art scenes. Alongside her practice as an artist, she has worked as an art teacher. From 1975 until 1977, she led a drawing workshop and, together with Miklós Erdély, ran the 'Kreativitási gyakorlatok' (Creativity Exercises) workshop at the Ganz-MÁVAG Művelődési Ház (Ganz-MÁVAG Culture House) in Budapest. Between 1987 and 1991, she taught at the Magyar Iparművészeti Főiskola, and since 1990 she has been teaching at the Magyar Képzőművészeti Főiskola. In 2011, she was invited to participate at the Istanbul Biennial, and in 2016 she had a solo exhibition at the White Cube in London. Since 2017 she has been the president of the Széchenyi Academy of Letters and Arts.

MÉHES, László (1944, Budapest), painter
From 1963 until 1967, he studied at the Magyar Képzőművészeti Főiskola. He developed his own figurative style at an early age, inspired by the surnaturalism of Tibor Csernus. He was influenced by pop art, and he developed his own procedure called '*monopoltypia*', involving the photographic effect of the imprints. His *Undressing Model* (1967) was denounced as a product of Western decadence, so he could only show his works to a small private audience. In 1969, he took part in the second 'Iparterv' exhibition; his work *Everyday* was the first instance of Hungarian hyperrealist painting. In 1970, he started making the ironic and critical *Lukewarm Water* series based on photographs from articles about Hungarian thermal baths. In 1971, he was exhibited at the Paris Youth Biennial. During his sojourn in Paris in 1972, he was influenced by Yves Klein; he began making nude female torsos combining his hyperrealist painterly vision and the use of a spray gun with methods of sculptural modelling (body imprints). In 1979, he settled in France. He lives in Torcy where he founded and leads an art school.

MÉHES, Lóránt Zuzu (1951, Szabadszállás), painter
He graduated at the Magyar Képzőművészeti Főiskola in 1979. In the early 1970s, he painted photorealist portraits and genre scenes while regularly participating in underground art events. His 1978 action was even covered by the French press in an article entitled 'Eyeglasses against Socialism'. Between 1981 and 1987 he collaborated with his friend János Vető as the artist duo Zuzu-Vető, creating rampantly eclectic 'postmodern social-impressionist neobarbaric' pieces (involving spray gun, felt-tip pen and applied textile objects) ironically appropriating and mocking political and cultural symbols. From 1984, he turned towards different religions; his mystical religious pictures (fusing the doctrines of Buddhism, Hinduism and Catholicism) feature decoratively painted banal religious symbols (*Heart of Mary*, *Holy Spirit*) and symbols (circle, triangle, fish) in a proliferating multitude of colours. Since the late 1990s, he has returned to photorealism; he paints his old photographs related to his personal memories, 'genre scenes' from his life.

MOLNÁR, Sándor (1936, Sajólád), painter
From 1955 until 1961, he studied at the Magyar Képzőművészeti Főiskola. From 1956, he painted abstract paintings. In 1958, he founded the so-called Zuglói kör. The members of the group (Imre Bak, István Nádler, Pál Deim) studied the theory of modern art and modern painting. In 1965, he became acquainted with Jean Bazaine in Paris. Metaphorically applying the four ancient elements and the seven stages of alchemy, in 1966 he developed his theory of yoga-painting as a creative and life programme, spanning five types and fifty years (earth-, water-, fire-, crystal- and air-pictures). His painting takes the formal construction of French lyrical abstraction as its point of departure; throughout the transformation of the image the figures and shapes come into contact, transforming and pervading each other. His ambition was to give rise to an up-to-date Eastern European art. His work was included at the 'Iparterv' exhibitions and shown at the Balatonboglári Kápolnaműterem. In 1986, he was guest lecturer at the Nimes School of Fine Arts. Between 1990 and 2005, he taught at the Magyar Képzőművészeti Főiskola.

NÁDLER, István (1938, Visegrád), painter
From 1958 until 1963, he studied painting at the Magyar Képzőművészeti Főiskola. On the invitation of the Károlyi Foundation, he took a study trip to Europe in 1964 and went to Paris in 1966. Early on, he painted lyrical, airy paintings, and then joined Kassák's historical Hungarian constructivist avant-garde and took on the era's neo-constructivist, hard-edge tendencies; he incorporated stylized folklore elements and Avar (Caucasian) motifs into his works. He participated in the 'Iparterv' exhibitions and was a member of the Pesti Műhely. In 1970, he worked at the Károlyi Foundation's art colony in Venice and in 1972 he was granted a scholarship by the Museum Folkwang, Essen. In the 1980s, music had a major role in the development of his painting; he discovered the motivic structures of folk art through Béla Bartók, while minimal music (Steve Reich) and traditional music from the Far East helped him to develop his gesture painting, coupled with structural abstraction, according to his own ideas. Malevich's cross has had a fundamental influence on his art.

ORSZÁG, Lili (1926, Uzhgorod, Ukraine – 1978, Budapest), painter, graphic artist
From 1945 until 1950, she studied at the Magyar Képzőművészeti Főiskola. Between 1950 and 1954 and from 1960 until her death, she worked as a stage- and costume designer at the Állami Bábszínház (State Puppet Theatre). Sublimating anxiety and persecution, and reflecting the influence of Magritte and de Chirico, her early surrealist works introduce her characteristic motifs: the prison-like wall, the tombstones and the female figures. Following a trip to Bulgaria, the influence of icon painting emerged in her work around 1957–59. After her trip to Prague in 1962, and the impact of its Jewish cemetery, she began creating collage-like paintings pervaded by Hebrew letters and archaic motifs (*Walls of Jerusalem*, 1962). From the mid-1960s, she fused the symbols of biblical (Jewish, Roman) cultures with imprints of printed electric circuit designs. In the 1970s, the classical and modern symbolism of the labyrinth became the organizing principle of her art, based on the logic of montage.

PÁTZAY, Pál (Kapuvár, 1896 – Budapest, 1979), sculptor
From 1912 until 1914, he studied at the Magyar Képzőművészeti Főiskola, from where he was expelled, and he then self-educated. Joining the circle focused on the journal *MA* (Today), he made small expressionist sculptures. He was imprisoned by the Horthy regime after the fall of the Hungarian Tanácsköztársaság (Republic of Councils) in 1919 for his assistance in the communist council's work. From the 1920s, he made decorative classicist sculptures. He was one of the founders of the Gresham kör. In 1927, he took a study trip to Paris, and between 1928 and 1930 he was at the Collegium Hungaricum in Rome on a scholarship. In 1937, he made the sculpture *Saint Stephen* for the Hungarian Pavilion at the Paris Expo; it was awarded the Diplôme d'honneur. In 1942, he made the official badge of the anti-war protest, the so-called Petőfi-plaquette; during the persecution of Jews in Hungary in 1944 he helped to hide people in his atelier. From 1945, he was an influential representative of the art scene, and between 1945 and 1975 he was a professor of the Magyar Képzőművészeti Főiskola. He denounced modernism and represented a kind of plastic, moderate but pedagogically doctrinaire academism.

PAUER, Gyula (1941, Budapest – 2012, Budapest), sculptor, conceptual artist
In the late 1950s, he studied ornamental sculpture under Alajos de Battista, and then began making sculptures in the style of Giacometti. In 1970, he presented his first *Pseudo* artworks at the Balatonboglári Kápolnaműterem exhibitions and then at a Budapest show disguised as a film shoot. These works manifest a conceptual way of thinking based on the ironical identification of the relation between reality and illusion, true and false, art and politics. His monumental conceptual work *Protest-Sign Forest*, created at the Artists' Colony of Nagyatád in 1978 and based on funny, philosophical and provocative texts, was destroyed by the authorities because of its political implications. Pervading the artist's entire oeuvre, the *Pseudo* concept appears in his life's work in the form of plans, texts, actions, installations, objects and paintings. In the 1970s–80s he worked as a set designer at the Kaposvár Theatre and later at the National Theatre, and for a number of films, eventually also as a production designer.

PINCZEHELYI, Sándor (1946, Szigetvár), painter, graphic artist
From 1966 until 1970, he studied Hungarian language and literature and graphic art at the Pécsi Tanárképző Főiskola (Teacher Training College of Pécs). Between 1969 and 1977, he worked as a poster designer at the Janus Pannonius Múzeum of Pécs and later became the director of the Pécsi Galéria until 1999. He was a member of the Pécsi Műhely and author of the neo-avant-garde group's inner communications channel (*Announcements*); he worked with printed graphics, painting and photography as well as crafts (enamel works). In the early 1970s, he made politically motivated conceptual works (*The Cobblestone is the Weapon of the Proletariat*, 1973), a series of cobblestones shaped like five-pointed stars (*Star*, 1972) and process art showing the phases of an event through photographs (*Sickle and Hammer I–IV*, 1973). An ironical travesty of the visual themes of Hungarian socialism is also present in his works from the 1980s (*RWG: Red-White-Green* cycle). In 1987, he founded the DOPP group, an association of poster designers. In 1992, he won a scholarship from the Collegium Hungaricum in Rome.

ST AUBY, Tamás (1944, Budapest), poet, happener
Born as Tamás Szentjóby, other 'after-egos' of the artist – who defines himself as a 'non-art artist' – include Tony Putr, St Turb, St Turba, St Aubsky and Szentyóby. He began his career in the early 1960s with political poetry contests within the Buta Költők Társasága (Dumb Poets' Circle). Together with Gábor Altorjay he did the first happening in Hungary. He organized action theatre, Fluxus concerts and poetry readings, made samizdat publications and put on radio

plays. In 1973–75, he made the film *Centaur*, which was instantly banned. Following his emigration in 1975, he settled in Switzerland and moved the headquarters of the IPUT (International Parallel Union of Telecommunications) – founded in 1968 under the cover-name *Parallel Course/Study Track* – to Geneva. He founded the Near-Eastern-European Free University for Unemployed Western Europeans and organized a 'Non-art Art Strike'. After his return to Hungary he started teaching at the Intermedia Department of the Magyar Képzőművészeti Főiskola. In 2009, he was exhibited at the Istanbul Biennial and in 2010 he had a solo exhibition at the Badischer Kunstverein in Karlsruhe. In 2012, he was invited to exhibit at documenta in Kassel.

SCHAÁR, Erzsébet (1908, Budafok – 1975, Budapest), sculptor
From 1924 until 1926, she studied sculpture at the Magyar Képzőművészeti Főiskola. In 1926, she took a study trip to Paris. She began her career focusing on the modelling of realist portraits. In the 1960s, she made expressive and gaunt figures resembling Giacometti's style. Later, she created her block-body figures and assembled scenes (scenes in front of a shop window, figures behind and in front of walls). She also included architectural elements in her art: she created box- and room-like spaces sectioned by chairs, doors and windows. In the late 1960s, she started applying female death masks onto human-size white blocks of polystyrene foam to represent people in her street scenes. In 1974, she summarized her oeuvre in *Street*, a monumental installation with multiple figures resembling a frozen scene.

SOMOGYI, József (1916, Hirm, Austria – 1993, Budapest), sculptor
Despite his initial interest in law, he turned towards art and, from 1936 until 1941, studied at the Magyar Képzőművészeti Főiskola. In 1945–63, he was a teacher at the Képző- és Iparművészeti Szakközépiskola (Secondary School of Fine and Applied Arts); in 1963–93, he taught at the Magyar Képzőművészeti Főiskola, and was also its rector between 1974 and 1987. Besides his pedagogical activity, he was also active in public life (president of the Magyar Képző- és Iparművészek Szövetsége [Association of Hungarian Artists], 1968–77; member of the Presidential Council, 1975–80). He caught the art scene's attention with his animal sculptures as early as the 1940s. His first Soviet-style socialist realist work was *The Smelter* (1953), followed by several monumental naturalist and figurative public statues in the 1960s (*János Szántó Kovács*, 1965). His sculpture is characterized by a simple modernity and geometrical construction, as well as profound emotional content and expressiveness pervading his austere figures. This is coupled with the rusticity of raw surfaces. In 1970, Somogyi and Gyula Hincz represented Hungary at the Venice Biennale.

SZABÓ, Ákos (1936, Budapest), painter
Following his piano studies, he studied painting at the Magyar Képzőművészeti Főiskola (his masters: János Kmetty and, later, Aurél Bernáth) from 1954 until 1960. Hungarian art criticism aligned him with the young surnaturalist artists around Tibor Csernus. His works were denounced by official critics and he had no chance of having a solo exhibition. At the time of his involuntary 'inner exile', he met Miklós Erdély and Sándor Altorjai, and they made a film together. Erdély interpreted his works as a typically Hungarian and socialist version of magic realism. In 1965, Kazimir Romanovicz, the owner of Galerie Lambert, invited him to exhibit in Paris, and he did not return to Hungary. In the 1960s in Paris, he experimented with a combination of biomorphic surrealism and photorealism. In the 1970s, however, he returned to the more traditional, academic versions of realism. He has been living in Normandy since 1995.

SZENES, Zsuzsa (1931, Budapest – 2001, Budapest), textile artist, graphic artist
From 1951 until 1955, she studied at the Magyar Iparművészeti Főiskola. Between 1959 and 1962, she worked at the Komplex Textile Studio designing unique textile patterns. From the early 1960s, she made grotesque graphics with a proliferous motif structure; her motifs (dolls, interiors, clocks, plants) and her lace-like line drawings also appeared in her textile works towards the end of the decade. By the mid-1970s, she was using textile art and techniques to create conceptual works of art; she covered a gas mask in braided wool (*What Used to Be a Commodity is Decoration Today*, 1975), a sentry box in striped knitwork (*Against the Cold in General*, 1978), and a chair and a rifle in a green-and-white striped material (*Cover*, 1976). In 1977, she was one of the founders of the Velemi Textilművészeti Alkotóműhely (Velem Workshop for Textile Art). From 1979, she also made performance pieces, photo works, environments and book illustrations related to textiles.

SZENTJÓBY, Tamás, *see* ST AUBY, Tamás

SZOMBATHY, Bálint (1950, Pačir, Serbia), artist, art critic
Engaged in visual poetry, mail art, installation, performance and graphic design, the intermedia artist and theoretical author is a key member of the neo-avant-garde art scene. He was one of the founders of the Bosch+Bosch group (1969–76), and the art editor of the neo-avant-garde journal *WOW* and later the journal *Új Symposion* (New Symposium). Under the alter-ego Art Lover, from 1980 he was the member of the neoist movement founded in Canada. In the mid-1970s, he joined the international mail-art and stamp-art movements (*Szombathy Art* logos, stamps of his own design). By transubstantiating erratic or irregular images from the fringes of art, he made electrographics, and in the 1990s he started integrating post-communist symbols into his works. He published studies in Hungarian and in foreign languages about Vojvodinese and international alternative art. He is the author of a number of monographs on artists. He received the Kassák Prize in 1989. He has been living in Hungary since 2000.

TOT, Amerigo (1909, Fehérvárcsurgó – 1984, Rome), sculptor
Born Imre Tóth, as a young man he came into conflict with radical right-wing protesters, for which he was imprisoned for three months in 1930. For a few months, he studied at the

Bauhaus in Dessau, then enlisted as a sailor in Hamburg. In 1933, he visited the Dresden school of Otto Dix; he was later arrested and interned by the Nazis, but he escaped to Rome. In the Second World War, he took part in the Italian partisan movement; he received his first commissions in Italy, including the frieze on the façade of the Termini railway station in Rome, 1949–53. After the war, he worked as a racing-car driver and harpoonist, and for a few years he managed a ceramics factory and participated in a number of films. In 1969, he had a solo exhibition at the Mücsarnok (as a legitimation of the Kádár regime, which wished to foster relations with émigré artists) in Budapest, and in 1978 a museum of his works opened in Pécs, the city György Aczél wished to turn into a cultural focal point. Tot was an adept artist but had no individual style (ranging from the archaic *Madonna of Csurgó* of 1969 to the nonfigurative model of *Seed* made in 1980 for the University of Gödöllő). In addition to his public works, he made drawings and photographic montages.

TÓT, Endre (1937, Sümeg), conceptual artist, painter
From 1959 until 1965, he studied mural art at the Magyar Képzőművészeti Főiskola. Later, he began experimenting with *art informel*, and then started practising colour calligraphy and lyrical abstract painting, made collages, and became influenced by pop art and minimal art. In 1968–69 his work was shown at the 'Iparterv' exhibitions. In 1971, he gave up painting and began making so-called idea or conceptual artworks. He developed self-identifying ideas (the *Rain* series using the '/' sign on a typewriter; the *Zero* and *Very Special Gladness* series are based on the '0' character) and distributed them through mail art, actions, films and other non-artistic media (rubber stamps, postcards, newspaper ads, telegraphs, stamps, posters, graffiti, signs, banners and Xeroxes). He carried out countless performances and actions. Since 1971, he has been regularly featured in international exhibitions. In 1978–79, he lived in Berlin on a DAAD scholarship and subsequently settled in Germany. He lives in Cologne.

TÓTH, Gábor (1950, Budapest), poet, action artist
From 1968 until 1971, he studied law at the ELTE. He has been active in several genres. In the late 1960s, he carried out and documented his actions without audience (*Reading*, 1967). He featured at Balatonboglári Kápolnaműterem events; in 1973, he organized the first exhibition of experimental poetry with Dóra Maurer. In his sound and action poetry, he used extraordinary 'instruments' (sandpaper, slurping, manual numbering machine). He also made land art. He has created photo concepts (*Self-manipulation*, 1975), films and pieces ironically mocking the analytical tendencies of conceptual art as well as its forerunners (Duchamp). He considers dimensionist poet Károly Tamkó Sirató to be his master (the dimensionists wished to bring art forms into the fourth dimension); his own dimensionist poetry in the mid-1970s fused dadaist and surrealist tones. His mail-art activity was dominated by unique slogans and ironic mottoes, related to art and the artist, which he would put on stamps, ads and stickers ('Beware, this might be a work of art').

VAJDA, Júlia (1913, Trenčín, Slovakia – 1982, Budakeszi), painter, graphic artist
Resettling from Bratislava to Hungary, in 1935 Júlia Richter became acquainted with Lajos Vajda, whom she married. From 1935 until 1939, she attended the Budapesti Iparművészeti Iskola (Budapest School of Arts and Crafts). Her early naturalist works became increasingly populated with surrealist elements inspired by her husband, but she was also profoundly influenced by icon painting and Russian orthodox religious art. From 1946, together with her second husband, József Jakovits, she participated in the exhibitions of the Európai Iskola and the Elvont Művészek Csoportja; her works from this time feature surrealist and enigmatic biblical paraphrases and slim, dancing chromosome-like figures. After 1948, the apartment at 1 Rottenbiller Street safeguarding Lajos Vajda's heritage – where Endre Bálint also worked along with József Jakovits – became an important place for Hungarian alternative art. In 1956–57 she stayed in Sweden and, between 1961 and 1963, in Paris. The legacy of Lajos Vajda is a defining trait in her art, but beyond the motif-led structure of surrealism and constructivism, she was also influenced by lyrical abstraction, of which she conceived a unique Hungarian version.

VAJDA, Lajos (1908, Zalaegerszeg – 1941, Budakeszi), painter
From 1928 until 1930, he studied at the Magyar Képzőművészeti Főiskola. In 1928, he joined Lajos Kassák's Munka kör (Work Circle) comprising avant-garde artists. Between 1930 and 1934, he lived in Paris; here he developed his characteristic visual language featuring tightly constructed and dynamic, socially sensitive photomontages, the folding out of flattened three-dimensional objects into the plane, and 'extended perspective'. In 1935, he became acquainted with his future wife, Júlia Vajda (née Richter). In 1935–36, with Dezső Korniss, he developed the 'Programme of Szentendre', which combined local traditions and the formal language of the avant-garde in order to lay the foundations of a new synthesis of Central and Eastern European art. After 1937 he became more and more introverted: his line drawings loosened up and he painted a dark world full of amorphous masks. From 1938, the masks and gnomes in his works turned into inner, otherworldly scenes, and colour gradually disappeared. The organic, black shapes of his charcoal drawings 'woven' onto packaging paper convey the inferno of the war and the forced labour service for Jews. Conscription to the latter led to his death.

VASARELY, Victor (1906, Pécs – 1997, Paris), painter, graphic artist
Born Győző Vásárhelyi, after graduating from secondary school he attended evening courses at the Medical University, then frequented a graphic art workshop influenced by Bauhaus. In 1930, he settled in Paris and worked in advertising design. The major surrealist works of his Paris period (*Zebra*, 1938) already showed a strong inclination towards op art, which would bring him world fame, while Hungarian cultural traditions crop up in his works even from the 1950s. Upon his initiative, in 1960 he exhibited together with Lajos Kassák at the Galerie Denise René in Paris;

they published *Kassák/Vasarely*, a joint graphic art album that linked the Eastern European ideals of the historical avant-garde (activism, constructivism) and the endeavours of Western European structuralist modernism (op art, concrete art). In 1969, a large-scale solo exhibition was arranged in Budapest for the internationally acclaimed, yet leftist, artist living in Paris. In 1976, a Victor Vasarely museum opened in Pécs as a permanent institution. In the same year, his own foundation's museum was inaugurated in Aix-en-Provence.

VETŐ, János (1953, Budapest), photographer, visual artist
As a child, he performed in theatres as an extra. In the late 1960s, he started taking photos at the concerts of alternative bands. His independent photographic work involved experimentation with sequences, then the deconstruction and reconstruction of the depicted image; he made so-called 'T-portraits', each composed of four detailed close-ups, of his friends and artists. From 1976 he collaborated with Tibor Hajas as his assistant and co-creator in putting together Hajas's photographic tableaus and shooting his films; he documented Hajas's performances and actions on stills, which were then published under joint authorship. In 1980, he founded Trabant, a band. In the mid-1980s he and Lóránt Méhes created belated but significant contributions to Hungarian pop art, using elements of urban folklore, graffiti and children's drawings, along with the methods and techniques of home-décor kitsch. He is based in Malmö.

VÍGH, Tamás (1926, Csillaghegy – 2010, Budapest), sculptor
During the Second World War, he was a shipyard worker, and then studied sculpture at the Magyar Képzőművészeti Főiskola from 1946 until 1952. His naturalistic diploma work (*Singing Youth*) was a great success but, taking the sculptor Béni Ferenczy's advice, from that point on he tried to measure up to his own set of values without compromise; many of his plans for public sculptures and monuments were rejected or never realized (*Monument of Pál Vásárhelyi*, 1967; *Tree of Life*, 1972). In the 1960s, he developed a unique sculptural style: made from creased and dented cast bronze or other metal sheets, they are slightly cubist and pop-art-like, and highlight positive/negative space through their structures. In the 1970s, he made expressive portraits with craggy surfaces and innovative medals (instead of the uniplanar form, the front and the back are bent so they work in unison). Between 1975 and 1986, he taught at the Magyar Képzőművészeti Főiskola. His work was a major contribution to reforming modern Hungarian sculpture.

VILT, Tibor (1905, Budapest – 1983, Budapest), sculptor
From 1925 until 1927, he studied at the Magyar Képzőművészeti Főiskola. Between 1928 and 1930, he was on a scholarship at the Collegium Hungaricum in Rome. He developed his individual style in 1936 (for instance, in the small, expressive sculpture *Thinker*), but until 1951 most of his commissions were for decorative limestone reliefs on buildings. He made a multifigure sculpture for the Ministry of Defence, and in 1955 he won the tender for a sculpture (*Electricity*) at the Tiszalök Power Plant. Defining himself as a 'professional sculptor', the artist created a series of small, heartrending sculptures and reliefs, which, just like his compositions inspired by the 1956 Hungarian revolution, could only be completed in plaster copies until the mid-1960s. In 1957, he was interned for his activity during the revolution. In the 1960s, he made small anthropomorphic sculptures, then large statues with torn and creased textures; from this point onwards, a younger generation of artists came to see him as a reformer of modern Hungarian sculpture.

Notes on Contributors

Edit András is an art historian living in Budapest and in Long Island, NY. Her main interest concerns Eastern and Central European art, gender issues, socially engaged art, public art, critical theories, post-socialist conditions and nationalism in the region. She has participated in several international conferences and workshops as an invited speaker and published numerous essays in collected volumes, catalogues and professional journals, including *Artmargins*, *e-flux*, *Idea*, *Third text* and *springerin*. She authored the books, *Kötéltánc* (Tightrope Dance, 2001), *Kulturális* átöltözés*: Művészet a szocializmus romjain* (Cultural Crossdressing, Art on the Ruins of Socialism, Budapest, 2009) and edited the anthology *Transitland: Video Art from Central and Eastern Europe 1989–2009* (Budapest, 2009). For further information, see http://editandras.arthistorian.hu.

Flóra Barkóczi is an art historian. She studied at Eötvös Loránd University, Budapest, and at Humboldt Universität in Berlin. Her MA thesis was *Photo Based Conceptual Art in Hungary in the 1970s: An Exhibition, Exposition – Photo/Art*. She worked in the Robert Capa Contemporary Photography Center in 2016–17, and was a board member of the Young Artists' Photo Studio. She began working for the acb ResearchLab in 2017.

Lóránt Bódi is a social scientist and PhD candidate at Atelier – Department of European Social Sciences and Historiography (ELTE, Budapest) working for the Research Centre of Humanities Institute of History of Hungarian Academy of Sciences. He studied at the University of ELTE and visited ZZF (Potsdam) and EHESS (Paris) as a researcher. His research focus is the politics of memory and the historical narratives during the post-war period and the Kádár era (1956–1989) in Hungary.

Notes on Contributors

Géza Boros is an art historian and art writer. He studied at the Eötvös Loránd University Faculty of Humanities, Budapest, where he earned a degree in Art History and Aesthetics in 1988. His research interests include the visual memory of the 1956 revolution in Hungary, political monuments and contemporary public art. His main focus of research is public monuments after 1945. He has published numerous essays and in 1997 a monography about the monument and memorial cult of the 1956 revolution in Hungary. He works at the Ludwig Museum – Museum of Contemporary Art, Budapest.

Kriszta Dékei, who compiled and edited the artists' biographies of the present volume, is an art historian and art writer. She studied literature and art history at Eötvös Loránd University Budapest. She received grants from the Hungarian Academy of Sciences and the Sasakawa Foundation, as well as the Ernő Kallai grant for art critics. She also worked for the Institute of Art History as a grant researcher. Since 2016, she has been working as a museologist at the Ludwig Museum Budapest – Museum of Contemporary Art. Her field of interest is contemporary art with a special focus on conceptual trends. She publishes in *Artmagazin*, *Artportal.hu*, *Balkon*, *Új Művészet*, *Műértő*, *exindex*, *revizor.hu*, and in *Magyar Narancs*.

Gábor Dobó holds an MA in Literary History (University of Florence and Eötvös Loránd University) and is a PhD candidate at Eötvös Loránd University, Budapest. He has been a researcher at the Kassák Museum since 2014. He studied at universities in Budapest, Florence and Angers. He is researching periodicals of the avant-garde, including the magazines of the Hungarian avant-garde. His doctoral research focuses on the international network of Lajos Kassák's magazine *Dokumentum* (Document) in 1926–27.

Dávid Fehér is an associate curator at the Museum of Fine Arts, Budapest, in the Department of Art after 1800, and a PhD candidate in the Department of Art History at Eötvös Loránd University, Budapest. His research focuses on the history of Hungary and Eastern Europe art in 1960–80, especially the reception of photorealism, pop art and conceptual art. His work on photorealism and his survey of the developments in pop art in Hungary and Eastern Europe have been published in the exhibition catalogues *East of Eden: Versions of Reality* (Ludwig Museum, Budapest) and *International Pop* (Walker Art Center, Minneapolis), respectively, as well as in major Hungarian journals. He publishes regularly in art journals and exhibition catalogues.

Maja and Reuben Fowkes are art historians and curators who are based in Budapest and London. They are founders of the Translocal Institute for Contemporary Art, a centre for transnational research into East European art and ecology based in Budapest that operates across the disciplinary boundaries of art history, contemporary art and ecological thought. Maja has a PhD from University College London, and Reuben's PhD is from Essex University. Recent publications include Maja Fowkes's *The Green Bloc: Neo-Avant-Garde Art and Ecology under Socialism* (CEU Press, 2015) and *River Ecologies: Contemporary Art and Environmental Humanities on the Danube* (Translocal Institute, 2015). Reuben Fowkes is a member of the editorial board of the journal *Third Text*. Their curatorial projects include the Experimental Reading Room (2014–16) and the River School (2013–15), as well as the exhibitions 'Revolutionary Trilogy' (2006–2009), 'Loophole to Happiness' (2011) and 'Walking without Footprints' (2015–16).

Péter György is the Head of the Film, Media and Cultural Studies Graduate Programme at Eötvös Loráng University, Budapest. Following the political transition in 1989, he was a founding member of Media Studies at Eötvös Loránd University; he has lectured at the New School for Social Research, New York, and has participated and published in numerous conferences and journals in Hungarian and in English. He received his Distinguished University Professorship in appreciation of his book on the philosophical issues of museum theory (also in English, 2008; Russian and Slovakian editions are forthcoming). His publications include a co-authored monograph on the European School (with Gábor Pataki, 1990), *The Spirit of Place, From Mauthausen to MoMA* (2008), *Apám helyett* (Instead of My Father, 2011), *Állatkert Kolozsváron* (A Zoo in Cluj, 2013), *Az eltörölt hely: Múzeum* (Wiped Out Place: The Museum, 2003).

Sándor Hornyik is an art historian and curator working for the Institute for Art History of the Research Centre for Humanities of the Hungarian Academy of Sciences as a senior research fellow. His research concerns the history and theory of avant-garde and neo-avant-garde art as well as the theoretical issues of contemporary art and visual culture. He published a book on the neo-avant-garde reception of modern natural sciences (*Avant-Garde Science?*, Budapest: Akadémiai Kiadó, 2008), and another on the intersections of visual studies and contemporary art (*Idegenek egy bűnös városban* [Aliens in a Sin City], Budapest: L'Harmattan, 2011). Between 2012 and 2014 he was the chief curator of MODEM (Museum of Modern Art Debrecen) where he curated several exhibitions dealing with socialist and post-socialist visual cultures, and he curated exhibitions in Maribor ('Foreign Matter', National Liberation Museum, 2012) and Riga ('Revolutionary Traditions', Riga Arts Space, 2011) as well.

Klara Kemp-Welch is a lecturer in 20th Century Modernism at the Courtauld Institute of Art in London, where she teaches modern and contemporary European and Latin American art. After completing her PhD in History of Art at University College London in 2008, she received a Leverhulme Early Career Fellowship, an Igor Zabel Working Grant and an AHRC Early Career Fellowship. Her first monograph, *Antipolitics in Central European Art: Reticence as Dissidence under Post-Totalitarian Rule* (London: I. B. Tauris, 2014), will be followed by a second, entitled *Networking the Bloc: International Relations and Experimental Art in Eastern Europe 1968–1981*, in autumn 2018.

Emese Kürti is an art historian, art writer and researcher, and head of acb ResearchLab in Budapest which was founded for the research, publication and display of the 1960s and 1970s. She holds a PhD in Film, Media and Contemporary Culture from Eötvös Loránd University, Budapest. Her dissertation suggests a new interpretation for the emerging neo-avant-garde based on experimental music in Hungary. She is the author of several essays related to neo-avant-garde culture and contemporary art. Her current research focuses on the experimental art of the 1960s and 1970s, and the poetical aspects of actionism. Her recent publications include *Screaming Hole: Poetry, Sound and Action as Intermedia Practice in the Work of Katalin Ladik* (Budapest: acb ResearchLab, 2017).

József Mélyi is an art historian, art writer and curator. Assistant professor at the Department of Art Theory of the Hungarian University of Fine Arts; since 2006 lecturer at the Moholy-Nagy University of Art and Design. Since the mid-1990s he has published several art reviews and criticism in Hungarian periodicals. His field of research is twentieth-century and contemporary art, primarily art in public spaces and institutional criticism. In 2000–2003 he was editor-in-chief of the online art journal *Exindex*. Curated exhibitions include: 'Kempelen – Man in the Machine' – 2007, Kunsthalle Budapest and ZKM, Karlsruhe; 'Amerigo Tot – Parallel Constructions' – 2009, Ludwig Museum – Museum of Contemporary Art, Budapest; 'Blow-ups – 1963. The Age of Jancsó's Cantata' – 2016, Új Budapest Galéria.

Katalin Orbán, who translated the majority of the present volume, has a PhD from Rutgers University and is currently Assistant Professor at the Art Theory and Media Institute of Eötvös Loránd University, Budapest. She writes on literature and visual culture, and her works on graphic narrative, reading and the politics of memory have appeared in the *Journal of Graphic Novels and Comics*, the 'Comics and Media' special issue of *Critical Inquiry*, *Representations*, and in her book *Ethical Diversions: The Post-Holocaust Narratives of Pynchon, Abish, DeLillo, and Spiegelman* (Routledge, 2013 [2005]). She previously taught in the interdisciplinary honours programme of the National University of Singapore and in the Writing Program of Harvard University, among others.

Júlia Perczel holds MA's in Social Science and Art History and is currently a PhD candidate in Network Science at the Central European University, Budapest. She studied and completed internships at Budapest, Tilburg and Stuttgart. Her main interest is the application of social and network science approaches to the understanding of contemporary art phenomena. Her doctoral research focuses on the impact of network structure and network-related dynamics on the processes of canon formation.

Magdalena Radomska is a post-Marxist art historian and historian of philosophy, and Assistant Professor at Adam Mickiewicz University in Poznan, Poland. She holds a PhD in art history, and has received scholarships at the Courtauld Institute of Art in London, the Hungarian Academy of Sciences in Budapest and the Eötvös Loránd University in Budapest. She was a director and lecturer for the course 'Writing Humanities after the Fall of Communism' in 2009 at the Central European University in Budapest. Her book *The Politics of Movements of Hungarian Neoavantgarde (1966–80)* was published in 2013. Currently she is researching post-communist art in post-communist Europe (National Science Centre grant) and criticism of capitalism in art (book forthcoming: *The Plural Subject: Art and Crisis after 2008*) and writing a monograph on post-Marxism. She is a member of the Polish AICA section, and editor of the magazine *Czas Kultury*. Radomska is working on the foundation the Piotr Piotrowski Centre for East-Central European Art History.

Edit Sasvári is an art historian and museum curator. Since 2010, she has been the director of the Kassák Museum in Budapest, dedicated to the historical avant-garde in Hungary. Her main research areas include modernism, the historical avant-garde, the neo-avant-garde, and cultural policy in the 1960s and 1970s. She has edited and contributed to numerous publications and catalogues, and curated several exhibitions. In 2003 she published the book (co-authored with Júlia Klaniczay) *Törvénytelen avantgárd. Galántai György balatonboglári kápolnaműterme, 1970–1973* (Illegal Avant-garde: The Balatonboglár Chapel Studio of György Galántai, 1970–1973). Between 2014 and 2016 she initiated and ran a research programme in the Kassák Museum entitled 'Hungarian Art in the 60s and 70s'.

Katalin Székely is an art historian and curator. She worked at the Ludwig Museum – Museum of Contemporary Art in 2008–2013, and is a PhD candidate in the Doctoral Programme in Film, Media and Contemporary Culture at Eötvös Loránd University. Her fields of research include new media practices in the neo-avant-garde in Hungary and East-Central Europe, and institutional critique in the East-Central European region from the early 1960s to the present. Since 2014, she has been a member of the curatorial team of the OFF-Biennale Budapest. Since November 2015 she has been working as a Programme Officer at the Open Society Archives, Budapest.

Merse Pál Szeredi is an art historian and curator working at the Kassák Museum in Budapest. He is currently a PhD candidate in Art History at the Eötvös Loránd University; his dissertation focuses on the international networks of the Hungarian avant-garde journal entitled *MA* (Today), edited by Lajos Kassák in Vienna between 1920 and 1925. He has curated several exhibitions at the Kassák Museum on the topic of Hungarian avant-garde journals edited by Lajos Kassák during the First World War and interwar period. Together with Gábor Dobó, he has organized two international conferences on new aspects in the research of East-Central European avant-garde arts in the 1920s. He has presented at international conferences, including those organized by the EAM and ESPRit. From 2016 to 2020, he is working as a researcher within the interdisciplinary research group at the Kassák Museum on Kassák's avant-garde journals.

Notes on Contributors

Hedvig Turai is an art historian and art writer. Currently she is working at the International Business School Budapest. Previously she worked at the Ludwig Museum Budapest – Contemporary Art Museum as a researcher and curator, taught in the Education Abroad Program Budapest run by the University of California, was a senior editor at Corvina publishing house and was a museologist at the Hungarian National Gallery. She holds a PhD from Eötvös Loránd University, Budapest (2000); her earlier publications include a monograph on the Hungarian painter Margit Anna (2002), and a co-edited book (with Zsófia Bán), *Exposed Memories: Family pictures in Private and Collective Memory* (2010). Her main interests are gender studies, the Holocaust in art and the Holocaust and gender.

Daniel Véri is an art and cultural historian, head of scientific affairs at the Ferenczy Museum Centre in Szentendre, Hungary. He holds a PhD in the history of art from Eötvös Loránd University (2016); his dissertation was dedicated to János Major, a major Jewish figure of the 1960s–70s Hungarian neo-avant-garde. Previously, he received MA degrees in art history (ELTE, 2009) and history (Central European University, 2010). His research interests include the cultural history of blood libels as well as Central European art from the 1945–89 period, and especially the artistic response to Jewish identity and the Holocaust.

Acknowledgments

The present volume is the outcome of a research programme entitled 'A magyar müvészet nemzetközi megismertetése' (Making Hungarian Art Internationally Known) run by Petőfi Irodalmi Múzeum – Kassák Múzeum between 2014 and 2016. Its publication is supported by the Prime Minister's Office, Hungary, and Péter Küllői.

We would like to express our gratitude to the Translocal Institute of Contemporary Art (founded by Maja and Reuben Fowkes) for jointly organizing an international conference, 'Contested Spheres: Actually Existing Artworlds under Socialism', within the framework of Kassák Múzeum's research programme. Special thanks are due to András Szántó and Péter Küllői, the initiators of the project, and to Ákos Birkás, for his intellectual support. We also thank the staff at Thames & Hudson, especially Roger Thorp and Mark Ralph, for their editorial and production expertise; and Barbara Szij, publishing assistant at Vince Books, for gathering all the photos in the book.

Picture Credits

l = left; r = right; t = top;
b = bottom; c = centre

2 Courtesy the artist
7 Courtesy the artist & Vintage Galéria, Budapest
18 Courtesy the artist
19t Photo: FORTEPAN/Magyar Rendőr
19b Photo: Tamás Papp, © Heirs of Tamás Papp, Courtesy of the heirs of Miklós Erdély and the Miklós Erdély Foundation
22tr Photo: FORTEPAN/Tamás Urbán
22b Photo: FORTEPAN/Gyula Nagy
24 Photo: Miklós Sulyok
30t Photo courtesy Gyula Várnai
30–1 Photo courtesy Zsolt Németh & ISD Dunaferr, Dunaújváros
32t Photo: FORTEPAN/Magyar Rendőr
32b Photo: Miklós Sulyok
33 Photo: Miklós Sulyok
44 Photo courtesy László Kiss
47br Courtesy Kolozsváry Collection, Győr
58 Courtesy the artist & acb Galéria, Budapest
64 Courtesy the artist & acb Galéria, Budapest
65 Courtesy the artist
67tl Courtesy the artist
67tr Photo: Zoltán Hasznos, Courtesy the artist
67b Photo: Ferenc Gelencsér
69br Photo: Déri Múzeum, Debrecen
71 Photo courtesy László Haris
76 Courtesy the artist
79l Courtesy Institute for the Research of the Avant-Garde, Zagreb
79r Photo courtesy János Gulyás
81t Courtesy Institute for the Research of the Avant-Garde, Zagreb
81b Photo: Bojan Brecelj, Courtesy Institute for the Research of the Avant-Garde, Zagreb
82 Courtesy László Beke
83t Courtesy László Beke
83b Photo: Zdzisław Holuka/Muzeum Współczesne, Wrocław, Courtesy the Lower Silesian Society for the Encouragement of Fine Arts
85 Photographer unknown, Courtesy Zakład Narodowy im. Ossolińskich, Wrocław
86 Photo: Vladimir Jakolić, Digitalna zbirka Hrvatske akademije znanosti i umjetnosti (DiZbi.HAZU), Zagreb
87 Photographer unknown
88 Photo: Éva Körner © IPUTNPU-Archives
89 Photo: Katalin Nádor, Courtesy Károly Kismányoky & Péter Kamarás
91 Courtesy the artist & Vintage Galéria, Budapest
94 Photo: Tamás Farkas, Courtesy Magyar Képzőművészeti Egyetem Könyvtár, Levéltár és Művészeti Gyűjtemény, Budapest
96t Photo: Károly Gink, Courtesy Magyar Képzőművészeti Egyetem Könyvtár, Levéltár és Művészeti Gyűjtemény, Budapest
96c Photographer unknown, Courtesy Magyar Képzőművészeti Egyetem Könyvtár, Levéltár és Művészeti Gyűjtemény, Budapest
96b Photo: Edit Molnár, Courtesy Biksady Galéria, Budapest
97 Photo courtesy Péter Forgács
98t Photo: Tamás Papp, © Heirs of Tamás Papp, Courtesy of the heirs of Miklós Erdély and the Miklós Erdély Foundation
98b Photo courtesy Zoltán Lábas
99 Photo: Tamás Papp, © Heirs of Tamás Papp, Courtesy of the heirs of Miklós Erdély and the Miklós Erdély Foundation
100 Photo: György Erdély, © Indigo Group, Courtesy of the Indigo Group and the Miklós Erdély Foundation
102t Courtesy Vintage Galéria, Budapest
102b Photo in the Miklós Erdély Estate, © Heirs of Miklós Erdély, Courtesy of the heirs of Miklós Erdély and the Miklós Erdély Foundation
104 Photo: Gábor Dobos, Courtesy Klára Palotai
108 Courtesy the heirs of Gábor Bódy & C^3 Kulturális és Kommunikációs Központ Alapítvány, Budapest
111 Photo courtesy Demeter Balla
112 Photo: Miklós Sulyok
116 Photo: Miklós Sulyok
117 Photo courtesy Tünde Kotricz/Köztérkép
118 Photo: Miklós Sulyok
119r Courtesy Virág Judit Galéria, Budapest
120t Courtesy Virág Judit Galéria, Budapest
121b Photo: Tihanyi-Bakos Fotóstúdió
122t Photo: Magyar Kereskedelmi és Vendéglátóipari Múzeum, Budapest
123t Photo courtesy Municipality of Hódmezővásárhely
123b Photo courtesy István Csuhai/Köztérkép
124–5 Photo: Miklós Sulyok
126 Photo: Miklós Sulyok
127 Courtesy Kieselbach Galéria, Budapest
128t Courtesy Virág Judit Galéria, Budapest
128b Photo: Zsuzsa Berényi, Courtesy Virág Judit Galéria, Budapest
132–3 Courtesy the artist
141tl Courtesy the artist
141tr Photo: Csanád Szesztay, Courtesy the artist
142c Courtesy the artist
142b Courtesy the artist
145t Photo: Miklós Sulyok
145b Photo: Dávid Kis
149t Courtesy Kieselbach Galéria, Budapest
149b Courtesy Kieselbach Galéria, Budapest
150t Photo: Ferenc Gelencsér
151 Courtesy the artist
152b Photo: Tihanyi-Bakos Fotóstúdió
153 Photo: Miklós Sulyok
154t Photo courtesy György Darabos/Art+Text Budapest
155 Photo: Miklós Sulyok
157t Photo: Tihanyi-Bakos Fotóstúdió
157b Photo: Miklós Sulyok
164 Courtesy Körmendi Galéria, Budapest
169 Courtesy the artist & acb Galéria, Budapest
170–1 Courtesy Kolozsváry Collection, Győr
175 Photo courtesy Demeter Balla
178 Photographer unknown
180 Photo courtesy Demeter Balla
183 Photographer unknown, Photo courtesy Péter Nemes
185 Photo: Attila Polgár, Photo courtesy HAP Galéria, Budapest
190t Courtesy Vintage Galéria, Budapest
190b Photo courtesy Gyula Kozák
191 Photo: Ferenc Kovács, © Heirs of Miklós Erdély, Courtesy of the heirs of Miklós Erdély and the Miklós Erdély Foundation
192 Photo: FORTEPAN/Róbert Hofbauer
194 Photo: László Magyar
197r Photo: Magyar Nemzeti Múzeum, Budapest
199 Photo courtesy the artist
200–1 Photo: FORTEPAN/Gyula Nagy
208b Photo: László Roboz, Budapest Főváros Levéltára, Courtesy László Beke
211 Photo: Miklós Sulyok
212–13 Photo: Tihanyi-Bakos Fotóstúdió

Picture Credits

215t Courtesy Kieselbach Galéria, Budapest
215b Courtesy the artist
216t Courtesy Vintage Galéria, Budapest
216bl Photo courtesy the owner & Dániel Véri
218 Photo: Steven Harris, Courtesy Steven Harris & Louise McCagg
221b Photo: Ferenc Kovács, © Heirs of Miklós Erdély, Courtesy of the heirs of Miklós Erdély and the Miklós Erdély Foundation
222l Courtesy the artist
222r Photo: Miklós Sulyok
228 Photo courtesy János Vető
232 Courtesy Vintage Galéria, Budapest
233 Courtesy Vintage Galéria, Budapest
236 Courtesy the artist
237 Photo: Tibor Gáyor, Courtesy the artist
238 Photo: László Kerekes, Courtesy the artist
240t Photo: Miklós Erdély Foundation © Heirs of Miklós Erdély, Courtesy of the heirs of Miklós Erdély and the Miklós Erdély Foundation
240b Courtesy the artist
241 Courtesy the artist & acb Galéria, Budapest
242 Courtesy the artist
243t Courtesy the artist & acb Galéria, Budapest
243b Courtesy the artist
250 Photo: Péter Moór
252–3 Photo: Ferenc Gelencsér
254 Photo: Péter Moór
255 Photo courtesy János Gulyás
256 Photo: Tihanyi-Bakos Fotóstúdió
260 Photo courtesy Gyula Kozák
261 Photo courtesy Gyula Kozák
263 Photo courtesy Gyula Kozák
264t Photo: Tihanyi-Bakos Fotóstúdió
264b Photo: Miklós Sulyok, Courtesy Municipality of Győr
266–7 Courtesy Kieselbach Galéria, Budapest
270t Courtesy Jarosław Kozłowski
270b Courtesy acb Galéria, Budapest
271 Photo: László Lugosi Lugo, © Heirs of Miklós Erdély, Courtesy of the heirs of Miklós Erdély and the Miklós Erdély Foundation
272 Courtesy Jarosław Kozłowski
274 Courtesy Jarosław Kozłowski
275t Courtesy Jarosław Kozłowski
275b Courtesy László Beke
276 Courtesy the artist
279 Photographer unknown, Courtesy Galeria Foksal, Warsaw
281t Photographer unknown, Courtesy Galeria Foksal, Warsaw
284 Courtesy László Beke
285b Courtesy the artist
290 Photo: Zoltán Bakos, Courtesy the artist
292 Photo: Gyula Zaránd, © IPUTNPU-Archives
294 Photographer unknown, © IPUTNPU-Archives
295 Courtesy acb Galéria, Budapest
297 Photo: Tibor Somogyi-Varga, Photo courtesy acb Galéria, Budapest
299 Photographer unknown, © Heirs of Miklós Erdély, Courtesy of the heirs of Miklós Erdély and the Miklós Erdély Foundation
300 Photographer unknown, Courtesy acb Galéria, Budapest
301 Photo: Tibor Somogyi-Varga, Courtesy acb Galéria, Budapest
302 Photo: Imre Póth, Courtesy acb Galéria, Budapest
304 Photo: Tibor Somogyi-Varga, Photo courtesy acb Galéria, Budapest
306 Photo: Zoltán Apró, Courtesy the artist
308–9 Photo courtesy acb Galéria, Budapest
310t Photo courtesy János Vető
310b Photo courtesy acb Galéria, Budapest
314 Photo: Ferenc Gelencsér
321 Photo courtesy Vintage Galéria, Budapest
322t Photo: László Lugosi Lugo, © Heirs of Miklós Erdély, Courtesy of the heirs of Miklós Erdély and the Miklós Erdély Foundation
322b Photo: Tamás St. Turba
323 Courtesy the artist
325 Photos: Csaba Aknay, Courtesy the artist & acb Galéria, Budapest
334 Photo: László Lugosi Lugo, © Heirs of Miklós Erdély, courtesy of the heirs of Miklós Erdély and the Miklós Erdély Foundation
336tl Photo: László Lugosi Lugo, © Heirs of Miklós Erdély, courtesy of the heirs of Miklós Erdély and the Miklós Erdély Foundation
336tr Photo: László Lugosi Lugo, © Heirs of Miklós Erdély courtesy of the heirs of Miklós Erdély and the Miklós Erdély Foundation
336b Photo: László Lugosi Lugo, © Heirs of Miklós Erdély, Courtesy of the heirs of Miklós Erdély and the Miklós Erdély Foundation
341b Courtesy the artist & Vintage Galéria, Budapest
342t Courtesy the artist
342b Courtesy the artist &Vintage Galéria, Budapest
344–5 Courtesy Vintage Galéria, Budapest
346 Photo courtesy Márk Pinczehelyi
349 Courtesy the heirs of Gábor Bódy & C[3] Kulturális és Kommunikációs Központ Alapítvány, Budapest
350 Photo courtesy © Kontakt: The Art Collection of Erste Group and ERSTE Foundation
351 Photo courtesy János Vető
353 Courtesy the heirs of Gábor Bódy & C[3] Kulturális és Kommunikációs Központ Alapítvány, Budapest
356 Courtesy the artist & Vintage Galéria, Budapest

Index

Page numbers in *italic* refer to the illustrations.

On the cover
Front: Dóra Maurer, *Seven Twists I–VI*, 1977–78
(detail; see page 342)
Back: Participating artists of the exhibition 'R', Budapesti Müszaki Egyetem (Budapest University of Technology), 1970
(see page 87)

Frontispiece
Endre Tót, *You Are The One Who Made Me Glad*, 1973–75
(see page 240)

Page 356
Details as for front cover (see above)

First published in the United Kingdom in 2018 by
Thames & Hudson Ltd, 181A High Holborn,
London WC1V 7QX

Hungarian edition first published in 2018 by Vince Books, Budapest

Published in association with the Petőfi Irodalmi Múzeum and the Kassák Múzeum, Budapest, and Vince Books, Budapest

Designed by Daly & Lyon
Artists' biographies compiled by Kriszta Dékei

British Library Cataloguing-in-Publication-Data
A catalogue record for this book is available from the British Library

ISBN 978-0-500-23978-0

Printed and bound in Slovenia by DZS-Grafik d.o.o.

PETŐFI IRODALMI MÚZEUM

KASSÁK MÚZEUM

VINCE